20 -80/202.

A HISTORY OF THE INQUISITION

BOOKS BY HENRY C. LEA

A HISTORY OF THE INQUISITION OF SPAIN. In four volumes,

A HISTORY OF AURICULAR CONFESSION AND INDULGENCES IN THE LATIN CHURCH. In three volumes,

AN HISTORICAL SKETCH OF SACERDOTAL CELIBACY IN THE CHRISTIAN CHURCH.

A FORMULARY OF THE PAPAL PENITENTIARY IN THE THIRTEENTH CENTURY. One volume, octavo.

SUPERSTITION AND FORCE. Essays on The Wager of Law, The Wager of Battle, The Ordeal, Torture.

STUDIES IN CHURCH HISTORY. The Rise of the Temporal Power, Benefit of Clergy, Excommunication, The Early Church and Slavery.

CHAPTERS FROM THE RELIGIOUS HISTORY OF SPAIN, CONNECTED WITH THE INQUISITION. Censorship of the Press, Mystics and Illuminati, Endemoniadas, El Santo Niño de la Guardia, Brianda de Bardaxi.

THE MORISCOS OF SPAIN, THEIR CONVERSION AND EXPULSION.

A HISTORY OF

THE INQUISITION

OF

THE MIDDLE AGES

BY

HENRY CHARLES LEA

IN THREE VOLUMES

VOLUME THREE

NEW YORK

RUSSELL & RUSSELL · PUBLISHERS

RUSSELL SCHOLARS' CLASSICS EDITION

Library of Congress Catalog Card Number 58 – 9830

First Printing, August 1955
Second Printing, March 1956
Third Printing, March 1958

MANUFACTURED IN THE UNITED STATES OF AMERICA

CONTENTS

BOOK III.—SPECIAL FIELDS OF INQUISITORIAL ACTIVITY

CHAPTER I.—THE SPIRITUAL FRANCISCANS.

CHAPTER II.—GUGLIELMA AND DOLCINO.

Chapter VII.—Witchcraft.

Chapter VIII.—Intellect and Faith.

Chapter IX.—Conclusion.

THE INQUISITION.

BOOK III.

SPECIAL FIELDS OF INQUISITORIAL ACTIVITY.

CHAPTER I.

THE SPIRITUAL FRANCISCANS.

In a former chapter we considered the Mendicants as an active agency in the suppression of heresy. One of the Orders, however, by no means restricted itself to this function, and we have now to examine the career of the Franciscans as the subjects of the spirit of persecuting uniformity which they did so much to render dominant.

While the mission of both Orders was to redeem the Church from the depth of degradation into which it had sunk, the Dominicans were more especially trained to take part in the active business of life. They therefore attracted the more restless and aggressive spirits; they accommodated themselves to the world, like the Jesuits of later days, and the worldliness which necessarily came with success awakened little antagonism within the organization. Power and luxury were welcomed and enjoyed. Even Thomas Aquinas, who, as we have seen, eloquently defended, against William of Saint-Amour, the superlative holiness of absolute poverty, subsequently admitted that poverty should be proportioned to the object which an Order was fitted to attain.*

---

* Th. Aquin. Summ. Sec. Sec. Q. clxxxviii. art. 7. ad 1.

III.—1

It was otherwise with the Franciscans. Though, as we have seen, the founders determined not to render the Order a simply contemplative one, the salvation of the individual through retreat from the world and its temptations bore a much larger part in their motives than in those of Dominic and his followers.* Absolute poverty and self-abnegation were its primal principles, and it inevitably drew to itself the intellects which sought a refuge from the temptations of life in self-absorbing contemplation, in dreamy speculation, and in the renunciation of all that renders life attractive to average human nature. As the organization grew in wealth and power there were necessarily developed within its bosom antagonisms in two directions. On the one hand, it nourished a spirit of mysticism, which, though recognized in its favorite appellation of the Seraphic Order, sometimes found the trammels of orthodoxy oppressive. On the other, the men who continued to cherish the views of the founders as to the supreme obligation of absolute poverty could not reconcile their consciences to the accumulation of wealth and its display in splendor, and they rejected the ingenious devices which sought to accommodate the possession of riches with the abnegation of all possession.

In fact, the three vows, of poverty, obedience, and chastity, were all equally impossible of absolute observance. The first was irreconcilable with human necessities, the others with human passions. As for chastity, the whole history of the Church shows the impracticability of its enforcement. As for obedience, in the

---

* Even the great Franciscan preacher, Berthold of Ratisbon (who died in 1272) will concede only qualified merit to those who labor to save the souls of their fellow-creatures, and such labors can easily be carried to excess. The duty which a man owes to his own soul, in prayer and devotion, is of much greater moment. — Beati Fr. Bertholdi a Ratisbona Sermones (Monachii, 1882, p. 29). See also his comparison of the contemplative with the active life. The former is Rachael, the latter is Leah, and is most perilous when wholly devoted to good works (Ib. pp. 44–5).

So the great Spiritual Franciscan, Pierre Jean Olivi—"Est igitur totius rationis summa, quod contemplatio est ex suo genere perfectior omni alia actione," though he admits that a lesser portion of time may allowably be devoted to the salvation of fellow-creatures.—Franz Ehrle, Archiv für Litteratur- und Kirchengeschichte, 1887, p. 503.

sense attached to it of absolute renunciation of the will, its in-compatibility with the conduct of human affairs was shown at an early period, when Friar Haymo of Feversham overthrew Gregory, the Provincial of Paris, and, not long afterwards, withstood the general Elias, and procured his deposition. As for poverty, we shall see to what inextricable complications it led, despite the efforts of successive popes, until the imperious will and resolute common-sense of John XXII. brought the Order from its seraphic heights down to the every-day necessities of human life—at the cost, it must be confessed, of a schism. The trouble was increased by the fact that St. Francis, foreseeing the efforts which would be made to evade the spirit of the Rule, had, in his Testament, strictly forbidden all alterations, glosses, and explanations, and had com-manded that these instructions should be read in all chapters of the Order. With the growth of the Franciscan legend, moreover, the Rule was held to be a special divine revelation, equal in authority to the gospel, and St. Francis was glorified until he became a being rather divine than human.*

Even before the death of the founder, in 1226, a Franciscan is found in Paris openly teaching heresies—of what nature we are not told, but probably the mystic reveries of an overwrought brain. As yet there was no Inquisition, and, as he was not sub-ject to episcopal jurisdiction, he was brought before the papal legate, where he asserted many things contrary to the orthodox faith, and was imprisoned for life. This foreshadowed much that was to follow, though there is a long interval before we hear again of similar examples.†

The more serious trouble concerning poverty was not long in developing itself. Next to St. Francis himself in the Order stood Elias. Before Francis went on his mission to convert the Soldan he had sent Elias as provincial beyond the sea, and on his return from the adventure he brought Elias home with him. At the first general chapter, held in 1221, Francis being too much en-

---

* Thom. de Eccleston de Adventu Minorum Coll. v.—S. Francis. Testament. (Opp. 1849, p. 48).—Nicolai. PP. III. Bull. *Exiit qui seminat* (Lib. v. Sexto xii. 3). —Lib. Sententt. Inq. Tolos. pp. 301, 303.

† Chron. Turonens. ann. 1326 (D. Bouquet, XVIII. 319). — Alberic. Trium Font. Chron. ann. 1228.

feebled to preside, Elias acted as spokesman and Francis sat at his feet, pulling his gown when he wanted anything said. In 1223 we hear of Cæsarius, the German provincial, going to Italy "to the blessed Francis or the Friar Elias." When, through infirmity or inability to maintain discipline, Francis retired from the generalate, Elias was vicar-general of the Order, to whom Francis submitted himself as humbly as the meanest brother, and on the death of the saint, in October, 1226, it was Elias who notified the brethren throughout Europe of the event, and informed them of the Stigmata, which the humility of Francis had always concealed. Although in February, 1227, Giovanni Parenti of Florence was elected general, Elias seems practically to have retained control. Parties were rapidly forming themselves in the Order, and the lines between them were ever more sharply drawn. Elias was worldly and ambitious; he had the reputation of being one of the ablest men of affairs in Italy; he could foresee the power attaching to the command of the Order, and he had not much scruple as to the means of attaining it. He undertook the erection of a magnificent church at Assisi to receive the bones of the humble Francis, and he was unsparing in his demands for money to aid in its construction. The very handling of money was an abomination in the eyes of all true brethren, yet all the provinces were called upon to contribute, and a marble coffer was placed in front of the building to receive the gifts of the pious. This was unendurable, and Friar Leo went to Perugia to consult with the blessed Gilio, who had been the third associate to join St. Francis, who said it was contrary to the precepts of the founder. "Shall I break it, then?" inquired Leo. "Yes," replied Gilio, "if you are dead, but if you are alive, let it alone, for you will not be able to endure the persecution of Elias." Notwithstanding this warning, Leo went to Assisi, and with the assistance of some comrades broke the coffer; Elias filled all Assisi with his wrath, and Leo took refuge in a hermitage.*

---

* Frat. Jordani Chron. c. 9, 14, 17, 31, 50 (Analecta Franciscana, Quaracchi, 1885, I. 4–6, 11, 16).—S. Francis. Testament. (Opp. p. 47); Ejusd. Epistt. vi., vii., viii. (Ib. 10–11).—Amoni Legenda S. Francisci, p. 106 (Roma, 1880).—Wadding. ann. 1229, No. 2.—Chron. Glassberger ann. 1227 (Analect. Franciscana II. p. 45).

When the edifice was sufficiently advanced, a general chapter
was held in 1230 to solemnize the translation of the saintly corpse.
Elias sought to utilize the occasion for his own election to the
generalate by summoning to it only those brethren on whose
support he could reckon, but Giovanni got wind of this and made
the summons general. Elias then caused the translation to be effected before the brethren had assembled ; his faction endeavored
to forestall the action of the chapter by carrying him from his
cell, breaking open the doors, and placing him in the general's
seat. Giovanni appeared, and after tumultuous proceedings his
friends obtained the upper hand ; the disturbers were scattered
among the provinces, and Elias retreated to a hermitage, where
he allowed his hair and beard to grow, and through this show of
sanctity obtained reconciliation to the Order. Finally, in the
chapter of 1232, his ambition was rewarded. Giovanni was deposed and he was elected general.*

These turbulent intrigues were not the only evidence of the
rapid degeneracy of the Order. Before Francis's Testament was
five years old his commands against evasions of the Rule by cunning interpretations had been disregarded. The chapter of 1231
had applied to Gregory IX. to know whether the Testament was
binding upon them in this respect, and he replied in the negative,
for Francis could not bind his successors. They also asked about
the prohibition to hold money and property, and Gregory ingeniously suggested that this could be effected through third parties, who could hold money and pay debts for them, arguing that
such persons should not be regarded as their agents, but as the
agents of those who gave the money or of those to whom it was
to be paid. These elusory glosses of the Rule were not accepted
without an energetic opposition which threatened a schism, and it
is easy to imagine the bitterness with which the sincere members
of the Order watched its rapid degeneracy ; nor was this bitterness
diminished by the use which Elias made of his position. His carnality and cruelty, we are told, convulsed the whole Order. His
rule was arbitrary, and for seven years, in defiance of the regulations, he held no general chapter. He levied exactions on all the

---

* Thomæ de Eccleston Collat. xii.—Jordani Chron. c. 61 (Analecta Franc. I.
19).—Chron. Anon. (Ib. I. 289).

provinces to complete the great structure at Assisi. Those who
resisted him were relegated to distant places. Even while yet only
vicar he had caused St. Anthony of Padua, who had come to Assisi to worship at the tomb of Francis, to be scourged to the blood,
when Anthony only expostulated with, "May the blessed God for-
give you, brethren !" Worse was the fate of Cæsarius of Speier,
who had been appointed Provincial of Germany in 1221 by St.
Francis himself, and had built up the Order to the north of the
Alps. He was the leader of the puritan malcontents, who were
known as Cæsarians, and he felt the full wrath of Elias. Thrown
into prison, he lay there in chains for two years. At length the
fetters were removed, and, early in 1239, his jailer having left the
door of his cell open, he ventured forth to stretch his cramped
limbs in the wintry sun. The jailer returned and thought that he
was attempting to escape. Fearing the pitiless anger of Elias, he
rushed after the prisoner and dealt him a mortal blow with a
cudgel. Cæsarius was the first, but by no means the last, martyr
who shed his blood for the strict observance of a Rule breathing
nothing but love and charity.*

The cup at last was full to overflowing. In 1237 Elias had
sent visitors to the different provinces whose conduct caused
general exasperation. The brethren of Saxony appealed to him
from their visitor, and, finding this fruitless, they carried their complaint to Gregory. The pope at length was roused to intervene.
A general chapter was convened in 1239, when, after a stormy
scene in presence of Gregory and nine cardinals, the pope finally
announced to Elias that his resignation would be received. Possibly in this there may have been political as well as ascetic motives. Elias was a skilful negotiator, and was looked upon with a
friendly eye by Frederic II., who forthwith declared that the dis-

---

* Gregor. PP. IX. Bull. *Quo elongati* (Pet. Rodulphii Hist. Seraph. Relig. Lib. II.
fol. 164–5).—Rodulphii op. cit. Lib. II. fol. 177.—Chron. Glassberger, ann. 1230,
1231 (Analecta II. 50, 56).—Frat. Jordani Chron. c. 18, 19, 61 (Analecta I. 7, 8,
19).—Franz Ehrle (Archiv für Litt.- u. Kirchengeschichte, 1886, p. 123).—Wadding. ann. 1239, No. 5.

The ingenious casuistry with which the Conventuals satisfied themselves that
the device of Gregory IX. enabled them to grow rich without transgressing the
Rule is seen in their defence before Clement VI., in 1311, as printed by Franz
Ehrle (Archiv für Litt.- u. Kirchengeschichte, 1887, pp. 107–8).

missal was done in his despite, for Elias was at the time engaged in an effort to heal the irremediable breach between the papacy and the empire. Certain it is that Elias at once took refuge with Frederic and became his intimate companion. Gregory made an effort to capture him by inviting him to a conference. Failing in this, a charge was brought against him of visiting poor women at Cortona without permission, and on refusing to obey a summons he was excommunicated.*

Thus already in the Franciscan Order there were established two well-defined parties, which came to be known as the Spirituals and the Conventuals, the one adhering to the strict letter of the Rule, the other willing to find excuses for its relaxation in obedience to the wants of human nature and the demands of worldliness. After the fall of Elias the former had the supremacy during the brief generalates of Alberto of Pisa, and Haymo of Feversham. In 1244 the Conventuals triumphed in the election of Crescenzio Grizzi da Jesi, under whom occurred what the Spirituals reckoned as the " Third Tribulation," for, in accordance with their apocalyptic speculations, they were to undergo seven tribulations before the reign of the Holy Ghost should usher in the Millennium. Crescenzio followed in the footsteps of Elias. Under Haymo, in 1242, there had been an attempt to reconcile with the Rule Gregory's declaration of 1231. Four leading doctors of the Order, with Alexander Hales at their head, had issued the *Declaratio Quatuor Magistrorum*, but even their logical subtlety had failed. The Order was constantly growing, it was constantly acquiring property,

---

* Jordani Chron. c. 62, 63 (Analecta I. 18–19).—Thomæ de Eccleston Collat. XII.—Chron. Glassberger, ann. 1239 (Analecta II. 60–1). — Huillard-Bréholles, Introd. p. DIII.; Ib. VI. 69–70.

Elias still managed to excite disturbance in the Order; he died excommunicate, and a zealous Franciscan guardian had his remains dug up and cast upon a dunghill. Frà Salimbene gives full details of his evil ways, and the tyrannous maladministration which precipitated his downfall. After his secession to Frederic II. a popular rhyme was current throughout Italy—

> " Hor attorna fratt Helya,
> Ke pres' ha la mala via."
>
> Salimbene Chronica, Parma, 1857, pp. 401–13.

Affò, however, asserts that he was absolved on his death-bed.—Vita del Beato Gioanni di Parma, Parma, 1777, p. 31. Cf. Chron. Glassberger ann. 1243–4.

and its needs were constantly increasing. A bull of Gregory IX. in 1239, authorizing the Franciscans of Paris to acquire additional land with which to enlarge their monastery of Saint-Germain-des-Près, is an example of what was going on all over Europe. In 1244, at the chapter which elected Crescenzio, the Englishman, John Kethene, succeeded, against the opposition of nearly the whole body of the assembly, in obtaining the rejection of Gregory's definition, but the triumph of the Puritans was short-lived. Crescenzio sympathized with the laxer party, and applied to Innocent IV. for relief. In 1245 the pope responded with a declaration in which he not only repeated the device of Gregory IX. by authorizing deposits of money with parties who were to be regarded as the agents of donors and creditors, but ingeniously assumed that houses and lands, the ownership of which was forbidden to the Order, should be regarded as belonging to the Holy See, which granted their use to the friars. Even papal authority could not render these transparent subterfuges satisfying to the consciences of the Spirituals, and the growing worldliness of the Order provoked continuous agitation. Crescenzio before taking the vows had been a jurist and physician, and there was further complaint that he encouraged the brethren in acquiring the vain and sterile science of Aristotle rather than in studying divine wisdom. Under Simone da Assisi, Giacopo Manfredo, Matteo da Monte Rubiano, and Lucido, seventy-two earnest brethren, finding Crescenzio deaf to their remonstrances, prepared to appeal to Innocent. He anticipated them, and obtained from the pope in advance a decision under which he scattered the recalcitrants in couples throughout the provinces for punishment. Fortunately his reign was short. Tempted by the bishopric of Jesi, he resigned, and in 1248 was succeeded by Giovanni Borelli, better known as John of Parma, who at the time was professor of theology in the University of Paris.*

---

* Thomæ de Ecclest. Collat. VIII., XII.—Wadding. ann. 1242, No. 2; ann. 1245, No. 16.—Potthast No. 10825.—Angeli Clarinens. Epist. Excusator (Franz Ehrle, Archiv für Litt.- u. Kirchengeschichte, 1885, p. 535; 1886, pp. 113, 117, 120).—Hist. Tribulation. (Ib. 1886, pp. 256 sqq.).

The *Historia Tribulationum* reflects the contempt of the Spirituals for human learning. Adam was led to disobedience by a thirst for knowledge, and returned to grace by faith and not by dialectics, or geometry or astrology. The evil in-

The election of John of Parma marked a reaction in favor of strict observance. The new general was inspired with a holy zeal to realize the ideal of St. Francis. The exiled Spirituals were recalled and allowed to select their own domiciles. During the first three years John visited on foot the whole Order, sometimes with two, and sometimes with only one companion, in the most humble guise, so that he was unrecognized, and could remain in a convent for several days, observing its character, when he would reveal himself and reform its abuses. In the ardor of his zeal he spared the feelings of no one. A lector of the Mark of Ancona, returning home from Rome, described the excessive severity of a sermon preached by him, saying that the brethren of the Mark would never have allowed any one to say such things to them; and when asked why the masters who were present had not interfered, he replied, "How could they? It was a river of fire which flowed from his lips." He suspended the declaration of Innocent IV. until the pontiff, better informed, could be consulted. It was, however, impossible for him to control the tendencies to relaxation of the Rule, which were ever growing stronger, and his efforts to that end only served to strengthen disaffection which finally grew to determined opposition. After consultation between some influential members of the Order it was resolved to bring before Alexander IV. formal accusations against him and the friends who surrounded him. The attitude of the Spirituals, in fact, fairly invited attack.*

To understand the position of the Spirituals at this time, and

---

dustry of the arts of Aristotle, and the seductive sweetness of Plato's eloquence are Egyptian plagues in the Church (Ib. 264–5). It was an early tradition of the Order that Francis had predicted its ruin through overmuch learning (Amoni, Legenda S. Francisci, App. cap. xi.).

Karl Müller (Die Anfänge des Minoritenordens, Freiburg, 1885, p. 180) asserts that the election of Crescenzio was a triumph of the Puritans, and that he was known for his flaming zeal for the rigid observance of the Rule. So far from this being the case, on the very night of his election he scolded the zealots (Th. Eccleston Collat. xii.), and the history of his generalate confirms the view taken of him by the Hist. Tribulationum. Affò (Vita di Gioanni di Parma, pp. 31–2) assumes that he endeavored to follow a middle course, and ended by persecuting the irreconcilables.

* Hist. Tribulat. (loc. cit. 1886, pp. 267–8, 274).—Affò, pp. 38–9, 54, 97–8.—Wadding. ann. 1256, No. 2.

subsequently, it is necessary to cast a glance at one of the most remarkable spiritual developments of the thirteenth century. Its opening years had witnessed the death of Joachim of Flora, a man who may be regarded as the founder of modern mysticism. Sprung from a rich and noble family, and trained for the life of a courtier under Roger the Norman Duke of Apulia, a sudden desire to see the holy places took him, while yet a youth, to the East, with a retinue of servitors. A pestilence was raging when he reached Constantinople, which so impressed him with the miseries and vanities of life that he dismissed his suite and continued his voyage as an humble pilgrim with a single companion. His legend relates that he fell in the desert overcome with thirst, and had a vision of a man standing by a river of oil, and saying to him, " Drink of this stream," which he did to satiety, and when he awoke, although previously illiterate, he had a knowledge of all Scripture. The following Lent he passed in an old well on Mount Tabor; in the night of the Resurrection a great splendor appeared to him, he was filled with divine light to understand the concordance of the Old and New Laws, and every difficulty and every obscurity vanished. These tales, repeated until the seventeenth century, show the profound and lasting impression which he left upon the minds of men.*

Thenceforth his life was dedicated to the service of God. Returning home, he avoided his father's house, and commenced preaching to the people ; but this was not permissible to a layman, so he entered the priesthood and the severe Cistercian Order. Chosen Abbot of Corazzo, he fled, but was brought back and forced to assume the duties of the office, till he visited Rome, in 1181, and obtained from Lucius III. permission to lay it down. Even the severe Cistercian discipline did not satisfy his thirst for austerity, and he retired to a hermitage at Pietralata, where his reputation for sanctity drew disciples around him, and in spite of his yearning for solitude he found himself at the head of a new Order, of which the Rule, anticipating the Mendicants in its urgency of poverty, was approved by Celestin III. in 1196. Already it had spread from the mother-house of San Giovanni in Fiore, and numbered several other monasteries.†

---

* Tocco, L'Eresia nel Medio Evo, Firenze, 1884, pp. 265–70. — Profetie dell' Abate Gioachino, Venezia, 1646, p. 8.

† Tocco, op. cit. pp. 271–81.—Cœlestin. PP. III. Epist. 279.

Joachim considered himself inspired, and though in 1200 he submitted his works unreservedly to the Holy See, he had no hesitation in speaking of them as divinely revealed. During his lifetime he enjoyed the reputation of a prophet. When Richard of England and Philip Augustus were at Messina, they sent for him to inquire as to the outcome of their crusade, and he is said to have foretold to them that the hour had not yet come for the deliverance of Jerusalem. Others of his fulfilled prophecies are also related, and the mystical character of the apocalyptic speculations which he left behind him served to increase, after his death, his reputation as a seer. His name became one customarily employed for centuries when any dreamer or sharper desired to attract attention, and quite a literature of forgeries grew up which were ascribed to him. Somewhat more than a century after his death we find the Dominican Pipino enumerating a long catalogue of his works with the utmost respect for his predictions. In 1319 Bernard Délicieux places unlimited confidence in a prophetical book of Joachim's in which there were representations of all future popes with inscriptions and symbols under them. Bernard points out the different pontiffs of his own period, predicts the fate of John XXII., and declares that for two hundred years there had been no mortal to whom so much was revealed as to Joachim. Cola di Rienzo found in the pseudo-prophecies of Joachim the encouragement that inspired his second attempt to govern Rome. The Franciscan tract *De ultima Ætate Ecclesiæ*, written in 1356, and long ascribed to Wickliff, expresses the utmost reverence for Joachim, and frequently cites his prophecies. The *Liber Conformitatum*, in 1385, quotes repeatedly the prediction ascribed to Joachim as to the foundation of the two Mendicant Orders, symbolized in those of the Dove and of the Crow, and the tribulations to which the former was to be exposed. Not long afterwards the hermit Telesforo da Cosenza drew from the same source prophecies as to the course and termination of the Great Schism, and the line of future popes until the coming of Antichrist—prophecies which attracted sufficient attention to call for a refutation from Henry of Hesse, one of the leading theologians of the day. Cardinal Peter d'Ailly speaks with respect of Joachim's prophecies concerning Antichrist, and couples him with the prophetess St. Hildegarda, while the rationalistic Cornelius Agrippa endeavors to explain his predictions by the occult powers of numbers. Human credulity preserved his reputation as a prophet to modern times, and until at least as late as the seventeenth century prophecies under his name were published, containing series of popes with symbolical figures, inscriptions, and explanations, apparently similar to the *Vaticinia Pontificum* which so completely possessed the confidence of Bernard Délicieux. Even in the seventeenth century the Carmelites printed the *Oraculum Angelicum* of Cyril, with its pseudo-Joachitic commentary, as a proof of the antiquity of their Order.*

Joachim's immense and durable reputation as a prophet was due not so much to his genuine works as to the spurious ones circulated under his name. These were numerous—Prophecies of Cyril, and of the Erythræan Sybil, Commentaries on Jeremiah, the *Vaticinia Pontificum*, the *De Oneribus Ecclesiæ* and *De Septem Temporibus Ecclesiæ*. In some of these, reference to Frederic II. would seem to indicate a period of composition about the year 1250, when the strife between the papacy and empire was at the hottest, and the current prophecies of Merlin were freely drawn upon in framing their exegesis. There can be little doubt that their authors were Franciscans of the Puritan party, and their fearless denunciations of existing evils show how impatient had grown the spirit of dissatisfaction. The apocalyptic prophecies

---

* Lib. Concordiæ Præf. (Venet. 1519).—Fr. Francisci Pipini Chron. (Muratori S. R. I. IX. 498–500).—Rog. Hovedens. ann. 1190.—MSS. Bib. Nat., fonds latin, No 4270, fol. 260-2.—Comba, La Riforma in Italia, I. 388.—Lechler's Wickliffe, Lorimer's Translation, II. 321.—Lib. Conformitat. Lib. I. Fruct. i. P. 2; Fruct. ix. P. 2 (fol. 12, 91).—Telesphori de magnis Tribulationibus Prœem.—Henric. de Hassia contra Vaticin. Telesphori c. xi. (Pez Thesaur. I. II. 521).—Franz Ehrle (Archiv für Lit.- u. Kirchengeschichte, 1886, p. 331).—P. d'Ailly Concord. Astron.Veritat. c. lix. (August. Vindel. 1490).—H. Cornel. Agripp. de Occult. Philosoph. Lib. II. c. ii.

The *Vaticinia Pontificum* of the pseudo-Joachim long remained a popular oracle. I have met with editions of Venice issued in 1589, 1600, 1605, and 1646, of Ferrara in 1591, of Frankfort in 1608, of Padua in 1625, and of Naples in 1660, and there are doubtless numerous others.

Dante represents Bonaventura as pointing out the saints—

> "Raban è quivi, e lucemi dallato
> Il Calavrese abate Giovacchino
> Di spirito profetico dotato."—(Paradiso XII.).

were freely interpreted as referring to the carnal worldliness which pervaded all orders in the Church; all are reprobate, none are elect; Rome is the Whore of Babylon, and the papal curia the most venal and extortionate of all courts; the Roman Church is the barren fig-tree, accursed by Christ, which shall be abandoned to the nations to be stripped. It would be difficult to exaggerate the bitterness of antagonism displayed in these writings, even to the point of recognizing the empire as the instrument of God which is to overthrow the pride of the Church. These outspoken utterances of rebellion excited no little interest, especially within the Order itself. Adam de Marisco, the leading Franciscan of England, sends to his friend Grosseteste, Bishop of Lincoln, some extracts from these works which have been brought to him from Italy. He speaks of Joachim as one justly credited with divine insight into prophetic mysteries; he asks to have the fragments returned to him after copying, and meanwhile commends to the bishop's consideration the impending judgments of Providence which are invited by the abounding wickedness of the time.[*]

Of Joachim's genuine writings the one which, perhaps, attracted the most attention in his own day was a tract on the nature of the Trinity, attacking the definition of Peter Lombard, and asserting that it attributed a Quaternity to God. The subtleties of theology were dangerous, and in place of proving the Master of Sentences a heretic, Joachim himself narrowly escaped. Thirteen years after his death, the great Council of Lateran, in 1215, thought his speculation sufficiently important to condemn it as erroneous in an elaborate refutation, which was carried into the canon law, and Innocent III. preached a sermon on the subject to the assembled fathers. Fortunately Joachim, in 1200, had expressly submitted all his writings to the judgment of the Holy See and had declared that he held the same faith as that of Rome. The council, therefore, refrained from condemning him personally

---

* Pseudo-Joachim de Oneribus Ecclesiæ c. iii., xv., xvi., xvii., xx., xxi., xxii., xxiii., xxx.—Ejusd. super Hieremiam c. i., ii., iii., etc.—Salimbene p. 107.—Monumenta Franciscana p. 147 (M. R. Series).

The author of the Commentary on Jeremiah had probably been disciplined for freedom of speech in the pulpit, for (cap. i.) he denounces as bestial a license to preach which restricts the liberty of the spirit, and only permits the preacher to dispute on carnal vices.

and expressed its approbation of his Order of Flora; but notwithstanding this the monks found themselves derided and insulted as the followers of a heretic, until, in 1220, they procured from Honorius III. a bull expressly declaring that he was a good Catholic, and forbidding all detraction of his disciples.*

His most important writings, however, were his expositions of Scripture composed at the request of Lucius III., Urban III., and Clement III. Of these there were three—the Concordia, the Decachordon, or *Psalterium decem Cordarum*, and the *Expositio in Apocalypsin*. In these his system of exegesis is to find in every incident under the Old Law the prefiguration of a corresponding fact in chronological order under the New Dispensation, and by an arbitrary parallelism of dates to reach forward and ascertain what is yet to come. He thus determines that mankind is destined to live through three states—the first under the rule of the Father, which ended at the birth of Christ, the second under that of the Son, and the third under the Holy Ghost. The reign of the Son, or of the New Testament, he ascertains by varied apocalyptic speculations is to last through forty-two generations, or 1260 years—for instance, Judith remained in widowhood three years and a half, or forty-two months, which is 1260 days, the great number representing the years through which the New Testament is to endure, so that in the year 1260 the domination of the Holy Ghost is to replace it. In the forty-second generation there will be a purgation which will separate the wheat from the chaff—such tribulations as man has never yet endured: fortunately they will be short, or all flesh would perish utterly. After this, religion will be renewed; man will live in peace and justice and joy, as in the Sabbath which closed the labors of creation; all shall know God, from sea to sea, to the utmost confines of the earth, and the glory of the Holy Ghost shall be perfect. In that final abundance of spiritual grace the observances of religion will be no longer

---

* Concil. Lateran. IV. c. 2.—Theiner Monument Slavor. Meridional. I. 63.—Lib. i. Sexto, 1, 2 (Cap. *Damnamus*). — Wadding. ann. 1256, No. 8, 9. — Salimbene Chron. p. 103.

Nearly half a century later Thomas Aquinas still considered Joachim's speculations on the Trinity worthy of elaborate refutation, and near the close of the fourteenth century Eymerich reproduces the whole controversy.—Direct. Inquisit. pp. 4–6, 15–17.

requisite. As the paschal lamb was superseded by the Eucharist, so the sacrifice of the altar will become superfluous. A new monastic Order is to arise which will convert the world; contemplative monachism is the highest development of humanity, and the world will become, as it were, one vast monastery.*

In this scheme of the future elevation of man, Joachim recognized fully the evils of his time. The Church he describes as thoroughly given over to avarice and greed; wholly abandoned to the lusts of the flesh, it neglects its children, who are carried off by zealous heretics. The Church of the second state, he says, is Hagar, but that of the third state will be Sarah. With endless amplitude he illustrates the progressive character of the relations between God and man in the successive eras. The first state, under God, was of the circumcision; the second, under Christ, is of the crucifixion; the third, under the Holy Ghost, will be of quietude and peace. Under the first was the order of the married; under the second, that of the priesthood; under the third will be that of monachism, which has already had its precursor in St. Benedict. The first was the reign of Saul, the second that of David, the third will be that of Solomon enjoying the plenitude of peace. In the first, man was under the law, in the second under grace, in the third he will be under ampler grace. The people of the first state are symbolized by Zachariah the priest, those of the second by John the Baptist, those of the third by Christ himself. In the first state there was knowledge, in the second piety, in the third will be plenitude of knowledge; the first state was servitude, the second was filial obedience, the third will be liberty; the first state was passed in scourging, the second in action, the third will be in contemplation; the first was in fear, the second in faith, the third will be in love; the first was of slaves, the second of freemen, the third will be of friends; the first was of old men, the second of youths, the third will be of children; the first was starlight, the second dawn, the third will be perfect day; the first was winter, the second opening spring, the third will be summer; the first brought forth nettles, the second roses, the third will bear lilies;

---

* Joachimi Concordiæ Lib. IV. c. 31, 34, 38; Lib. V. c. 58, 63, 65, 67, 68, 74, 78, 89, 118.

Joachim was held to have predicted the rise of the Mendicants (v. 43), but his anticipations looked wholly to contemplative monachism.

the first was grass, the second grain in the ear, the third will be
the ripened wheat; the first was water, the second wine, the third
will be oil.   Finally, the first belongs to the Father, creator of all
things, the second to the Son, who assumed our mortal clay, the
third will belong to the pure Holy Spirit.*

It is a very curious fact that while Joachim's metaphysical
subtleties respecting the Trinity were ostentatiously condemned
as a dangerous heresy, no one seems at the time to have recognized
the far more perilous conclusions to be drawn from these apocalyptic reveries.   So far from being burned as heretical, they were
prized by popes, and Joachim was honored as a prophet until his
audacious imitators and followers developed the revolutionary doctrines to which they necessarily led.   To us, for the moment, their
chief significance lies in the proof which they afford that the most
pious minds confessed that Christianity was practically a failure.
Mankind had scarce grown better under the New Law.   Vices
and passions were as unchecked as they had been before the coming of the Redeemer.   The Church itself was worldly and carnal;
in place of elevating man it had been dragged down to his level;
it had proved false to its trust and was the exemplar of evil rather
than the pattern of good.   To such men as Joachim it was impossible that crime and misery should be the ultimate and irremediable condition of human life, and yet the Atonement had thus far
done little to bring it nearer to the ideal.   Christianity, therefore,
could not be a finality in man's existence upon earth; it was
merely an intermediate condition, to be followed by a further development, in which, under the rule of the Holy Ghost, the law
of love, fruitlessly inculcated by the gospel, should at last become
the dominant principle, and men, released from carnal passions,

---

* Joachimi Concordiæ Lib. I. Tract. ii. c. 6; IV. 25, 26, 33; v. 2, 21, 60, 65,
66, 84.

The Commission of Anagni in 1255 by a strained interpretation of a passage
in the Concordia (II. i. 7) accused Joachim of having justified the schism of the
Greeks (Denifle, Archiv f. Litt.- u. K. 1885, p. 120).   So far was he from this
that he never loses an occasion of decrying the Oriental Church, especially for
the marriage of its priests (e. g., v. 70, 72).   Yet when he asserted that Antichrist
was already born in Rome, and it was objected to him that Babylon was assigned
as the birthplace, he had no hesitation in saying that Rome was the mystical
Babylon.—Rad. de Coggeshall Chron. (Bouquet, XVIII. 76).

should realize the glad promises so constantly held out before them and so miserably withheld in the performance.   Joachim himself might seek to evade these deductions from his premises, yet others could not fail to make them, and nothing could be more audaciously subversive of the established spiritual and temporal order of the Church.

Yet for a time his speculations attracted little attention and no animadversion.   It is possible that the condemnation of his theory of the Trinity may have cast a shadow over his exegetical works and prevented their general dissemination, but they were treasured by kindred spirits, and copies of them were carried into various lands and carefully preserved.   Curiously enough, the first response which they elicited was from the bold heretics known as the Amaurians, whose ruthless suppression in Paris, about the year 1210, we have already considered.   Among their errors was enumerated that of the three Eras, which was evidently derived from Joachim, with the difference that the third Era had already commenced.   The power of the Father only lasted under the Mosaic Law; with the advent of Christ all the sacraments of the Old Testament were superseded.   The reign of Christ has lasted till the present time, but now commences the sovereignty of the Holy Ghost; the sacraments of the New Testament—baptism, the Eucharist, penitence, and the rest—are obsolete and to be discarded, and the power of the Holy Ghost will operate through the persons in whom it is incarnated.   The Amaurians, as we have seen, promptly disappeared, and the derivative sects—the Ortlibenses, and the Brethren of the Free Spirit—seem to have omitted this feature of the heresy.   At all events, we hear nothing more of it in that quarter.*

Gradually, however, the writings of Joachim obtained currency, and with the ascription to him of the false prophecies which appeared towards the middle of the century his name became more widely known and of greater authority.   In Provence and Languedoc, especially, his teachings found eager reception.   Harried successively by the crusades and the Inquisition, and scarce as yet fairly reunited with the Church, those regions furnished an

---

* Rigord. de Gest. Phil. Aug. ann. 1210.—Guillel. Nangiac. ann. 1210.—Cæsar. Heisterb. dist. v. c. xxii.

ample harvest of earnest minds which might well seek in the hoped-for speedy realization of Joachim's dreams compensation for the miseries of the present. Nor did those dreams lack an apostle of unquestionable orthodoxy. Hugues de Digne, a hermit of Hyères, had a wide reputation for learning, eloquence, and sanctity. He had been Franciscan Provincial of Provence, but had laid down that dignity to gratify his passion for austerity, and his sister, St. Douceline, lived in a succession of ecstasies in which she was lifted from the ground. Hugues was intimate with the leading men of the Order; Alexander Hales, Adam de Marisco, and the general, John of Parma, are named as among his close friends. With the latter, especially, he had the common bond that both were earnest Joachites. He possessed all the works of Joachim, genuine and spurious, he had the utmost confidence in their prophecies, which he regarded as divine inspiration, and he did much to extend the knowledge of them, which was not difficult, as he himself had the reputation of a prophet.[*]

The Spiritual section of the Franciscans was rapidly becoming leavened with these ideas. To minds inclined to mysticism, filled with unrest, dissatisfied with the existing unfulfilment of their ideal, and longing earnestly for its realization, there might well be an irresistible fascination in the promises of the Calabrian abbot, of which the term was now so rapidly approaching. If these Joachitic Franciscans developed the ideas of their teacher with greater boldness and definiteness, their ardor had ample excuse. They were living witnesses of the moral failure of an effort from which everything had been expected for the regeneration of humanity. They had seen how the saintly teachings of Francis and the new revelation of which he had been the medium were perverted by worldly men to purposes of ambition and greed; how the Order, which should have been the germ of human redemption, was growing more and more carnal, and how its saints were martyred by their fellows. Unless the universe were a failure, and the promises of God were lies, there must be a term to

---

[*] Salimbene Chron. pp. 97-109, 124, 318-20.—Chron. Glassberger ann. 1286. —Vie de Douceline (Meyer, Recueil d'anciens Textes, pp. 142-46).

Salimbene, in enumerating the special intimates of John of Parma, characterizes several of them as "great Joachites."

human wickedness; and as the Gospel of Christ and the Rule of Francis had not accomplished the salvation of mankind, a new gospel was indispensable. Besides, Joachim had predicted that there would arise a new religious Order which would rule the world and the Church in the halcyon age of the Holy Ghost. They could not doubt that this referred to the Franciscans as represented by the Spiritual group, which was striving to uphold in all its strictness the Rule of the venerated founder.*

Such, we may presume, were the ideas which were troubling the hearts of the earnest Spirituals as they pondered over the prophecies of Joachim. In their exaltation many of them were themselves given to ecstasies and visions full of prophetic insight. Prominent members of the Order had openly embraced the Joachitic doctrines, and his prophecies, genuine and spurious, were applied to all events as they occurred. In 1248 Salimbene, the chronicler, who was already a warm believer, met at the Franciscan convent of Provins (Champagne) two ardent condisciples, Gherardo da Borgo San Donnino and Bartolommeo Ghiscolo of Parma. St. Louis was just setting forth on his ill-starred Egyptian crusade. The Joachites had recourse to the pseudo-Joachim on Jeremiah, and foretold that the expedition would be a failure, that the king would be taken prisoner, and that pestilence would decimate the host. This was not calculated to render them popular; the peace of the good brethren was sadly broken by quarrels, and the Joachites found it advisable to depart. Salimbene went to Auxerre, Ghiscolo to Sens, and Gherardo to Paris, where his learning secured for him admission to the university as the representative of Sicily, and he obtained a chair in theology. Here for four years he pursued his apocalyptic studies.†

---

* Protocoll. Commiss. Anagniæ (Denifle, Archiv für Litteratur- und Kirchengeschichte, 1885, pp. 111–12).

† Hist. Tribulat. (ubi sup. pp. 178–9).—Salimbene, pp. 102, 233.

According to the exegesis of the Joachites, Frederic II. was to attain the age of seventy. When he died, in 1250, Salimbene refused to believe it, and remained incredulous until Innocent IV., in his triumphal progress from Lyons, came to Ferrara, nearly ten months afterwards, and exchanged congratulations upon it. Salimbene was present, and Frà Gherardino of Parma turned to him and said, "You know it now; leave your Joachim and apply yourself to wisdom" (Ib. pp. 107, 227).

Suddenly, in 1254, Paris was startled with the appearance of a book under the title of " The Everlasting Gospel "—a name derived from the Apocalypse—" And I saw another angel fly in the midst of heaven, having the everlasting gospel to preach unto them that dwell on the earth, and to every nation, and kindred, and tongue, and people " (Rev. xiv. 6). It consisted of Joachim's three undoubted works, with explanatory glosses, preceded by a long Introduction, in which the hardy author developed the ideas of the prophet audaciously and uncompromisingly. The daring venture had an immediate and immense popular success, which shows how profoundly the conviction which prompted it was shared among all classes. The rhymes of Jean de Meung indicate that the demand for it came from the laity rather than the clergy, and that it was sought by women as well as by men—

> " Ung livre de par le grant diable
> Dit l'Évangile pardurable . . .
> A Paris n'eust home ne feme
> Au parvis devant Nostre-Dame
> Qui lors avoir ne le péust
> A transcrire, s'il li pléust." *

Nothing more revolutionary in spirit, more subversive of the established order of the Church, can be conceived than the assertions which thus aroused popular sympathy and applause. Joachim's computations were accepted, and it was assumed absolutely that in six years, in 1260, the reign of Christ would end and the reign of the Holy Ghost begin. Already, in 1200, the spirit of life had abandoned the Old and New Testaments in order to give place to the Everlasting Gospel, consisting of the Concordia,

---

* Renan, Nouvelles Études, p. 296.

Joachim had already used the term Everlasting Gospel to designate the spiritual interpretation of the Evangelists, which was henceforth to rule the world. His disciple naturally considered Joachim's commentaries to be this spiritual interpretation, and that they constituted the Everlasting Gospel to which he furnished a Gloss and Introduction. The Franciscans were necessarily the contemplative Order intrusted with its dissemination. (See Denifle, Archiv für Litteratur- etc., 1885, pp. 54–59, 61.) According to Denifle (pp. 67–70) the publication of Gherardo consisted only of the Introduction and the Concordia. The Apocalypse and the Decachordon were to follow, but the venturesome enterprise was cut short.

the Expositio, and the Decachordon—the development and spiritualization of all that had preceded it. Even as Joachim had dwelt on the ascending scale of the three Eras, so the author of the Introduction characterized the progressive methods of the three Scriptures. The Old Testament is the first heaven, the New Testament the second heaven, the Everlasting Gospel the third heaven. The first is like the light of the stars, the second like that of the moon, and the third like that of the sun; the first is the porch, the second the holy place, and the third the Holy of Holies; the first is the rind, the second the nut, the third the kernel; the first is earth, the second water, the third fire; the first is literal, the second spiritual, and the third is the law promised in Jeremiah xxxi. The preaching and dissemination of this supreme and eternal law of God is committed to the barefooted Order (the Franciscans). At the threshold of the Old Law were three men, Abraham, Isaac, and Jacob: at that of the New Law were three others, Zachariah, John the Baptist, and Christ: and at that of the coming age are three, the man in linen (Joachim), the Angel with the sharp sickle, and the Angel with the sign of the living God (Francis). In the blessed coming reign of the Holy Ghost men will live under the law of love, as in the first Era they lived in fear, and in the second in grace. Joachim had argued against the continuance of the sacraments; Gherardo regarded them as symbols and enigmas, from which man would be liberated in the time to come, for love would replace all the observances founded upon the second Dispensation. This was destructive of the whole sacerdotal system, which was to be swept away and relegated to the limbo of the forgotten past; and scarce less revolutionary was his bold declaration that the Abomination of Desolation would be a pope tainted with simony, who, towards the end of the sixth age, now at hand, would obtain the papacy.*

---

* Protocol. Commiss. Anagniæ (H. Denifle Archiv für Litt.- etc., 1885, pp. 99–102, 109, 126, 135–6).

It appears to me that Father Denifle's laborious research has sufficiently proved that the errors commonly ascribed to the Everlasting Gospel (D'Argentré I. i. 162–5; Eymeric. Direct. Inq. P. ii. Q. 9; Hermann. Korneri Chron. ap. Eccard. Corp. Hist. Med. Ævi. II. 849–51) are the strongly partisan accusations sent to Rome by William of St. Amour (ubi sup. pp. 76–86) which have led to

The authorship of this bold challenge to an infallible Church was long attributed to John of Parma himself, but there would seem little doubt that it was the work of Gherardo—the outcome of his studies and reveries during the four years spent in the University of Paris, although John of Parma possibly had a hand in it. Certainly, as Tocco well points out, he at least sympathized with it, for he never punished the author, in spite of the scandal which it brought upon the Order, and Bernard Gui tells us that at the time it was commonly ascribed to him. I have already related with what joy William of Saint Amour seized upon it in the quarrel between the University and the Mendicants, and the advantage it momentarily gave the former. Under existing circumstances it could have no friends or defenders. It was too reckless an onslaught on all existing institutions, temporal and spiritual. The only thing to be done with it was to suppress it as quietly as possible. Consideration for the Franciscan Order demanded this, as well as the prudence which counselled that attention should not be unduly called to it, although hundreds of victims had been burned for heresies far less dangerous. The commission which sat at Anagni in July, 1255, for its condemnation had a task over which there could be no debate, but I have already pointed out the contrast between the reserve with which it was suppressed and the vindictive clamor with which Saint Amour's book against the Mendicants was ordered to be burned.*

---

exaggerated misconceptions of its rebellious tendencies. Father Denifle, however, proceeds to state that the result of the commission of Anagni (July, 1255) was merely the condemnation of the views of Gherardo, and that the works of Joachim (except his tract against Peter Lombard) have never been condemned by the Church. Yet when the exaggerations of William of St. Amour are thrown aside, there is in reality little in principle to distinguish Joachim from Gherardo; and if the former was not condemned it was not the fault of the Commission of Anagni, which classed both together and energetically endeavored to prove Joachim a heretic, even to showing that he never abandoned his heresy on the Trinity (ubi sup. pp. 137–41).

Yet if there was little difference in the letter, there was a marked divergence in spirit between Joachim and his commentator—the former being constructive and the latter destructive as regards the existing Church. See Tocco, Archivio Storico Italiano, 1886.

* Matt. Paris ann. 1256 (Ed. 1644, p. 632).—Salimbene, p. 102.—Bern. Guidon.

The Spiritual section of the Franciscans was fatally compromised, and the worldly party, which had impatiently borne the strict rule of John of Parma, saw its opportunity of gaining the ascendency. Led by Bernardo da Bessa, the companion of Bonaventura, formal articles of accusation were presented to Alexander IV. against the general. He was accused of listening to no explanations of the Rule and Testament, holding that the privileges and declarations of the popes were of no moment in comparison. It was not hinted that he was implicated in the Everlasting Gospel, but it was alleged that he pretended to enjoy the spirit of prophecy and that he predicted a division of the Order between those who procured papal relaxations and those who adhered to the Rule, the latter of whom would flourish under the dew of heaven and the benediction of God. Moreover, he was not orthodox, but defended the errors of Joachim concerning the Trinity, and his immediate comrades had not hesitated, in sermons and tracts, to praise Joachim immoderately and to assail the leading men of the Order. In this, as in the rest of the proceedings, the studied silence preserved as to the Everlasting Gospel shows how dangerous was the subject, and how even the fierce passions of the strife shrank from compromising the Order by admitting that any of its members were responsible for that incendiary production.*

Vit. Alex. PP. IV. (Muratori S. R. I. III. I. 593). Cf. Amalr. Auger. Vit. Alex. PP. IV. (Ib. III. II. 404).

For the authorship of the Everlasting Gospel, see Tocco, L'Heresia nel Medio Evo, pp. 473-4, and his review of Denifle and Haupt, Archivio Storico Italiano, 1886; Renan, pp. 248, 277; and Denifle, ubi sup. pp. 57-8.

One of the accusations brought against William of Saint Amour was that he complained of the delay in condemning the Everlasting Gospel, to which he replied with an allusion to the influence of those who defended the errors of Joachim.—Dupin, Bib. des Auteurs Éccles. T. X. ch. vii.

Thomas of Cantimpré assures us that Saint Amour would have won the day against the Mendicant Orders but for the learning and eloquence of Albertus Magnus.—Bonum Universale, Lib. II. c. ix.

* Wadding. ann. 1256, No. 2.—Affò (Lib. II. c. iv.) argues that John of Parma's resignation was wholly spontaneous, that there were no accusations against him, and that both the pope and the Franciscans were with difficulty persuaded to let him retire. He quotes Salimbene (Chronica p. 137) as to the reluctance of the chapter to accept his resignation, but does not allude to the assertion of the same authority that John was obnoxious to Alexander and to many of the ministers of the Order by reason of his too zealous belief in Joachim (Ib. p. 131).

Alexander was easily persuaded, and a general chapter was held in the Araceli, February 2, 1257, over which he personally presided. John of Parma was warned to resign, and did so, pleading age, weariness, and disability. After a decent show of resistance his resignation was accepted and he was asked to nominate a successor. His choice fell upon Bonaventura, then only thirty-four years of age, whose participation in the struggle with the University of Paris had marked him as the most promising man in the Order, while he was not identified with either faction. He was duly elected, and the leaders of the movement required him to proceed against John and his adherents. Bonaventura for a while hesitated, but at length consented. Gherardo refused to recant, and Bonaventura sent for him to come to Paris. In passing through Modena he met Salimbene, who had cowered before the storm and had renounced Joachitism as a folly. The two friends had a long colloquy, in which Gherardo offered to prove that Antichrist was already at hand in the person of Alonso the Wise of Castile. He was learned, pure-minded, temperate, modest, amiable—in a word, a most admirable and lovable character; but nothing could wean him from his Joachitic convictions, though in his trial discreet silence, as usual, was observed about the Everlasting Gospel, and he was condemned as an upholder of Joachim's Trinitarian speculations. Had he not been a Franciscan he would have been burned. It was a doubtful mercy which consigned him to a dungeon in chains and fed him on bread and water for eighteen years, until his weary life came to an end. He never wavered to the last, and his remains were thrust into a corner of the garden of the convent where he died. The same fate awaited his comrade Leonardo, and also another friar named Piero de' Nubili, who refused to surrender a tract of John of Parma's.*

---

* Wadding. ann. 1256, No. 3–5.—Salimbene, pp. 102, 233–6.—Hist. Tribulat. (Archiv für L. u. K. 1886, p. 285).—Although Salimbene prudently abandoned Joachitism, he never outgrew his belief in Joachim's prophetic powers. Many years later he gives as a reason for suspecting the Segarellists, that if they were of God, Joachim would have predicted them as he did the Mendicants (Ib. 123–4).

The silence of the Historia Tribulationum with respect to the Everlasting Gospel is noteworthy. By common consent that dangerous work seems to be ignored by all parties.

Then John himself was tried by a special court, to preside over which Alexander appointed Cardinal Caietano, afterwards Nicholas III.   The accused readily retracted his advocacy of Joachim, but his bearing irritated the judges, and, with Bonaventura's consent, he would have shared the fate of his associates but for the strenuous intercession of Ottoboni, Cardinal of S. Adrian, afterwards Adrian V.   Bonaventura gave him the option of selecting a place of retreat, and he chose a little convent near Rieti.   There he is said to have lived for thirty-two years the life of an angel, without abandoning his Joachitic beliefs.   John XXI., who greatly loved him, thought of making him a cardinal in 1277, but was prevented by death.   Nicholas III., who had presided at his trial, a few years later offered him the cardinalate, so as to be able to enjoy his advice, but he quietly answered, " I could give wholesome counsel if there were any one to listen to me, but in the Roman court there is little discussed but wars and triumphs, and not the salvation of souls."   In 1289, however, notwithstanding his extreme age, he accepted from Nicholas IV. a mission to the Greek Church, but he died at Camerino soon after setting out. Buried there, he speedily shone in miracles; he became the object of a lasting cult, and in 1777 he was formally beatified, in spite of the opposition arising from his alleged authorship of the Introduction to the Everlasting Gospel.*

The faith of the Joachites was by no means broken by these reverses.   William of Saint Amour thought it necessary to return to the charge with another bitter tract directed against them.   He shares their belief in the impending change, but declares that in place of being the reign of love under the Holy Ghost, it will be the reign of Antichrist, whom he identifies with the Friars.   Persecution, he says, had put an end to the open defence of the pestiferous doctrine of the Everlasting Gospel, but it still had many believers in secret.   The south of France was the headquarters of the sect.   Florent, Bishop of Acre, had been the official prosecutor before the Commission of Anagni in 1255.   He was rewarded with the archbishopric of Arles in 1262, and in 1265 he held a provin-

---

* Wadding. ann. 1256, No. 6; ann. 1289, No. 26.—Hist. Tribulat. (loc. cit. p. 285).—Salimbene Chron. pp. 131-33, 317.—Tocco, pp. 476-77.—P. Rodulphii Hist. Seraph. Relig. Lib. I. fol. 117.—Affò, Lib. III. c. x.

cial synod with the object of condemning the Joachites, who were
still numerous in his province. An elaborate refutation of the
errors of the Everlasting Gospel was deemed necessary; it was
deplored that many learned men still suffered themselves to be
misled by it, and that books containing it were written and eagerly
passed from hand to hand. The anathema was decreed against
this, but no measures of active persecution seem to have been
adopted, nor do we hear of any steps taken by the Inquisition to
suppress the heresy. As we shall see hereafter, the leaven long
remained in Languedoc and Provence, and gave a decided impress
to the Spiritual Franciscanism of those regions. It mattered little
that the hoped-for year 1260 came and passed away without the
fulfilment of the prophecy. Earnest believers can always find excuses for such errors in computation, and the period of the advent
of the Holy Ghost could be put off from time to time, so as always
to stimulate hope with the prospect of emancipation in the near
future.*

Although the removal of John of Parma from the generalate
had been the victory of the Conventuals, the choice of Bonaventura might well seem to give to the Spirituals assurance of continued supremacy. In his controversy with William of Saint
Amour he had taken the most advanced ground in denying that
Christ and the apostles held property of any kind, and in identifying poverty with perfection. " Deep poverty is laudable; this is
true of itself: therefore deeper poverty is more laudable, and the
deepest, the most laudable. But this is the poverty of him who
neither in private nor in common keeps anything for himself. . . .
To renounce all things, in private or in common, is Christian perfection, not only sufficient but abundant: it is the principal counsel of evangelical perfection, its fundamental principle and sublime
foundation." Not only this, but he was deeply imbued with mysticism and was the first to give authoritative expression to the
Illuminism which subsequently gave the Church so much trouble.

---

* Lib. de Antichristo P. I. c. x., xiii., xiv. (Martene Ampl. Coll. IX. 1273,
1313, 1325–35).—Thomæ Aquinat. Opusc. contra Impugn. Relig. c. xxiv. 5, 6.—
Concil. Arelatens. ann. 1260 (1265) c. 1 (Harduin. VII. 509–12).—Fisquet, La
France Pontificale, Métropole d'Aix, p. 577.—Renan, p. 254.

His *Mystica Theologia* is in sharp contrast to the arid scholastic theology of the day as represented by Thomas Aquinas. The soul is brought face to face with God; its sins are to be repented of in the silent watches of the night, and it is to seek God through its own efforts. It is not to look to others for aid or leadership, but, depending on itself, strive for the vision of the Divine. Through this Path of Purgation it ascends to the Path of Illumination, and is prepared for the reception of the Divine Radiance. Finally it reaches the Third Path, which leads to union with the Godhead and participation in Divine Wisdom. Molinos and Madame Guyon indulged in no more dangerous speculations; and the mystic tendencies of the Spirituals received a powerful stimulus from such teachings.*

It was inevitable that the strife within the Order between property and poverty should grow increasingly bitter. Questions were constantly arising which showed the incompatibility of the vows as laid down by St. Francis with the functions of an organization which had grown to be one of the leading factors of a wealthy and worldly Church. In 1255 we find the sisters of the monastery of St. Elizabeth complaining to Alexander IV. that when property was given or bequeathed to them the ecclesiastical authorities enforced on them the observance of the Rule, by compelling them to part with it within a year by sale or gift, and the pope graciously promised that no such custom should be enforced in future. About the same time John of Parma complained that when his friars were promoted to the episcopate they carried away with them books and other things of which they had properly only the use, being unable to own anything under peril of their souls. Again Alexander graciously replied that friars, on promotion, must deliver to the provincial everything which they had in their hands. Such troubles must have been of almost daily occurrence, and it was inevitable that the increasing friction should result in schism. When the blessed Gilio, the third disciple who joined St. Francis, was taken to Assisi to view the splendid buildings erected in honor of the humble Francis, and was carried through three magnificent churches, connected with a vast refec-

---

* S. Bonavent. de Paup. Christi Art. i. No. i., ii.—Ejusd. Mystic. Theol. cap. i. Partic. 2; cap. ii. Partic. 1, 2; Cap. iii. Partic. 1.

tory, a spacious dormitory, and other offices and cloisters, adorned
with lofty arches and spacious portals, he kept silent until one of
his guides pressed him for an expression of admiration. "Brethren," he then said, "there is nothing lacking except your wives."
This seemed somewhat irrelevant, till he explained that the vows
of poverty and chastity were equally binding, and now that one
was set aside the other might as well follow. Salimbene relates
that in the convent of Pisa he met Frà Boncampagno di Prato,
who, in place of the two new tunics per year distributed to each
of the brethren, would only accept one old one, and who declared
that he could scarce satisfy God for taking that one. Such exaggerated conscientious sensitiveness could not but be peculiarly
exasperating to the more worldly members.*

The Conventuals had lost no time in securing the results of
their victory over John of Parma. Scarce had his resignation been
secured, and before Bonaventura could arrive from Paris they
obtained from Alexander, February 20, 1257, a repetition of the
declaration of Innocent IV. which enabled the Order to handle
money and hold property through the transparent device of agents
and the Holy See. The disgust of the Puritan party was great,
and even the implicit reverence prescribed for the papacy could
not prevent ominous mutterings of disobedience, raising questions
as to the extent of the papal power to bind and to loose, which in
time were to ripen into open rebellion. The Rule had been proclaimed a revelation equal in authority to the gospel, and it might
well be asked whether even the successor of St. Peter could set it
aside. It was probably about this time that Berthold of Ratisbon,
the most celebrated Franciscan preacher of his day, in discoursing
to his brethren on the monastic state, boldly declared that the
vows of poverty, obedience, and chastity were so binding that
even the pope could not dispense for them. This, in fact, was
admitted on all sides as a truism. About 1290 the Dominican
Provincial of Germany, Hermann of Minden, in an encyclical, alludes to it as a matter of course, but in little more than a quarter
of a century we shall see that such utterances were treated as heresy, and were sternly suppressed with the stake.†

---

* Wadding. Regest. Alex. PP. IV. No. 39-41; Annal. ann. 1262, No. 36.—
Salimbene, p. 122.

† Wadding. ann. 1256, No. 4; Regest. Alex. PP. IV. No. 66.—Bertholdi a

Bonaventura, as we have seen, honestly sought to restrain the growing laxity of the Order. Before leaving Paris he addressed, April 23, 1257, an encyclical letter to the provincials, calling their attention to the prevalent vices of the brethren and the contempt to which they exposed the whole Order. Again, some ten years later, at the instance of Clement IV., he issued another similar epistle, in which he strongly expressed his horror at the neglect of the Rule shown in the shameless greed of so many members, the importunate striving for gain, the ceaseless litigation caused by their grasping after legacies and burials, and the splendor and luxury of their buildings. The provincials were instructed to put an end to these disorders by penance, imprisonment, or expulsion; but however earnest in his zeal Bonaventura may have been, and however self-denying in his own life, he lacked the fiery energy which enabled John of Parma to give effect to his convictions. How utter was the prevailing degeneracy is seen in the complaint presented in 1265 to Clement IV., that in many places the ecclesiastical authorities held that the friars, being dead to the world, were incapable of inheritance. Relief was prayed from this, and Clement issued a bull declaring them competent to inherit and free to hold their inheritances, or to sell them, and to use the property or its price as might to them seem best.*

The question of poverty evidently was one incapable of per-

Ratispona Sermones, Monachii, 1882, p. 68. — H. Denifle, Archiv für Litt.- u. Kirchengeschichte, 1886, p. 649.

To the true Franciscan the Rule and the gospel were one and the same. According to Thomas of Celano, "Il perfetto amatore dell' osservanza del santo vangelio e della professione della nostra regola, che non è altro che perfetta osservanza del vangelio, questo [Francesco] ardentissimamente amava, e quelli che sono e saranno veri amatori, donò a essi singular benedizione. Veramente, dicea, questa nostra professione a quelli che la seguitano, esser libro di vita, speranza di salute, arra di gloria, melodia del vangelio, via di croce, stato di perfezione, chiave di paradiso, e patto di eterna pace."—Amoni, Legenda S. Francisci, App. c. xxix.

* S. Bonavent. Opp. I. 485-6 (Ed. 1584).—Wadding. ann. 1257, No. 9; Regest. Clem. PP. IV. No. I.

Pierre Jean Olivi states that he himself heard Bonaventura declare in a chapter held in Paris that he would, at any moment, submit to be ground to powder if it would bring the Order back to the condition designed by St. Francis.— Franz Ehrle, Archiv für L. u. K. 1887, p. 517.

manent and satisfactory settlement.   Dissension in the Order
could not be healed.   In vain Gregory X., about 1275, was appealed to, and decided that the injunction of the Rule against the
possession of property, individually or in common, was to be strictly observed.   The worldly party continued to point out the in-
compatibility of this with the necessities of human nature; they
declared it to be a tempting of God and a suicide of the individual; the quarrel continually grew more bitterly envenomed, and
in 1279 Nicholas III. undertook to settle it with a formal declaration which should forever close the mouths of all cavillers.   For
two months he secretly labored at it in consultation with the two
Franciscan cardinals, Palestrina and Albano, the general, Bonagrazia, and some of the provincials.   Then it was submitted to a
commission in which was Benedetto Caietano, afterwards Boniface VIII.   Finally it was read and adopted in full consistory,
and it was included, twenty years later, in the additions to the
canon law compiled and published by order of Boniface.   No utterance of the Holy See could have more careful consideration
and more solemn authority than the bull known as *Exiit qui seminat*, which was thus ushered into the world, and which subsequently became the subject of such deadly controversy.*

It declares the Franciscan Rule to be the inspiration of the
Holy Ghost through St. Francis.   The renunciation of property,
not only individual but in common, is meritorious and holy.   Such
absolute renunciation of possession had been practised by Christ
and the apostles, and had been taught by them to their disciples;
it is not only meritorious and perfect, but lawful and possible, for
there is a distinction between use, which is permitted, and ownership, which is forbidden.   Following the example of Innocent IV.
and Alexander IV., the proprietorship of all that the Franciscans
use is declared to be vested, now and hereafter, in the Roman
Church and pontiff, which concede to the friars the usufruct
thereof.   The prohibition to receive and handle money is to be
enforced, and borrowing is especially deprecated; but, when necessity obliges, this may be effected through third parties, although
the brethren must abstain from handling the money or administering or expending it.   As for legacies, they must not be left

---

* Lib. v. Sexto xii. 3.—Wadding. ann. 1279, No. 11.

directly to the friars, but only for their use; and minute regulations are drawn up for exchanging or selling books and utensils. The bull concludes with instructions that it is to be read and taught in the schools, but no one, under pain of excommunication and loss of office and benefice, shall do anything but expound it literally—it is not to be glossed or commented upon, or discussed, or explained away. All doubts and questions shall be submitted directly to the Holy See, and any one disputing or commenting on the Franciscan Rule or the definitions of the bull shall undergo excommunication, removable only by the pope.

Had the question been capable of permanent settlement in this sense, this solemn utterance would have put an end to further trouble. Unluckily, human nature did not cease to be human nature, with its passions and necessities, on crossing the threshold of a Franciscan convent. Unluckily, papal constitutions were as cobwebs when they sought to control the ineradicable vices and weakness of man. Unluckily, moreover, there were consciences too sensitive to be satisfied with fine-drawn distinctions and subtleties ingeniously devised to evade the truth. Yet the bull *Exiit qui seminat* for a while relieved the papacy from further discussion, although it could not quiet the intestine dissensions of the Order. There was still a body of recalcitrants, not numerous, it is true, but eminent for the piety and virtue of its members, which could not be reconciled by these subterfuges. These recalcitrants gradually formed themselves into two distinct bodies, one in Italy, and the other in southern France. At first there is little to distinguish them apart, and for a long while they acted in unison, but there gradually arose a divergence between them, which in the end became decisively marked, owing to the greater influence exercised in Languedoc and Provence by the traditions of Joachim and the Everlasting Gospel.

We have seen how the thirst for ascetic poverty, coupled in many cases, doubtless, with the desire to escape from the sordid cares of daily life, led thousands to embrace a career of wandering mendicancy. Sarabites and *circumcelliones*—vagrant monks, subjected to no rule—had been the curse of the Church ever since the invention of cenobitism; and the exaltation of poverty in the thirteenth century had given a new impulse to the crowds who

preferred the idleness of the road or of the hermitage to the re-
straints and labor of civilized existence. It was in vain that the
Lateran Council had prohibited the formation of new and unauthorized Orders. The splendid success of the Mendicants had
proved too alluring, and others were formed on the same basis,
without the requisite preliminary of the papal approval. The
multitudes of holy beggars were becoming a serious nuisance, oppressive to the people and disgraceful to the Church. When Gregory X. summoned the General Council of Lyons, in 1274, this was
one of the evils to be remedied. The Lateran canon prohibiting
the formation of unauthorized Orders was renewed. Gregory proposed to suppress all the congregations of hermits, but, at the instance of Cardinal Richard, the Carmelites and Augustinians were
allowed to exist on sufferance until further order, while the audacity of other associations, not as yet approved, was condemned,
especially that of the mendicants, whose multitude was declared
to exceed all bounds. Such mendicant Orders as had been confirmed since the Council of Lateran were permitted to continue,
but they were instructed to admit no new members, to acquire no
new houses, and not to sell what they possessed without special
license from the Holy See. Evidently it was felt that the time
had come for decisive measures to check the tide of saintly mendicancy.*

Some vague and incorrect rumors of this legislation penetrating to Italy, led to an explosion which started one of the most
extraordinary series of persecutions which the history of human
perversity affords. On the one hand there is the marvellous constancy which endured lifelong martyrdom for an idea almost unintelligible to the modern mind; on the other there is the seemingly causeless ferocity, which appears to persecute for the mere
pleasure of persecution, only to be explained by the bitterness of
the feuds existing within the Order, and the savage determination
to enforce submission at every cost.

It was reported that the Council of Lyons had decreed that
the Mendicants could hold property. Most of the brethren acquiesced readily enough, but those who regarded the Rule as divine
revelation, not to be tampered with by any earthly authority, de-

---

* Concil. Lugdunens. II. c. 23 (Harduin. VII. 715).—Salimbene, pp. 110–11.

clared that it would be apostasy, and a thing not to be admitted under any circumstances. Several disputations were held which only confirmed each side in its views. One point which gave rise to peculiar animosity was the refusal of the Spirituals to take their turns in the daily rounds in quest of moneyed alms, which had grown to be the custom in most places; and it is easy to imagine the bitter antagonism to which this disobedience must have led. It shows how strained were the relations between the factions that proceedings for heresy were forthwith commenced against these zealots. The rumor proved false, the excitement died away, and the prosecutions were allowed to slumber for a few years, when they were revived through fear that these extreme opinions, if left unpunished, might win over the majority. Liberato da Macerata, Angelo da Cingoli (il Clareno), Traymondo, Tommaso da Tollentino, and one or two others whose names have not reached us were the obdurate ones who would make no concession, even in theory. Angelo, to whom we owe an account of the matter, declared that they were ready to render implicit obedience, that no offence was proved against them, but that nevertheless they were condemned, as schismatics and heretics, to perpetual imprisonment in chains. The sentence was inhumanly harsh. They were to be deprived of the sacraments, even upon the death-bed, thus killing soul as well as body; during life no one was to speak with them, not even the jailer who brought the daily pittance of bread and water to their cells, and examined their fetters to see that they were attempting no escape. As a warning, moreover, the sentence was ordered to be read weekly in all the chapters, and no one was to presume to criticise it as unjust. This was no idle threat, for when Friar Tommaso da Casteldemilio heard it read and said it was displeasing to God, he was cast into a similar prison, where he rotted to death in a few months. The fierce spirits in control of the Order were evidently determined that at least the vow of obedience should be maintained.*

---

* Angel. Clarinens. Epist. Excusat. (Archiv für Litt.- u. Kirchengeschichte, 1885, pp. 523–4).—Histor. Tribulation. (Ibid. 1886, pp. 302–4).—Ubertini Responsio (Ibid. 1887, p. 68). — Cf. Rodulphii Hist. Seraph. Relig. Lib. ii. fol. 180.

For the first time the development and history of the Spiritual Franciscans can now be traced with some accuracy, thanks to Franz Ehrle, S. J., who has

The prisoners seem to have lain in jail until after the election to the generalate of Raymond Gaufridi, at Easter, 1289. Visiting the Mark of Ancona, where they were incarcerated, he investigated the case, blamed severely the perpetrators of the injustice, and set the martyrs free in 1290. The Order had been growing more lax in its observance than ever, in spite of the bull *Exiit qui seminat.* Matteo d'Acquasparta, who was general from 1287 to 1289, was easy and kindly, well-intentioned but given to self-indulgence, and by no means inclined to the effort requisite to enforce the Rule. Respect for it, indeed, was daily diminishing. Coffers were placed in the churches to receive offerings; bargains were made as to the price of masses and for the absolution of sinners; boys were stationed at the church-doors to sell wax tapers in honor of saints; the Friars habitually begged money in the streets, accompanied by boys to receive and carry it; the sepulture of the rich was eagerly sought for, leading to disgraceful quarrels with the heirs and with the secular clergy. Everywhere there was self-seeking and desire for the enjoyment of an idle and luxurious life. It is true that lapses of the flesh were still rigidly punished, but these cases were sufficiently frequent to show that ample cause for scandal arose from the forbidden familiarity with women which the brethren permitted themselves. So utter was the general demoralization that Nicholas, the Provincial of France, even dared to write a tract calling in question the bull *Exiit qui seminat* and its exposition of the Rule. As this was in direct contravention of the bull itself, Acquasparta felt compelled to condemn the work and to punish its author and his supporters, but the evil continued to work. In the Mark of Ancona and in some other places the reaction against asceticism was so strong that the Testament of the revered Francis was officially ordered to be burned. It was the main bulwark of the Spirituals against relaxation of the Rule, and in one instance it was actually burned on the head of a friar, N. de Recanate, who presumably had made himself obnoxious by insisting on its authority.*

---

printed the most important documents relating to this schism in the Order, elucidated with all the resources of exact research. My numerous references to his papers show the extent of my indebtedness to his labors.

* Histor. Tribulat. (loc. cit. 1886, p. 305). — Ubertin/ Responsio (Ibid. 1887, pp. 69, 77).—Articuli Transgressionum (Ibid. 1887, pp. 105–7).—Wadding. ann.

Raymond Gaufridi was earnestly desirous of restoring discipline, but the relaxation of the Order had grown past curing. His release of the Spirituals at Ancona caused much murmuring; he was ridiculed as a patron of fantastic and superstitious men, and conspiracies were set on foot which never ceased till his removal was effected in 1295. It was perhaps to conjure these attempts that he sent Liberato, Angelo, Tommaso, and two kindred spirits named Marco and Piero to Armenia, where they induced King Haito II. to enter the Franciscan Order, and won from him the warmest eulogies. Even in the East, however, the hatred of their fellow-missionaries was so earnest and so demonstrative that they were forced to return in 1293. On their arrival in Italy the provincial, Monaldo, refused to receive them or to allow them to remain until they could communicate with Raymond, declaring that he would rather entertain fornicators.*

The unreasoning wrath which insisted on these votaries of poverty violating their convictions received a check when, in 1294, the choice of the exhausted conclave fell by chance on the hermit Pier Morrone, who suddenly found his mountain burrow transformed into the papal palace. Celestin V. preserved in St. Peter's chair the predilection for solitude and maceration which had led him to the life of the anchorite. To him Raymond referred the Spirituals, whom he seemed unable to protect. Celestin listened to them kindly and invited them to enter his special Order—the Celestinian Benedictines—but they explained to him the difference of their vows, and how their brethren detested the observance of the Rule. Then in public audience he ordered them to observe strictly the Rule and Testament of Francis; he released them from obedience to all except himself and to Liberato, whom he made their chief; Cardinal Napoleone Orsini was declared their protector, and the abbot of the Celestinians was ordered to provide

---

1289, No. 22–3.—Ubertini Declaratio (Archiv, 1887, pp. 168–9).—Dante contrasts Acquasparta with Ubertino da Casale, of whom we shall see more presently—

"Ma non sia da Casal ne d'Acquasparta
La onde vegnon tali alla Scrittura
Ch' uno la fugge e l'altro la coarta."—(Paradiso XII.).

* Hist. Tribulat. (loc. cit. 1886, pp. 306–8).—Angel. Clarinens. Epist. (Ibid. 1885, pp. 524–5).—Wadding. ann. 1292, No. 14.

them with hermitages. Thus they were fairly out of the Order; they were not even to call themselves Minorites or Franciscans, and it might be supposed that their brethren would be as glad to get rid of them and their assumption of superior sanctity as they were to escape from oppression.*

Yet the hatred provoked by the quarrel was too deep and bitter to spare its victims, and the breathing-space which they enjoyed was short. Celestin's pontificate came to an abrupt termination. Utterly unfitted for his position, speedily made the tool of designing men, and growing weary of the load which he felt himself unable to endure, after less than six months he was persuaded to abdicate, in December, 1294, and was promptly thrown into prison by his successor, Boniface VIII., for fear that he might be led to reconsider an abdication the legality of which might be questioned. All of Celestin's acts and grants were forthwith annulled, and so complete was the obliteration of everything that he had done, that even the appointment of a notary is found to require confirmation and a fresh commission. Boniface's contempt for the unworldly enthusiasm of asceticism did not lead him to make any exception in favor of the Spirituals. To him the Franciscan Order was merely an instrument for the furtherance of his ambitious schemes, and its worldliness was rather to be stimulated than repressed. Though he placed in his Sixth Book of Decretals the bull *Exiit qui seminat*, his practical exposition of its provisions is seen in two bulls issued July 17, 1296, by one of which he assigns to the Franciscans of Paris one thousand marks, to be taken from the legacies for pious uses, and by the other he converts to them a legacy of three hundred livres bequeathed by Ada, lady of Pernes, for the benefit of the Holy Land. Under such auspices the degradation of the Order could not but be rapid. Before his first year was out, Boniface had determined upon the removal of the general, Raymond. October 29, 1295, he offered the latter the bishopric of Pavia, and on his protesting that he had not strength for the burden, Boniface said that he could not be fit for the heavier load of the generalate, of which he relieved him on the spot. We can understand the insolence which led a party of the

---

* Angel. Clarin. Epist. (op. cit. 1885, p. 526); Hist. Tribulationum (Ib. 1886, pp. 308-9).

Conventual faction to visit Celestin in his prison and taunt and insult him for the favor which he had shown to the Spirituals. A prosecution for heresy which Boniface ordered, in March, 1295, against Frà Pagano di Pietra-Santa was doubtless instigated by the same spirit.*

More than this. To Boniface's worldly, practical mind the hordes of wandering mendicants, subjected to no authority, were an intolerable nuisance, whether it arose from ill-regulated asceticism or idle vagabondage. The decree of the Council of Lyons had failed to suppress the evil, and, in 1496 and 1497, Boniface issued instructions to all bishops to compel such wanderers or hermits, popularly known as Bizochi, either to lay aside their fictitious religious habits and give up their mode of life, or to betake themselves to some authorized Order. The inquisitors were instructed to denounce to the bishops all suspected persons, and if the prelates were remiss, to report them to the Holy See. One remarkable clause gives special authority to the inquisitors to prosecute such of these Bizochi as may be members of their own Orders, thus showing that there was no heresy involved, as otherwise the inquisitors would have required no additional powers.†

The following year Boniface proceeded to more active measures. He ordered the Franciscan, Matteo da Chieti, Inquisitor of Assisi, to visit personally the mountains of the Abruzzi and Mark of Ancona and to drive from their lurking-places the apostates from various religious Orders and the Bizochi who infested those regions. His previous steps had probably been ineffective, and possibly also he may have been moved to more decisive action by the rebellious attitude of the Spirituals and proscribed mendicants. Not only did they question the papal authority, but they were beginning to argue that the papacy itself was vacant. So far from being content with the bull *Exiit qui seminat*, they held that its author, Nicholas III., had been deprived by God of the papal functions, and consequently that he had had no legitimate successors. Thereafter there had been no true ordinations of priest and prelate, and the real Church consisted in themselves alone. To rem-

---

* Hist. Tribulat. (loc. cit. 1886, pp. 309–10).—Faucon et Thomas, Registres de Boniface VIII. No. 37, 1232, 1233, 1292, 1825.—Wadding. ann. 1295, No. 14.

† Franz Ehrle, Archiv für L. u. K. 1886, pp. 157–8.

edy this, Frère Matthieu de Bodici came from Provence, bringing
with him the books of Pierre Jean Olivi, and in the Church of St.
Peter in Rome he was elected pope by five Spirituals and thirteen
women. Boniface promptly put the Inquisition on their track,
but they fled to Sicily, which, as we shall see, subsequently became the headquarters of the sect.*

Friar Jordan, to whom we are indebted for these details, assumes that Liberato and his associates were concerned in this
movement. The dates and order of events are hopelessly confused, but it would rather seem that the section of the Spirituals
represented by Liberato kept themselves aloof from all such revolutionary projects. Their sufferings were real and prolonged, but
had they been guilty of participating in the election of an antipope they would have had but the choice between perpetual imprisonment and the stake. They were accused of holding that
Boniface was not a lawful pope, that the authority of the Church
was vested in themselves alone, and that the Greek Church was
preferable to the Latin—in other words of Joachitism—but Angelo
declares emphatically that all this was untrue, and his constancy
of endurance during fifty years of persecution and suffering entitles his assertion to respect. He relates that after their authorization by Celestin V. they lived as hermits in accordance with the
papal concession, sojourning as paupers and strangers wherever
they could find a place of retreat, and strictly abstaining from
preaching and hearing confessions, except when ordered to do so
by bishops to whom they owed obedience. Even before the resignation of Celestin, the Franciscan authorities, irritated at the escape of their victims, disregarded the papal authority and endeavored with an armed force to capture them. Celestin himself
seems to have given them warning of this, and the zealots, recognizing that there was no peace for them in Italy, resolved to ex-
patriate themselves and seek some remote spot where they could
gratify their ascetic longings and worship God without human

---

* Raynald. ann. 1297, No. 55.—Jordani Chron. cap. 236, Partic. 3 (Muratori,
Antiq XI. 766).

So far was Pierre Jean Olivi from participating in these rebellious movements
that he wrote a tract to prove the legality of Celestin's abdication and Boniface's
succession (Franz Ehrle, Archiv f. L. u. K. 1887, p. 525).

interference. They crossed the Adriatic and settled on a desert island off the Achaian coast. Here, lost to view, they for two years enjoyed the only period of peace in their agitated lives; but at length news of their place of retreat reached home, and forthwith letters were despatched to the nobles and bishops of the mainland accusing them of being Cathari, while Boniface was informed that they did not regard him as pope, but held themselves to be the only true Church. In 1299 he commissioned Peter, Patriarch of Constantinople, to try them, when they were condemned without a hearing, and he ordered Charles II. of Naples, who was overlord of the Morea, to have them expelled, an order which Charles transmitted to Isabelle de Villehardouin, Princess of Achaia. Meanwhile the local authorities had recognized the falsity of the accusations, for the refugees celebrated mass daily and prayed for Boniface as pope, and were willing to eat meat, but this did not relieve them from surveillance and annoyance, one of their principal persecutors being a certain Geronimo, who came to them with some books of Olivi's, and whom they were forced to eject for immorality, after which he turned accuser and was rewarded with the episcopate.*

The pressure became too strong, and the little community gradually broke up. An intention to accompany Frà Giovanni da Monte on a mission to Tartary had to be abandoned on account of the excommunication consequent upon the sentence uttered by the Patriarch of Constantinople. Liberato sent two brethren to appeal to Boniface, and then two more, but they were all seized and prevented from reaching him. Then Liberato himself departed secretly and reached Perugia, but the sudden death of Boniface (October 11, 1303) frustrated his object. The rest returned at various times, Angelo being the last to reach Italy, in 1305. He found his brethren in evil plight. They had been cited by the Dominican inquisitor, Tommaso di Aversa, and had obediently presented themselves. At first the result was favorable. After an examination lasting several days, Tommaso pronounced them

---

* Angel. Clarin. Epist. (Archiv für Litt.- u. Kirchengeschichte, 1885, pp. 522–3, 527–9).—Hist. Tribulat. (Ibid. 1886, pp. 314–18).—Franz Ehrle (Ibid. 1886, p. 335.

Franz Ehrle identifies the refuge of the Spirituals with the island of Trixonia in the Gulf of Corinth (Ibid. 1886, pp. 313–14).

orthodox, and dismissed them, saying publicly, " Frà Liberato, 1 swear by Him who created me that never the flesh of a poor man could be sold for such a price as I could get for yours. Your brethren would drink your blood if they could." He even conducted them in safety back to their hermitages, and when the rage of the Conventuals was found to be unappeasable he gave them the advice that they should leave the kingdom of Naples that night and travel by hidden ways to the pope ; if they could bring letters from the latter, or from a cardinal, he would defend them as long as he held the office. The advice was taken ; Liberato left Naples that night, but fell sick on the road and died after a lingering illness of two years. Meanwhile, as we shall see hereafter, the exploits of Dolcino in Lombardy were exciting general terror, which rendered all irregular fraternities the object of suspicion and dread. The Conventuals took advantage of this and incited Frà Tommaso to summon before him all who wore unauthorized religious habits. The Spirituals were cited again, to the number of forty-two, and this time they did not escape so easily. They were condemned as heretics, and when Andrea da Segna, under whose protection they had lived, interposed in their favor, Tommaso carried them to Trivento, where they were tortured for five days. This excited the compassion of the bishop and nobles of the town, so they were transferred to Castro Mainardo, a solitary spot, where for five months they were afflicted with the sharpest torments. Two of the younger brethren yielded and accused themselves and their comrades, but revoked when released. Some of them died, and finally the survivors were ordered to be scourged naked through the streets of Naples and were banished the kingdom, although no specific heresy was alleged against them in the sentence. Through all this the resolution of the little band never faltered. Convinced that they alone were on the path of salvation, they would not be forced back into the Order. On the death of Liberato, Angelo was chosen as their leader, and amid persecution and obloquy they formed a congregation in the Mark of Ancona, known as the Clareni, from the surname of their chief, and under the protection of the cardinal, Napoleone Orsini.[*]

---

[*] Angel. Clarin. Epist. (op. cit. 1885, 529–31).—Hist. Tribulat. (Ib. 1886, 320–6).—Wadding. ann. 1302, No. 8 ; 1307, No. 2–4.

This group had not been by any means alone in opposing the laxity of the Conventuals, although it was the only one which succeeded in throwing off the yoke of its opponents. The Spirituals were numerous in the Order, but the policy of Boniface VIII. led him to support the efforts of the Conventuals to keep them in subjection. Jacopone da Todi, the author of the Stabat Mater, was perhaps the most prominent of these, and his savage verses directed against the pope did not tend to harmonize the troubles. After the capture of Palestrina, in 1298, Boniface threw him into a foul dungeon, where he solaced his captivity with canticles full of the mystic ardor of divine love. It is related that Boniface once, passing the grating of his cell, jeeringly called to him, "Jacopo, when will you get out?" and was promptly answered, "When you come in." In a sense the prophecy proved true, for one of the first acts of Benedict XI., in December, 1303, was to release Jacopone from both prison and excommunication.[*]

Frà Corrado da Offida was another prominent member of the Spiritual group. He had been a friend of John of Parma; for fifty-five years he wore but a single gown, patched and repatched as necessity required, and this with his rope girdle constituted his sole worldly possessions. In the mystic exaltation which characterized the sect he had frequent visions and ecstasies, in which he was lifted from the ground after the fashion of the saints. When Liberato and his companions were in their Achaian refuge he designed joining them with Jacopo de' Monti and others, but the execution of the project was in some way prevented.[†]

---

[*] Cantù, Eretici d' Italia, I. 129.—Comba, La Riforma in Italia, I. 314.

A specimen of Jacopone's attacks on Boniface will show the temper of the times—

"Ponesti la tua lingua
Contra religione
A dir blasfemia
Senza niun cagione.

O pessima avarizia
Sete induplicata,
Bever tanta pecunia
E non esser saziata!"

(Comba, op. cit. 312.)

There is doubtless foundation for the story related by Savonarola in a sermon, that Jacopone was once brought into the consistory of cardinals and requested to preach, when he solemnly repeated thrice, "I wonder that in consequence of your sins the earth does not open and swallow you."—Villari, Frà Savonarola, II. Ed. T. II. p. 3.

[†] Hist. Tribulat. (loc. cit. pp. 311–13).

Such men, filled with the profoundest conviction of their holy calling, were not to be controlled by either kindness or severity. It was in vain that the general, Giovanni di Murro, at the chapter of 1302, held in Genoa, issued a precept deploring the abandonment, by the Order, of holy poverty, as shown by the possession of lands and farms and vineyards, and the assumption by friars of duties which involved them in worldly cares and strife and litigation. He ordered the sale of all property, and forbade the members of the Order from appearing in any court. Yet while he was thus rigid as to the ownership of property, he was lax as to its use, and condemned as pernicious the doctrine that the vow of poverty involved restriction in its enjoyment. He was, moreover, resolved on extinguishing the schism in the Order, and his influence with Boniface was one of the impelling causes of the continued persecution of the Spirituals. They stubbornly rejected all attempts at reconciliation, and placed a true estimate on these efforts of reform. Before the year was out Giovanni was created Cardinal Bishop of Porto, and was allowed to govern the Order through a vicar; the reforms were partially enforced in some provinces for a short time; then they fell into desuetude, and matters went on as before.*

In France, where the influence of Joachim and the Everlasting Gospel was much more lasting and pronounced than in Italy, the career of the Spirituals revolves around one of the most remarkable personages of the period—Pierre Jean Olivi. Born in 1247, he was placed in the Franciscan Order at the age of twelve, and was trained in the University of Paris, where he obtained the baccalaureate. His grave demeanor, seasoned with a lively wit, his irreproachable morals, his fervid eloquence, and the extent of his learning won for him universal respect, while his piety, gentleness, humility, and zeal for holy poverty gained for him a reputation for sanctity which assigned to him the gift of prophecy. That such a man should attach himself to the Spirituals was a matter of course, and equally so was the enmity which he excited by unsparing reproof of the laxity of observance into which the Order had declined. In his voluminous writings he taught that absolute

---

* Wadding. ann. 1302, No. 1-3, 7; ann. 1310, No. 9.—Franz Ehrle (Archiv für Litt.- u. K. 1886, p. 385).

poverty is the source of all the virtues and of a saintly life; that
the Rule prohibited all proprietorship, whether individual or in common, and that the vow bound the members to the most sparing use
of all necessaries, the meanest garments, the absence of shoes, etc.,
while the pope had no power to dispense or absolve, and much less
to order anything contrary to the Rule. The convent of Béziers,
to which he belonged, became the centre of the Spiritual sect, and
the devotion which he excited was shared by the population at
large, as well as by his brethren. The temper of the man was
shown when he underwent his first rebuke. In 1278 some writings
of his in praise of the Virgin were considered to trench too closely on Mariolatry. The Order had not yet committed itself to
this, and complaint was made to the general, Geronimo d'Ascoli,
afterwards Nicholas IV., who read the tracts and condemned him
to burn them with his own hands. Olivi at once obeyed without
any sign of perturbation, and when his wondering brethren asked
how he could endure such mortification so tranquilly, he replied
that he had performed the sacrifice with a thoroughly placid mind;
he had not felt more pleasure in writing the tracts than in burning them at the command of his superior, and the loss was nothing, for if necessary he could easily write them again in better
shape. A man so self-centred and imperturbable could not fail to
impress his convictions on those who surrounded him.*

What his convictions really were is a problem not easily solved
at the present day. The fierce antagonisms which he excited by
his fiery onslaughts on individuals as well as on the general laxity
of the Order at large, caused his later years to be passed in a series
of investigations for heresy. At the general chapter of Strassburg, in 1282, his writings were ordered to be examined. In 1283
Bonagrazia di S. Giovanni, the general, came to France, collected
and placed them all in the hands of seven of the leading members of
the Order, who found in them propositions which they variously

---

* Wadding. ann. 1278, No. 27-8.—Franz Ehrle, Archiv f. L. u. K. 1887, pp.
505-11, 528-9.

When Geronimo d'Ascoli attained the papacy he was urged to prosecute Olivi,
but refused, expressing the highest consideration for his talents and piety, and
declaring that his rebuke had been merely intended as a warning (Hist. Trib.
loc. cit. 1886, p. 289).

characterized as false, heretical, presumptuous, and dangerous, and
ordered the tracts containing them to be surrendered by all possessing them.   Olivi subscribed to the judgment in 1284, although
he complained that he had not been permitted to appear in person
before his judges and explain the censured passages, to which
distorted meanings had been applied.   With some difficulty he
procured copies of his inculpated writings and proceeded to justify himself.   Still the circle of his disciples continued to increase;
incapable of the self-restraint of their master, and secretly imbued
with Joachitic doctrines, they were not content with the quiet
propagation of their principles, but excited tumults and seditions.
Olivi was held responsible.   The chapter held at Milan in 1285
elected as general minister Arlotto di Prato, one of the seven who
had condemned him, and issued a decree ordering a strict perqui-
sition and seizure of his writings.   The new general, moreover,
summoned him to Paris for another inquisition into his faith,
of which the promoters were two of the members of the previous
commission, Richard Middleton and Giovanni di Murro, the future
general.   The matter was prolonged until 1286, when Arlotto
died, and nothing was done.   Matteo d'Acquasparta vouched for
his orthodoxy in appointing him teacher in the general school of
the Order at Florence.   Raymond Gaufridi, who succeeded Matteo
d'Acquasparta in 1290, was a friend and admirer of Olivi, but could
not prevent fresh proceedings, though he appointed him teacher
at Montpellier.   Excitement in Languedoc had reached a point
which led Nicholas IV., in 1290, to order Raymond to suppress
the disturbers of the peace.   He commissioned Bertrand de Cigotier, Inquisitor of the Comtat Venaissin, to investigate and report,
in order that the matter might be brought before the next general chapter, to be held in Paris.   In 1292, accordingly, Olivi appeared before the chapter, professed his acceptance of the bull
Exiit qui seminat, asserted that he had never intentionally taught
or written otherwise, and revoked and abjured anything that he
might inadvertently have said in contradiction of it.   He was dismissed in peace, but twenty-nine of his zealous and headstrong
followers, whom Bertrand de Cigotier had found guilty, were duly
punished.   His few remaining years seem to have passed in comparative peace.   Two letters written in 1295, one to Corrado da
Offida and the other to the sons of Charles II. of Naples, then

held as hostages in Catalonia, who had asked him to visit them, show that he was held in high esteem, that he desired to curb the fanatic zeal of the more advanced Spirituals, and that he could not restrain himself from apocalyptic speculation. On his deathbed, in 1298, he uttered a confession of faith in which he professed absolute submission to the Roman Church and to Boniface as its head. He also submitted all his works to the Holy See, and made a declaration of principles as to the matters in dispute within the Order, which contained nothing that Bonaventura would not have signed, or Nicholas III. would have impugned as contrary to the bull *Exiit*, although it sharply rebuked the money-getting practices and relaxation of the Order.*

He was honorably buried at Narbonne, and then the controversy over his memory became more lively than ever, rendering it almost impossible to determine his responsibility for the opinions which were ascribed to him by both friends and foes. That his bones became the object of assiduous cult, in spite of repeated prohibitions, that innumerable miracles were worked at his tomb, that crowds of pilgrims flocked to it, that his feast-day became one of the great solemnities of the year, and that he was regarded as one of the most efficient saints in the calendar, only shows the popular estimate of his virtues and the zeal of those who regarded

---

* Wadding. ann. 1282, No. 2; ann. 1283, No. 1; ann. 1285, No. 5; ann. 1290, No. 11; ann. 1292, No. 13; ann. 1297, No. 33–4.—Chron. Glassberger ann. 1283.— Hist. Tribulat. (loc. cit. pp. 294–5).—Franz Ehrle, Archiv, 1886, pp. 383, 389; 1887, pp. 417–27, 429, 433, 438, 534.—Raym. de Fronciacho (Archiv, 1887, p. 15).

Olivi's death is commonly assigned to 1297, but the *Transitus Sancti Patris*, which was one of the books most in vogue among his disciples, states that it occurred on Friday, March 14, 1297 (Bernard. Guidon. Practica P. v.); Friday fell on March 14 in 1298, and the common habit of commencing the year with Easter explains the substitution of 1297 for 1298.

His bones are generally said to have been dug up and burned a few months after interment, by order of the general, Giovanni di Murro (Tocco, op. cit. p. 503). Wadding, indeed, asserts that they were twice exhumed (ann. 1297, No. 36). Eymerich mentions a tradition that they were carried to Avignon and thrown by night into the Rhone (Eymerici Direct. Inquis. p. 313). The cult of which they were the object shows that this could not have been the case, and Bernard Gui, the best possible authority, in commenting on the *Transitus* states that they were abstracted in 1318 and hidden no one knows where—doubtless by disciples to prevent the impending profanation of exhumation.

themselves as his disciples.   Certain it is that the Council of Vienne,
in 1312, treated his memory with great gentleness.   While it condemned with merciless severity the mystic extravagances of the
Brethren of the Free Spirit, it found only four errors to note in
the voluminous writings of Olivi—errors of merely speculative interest, such as are frequent among the schoolmen of the period—
and these it pointed out without attributing them to him or even
mentioning his name.   These his immediate followers denied his
holding, although eventually one of them, curiously enough, became a sort of shibboleth among the Olivists.   It was that Christ
was still alive on the cross when pierced by the lance, and was
based on the assertion that the relation in Matthew originally differed in this respect from that in John, and had been altered to
secure harmony.   All other questions relating to the teachings of
Olivi the council referred to the Franciscans for settlement, showing that they were deemed of minor importance, after they had
been exhaustively debated before it by Bonagrazia da Bergamo in
attack and Ubertino da Casale in defence.   Thus the council condemned neither his person nor his writings; that the result was
held as vindicating his orthodoxy was seen when, in 1313, his feast-
day was celebrated with unexampled enthusiasm at Narbonne, and
was attended by a concourse equal to that which assembled at the
anniversary of the Portiuncula.   Moreover, after the heat of the
controversy had passed away, the subsequent condemnation of his
writings by John XXII. was removed by Sixtus IV., towards the
end of the fifteenth century.   Olivi's teachings may therefore fairly
be concluded to have contained no very revolutionary doctrines.
In fact, shortly after his death all the Franciscans of Provence
were required to sign an abjuration of his errors, among which
was enumerated the one respecting the wound of Christ, but nothing was said respecting the graver aberrations subsequently attributed to him.*

---

* Wadding. ann. 1291, No. 13; 1297, No. 35; 1312, No. 4.—Lib. Sententt.
Inq. Tolos. pp. 306, 319.—Coll. Doat. XXVII. fol. 7 sqq.—Lib. i. Clement. i. 1.—
Tocco, op. cit. pp. 509–10.—MSS. Bib. Nat. No. 4270, fol. 168.—Franz Ehrle
(ubi sup. 1885, p. 544; 1886, pp. 389–98, 402–5; 1887, pp. 449, 491).—Raymond de
Fronciacho (Archiv, 1887, p. 17).

The traditional wrath of the Conventuals was still strong enough in the year
1500 to lead the general chapter held at Terni to forbid, under pain of imprison-

On the other hand he was unquestionably the heresiarch of the Spirituals, both of France and Italy, regarded by them as the direct successor of Joachim and Francis. The *Historia Tribulationum* finds in the pseudo-Joachitic prophecies a clear account of all the events in his career. Enthusiastic Spirituals, who held the revolutionary doctrines of the Everlasting Gospel, testified before the Inquisition that the third age of the Church had its beginning in Olivi, who thus supplanted St. Francis himself. He was inspired of heaven; his doctrine had been revealed to him in Paris, some said, while he was washing his hands; others that the illumination came to him from Christ while in church, at the third hour of the day. Thus his utterances were of equal authority with those of St. Paul, and were to be obeyed by the Church without the change of a letter. It is no wonder that he was held accountable for the extravagances of those who regarded him with such veneration and recognized him as their leader and teacher.*

When Olivi died, his former prosecutor, Giovanni di Murro, was general of the Order, and, strong as were his own ascetic convictions, he lost no time in completing the work which he had previously failed to accomplish. Olivi's memory was condemned as that of a heretic, and an order was issued for the surrender of all his writings, which was enforced with unsparing rigor, and continued by his successor, Gonsalvo de Balboa. Pons Botugati, a friar eminent for piety and eloquence, refused to surrender for burning some of the prohibited tracts, and was chained closely to the wall in a damp and fetid dungeon, where bread and water were sparingly flung to him, and where he soon rotted to death in filth, so that when his body was hastily thrust into an unconsecrated grave it was found that already the flesh was burrowed through by worms. A number of other recalcitrants were also imprisoned with almost equal harshness, and in the next general chapter the reading of all of Olivi's works was formally prohibited. That much incendiary matter was in circulation, attributed directly or indirectly to him, is shown by a catalogue of Olivist tracts, treating of such dangerous questions as the power of the pope to

---

ment, any member of the Order from possessing any of Olivi's writings.—Franz Ehrle (ubi sup. 1887, pp. 457-8).

* Hist. Tribulat. (loc. cit. p. 988-9).—Coll. Doat, XXVII. fol. 7 sqq.—Lib. Sententt. Inq. Tolos. pp. 306, 308.—Bernard. Guidon. Practica P. v.

dispense from vows, his right to claim implicit obedience in matters concerning faith and morals, and other similar mutterings of
rebellion.*

The work of Olivi which called forth the greatest discussion,
and as to which the evidences are peculiarly irreconcilable, was
his Postil on the Apocalypse. It was from this that the chief
arguments were drawn for his condemnation. In an inquisitorial
sentence of 1318 we learn that his writings were then again under
examination by order of John XXII.; that they were held to be
the source of all the errors which the sectaries were then expiating
at the stake, and that principal among them was his work on the
Apocalypse, so that, until the papal decision, no one was to hold
him as a saint or a Catholic. When the condemnatory report of
eight masters of theology came, in 1319, the Spirituals held that
the outrage thus committed on the faith deprived of all virtue the
sacrament of the altar. No formal judgment was rendered, however, until February 8, 1326, when John XXII. finally condemned
the Postil on the Apocalypse after a careful scrutiny in the Consistory, and the general chapter of the Order forbade any one to
read or possess it. One of the reports of the experts upon it has
reached us. It is impossible to suppose that they deliberately
manufactured the extracts on which their conclusions are based,
and these extracts are quite sufficient to show that the work was
an echo of the most dangerous doctrines of the Everlasting Gospel. The fifth age is drawing to an end, and, under the figure of
the mystical Antichrist, there are prophecies about the pseudo-pope,
pseudo-Christs, and pseudo-prophets in terms which clearly allude
to the existing hierarchy. The pseudo-pope will be known by his
heresies concerning the perfection of evangelical poverty (as we
shall see was the case with John XXII.), and the pseudo-Joachim's
prophecies concerning Frederic II. are quoted to show how prelates and clergy who defend the Rule will be ejected. The carnal
church is the Great Whore of Babylon; it makes drunken and

---

* Hist. Tribulat. (loc. cit. pp. 300–1).—Tocco, pp. 489–91, 503–4.

Wadding (ann. 1297, No. 33–5) identifies Pons Botugati with St. Pons Car-
bonelli, the illustrious teacher of St. Louis of Toulouse. Franz Ehrle (Archiv
für L. u. K. 1886, p. 300) says he can find no evidence of this, and the author
of the *Hist. Tribulat.*, in his detailed account of the affair, would hardly have
omitted a fact so serviceable to his cause.

corrupts the nations with its carnalities, and oppresses the few remaining righteous, as under Paganism it did with its idolatries. In forty generations from the harvest of the apostles there will be a new harvest of the Jews and of the whole world, to be garnered by the Evangelical Order, to which all power and authority will be transferred. There are to be a sixth and a seventh age, after which comes the Day of Judgment. The date of this latter cannot be computed, but at the end of the thirteenth century the sixth age is to open. The carnal church, or Babylon, will expire, and the triumph of the spiritual church will commence.*

It has been customary for historians to assume that this resurrection of the Everlasting Gospel was Olivi's work, though it is evident from the closing years of his career that he could not have been guilty of uttering such inflammatory doctrines, and this is confirmed by the silence of the Council of Vienne concerning them, although it condemned his other trifling errors after a thorough debate on the subject by his enemies and friends. In fact, Bonagrazia, in the name of the Conventuals, bitterly attacked his memory and adduced a long list of his errors, including cursorily certain false and fantastic prophecies in the Postil on the Apocalypse and his stigmatizing the Church as the Great Whore. Had such passages as the above existed they would have been set forth at length and defence would have been impossible. Ubertino in reply, however, boldly characterized the assertion as most mendacious and impious; Olivi, he declared, had always spoken most reverently of the Church and Holy See; the Postil itself closed with a submission to the Roman Church as the universal mistress, and in the body of the work the Holy See was repeatedly alluded to as the seat of God and of Christ; the Church Militant and the Church Triumphant are spoken of as the seats of God which will last to the end, while the reprobate are Babylon and the Great Whore. It is impossible that Ubertino can have quoted these passages falsely, for Bonagrazia would have readily overwhelmed him with confusion, and the Council of Vienne would have rendered a far different judgment. We know from undoubted sources that

---

* Baluz. et Mansi II. 249-50.—Bern. Guidon. Pract. P. v.—Doat, XXVII. fol. 7 sqq.—Bern. Guidon. Vit. Johann. PP. XXII. (Muratori S. R. I. III. II. 491).—Wadding. ann. 1325, No. 4.—Alvar. Pelag. de Planctu Eccles. Lib. II. art. 59.—Baluz. et Mansi II. 266-70.

III.—4

the revolutionary doctrines commonly attributed to Olivi were entertained by those who considered themselves and were considered to be his disciples, and we can only assume that in their misguided zeal they interpolated his Postil, and gave to their own mystic dreams the authority of his great name.*

After the death of Olivi the Franciscan officials seem to have felt themselves unable to suppress the sect which was spreading and organizing throughout Languedoc. For some reason not apparent, unless it may have been jealousy of the Dominicans, the aid of the Inquisition was not called in, and the inquisitors withheld their hands from offenders of the rival Order. The regular church authorities, however, were appealed to, and in 1299 Gilles, Archbishop of Narbonne, held at Béziers a provincial synod, in which were condemned the Beguines of both sexes who under the lead of learned men of an honorable Order (the Franciscans) engaged in religious exercises not prescribed by the Church, wore vestments distinguishing them from other folk, performed novel penances and abstinences, administered vows of chastity, often not observed, held nocturnal conventicles, frequented heretics, and proclaimed that the end of the world was at hand, and that already the reign of Antichrist had begun. From them many scandals had already arisen, and there was danger of more and greater troubles. The bishops were therefore ordered, in their several dioceses, to investigate these sectaries closely and to suppress them. We see from this that there was rapidly growing up a new heresy based upon the Everlasting Gospel, with the stricter Franciscans as a nucleus, but extending among the people. For this popular propaganda the Tertiary Order afforded peculiar facilities, and we shall find hereafter that the Beguines, as they were generally called, were to a great extent Tertiaries, when not full members of the Order. There was nothing, however, to tempt the cupidity

---

* Franz Ehrle (Archiv f. L. u. K. 1886, pp. 368–70, 407–9).—Wadding. ann. 1297, No. 36–47.—Baluz. et Mansi II. 276.

Tocco (Archivio Storico Italiano, T. XVII. No. 2.—Cf. Franz Ehrle, Archiv für L. u. K. 1887, p. 493) has recently found in the Laurentian Library a MS. of Olivi's Postil on the Apocalypse. It contains all the passages cited in the condemnation, showing that the commission which sat in judgment did not invent them, but as it is of the fifteenth century it does not invalidate the suggestion that his followers interpolated his work after his death.

of the episcopal officials to the prosecution of those whose principal belief consisted in the renunciation of all worldly goods, and
it is not likely that they showed themselves more diligent in their
duties than we have seen them when greater interests were at
stake. The action of the council may therefore be safely assumed
as wasted, except as justifying persecution within the Order. The
lay Beguines doubtless enjoyed practical immunity, while the
Spiritual Friars continued to endure the miseries at the hands of
their superiors for which monastic life afforded such abundant
opportunities. Thus, at Villefranche, when Raymond Auriole
and Jean Prime refused to admit that their vows permitted a
liberal use of the things of the world, they were imprisoned in
chains and starved till Raymond died, deprived of the sacraments
as a heretic, and Jean barely escaped with his life.*

Thus passed away the unfortunate thirteenth century—that
age of lofty aspirations unfulfilled, of brilliant dreams unsubstantial as visions, of hopes ever looking to fruition and ever disappointed. The human intellect had awakened, but as yet the human conscience slumbered, save in a few rare souls who mostly
paid in disgrace or death the penalty of their precocious sensitiveness. That wonderful century passed away and left as its legacy
to its successor vast progress, indeed, in intellectual activity, but
on the spiritual side of the inheritance a dreary void. All efforts
to elevate the ideals of man had miserably failed. Society was
harder and coarser, more carnal and more worldly than ever, and
it is not too much to say that the Inquisition had done its full
share to bring this about by punishing aspirations, and by teaching that the only safety lay in mechanical conformity, regardless
of abuses and unmindful of corruption. The results of that hundred years of effort and suffering are well symbolized in the two
popes with whom it began and ended—Innocent III. and that
pinchbeck Innocent, Boniface VIII., who, in the popular phrase
of the time, came in like a fox, ruled like a lion, and died like
a dog. In intellect and learning Boniface was superior to his
model, in imperious pride his equal, in earnestness, in self-devo-

---

* Concil. Biterrens. ann. 1299 c. 4 (Martene Thesaur. IV. 226).—Ubertini
Declaratio (Archiv f. Litt.- u. K. 1887, pp. 183-4).

tion, in loftiness of aim, in all that dignifies ambition, immeasurably his inferior. It is no wonder that the apocalyptic speculations of Joachim should acquire fresh hold on the minds of those
who could not reconcile the spiritual desert in which they lived
with their conception of the merciful providence of God. To such
men it seemed impossible that he could permit a continuance of
the cruel wickedness which pervaded the Church, and through it
infected society at large. This was plainly beyond the power of
a few earnest zealots to cure, or even to mitigate, so the divine
interposition was requisite to create a new earth, inhabited only
by the few virtuous Elect, under a reign of ascetic poverty and
all-embracing love.

One of the most energetic and impetuous missionaries of these
beliefs was Arnaldo de Vilanova, in some respects, perhaps, the
most remarkable man of his time, whom we have only of late
learned to know thoroughly, from the researches of Señor Pelayo.
As a physician he stood unrivalled. Kings and popes disputed
his services, and his voluminous writings on medicine and hygiene
were reprinted in collective editions six times during the sixteenth
century, besides numerous issues of special treatises. As a chem-
ist he is more doubtfully said to have left his mark in several
useful discoveries. As an alchemist he had the repute of producing ingots of gold in the court of Robert of Naples, a great
patron of the science, and his treatises on the subject were included in collections of such works printed as lately as the eighteenth century. A student of both Arabic and Hebrew, he translated from Costa ben Luca treatises on incantations, ligatures, and
other magic devices. He wrote on astronomy and on oneiro-
mancy, for he was an expert expounder of dreams, and also on
surveying and wine-making. He draughted laws for Frederic of
Trinacria which that enlightened monarch promulgated and enforced, and his advice to Frederic and his brother Jayme II. of
Aragon on their duties as monarchs stamps him as a conscientious
statesman. When Jayme applied to him for the explanation of a
mysterious dream he not only satisfied the king with his exposition, but proceeded to warn him that his chief duty lay in administering justice, first to the poor, and then to the rich. When
asked how often he gave audience to the poor, Jayme answered,
once a week, and also when he rode out for pleasure. Arnaldo

sternly reproved him; he was earning damnation; the rich had
access to him every day, morning, noon, and night, the poor but
seldom; he made of God the hog of St. Anthony, which received
only the refuse rejected by all. If he wished to earn salvation he
must devote himself to the welfare of the poor, without which, in
spite of the teachings of the Church, neither psalms, nor masses,
nor fasting, nor even alms would suffice. To Jayme he was not
only physician but counsellor, venerable and much beloved, and
he was repeatedly employed on diplomatic missions by the kings
of both Aragon and Sicily.*

Multifarious as were these occupations, they consumed but a
portion of his restless activity. In dedicating to Robert of Naples
his treatise on surveying, he describes himself—

> "Yeu, Arnaut de Vilanova . . .
> Doctor en leys et en decrets,
> Et en siensa de strolomia,
> Et en l'art de medicina,
> Et en la santa teulogia "—

and, although a layman, married, and a father, his favorite field of
labor was theology, which he had studied with the Dominicans of
Montpellier. In 1292 he commenced with a work on the Tetra-
grammaton, or ineffable name of Jehovah, in which he sought to
explain by natural reasons the mystery of the Trinity. Embarked
in such speculations he soon became a confirmed Joachite. To a
man of his lofty spiritual tendencies and tender compassion for his
fellows, the wickedness and cruelty of mankind were appalling, and
especially the crimes of the clergy, among whom he reckoned the
Mendicants as the worst. Their vices he lashed unsparingly, and
he naturally fell in with the speculations of the pseudo-Joachitic
writings, anticipating the speedy advent of Antichrist and the Day
of Judgment. In numberless works composed in both Latin and
the vernacular he commented upon and popularized the Joachitic
books, even going so far as to declare that the revelation of Cyril
was more precious than all Scripture. Such a man naturally
sympathized with the persecuted Spirituals. He boldly undertook
their defence in sundry tracts, and when, in 1309, Frederic of Tri-

---

* Pelayo, Heterodoxos Españoles, I. 450–61, 475, 590–1, 726–7, 772.—M. Flac.
Illyr. Cat. Test. Veritatis, pp. 1732 sqq. (Ed. 1603).

nacria applied to him to expound his dream, he seized the opportunity
to invoke the monarch's commiseration for their sufferings, by explaining to him how, when they sought to appeal to the Holy See,
their brethren persecuted and slew them, and how evangelical poverty was treated as the gravest of crimes. He used his influence
similarly at the court of Naples, thus providing for them, as we
shall see, a place of refuge in their necessity.*

With his impulsive temperament it was impossible for him to
hold aloof from the bitter strife then raging. Before the thirteenth century was out he addressed letters to the Dominicans and
Franciscans of Paris and Montpellier, to the Kings of France and
Aragon, and even to the Sacred College, announcing the approaching end of the world; the wicked Catholics, and especially the
clergy, were the members of the coming Antichrist. This aroused
an active controversy, in which neither party spared the other.
After a war of tracts the Catalan Dominicans formally accused
him before the Bishop of Girona, and he responded that they had
no standing in court, as they were heretics and madmen, dogs and
jugglers, and he cited them to appear before the pope by the following Lent. It could only have been the royal favor which preserved him from the fate at the stake of many a less audacious
controversialist; and when, in 1300, King Jayme sent him on a mission to Philippe le Bel, he boldly laid his work on the advent of
Antichrist before the University of Paris. The theologians looked
askance on it, and, in spite of his ambassadorial immunity, on the
eve of his return he was arrested without warning by the episcopal Official. The Archbishop of Narbonne interposed in vain, and
he was bailed out on security of three thousand livres, furnished by
the Viscount of Narbonne and other friends. Brought before the
masters of theology, he was forced by threats of imprisonment to
recant upon the spot, without being allowed to defend himself,
and one can well believe his statement that one of his most eager
judges was a Franciscan, whose zeal was doubtless inflamed by the
portentous appearance of another Olivi from the prolific South.†

A formal appeal to Boniface was followed by a personal visit

---

* Pelayo, I. 454, 458, 464–6, 468–9, 730–1, 779.—Franz Ehrle, Archiv für Litt.-
und Kirchengeschichte, 1886, 327–8.

† Pelayo, I. 460, 464–8, 739–45.

to the papal court. Received at first with jeers, his obstinacy provoked repression. As a relapsed, he might have been burned, but
he was only imprisoned and forced to a second recantation, in
spite of which Philippe le Bel, at the assembly of the Louvre in
1303, in his charges of heresy against Boniface asserted that the
pope had approved a book of Arnaldo's which had already been
burned by himself and by the University of Paris. Boniface, in
fact, in releasing him, imposed on him silence on theologic matters,
though appreciating his medical skill and appointing him papal
physician. For a while he kept his peace, but a call from heaven
forced him to renewed activity, and he solemnly warned Boniface
of the divine vengeance if he remained insensible to the duty
of averting the wrath to come by a thorough reformation of the
Church. The catastrophe of Anagni soon followed, and Arnaldo,
who had left the papal court, naturally regarded it as a confirmation of his prophecy, and looked upon himself as an envoy of God.
With a fierce denunciation of clerical corruptions he repeated the
warning to Benedict XI., who responded by imposing a penance
on him and seizing all his apocalyptic tracts. In about a month
Benedict, too, was dead, and Arnaldo announced that a third message would be sent to his successor, "though when and by whom
has not been revealed to me, but I know that if he heeds it divine
power will adorn him with its sublimest gifts; if he rejects it, God
will visit him with a judgment so terrible that it will be a wonder
to all the earth." *

For some years we know nothing of his movements, although
his fertile pen was busily employed with little intermission, and the
Church vainly endeavored to suppress his writings. In 1305 Fray
Guillermo, Inquisitor of Valencia, excommunicated and ejected
from church Gambaldo de Pilis, a servant of King Jayme, for
possessing and circulating them. The king applied to Guillermo
for his reasons, and, on being refused, angrily wrote to Eymerich,
the Dominican general. He declared that Arnaldo's writings were

---

* Pelayo, I. 470-4, 729, 734.—D'Argentré I. II. 417.—Du Puy, Histoire du
Differend, Pr. 103.

One of the charges against Bernard Délicieux, in 1319, was that of sending to
Arnaldo certain magic writings to encompass the death of Benedict. A witness
was found to swear that this was the cause of Benedict's death.—MSS. Bib. Nat.,
fonds latin, No. 4270, fol. 12, 50, 51, 61.

eagerly read by himself, his queen and his children, by archbishops and bishops, by the clergy and the laity. He demanded that the sentence be revoked as uncanonical, else he would punish Fray Guillermo severely and visit with his displeasure all the Dominicans of his dominions. It was probably this royal favor which saved Arnaldo when he came near being burned at Santa Christina, and escaped with no worse infliction than being stigmatized as a necromancer and enchanter, a heretic and a pope of the heretics.*

When the persecution of the Spirituals of Provence was at its height, Arnaldo procured from Charles the Lame of Naples, who was also Count of Provence, a letter to the general, Gerald, which for a time put a stop to it. In 1309 we find him at Avignon, on a mission from Jayme II., well received by Clement V., who prized highly his skill as a physician. He used effectively this position by secretly persuading the pope to send for the leaders of the Spirituals, in order to learn from them orally and in writing of what they complained and what reformation they desired in their Order. With regard to his own affairs he was not so fortunate. At a public hearing before the pope and cardinals, in October, 1309, he predicted the end of the world within the century, and the advent of Antichrist within its first forty years; he dwelt at much length on the depravity of clergy and laity, and complained bitterly of the persecution of those who desired to live in evangelical poverty. All this was to be expected of him, but he added the incredible indiscretion of reading a detailed account of the dreams of Jayme II. and Frederic of Trinacria, their doubts and his explanations and exhortations—matters, all of them, as sacredly confidential as the confession of a penitent. Cardinal Napoleone Orsini, the protector of the Spirituals, wrote to Jayme congratulating him on his piety as revealed by that wise and illuminated man, inflamed with the love of God, Master Arnaldo, but this effort to conjure the tempest was unavailing. The Cardinal of Porto and Ramon Ortiz, Dominican Provincial of Aragon, promptly reported to Jayme that he and his brother had been represented as wavering in the faith and as believers in dreams, and advised him no longer to employ as his envoy such a heretic as Arnaldo. Jayme's pride was deeply wounded. It was in vain that Clement

---

* Pelayo, I. 481, 772.

assured him that he had paid no attention to Arnaldo's discourse;
the king wrote to the pope and cardinals and to his brother denying the story of his dream and treating Arnaldo as an impostor.
Frederic was less susceptible : he wrote to Jayme that the story
could do them no harm, and that the real infamy would lie in
abandoning Arnaldo in his hour of peril.   Arnaldo took refuge
with him, and not long afterwards was sent by him again to Avignon on a mission, but perished during the voyage.   The exact date
of his death is unknown, but it was prior to February, 1311.   For
selfish reasons Clement mourned his loss, and issued a bull announcing that Arnaldo had been his physician and had promised
him a most useful book which he had written; he had died without doing so, and now Clement summoned any one possessing the
precious volume to deliver it to him.*

The interposition of Arnaldo offered to the Spirituals an unexpected prospect of deliverance.   From Languedoc to Venice and
Florence they were enduring the bitterest persecution from their
superiors; they were cast into dungeons where they starved to
death, and were exposed to the infinite trials for which monastic
life afforded such abundant opportunities, when Arnaldo persuaded
Clement to make an energetic effort to heal the schism in the Order and to silence the accusations which the Conventuals brought
against their brethren.   An occasion was found in an appeal from
the citizens of Narbonne setting forth that the books of Olivi had
been unjustly condemned, that the Rule of the Order was disregarded, and those who observed it were persecuted, and further
praying that a special cult of Olivi's remains might be permitted.
A commission of important personages was formed to investigate
the faith of Angelo da Clarino and his disciples, who still dwelt in
the neighborhood of Rome, and who were pronounced good Catholics.   Such leading Spirituals as Raymond Gaufridi, the former
general, Ubertino da Casale, the intellectual leader of the sect,
Raymond de Giniac, former Provincial of Aragon, Gui de Mirepoix, Bartolommeo Sicardi, and others were summoned to Avignon,

---

* Hist. Tribulationum (Archiv für Litt.- u. K. 1886, I. 129).—Pelayo, I. 481–
3, 773, 776.— Wadding. ann. 1312, No. 7.— Cf. Trithem. Chron. Hirsaug. ann.
1310; P. Langii Chron. Citicens. ann. 1320.

where they were ordered to draw up in writing the points which they deemed requisite for the reformation of the Order. To enable them to perform this duty in safety they were taken under papal protection by a bull which shows in its minute specifications how real were the perils incurred by those who sought to restore the Order to its primitive purity. Apparently stimulated by these warnings, the general, Gonsalvo, at the Chapter of Padua in 1310, caused the adoption of many regulations to diminish the luxury and remove the abuses which pervaded the Order, but the evil was too deep-seated. He was resolved, moreover, on reducing the Spirituals to obedience, and the hatred between the two parties grew bitterer than ever.*

The articles of complaint, thirty-five in number, which the Spirituals laid before Clement V. in obedience to his commands formed a terrible indictment of the laxity and corruption which had crept into the Order. It was answered but feebly by the Conventuals, partly by denying its allegations, partly by dialectical subtleties to prove that the Rule did not mean what it said, and partly by accusing the Spirituals of heresy. Clement appointed a commission of cardinals and theologians to hear both sides. For two years the contest raged with the utmost fury. During its continuance Raymond Gaufridi, Gui de Mirepoix, and Bartolommeo Sicardi died—poisoned by their adversaries, according to one account, worn out with ill-treatment and insult according to another. Clement had temporarily released the delegates of the Spirituals from the jurisdiction of their enemies, who had the audacity, March 1, 1311, to enter a formal protest against his action, alleging that they were excommunicated heretics under trial, who could not be thus protected. In this prolonged discussion the opposing leaders were Ubertino da Casale and Bonagrazia (Bon-

----

* Franz Ehrle (Archiv für Litt.- u. K. 1886, pp. 380–1, 384, 386 ; 1887, p. 36).— Raym. de Fronciacho (Ib. 1887, p. 18).—Eymerich p. 316.—Angeli Clarini Litt. Excus. (Archiv, 1885, pp. 531–2).—Wadding. ann. 1210, No. 6.—Regest. Clement. PP. V. T. V. pp. 379 sqq. Romæ, 1887).

At the same time that the general, Gonsalvo, was seeking to repress the acquisitiveness of the friars they were procuring from the Emperor Henry VII. a decree annulling a local statute of Nuremberg which forbade any citizen from giving them more than a single gold piece at a time, or a measure of corn.— Chron. Glassberger ann. 1310.

cortese) da Bergamo. The former, while absorbed in devotion on Mont' Alverno, the scene of St. Francis's transfiguration, had been anointed by Christ and raised to a lofty degree of spiritual insight. His reputation is illustrated by the story that while laboring with much success in Tuscany he had been summoned to Rome by Benedict XI. to answer some accusations brought against him. Soon afterwards the people of Perugia sent a solemn embassy to the pope with two requests—one that Ubertino be restored to them, the other that the pope and cardinals would reside in their city—whereat Benedict smiled and said, "I see you love us but a little, since you prefer Frà Ubertino to us." He was a Joachite, moreover, who did not hesitate to characterize the abdication of Celestin as a horrible innovation, and the accession of Boniface as a usurpation. Bonagrazia was perhaps superior to his opponent in learning and not his inferior in steadfast devotion to what he deemed the truth, though Ubertino characterized him as a lay novice, skilled in the cunning tricks of the law. We shall see hereafter his readiness to endure persecution in defence of his own ideal of poverty; and the antagonism of two such men upon the points at issue between them is the most striking illustration of the impracticable nature of the questions which raised so heated a strife and cost so much blood.*

The Spirituals failed in their efforts to obtain a decree of separation which should enable them, in peace, to live according to their interpretation of the Rule, but in other respects the decision of the commission was wholly in their favor, in spite of the persistent effort of the Conventuals to divert attention from the real questions at issue to the assumed errors of Olivi. Clement accepted the decision, and in full consistory, in presence of both parties, ordered them to live in mutual love and charity, to bury the past in oblivion, and not to insult each other for past differences. Ubertino replied, "Holy Father, they call us heretics and defenders of heresy; there are whole books full of this in your archives and those of the Order. They must either allege these things

---

* Archiv für L. u. K. 1887, pp. 93 sqq.—Hist. Tribulat. (Ibid. 1886, pp. 130, 132–4).—Ehrle (Ibid. 1866, pp. 366, 380).—Wadding. ann. 1310, No. 1–5.—Chron. Glassberger ann. 1310.—Ubertini de Casali Tract. de septem Statibus Ecclesiæ c. iv.

and let us defend ourselves, or they must recall them. Otherwise there can be no peace between us." To this Clement rejoined, "We declare as pope, that from what has been stated on both sides before us, no one ought to call you heretics and defenders of heresy. What exists to that effect in our archives or elsewhere we wholly erase and pronounce to be of no validity against you." The result was seen in the Council of Vienne (1311–12), which adopted the canon known as *Exivi de Paradiso*, designed to settle forever the controversy which had lasted so long. Angelo da Clarino declares that this was based wholly upon the propositions of Ubertino; that it was the crowning victory of the Spirituals, and his heart overflows with joy when he communicates the good news to his brethren. It determined, he says, eighty questions concerning the interpretation of the Rule; hereafter those who serve the Lord in hermitages and are obedient to their bishops are secured against molestation by any person. The inquisitors, he further stated, were placed under control of the bishops, which he evidently regarded as a matter of special importance, for in Provence and Tuscany the Inquisition was Franciscan, and thus in the hands of the Conventuals. We have seen that Clement delayed issuing the decrees of the council. He was on the point of doing so, after careful revision, when his death, in 1314, followed by a long interregnum, caused a further postponement. John XXII. was elected in August, 1316, but he, too, desired time for further revision, and it was not until November, 1317, that the canons were finally issued. That they underwent change in this process is more than probable, and the canon *Exivi de Paradiso* was on a subject peculiarly provocative of alteration. As it has reached us it certainly does not justify Angelo's pæan of triumph. It is true that it insists on a more rigid compliance with the Rule. It forbids the placing of coffers in churches for the collection of money; it pronounces the friars incapable of enjoying inheritances; it deprecates the building of magnificent churches, and convents which are rather palaces; it prohibits the acquisition of extensive gardens and great vineyards, and even the storing up of granaries of corn and cellars of wine where the brethren can live from day to day by beggary; it declares that whatever is given to the Order belongs to the Church of Rome, and that the friars have only the use of it, for they can hold noth-

ing, either individually or in common. In short, it fully justified
the complaints of the Spirituals and interpreted the Rule in accordance with their views, but it did not, as Angelo claimed, allow them to live by themselves in peace, and it subjected them to
their superiors. This was to remand them into slavery, as the
great majority of the Order were Conventuals, jealous of the assumption of superior sanctity by the Spirituals, and irritated by
their defeat and by the threatened enforcement of the Rule in all
its rigidity. This spirit was still further inflamed by the action
of the general, Gonsalvo, who zealously set to work to carry out
the reforms prescribed by the canon *Exivi*. He traversed the
various provinces, pulling down costly buildings and compelling
the return of gifts and legacies to donors and heirs. This excited
great indignation among the laxer brethren, and his speedy death,
in 1313, was attributed to foul play. The election of his successor, Alessandro da Alessandria, one of the most earnest of the
Conventuals, showed that the Order at large was not disposed to
submit quietly to pope and council.*

As might have been expected, the strife between the parties
became bitterer than ever. Clement's leaning in favor of asceticism is shown by his canonization, in 1313, of Celestin V., but when
the Spirituals applied to him for protection against their brethren
he contented himself with ordering them to return to their convents and commanding them to be kindly treated. These commands were disregarded. Mutual hatreds were too strong for
power not to be abused. Clement did his best to force the Conventuals to submission; as early as July, 1311, he had ordered
Bonagrazia to betake himself to the convent of Valcabrère in
Comminges, and not to leave it without special papal license. At
the same time he summoned before him Guiraud Vallette, the
Provincial of Provence, and fifteen of the principal officials of the
Order throughout the south of France, who were regarded as the
leaders in the oppression of the Spirituals. In public consistory

---

* Ubertini Responsio (Archiv für L. u. K. 1887, p. 87).—Baluz. et Mansi II.
278.—Franz Ehrle (Archiv für L. u. K. 1885, pp. 541-2, 545 ; 1886, p. 362).—
Hist. Tribulat. (Ibid. 1886, pp. 138-41).—C. 1, Clement. v. 11.—Wadding. ann.
1312, No. 9 ; ann. 1313, No. 1.—Chron. Glassberger ann. 1312.—Alvar. Pelag. de
Planct. Eccles. Lib. II. art. 67.

he repeated his commands, scolded them for disobedience and rebellion, dismissed from office those who had positions, and declared
ineligible those who were not officials. Those whom he ejected he
replaced with suitable persons whom he strictly commanded to
preserve the peace and show favor to the sorely afflicted minority.
In spite of this the scandals and complaints continued, until the
general, Alessandro, granted to the Spirituals the three convents
of Narbonne, Béziers, and Carcassonne, and ordered that the
superiors placed over them should be acceptable. The change
was not effected without the employment of force, in which the
Spirituals had the advantage of popular sympathy, and the convents thus favored became houses of refuge for the discontented
brethren elsewhere. Then for a while there seems to have been
quiet, but with Clement's death, in 1314, the turmoil commenced
afresh. Bonagrazia, under pretext of sickness, hastened to leave
his place of confinement, and joined eagerly in the renewed disturbance; the dismissed officials again made their influence felt;
the Spirituals complained that they were abused and defamed in
private and in public, pelted with mud and stones, deprived of
food and even of the sacraments, despoiled of their habits, and
scattered to distant places or imprisoned.*

It is possible that Clement might have found some means of
dissolving the bonds between these irreconcilable parties, but for
the insubordination of the Italian Spirituals. These grew impatient during the long conferences which preceded the Council
of Vienne. Subjected to daily afflictions and despairing of rest
within the Order, they eagerly listened to the advice of a wise and
holy man, Canon Martin of Siena, who assured them that, however few their numbers, they had a right to secede and elect their
own general. Under the lead of Giacopo di San Gemignano they
did so, and effected an independent organization. This was rank
rebellion and greatly prejudiced the case of the Spirituals at Avignon. Clement would not listen to anything that savored of concessions to those who thus threw off their pledged obedience. He
promptly sent commissions for their trial, and they were duly ex-

---

* Jordan. Chron. c. 326 Partic. iii. (Muratori Antiq. XI. 767).—Hist. Tribulat.
(Archiv, 1886, 140–1).—Franz Ehrle (Ibid. 1886, pp. 158–64; 1887, pp. 33, 40).—
Raym. de Fronciacho (Ib. 1887, p. 27).

communicated as schismatics and rebels, founders of a superstitious sect, and disseminators of false and pestiferous doctrines.
Persecution against them raged more furiously than ever. In
some places, supported by the laity, they ejected the Conventuals
from their houses and defended themselves by force of arms, disregarding the censures of the Church which were lavished on them.
Others made the best of their way to Sicily, and others again,
shortly before Clement's death, sent letters to him professing submission and obedience, but the friends of the Spirituals feared to
compromise themselves by even presenting them. After the accession of John XXII. they made another attempt to reach the
pope, but by that time the Conventuals were in full control and
threw the envoys into prison as excommunicated heretics. Such
of them as were able to do so escaped to Sicily. It is worthy of
note that everywhere the virtues and sanctity of these so-called
heretics won for them popular favor, and secured them protection
more or less efficient, and this was especially the case in Sicily.
King Frederic, mindful of the lessons taught him by Arnaldo de
Vilanova, received the fugitives graciously and allowed them to
establish themselves, in spite of repeated remonstrances on the
part of John XXII. There Henry da Ceva, whom we shall meet
again, had already sought refuge from the persecution of Boniface
VIII. and had prepared the way for those who were to follow.
In 1313 there are allusions to a pope named Celestin whom the
" Poor Men " in Sicily had elected, with a college of cardinals, who
constituted the only true Church and who were entitled to the
obedience of the faithful. Insignificant as this movement may
have seemed at the time, it subsequently aided the foundation of
the sect known as Fraticelli, who so long braved with marvellous
constancy the unsparing rigor of the Italian Inquisition.*

Into these dangerous paths of rebellion the original leaders of

---

* Hist. Tribulat. (loc. cit. pp. 139–40).—Lami, Antichità Toscane, pp. 596–99.
—Franz Ehrle, Archiv, 1885, pp. 156–8.— Joann. S. Victor. Chron. ann. 1319
(Muratori S. R. I. III. ii. 479).—Wadding. ann. 1313, No. 4–7.—D'Argentré I. i.
297.—Arch. de l'Inq. de Carcass. (Doat, XXVII. fol. 7 sqq.).—Raym. de Fronciacho (Archiv, 1887, p. 31).

Frà Francesco del Borgo San Sepolcro, who was tried by the Inquisition at
Assisi in 1311 for assuming gifts of prophecy, was probably a Tuscan Joachite
who refused submission (Franz Ehrle, Archiv für L. u. K. 1887, p. 11).

the Italian Spirituals were not obliged to enter, as they were released from subjection to the Conventuals, and could afford to remain in obedience to Rome.   Angelo da Clarino writes to his disciples that torment and death wore preferable to separation from
the Church and its head; the pope was the bishop of bishops, who
regulated all ecclesiastical dignities; the power of the keys is from
Christ, and submission is due in spite of persecution.   Yet, together
with these appeals are others which show how impracticable was
the position created by the belief in St. Francis as a new evan-
gelist whose Rule was a revelation.   If kings or prelates command what is contrary to the faith, then obedience is due to
God, and death is to be welcomed.   Francis placed in the Rule
nothing but what Christ bade him write, and obedience is due to
it rather than to prelates.   After the persecution under John
XXII. he even quotes a prophecy attributed to Francis, to the
effect that men would arise who would render the Order odious,
and corrupt the whole Church; there would be a pope not canonically elected who would not believe rightly as to Christ and the
Rule; there would be a split in the Order, and the wrath of God
would visit those who cleaved to error.   With clear reference to
John, he says that if a pope condemns evangelical truth as an
error he is to be left to the judgment of Christ and the doctors;
if he excommunicates as heresy the poverty of the Gospel, he is
excommunicate of God and is a heretic before Christ.   Yet, though
his faith and obedience were thus sorely tried, Angelo and his followers never attempted a schism.   He died in 1337, worn out with
sixty years of tribulation and persecution—a man of the firmest
and gentlest spirit, of the most saintly aspirations, who had fallen
on evil days and had exhausted himself in the hopeless effort to
reconcile the irreconcilable.   Though John XXII. had permitted
him to assume the habit and Rule of the Celestins, he was obliged
to live in hiding, with his abode known only to a few faithful
friends and followers, of some of whom we hear as on trial before
the Inquisition as Fraticelli, in 1334.   It was in the desert hermitage of Santa Maria di Aspro in the Basilicata; but three days
before his death a rumor spread that a saint was dying there, and
such multitudes assembled that it was necessary to place guards
at the entrance of his retreat, and admit the people two by two to
gaze on his dying agonies.   He shone in miracles, and was finally

beatified by the Church, which through the period of two generations had never ceased to trample on him, but his little congregation, though lost to sight in the more aggressive energy of the Fraticelli, continued to exist, even after the tradition of self-abnegation was taken up under more fortunate auspices by the Observantines, until it was finally absorbed into the latter in the reorganization of 1517 under Leo X.*

In Provence, even before the death of Clement V., there were ardent spirits, nursing the reveries of the Everlasting Gospel, who were not satisfied with the victory won at the Council of Vienne. When, in 1311, the Conventuals assailed the memory of Olivi, one of their accusations was that he had given rise to sects who claimed that his doctrine was revealed by Christ, that it was of equal authority with the gospel, that since Nicholas III. the papal supremacy had been transferred to them, and they consequently had elected a pope of their own. This Ubertino did not deny, but only argued that he knew nothing of it; that if it were true Olivi was not responsible, as it was wholly opposed to his teaching, of which not a word could be cited in support of such insanity. Yet, undoubtedly there were sectaries calling themselves disciples of Olivi among whom the revolutionary leaven was working, and they could recognize no virtue or authority in the carnal and worldly Church. In 1313 we hear of a Frère Raymond Jean, who, in a public sermon at Montréal, prophesied that they would suffer persecution for the faith, and when, after the sermon, he was asked what he meant, boldly replied in the presence of several persons, "The enemies of the faith are among ourselves. The Church which governs us is symbolled by the Great Whore of the Apocalypse, who persecutes the poor and the ministers of Christ. You see we do not dare to walk openly before our brethren." He added that the only true pope was Celestin, who had been elected in Sicily, and his organization was the only true Church.†

Thus the Spirituals were by no means a united body. When

---

* Franz Ehrle (Archiv f. L. u. K. 1885, pp. 534-9, 553-5, 558-9, 561, 563-4, 566-9; 1887, p. 406).—S. Francisci Prophet. xiv. (Opp. Ed. 1849, pp. 270-1).— Chron. Glassberger ann. 1502, 1506, 1517.

† Franz Ehrle (Archiv für Litt.- u. K. 1886, pp. 371, 411).—Arch. de l'Inq. de Carcassonne (Doat, XXVII. fol. 7 sqq.).

once the trammels of authority had been shaken off, there was among them too much individuality and too ardent a fanaticism for them to reach precisely the same convictions, and they were fractioned into little groups and sects which neutralized what slender ability they might otherwise have had to give serious trouble to the powerful organization of the hierarchy. Yet, whether their doctrines were submissive like those of Angelo, or revolutionary like those of Raymond Jean, they were all guilty of the unpardonable crime of independence, of thinking for themselves where thought was forbidden, and of believing in a higher law than that of papal decretals. Their steadfastness was soon to be put to the test. In 1314 the general, Alessandro, died, and after an interval of twenty months Michele da Cesena was chosen as his successor. To the chapter of Naples which elected him the Spirituals of Narbonne sent a long memorial reciting the wrongs and afflictions which they had endured since the death of Clement had deprived them of papal protection. The nomination of Michele might seem to be a victory over the Conventuals. He was a distinguished theologian, of resolute and unbending temper, and resolved on enforcing the strict observance of the Rule. Within three months of his election he issued a general precept enjoining rigid obedience to it. The vestments to be worn were minutely prescribed, money was not to be accepted except in case of absolute necessity; no fruits of the earth were to be sold; no splendid buildings to be erected; meals were to be plain and frugal; the brethren were never to ride, nor even to wear shoes except under written permission of their convents when exigency required it. The Spirituals might hope that at last they had a general after their own heart, but they had unconsciously drifted away from obedience, and Michele was resolved that the Order should be a unit, and that all wanderers should be driven back into the fold.*

A fortnight before the issuing of this precept the long inter-regnum of the papacy had been closed by the election of John XXII. There have been few popes who have so completely embodied the ruling tendencies of their time, and few who have exerted so large an influence on the Church, for good or for evil.

---

* Franz Ehrle (loc. cit. 1886, pp. 160–4).—Wadding. ann. 1316, No. 5.

Sprung from the most humble origin, his abilities and force of character had carried him from one preferment to another, until he reached the chair of St. Peter. He was short in stature but robust in health, choleric and easily moved to wrath, while his enmity once excited was durable, and his rejoicing when his foes came to an evil end savored little of the Christian pastor. Persistent and inflexible, a purpose once undertaken was pursued to the end regardless of opposition from friend or enemy. He was especially proud of his theologic attainments, ardent in disputation, and impatient of opposition. After the fashion of the time he was pious, for he celebrated mass almost every day, and almost every night he arose to recite the Office or to study. Among his good works is enumerated a poetical description of the Passion of Christ, concluding with a prayer, and he gratified his vanity as an author by proclaiming many indulgences as a reward to all who would read it through. His chief characteristics, however, were ambition and avarice. To gratify the former he waged endless wars with the Visconti of Milan, in which, as we are assured by a contemporary, the blood shed would have incarnadined the waters of Lake Constance, and the bodies of the slain would have bridged it from shore to shore. As for the latter, his quenchless greed displayed an exhaustless fertility of resource in converting the treasures of salvation into current coin. He it was who first reduced to a system the "Taxes of the Penitentiary," which offered absolution at fixed prices for every possible form of human wickedness, from five grossi for homicide or incest, to thirty-three grossi for ordination below the canonical age. Before he had been two years in the papacy he arrogated to himself the presentation to all the collegiate benefices in Christendom, under the convenient pretext of repressing simony, and then from their sale we are told that he accumulated an immense treasure. Another still more remunerative device was the practice of not filling a vacant episcopate from the ranks, but establishing a system of promotion from a poorer see to a richer one, and thence to archbishoprics, so that each vacancy gave him the opportunity of making numerous changes and levying tribute on each. Besides these regular sources of unhallowed gains he was fertile in special expedients, as when, in 1326, needing money for his Lombard wars, he applied to Charles le Bel for authority to levy a subsidy on the churches of France,

Germany being for the time cut off by his quarrel with Louis of Bavaria. Charles at first refused, but finally agreed to divide the spoils, and granted the power in consideration of a papal grant to him of a tithe for two years—as a contemporary remarks, " *et ainsi saincte yglise, quant l'un le tont, l'autre l'escorche.*" John proceeded to extort a large sum; from some he got a full tithe, from others a half, from others again as much as he could extract, while all who held benefices under papal authority had to pay a full year's revenue. His excuse for this insatiable acquisitiveness was that he designed the money for a crusade, but as he lived to be a nonagenary without executing that design, the contemporary Villani is perhaps justified in the cautious remark—" Possiby he had such intention." Though for the most part parsimonious, he spent immense sums in advancing the fortunes of his nephew—or son—the Cardinal-legate Poyet, who was endeavoring to found a principality in the north of Italy. He lavished money in making Avignon a permanent residence for the papacy, though it was reserved for Benedict XII. to purchase and enlarge the enormous palace-fortress of the popes. Yet after his death, when an inventory of his effects came to be made, there was found in his treasury eighteen millions of gold florins, and jewels and vestments estimated at seven millions more. Even in mercantile Florence, the sum was so incomprehensible that Villani, whose brother was one of the appraisers, feels obliged to explain that each million is a thousand thousands. When we reflect upon the comparative poverty of the period and the scarcity of the precious metals, we can estimate how great an amount of suffering was represented by such an accumulation, wrung as it was, in its ultimate source, from the wretched peasantry, who gleaned at the best an insufficient subsistence from imperfect agriculture. We can, perhaps, moreover, imagine how, in its passage to the papal treasury, it represented so much of simony, so much of justice sold or denied to the wretched litigants in the curia, so much of purgatory remitted, and of pardons for sins to the innumerable applicants for a share of the Church's treasury of salvation.*

* Villani, Chronica, Lib. XI. c. 20.—Chron. Glassberger ann. 1334.—Vitodurani Chron. (Eccard. Corp. Hist. Med. Ævi I. 1806–8).—Friedrich, Statut. Synod. Wratislav., Hannoveræ, 1827, pp. 37, 38, 41.—Grandes Chroniques. V. 300.— Guillel. Nangiac. Contin. ann. 1326.—The collection of papal briefs relating to

The permanent evil which he wrought by his shameless traffic in benefices, and the reputation which he left behind him, are visible in the bitter complaints which were made at the Council of Siena, a century later, by the deputies of the Gallican nation. They refer to his pontificate as that in which the Holy See reserved all benefices to itself, when graces, expectatives, etc., were publicly sold to the highest bidder, without regard to qualification, so that in France many benefices were utterly ruined by reason of the insupportable burdens laid upon them. It is no wonder, therefore, that when St. Birgitta of Sweden was applied to, in the latter half of the fourteenth century, by some Franciscans to learn whether John's decretals on the subject of the poverty of Christ were correct, and she was vouchsafed two visions of the Virgin to satisfy their scruples, the Virgin reported that his decretals were free from error, but discreetly announced that she was not at liberty to say whether his soul was in heaven or in hell. Such was the man to whom the cruel irony of fate committed the settlement of the delicate scruples which vexed the souls of the Spirituals.*

John had been actively engaged in the proceedings of the Council of Vienne, and was thoroughly familiar with all the details of the question. When, therefore, the general, Michele, shortly after his accession, applied to him to restore unity in the distracted Order, his imperious temper led him to take speedy and vigorous action. King Frederic of Trinacria was ordered to seize the refugees in his dominions, and deliver them to their superiors to be disciplined. Bertrand de la Tour, the Provincial of Aquitaine, was instructed to reduce to obedience the rebels of the convents

---

Saxony recently printed by Schmidt (Päbstliche Urkunden und Regesten, pp. 87–295) will explain the immense sums raised by John XXII. from the sale of canonries. It is within bounds to say that more than half the letters issued during his pontificate are appointments of this kind.

The accounts of the papal collector for Hungary in 1320 show the thoroughness with which the first-fruits of every petty benefice were looked after, and the enormous proportion consumed in the process. The collector charges himself with 1913 gold florins received, of which only 732 reached the papal treasury. (Theiner, Monumenta Slavor. Meridional. I. 147).

* Jo. de Ragusio Init. et Prosecut. Basil. Concil. (Monument. Concil. Sæc. XV. T. I. p. 32).—Revelat. S. Brigittæ Lib. vii. c. viii.

of Béziers, Narbonne, and Carcassonne.   Bertrand at first tried
persuasion.   The outward sign of the Spirituals was the habit.
They wore smaller hoods, and gowns shorter, narrower, and coarser
than the Conventuals ; and, holding this to be in accordance with
the precedent set by Francis, it was as much an article of faith
with them as the absence of granaries and wine-cellars and the
refusal to handle money.   When he urged them to abandon these
vestments they therefore replied that this was one of the matters
in which they could not render obedience.   Then he assumed a
tone of authority under the papal rescript, and they rejoined by
an appeal to the pope better informed, signed by forty-five friars
of Narbonne, and fifteen of Béziers.   On receipt of the appeal,
John peremptorily ordered, April 27, 1317, all the appellants to
present themselves before him within ten days, under pain of excommunication.   They set forth, seventy-four in number, with
Bernard Délicieux at their head, and on reaching Avignon did not
venture to lodge in the Franciscan convent, but bivouacked for
the night on the public place in front of the papal doors.*

They were regarded as much more dangerous rebels than the
Italian Spirituals.   The latter had already had a hearing in which
Ubertino da Casale confuted the charges brought against them,
and he, Goffrido da Cornone, and Philippe de Caux, while expressing sympathy and readiness to defend Olivi and his disciples, had
plainly let it be seen that they regarded themselves as not personally concerned with them.   John drew the same distinction ;
and though Angelo da Clarino was for a while imprisoned on the
strength of an old condemnation by Boniface VIII., he was soon
released and permitted to adopt the Celestin habit and Rule.
Ubertino was told that if he would return for a few days to the
Franciscan convent proper provision would be made for his future.   To this he significantly replied, " After staying with the
friars for a single day I will not require any provision in this
world from you or any one else," and he was permitted to transfer himself to the Benedictine Order, as were likewise several
others of his comrades.   He had but a temporary respite, how-

---

* Wadding. ann. 1317, No. 9–14. — Hist. Tribulation. (Archiv für L. u. K.
1886, p. 142).—Joann. S. Victor. Chron. ann. 1311, 1316 (Muratori S. R. I. III. II.
460, 478).

ever, and we shall see hereafter that in 1325 he was obliged to take refuge with Louis of Bavaria.*

The Olivists were not to escape so easily. The day after their arrival they were admitted to audience. Bernard Délicieux argued their case so ably that he could only be answered by accusing him of having impeded the Inquisition, and John ordered his arrest. Then François Sanche took up the argument, and was accused of having vilified the Order publicly, when John delivered him to the Conventuals, who promptly imprisoned him in a cell next to the latrines. Then Guillaume de Saint-Amand assumed the defence, but the friars accused him of dilapidation and of deserting the Convent of Narbonne, and John ordered his arrest. Then Geoffroi attempted it, but John interrupted him, saying, "We wonder greatly that you demand the strict observance of the Rule, and yet you wear five gowns." Geoffroi replied, "Holy Father, you are deceived, for, saving your reverence, it is not true that I wear five gowns." John answered hotly, "Then we lie," and ordered Geoffroi to be seized until it could be determined how many gowns he wore. The terrified brethren, seeing that their case was prejudged, fell on their knees, crying, "Holy Father, justice, justice!" and the pope ordered them all to go to the Franciscan convent, to be guarded till he should determine what to do with them. Bernard, Guillaume, and Geoffroi, and some of their comrades were subjected to harsh imprisonment in chains by order of the pope. Bernard's fate we have already seen. As to the others, an inquisition was held on them, when all but twenty-five submitted, and were rigorously penanced by the triumphant Conventuals.†

The twenty-five recalcitrants were handed over to the Inquisition of Marseilles, under whose jurisdiction they were arrested. The inquisitor was Frère Michel le Moine, one of those who had been degraded and imprisoned by Clement V. on account of their zeal in persecuting the Spirituals. Now he was able to glut his revenge. He had ample warrant for whatever he might please to do, for John had not waited to hear the Spirituals before condemning them. As early as February 17, he had ordered the inquisi-

---

* Hist. Tribulat. (ubi sup. pp. 142–44, 151–2).—Franz Ehrle, Archiv, 1887, p. 546.

† Hist. Tribulat. (Ibid. pp. 145–6).—Raym. de Fronciacho (Ib. 1887, p. 29).

tors of Languedoc to denounce as heretics all who styled themselves Fraticelli or *Fratres de paupere vita*. Then, April 13, he
had issued the constitution *Quorumdam*, in which he had definitely settled the two points which had become the burning questions
of the dispute—the character of vestments to be worn, and the
legality of laying up stores of provisions in granaries, and cellars
of wine and oil. These questions he referred to the general of
the Order with absolute power to determine them. Under Michele's instructions, the ministers and guardians were to determine
for each convent what amount of provisions it required, what portion might be stored up, and to what extent the friars were to beg
for it. Such decisions were to be implicitly followed without
thinking or asserting that they derogated from the Rule. The
bull wound up with the significant words, " Great is poverty,
but greater is blamelessness, and perfect obedience is the greatest
good." There was a hard common-sense about this which may
seem to us even commonplace, but it decided the case against the
Spirituals, and gave them the naked alternative of submission or
rebellion.*

This bull was the basis of the inquisitorial process against the
twenty-five recalcitrants. The case was perfectly clear under it,
and in fact all the proceedings of the Spirituals after its issue had
been flagrantly contumacious—their refusal to change their vestments, and their appeal to the pope better informed. Before
handing them over to the Inquisition they had been brought before Michele da Cesena, and their statements to him when read
before the consistory had been pronounced heretical and the authors subject to the penalty of heresy. Efforts of course had been
made to secure their submission, but in vain, and it was not until
November 6, 1317, that letters were issued by John and by Michele
da Cesena to the Inquisitor Michel, directing him to proceed with
the trial. Of the details of the process we have no knowledge,
but it is not likely that the accused were spared any of the rigors
customary in such cases, when the desire was to break the spirit
and induce compliance. This is shown, moreover, in the fact that
the proceedings were protracted for exactly six months, the sentence being rendered on May 7, 1318, and by the further fact that

---

* Coll. Doat, **XXXIV.** 147.—Extrav. Joann. **XXII**. Tit. **XIV**. cap. 1.

most of the culprits were brought to repentance and abjuration. Only four of them had the physical and mental endurance to persevere to the last—Jean Barrani, Déodat Michel, Guillem Sainton, and Pons Rocha—and these were handed over the same day to the secular authorities of Marseilles and duly burned. A fifth, Bernard Aspa, who had said in prison that he repented, but who refused to recant and abjure, was mercifully condemned to prison for life, though under all inquisitorial rules he should have shared the fate of his accomplices. The rest were forced to abjure publicly and to accept the penances imposed by the inquisitor, with the warning that if they failed to publish their abjuration wherever they had preached their errors they would be burned as relapsed.*

Although in the sentence the heresy of the victims is said to have been drawn from the poisoned doctrine of Olivi, and though the inquisitor issued letters prohibiting any one from possessing or reading his books, there is no allusion to any Joachite error. It was simply a question of disobedience to the bull *Quorumdam*. They affirmed that this was contrary to the Gospel of Christ, which forbade them to wear garments of other fashion than that which they had adopted, or to lay up stores of corn and wine. To this the pope had no authority to compel them; they would not obey him, and this they declared they would maintain until the Day of Judgment. Frivolous as the questions at issue undoubtedly were, it was on the one hand a case of conscience from which reason had long since been banished by the bitterness of controversy, and on the other the necessity of authority compelling obedience. If private judgment were allowed to set aside the commands of a papal decretal, the moral power of the papacy was gone, and with it all temporal supremacy. Yet, underlying all this was the old Joachitic leaven which taught that the Church of Rome had no spiritual authority, and thus that its decrees were not binding on the elect. When Bernard Délicieux was sent, in 1319, from Avignon to Castelnaudari for trial, on the road he talked freely with his escort and made no secret of his admiration for Joachim, even going so far as to say that he had erased from his copy of the Decretum the Lateran canon condemning Joachim's Trinitarian

---

* Baluz. et Mansi II. 248–51.—Hist. Tribulat. (loc. cit. p. 147).

error, and that if he were pope he would abrogate it. The influence of the Everlasting Gospel is seen in the fact that of those
who recanted at Marseilles and were imprisoned, a number fled to
the Infidel, leaving behind them a paper in which they defiantly
professed their faith, and prophesied that they would return triumphantly after the death of John XXII.*

Thus John, ere yet his pontificate was a year old, had succeeded in creating a new heresy—that which held it unlawful for
Franciscans to wear flowing gowns or to have granaries and cellars.
In the multiform development of human perversity there has been
perhaps none more deplorably ludicrous than this, that man should
burn his fellows on such a question, or that men should be found
dauntless enough to brave the flames for such a principle, and to
feel that they were martyrs in a high and holy cause. John probably, from the constitution of his mind and his training, could not
understand that men could be so enamoured of holy poverty as to
sacrifice themselves to it, and he could only regard them as obstinate rebels, to be coerced into submission or to pay the penalty.
He had taken his stand in support of Michele da Cesena's authority, and resistance, whether active or passive, only hardened him.

The bull *Quorumdam* had created no little stir. A defence of
it, written by an inquisitor of Carcassonne and Toulouse, probably
Jean de Beaune, shows that its novel positions had excited grave
doubts in the minds of learned men, who were not convinced of its
orthodoxy, though not prepared to risk open dissent. There is also
an allusion to a priest who persisted in maintaining the errors
which it condemned and who was handed over to the secular arm,

---

* Raym. de Fronciacho (Archiv f. L. u. K. 1887, p. 31).—Baluz. et Mansi
II. 248–51, 271–2.— Joann. S. Victor. Chron. ann. 1319 (Muratori S. R. I. III. II.
478–9).—MSS. Bib. Nat., fonds latin, No. 4270, fol. 188, 262. Bernard, however,
in his examination, denied these allegations as well as Olivi's tenet that Christ
was alive when lanced upon the Cross, although he said some MSS. of St. Mark
so represented him (fol. 167–8).

Of the remainder of those who were tried at Marseilles the fate is uncertain.
From the text it appears that at least some of them were imprisoned. Others
were probably let off with lighter penances, for in 1325 Blaise Boerii, a shoe-
maker of Narbonne, when on trial before the Inquisition of Carcassonne, confessed that he had visited, in houses at Marseilles, three of them at one time and
four at another, and had received them in his own house and had conducted
them on their way.—Doat, XXVII. 7 sqq.

but who recanted ere the fagots were lighted and was received to penance. To silence discussion, John assembled a commission of thirteen prelates and doctors, including Michele da Cesena, who after due consideration solemnly condemned as heretical the propositions that the pope had no authority to issue the bull, and that obedience was not due to prelates who commanded the laying aside of short and narrow vestments and the storing up of corn and wine. All this was rapidly creating a schism, and the bull *Sancta Romana*, December 30, 1317, and *Gloriosam ecclesiam*, January 23, 1318, were directed against those who under the names of Fraticelli, Beguines, Bizochi, and *Fratres de paupere vita*, in Sicily, Italy, and the south of France, were organizing an independent Order under the pretence of observing strictly the Rule of Francis, receiving multitudes into their sect, building or receiving houses in gift, begging in public, and electing superiors. All such are declared excommunicate *ipso facto*, and all prelates are commanded to see that the sect is speedily extirpated.*

Among the people, the cooler heads argued that if the Franciscan vow rendered all possession sinful it was not a vow of holiness, for in things in which use was consumption, such as bread and cheese, use passed into possession. He who took such a vow, therefore, by the mere fact of living broke that vow, and could not be in a state of grace. The supreme holiness of poverty, however, had been so assiduously preached for a hundred years that a large portion of the population sympathized with the persecuted Spirituals; many laymen, married and unmarried, joined them as Tertiaries, and even priests embraced their doctrines. There speedily grew up a sect, by no means confined to Franciscans, to replace the fast-vanishing Cathari as an object for the energies of the Inquisition. It is the old story over again, of persecuted saints with the familiars ever at their heels, but always finding refuge and hiding-place at the hands of friendly sympathizers. Pierre Trencavel, a priest of Béziers, may be taken as an example. His name recurs frequently in the examinations before the Inquisition as that of one of the principal leaders of the sect. Caught at last, he was thrown into the prison of Carcassonne, but managed to escape,

---

* Baluz. et Mansi II. 270-1, 274-6.—Extravagant. Joann. XXII. Tit. vii.— Mag. Bull. Roman. I. 193.

when he was condemned in an *auto de fé* as a convicted heretic. Then a purse was raised among the faithful to send him to the East. After an absence of some years he returned and was as active as ever, wandering in disguise throughout the south of France and assiduously guarded by the devotees. What was his end does not appear, but he probably perished at length at the stake as a relapsed heretic, for in 1327 we find him and his daughter Andrée in the pitiless hands of Michel of Marseilles. Jean du Prat, then Inquisitor of Carcassonne, wanted them, in order to extort from them the names of their disciples and of those who had sheltered them. Apparently Michel refused to surrender them, and a peremptory order from John XXII. was requisite to obtain their transfer. In 1325 Bernard Castillon of Montpellier confesses to harboring a number of Beguines in his house, and then to buying a dwelling for them in which he visited them. Another culprit acknowledges to receiving many fugitives in his house at Montpellier. There was ample sympathy for them and ample occasion for it.*

The burning of the four martyrs of Marseilles was the signal for active inquisitorial work. Throughout all the infected region the Holy Office bent its energies to the suppression of the new heresy; and as previously there had been no necessity for concealing opinions, the suspects were readily laid hold of. There was

---

* Guill. Nangiac. Contin. ann. 1317.—Coll. Doat, XXVII. 7 sqq., 170; XXXV. 18.—Lib. Sententt. Inq. Tolos. pp. 301, 312, 381.

The case of Raymond Jean illustrates the life of the persecuted Spirituals. As early as 1312 he had commenced to denounce the Church as the Whore of Babylon, and to prophesy his own fate. In 1317 he was one of the appellants who were summoned to Avignon, where he submitted. Remitted to the obedience of his Order, he was sent by his superior to the convent of Anduse, where he remained until he heard the fate of his stancher companions at Marseilles, when he fled with a comrade. Reaching Béziers, they found refuge in a house where, in company with some female apostates from the Order, they lay hid for three years. After this Raymond led a wandering life, associating for a while with Pierre Trencavel. At one time he went beyond seas; then returning, he adopted the habit of a secular priest and assumed the cure of souls, sometimes in Gascony and again in Rodez or east of the Rhone. Captured at last in 1325 and brought before the Inquisition of Carcassonne, after considerable pressure he was induced to recant. His sentence is not given, but doubtless it was perpetual imprisonment.—Doat, XXVII. 7 sqq.

thus an ample harvest, and the rigor of the inquisition set on foot
is shown by the order issued in February, 1322, by John XXII.,
that all Tertiaries in the suspected districts should be summoned
to appear and be closely examined. This caused general terror.
In the archives of Florence there are preserved numerous letters
to the papal curia, written in February, 1322, by the magistrates
and prelates of the Tuscan cities, interceding for the Tertiaries, and
begging that they shall not be confounded with the new sect of
Beguines. This is doubtless a sample of what was occurring
everywhere, and the all-pervading fear was justified by the daily
increasing roll of martyrs. The test was simple. It was whether
the accused believed that the pope had power to dispense with
vows, especially those of poverty and chastity. As we have seen,
it was a commonplace of the schools, which Aquinas proved beyond
cavil, that he had no such power, and even as recently as 1311
the Conventuals, in arguing before Clement V., had admitted that
no Franciscan could hold property or take a wife under command
from the pope; but things had changed in the interval, and now
those who adhered to the established doctrine had the alternative
of recantation or the stake. Of course but a small portion of the
culprits had the steadfastness to endure to the end against the persuasive methods which the Inquisition knew so well how to employ,
and the number of the victims who perished shows that the sect
must have been large. Our information is scanty and fragmentary, but we know that at Narbonne, where the bishops at first
endeavored to protect the unfortunates, until frightened by the
threats of the inquisitors, there were three burned in 1319, seventeen
in Lent, 1321, and several in 1322. At Montpellier, persecution
was already active in 1319. At Lunel there were seventeen burned;
at Béziers, two at one time and seven at another; at Pézénas, several, with Jean Formayron at their head; in Gironde, a number in
1319; at Toulouse, four in 1322, and others at Cabestaing and Lo-
dève. At Carcassonne there were burnings in 1319, 1320, and 1321,
and Henri de Chamay was active there between 1325 and 1330.
A portion of his trials are still extant, with very few cases of burning, but Mosheim had a list of one hundred and thirteen persons
executed at Carcassonne as Spirituals from 1318 to about 1350.
All these cases were under Dominican inquisitors, and the Franciscans were even more zealous, if we may believe Wadding's boast

that in 1323 there were one hundred and fourteen burned by Franciscan inquisitors alone.   The Inquisition at Marseilles, in fact, which was in Franciscan hands, had the reputation of being excessively severe with the recalcitrant brethren of the Order.   In a case occurring in 1329 Frère Guillem de Salvelle, the Guardian of Béziers, states that their treatment there was very harsh and the imprisonment of the most rigorous description.   Doubtless Angelo da Clarino has justification for the assertion that the Conventuals improved their triumph over their antagonists like mad dogs and wolves, torturing, slaying, and ransoming without mercy.   Trivial as may seem to us the cause of quarrel, we cannot but respect the simple earnestness which led so many zealots to seal their convictions with their blood.   Many of them, we are told, courted martyrdom and eagerly sought the flames.   Bernard Léon of Montréal was burned for persistently declaring that, as he had vowed poverty and chastity, he would not obey the pope if ordered to take a wife or accept a prebend.*

Ferocious persecution such as this of course only intensified the convictions of the sufferers and their antagonism to the Holy See. So far as regards the ostensible subject of controversy, we learn from Pierre Tort, when he was before the Inquisition of Toulouse in 1322, that it was allowable to lay in stores of corn and wine sufficient for eight or fifteen days, while of salt and oil there might be provision for half a year.   As to vestments, Michele da Cesena had exercised the power conferred on him by the bull *Quorumdam* by issuing, in 1317, a precept requiring the gown to be made of coarse stuff, reaching down to cover only half the foot, while the cord was to be of hemp and not of flax.   Although he seems to have left the burning question of the hood untouched, this regulation might have satisfied reasonable scruples, but it was a case of conscience which admitted of no compromise.   The Spirituals declared that they were not bound to abandon the still shorter and

---

* Raynald ann. 1322, No. 51.—Archivio di Firenze, Prov. del Convento di Santa Croce, Feb. 1322.—S. Th. Aquin. Summ. Sec. Sec. Q. LXXXVIII. Art. xi.; Q. CLXXXVI. Art. viii. ad 3.—Franz Ehrle (Archiv für Litt.- u. Kirchengeschichte, 1887, p. 156).—Lib. Sententt. Inq. Tolos. pp. 300, 313, 381-93.—Coll. Doat, XXVII., XXVIII.—Mosheim de Beghardis pp. 499, 632.—Vaissette, IV. 182-3.— Wadding. ann. 1317, No. 45.—Hist. Tribulat. (loc. cit. p. 149).—Arch. de l' Inq. de Carcass. (Doat, XXVII. 162).—Johann. S. Victor. Chron. ann. 1316-19.

more ungainly gowns which their tradition attributed to St. Francis, no matter what might be commanded by pope or general, and so large was the importance attributed to the question that in the popular belief the four martyrs of Marseilles were burned because they wore the mean and tightly-fitting garments which distinguished the Spirituals.*

Technically they were right, for, as we have seen above, it had hitherto been generally admitted that the pope could not dispense for vows; and when Olivi developed this to the further position that he could not order anything contrary to an evangelical vow, it was not reckoned among his errors condemned by the Council of Vienne. While all this, however, had been admitted as a theoretical postulate, when it came to be set up against the commands of such a pope as John XXII. it was rebellious heresy, to be crushed with the sternest measures. At the same time it was impossible that the sufferers could recognize the authority which was condemning them to the stake. Men who willingly offered themselves to be burned because they asserted that the pope had no power to dispense from the observance of vows; who declared that if there were but one woman in the world, and if she had taken a vow of chastity, the pope could give her no valid dispensation, even if it were to prevent the human race from coming to an end; who asserted that John XXII. had sinned against the gospel of Christ when he had attempted to permit the Franciscans to have granaries and cellars; who held that although the pope might have power over other Orders he had none over that of St. Francis, because his Rule was divine revelation, and not a word in it could be altered or erased—such men could only defend themselves against the pope by denying the source of his authority. All the latent Joachitic notions which had been dormant were vivified and became the leading principles of the sect. John XXII., when he issued the bull *Quorumdam*, became the mystical Antichrist, the forerunner of the true Antichrist. The Roman Church was the carnal Church; the Spirituals would form the new Church, which would fight with Antichrist, and, under the guidance of the Holy Ghost, would usher in the new age when man would

---

* Lib. Sententt. Inq. Tolosan. pp. 320, 325.—Wadding. ann. 1317, No. 23.—Coll. Doat, XXVII. 7 sqq.

be ruled by love and poverty be universal. Some of them placed this in 1325, others in 1330, others again in fourteen years from 1321. Thus the scheme of the Everlasting Gospel was formally adopted and brought to realization. There were two churches— one the carnal Church of Rome, the Whore of Babylon, the Synagogue of Satan, drunk with the blood of the saints, over which John XXII. pretended to preside, although he had forfeited his station and become a heretic of heretics when he consented to the death of the martyrs of Marseilles. The other was the true Church, the Church of the Holy Ghost, which would speedily triumph through the arms of Frederic of Trinacria. St. Francis would be resurrected in the flesh, and then would commence the third age and the seventh and last state of mankind. Meanwhile, the sacraments were already obsolete and no longer requisite for salvation. It is to this period of frenzied exaltation that we may doubtless attribute the interpolations of Olivi's writings.[*]

This new Church had some sort of organization. In the trial of Naprous Boneta at Carcassonne, in 1325, there is an allusion to a Frère Guillem Giraud, who had been ordained by God as pope in place of John XXII., whose sin had been as great as Adam's, and who had thus been deposed by the divine will. There were not lacking saints and martyrs, besides Francis and Olivi. Fragments of the bodies and bones of those who perished at the stake were treasured up as relics, and even pieces of the stakes at which they suffered. These were set before altars in their houses, or carried about the person as amulets. In this cult, the four martyrs of Marseilles were pre-eminently honored; their suffrages with God were as potent as those of St. Laurence or St. Vincent, and in them Christ had been spiritually crucified on the four arms of the cross. One poor wretch, who was burned at Toulouse in 1322, had inserted in his litany the names of seventy Spirituals who had suffered; he invoked them among the other saints, attaching equal importance to their intervention; and this was doubtless a customary and recognized form of devotion. Yet this cult was simpler than that of the orthodox Church, for it was held that the

---

[*] Lib. Sententt. Inq. Tolosan. pp. 298–99, 302–6, 316.—Bern. Guidon. Practica P. v.—Doat, XXVII. 7 sqq.—Johann. S. Victor. Chron. ann. 1316–19 (Muratori S. R. I. III. II. 478–9).

saints needed no oblations, and if a man had vowed a candle to one of them or to the Virgin, or a pilgrimage to Compostella, it would be better to give to the poor the money that it would cost.*

The Church composed of these enthusiastic fanatics broke off all relations with the Italian Spirituals, whose more regulated zeal seemed lukewarmness and backsliding. The prisoners who were tried by Bernard Gui in 1322 at Toulouse described the Franciscan Order as divided into three fragments—the Conventuals, who insisted on having granaries and cellars, the Fraticelli under Henry da Ceva in Sicily, and the Spirituals, or Beguines, then under persecution. The two former groups they said did not observe the Rule and would be destroyed, while their own sect would endure to the end of the world. Even the saintly and long-suffering Angelo da Clarino was denounced as an apostate, and there were hot-headed zealots who declared that he would prove to be the mystical Antichrist. Others were disposed to assign this doubtful honor, or even the position of the greater Antichrist, to Felipe of Majorca, brother of that Ferrand whom we have seen offered the sovereignty of Carcassonne. Felipe's thirst for asceticism had led him to abandon his brother's court and become a Tertiary of St. Francis. Angelo alludes to him repeatedly, with great admiration, as worthy to rank with the ancient perfected saints. In the stormy discussions soon after John's accession he had intervened in favor of the Spirituals, petitioning that they be allowed to form a separate Order. After taking the full vows, he renewed this supplication in 1328, but it was refused in full consistory, after which we hear of him wandering over Europe and living on beggary. In 1341, with the support of Robert of Naples, he made a third application, which Benedict XII. rejected for the reason that he was a supporter and defender of the Beguines, whom he had justified after their condemnation by publicly asserting many enormous heretical lies about the Holy See. Such were the men whose self-devotion seemed to these fiery bigots so tepid as to render them objects of detestation.†

---

* Doat, XXVII. 7 sqq.—Lib. Sententt. Inq. Tolos. pp. 305, 307, 310, 383–5.— Bern. Guidon. Practica P. v.

† Lib. Sententt. Inq. Tolos. pp. 303, 309, 326, 330.—Bern. Guidon. Practica P. v.—Franz Ehrle (op. cit. 1885, pp. 540, 543, 557).—Raym. de Fronciacho (Ib.

III.—6

The heights of exaltation reached in their religious delirium are illustrated by the career of Naprous Boneta, who was reverenced in the sect as an inspired prophetess. As early as 1315 she had fallen into the hands of the Inquisition at Montpellier, and had been thrown into prison, to be subsequently released. She and her sister Alissette were warmly interested in the persecuted Spirituals, and gave refuge to many fugitives in their house. As persecution grew hotter, her exaltation increased. In 1320 she commenced to have visions and ecstasies, in which she was carried to heaven and had interviews with Christ. Finally, on Holy Thursday, 1321, Christ communicated to her the Divine Spirit as completely as it had been given to the Virgin, saying, "The Blessed Virgin Mary was the giver of the Son of God: thou shalt be the giver of the Holy Ghost." Thus the promises of the Everlasting Gospel were on the point of fulfilment, and the Third Age was about to dawn. Elijah, she said, was St. Francis, and Enoch was Olivi; the power granted to Christ lasted until God gave the Holy Spirit to Olivi, and invested him with as much glory as had been granted to the humanity of Christ. The papacy has ceased to exist, the sacraments of the altar and of confession are superseded, but that of matrimony remains. That of penitence, indeed, still exists, but it is purely internal, for heartfelt contrition works forgiveness of sins without sacerdotal intercession or the imposition of penance. One remark, which she casually made when before her judges, is noteworthy as manifesting the boundless love and charity of these poor souls. The Spirituals and lepers, she said, who had been burned were like the innocents massacred by Herod—it was Satan who procured the burning of the Spirituals and lepers. This alludes to the hideous cruelties which, as we have seen, were perpetrated on the lepers in 1321 and 1322, when the whole of France went mad with terror over a rumored poisoning of the wells by these outcasts, and when, it seems, the Spirituals were wise enough and humane enough to sympathize with them and condemn their murder. Naprous, at length, was brought before Henri de Chamay,

---

1887, p. 29.—Guillel. Nangiac. Contin. ann. 1330.—Wadding. ann. 1341, No. 21, 23.

A subdivision of the Italian Fraticelli took the name of Brethren of Fray Felipe de Mallorca (Tocco, Archivio Storico Napoletano, 1887, Fasc. 1).

the Inquisitor of Carcassonne, in 1325. Sincere in the belief of
her divine mission, she spontaneously and fearlessly related her
history and stated her faith, and in her replies to her examiners
she was remarkably quick and intelligent. When her confession
was read over to her she confirmed it, and to all exhortations to
retract she quietly answered that she would live and die in it as
the truth. She was accordingly handed over to the secular arm
and sealed her convictions with her blood.*

Extravagances of belief such as this were not accompanied with
extravagance of conduct. Even Bernard Gui has no fault to find
with the heretics' mode of life, except that the school of Satan
imitated the school of Christ, as laymen imitate like monkeys the
pastors of the Church. They all vowed poverty and led a life of
self-denial, some of them laboring with their hands and others begging by the wayside. In the towns and villages they had little
dwellings which they called Houses of Poverty, and where they
dwelt together. On Sundays and feast-days their friends would
assemble and all would listen to readings from the precepts and
articles of faith, the lives of the saints, and their own religious
books in the vulgar tongue—mostly the writings of Olivi, which
they regarded as revelations from God, and the " *Transitus Sancti
Patris*," which was a legendary account of his death. The only
external signs by which Bernard says they were to be recognized
were that on meeting one another, or entering a house, they would
say, " Blessed be Jesus Christ," or " Blessed be the name of the
Lord Jesus Christ." When praying in church or elsewhere they
sat with hooded heads and faces turned to the wall, not standing
or kneeling, or striking their hands, as was customary with the
orthodox. At dinner, after asking a blessing, one of them would
kneel and recite *Gloria in excelsis*, and after supper, *Salve Regina*.
This was all inoffensive enough, but they had one peculiarity to
which Bernard as an inquisitor took strong exceptions. When on
trial they were ready enough to confess their own faith, but nothing would induce them to betray their associates. In their simplicity they held that this would be a violation of Christian charity
to which they could not lawfully be compelled, and the inquisitor
wasted infinite pains in the endeavor to show that it is charity to

* Coll. Doat, XXVII. 7 sqq., 95.

one's neighbor, and not an injury, to give him a chance of conversion.*

Evidently these poor folk would have been harmless enough if let alone, and their persecution could only be justified by the duty of the Church to preserve erring souls from perdition. A sect based upon the absolute abnegation of property as its chief principle, and the apocalyptic reveries of the Everlasting Gospel, could never become dangerous, though it might be disagreeable, from its mute—or perhaps vivacious—protest against the luxury and worldliness of the Church. Even if let alone it would probably soon have died out. Springing as it did in a region and at a period in which the Inquisition was thoroughly organized, it had no chance of survival, and it speedily succumbed under the ferocious energy of the proceedings brought to bear against it. Yet we cannot fix with any precision the date of its extinction. The records are imperfect, and those which we possess fail to draw a distinction between the Spirituals and the orthodox Franciscans, who, as we shall see, were driven to rebellion by John XXII. on the question of the poverty of Christ. This latter dogma became one of so much larger importance that the dreams of the Spirituals were speedily lost to view, and in the later cases it is reasonable to assume that the victims were Fraticelli. Still, there are several prosecutions on record at Carcassonne in 1329, which were doubtless of Spirituals. One of them was of Jean Roger, a priest who had stood in high consideration at Béziers; he had been an associate of Pierre Trencavel in his wanderings, and the slight penance imposed on him would seem to indicate that the ardor of persecution was abating, though we learn that the bones of the martyrs of Marseilles were still handed around as relics. John XXII. was not disposed to connive at any relaxation of rigor, and in February, 1331, he reissued his bull *Sancta Romana*, with a preface addressed to bishops and inquisitors in which he assumes that the sect is flourishing as vigorously as ever, and orders the most active measures taken for its suppression. Doubtless there were subsequent prosecutions, but the sect as a distinctive one faded out of sight.†

During the period of its active existence it had spread across

---

* Bern. Guidon. Practica P. v.   † Doat, XXVII. 156, 170, 178, 215; XXXII. 147.

the Pyrenees into Aragon. Even before the Council of Béziers, in 1299, took official cognizance of the nascent heresy, the bishops of Aragon, assembled at Tarragona in 1297, instituted repressive measures against the Beguines who were spreading errors throughout the kingdom, and all Franciscan Tertiaries were subjected to supervision. Their books in the vulgar tongue were especially dreaded, and were ordered to be surrendered. These precautions did not avert the evil. As we have seen, Arnaldo de Vilanova became a warm advocate of the Spirituals; his indefatigable pen was at their service, his writings had wide circulation, and his influence with Jayme II. protected them. With his death and that of Clement V. persecution commenced. Immediately after the latter event, in 1314, the Inquisitor Bernardo de Puycerda, one of Arnaldo's special antagonists, undertook their suppression. At their head stood a certain Pedro Oler, of Majorca, and Fray Bonato. They were obstinate, and were handed over to the secular arm, when all were burned except Bonato, who recanted on being scorched by the flames. He was dragged from the burning pile, cured, and condemned to perpetual imprisonment, but after some twenty years he was found to be still secretly a Spiritual, and was burned as a relapsed in 1335. Emboldened by the accession of John XXII., in November, 1316, Juan de Llotger, the inquisitor, and Jofre de Cruilles, provost of the vacant see of Tarragona, called together an assembly of Dominicans, Franciscans, and Cistercians, who condemned the apocalyptic and spiritualistic writings of Arnaldo, which were ordered to be surrendered within ten days under pain of excommunication. The persecution continued. Durán de Baldach was burned as a Spiritual, with a disciple, in 1325. About the same time John XXII. issued several bulls commanding strict inquisition to be made for them throughout Aragon, Valencia, and the Balearic Isles, and subjecting them to the jurisdiction of the bishops and inquisitors in spite of any privileges or immunities which they might claim as Franciscans. The heresy, however, seems never to have obtained any firm foothold on Spanish soil. Yet it penetrated even to Portugal, for Alvaro Pelayo tells us that there were in Lisbon some pseudo-Franciscans who applauded the doctrine that Peter and his successors had not received from Christ the power which he held on earth.*

---

* Concil. Tarraconens. ann. 1297 c. 1–4 (Martene Ampl. Coll. VII. 305–6).—

A somewhat different development of the Joachitic element is seen in the Franciscan Juan de Pera-Tallada or de Rupescissa, better known perhaps through Froissart as Jean de la Roche-taillade. As a preacher and missionary he stood pre-eminent, and his voice was heard from his native Catalonia to distant Moscow. Somewhat given to occult science, various treatises on alchemy have been attributed to him, among which Pelayo tells us that it is difficult to distinguish the genuine from the doubtful. Not only in this did he follow Arnaldo de Vilanova, but in mercilessly lashing the corruptions of the Church, and in commenting on the prophecies of the pseudo-Joachim. No man of this school seemed able to refrain from indulging in prophecy himself, and Juan gained wide reputation by predictions which were justified by the event, such as the battle of Poitiers and the Great Schism. Perhaps this might have been forgiven had he not also foretold that the Church would be stripped of the superfluities which it had so shockingly abused. One metaphor which he employed was largely quoted. The Church, he said, was a bird born without feathers, to which all other fowls contributed plumage, which they would reclaim in consequence of its pride and tyranny. Like the Spirituals he looked fondly back to the primitive days before Constantine, when in holy poverty the foundations of the faith were laid. He seems to have steered clear of the express heresy as to the poverty of Christ, and when he came to Avignon, in 1349, to proclaim his views, although several attempts to burn him were ineffectual, he was promptly thrown into jail. He was " *durement grand clerc*," and his accusers were unable to convict him, but he was too dangerous a man to be at large, and he was kept in confinement. When he was finally liberated is not stated, but if Pelayo is correct in saying that he returned home at the age of ninety he must have been released after a long incarceration.*

Eymeric. pp. 265–6.—Raynald. ann. 1325, No. 20.—Mosheim de Beghardis p. 641.—Pelayo, Heterodoxos Españoles, I. 777–81, 783.—For the fate of Arnaldo de Vilanova's writings in the Index Expurgatorius, see Reusch, Der Index der verbotenen Bücher, I. 33–4. Two of the tracts condemned in 1316 have been found, translated into Italian, in a MS. of the Magliabecchian Library, by Prof. Tocco, who describes them in the Archivio Storico Italiano, 1886, No. 6, and in the Giornale Storico della Lett. Ital. VIII. 3.

* Pelayo, Heterodoxos Españoles, I. 500–2.—Jo. de Rupesciss. Vade mecum

The ostensible cause of his punishment was his Joachitic speculation as to Antichrist, though, as Wadding observes, many holy men did the same without animadversion, like St. Vicente Ferrer, who in 1412 not only predicted Antichrist, but asserted that he was already nine years old, and who was canonized, not persecuted. Milicz of Cremsier also, as we have seen, though persecuted, was acquitted. Fray Juan's reveries, however, trenched on the borders of the Everlasting Gospel, although keeping within the bounds of orthodoxy. In his prison, in November, 1349, he wrote out an account of a miraculous vision vouchsafed him in 1345, in return for continued prayer and maceration. Louis of Bavaria was the Antichrist who would subjugate Europe and Africa in 1366, while a similar tyrant would arise in Asia. Then would come a schism with two popes; Antichrist would lord it over the whole earth and many heretical sects would arise. After the death of Antichrist would follow fifty-five years of war; the Jews would be converted, and with the destruction of the kingdom of Antichrist the Millennium would open. Then the converted Jews would possess the world, all would be Tertiaries of St. Francis, and the Franciscans would be models of holiness and poverty. The heretics would take refuge in inaccessible mountains and the islands of the sea, whence they would emerge at the close of the Millennium; the second Antichrist would appear and bring a period of great suffering, until fire would fall from heaven and destroy him and his followers, after which would follow the end of the world and the Day of Judgment.*

Meditation in prison seems to have modified somewhat his prophetic vision, and in 1356 he wrote his *Vade mecum in Tribulatione*, in which he foretold that the vices of the clergy would lead to the speedy spoliation of the Church; in six years it would be reduced to a state of apostolical poverty, and by 1370 would commence the process of recuperation which would bring all mankind under the domination of Christ and of his earthly representative.

(Fascic. Rer. Expetend. et Fugiend. II. 497).—Froissart, Liv. I. P. ii. ch. 124; Liv. III. ch. 27.—Rolewink Fascic. Temp. ann. 1364.—Mag. Chron. Belgic. (Pistorii III. 336).—Meyeri Annal. Flandr. ann. 1359. — Henr. Rebdorff. Annal. ann. 1351.—Paul Æmylii de Reb. Gest. Francor. (Ed. 1569, pp. 491-2).—M. Flac. Illyr. Cat. Test. Veritat. Lib. XVIII. p. 1786 (Ed. 1608).

* Wadding. ann. 1357, No. 17.—Pelayo, op. cit. I. 501-2.

During the interval there would be a succession of the direst calamities. From 1360 to 1365 the worms of the earth would arise and destroy all beasts and birds; tempest and deluge and earthquake, famine and pestilence and war would sweep away the wicked; in 1365 Antichrist would come, and such multitudes would apostatize that but few faithful would be left. His reign would be short, and in 1370 a pope canonically elected would bring mankind to Christianity, after which all cardinals would be chosen from the Greek Church. During these tribulations the Franciscans would be nearly exterminated, in punishment for their relaxation of the Rule, but the survivors would be reformed and the Order would fill the earth, innumerable as the stars of heaven; in fact, two Franciscans of the most abject poverty were to be the Elias and Enoch who would conduct the Church through that disastrous time. Meanwhile he advised that ample store should be made in mountain caves of beans and honey, salt meats, and dried fruits by those who desired to live through the convulsions of nature and society. After the death of Antichrist would come the Millennium; for seven hundred years, or until about A.D. 2000, mankind would be virtuous and happy, but then would come a decline; existing vices, especially among the clergy, would be revived, preparatory to the advent of Gog and Magog, to be followed by the final Antichrist. It shows the sensitiveness of the hierarchy that this harmless nympholepsy was deemed worthy of severe repression.*

The influence of the Everlasting Gospel was not yet wholly exhausted. I have alluded above to Thomas of Apulia, who in 1388 insisted on preaching to the Parisians that the reign of the Holy Ghost had commenced, and that he was the divinely commissioned envoy sent to announce it, when his mission was humanely cut short by confining him as a madman. Singularly identical in all but the result was the career of Nicholas of Buldesdorf, who, about 1445, proclaimed that God had commanded him to announce that the time of the New Testament had passed away, as that of the Old had done; that the Third Era and Seventh Age of the world had come, under the reign of the Holy Ghost, when man would be restored to the state of primal innocence; and that he was the Son of God deputed to spread the glad tidings. To

---

* Fascic. Rer. Expetend. et Fugiend. II. 494–508.

the council still sitting at Basle he sent various tracts containing these doctrines, and he finally had the audacity to appear before it in person. His writings were promptly consigned to the flames and he was imprisoned. Every effort was made to induce him to recant, but in vain. The Basilian fathers were less considerate of insanity than the Paris doctors, and Nicholas perished at the stake in 1446.*

A last echo of the Everlasting Gospel is heard in the teaching of two brothers, John and Lewin of Würzburg, who in 1466 taught in Eger that all tribulations were caused by the wickedness of the clergy. The pope was Antichrist, and the cardinals and prelates were his members. Indulgences were useless and the ceremonies of the Church were vanities, but the time of deliverance was at hand. A man was already born of a virgin, who was the anointed of Christ and would speedily come with the third Evangel and bring all the faithful into the fold. The heresy was rapidly and secretly spreading among the people, when it was discovered by Bishop Henry of Ratisbon. The measures taken for its suppression are not recorded, and the incident is only of interest as showing how persistently the conviction reappeared that there must be a final and higher revelation to secure the happiness of man in this world and his salvation in the next.†

---

* Füesslins neue u. unpartheyische Kirchen- u. Ketzerhistorie, Frankfurt, 1772, II. 63-66.

† Chron. Glassberger ann. 1466 (Analecta Franciscana II. 422-6).

CHAPTER II.

GUGLIELMA AND DOLCINO.

THE spiritual exaltation which produced among the Franciscans the developments described in the last chapter was by no means confined to the recognized members of that Order. It manifested itself in even more irregular fashion in the little group of sectaries known as Guglielmites, and in the more formidable demonstration of the Dolcinists, or Apostolic Brethren.

About the year 1260 there came to Milan a woman calling herself Guglielma. That she brought with her a son shows that she had lived in the world, and was doubtless tried with its vicissitudes, and as the child makes no further appearance in her history, he probably died young. She had wealth, and was said to be the daughter of Constance, queen and wife of the King of Bohemia. Her royal extraction is questionable, but the matter is scarce worth the discussion which it has provoked.* She was a woman of pre-eminent piety, who devoted herself to good works, without practising special austerities, and she gradually attracted around her a little band of disciples, to whom such of her utterances as have been recorded show that she gave wholesome ethical instruction.

---

* Constance, daughter of Bela III. of Hungary, was second wife of Ottokar I. of Bohemia, who died in 1230 at the age of eighty. She died in 1240, leaving three daughters, Agnes, who founded the Franciscan convent of St. Januarius in Prague, which she entered May 18, 1236; Beatrice, who married Otho the Pious, of Brandenburg, and Ludomilla, who married Louis I. of Bavaria. Guglielma can scarce have been either of these (Art de Ver. les Dates, VIII. 17). Her disciple, Andrea Saramita, testified that after her death he journeyed to Bohemia to obtain reimbursement of certain expenses; he failed in his errand, but verified her relationship to the royal house of Bohemia (Andrea Ogniben, I Guglielmiti del Secolo XIII., Perugia, 1867, pp. 10–11).—On the other hand, a German contemporary chronicler asserts that she came from England (Annal. Dominican. Colmariens. ann. 1301—Urstisii III. 33).

They adopted the style of plain brown garment which she habitually wore, and seem to have formed a kind of unorganized congregation, bound together only by common devotion to her.*

At that period it was not easy to set bounds to veneration; the spiritual world was felt to be in the closest relation with the material, and the development of Joachitism shows how readily received were suggestions that a great change was impending, and a new era about to open for mankind. Guglielma's devotees came to regard her as a saint, gifted with thaumaturgic power. Some of her disciples claimed to be miraculously cured by her—Dr. Giacobbe da Ferno of an ophthalmic trouble, and Albertono de' Novati of a fistula. Then it was said that she had received the supereminent honor of the Stigmata, and although those who prepared her body for the grave could not see them, this was held to be owing to their unworthiness. It was confidently predicted that she would convert the Jews and Saracens, and bring all mankind into unity of faith. At last, about 1276, some of the more enthusiastic disciples began to whisper that she was the incarnation of the Holy Ghost, in female form—the Third Person of the Trinity, as Christ was of the Second, in the shape of a man. She was very God and very man; it was not alone the body of Christ which suffered in the Passion, but also that of the Holy Ghost, so that her flesh was the same as that of Christ. The originators of this strange belief seem to have been Andrea Saramita, a man of standing in Milan, and Suor Maifreda di Pirovano, an Umiliata of the ancient convent of Biassono, and a cousin of Matteo Visconti. There is no probability that Guglielma countenanced these absurd stories. Andrea Saramita was the only witness who asserted that he had them from her direct, and he had a few days before testified to the contrary. The other immediate disciples of Guglielma stated that she made no pretensions to any supernatural character. When people would ask her to cure them or relieve them of trouble she would say, "Go, I am not God." When told of the strange beliefs entertained of her she strenuously asserted that she was only a miserable woman and a vile worm. Marchisio Secco, a monk of Chiaravalle, testified that he had had a dispute with Andrea on the subject, and they agreed to refer it to her, when she indig-

---

* Ogniben, op. cit. pp. 56, 73–5, 103–4.

nantly replied that she was flesh and bone, that she had brought a son with her to Milan, and that if they did not do penance for uttering such words they would be condemned to hell. Yet, to minds familiar with the promises of the Everlasting Gospel, it might well seem that the era of the Holy Ghost would be ushered in with such an incarnation.*

Guglielma died August 24, 1381, leaving her property to the great Cistercian house of Chiaravalle, near Milan, where she desired to be buried. There was war at the time between Milan and Lodi; the roads were not safe, and she was temporarily interred in the city, while Andrea and Dionisio Cotta went to the Marquis of Montferrat to ask for an escort of troops to accompany the cortége. The translation of the body took place in October, and was conducted with great splendor. The Cistercians welcomed the opportunity to add to the attractions and revenues of their establishment. At that period the business of exploiting new saints was exceedingly profitable, and was prosecuted with corresponding energy. Salimbene complains bitterly of it in referring to a speculation made in 1279, at Cremona, out of the remains of a drunken vintner named Alberto, whose cult brought crowds of devotees with offerings, to the no small gain of all concerned. Such things, as we have seen in the case of Armanno Pongilupo and others, were constantly occurring, though Salimbene declares that the canons forbade the veneration of any one, or picturing him as a saint, until the Roman Church had authoritatively passed upon his claims. In this Salimbene was mistaken. Zanghino Ugolini, a much better authority, assures us that the worship of uncanonized saints was not heretical, if it were believed that their miracles were worked by God at their intercession, but if it were believed that they were worked by the relics without the assent of God, then the Inquisition could intervene and punish; but so long as a saint was uncanonized his cult was at the discretion of the bishop, who could at any time command its cessation, and the

---

* Ogniben, op. cit. pp. 12, 20–1, 35–7, 69, 70, 74, 76, 82, 84–6, 101, 104–6, 116.

Dr. Andrea Ogniben, to whom we are indebted for the publication of the fragmentary remains of the trial of the Guglielmites, thinks that Maifreda di Pirovano was a cousin of Matteo Visconti, through his mother, Anastasia di Pirovano (op. cit. p. 23). The Continuation of Nangis calls her his half-sister (Guillel. Nangiac. Contin. ann. 1317).

mere fact that miracles were performed was no evidence, as they are frequently the work of demons to deceive the faithful.*

In this case the Archbishop of Milan offered no interference, and the worship of Guglielma was soon firmly established. A month after the translation Andrea had the body exhumed and carried into the church, where he washed it with wine and water and arrayed it in a splendid embroidered robe. The washings were carefully preserved, to be used as a chrism for the sick; they were placed on the altar of the nunnery of Biassono, and Maifreda employed them in anointing the affected parts of those who came to be healed. Presently a chapel with an altar arose over her tomb, and tradition still points out at Chiaravalle the little oratory where she is said to have lain, and a portrait on the wall over the vacant tomb is asserted to be hers. It represents her as kneeling before the Virgin, to whom she is presented by St. Bernard, the patron of the abbey; a crowd of other figures is around her, and the whole indicates that those who dedicated it to her represented her as merely a saint, and not as an incarnation of the Godhead. Another picture of her was placed by Dionisio Cotta in the Church of St. Maria fuori di Porta Nuova, and two lamps were kept burning before it to obtain her suffrage for the soul of his brother interred there. Other pictures were hung in the Church of S. Eufemia and in the nunnery of Biassono. In all this the good monks of Chiaravalle were not remiss. They kept lighted lamps before her altar. Two feast-days were assigned to her—the anniversaries of her death and of her translation—when the devotees would assemble at the abbey, and the monks would furnish a simple banquet, outside of the walls—for the Cistercian rules forbade the profanation of a woman's presence within the sacred enclosure—and some of the monks would discourse eloquently upon the saintliness of Guglielma, comparing her to other saints and to the moon and stars, and receiving such oblations as the piety of the worshippers would offer. Nor was this the only gain to the abbey. Giacobbe de' Novati, one of the believers, belonged to one of the noblest families of Milan, and at his castle the Guglielmites

---

* Ogniben, op. cit. pp. 30, 44, 115.—Salimbene Chronica, pp. 274-6.—Chron. Parmens. ann. 1279 (Muratori S. R. I. IX. 791-2).—Zanchini Tract. de Hæret. c. xxii.

were wont to assemble. When he died he instituted the abbey
as his heir, and the inheritance could not have been inconsiderable. There were, doubtless, other instances of similar liberality
of which the evidences have not reached us.*

All this was innocent enough, but within the circle of those
who worshipped Guglielma there was a little band of initiated
who believed in her as the incarnation of the Holy Ghost. The
history of the Joachites has shown us the readiness which existed
to look upon Christianity as a temporary phase of religion, to
be shortly succeeded by the reign of the Holy Ghost, when the
Church of Rome would give place to a new and higher organization. It was not difficult, therefore, for the Guglielmites to persuade themselves that they had enjoyed the society of the Para-
clete, who was shortly to appear, when the Holy Spirit would be
received in tongues of flame by the disciples, the heathen and the
Jew would be converted, and there would be a new church usher-
ing in the era of love and blessedness, for which man had been
sighing through the weary centuries. Of this doctrine Andrea
was chief apostle. He claimed to be the first and only spiritual
son of Guglielma, from whom he had received the revelation, and
he embroidered it to suit the credulity of the disciples. The Archangel Raphael had announced to the blessed Constance the incarnation in her of the Holy Ghost; a year afterwards, Guglielma
was born on the holy day of Pentecost; she had chosen the form
of a woman, for if she had come as man she would have died like
Christ, and the whole world would have perished. On one occasion, in her chamber, she had changed a chair into an ox, and had
told him to hold it if he could, but when he attempted to do so it
disappeared. The same indulgences were obtainable by visiting
her tomb at Chiaravalle as by a pilgrimage to the Holy Sepulchre.
Wafers which had been consecrated by laying them on the tomb
were eagerly partaken of by the disciples, as a new form of communion. Besides the two regular feast-days, there was a third for
the initiated, significantly held on Pentecost, the day when she
was expected to reappear. Meanwhile, the devotion of the faithful was stimulated by stories of her being in communication with

---

* Ogniben, op. cit. **pp. 20–1, 25–6, 31, 36, 49–50, 56–7, 61, 72–3, 74, 93–4, 104,.
116.**—Tamburini, **Storia dell' Inquisizione, II. 17–18.**

her representatives, both in her own form and in that of a dove. How slight was the evidence required for believers was seen in an incident which gave them great comfort in 1293. At a banquet in the house of Giacobbe da Ferno, a warm discussion arose between those who doubted and those whose convictions were decided. Carabella, wife of Amizzone Toscano, one of the earnest believers, was sitting on her mantle, and when she arose she found three knots in the cords which had not been there before. This was at once pronounced a great miracle, and was evidently regarded as a full confirmation of the truth.*

If it were not for the tragedy which followed there would be nothing to render Guglielmitism other than a jest, for the Church which was to replace the massive structure of Latin Christianity was as ludicrous in its conception as these details of its faith. The Gospels were to be replaced by sacred writings produced by Andrea, of which he had already prepared several, in the names of some of the initiated—" The Epistle of Sibilia to the Novaresi," " The Prophecy of Carmeo the Prophet to all Cities and Nations," and an account of Guglielma's teachings commencing, " In that time the Holy Ghost said to his disciples." Maifreda also composed litanies of the Holy Ghost and prayers for the use of the Church. When, on the second advent of Guglielma, the papacy was to pass away, Maifreda was to become pope, the vicar of the Holy Ghost, with the keys of heaven and hell, and baptize the Jew and the Saracen. A new college of cardinals was to be formed, of whom only one appears to have been selected—a girl named Taria, who, to judge from her answers when before the Inquisition, and the terms of contempt in which she is alluded to by some of the sect, was a worthy representative of the whole absurd scheme. While awaiting her exaltation to the papacy Maifreda was the object of special veneration. The disciples kissed her hands and feet, and she gave them her blessing. It was probably the spiritual excitement caused by the jubilee proclaimed by Boniface VIII., attracting pilgrims to Rome by the hundred thousand to gain the proffered indulgences, which led the Guglielmites to name the Pentecost of 1300 for the advent of the Holy Ghost. With a curious manifestation of materialism, the worshippers pre-

* Ogniben, op. cit. pp. 21, 25, 30, 36, 55. 70, 72, 96, 101.

pared splendid garments for the adornment of the expected God—
a purple mantle with a silver clasp costing thirty pounds of ter-
zioli, gold-embroidered silks and gilt slippers—while Pietra de' Al-
zate contributed forty-two dozen pearls, and Catella de' Giorgi
gave an ounce of pearls. In preparation for her new and holy
functions, Maifreda undertook to celebrate the mysteries of the
mass. During the solemnities of Easter, in sacerdotal vestments,
she consecrated the host, while Andrea in a dalmatic read the
Gospel, and she administered communion to those present. When
should come the resurrection of Guglielma, she was to repeat the
ceremony in S. Maria Maggiore, and the sacred vessels were already prepared for this, on an extravagant scale, costing more
than two hundred lire.*

The sums thus lavished show that the devotees belonged to
the wealthy class. What is most noteworthy, in fact, in the whole
story, is that a belief so absurd should have found acceptance
among men of culture and intelligence, showing the spirit of unrest that was abroad, and the readiness to accept any promise,
however wild, of relief from existing evils. There were few more
prominent families in Milan than the Garbagnati, who were Ghibellines and closely allied with the Visconti. Gasparo Garbagnate
filled many positions of importance, and though his name does not
appear among the sectaries, his wife Benvenuta was one of them,
as well as his two sons, Ottorino and Francesco, and Bella, the
wife of Giacobbe. Francesco was a man of mark as a diplomat
and a lawyer. Sent by Matteo Visconti in 1309 on a mission to
the Emperor Henry VII., he won high favor at the imperial court
and obtained the objects for which he had been despatched. He
ended his career as a professor of jurisprudence in the renowned
University of Padua. Yet this man, presumably learned and cool-
headed, was an ardent disciple, who purchased gold-embroidered
silks for the resurrection of Guglielma, and composed prayers in
her honor. One of the crimes for which Matteo was condemned
in 1323 by the Inquisition was retaining in his service this Francesco Garbagnate, who had been sentenced to wear crosses for his
participation in the Guglielmite heresy; and when John XXII., in

---

* Ogniben, op. cit. pp. 17, 20, 22, 23, 30, 34, 37, 40, 42, 47, 54, 62, 72, 80, 90,
94, 96.

1324, confirmed the sentence, he added that Matteo had terrorized the inquisitors to save his son Galeazzo, who was also a Guglielmite.*

When the heresy became known popular rumor of course attributed to it the customary practices of indiscriminate sexual indulgence which were ascribed to all deviations from the faith. In the legend which was handed down by tradition there appears the same story as to its discovery which we have seen told at Cologne about the Brethren of the Free Spirit—of the husband tracking his wife to the nocturnal rendezvous, and thus learning the obscene practices of the sect. In this case the hero of the tale is Corrado Coppa, whose wife Giacobba was an earnest believer.† It is sufficient to say that the official reports of the trial, in so far as they have reached us, contain no allusions whatever to any licentious doctrines or practices. The inquisitors wasted no time on inquiries in that direction, showing that they knew there was nothing of the kind to reward investigation.

Numerically speaking, the sect was insignificant. It is mentioned that on one occasion, at a banquet in honor of Guglielma, given by the monks of Chiaravalle, there were one hundred and twenty-nine persons present, but these doubtless included many who only reverenced her as a saint. The inner circle of the initiated was apparently much smaller. The names of those inculpated in the confessions before the Inquisition amount only to about thirty, and it is fair to assume that the number of the sectaries at no time exceeded thirty-five or forty.‡

It is not to be supposed that this could go on for nearly twenty years and wholly escape the vigilance of the Milanese inquisitors. In 1284, but a few years after Guglielma's death, two of the disciples, Allegranza and Carabella, incautiously revealed the mysteries of their faith to Belfiore, mother of Frà Enrico di Nova, who at once conveyed it to the inquisitor, Frà Manfredo di Donavia. Andrea was forthwith summoned, with his wife Riccadona, his sister, Migliore, and his daughter, Fiordebellina; also Maifreda,

---

* Ogniben, op. cit. pp. 65–7, 83–4, 90–1, 110.—Ughelli, T. IV. pp. 286–93 (Ed. 1652).—Raynald. ann. 1324, No. 7–11.

† Philip. Bergomat. Supplem. Chron. ann. 1298.—Bern. Corio Hist. Milanes. ann. 1300.

‡ Ogniben, op. cit. pp. 1, 2, 34, 74, 110.—Tamburini, op. cit. II. 67–8.

III.—7

Bellacara de' Carentani, Giacobba dei Bassani, and possibly some others. They readily abjured and were treated with exceptional mildness, for Frà Manfredo absolved them by striking them over the shoulders with a stick, as a symbol of the scourging which as penitents they had incurred. He seems to have attached little importance to the matter, and not to have compelled them to reveal their accomplices. Again, in 1295 and 1296, there was an investigation made by the Inquisitor Frà Tommaso di Como, of which no details have reached us, but which evidently left the leaders unharmed.*

We do not know what called the attention of the Inquisition to the sect in the spring of 1300, but we may conjecture that the expected resurrection of Guglielma at the coming Pentecost, and the preparations made for that event, caused an agitation among the disciples leading possibly to incautious revelations. About Easter (April 10) the inquisitors summoned and examined Maifreda, Giacobba dei Bassani, and possibly some others, but without result. Apparently, however, they were watched, secret information was gathered, and in July the Holy Office was ready to strike effectively. On July 18 a certain Frà Ghirardo presented himself to Lanfranco de' Amizzoni and revealed the whole affair, with the names of the principal disciples. Andrea sought him out and endeavored to learn what he had said, but was merely told to look to himself, for the inquisitors were making many threats. On the 20th Andrea was summoned; his assurances that he had never heard that Guglielma was regarded as more than an ordinary saint were apparently accepted, and he was dismissed with orders to return the next day and meanwhile to preserve absolute secrecy.†

Andrea and Maifreda were thoroughly frightened; they begged the disciples, if called before the inquisitors, to preserve silence with regard to them, as otherwise they could not escape death. It is a peculiar illustration of the recognized hostility between the two Mendicant Orders that the first impulse was to seek assistance from the Franciscans. No sooner were the citations issued than Andrea, with the Doctor Beltramo da Ferno, one of the ear-

---

* Ogniben, pp. 14, 23, 33, 36, 39, 60, 72, 101, 110, 114.

† Ibid. pp. 13, 30–33, 39.

nest believers, went to the Franciscan convent, where they learned
from Frà Daniele da Ferno that Frà Guidone de Cocchenato and
the rest of the inquisitors had no power to act, as their commissions had been annulled by the pope, and that Frà Pagano di Pietra Santa had a bull to that effect. Some intrigue would seem to
be behind this, which it would be interesting to disentangle, for
we meet here with old acquaintances. Frà Guidone is doubtless
the same inquisitor whom we have seen in 1279 participating in
the punishment of Corrado da Venosta, and Frà Pagano has come
before us as the subject of a prosecution for heresy in 1295. Possibly it was this which now stimulated his zeal against the inquisitors, for when the Guglielmites called upon him the next day he
produced the bull and urged them to appear, and thus afford him
evidence that the inquisitors were discharging their functions—
evidence for which he said that he would willingly give twenty-
five lire. It is a striking proof of the impenetrable secrecy in
which the operations of the Inquisition were veiled that he had
been anxiously and vainly seeking to obtain testimony as to who
were really discharging the duties of the tribunal; when, latterly,
a heretic had been burned at Balsemo he had sent thither to find
out who had rendered the sentence, but was unable to do so.
Then the Guglielmites applied to the Abbot of Chiaravalle and to
one of his monks, Marchisio di Veddano, himself suspected of Guglielmitism. These asked to have a copy of the bull, and one was
duly made by a notary and given to them, which they took to the
Archbishop of Milan at Cassano, and asked him to place the investigation of the matter in their hands. He promised to intervene, but if he did so he was probably met with the information,
which had been speedily elicited from the culprits, that they held
Boniface VIII. not to be pope, and consequently that the archbishop whom he had created was not archbishop. Either in this
or in some other way the prelate's zeal was refrigerated, and he
offered no opposition to the proceedings.*

---

* Ogniben, pp. 21, 40, 42, 78–9.

Dionese de' Novati deposed (p. 93) that Maifreda was in the habit of saying
that Boniface was not truly pope, and that another pontiff had been created.
We have seen that the Spiritual Franciscans had gone through the form of
electing a new pope. There was not much in common between them and the
Guglielmites, and yet this would point to some relations as existing.

The Inquisition was well manned, for, besides Frà Guidone, whose age and experience seem to have rendered him the leading actor in the tragedy, and Lanfranco, who took little part in it, we meet with a third inquisitor, Rainerio di Pirovano, and in their absence they are replaced with deputies, Niccolò di Como, Niccolò di Varenna, and Leonardo da Bergamo. They pushed the matter with relentless energy. That torture was freely used there can be no doubt. No conclusion to the contrary can be drawn from the absence of allusion to it in the depositions of the accused, for this is customary. Not only do the historians of the affair speak without reserve of its employment, but the character of the successive examinations of the leading culprits indicates it unerringly—the confident asseverations at first of ignorance and innocence, followed, after a greater or less interval, with unreserved confession. This is especially notable in the cases of those who had abjured in 1284, such as Andrea, Maifreda, and Giacobba, who, as relapsed, knew that by admitting their persistent heresy they were condemning themselves to the flames without hope of mercy, and who therefore had nothing to gain by confession, except exemption from repetition of torment.*

The documents are too imperfect for us to reconstruct the process and ascertain the fate of all of those implicated. In Languedoc, after all the evidence had been taken, there would have been an assembly held in which their sentences would have been determined, and at a solemn Sermo these would have been promulgated, and the stake would have received its victims. Much less formal were the proceedings at Milan. The only sentence of which we have a record was rendered August 23 in an assembly where the archbishop sat with the inquisitors and Matteo Visconti appears among the assessors; and in this the only judgment was on Suor Giacobba dei Bassani, who, as a relapsed, was necessarily handed over to the secular arm for burning. It would seem that

---

* Compare Andrea's first examination, July 20 (Ogniben, op. cit. pp. 8–13), and his second, Aug. 10 (pp. 56–7), with his defiant assertion of his belief, Aug. 13 (pp. 68–72). So, Maifreda's first interrogatory, July 31 (pp. 23–6), with her confession, Aug. 6, and revelation of the names of her worshippers (pp. 33–5). Also, Giacobba dei Bassani's denial, Aug. 3, and confession, Aug. 11 (p. 39). It is the same with those not relapsed. See Suor Agnese dei Montanari's flat denial, Aug. 3, and her confession, Aug. 11 (pp. 37–8).

even before this Ser Mirano di Garbagnate, a priest deeply implicated, had been burned. Andrea was executed probably between
September 1 and 9, and Maifreda about the same time—but we
know nothing about the date of the other executions, or of the
exhumation and cremation of Guglielma's bones—while the examinations of other disciples continued until the middle of October.
Another remarkable peculiarity is that for the minor penalties
the inquisitors called in no experts and did not even consult the
archbishop, but acted wholly at their own discretion, a single
frate absolving or penancing each individual as he saw fit. The
Lombard Inquisition apparently had little deference for the episcopate, even of the Ambrosian Church.*

Yet the action of the Inquisition was remarkable for its mildness, especially when we consider the revolutionary character of
the heresy. The number of those absolutely burned cannot be
definitely stated, but it probably did not exceed four or five.
These were the survivors of those who had abjured in 1284, for
whom, as relapsed and obstinate heretics, there could be no mercy
The rest were allowed to escape with penalties remarkably light.
Thus Sibilia Malcolzati had been one of the most zealous of the
sect; in her early examinations she had resolutely perjured herself, and it had cost no little trouble to make her confess, yet
when, on October 6, she appeared before Frà Rainerio and begged
to be relieved from the excommunication which she had incurred,
he was moved by her prayers and assented, on the ordinary conditions that she would stand to the orders of the Church and
Inquisition, and perform the obligations laid upon her. Still more
remarkable is the leniency with which two sisters, Catella and
Pietra Oldegardi, were treated, for Frà Guidone absolved them on
their abjuring their heresy, contenting himself with simply referring them to their confessors for the penance which they were to
perform. The severest punishment recorded for any except the
relapsed was the wearing of crosses, and these, imposed in September and October, were commuted in December for a fine of
twenty-five lire, payable in February—showing that confiscation
was not a part of the penalty. Even Taria, the expectant cardinal
of the New Dispensation, was thus penanced and relieved. Im-

---

* Ogniben, pp. 19–20, 77, 91.

mediately after Andrea's execution an examination of his wife
Riccadona, as to the furniture in her house and the wine in her
cellar, shows that the Inquisition was prompt in looking after the
confiscations of those condemned to death; and the fragment of
an interrogatory, February 12, 1302, of Marchisio Secco, a monk
of Chiaravalle, indicates that it was involved in a struggle with
the abbey to compel the refunding of the bequest of Guglielma,
as the heresy for which she had been condemned, of course, rendered void all dispositions of her property. How this resulted we
have no means of knowing, but we may feel assured that the abbey was forced to submit; indeed, the complicity of the monks
with the heretics was so clearly indicated that we may wonder
none of their names appear in the lists of those condemned.*

Thus ended this little episode of heresy, of no importance in
its origin or results, but curious from the glimpse which it affords
into the spiritual aberrations of the time, and the procedure of
the Lombard Inquisition, and noteworthy as a rare instance of
inquisitorial clemency.†

---

* Ogniben, pp. 42–4, 63, 67–8, 81–2, 91–2, 95–6, 97, 100, 110, 113, 115–16.

† Spiritual eccentricities, such as those of the Guglielmites, are not to be
regarded as peculiar to any age or any condition of civilization. The story of
Joanna Southcote is well known, and the Southcottian Church maintained its
existence in London until the middle of the present century. In July, 1886, the
American journals reported the discovery, in Cincinnati, of a sect even more
closely approximating to the Guglielmites, and about as numerous, calling themselves Perfectionists, and believing in two married sisters—a Mrs. Martin as an
incarnation of God, and a Mrs. Brooke as that of Christ. Like their predecessors in Milan the sect is by no means confined to the illiterate, but comprises
people of intelligence and culture who have abandoned all worldly occupation
in the expectation of the approaching Millennium—the final era of the Everlasting Gospel. The exposure for a time broke up the sect, of which some members departed, while others, with the two sisters, joined a Methodist church.
Their faith was not shaken, however, and in June, 1887, the church expelled
them after an investigation. One of the charges against them was that they
held the Church of the present day to be Babylon and the abomination of the
earth. England has also recently had a similar experience in a peasant woman
of not particularly moral life who for some fifteen years, until her death, September 18, 1886, was regarded by her followers as a new incarnation of Christ.
Her own definition of herself was, " I am the second appearing and incarnation
of Jesus, the Christ of God, the Bride, the Lamb's Wife, the God-Mother and
Saviour, Life from Heaven," etc., etc. She signed herself " Jesus, First and

About the time when Guglielma settled in Milan, Parma witnessed the commencement of another abnormal development of the great Franciscan movement. The stimulus which monachism had received from the success of the Mendicant Orders, the exaltation of poverty into the greatest of virtues, the recognition of beggary as the holiest mode of life, render it difficult to apportion between yearnings for spiritual perfection and the attractions of idleness and vagabondage in a temperate climate the responsibility for the numerous associations which arose in imitation of the Mendicants. The prohibition of unauthorized religious orders by the Lateran Council was found impossible of enforcement. Men would herd together with more or less of organization in caves and hermitages, in the streets of cities, and in abandoned dwellings and churches by the roadsides. The Carmelites and Augustinian hermits won recognition after a long struggle, and became established Orders, forming, with the Franciscans and Dominicans, the four Mendicant religions. Others, less reputable, or more independent in spirit, were condemned, and when they refused to disband they were treated as rebels and heretics. In the tension of the spiritual atmosphere, any man who would devise and put in practice a method of life assimilating him most nearly to the brutes would not fail to find admirers and followers; and, if he possessed capacity for command and organization, he could readily mould them into a confraternity and become an object of veneration, with an abundant supply of offerings from the pious.

The year 1260 was that in which, according to Abbot Joachim, the era of the Holy Ghost was to open. The spiritual excitement which pervaded the population was seen in the outbreak of the Flagellants, which filled northern Italy with processions of penitents scourging themselves, and in the mutual forgiveness of injuries, which brought an interval of peace to a distracted land. In such a condition of public feeling, gregarious enthusiasm is easily directed to whatever responds to the impulse of the moment, and

---

Last, Mary Ann Girling." At one time her sect numbered a hundred and seventy-five members, some of them rich enough to make it considerable donations, but under the petty persecution of the populace it dwindled latterly to a few, and finally dispersed. Aberrations of this nature belong to no special stage of intellectual development. The only advance made in modern times is in the method of dealing with them.

the self-mortification of a youth of Parma, called Gherardo Segarelli, found abundant imitators. Of low extraction, uncultured
and stupid, he had vainly applied for admission into the Franciscan
Order. Denied this, he passed his days vacantly musing in the
Franciscan church. The beatitude of ecstatic abstraction, carried
to the point of the annihilation of consciousness, has not been confined to the Tapas and Samadhi of the Brahman and Buddhist.
The monks of Mt. Athos, known as Umbilicani from their pious
contemplation of their navels, knew it well, and Jacopone da Todï
shows that its dangerous raptures were familiar to the zealots of
the time.* Segarelli, however, was not so lost to external im-
pressions but that he remarked in the scriptural pictures which
adorned the walls the representations of the apostles in the habits
which art has assigned to them. The conception grew upon him
that the apostolic life and vestment would form the ideal religious
existence, superior even to that of the Franciscans which had been
denied to him. As a preliminary, he sold his little property ; then,
mounting the tribune in the Piazza, he scattered the proceeds among
the idlers sunning themselves there, who forthwith gambled it
away with ample floods of blasphemy. Imitating literally the
career of Christ, he had himself circumcised ; then, enveloped in
swaddling clothes, he was rocked in a cradle and suckled by a
woman. His apprenticeship thus completed, he embarked on the
career of an apostle, letting hair and beard grow, enveloped in a
white mantle, with the Franciscan cord around his waist, and sandals on his feet. Thus accoutred he wandered through the streets
of Parma crying at intervals " *Penitenzagite*," which was his ignorant rendering of " *Penitentiam agite !*"—the customary call to
repentance.†

For a while he had no imitators. In search of disciples he wandered to the neighboring village of Collechio, where, standing at
the roadside, he shouted " Enter my vineyard !" The passers-by
who knew his crazy ways paid no attention to him, but strangers
took his call to be an invitation to help themselves from the

---

*   "O glorioso stare   Annichilarsi bene
        In nihil quietato !   Non è potere humano
        Lo' intelletto posato   Anzi è virtù divina !"
        E l'affetto dormire !
                                   (Comba, La Riforma in Italia, I. 310.)

† Salimbene, pp. 112–13.

ripening grapes of an adjacent vineyard, which they accordingly stripped. At length he was joined by a certain Robert, a servant of the Franciscans, who, as Salimbene informs us, was a liar and a thief, too lazy to work, who flourished for a while in the sect as Frà Glutto, and who finally apostatized and married a female hermit. Gherardo and Glutto wandered through the streets of Parma in their white mantles and sandals, calling the people to repentance. They gathered associates, and the number rapidly grew to three hundred. They obtained a house in which to eat and sleep, and lacked for nothing, for alms came pouring in upon them more liberally than on the regular Mendicants. These latter wondered greatly, for the self-styled Apostles gave nothing in return—they could not preach, or hear confessions, or celebrate mass, and did not even pray for their benefactors. They were mostly ignorant peasants, swineherds and cowherds, attracted by an idle life which was rewarded with ample victuals and popular veneration. When gathered together in their assemblies they would gaze vacantly on Segarelli and repeat at intervals in honor of him, "Father! Father! Father!" *

When the Council of Lyons, in 1274, endeavored to control the pest of these unauthorized mendicant associations, it did not disperse them, but contented itself with prohibiting the reception of future members, in the expectation that they would thus gradually become extinguished. This was easily eluded by the Apostles, who, when a neophyte desired to join them, would lay before him a habit and say, "We do not dare to receive you, as this is prohibited to us, but it is not prohibited to you; do as you think fit." Thus, in spite of papal commands, the Order increased and multiplied, as we are told, beyond computation. In 1284 we hear of seventy-two postulants in a body passing through Modena and Reggio to Parma to be adopted by Segarelli, and a few days afterwards twelve young girls came on the same errand, wrapped in their mantles and styling themselves Apostolesses. Imitating Dominic and Francis, Segarelli sent his followers throughout Europe and beyond seas to evangelize the world. They penetrated far, for already in 1287 we find the Council of Würzburg stigmatizing the wandering Apostles as tramps, and forbidding any one

---

* Salimbene, pp. 114–16.

to give them food on account of their religious aspect and unusual
dress.   Pedro de Lugo (Galicia), who abjured before the Inquisition
of Toulouse in 1322, testified that he had been inducted in the sect
twenty years previous by Richard, an Apostle from Alessandria in
Lombardy, who was busily spreading the heresy beyond Compostella.*

Notwithstanding the veneration felt by the brethren for Segarelli he steadily refused to assume the headship of the Order, saying that each must bear his own burden.   Had he been an active
organizer, with the material at his disposition, he might have given
the Church much trouble, but he was inert and indisposed to abandon his contemplative self-indulgence.   He seems to have hesitated
somewhat as to the form which the association should assume, and
consulted Alberto of Parma, one of the seven notaries of the curia,
whether they should select a superior.   Alberto referred him to
the Cistercian Abbot of Fontanaviva, who advised that they should
not found houses, but should continue to wander over the land
wrapped in their mantles, and they would not fail of shelter by
the charitable.   Segarelli was nothing loath to follow his counsel,
but a more energetic spirit was found in Guidone Putagi, brother
of the Podestà of Bologna, who entered the Order with his sister
Tripia.   Finding that Segarelli would not govern, he seized command and for many years conducted affairs, but he gave offence
by abandoning the poverty which was the essence of the association.   He lived splendidly, we are told, with many horses, lavish-
ing money like a cardinal or papal legate, till the brethren grew
tired and elected Matteo of Ancona as his successor.   This led to
a split.   Guidone retained possession of the person of Segarelli,
and carried him to Faenza.   Matteo's followers came there and
endeavored to seize Segarelli by force ; the two parties came to
blows and the Anconitans were defeated.   Guidone, however, was
so much alarmed for his safety that he left the Apostles and joined
the Templars.†

Bishop Opizo of Parma, a nephew of Innocent IV., had a liking

---

* Concil. Lugdun. ann. 1274 c. 23.—Salimbene, pp. 117, 119, 329–30.—Concil. Herbipolens. ann. 1287 (Harduin. VII. 1141).—Lib. Sententt. Inq. Tolosan.
p. 360.

† Salimbene, pp. 114–16.

for Segarelli, and for his sake protected the Apostles, which serves to account for their uninterrupted growth. In 1286, however, three of the brethren misbehaved flagrantly at Bologna, and were summarily hanged by the podestà. This seems to have drawn attention to the sectaries, for about the same time Honorius IV. issued a bull especially directed against them. They were commanded to abandon their peculiar vestments and enter some recognized order; prelates were required to enforce obedience by imprisonment, with recourse, if necessary, to the secular arm, and the faithful at large were ordered not to give them alms or hospitality. The Order was thus formally proscribed. Bishop Opizo hastened to obey. He banished the brethren from his diocese and imprisoned Segarelli in chains, but subsequently relenting kept him in his palace as a jester, for when filled with wine the Apostle could be amusing.*

For some years we hear little of Segarelli and his disciples. The papal condemnation discouraged them, but it received scant obedience. Their numbers may have diminished, and public charity may have been to some extent withdrawn, but they were still numerous, they continued to wear the white mantle, and to be supported in their wandering life. The best evidence that the bull of Honorius failed in its purpose is the fact that in 1291 Nicholas IV. deemed its reissue necessary. They were now in open antagonism to the Holy See—rebels and schismatics, rapidly ripening into heretics, and fair subjects of persecution. Accordingly, in 1494, we hear of four of them—two men and two women—burned at Parma, and of Segarelli's condemnation to perpetual imprisonment by Bishop Opizo. There is also an allusion to an earnest missionary of the sect, named Stephen, dangerous on account of the eloquence of his preaching, who was burned by the Inquisition. Segarelli had saved his life by abjuration, possibly after a few years he may have been released, but he did not abandon his errors; the Inquisitor of Parma, Frà Manfredo, convicted him as a relapsed heretic, and he was burned in Parma in 1300. An active persecution followed of his disciples. Many were apprehended by the Inquisition

---

* Salimbene, pp. 117, 371.—Mag. Bull. Rom. I. 158.—At the same time Honorius approved the Orders of the Carmelites and of St. William of the Desert (Raynald. ann. 1286, No. 36, 37).

and subjected to various punishments, until Parma congratulated itself that the heresy was fairly stamped out.*

Persecution, as usual, had the immediate effect of scattering the heretics, of confirming them in the faith, and of developing the heresy into a more decided antagonism towards the Church. Segarelli's disciples were not all ignorant peasants. In Tuscany a Franciscan of high reputation for sanctity and learning was in secret an active missionary, and endeavored even to win over Ubertino da Casale. Ubertino led him on and then betrayed him, and when we are told that he was forced to reveal his followers, we may assume that he was subjected to the customary inquisitorial processes. This points to relationship between the Apostles and the disaffected Franciscans, and the indication is strengthened by the anxiety of the Spirituals to disclaim all connection. The Apostles were deeply tinged with Joachitism, and the Spirituals endeavor to hide the fact by attributing their errors to Joachim's detested heretic imitator, the forgotten Amaury. The Conventuals, in fact, did not omit this damaging method of attack, and in the contest before Clement V. the Spirituals were obliged to disavow all connection with Dolcinism.†

We know nothing of any peculiar tenets taught by Segarelli. From his character it is not likely that he indulged in any recondite speculations, while the toleration which he enjoyed until near the end of his career probably prevented him from formulating any revolutionary doctrines. To wear the habit of the association, to live in absolute poverty, without labor and depending on daily charity, to take no thought of the morrow, to wander without a home, calling upon the people to repent, to preserve the strictest chastity, was the sum of his teaching, so far as we know, and this remained to the last the exterior observance of the Apostles. It was rigidly enforced. Even the austerity of the Franciscans allowed the friar two gowns, as a concession to health and comfort, but the Apostle could have but one, and if he desired it washed he

---

* Mag. Bull. Rom. I. 158.—Chron. Parmens. ann. 1294 (Muratori S. R. I. IX. 826).—Hist. Tribulat. (Archiv für Litt.- u. Kirchengeschichte, 1886, p. 130).— Addit. ad Hist. Frat. Dulcini (Muratori IX. 450).

† Hist. Tribulat. (ubi sup.).—Ubertini Responsio (Archiv f. L. u. K. 1887, p. 51).

had to remain covered in bed until it was dried. Like the Waldenses and Cathari, the Apostles seem to have considered the use of the oath as unlawful. They were accused, as usual, of inculcating promiscuous intercourse, and this charge seemed substantiated by the mingling of the sexes in their wandering life, and by the crucial test of continence to which they habitually exposed themselves, in imitation of the early Christians, of lying together naked; but the statement of their errors drawn up by the inquisitors who knew them, for the instruction of their colleagues, shows that license formed no part of their creed, though it would not be safe to say that men and women of evil life may not have been attracted to join them by the idleness and freedom from care of their wandering existence.*

By the time of Gherardo's death, however, persecution had been sufficiently sharp and long-continued to drive the Apostles into denying the authority of the Holy See and formulating doctrines of pronounced hostility to the Church. An epistle written by Frà Dolcino, about a month after Segarelli's execution, shows that minds more powerful than that of the founder had been at work framing a body of principles suited to zealots chafing under the domination of a corrupt church, and eagerly yearning for a higher theory of life than it could furnish. Joachim had promised that the era of the Holy Ghost should open with the year 1260. That prophecy had been fulfilled by the appearance of Segarelli, whose mission had then commenced. Tacitly accepting this coincidence, Dolcino proceeds to describe four successive states of the Church. The first extends from the Creation to the time of Christ; the second from Christ to Silvester and Constantine, during which the Church was holy and poor; the third from Silvester to Segarelli, during which the Church declined, in spite of the reforms introduced by Benedict, Dominic, and Francis, until it had wholly lost

---

* Salimbene, pp. 113, 117, 121.—Lib. Sententt. Inq. Tolos. pp. 360-1.—Muratori S. R. I. IX. 455-7.—Bern. Guidon. Practica P. v. —Eymeric. P. II. Q. 11.

The test of continence was regarded with horror by the inquisitors, and yet when practised by St. Aldhelm it was considered as proof of supereminent sanctity (Girald. Cambrens. Gemm. Eccles. Dist. II. c. xv.). The coincidence, in fact, is remarkable between the perilous follies of the Apostles and those of the Christian zealots of the third century, as described and condemned by Cyprian (Epist. IV. ad Pompon.).

the charity of God.   The fourth state was commenced by Segarelli, and will last till the Day of Judgment.   Then follow prophecies which seem to be based on those of the Pseudo-Joachim's
Commentaries on Jeremiah.   The Church now is honored, rich,
and wicked, and will so remain until all clerks, monks, and friars
are cut off with a cruel death, which will happen within three
years.   Frederic, King of Trinacria, who had not yet made his
peace with the Holy See, was regarded as the coming avenger, in
consequence, doubtless, of his relations with the Spirituals and his
tendencies in their favor.   The epistle concludes with a mass of
Apocalyptical prophecies respecting the approaching advent of
Antichrist, the triumph of the saints, and the reign of holy poverty and love, which is to follow under a saintly pope.   The seven
angels of the churches are declared to be Benedict, of Ephesus ;
Silvester, of Pergamus; Francis, of Sardis ; Dominic, of Laodicea ;
Segarelli, of Smyrna ; Dolcino himself, of Thyatira ; and the holy
pope to come, of Philadelphia.   Dolcino announces himself as the
special envoy of God, sent to elucidate Scripture and the prophecies, while the clergy and the friars are the ministers of Satan,
who persecute now, but who will shortly be consumed, when he
and his followers, with those who join them, will prevail till the
end.*

Segarelli had perished at the stake, July 18, and already in
August here was a man assuming with easy assurance the dangerous position of heresiarch, proclaiming himself the mouthpiece of
God, and promising his followers speedy triumph in reward for
what they might endure under his leadership.   Whether or not
he believed his own prophecies, whether he was a wild fanatic or
a skilful charlatan, can never be absolutely determined, but the
balance of probability lies in his truthfulness.   With all his gifts
as a born leader of men, it is safe to assert that if he had not believed in his mission he could not have inspired his followers with
the devotion which led them to stand by him through sufferings
unendurable to ordinary human nature ; while the cool sagacity
which he displayed under the most pressing emergencies must

---

* Muratori IX. 449–53.—Guill. Nangiac. Contin. ann. 1306.—R. Fran. Pipini
Chron. cap. xv. (Muratori, IX. 599).—Cf. Lib. Sententt. Inq. Tolos. p. 360.—
Pelayo, Heterodoxos Españoles, I. 720.

have been inflamed by apocalyptic visions ere he could have embarked in an enterprise in which the means were so wholly inadequate to the end—ere he could have endeavored single-handed to overthrow the whole majestic structure of the theocratic church and organized feudalism. Dante recognized the greatness of Dolcino when he represents him as the only living man to whom Mahomet from the depths of hell deigns to send a message, as to a kindred spirit. The good Spiritual Franciscans, who endured endless persecution without resistance, could only explain his career by a revelation made to a servant of God beyond the seas, that he was possessed by a malignant angel named Furcio.*

The paternity of Dolcino is variously attributed to Giulio, a priest of Trontano in the Val d'Ossola, and to Giulio, a hermit of Prato in the Valsesia, near Novara. Brought as a child to Vercelli, he was bred in the church of St. Agnes by a priest named Agosto, who had him carefully trained. Gifted with a brilliant intellect, he soon became an excellent scholar, and, though small of stature, he was pleasant to look upon and won the affection of all. In after-times it was said that his eloquence and persuasiveness were such that no one who once listened to him could ever throw off the spell. His connection with Vercelli came to a sudden end. The priest lost a sum of money and suspected his servant Patras. The man took the boy and by torturing him forced him to confess the theft—rightly or wrongly. The priest interfered to prevent the matter from becoming public, but shame and terror caused Dolcino to depart in secret, and we lose sight of him until we hear of him in Trent, at the head of a band of Apostles. He had joined the sect in 1291; he must early have taken a prominent position in it, for he admitted in his final confession that he had thrice been in the hands of the Inquisition, and had thrice abjured. This he could do without forfeiting his position, for it was one of the principles of the sect, which greatly angered the inquisitors, that deceit was lawful when before the Inquisition; that

* Hist. Tribulat. (ubi sup.).

    Or dì a Frà Dolcin dunque che s' armi,
      Tu che forse vedrai il sole in breve,
      S' egli non vuol quì tosto seguitarmi;
   Sì di vivanda, che stretta di neve
      Non rechi la vittoria al Noarese,
      Ch' altrimenti acquistar non saria lieve.—INFERNO, XXVIII.

oaths could then be taken with the lips and not with the heart; but that if death could not be escaped, then it was to be endured cheerfully and patiently, without betraying accomplices.*

For three years after his epistle of August, 1300, we know nothing of Dolcino's movements, except that he is heard of in Milan, Brescia, Bergamo, and Como, but they were busy years of propagandism and organization. The time of promised liberation came and passed, and the Church was neither shattered nor amended. Yet the capture of Boniface VIII. at Anagni, in September, 1303, followed by his death, might well seem to be the beginning of the end, and the fulfilment of the prophecy. In December, 1303, therefore, Dolcino issued a second epistle, in which he announced as a revelation from God that the first year of the tribulations of the Church had begun in the fall of Boniface. In 1304 Frederic of Trinacria would become emperor, and would destroy the cardinals, with the new evil pope whom they had just elected; in 1305 he would carry desolation through the ranks of all prelates and ecclesiastics, whose wickedness was daily increasing. Until that time the faithful must lie hid to escape persecution, but then they would come forth, they would be joined by the Spirituals of the other orders, they would receive the grace of the Holy Ghost, and would form the new Church which would endure to the end. Meanwhile he announced himself as the ruler of the Apostolic Congregation, consisting of four thousand souls, living without external obedience, but in the obedience of the Spirit. About a hundred, of either sex, were organized in control of the brethren, and he had four principal lieutenants, Longino Cattaneo da Bergamo, Federigo da Novara, Alberto da Otranto, and Valderigo da Brescia. Superior to these was his dearly-loved sister in Christ, Margherita. Margherita di Trank is described to us as a woman of noble birth, considerable fortune, and surpassing beauty, who had been educated in the convent of St. Catharine at Trent. Dolcino had been the agent of the convent, and had thus made her acquaintance. Infatuated with him, she fled with him, and remained constant to the last. He always maintained that their relations

---

* Benvenuto da Imola (Muratori Antiq. III. 457–9).—Bescapè, La Novara Sacra, Novara, 1878, p. 157.—Baggiolini, Dolcino e i Patarini, Novara, 1838, pp. 35–6.— Hist. Dulcin. Hæresiarch. (Muratori. S. R. I. IX. 436–7).—Addit. ad Hist. (Ibid. 457, 460).

were purely spiritual, but this was naturally doubted, and the churchmen asserted that she bore him a child whose birth was represented to the faithful as the operation of the Holy Ghost.*

Although in this letter of December, 1303, Dolcino recognizes the necessity of concealment, perhaps the expected approaching fruition of his hopes may have encouraged him to relax his precautions. Returning in 1304 to the home of his youth with a few sectaries clad in the white tunics and sandals of the Order, he commenced making converts in the neighborhood of Gattinara and Serravalle, two villages of the Valsesia, a few leagues above Vercelli. The Inquisition was soon upon the track, and, failing to catch him, made the people of Serravalle pay dearly for the favor which they had shown him. Deep-seated discontent, both with the Church and their feudal lords, can alone explain the assistance which Dolcino received from the hardy population of the foot-hills of the Alps, when he was forced to raise openly the standard of revolt. A short distance above Serravalle, on the left bank of the Sesia, a stream fed by the glaciers of Monte Rosa, lay Borgo di Sesia, in the diocese of Novara. Thither a rich husbandman, much esteemed by his neighbors, named Milano Sola, invited Dolcino, and for several months he remained there undisturbed, making converts and receiving his disciples, whom he seems to have summoned from distant parts, as though resolved to make a stand and take advantage of the development of his apocalyptic prophecies. Preparations made to dislodge him, however, convinced him that safety was only to be found in the Alps, and under the guidance of Milano Sola the Apostles moved up towards the head-waters of the Sesia, and established themselves on a mountain crest, difficult of access, where they built huts. Thus passed the year 1304. Their numbers were not inconsiderable—some fourteen hundred of both sexes —inflamed with religious zeal, regarding Dolcino as a prophet whose lightest word was law. Thus contumaciously assembled in defiance of the summons of the Inquisition, they were in open rebellion

---

* Corio, Hist. Milanesi, ann. 1307.—Benv. da Imola, loc. cit.—Additamentum (Muratori IX. 454–55, 459).—Baggiolini, pp. 36–7.

Dolcino's two epistles were formally condemned by the Bishop of Parma and Frà Manfredo, the inquisitor, and must therefore have been circulated outside of the sect (Eymeric. Direct. Inq. P. II. Q. 29).

III.—8

against the Church. The State also soon became their enemy, for as the year 1305 opened, their slender stock of provisions was exhausted and they replenished their stores by raids upon the lower valleys.*

The Church could not afford to brook this open defiance, to say nothing of the complaints of rapine and sacrilege which filled the land, yet it shows the dread which Dolcino already inspired that recourse was had to the pope, under whose auspices a formal crusade was preached, in order to raise a force deemed sufficient to exterminate the heretics. One of the early acts of Clement V. after his election, June 5, 1305, was to issue bulls for this purpose, and the next step was to hold an assembly, August 24, where a league was formed and an agreement signed pledging the assembled nobles to shed the last drop of their blood to destroy the Gazzari, who had been driven out of Sesia and Biandrate, but had not ceased to trouble the land. Armed with the papal commissions, Rainerio, Bishop of Vercelli, and the inquisitors raised a considerable force and advanced to the mountain refuge of the Apostles. Dolcino, seeing the futility of resistance, decamped by night and established his little community on an almost inaccessible mountain, and the crusaders, apparently thinking them dispersed, withdrew. Dolcino was now fairly at bay; the only hope of safety lay in resistance, and since the Church was resolved on war, he and his followers would at least sell their lives as dearly as they could. His new retreat was on the Parete Calvo—the Bare Wall—whose name sufficiently describes its character, a mountain overlooking the village of Campertogno. On this stronghold the Apostles fortified themselves and constructed such habitations as they could, and from it they ravaged the neighboring valleys for subsistence. The Podestà of Varallo assembled the men of the Valsesia to dislodge them, but Dolcino laid an ambush for him, attacked him with stones and such other weapons as the Apostles chanced to have, and took him prisoner with most of his men, obtaining ransoms which enabled the sectaries to support life for a while longer. Their depredations continued till all the land within striking distance was reduced to a desert, the churches despoiled, and the inhabitants driven off.†

---

* Hist. Dulcin. (Muratori IX. 428–9).—Bescapè, loc. cit.

† Hist. Dulcin. (Muratori IX. 430–1).—Bescapè. loc. cit.

The winter of 1305–6 put to the test the endurance of the heretics on their bare mountain-top. As Lent came on they were reduced to eating mice and other vermin, and hay cooked in grease. The position became untenable, and on the night of March 10, compelled by stern necessity to abandon their weaker companions, they left the Parete Calvo, and, building paths which seemed impossible over high mountains and through deep snows, they established themselves on Monte Rubello, overlooking the village of Triverio, in the diocese of Vercelli. By this time, through want and exhaustion, their numbers were reduced to about a thousand, and the sole provisions which they brought with them were a few scraps of meat. With such secrecy and expedition had the move been executed that the first intimation that the people of Triverio had of the neighborhood of the dreaded heretics was a foray by night, in which their town was ravaged. We do not hear that any of the unresisting inhabitants were slain, but we are told that thirty-four of the Apostles were cut off in their retreat and put to death. The whole region was now alarmed, and the Bishop of Vercelli raised a second force of crusaders, who bravely advanced to Monte Rubello. Dolcino was rapidly learning the art of war; he made a sally from his stronghold, though again we learn that some of his combatants were armed only with stones, and the bishop's troops were beaten back with the loss of many prisoners who were exchanged for food.*

The heretic encampment was now organized for permanent occupation. Fortifications were thrown up, houses built, and a well dug. Thus rendered inexpugnable, the hunted Apostles were in safety from external attack, and on their Alpine crag, with all mankind for enemies, they calmly awaited in their isolation the fulfilment of Dolcino's prophecies. Their immediate danger was starvation. The mountain-tops furnished no food, and the remains of the episcopal army stationed at Mosso maintained a strict blockade. To relieve himself, early in May, Dolcino by a clever stratagem lured them to an attack, set upon them from an ambush, and dispersed them, capturing many prisoners, who, as before, were exchanged for provisions. The bishop's resources were exhausted. Again he appealed to Clement V., who graciously

---

* Hist. Dulcin. (Muratori IX. 430–2).

anathematized the heretics, and offered plenary indulgence to all who would serve in the army of the Lord for thirty days against them, or pay a recruit for such service. The papal letters were published far and wide, the Vercellese ardently supported their aged bishop, who personally accompanied the crusade; a large force was raised, neighboring heights were seized and machines erected which threw stones into the heretic encampment and demolished their huts. A desperate struggle took place for the possession of one commanding eminence, where mutual slaughter so deeply tinged the waters of the Riccio that its name became changed to that of Rio Carnaschio, and so strong was the impression made upon the popular mind that within the last century it would have fared ill with any sceptical traveller who should aver within hearing of a mountaineer of the district that its color was the same as that of the neighboring torrents.*

This third crusade was as fruitless as its predecessors. The assailants were repulsed and fell back to Mosso, Triverio, and Crevacore, while Dolcino, profiting by experience, fortified and garrisoned six of the neighboring heights, from which he harried the surrounding country and kept his people supplied with food. To restrain them the crusaders built two forts and maintained a heavy force within them, but to little purpose. Mosso, Triverio, Cassato, Flecchia, and other towns were burned, and the accounts of the wanton spoliation and desecration of the churches show how thoroughly antisacerdotal the sect had become. Driven to desperation, the ancient loving-kindness of their creed gave place to the cruelty which they learned from their assailants. To deprive them of resources it was forbidden to exchange food with them for prisoners, and their captives were mercilessly put to death. According to the contemporary inquisitor to whom we are indebted for these details, since the days of Adam there had never been a sect so execrable, so abominable, so horrible, or which in a time so short accomplished so much evil. The worst of it was that Dolcino infused into his followers his own unconquerable spirit. In male attire the women accompanied the men in their expeditions. Fanaticism rendered them invincible, and so great was the terror which they inspired that the faithful fled from the

---

* Hist. Dulcin (Muratori IX. 432–4.)—Baggiolini, p. 131.

faces of these dogs, of whom we are told a few would put to flight a host and utterly destroy them. The land was abandoned by the inhabitants, and in December, seized with a sudden panic, the crusaders evacuated one of the forts, and the garrison of the other, amounting to seven hundred men, was rescued with difficulty.*

Dolcino's fanaticism and military skill had thus triumphed in the field, but the fatal weakness of his position lay in his inability to support his followers. This was clearly apprehended by the Bishop of Vercelli, who built five new forts around the heretic position; and when we are told that all the roads and passes were strictly guarded so that no help should reach them, we may infer that, in spite of the devastation to which they had been driven, they still had friends among the population. This policy was successful. During the winter of 1306–7 the sufferings of the Apostles on their snowy mountain-top were frightful. Hunger and cold did their work. Many perished from exhaustion. Others barely maintained life on grass and leaves, when they were fortunate enough to find them. Cannibalism was resorted to; the bodies of their enemies who fell in successful sorties were devoured, and even those of their comrades who succumbed to starvation. The pious chronicler informs us that this misery was brought upon them by the prayers and vows of the good bishop and his flock.†

To this there could be but one ending, and even the fervid genius of Dolcino could not indefinitely postpone the inevitable. As the dreary Alpine winter drew to an end, towards the close of March, the bishop organized a fourth crusade. A large army was raised to deal with the gaunt and haggard survivors; hot fighting occurred during Passion Week, and on Holy Thursday (March 23, 1307) the last entrenchments were carried. The resistance had been stubborn, and again the Rio Carnaschio ran red with blood. No quarter was given. " On that day more than a thousand of the heretics perished in the flames, or in the river, or by the sword, in the cruellest of deaths. Thus they who made sport of God the Eternal Father and of the Catholic faith came, on the day of the Last Supper, through hunger, steel, fire, pestilence, and all wretchedness, to shame and disgraceful death, as they deserved."

---

* Hist. Dulcin. (Muratori IX. 434, 437–8).
† Hist. Dulcin. (Ib. 439–40).

Strict orders had been given by the bishop to capture alive Dolcino and his two chief subordinates, Margherita and Longino Cattaneo, and great were the rejoicings when they were brought to him on Saturday, at the castle of Biella.*

No case could be clearer than theirs, and yet the bishop deemed it necessary to consult Pope Clement—a perfectly superfluous ceremony, explicable perhaps, as Gallenga suggests, by the opportunity which it afforded of begging assistance for his ruined diocese and exhausted treasury. Clement's avarice responded in a niggardly fashion, though the extravagant pæan of triumph in which the pope hastened to announce the glad tidings to Philippe le Bel on the same evening in which he received them shows how deep was the anxiety caused by the audacious revolt of the handful of Dolcinists. The Bishops of Vercelli, Novara, and Pavia, and the Abbot of Lucedio were granted the first fruits of all benefices becoming vacant during the next three years in their respective territories, and the former, in addition, was exempted during life from the exactions of papal legates, with some other privileges. While awaiting this response the prisoners were kept, chained hand and foot and neck, in the dungeon of the Inquisition at Vercelli, with numerous guards posted to prevent a rescue, indicating a knowledge that there existed deep popular sympathy for the rebels against State and Church. The customary efforts were made to procure confession and abjuration, but while the prisoners boldly affirmed their faith they were deaf to all offers of reconciliation. Dolcino even persisted in his prophecies that Antichrist would appear in three years and a half, when he and his followers would be translated to Paradise; that after the death of Antichrist he would return to the earth to be the holy pope of the new church, when all the infidels would be converted. About two months passed away before Clement's orders were received, that they should be tried and punished at the scene of their crimes. The customary assembly of experts was convened in Vercelli; there could be no doubt as to their guilt, and they were abandoned to

---

* Hist. Dulcin. (Muratori IX. 439).

Ptolemy of Lucca, who is good contemporaneous authority, puts the number of those captured with Dolcino at one hundred and fifty, and of those who perished through exposure and by the sword at only about three hundred. —Hist. Eccles. Lib. xxiv. (Muratori XI. 1227).

the secular arm. For the superfluous cruelty which followed the Church was not responsible; it was the expression of the terror of the secular authorities, leading them to repress by an awful example the ever-present danger of a peasant revolt. On June 1, 1307, the prisoners were brought forth. Margherita's beauty moved all hearts to compassion, and this, coupled with the reports of her wealth, led many nobles to offer her marriage and pardon if she would abjure, but, constant to her faith and to Dolcino, she preferred the stake. She was slowly burned to death before his eyes, and then commenced his more prolonged torture. Mounted on a cart, provided with braziers to keep the instruments of torment heated, he was slowly driven along the roads through that long summer day and torn gradually to pieces with red-hot pincers. The marvellous constancy of the man was shown by his enduring it without rewarding his torturers with a single change of feature. Only when his nose was wrenched off was observed a slight shiver in the shoulders, and when a yet crueller pang was inflicted, a single sigh escaped him. While he was thus dying in lingering torture Longino Cattaneo, at Biella, was similarly utilized to afford a salutary warning to the people. Thus the enthusiasts expiated their dreams of the regeneration of mankind.*

Complete as was Dolcino's failure, his character and his fate left an ineffaceable impression on the population. The Parete Calvo, his first mountain refuge, was considered to be haunted by evil spirits, whom he had left to guard a treasure buried in a cave, and who excited such tempests when any one invaded their domain that the people of Triverio were forced to maintain guards to warn off persistent treasure-seekers. Still stronger was the

---

* Mariotti (A. Galenga), Frà Dolcino and his Times, London, 1853, pp. 287–88.—Regest. Clement. PP. V. T. II. pp. 79–82, 88 (Ed. Benedictina, Romæ,1886). —Mosheims Ketzergeschichte I. 395.—Ughelli, Italia Sacra, Ed. 1652, IV. 1104–8.—Hist. Dulcin. (Muratori IX. 436, 440).—Benv. da Imola (Muratori Antiq. III. 460).—Bernard. Guidon. Vit. Clement. PP. V. (Muratori III. I. 674).—Bescapè, loc. cit.

The punishment inflicted on Dolcino and Longino was not exceptional. By a Milanese statute of 1393 all secret attempts upon the life of any member of a family with whom the criminal lived were subject to a penalty precisely the same in all details, except that it ended by attaching the offender to a wheel and leaving him to perish in prolonged agony.—Antiqua Ducum Mediolani Decreta, p. 187 (Mediolani, 1654).

influence which he exerted upon his fastness on Monte Rubello. It became known as the Monte dei Gazzari, and to it, as to an accursed spot, priests grew into the habit of consigning demons whom they exorcised on account of hail-storms. The result of this was that the congregated spirits caused such fearful tempests that the neighboring lands were ruined, the harvests were yearly destroyed, and the people reduced to beggary. Finally, as a cure, the inhabitants of Triverio vowed to God and to St. Bernard that if they were relieved they would build on the top of the mountain a chapel to St. Bernard. This was done, and the mountain thus acquired its modern name of Monte San Bernardo. Every year on June 15, the feast of St. Bernard, one man from every hearth in the surrounding parishes marched with their priests in solemn procession, bearing crosses and banners, and celebrating solemn services, in the presence of crowds assembled to gain the pardons granted by the pope, and to share in a distribution of bread provided by a special levy made on the parishes of Triverio and Portola. This custom lasted till the French invasion under Napoleon. Renewed in 1815, it was discontinued on account of the disorders which attended it. Again resumed in 1839, it was accompanied with a hurricane which is still in the Valsesia attributed to the heresiarch, and even to the present day the mountaineers see on the mountain-crest a procession of Dolcinists during the night before its celebration. Dolcino's name is still remembered in the valleys as that of a great man who perished in the effort to free the populations from temporal and spiritual tyranny.*

Dolcino and his immediate band of followers were thus exterminated, but there remained the thousands of Apostles, scattered throughout the land, who cherished their belief in secret. Under the skilful hand of the Inquisition, the harmless eccentricities of Segarelli were hardened and converted into a strongly antisacerdotal heresy, antagonistic to Rome, precisely as we have seen the same result with the exaggerated asceticism of the Olivists. There was much in common between the sects, for both drew their inspiration from the Everlasting Gospel. Like the Olivists, the Apostles held that Christ had withdrawn his authority from the

* A. Artiaco (Rivista Cristiana, 1877, 145–51).—Hist. Dulcin. (Muratori IX. 441–2).—Baggiolini, pp. 165–71.

Church of Rome on account of its wickedness; it was the Whore of Babylon, and all spiritual power was transferred to the Spiritual Congregation, or Order of Apostles, as they styled themselves. As time passed on without the fulfilment of the apocalyptic promises, as Frederic of Trinacria did not develop into a deliverer, and as Antichrist delayed his appearance, they seem to have abandoned these hopes, or at least to have repressed their expression, but they continued to cherish the belief that they had attained spiritual perfection, releasing them from all obedience to man, and that there was no salvation outside of their community. Antisacerdotalism was thus developed to the fullest extent. There seems to have been no organization in the Order. Reception was performed by the simplest of ceremonies, either in church before the altar or in any other place. The postulant stripped himself of all his garments, in sign of renunciation of all property and of entering into the perfect state of evangelical poverty; he uttered no vows, but in his heart he promised to live henceforth in poverty. After this he was never to receive or carry money, but was to live on alms spontaneously offered to him, and was never to reserve anything for the morrow. He made no promise of obedience to mortal man, but only to God, to whom alone he was subject, as were the apostles to Christ. Thus all the externals of religion were brushed aside. Churches were useless; a man could better worship Christ in the woods, and prayer to God was as effective in a pigsty as in a consecrated building. Priests and prelates and monks were a detriment to the faith. Tithes should only be given to those whose voluntary poverty rendered it superfluous. Though the sacrament of penitence was not expressly abrogated, yet the power of the keys was virtually annulled by the principle that no pope could absolve for sin unless he were as holy as St. Peter, living in perfect poverty and humility, abstaining from war and persecution, and permitting every one to dwell in liberty; and, as all prelates, from the time of Silvester, had been seducers and prevaricators, excepting only Frà Pier di Morrone (Celestin V.), it followed that the indulgences and pardons so freely hawked around Christendom were worthless. One error they shared with the Waldenses—the prohibition of oaths, even in a court of justice.*

---

* Addit. ad Hist. Dulcin. (Muratori IX. 455–7).—Bern. Guidon. Pract. P. v.

The description which Bernard Gui gives of the Apostles, in order to guide his brother inquisitors in their detection, shows how fully they carried into practice the precepts of their simple creed. They wore a special habit, closely approaching a conventual garb — probably the white mantle and cord adopted by Segarelli. They presented all the exterior signs of saintliness. As they wandered along the roads and through the streets they sang hymns, or uttered prayers and exhortations to repentance. Whatever was spontaneously set before them they ate with thankfulness, and when appetite was satisfied they left what might remain and carried nothing with them. In their humble fashion they seem to have imitated the apostles as best they could, and to have carried poverty to a pitch which Angelo da Clarino himself might have envied. Bernard Gui, in addition, deplores their intractable obstinacy, and adduces a case in which he had kept one of them in prison for two years, subjecting him to frequent examination, before he was brought to confession and repentance — by what gentle persuasives we may readily guess.*

All this may seem to us the most harmless of heresies, and yet the impression produced by the exploits of Dolcino caused it to be regarded as one of the most formidable; and the earnestness of the sectaries in making converts was rendered dangerous by their drawing their chief arguments from the evil lives of the clergy. When the Brethren of the Free Spirit were condemned in the Clementines, Bernard Gui wrote earnestly to John XXII., urging that a clause should be inserted including the Apostles, whom he described as growing like weeds and spreading from Italy to Languedoc and Spain. This is probably one of the exaggerations customary in such matters, but about this time a Dolcinist named Jacopo da Querio was discovered and burned in Avignon. In 1316 Bernard Gui found others within his own district, when his energetic proceedings soon drove the poor wretches across the Pyrenees, and he addressed urgent letters to all the prelates of Spain, describing them and calling for their prompt extermination, which resulted, as mentioned in a former chapter, in the apprehension of five of the heretics at far-off Compostella, doubtless the remnants of the disciples of the Apostle Richard. Possibly

---

* Bernard. Guidon. Practica P. v.

this may have driven some of them back to France for safety, for in the *auto* of September, 1322, at Toulouse, there figures the Galician already referred to named Pedro de Lugo, who had been strenuously labored with for a year in prison, and on his abjuration was incarcerated for life on bread and water. In the same *auto* there was another culprit whose fate illustrates the horror and terror inspired by the doctrines of the Dolcinists. Guillem Ruffi had been previously forced to abjuration as a Beguine, and subsequently had betrayed two of his former associates, one of whom had been burned and the other imprisoned. This would seem to be sufficient proof of his zeal for orthodoxy, and yet, when he happened to state that in Italy there were Fraticelli who held that no one was perfect who could not endure the test of continence above alluded to, adding that he had tried the experiment himself with success, and had taught it to more than one woman, this was considered sufficient, and without anything further against him he was incontinently burned as a relapsed heretic.*

In spite of Bernard Gui's exaggerated apprehensions, the sect, although it continued to exist for some time, gave no further serious trouble. The Council of Cologne in 1306 and that of Trèves in 1310 allude to the Apostles, showing that they were not unknown in Germany. Yet about 1335 so well-informed a writer as Alvar Pelayo speaks of Dolcino as a Beghard, showing how soon the memory of the distinctive characteristics of the sect had faded away. At this very time, however, a certain Zoppio was secretly spreading the heresy at Rieti, where it seems to have found numerous converts, especially among the women. Attention being called to it, Frà Simone Filippi, inquisitor of the Roman province, hastened thither, seized Zoppio, and after examining him delivered him to the authorities for safe-keeping. When he desired to proceed with the trial the magistrates refused to surrender the prisoner, and abused the inquisitor. Benedict XII. was appealed to, who scolded roundly the recalcitrant officials for defending a heresy so horrible that decency forbids his describing it; he threat-

---

* Addit. ad Hist. Dulcin. (Muratori IX. 458).—Bernard. Guidon. Practica P. v. —Bernard. Guidon. Gravam. (Doat, XXX. 120–4).—Raym. de Fronciacho (Archiv für Litt.- u. K. 1887, p. 10.—Lib. Sententt. Inq. Tolos. pp. 360–3, 381.

ened them with exemplary punishment for continued contumacy, and promised that, if they were afraid of damage to the reputation of their women, the latter should be mildly treated and spared humiliating penance on giving information as to their associates.*

After a long interval we hear of the Apostles again in Languedoc, where, in 1368, the Council of Lavaur calls attention to them as wandering through the land in spite of the condemnation of the Holy See, and disseminating errors under an appearance of external piety, wherefore they are ordered to be arrested and punished by the episcopal courts. In 1374 the Council of Narbonne deemed it necessary to repeat this injunction; and we have seen that in 1402 and 1403 the zeal of the Inquisitor Eylard was rewarded in Lubec and Wismar by the capture and burning of two Apostles. This is the last authentic record of a sect which a hundred years before had for a brief space inspired so wide a terror.†

Closely allied with the Dolcinists, and forming a link between them and the German Brethren of the Free Spirit, were some Italian heretics known as followers of the Spirit of Liberty, of whom a few scattered notices have reached us. They seem to have avoided the pantheism of the Germans, and did not teach the return of the soul to its Creator, but they adopted the dangerous tenet of the perfectibility of man, who in this life can become as holy as Christ. This can be accomplished by sins as well as by virtues, for both are the same in the eye of God, who directs all things and allows no human free-will. The soul is purified by sin, and the greater the pleasure in carnal indulgences the more nearly they represent God. There is no eternal punishment, but

---

* Concil. Coloniens. ann. 1306 c. 1, 2 (Hartzheim IV. 100, 102).—Concil. Trevirens. ann. 1310 c. 50 (Martene Thesaur. IV. 250).—Alvar. Pelag. de Planctu Eccles. Lib. ɪɪ. art. lii. (fol. 166, 172, Ed. 1517).—Wadding. ann. 1335, No. 8–9.—Raynald. ann. 1335, No. 62.

† Concil. Vaurens. ann. 1368 c. 24; Concil. Narbonn. ann. 1374 c. 5 (Harduin. VII. 1818, 1880).—Herman. Corneri Chron. ann. 1260, 1402 (Eccard. Corp. Hist. Med. Ævi II. 906, 1185).

I have already referred (Vol. II. p. 429) to the persecution at Prague, in 1315, of some heretics whom Dubravius qualifies as Dolcinists, but who probably were Waldenses and Luciferans.

souls not sufficiently purified in this life undergo purgation until admitted to heaven.*

We first hear of these sectaries as appearing among the Franciscans of Assisi, where, under active proceedings, seven of the friars confessed, abjured, and were sentenced to perpetual prison. When, in 1309, Clement V. sought to settle the points in dispute between the Spirituals and Conventuals, the first of the four preliminary questions which he put to the contending factions related to the connection between the Order and this heresy, of which both sides promptly sought to clear themselves. The next reference to them is in April, 1311, when they were said to be multiplying rapidly in Spoleto, among both ecclesiastics and laymen, and Clement sent thither Raimundo, Bishop of Cremona, to stamp out the new heresy. The effort was unavailing, for in 1327, at Florence, Donna Lapina, belonging to the sect "of the Spirit" whose members believed themselves impeccable, was condemned by Frà Accursio, the inquisitor, to confiscation and wearing crosses; and in 1329 Frà Bartolino da Perugia, in announcing a general inquisition to be made of the province of Assisi, enumerates the new heresy of the Spirit of Liberty among those which he proposes to suppress. More important was the case of Domenico Savi of Ascoli, who was regarded as a man of the most exemplary piety. In 1337 he abandoned wife and children for a hermit's life, and the bishop built for him a cell and oratory. This gave him still greater repute, and his influence was such that when he began to disseminate the doctrines of the Spirit of Liberty, which he undertook by means of circulating written tracts, the number of his followers is reckoned at ten thousand. It was not long before this attracted the attention of the Inquisition. He was tried, and recanted, while his writings were ordered to be burned. His convictions, however, were too strong to allow him to remain orthodox. He relapsed, was tried a second time, appealed to the pope, and was finally condemned by the Holy See in 1344, when he was handed over to the secular arm and burned at Ascoli. As nothing is said

---

* MS. Bibl. Casanatense A. IV. 49.—I owe the communication of this document to the kindness of M. Charles Molinier. See also Amati, Archivio Storico Italiano, No. 38, p. 14.

For the connection between these heretics and the Dolcinists, compare Archiv für Lit.- u. Kirchengeschichte, 1886, p. 131, with 1887, pp. 123–4.

about the fate of his disciples it may be assumed that they escaped
by abjuration. He is usually classed with the Fraticelli, but the
errors attributed to him bear no resemblance to those of that sect,
and are evidently exaggerations of the doctrines of the Spirit of
Liberty.*

Before dismissing the career of Dolcino, it may be worth while
to cast a passing glance at that of a modern prophet which, like
the cases of the modern Guglielmites, teaches us that such spiritual
phenomena are common to all ages, and that even in our colder
and more rationalistic time the mysteries of human nature are the
same as in the thirteenth century.

Dolcino merely organized a movement which had been in progress for nearly half a century, and which was the expression of
a widely diffused sentiment. David Lazzaretti of Arcidosso was
both founder and martyr. A wagoner in the mountains of southern Tuscany, his herculean strength and ready speech made him
widely known throughout his native region, when a somewhat
wild and dissipated youth was suddenly converted into an ascetic
of the severest type, dwelling in a hermitage on Monte Labbro, and
honored with revelations from God. His austerities, his visions,
and his prophecies soon brought him disciples, many of whom
adopted his mode of life, and the peasants of Arcidosso revered
him as a prophet. He claimed that, as early as 1848, he had been
called to the task of regenerating the world, and that his sudden
conversion was caused by a vision of St. Peter, who imprinted on
his forehead a mark $(O+C)$ in attestation of his mission. He
was by no means consistent in his successive stages of development. A patriot volunteer in 1860, he subsequently upheld the
cause of the Church against the assaults of heretic Germany, but
in 1876 his book, "My Struggle with God," reveals his aspirations
towards the headship of a new faith, and describes him as carried
to heaven and discoursing with God, though he still professed
himself faithful to Rome and to the papacy. The Church dis-
dained his aid and condemned his errors, and he became a heresi-

---

* Archiv für Litt.- u. Kirchengeschichte, 1887, pp. 51, 144–5.—Raynald. ann.
1311, No. 66–70 ; ann. 1318, No. 44.—Archiv. di Firenze, Prov. S. Maria Novella,
1327, Ott. 31.—Franz Ehrle, Archiv für Lit.- u. Kirchengeschichte, 1885, p. 160.
—D'Argentré I. i. 336–7.—Cantù, Eretici d'Italia, I. 133..

arch. In the spring of 1878 he urged the adoption of sacerdotal marriage, he disregarded fast-days, administered communion to his disciples in a rite of his own, and composed for them a creed of which the twenty-fourth article was, " I believe that our founder, David Lazzaretti, the anointed of the Lord, judged and condemned by the Roman curia, is really Christ, the leader and the judge." That the people accepted him is seen in the fact that for three successive Sundays the priest of Arcidosso found his church without a worshipper. David founded a " Society of the Holy League, or Christian Brotherhood," and proclaimed the coming Republic or Kingdom of God, when all property should be equally divided. Even this communism did not frighten off the small proprietors who constituted the greater portion of his following. There was general discontent, owing to a succession of unfortunate harvests and the increasing pressure of taxation, and when, on August 14, 1878, he announced that he would set out with his disciples peacefully to inaugurate his theocratic republic, the whole population gathered on Monte Labbro. After four days spent in religious exercises the extraordinary crusade set forth, consisting of all ages and both sexes, arrayed in a fantastic uniform of red and blue, and bearing banners and garlands of flowers with which to revolutionize society. Its triumphal march was short. At the village of Arcidosso its progress was disputed by a squad of nine carabineers, who poured volleys into the defenceless crowd. Thirty-four of the Lazzarettists fell, killed and wounded, and among them David himself, with a bullet in his brain.* Whether he was enthusiast or impostor may remain an open question. Travel and study had brought him training; he was no longer a rude moun-

---

* Barzellotti, David Lazzaretti di Arcidosso detto il Santo. Bologna, 1885.

Somewhat similar is the career of an ex-sergeant of the Italian army named Gabriele Donnici, who has founded in the Calabrian highlands a sect dignifying itself with the title of the Saints. Gabriele is a prophet announcing the advent of a new Messiah, who is to come not as a lamb, but as a lion breathing vengeance and armed with bloody scourges. He and his brother Abele were tried for the murder of the wife of the latter, Grazia Funaro, who refused to submit to the sexual abominations taught in the sect. They were condemned to hard labor and imprisonment, but were discharged on appeal to the Superior Court of Cosenza. Other misdeeds of the sectaries are at present occupying the attention of the Italian tribunals.—Rivista Cristiana, 1887, p. 57.

tain peasant, but could estimate the social forces against which he raised the standard of revolt, and could recognize that they were insuperable save to an envoy of God.   Possibly on the slopes of Monte Amiata his memory may linger like that of Dolcino in the Valsesia; certain it is that many of his disciples long expected his resurrection.

CHAPTER III.

THE FRATICELLI.

WE have seen how John XXII. created and exterminated the heresy of the Spiritual Franciscans, and how Michele da Cesena enforced obedience within the Order as to the question of granaries and cellars and the wearing of short and narrow gowns. The settlement of the question, however, on so illogical a basis as this was impossible, especially in view of the restless theological dogmatism of the pope and his inflexible determination to crush all dissidence of opinion. Having once undertaken to silence the discussions over the rule of poverty which had caused so much trouble for nearly a century, his logical intellect led him to carry to their legitimate conclusions the principles involved in his bulls *Quorumdam, Sancta Romana,* and *Gloriosam Ecclesiam,* while his thorough worldliness rendered him incapable of anticipating the storm which he would provoke. A character such as his was unable to comprehend the honest inconsistency of men like Michele and Bonagrazia, who could burn their brethren for refusing to have granaries and cellars, and who, at the same time, were ready to endure the stake in vindication of the absolute poverty of Christ and the apostles, which had so long been a fundamental belief of the Order, and had been proclaimed as irrefragable truth in the bull *Exiit qui seminat.*

In fact, under a pope of the temperament of John, the orthodox Franciscans had a narrow and dangerous path to tread. The Spirituals were burned as heretics because they insisted on following their own conception of the Rule of Francis, and the distinction between this and the official recognition of the obligation of poverty was shadowy in the extreme. The Dominicans were not slow to recognize the dubious position of their rivals, nor averse to take advantage of it. If they could bring the received doctrines of the Franciscan Order within the definition of the new

III.—9

heresy they would win a triumph that might prove permanent. The situation was so artificial and so untenable that a catastrophe was inevitable, and it might be precipitated by the veriest trifle.

In 1321, when the persecution of the Spirituals was at its height, the Dominican inquisitor, Jean de Beaune, whom we have seen as the colleague of Bernard Gui and the jailer of Bernard Délicieux, was engaged at Narbonne in the trial of one of the proscribed sect. To pass judgment he summoned an assembly of experts, among whom was the Franciscan Berenger Talon, teacher in the convent of Narbonne. One of the errors which he represented the culprit as entertaining was that Christ and the apostles, following the way of perfection, had held no possessions, individually or in common. As this was the universal Franciscan doctrine, we can only regard it as a challenge when he summoned Frère Berenger to give his opinion respecting it. Berenger thereupon replied that it was not heretical, having been defined as orthodox in the decretal *Exiit*, when the inquisitor hotly demanded that he should recant on the spot. The position was critical, and Berenger, to save himself from prosecution, interjected an appeal to the pope. He hastened to Avignon, but found that Jean de Beaune had been before him. He was arrested; the Dominicans everywhere took up the question, and the pope allowed it to be clearly seen that his sympathies were with them. Yet the subject was a dangerous one for disputants, as the bull *Exiit* had anathematized all who should attempt to gloss or discuss its decisions; and, as a preliminary to reopening the question, John was obliged, March 26, 1322, to issue a special bull, *Quia nonnunquam*, wherein he suspended, during his pleasure, the censures pronounced in *Exiit qui seminat*. Having thus intimated that the Church had erred in its former definition, he proceeded to lay before his prelates and doctors the significant question whether the pertinacious assertion that Christ and the apostles possessed nothing individually or in common was a heresy.[*]

The extravagances of the Spirituals had borne their fruit, and there was a reaction against the absurd laudation of poverty which had grown to be a fetich. This bore hard on those who had been

---

[*] Nicholaus Minorita (Baluz. et Mansi III. 207).—Chron. Glassberger ann. 1321.—Wadding. ann. 1321, No. 16–19; ann. 1322, No. 49–50.

conscientiously trained in the belief that the abnegation of property was the surest path to salvation; but the follies of the ascetics had become uncomfortable, if not dangerous, and it was necessary for the Church to go behind its teachings since the days of Antony and Hilarion and Simeon Stylites, to recur to the common-sense of the gospel, and to admit that, like the Sabbath, religion was made for man and not man for religion. In a work written some ten years after this time, Alvar Pelayo, papal penitentiary and himself a Franciscan, treats the subject at considerable length, and doubtless represents the views which found favor with John. The anchorite should be wholly dead to the world and should never leave his hermitage; memorable is the abbot who refused to open his door to his mother for fear his eye should rest upon her, and not less so the monk who, when his brother asked him to come a little way and help him with a foundered ox, replied, "Why dost thou not ask thy brother who is yet in the world?" "But he has been dead these fifteen years!" "And I have been dead to the world these twenty years!" Short of this complete renunciation, all men should earn their living by honest labor. In spite of the illustrious example of the sleepless monks of Dios, the apostolic command "Pray without ceasing" (Thessal. v. 17) is not to be taken literally. The apostles had money and bought food (John IV. 8), and Judas carried the purse of the Lord (John XII. 6). Better than a life of beggary is one blessed by honest labor, as a swineherd, a shepherd, a cowherd, a mason, a blacksmith, or a charcoal-burner, for a man is thus fulfilling the purpose of his creation. It is a sin for the able-bodied to live on charity, and thus usurp the alms due to the sick, the infirm, and the aged. All this is a lucid interval of common-sense, but what would Aquinas or Bonaventura have said to it, for it sounds like the echo of their great antagonist, William of Saint-Amour?*

---

* Alvar. Pelag. de Planctu Ecclesiæ Lib. I. Art. 51. fol. 165-9.

In fact, the advocates of poverty did not miss the easy opportunity of stigmatizing their antagonists as followers of William of Saint-Amour. See Tocco, "Un Codice della Marciana," Venezia, 1887, pp. 12, 39 (Ateneo Veneto, 1886–1887).

The MS. of which Professor Tocco has here printed the most important portions, with elucidatory notes, is a collection of the responses made to the question submitted for discussion by John XXII. as to the poverty of Christ and the

It was inevitable that the replies to the question submitted by John should be adverse to the poverty of Christ and the apostles. The bishops were universally assumed to be the representatives of the latter, and could not be expected to relish the assertion that their prototypes had been commanded by Christ to own no property. The Spirituals had made a point of this. Olivi had proved not only that Franciscans promoted to the episcopate were even more bound than their brethren to observe the Rule in all its strictures, but that bishops in general were under obligation to live in deeper poverty than the members of the most perfect Order. Now that there was a chance of justifying their worldliness and luxury, it was not likely to be lost. Yet John himself for a while held his own opinion suspended. In a debate before the consistory, Ubertino da Casale, the former leader of the orthodox Spirituals, was summoned to present the Franciscan view of the poverty of Christ, in answer to the Dominicans, and we are told that John was greatly pleased with his argument. Unluckily, at the General Chapter held at Perugia, May 30, 1322, the Franciscans appealed to Christendom at large by a definition addressed to all the faithful, in which they proved that the absolute poverty of Christ was the accepted doctrine of the Church, as set forth in the bulls *Exiit* and *Exivi de Paradiso*, and that John himself had approved of these in his bull *Quorumdam*. Another and more comprehensive utterance to the same effect received the signatures of all the Franciscan masters and bachelors of theology in France and England. With a disputant such as John this was an act of

---

apostles. They are significant of the general reaction against the previously prevailing dogma, and of the eagerness with which, as soon as the free expression of opinion was safe, the prelates repudiated a doctrine condemnatory of the temporalities so industriously accumulated by all classes of ecclesiastics. There were but eight replies affirming the poverty of Christ, and these were all from Franciscans—the Cardinals of Albano and San Vitale, the Archbishop of Salerno, the Bishops of Caffa, Lisbon, Riga, and Badajoz, and an unknown master of the Order. On the other side there were fourteen cardinals, including even Napoleone Orsini, the protector of the Spirituals, and a large number of archbishops, bishops, abbots, and doctors of theology. It is doubtless true, however, that the fear of offending the pope was a factor in producing this virtual unanimity—a fear not unreasonable, as was shown by the disgrace and persecution of those who maintained the poverty of Christ.—(Tocco, *ubi sup.* p. 35).

more zeal than discretion. His passions were fairly aroused, and
he proceeded to treat the Franciscans as antagonists. In December of the same year he dealt them a heavy blow in the bull *Ad
conditorem*, wherein with remorseless logic he pointed out the fallacy of the device of Innocent IV. for eluding the provisions of
the Rule by vesting the ownership of property in the Holy See and
its use in the Friars. It had not made them less eager in acquisitiveness, while it had led them to a senseless pride in their own asserted superiority of poverty. He showed that use and consumption as conceded to them were tantamount to ownership, and that
pretended ownership subject to such usufruct was illusory, while
it was absurd to speak of Rome as owning an egg or a piece of
cheese given to a friar to be consumed on the spot. Moreover, it
was humiliating to the Roman Church to appear as plaintiff or defendant in the countless litigations in which the Order was involved, and the procurators who thus appeared in its name were
said to abuse their position to the injury of many who were de-
frauded of their rights. For these reasons he annulled the provisions of Nicholas III., and declared that henceforth no ownership in the possessions of the Order should inhere in the Roman
Church and no procurator act in its name.*

The blow was shrewdly dealt, for though the question of the
poverty of Christ was not alluded to, the Order was deprived of
its subterfuge, and was forced to admit practically that ownership
of property was a necessary condition of its existence. Its members, however, had too long nursed the delusion to recognize its
fallacy now, and in January, 1323, Bonagrazia, as procurator specially commissioned for the purpose, presented to the pope in full
consistory a written protest against his action. If Bonagrazia
had not arguments to adduce he had at least ample precedents to
cite in the long line of popes since Gregory IX., including John
himself. He wound up by audaciously appealing to the pope, to

---

* Franz Ehrle, Archiv für Litt.- u. K. 1887, pp. 511–12.—Baluz et Mansi II.
279–80.—Nicholaus Minorita (Ibid. III. 208–13).

Curiously enough, in this John did exactly what his special antagonists, the
Spirituals, had desired. Olivi had long before pointed out the scandal of an
Order vowed to poverty litigating eagerly for property and using the transparent cover of papal procurators (Hist. Tribulat. ap. Archiv für Litt.- u. K. 1886,
p. 298).

Holy Mother Church, and to the apostles, and though he concluded by submitting himself to the decisions of the Church, he could not escape the wrath which he had provoked. It was not many years since Clement V. had confined him for resisting too bitterly the extravagance of the Spirituals : he still consistently occupied the same position, and now John cast him into a foul and dismal dungeon because he had not moved with the world, while the only answer to his protest was taking down from the church doors the bull *Ad conditorem* and replacing it with a revised edition, more decided and argumentative than its predecessor.*

All this did not conduce to a favorable decision of the question as to the poverty of Christ. John was now fairly enlisted against the Franciscans, and their enemies lost no opportunity of inflaming his passions. He would listen to no defence of the decision of the Chapter of Perugia. In consistory a Franciscan cardinal and some bishops timidly ventured to suggest that possibly there might be some truth in it, when he angrily silenced them—" You are talking heresy "—and forced them to recant on the spot. When he heard that the greatest Franciscan schoolman of the day, William of Ockham, had preached that it was heretical to affirm that Christ and the apostles owned property, he promptly wrote to the Bishops of Bologna and Ferrara to investigate the truth of the report, and if it was correct to cite Ockham to appear before him at Avignon within a month. Ockham obeyed, and we shall hereafter see what came of it.†

The papal decision on the momentous question was at last put forth, November 12, 1323, in the bull *Cum inter nonnullos*. In this there was no wavering or hesitation. The assertion that Christ and the apostles possessed no property was flatly declared to be a perversion of Scripture ; it was denounced for the future as erroneous and heretical, and its obstinate assertion by the Franciscan chapter was formally condemned. To the believers in the supereminent holiness of poverty, it was stunning to find themselves cast out as heretics for holding a doctrine which for generations had passed as an incontrovertible truth, and had repeatedly received the sanction of the Holy See in its most solemn form

---

* Nicholaus Minorita (Bal. et Mansi III. 213–24).

† Wadding. ann. 1323, No. 3, 15.

of ratification. Yet there was no help for it, and unless they were prepared to shift their belief with the pope, they could only expect to be delivered in this world to the Inquisition and in the next to Satan.*

Suddenly there appeared a new factor in the quarrel, which speedily gave it importance as a political question of the first magnitude. The sempiternal antagonism between the papacy and the empire had been recently assuming a more virulent aspect than usual under the imperious management of John XXII. Henry VII. had died in 1313, and in October, 1314, there had been a disputed election. Louis of Bavaria and Frederic of Austria both claimed the kaisership. Since Leo III., in the year 800, had renewed the line of Roman emperors by crowning Charlemagne, the ministration of the pope in an imperial coronation had been held essential, and had gradually enabled the Holy See to put forward undefined claims of a right to confirm the vote of the German electors. For the enforcement of such claims a disputed election gave abundant opportunity, nor were there lacking other elements to complicate the position. The Angevine papalist King of Naples, Robert the Good, had dreams of founding a great Italian Guelf monarchy, to which John XXII. lent a not unfavorable ear; especially as his quarrel with the Ghibelline Visconti of Lombardy was becoming unappeasable. The traditional enmity between France and Germany, moreover, rendered the former eager in everything that could cripple the empire, and French influence was necessarily dominant in Avignon. It would be foreign to our purpose to penetrate into the labyrinth of diplomatic intrigue which speedily formed itself around these momentous questions. An alliance between Robert and Frederic, with the assent of the pope, seemed to give the latter assurance of recognition, when the battle of Mühldorf, September 28, 1322, decided the question. Frederic was a prisoner in the hands of his rival, and there could be no further doubt as to which of them should reign in Germany. It did not follow, however, that John would consent to place the imperial crown on the head of Louis.†

---

* Nicholaus Minorita (Bal. et Mansi III. 224).

† Carl Müller, Der Kampf Ludwigs des Baiern mit der römischen Curie, § 4. —Felten, Die Bulle *Ne pretereat*, Trier, 1885.—Preger, Die Politik des Pabstes Johann XXII., München, 1885, pp. 44–6.

So far was he from contemplating any such action that he still insisted on deciding between the claims of the competitors. Louis contemptuously left his pretensions unanswered and proceeded to settle matters by concluding a treaty with his prisoner and setting him free. Moreover, he intervened effectually in the affairs of Lombardy, rescued the Visconti from the Guelf league which was about to overwhelm them, and ruined the plans of the cardinal legate, Bertrand de Poyet, John's nephew or son, who was carving out a principality for himself. It would have required less than this to awaken the implacable hostility of such a man as John, whose only hope for the success of his Italian policy now lay in dethroning Louis and replacing him with the French king, Charles le Bel. He rushed precipitately to the conflict and proclaimed no quarter. October 8, 1323, in the presence of a vast multitude, a bull was read and affixed to the portal of the cathedral of Avignon, which declared not only that no one could act as King of the Romans until his person had been approved by the pope, but repeated a claim, already made in 1317, that until such approval the empire was vacant, and its government during the interregnum belonged to the Holy See. All of Louis's acts were pronounced null and void; he was summoned within three months to lay down his power and submit his person to the pope for approval, under pain of the punishments which he had incurred by his rebellious pretence of being emperor; all oaths of allegiance taken to him were declared annulled; all prelates were threatened with suspension, and all cities and states with excommunication and interdict if they should continue to obey him. Louis at first received this portentous missive with singular humility. November 12 he sent to Avignon envoys, who did not arrive until January 2, 1324, to ask whether the reports which he had heard of the papal action were true, and if so to request a delay of six months in which to prove his innocence. To this John, on January 7, gave answer extending the term only two months from that day. Meanwhile Louis had taken heart, possibly encouraged by the outbreak of the quarrel between John and the Franciscans, for the date of the credentials of the envoys, November 12, was the same as that of the bull *Cum inter nonnullos*. On December 18, he issued the Nuremberg Protest, a spirited vindication of the rights of the German nation and empire against the new pretensions of the papacy; he demanded the assembling of a general council before which he would make good his claims; it was his duty, as the head of the empire, to maintain the purity of the faith against a pope who was a fautor of heretics. It shows how little he yet understood about the questions at issue that to sustain this last charge he accused John of unduly protecting the Franciscans against universal complaints that they habitually violated the secrecy of the confessional, this being apparently his version of the papal condemnation of John of Poilly's thesis that confession to a Mendicant friar was insufficient.*

If Louis at first thought to gain strength by thus utilizing the jealousy and dislike felt by the secular clergy towards the Mendicants, he soon realized that a surer source of support was to be found in espousing the side of the Franciscans in the quarrel forced upon them by John. The two months' delay granted by John expired March 7 without Louis making an appearance, and on March 25 the pope promulgated against him a sentence of excommunication, with a threat that he should be deprived of all rights if he did not submit within three months. To this Louis speedily rejoined in a document known as the Protest of Sachsenhausen, which shows that since December he had put himself in communication with the disaffected Franciscans, had entered into alliance with them, and had recognized how great was the advantage of posing as the defender of the faith and assailing the pope with the charge of heresy. After paying due attention to John's assaults on the rights of the empire, the Protest takes up the question of his recent bulls respecting poverty and argues them in much detail. John had declared before Franciscans of high standing that for forty years he had regarded the Rule of Francis as fantastic and impossible. As the Rule was revealed by Christ, this alone proves him to be a heretic. Moreover, as the Church is infallible in its definitions of faith, and as it has repeatedly, through Honorius III., Innocent IV., Alexander IV., Innocent V., Nicholas III., and Nicholas IV., pronounced in favor of the poverty of Christ and the apostles, John's condemnation of this tenet abundantly shows him

---

* Carl Müller, op. cit. § 5.—Preger, Politik des Pabstes Johann XXII. (München, 1885, pp. 7, 54).—Martene Thesaur. II. 644-51.—Raynald. ann. 1323, No. 34-5.

to be a heretic. His two constitutions, *Ad conditorem* and *Cum inter nonnullos*, therefore, have cut him off from the Church as a manifest heretic teaching a condemned heresy, and have disabled him from the papacy; all of which Louis swore to prove before a general council to be assembled in some place of safety.*

John proceeded with his prosecution of Louis by a further declaration, issued July 11, in which, without deigning to notice the Protest of Sachsenhausen, he pronounced Louis to have forfeited by his contumacy all claim to the empire; further obstinacy would deprive him of his ancestral dukedom of Bavaria and other possessions, and he was summoned to appear October 1, to receive final sentence. Yet John could not leave unanswered the assault upon his doctrinal position, and on November 10 he issued the bull *Quia quorumdam*, in which he argued that he had exercised no undue power in contradicting the decisions of his predecessors: he declared it a condemned heresy to assert that Christ and the apostles had only simple usufruct, without legal possession, in the things which Scripture declared them to have possessed, for if this were true it would follow that Christ was unjust, which is blasphemy. All who utter, write, or teach such doctrines fall into condemned heresy, and are to be avoided as heretics.†

Thus the poverty of Christ was fairly launched upon the world as a European question. It is a significant illustration of the intellectual condition of the fourteenth century that in the subsequent

---

* Martene Thesaur. II. 652–9.—Nich. Minorita (Bal. et Mansi III. 224–33).

The date of the Protest of Sachsenhausen is not positively known, but it was probably issued in April or May, 1324 (Müller, op. cit. I. 357–8). Its authorship is ascribed by Preger to Franz von Lautern, and Ehrle has shown that much of its argumentation is copied literally from the writings of Olivi (Archiv für Litt.-u. Kirchengeschichte, 1887, 540). When there were negotiations for a settlement in 1336, Louis signed a declaration prepared by Benedict XII., in which he was made to say that the portions concerning the poverty of Christ were inserted without his knowledge by his notary, Ulric der Wilde for the purpose of injuring him (Raynald ann. 1336, No. 31–5); but he accompanied this self-abasing statement with secret instructions of a very different character (Preger, Kirchenpolitische Kampf, p. 12).

† Martene Thesaur. II. 660–71.—Nich. Minorita (Bal. et Mansi III. 233–6).

Even in far-off Ireland the bull of July 11, depriving Louis of the empire, was read in all the churches in English and Irish.—Theiner, Monument. Hibern. et Scotor. No. 456, p. 230.

stages of the quarrel between the papacy and the empire, involving the most momentous principles of public law, those principles,
in the manifestoes of either side, assume quite a subordinate position. The shrewd and able men who conducted the controversy
evidently felt that public opinion was much more readily influenced by accusations of heresy, even upon a point so trivial and
unsubstantial, than by appeals to reason upon the conflicting jurisdictions of Church and State.* Yet, as the quarrel widened and
deepened, and as the stronger intellects antagonistic to papal pretensions gathered around Louis, they were able, in unwonted liberty of thought and speech, to investigate the theory of government and the claims of the papacy with unheard-of boldness.
Unquestionably they aided Louis in his struggle, but the spirit of
the age was against them. Spiritual authority was still too awful for successful rebellion, and when Louis passed away affairs
returned to the old routine, and the labors of the men who had
waged his battle in the hope of elevating humanity disappeared,
leaving but a doubtful trace upon the modes of thought of the
time.

The most audacious of these champions was Marsiglio of Padua.
Interpenetrated with the principles of the imperial jurisprudence,
in which the State was supreme and the Church wholly subordinated, he had seen in France how the influence of the Roman law
was emancipating the civil power from servitude, and perhaps in
the University of Paris had heard the echoes of the theories of
Henry of Ghent, the celebrated Doctor Solemnis, who had taught
the sovereignty of the people over their princes. He framed a
conception of a political organization which should reproduce that
of Rome under the Christian emperors, with a recognition of the
people as the ultimate source of all civil authority. Aided by Jean
de Jandun he developed these ideas with great hardihood and
skill in his "*Defensor Pacis*," and in 1326, when the strife between John and Louis was at its hottest, the two authors left
Paris to lay the result of their labors before the emperor. In a
brief tract, moreover, "*De translatione imperii*," Marsiglio subse-

---

* See the documents in the second prosecution of Louis by John, where the
accusations against him constantly commence with his pertinacious heresy in
maintaining the condemned doctrine of the poverty of Christ.—Martene Thesaur.
II. 682 sqq. Cf. Guill. Nangiac. Contin. ann. 1328.

quently sketched the manner in which the Holy Roman Empire
had arisen, showing the ancient subjection of the Holy See to the
imperial power, and the baselessness of the papal claims to confirm
the election of the emperors.   John XXII. had no hesitation in
condemning the daring authors as heretics, and the protection
which Louis afforded them added another count to the indictment
against him for heresy.   Unable to wreak vengeance upon them,
all who could be supposed to be their accomplices were sternly
dealt with.   A certain Francesco of Venice, who had been a student with Marsiglio at Paris, was seized and carried to Avignon
on a charge of having aided in the preparation of the wicked book,
and of having supplied the heresiarch with money.   Tried before
the Apostolic Chamber, he stoutly maintained that he was ignorant of the contents of the "*Defensor Pacis*," that he had deposited money with Marsiglio, as was customary with scholars, and
that Marsiglio had left Paris owing him thirteen sols parisis.   Jean
de Jandun died in 1328, and Marsiglio not later than 1343, thus
mercifully spared the disappointment of the failure of their theories.   In so far as purely intellectual conceptions had weight in
the conflict they were powerful allies for Louis.   In the "*Defensor Pacis*" the power of the keys is argued away in the clearest
dialectics.   God alone has power to judge, to absolve, to condemn.
The pope is no more than any other priest, and a priestly sentence
may be the result of hatred, favor, or injustice, of no weight with
God.   Excommunication, to be effective, must not proceed from
the judgment of a single priest, but must be the sentence of the
whole community, with full knowledge of all the facts.   It is no
wonder that when, in 1376, a French translation of the work appeared in Paris it created a profound sensation.   A prolonged
inquest was held, lasting from September to December, in which
all the learned men in the city were made to swear before a notary
as to their ignorance of the translator.*

---

* Altmayer, Les Précurseurs de la Réforme aux Pays-Bas, Bruxelles, 1886, I.
38. — Guillel. Nangiac. Contin. ann. 1326. — Fasciculus Rer. Expetendarum et
Fugiend. II. 55, Ed. 1690. — D'Argentré, I. ɪ. 304–11, 397–400.—Baluz. et Mansi
II. 280–1. — Martene Thesaur. II. 704–16. — Preger, Kirchenpolitische Kampf,
pp. 34, 65.—Defensor. Pacis II. 6.

The manner in which Fritsche Closener, a contemporary priest of Strassburg,
speaks of the *Defensor Pacis* shows what an impression it made, and that even

More vehement and more fluent as a controversialist was the great schoolman, William of Ockham. When the final breach came between the papacy and the rigid Franciscans he was already under inquisitorial trial for his utterances. Escaping from Avignon with his general, Michele, he found refuge, like the rest, with Louis, whose cause he strengthened by skilfully linking the question of Christ's poverty with that of German independence. Those who refused to accept a papal definition on a point of faith could only justify themselves by proving that popes were fallible and their power not unlimited. Thus the strife over the narrow Franciscan dogmatism on poverty broadened until it embraced the great questions which had disturbed the peace of Europe since the time of Hildebrand, nearly three centuries before. In 1324 Ockham boasted that he had set his face like flint against the errors of the pseudo-pope, and that so long as he possessed hand, paper, pens, and ink, no abuse or lies or persecution or persuasion would induce him to desist from attacking them. He kept his promise literally, and for twenty years he poured forth a series of controversial works in defence of the cause to which he had devoted his life. Without embracing the radical doctrines of Marsiglio on the popular foundation of political institutions, he practically reached the same outcome. While admitting the primacy of the pope, he argued that a pope can fall into heresy, and so, indeed, can a general council, and even all Christendom. The influence of the Holy Ghost did not deprive man of free-will and prevent him from succumbing to error, no matter what might be his station. There was nothing sure but Scripture; the poorest and meanest peasant might adhere to Catholic truth revealed to him by God, while popes and councils erred. Above the pope is the general council representing the whole Church. A pope refusing to entertain an appeal to a general council, declining to assemble it, or arrogating its authority to himself is a manifest heretic, whom it is the duty of the bishops to depose, or, if the bishops refuse, then that of the emperor, who is supreme over the earth. But it was not only by the enunciation of general princi-

---

a portion of the clergy was not averse to its conclusions.—Closeners Chronik (Chroniken der deutschen Städte VIII. 70.—Cf. Chron. des Jacob von Königs-hofen, Ib. p. 473).

ples that he carried on the war; merciless were his assaults on the errors and inconsistencies of John XXII., who was proved guilty of seventy specific heresies. Thus to the bitter end his dauntless spirit kept up the strife; one by one his colleagues died and submitted, and he was left alone, but he continued to shower ridicule on the curia and its creatures in his matchless dialectics. Even the death of Louis and the hopeless defeat of his cause did not stop his fearless pen. Church historians claim that in 1349 he at last made his peace and was reconciled, but this is more than doubtful, for Giacomo della Marca classes him with Michele and Bonagrazia as the three unrepentant heretics who died under excommunication. It is not easy to determine with accuracy what influence was exercised by the powerful intellects which England, France, and Italy thus contributed to the defence of German independence. Possibly they may have stimulated Wickliff to question the foundation of papal power and the supremacy of the Church over the State, leading to Hussite insubordination. Possibly, too, they may have contributed to the movement which in various development emboldened the Councils of Constance and Basle to claim superiority over the Holy See, the Gallican Church to assert its liberties, and England to frame the hostile legislation of the Statutes of Provisors and Præmunire. If this be so, the hopeless entanglements of German politics caused them to effect less in their own chosen battle-field than in lands far removed from the immediate scene of conflict.*

This rapid glance at the larger aspects of the strife has been necessary to enable us to follow intelligently the vicissitudes of the discussion over the poverty of Christ, which occupied in the struggle a position ludicrously disproportionate to its importance. For some time after the issue of the bulls *Cum inter nonnullos* and *Quia quorumdam* there was a sort of armed neutrality between John and the heads of the Franciscan Order. Each seemed to be afraid of taking a step which should precipitate a conflict, doubt-

---

* Martene Thesaur. II. 749-52.—Tocco, L'Eresia nel Medio Evo, pp. 532-555. —Preger, Der Kirchenpolitische Kampf, pp. 8-9.—Carl Müller, op. cit. II. 251-2.—Trithem. Chron. Hirsaug. ann. 1323.—Raynald. ann. 1349, No. 16-17.—Jac. de Marchia Dial. (Bal. et Mansi II. 600).

less secretly felt by both sides to be inevitable. Still there was a little skirmishing for position. In 1325 Michele had summoned the general chapter to assemble at Paris, but he feared that an effort would be made to annul the declarations of Perugia, and that John would exercise a pressure by means of King Charles le Bel, whose influence was great through the number of benefices at his disposal. Suddenly, therefore, he transferred the call to Lyons, where considerable trouble was experienced through the efforts of Gerard Odo, a creature of the pope, and subsequently the successor of Michele, to obtain relaxations of the Rule as regarded poverty. Still the brethren stood firm, and these attempts were defeated, while a constitution threatening with imprisonment all who should speak indiscreetly and disrespectfully of John XXII. and his decretals indicates the passions which were seething under the surface. Not long after this we hear of a prosecution suddenly commenced against our old acquaintance Ubertino da Casale, in spite of his Benedictine habit and his quiet residence in Italy. He seems to have been suspected of having furnished the arguments on the subject of the poverty of Christ in the Protest of Sachsenhausen, and, September 16, 1325, an order was sent for his arrest, but he got wind of it and escaped to Germany—the first of the illustrious band of refugees who gathered around Louis of Bavaria, though he appears to have made his peace in 1330. John seems to have at last grown restive at the tácit insubordination of the Franciscans, who did not openly deny his definitions as to the poverty of Christ, but whom he knew to be secretly cherishing in their hearts the condemned doctrine. In 1326 Michele issued decrees subjecting to a strict censorship all writings by the brethren and enforcing one of the rules which prohibited the discussion of doubtful opinions, thus muzzling the Order in the hope of averting dissension; but it was not in John's nature to rest satisfied with silence which covered opposition, and in August, 1327, he advanced to the attack. In the bull *Quia nonnunquam,* addressed to archbishops and inquisitors, he declared that many still believed in the poverty of Christ in spite of his having pronounced such belief a heresy, and that those who entertained it should be treated as heretics. He therefore now orders the prelates and inquisitors to prosecute them vigorously, and though the Franciscans are not specially named, the clause which deprives the accused of all papal

privileges and subjects them to the ordinary jurisdictions sufficiently shows that they were the object of the assault. It is quite
possible that this was provoked by some movement among the remains of the moderate Spirituals of Italy—men who came to be
known as Fraticelli—who had never indulged in the dangerous
enthusiasms of the Olivists, but who were ready to suffer martyrdom in defence of the sacred principles of poverty. Such men
could not but have been at once excited by the papal denial of
Christ's poverty, and encouraged by finding the Order at large
driven into antagonism with the Holy See. Sicily had long been
a refuge for the more zealous when forced to flee from Italy. At
this time we hear of their crossing back to Calabria, and of John
writing to Niccolò da Reggio, the Minister of Calabria, savage instructions to destroy them utterly. Lists are to be made out and
sent to him of all who show them favor, and King Robert is appealed to for aid in the good work. Robert, in spite of his close
alliance with the pope, and the necessity of the papal favor for his
ambitious plans, was sincerely on the side of the Franciscans. He
seems never to have forgotten the teachings of Arnaldo de Vilanova, and as his father, Charles the Lame, had interfered to protect
the Spirituals of Provence, so now both he and his queen did what
they could with the angry pope to moderate his wrath, and at the
same time he urged the Order to stand firm in defence of the Rule.
In the protection which he afforded he did not discriminate closely
between the organized resistance of the Order under its general,
and the irregular mutiny of the Fraticelli. His dominions, as well
as Sicily, served as a refuge for the latter. With the troubles
provoked by John their numbers naturally grew. Earnest spirits,
dissatisfied with Michele's apparent acquiescence in John's new
heresy, would naturally join them. They ranged themselves under Henry da Ceva, who had fled to Sicily from persecution under Boniface VIII.; they elected him their general minister and
formed a complete independent organization, which, when John
triumphed over the Order, gathered in its recalcitrant fragments
and constituted a sect whose strange persistence under the fiercest
persecution we shall have to follow for a century and a half.*

---

* Wadding. ann. 1317, No. 9; ann. 1318, No. 8; ann. 1323, No. 16; ann. 1325,
No. 6; ann. 1331, No. 3.—Chron. Glassberger ann. 1325, 1326, 1330.—Raynald. ann.

On the persecution of these insubordinate brethren Michele da Cesena could afford to look with complacency, and he evidently desired to regard the bull of August, 1327, as directed against them. He maintained his attitude of submission. In June the pope had summoned him from Rome to Avignon, and he had excused himself on the ground of sickness. His messengers with his apologies were graciously received, and it was not until December 2 that he presented himself before John. The pope subsequently declared that he had been summoned to answer for secretly encouraging rebels and heretics, and doubtless the object was to be assured of his person, but he was courteously welcomed, and the ostensible reason given for sending for him was certain troubles in the provinces of Assisi and Aragon, in which Michele obediently changed the ministers. Until April, 1328, he remained in the papal court, apparently on the best of terms with John.[*]

Meanwhile the quarrel between the empire and the papacy had been developing apace. In the spring of 1326 Louis suddenly and without due preparation undertook an expedition to Italy, at the invitation of the Ghibellines, for his imperial coronation. When he reached Milan in April to receive the iron crown John sternly forbade his further progress, and on this being disregarded, proceeded to excommunicate him afresh. Thus commenced another prolonged series of citations and sentences for heresy, including the preaching of a crusade with Holy Land indulgences against the impenitent sinner. Unmoved by this, Louis slowly made his way to Rome, which he entered January 7, 1327, and where he was crowned on the 17th, in contemptuous defiance of papal prerogative, by four syndics elected by the people, after which, according to usage, he exchanged the title of King of the Romans for that of Emperor. As the defender of the faith he proceeded to try the pope on the charge of heresy, based upon his denial of the poverty of Christ. April 14 he promulgated a law authorizing the prosecution and sentence *in absentia* of those notoriously defamed for treason or heresy, thus imitating the papal injustice of

1325, No. 20, 27.—Franz Ehrle (Archiv für L. u. K. 1886, p. 151).—Martene Thesaur. II. 752–3.—Vitoduran. Chron. (Eccard. Corp. Hist. I. 1799).—D'Argentré, I. I. 297.—Eymeric. pp. 291–4.

[*] Martene Thesaur. II. 749.—Baluz. et Mansi III. 315–16.—Nicholaus Minorita (Baluz. et Mansi III. 238–40).

III.—10

which he himself complained bitterly; and, on the 17th, sentence
of deposition was solemnly read to the assembled people before
the basilica of St. Peter. It recited that it was rendered at the
request of the clergy and people of Rome; it recapitulated the
crimes of the pope, whom it stigmatized as Antichrist; it pronounced him a heretic on account of his denying the poverty of
Christ, deposed him from the papacy, and threatened confiscation
on all who should render him support and assistance.*

As a pope was necessary to the Church, and as the college of
cardinals were under excommunication as fautors of heresy, recourse was had to the primitive method of selection: some form
of election by the people and clergy of Rome was gone through
on May 12, and a new Bishop of Rome was presented to the
Christian world in the person of Pier di Corbario, an aged Franciscan of high repute for austerity and eloquence. He was Minister of the province of the Abruzzi and papal penitentiary. He
had been married, his wife was still living, and he was said to
have entered the Order without her consent, which rendered him
"irregular" and led to an absurd complication, for the woman,
who had never before complained of his leaving her, now came
forward and put in her claims to be bought off. He assumed the
name of Nicholas V., a college of cardinals was readily created
for him, he appointed nuncios and legates and proceeded to degrade the Guelfic bishops and replace them with Ghibellines. In
the confusion attendant upon these revolutionary proceedings it
can be readily imagined that the Fraticelli emerged from their
hiding-places and indulged in glowing anticipations of the future
which they fondly deemed their own.†

Although the Franciscan prefect of the Roman province assembled a chapter at Anagni which pronounced against Pier di
Corbario, and ordered him to lay aside his usurped dignity, it was
impossible that the Order should escape responsibility for the rebellion, nor is it likely that Michele da Cesena was not privy to
the whole proceeding. He had remained quietly at Avignon, and

---

* Chron. Sanens. (Muratori S. R. I. XV. 77, 79).—Martene Thesaur. II. 684–
723.—Nicholaus Minorita (Bal. et Mansi III. 240–3).

† Nicholaus Minorita (Bal. et Mansi III. 243).—Ptolomæi Lucensis Hist.
Eccles. cap. 41 (Muratori S. R. I. XI. 1210).—Chron. Sanens. (Muratori XV. 80).
—Wadding. ann. 1328, No. 2–4, 8–11.

John had manifested no abatement of cordiality until April 9, when, on being summoned to an audience, the pope attacked him on the subject of the Chapter of Perugia, which six years before had asserted the poverty of Christ and the apostles. Michele stoutly defended the utterances of the chapter, saying that if they were heretical then Nicholas IV. and the other popes who had affirmed the doctrine were heretics. Then the papal wrath exploded. Michele was a headstrong fool, a fautor of heretics, a serpent nourished in the bosom of the Church; and when the stream of invective had exhausted itself he was placed under constructive arrest, and ordered not to leave Avignon without permission, under pain of excommunication, of forfeiture of office, and of future disability. A few days later, on April 14, in the secrecy of the Franciscan convent, he relieved his feelings by executing a solemn notarial protest, in the presence of William of Ockham, Bonagrazia, and other trusty adherents, in which he recited the circumstances, argued that the pope either was a heretic or no pope, for either his present utterances were erroneous or else Nicholas IV. had been a heretic; in the latter case Boniface VIII. and Clement V., who had approved the Bull *Exiit qui seminat*, were likewise heretics, their nominations of cardinals were void, and the conclave which elected John was illegal. He protested against whatever might be done in derogation of the rights of the Order, that he was in durance and in just fear, and that what he might be forced to do would be null and void. The whole document is a melancholy illustration of the subterfuges rendered necessary by an age of violence.[*]

Michele was detained in Avignon while the general chapter of the Order was held at Bologna, to which John sent Bertrand, Bishop of Ostia, with instructions to have another general chosen. The Order, however, was stubborn. It sent a somewhat defiant message to the pope and re-elected Michele, requesting him moreover to indicate Paris as the next place of assemblage, to be held, according to rule, in three years, to which he assented. In view of the drama which was developing in Rome he might reasonably fear for liberty or life. Preparations were made for his escape. A galley, furnished, according to John, by the Emperor Louis, but according to other and more trustworthy accounts, by Genoese

---

[*] Nicholaus Minorita (Bal. et Mansi III. 238–40).

refugees, was sent to Aigues-mortes. Thither he fled, May 26, accompanied by Ockham and Bonagrazia. The Bishop of Porto, sent by John in hot haste after him, had an interview with him on the deck of his galley, but failed to induce him to return. He reached Pisa on June 9, and there ensued a war of manifestoes of unconscionable length, in which Michele was pronounced excommunicate and deposed, and John was proved to be a heretic who had rightfully forfeited the papacy. Michele could only carry on a wordy conflict, while John could act. Bertrand de la Tour, Cardinal of San Vitale, was appointed Vicar-general of the Order, another general chapter was ordered to assemble in Paris, June, 1329, and preparations were made for it by removing all provincials favorable to Michele, and appointing in their places men who could be relied on. Out of thirty-four who had met in Bologna only fourteen were seen in Paris; Michele was deposed and Gerard Odo was elected in his place; but even under this pressure no declaration condemning the poverty of Christ could be obtained from the chapter. The mass of the Order, reduced to silence, remained faithful to the principles represented by its deposed general, until forced to acquiescence by the arbitrary measures so freely employed by the pope and the examples made of those who dared to express opposition. Still John was not disposed to relax the Franciscan discipline, and when, in 1332, Gerard Odo, in the hope of gaining a cardinal's hat, persuaded fourteen provincial ministers to join him in submitting a gloss which would have virtually annulled the obligation of poverty, his only reward was the ridicule of the pope and sacred college.*

---

* Nicholaus Minorita (Baluz. et Mansi III. 243–349).—Jac. de Marchia Dial. (Ibid. II. 598).—Chron. Sanens. (Muratori S. R. I. XV. 81).—Vitodurani Chron. (Eccard. Corp. Hist. I. 1799–1800).—Martene Thesaur. II. 757–60.—Alvar. Pelag. De Planctu Eccles. Lib. II. art. 67.

The career of Cardinal Bertrand de la Tour illustrates the pliability of conscience requisite to those who served John XXII. He was a Franciscan of high standing. As Provincial of Aquitaine he had persecuted the Spirituals. Elevated to the cardinalate, when John called for opinions on the question of the poverty of Christ he had argued in the affirmative. In conjunction with Vitale du Four, Cardinal of Albano, he had secretly drawn up the declaration of the Chapter of Perugia which so angered the pope, but when the latter made up his mind that Christ had owned property, the cardinal promptly changed his

The settlement of the question depended much more upon political than upon religious considerations. Louis had abandoned Rome and established himself in Pisa with his pope, his cardinals, and his Franciscans, but the Italians were becoming tired of their kaiser. It mattered little that in January, 1329, he indulged in the childish triumph of solemnly burning John XXII. in effigy; he was obliged soon after to leave the city, and towards the end of the year he returned to Germany, carrying with him the men who were to defend his cause with all the learning of the schools, and abandoning to their fate those of his partisans who were unable to follow him.* The proceedings which ensued at Todi will serve to show how promptly the Inquisition tracked his retreating footsteps, and how useful it was as a political agency in reducing rebellious communities to submission.

The Todini were Ghibelline. In 1327, when John XXII. had ordered Francisco Damiani, Inquisitor of Spoleto, to proceed vigorously against Mucio Canistrario of Todi as a rebel against the Church, and Mucio had accordingly been imprisoned, the people had risen in insurrection and liberated the captive, while the inquisitor had been forced to fly for his life. In August, 1328, they had welcomed Louis as emperor and Pier di Corbario as pope, and had ordered their notaries to use the regnal years of the latter in their instruments; they had, moreover, attacked and taken the Guelf city of Orvieto and, like all the cities which adhered to Louis, they had expelled the Dominicans. In August, 1329, abandoned by Louis, proceedings were commenced against them by the Franciscan, Frà Bartolino da Perugia, the inquisitor, who announced his intention of making a thorough inquest of the whole district of Assisi against all Patarins and heretics, against those who assert things not to be sins which the Church teaches to be sins, or are minor sins which the Church holds to be greater, against those who understand the Scriptures in a sense different from what the Holy Spirit demands, against those who talk against the state and observance of the Roman Church and its

---

convictions, and was now engaged in persecuting those who adhered to the belief which he had prescribed for them.—Tocco, Un Codice della Marciana, pp. 40, 43, 45.

* Chron. Cornel. Zantfliet (Martene Ampl. Coll. V. 187).—Villani, Lib. x. c. 126, 144.

teachings, and against those who have detracted from the dignity and person of the pope and his constitutions. Under this searching examinations were made as to the acts of the citizens during the visit of Louis, any sign of respect paid to him being regarded as a crime, and two sets of prosecutions were commenced—one against the Ghibellines of the city and the other against the "rebellious" Franciscans. These latter were summoned to reply to five articles—1, If they believed in, favored, or adhered to the Bavarian and the intrusive antipope; 2, If they had marched with a cross to meet these heretics on their entrance into Todi; 3, If they had obeyed or done reverence to the Bavarian as emperor or to P. di Corbario as pope; 4, If they had taught or preached that the constitutions of John were heretical or himself a heretic; 5, If, after Michele da Cesena was condemned and deposed for heresy, they had adhered to him and his errors. These interrogations show how conveniently the religious and political questions were mingled together, and how thorough was the investigation rendered possible by the machinery of the Inquisition. The proceedings dragged on, and, July 1, 1330, John condemned the whole community as heretics and fautors of heresy. July 7 he sent this sentence to the legate, Cardinal Orsini, with instructions to cite the citizens peremptorily and to try them, according to the inquisitorial formula, "*summarie et de plano et sine strepitu et figura.*" Under this the Todini finally made submission, the cardinal sent Frà Bartolino and his colleague thither, and the city was reconciled, subject to the papal approval. They had been obliged to make a gift of ten thousand florins to Louis, and now a fine of equal amount was levied upon them, besides one hundred lire imposed on each of one hundred and thirty-four citizens. Apparently the terms exacted were not satisfactory to John, for a papal brief of July 20, 1331, declared the submission of the citizens deceitful, and ordered the interdict renewed. The last document which we have in the case is one of June 1, 1332, in which the legate sends to the Bishop of Todi a list of one hundred and ninety-seven persons, including Franciscans, parish priests, heads of religious houses, nobles, and citizens, who are ordered to appear before him at Orvieto on June 15, to stand trial on the inquisitions which have been found against them. That the proceedings were pushed to the bitter end there can be no doubt, for when in this year the

General Gerard Odo proposed to revoke the commission of Frà Bartolino, John intervened and extended it for the purpose of enabling him to continue the prosecutions to a definite sentence. This is doubtless a fair specimen of the minute persecution which was going on wherever the Ghibellines were not strong enough to defend themselves by force of arms.*

As for the unhappy antipope, his fate was even more deplorable. Confided at Pisa by Louis to the care of Count Fazio da Doneratico, the leading noble of the city, he was concealed for a while in a castle in Maremma. June 18, 1329, the Pisans rose and drove out the imperialist garrison, and in the following January they were reconciled to the Church. A part of the bargain was the surrender of Pier di Corbario, to whom John promised to show himself a kind father and benevolent friend, besides enriching Fazio for the betrayal of his trust. After making public abjuration of his heresies in Pisa, Pier was sent, guarded by two state galleys, to Nice, where he was delivered to the papal agents. In every town on the road to Avignon he was required publicly to repeat his abjuration and humiliation. August 25, 1330, with a halter around his neck, he was brought before the pope in public consistory. Exhausted and broken with shame and suffering, he flung himself at his rival's feet and begged for mercy, abjuring and anathematizing his heresies, and especially that of the poverty of Christ. Then, in a private consistory, he was made again to confess a long catalogue of crimes, and to accept such penance as might be awarded him. No humiliation was spared him, and nothing was omitted to make his abject recantation complete. Having thus rendered him an object of contempt and deprived him of all further power of harm, John mercifully spared him bodily torment. He was confined in an apartment in the papal palace, fed from the papal table, and allowed the use of books, but no one was admitted to see him without a special papal order. His wretched life soon came to an end, and when he died, in 1333, he was buried in the Franciscan habit. Considering the ferocity of the age, his treatment is one of the least discreditable acts in the career of John XXII. It was hardly to be expected, after the

---

* Franz Ehrle (Archiv für L. u K. 1885, pp. 159–64; 1886, pp. 653–69).— Archivio Storico Italiano, 1 Ott. 1865, pp. 10–21.—Ripoll II. 180.—Wadding. ann. 1326, No. 9; 1327, No. 3–4; 1331, No. 4; 1332, No. 5.

savage vindictiveness of the Ernulphine curse which he had published, April 20, 1329, on his already fallen rival—"May he in this life feel the wrath of Peter and Paul, whose church he has sought to confound! May his dwelling-place be deserted, and may there be none to live under his roof! May his children be orphans, and his wife a widow! May they be driven forth from their hearth-stones to beggary! May the usurer devour their substance, and strangers seize the work of their hands! May the whole earth fight against him, may the elements be his enemies, may the merits of all the saints at rest confound him and wreak vengeance on him through life!" *

During the progress of this contest public opinion was by no means unanimous in favor of John, and the Inquisition was an efficient instrumentality in repressing all expression of adverse sentiments. In 1328, at Carcassonne, a certain Germain Frevier was tried before it for blaspheming against John, and stigmatizing his election as simoniacal because he had promised never to set foot in stirrup till he should set out for Rome. Germain, moreover, had declared that the Franciscan pope was the true pope, and that if he had money he would go there and join him and the Bavarian. Germain was not disposed to martyrdom; at first he denied, then, after being left to his reflections in prison for five months, he pleaded that he had been drunk and knew not what he was saying; a further delay showed him that he was helpless, he confessed his offences and begged for mercy.†

Another case, in 1329, shows us what were the secret feelings of a large portion of the Franciscan Order, and the means required to keep it in subordination. Before the Inquisition of Carcassonne, Frère Barthelémi Bruguière confessed that in saying mass and coming to the prayer for the pope he had hesitated which of the two popes to pray for, and had finally desired his prayer to be for whichever was rightfully the head of the Church. Many of his brethren, he said, were in the habit of wishing that God would give John XXII. so much to do that he would forget the

---

* Villani, Lib. x. c. 131, 142, 160.—Guill. Nangiac. Contin. ann. 1330.—Wadding. ann. 1330, No. 9.—Martene Thesaur. II. 736–70; 806–15.—Chron. Cornel. Zantfliet ann. 1330 (Martene Ampl. Coll. V. 194–8).

† Archives de l'Inq. de Carcassonne (Doat, XXVII. 7 sqq.).

Franciscans, for it seemed to them that his whole business was to afflict them. It was generally believed among them that their general, Michele, had been unjustly deposed and excommunicated. In a large assembly of friars he had said, "I wish that antipope was a Dominican, or of some other Order," when another rejoined, "I rejoice still more that the antipope is of our Order, for if he was of another we should have no friend, and now at least we have the Italian," whereat all present applauded. For a while Frère Barthelémi held out, but imprisonment with threats of chains and fasting broke down his resolution, and he threw himself upon the mercy of the inquisitor, Henri de Chamay. That mercy consisted in a sentence of harsh prison for life, with chains on hands and feet and bread and water for food. Possibly the Dominican inquisitor may have felt pleasure in exhibiting a Franciscan prisoner, for he allowed Barthelémi to retain his habit; and it shows the minute care of John's vindictiveness that a year later he wrote expressly to Henri de Chamay reciting that, as the delinquent had been expelled from the Order, the habit must be stripped from him and be delivered to the Franciscan authorities.*

In Germany the Franciscans for the most part remained faithful to Michele and Louis, and were of the utmost assistance to the latter in the struggle. The test was the observance of the interdict which for so many years suspended divine service throughout the empire, and was a sore trial to the faithful. To a great extent this was disregarded by the Franciscans. It was to little purpose that, in January, 1331, John issued a special bull directed against them, deprived of all privileges and immunities those who recognized Louis as emperor and celebrated services in interdicted places, and ordered all prelates and inquisitors to prosecute them. On the other hand, Louis was not behindhand in enforcing obedience by persecution wherever he had the power. An imperial brief of June, 1330, addressed to the magistrates of Aix, directs them to assist and protect those teachers of the truth, the Franciscans Siegelbert of Landsberg and John of Royda, and to imprison all their brethren whom they may designate as rebels to the empire and to the Order until the general, Michele, shall decide what is to be done with them. This shows that even in Ger-

---

* Doat, XXVII. 202–3, 229; XXXV. 87.

many the Order was not unanimous, but doubtless the honest Franciscan, John of Winterthur, reflects the feelings of the great body when he says that the reader will be struck with horror and stupor on learning the deeds with which the pope convulsed the Church. Inflamed by some madness, he sought to argue against the poverty of Christ, and when the Franciscans resisted him he persecuted them without measure. The Dominicans encouraged him, and he largely rewarded them. The traditional enmity between the Orders found ample gratification. The Dominicans, to excite contempt for the Franciscans, exhibited paintings of Christ with a purse, putting in his hand to take out money; nay, to the horror of the faithful, on the walls of their monasteries, in the most frequented places, they pictured Christ hanging on the cross with one hand nailed fast, and with the other putting money in a pouch suspended from his girdle. Yet rancor and religious zeal did not wholly extinguish patriotism among the Dominicans; they were, moreover, aggrieved by the sentence of heresy passed upon Master Eckart, which may perhaps explain the fact that Tauler supported Louis, as also did Margaret Ebner, one of the Friends of God, and the most eminent Dominican sister of the day. It is true that many Dominican convents were closed for years, and their inmates scattered and exiled for persistently refusing to celebrate, but others complied unwillingly with the papal mandates. At Landshut they had ceased public service, but when the emperor came there they secretly arranged with the Duke of Teck to assail their house with torches and threaten to burn it down, so that they might have the excuse of constraint for resuming public worship, and the comedy was successfully carried out. In fact, the General Chapter of 1328 complained that in Germany the brethren in many places were notably negligent in publishing the papal bulls about Louis.*

All this, however, was but an episode in the political struggle, which was to be decided by the rivalries between the houses of Wittelsbach, Hapsburg, and Luxemburg, and the intrigues of France. Louis gradually succeeded in arousing and centring

---

* Martene Thesaur. II. 826-8.—Carl Müller, op. cit. I. 239.—Vitodurani Chron. (Eccard. Corp. Hist. I. 1798, 1800, 1844-5, 1871).—Andreas Ratisponens. Chron. ann. 1336 (Ibid. I. 2103-4).—Preger, Der Kirchenpolitische Kampf, pp. 42-5.— Denifle, Archiv für Litt.- u. Kirchengeschichte, 1886, p. 624.

upon himself the national spirit, aided therein by the arrogant disdain with which John XXII. and his successors received his repeated offers of qualified submission. When, in 1330, Louis had temporarily secured the support of John of Luxemburg, King of Bohemia, and the Duke of Austria, and they offered themselves as sureties that he would fulfil what might be required of him, provided the independence of the empire was recognized, John retorted that Louis was a heretic and thus incapacitated; he was a thief and a robber, a wicked man who consorted with Michele, Ockham, Bonagrazia, and Marsiglio; not only had he no title to the empire, but the state of Christendom would be inconceivably deplorable if he were recognized. After the death of John in December, 1334, another attempt was made, but it suited the policy of France and of Bohemia to prolong the strife, and Benedict XII. was as firm as his predecessor. Louis was at all times ready to sacrifice his Franciscan allies, but the papacy demanded the right practically to dictate who should be emperor, and by a skilful use of appeals to the national pride Louis gradually won the support of an increasing number of states and cities. In 1338 the convention of Rhense and the Reichstag of Frankfort formally proclaimed as a part of the law of the empire that the choice of the electors was final, and that the papacy had no confirmatory power. The interdict was ordered not to be observed, and in all the states adhering to Louis ecclesiastics were given the option of resuming public worship within eight days or of undergoing a ten years' exile. It was some relief to them in this dilemma that the Roman curia sold absolutions in such cases for a florin.*

In the strife between Louis and the papacy the little colony of Franciscan refugees at Munich was of the utmost service to the imperial cause, but their time was drawing to an end. Michele da Cesena died November 29, 1342, his latest work being a long manifesto proving that John had died an unrepentant heretic, and that his successors in defending his errors were likewise heretics; if but one man in Christendom holds the true faith, that man in

---

* Martene Thesaur. II. 800–6.— Raynald. ann. 1336, No. 31–5.—Vitoduran. Chron. (Eccard. Corp. Hist. I. 1842–5, 1910). — Preger, Der Kirchenpolitische Kampf, p. 33.—Hartzheim IV. 323–32.—H. Mutii Germ. Chron. ann. 1338 (Pistorii Germ. Scriptt. II. 878–81).

himself is the Church. The dithyrambic palinode which passes as his death-bed recantation is clearly a forgery, and there can be no doubt that Michele persisted to the end. When dying he handed the seal of the Order over to William of Ockham, who used it as Vicar-general; he had already, in April, 1342, appointed two citizens of Munich, John Schito and Grimold Treslo, as syndics and procurators of the Order, the latter of whom subsequently assumed the generalate. Bonagrazia died in June, 1347, declaring with the last breath of his indomitable soul that the cause of Louis was righteous. The date of William of Ockham's death is uncertain, but it occurred between 1347 and 1350.*

Thus dropped off, one by one, the men who had so gallantly defended the doctrine of the poverty of Christ. As regards the political conceptions which were the special province of Marsiglio and Ockham, their work was done, and they could exercise no further influence over the uncontrollable march of events. With the death of Benedict XII., in 1342, Louis made renewed efforts for pacification, but John of Bohemia was intriguing to secure the succession for his house, and they were fruitless, except to strengthen Louis by demonstrating the impossibility of securing terms tolerable to the empire. Still the intrigue went on, and in July, 1346, the three ecclesiastical electors, Mainz, Trèves, and Cologne, with Rodolph of Saxony, and John of Bohemia, assembled at Rhense under the impulsion of Clement VI. and elected the son of John, Charles Margrave of Moravia, as a rival king of the Romans. The movement, however, had no basis of popular support, and when Louis hastened to the Rhinelands all the cities and nearly all the princes and nobles adhered to him. Had the election been postponed for a few weeks it would never have taken place, for the next month occurred the battle of Crécy, where the gallant knight, John of Bohemia, died a chivalrous death, Charles, the newly-elected king, saved his life by flight, and French influence was temporarily eclipsed. Thus unauspiciously commenced, the reign of Charles IV. had little promise of duration, when, in Octo-

---

* Vitoduran Chron. (Eccard. I. 1844).—Sächsische Weltchronik, dritte bairisch Fortsetzung No. 9 (Pertz II. 346).—Baluz. et Mansi III. 349–55.—Muratori S. R. I. III. ii. 513–27.—Jac. de Marchia Dial. (Bal. et Mansi II. 600).—Preger, op. cit. pp. 35–6.—Carl Müller, op. cit. I. 370–2.—Chron. Glassberger ann. 1342, 1347.

ber, 1347, Louis, while indulging in his favorite pastime of hunting, was struck with apoplexy and fell dead from his horse. The hand of God might well be traced in the removal of all the enemies of the Holy See, and Charles had no further organized opposition to dread.*

Desirous of obtaining the fullest advantage from this unlooked-for good-fortune, Clement VI. commissioned the Archbishop of Prague and the Bishop of Bamberg to reconcile all communities and individuals who had incurred excommunication by supporting the Bavarian, with a formula of absolution by which they were obliged to swear that they held it heresy for an emperor to depose a pope, and that they would never obey an emperor until he had been approved by the pope. This excited intense disgust, and in many places it could not be enforced. The teachings of Marsiglio and Ockham had at least borne fruit in so far that the papal pretensions to virtually controlling the empire were disdainfully rejected. The German spirit thus aroused is well exemplified by what occurred at Basle, a city which had observed the interdict and was eager for its removal. When Charles and the Bishop of Bamberg appeared before the gates they were received by the magistrates and a great crowd of citizens. Conrad of Barenfels, the burgomaster, addressed the bishop: "My Lord of Bamberg, you must know that we do not believe, nor will we confess, that our late lord, the Emperor Louis, ever was a heretic. Whomsoever the electors or a majority of them shall choose as King of the Romans we will hold as such, whether he applies to the pope or not, nor will we do anything else that is contrary to the rights of the empire. But if you have power from the pope and are willing to remit all our sins, so be it." Then, turning to the people, he called out, "Do you give to me and to Conrad Münch power to ask for the absolution of your sins?" The crowd shouted assent; the two Conrads took an oath in accordance with this; divine services were resumed, and the king and bishop entered the town.†

---

* Schmidt, Päbstliche Urkunden und Regesten, p. 362. — Henr. Rebdorff. Annal. ann. 1346–7 (Freher et Struv. I. 626–8).

† Henr. Rebdorff. Annal. ann. 1347 (Freher et Struv. I. 628).—Matthiæ Neuburg. (Albert. Argentinens.) Chron. ann. 1348 (Urstisii II. 142–3).—Preger, Der Kirchenpolitische Kampf, pp. 56–60.

Yet the question as to the poverty of Christ, which had been put forward by John and Louis as the ostensible cause of quarrel, and which had been so warmly embraced by a portion at least of the German Franciscans, sank completely out of sight north of the Alps with the death of Louis and the extinction of the Munich colony of refugees. Germany had her own hordes of mendicants, regular and irregular, in the Beguines and Beghards, who seem to have troubled themselves but little about points so purely speculative; and though we occasionally hear of Fraticelli in those regions, it is rather as a convenient name employed by monkish chroniclers than as really representing a distinctive sect.

It was otherwise in the South, and especially in Italy, the native home of Franciscanism and of the peculiar influences which moulded the special ascetic development of the Order. There the impulses which had led the earlier Spirituals to endure the extremity of persecution in vindication of the holiness of absolute poverty were still as strong as ever. Under Boniface and Clement and during the earlier years of John its professors had lain in hiding or had sought the friendly refuge of Sicily. In the confusion of the Franciscan schism they had emerged and multiplied. With the downfall of the antipope and the triumph of John they were once more proscribed. In the quarrel over the poverty of Christ, that tenet had naturally become the distinguishing mark of the sectaries, and its condemnation by John necessarily entailed the consequence of denying the papal authority and asserting the heresy of the Holy See. Yet there can be no doubt that among the austerer members of the orthodox Order who accepted the definitions of the papacy there was much sympathy felt for the rebellious dissidents. Resistance to the imperious will of John XXII. having failed, there were abundant stories of visions and miracles circulated from convent to convent, as to the wrath of God and of St. Francis visited upon those who infringed upon the holy vow of poverty. The *Liber Conformitatum* is manifestly the expression of the aspirations of those who wished to enforce the Rule in all its strictness as the direct revelation of the Holy Spirit. Such men felt that the position of their proscribed brethren was logically correct, and they were unable to reconcile the decrees of Nicholas III. with those of John XXII. One of these, described as a man much beloved of God, applied to St. Birgitta to resolve his doubts, whereupon she had two visions in which the Virgin sent him her commands to say to all who believed that the pope was no pope, and that priests do not truly consecrate the host in the mass, that they were heretics filled with diabolical iniquity. All this points to a strong secret sympathy with the Fraticelli which extended not only among the people, but among the friars and occasionally even among the prelates, explaining the ability of the sectaries to maintain their existence from generation to generation in spite of almost unremitting persecution by the Inquisition.*

In 1335, one of the earliest cares of Benedict XII. after his accession was the repression of these *Fratres de paupere Vita*, as they styled themselves. They still in many places publicly displayed their contumacy by wearing the short and narrow gowns of the Spirituals. They still held Michele to be their general, insulted the memory of John XXII., and were earnestly and successfully engaged in proselytism. Moreover, they were openly protected by men of rank and power. All the inquisitors, from Treviso and Lombardy to Sicily, were commanded to free the Church from these impious hypocrites by vigorous action, and directions were sent to the prelates to lend efficient assistance. There were some, at least, of the latter who did not respond, for in 1336 Francesco, Bishop of Camerino, and Giacopo, Bishop of Firmo, were summoned to answer for favoring the sectaries and permitting them to live in their dioceses. The whole Order, in fact, was still infected with these dangerous doctrines, and could not be brought to view the dissidents with proper abhorrence. Benedict complained that in the kingdom of Naples many Franciscan convents gave shelter to these perverse brethren, and in a bull regulating the Order issued this same year he alludes to those among them who wear peculiar vestments and, under a pretended exterior of sanctity, maintain heresies condemned by the Church of Rome; all such, together with those who protect them, are to be imprisoned until they submit. It was not always easy to enforce obedience to these mandates. The Bishop of Camerino was stubborn, and the next year, 1337, Frà Giovanni di Borgo, the inquisitor of

---

* Wadding. ann. 1330, No. 14–15.—Alvar. Pelag. de Planct. Eccles. Lib. II. art. 51 (fol. 169 *a*).—Lib. Conformitatum Lib. I. Fruct. ix. p. ii.—Revel. S. Brigittæ Lib. VII. c. 8.

the Mark of Ancona, was instructed to proceed severely against him and other fautors of these heretics. By his active operations Frà Giovanni incurred the ill-will of the nobles of his district, who had sufficient influence with the general, Gerard Odo, to procure his replacement by his associate Giacomo and subsequently by Simone da Ancona, but the Cardinal Legate Bertrand intervened, and Benedict restored him with high encomiums on his efficiency. Although persecution was thus active, it is probable that few of the sectaries had the spirit of martyrdom, and that they recanted under pressure, but there was no hesitation in inflicting the full punishment of heresy on those who were persistent. June 3, 1337, at Venice, Frà Francesco da Pistoia was burned for pertinaciously asserting the poverty of Christ in contempt of the definitions of John XXII., nor was he the only victim.*

The test of heresy, as I have said, was the assertion that Christ and the apostles held no property. This appears from the abjuration of Frà Francesco d' Ascoli in 1344, who recants that belief and declares that in accordance with the bulls of John XXII. he holds it to be heretical. That such continued to be the customary formula appears from Eymerich, who instructs his inquisitor to make the penitent declare under oath, " I swear that I believe in my heart and profess that our Lord Jesus Christ and his apostles while in this mortal life held in common the things which Scripture declares them to have had, and that they had the right of giving, selling, and alienating them." †

The heresy was thus so purely an artificial one, created by the Holy See, that perhaps it is not difficult to understand the sympathy excited by these poor and self-denying ascetics, who bore all the external marks of what the Church had for ages taught to be exceeding holiness. Camerino continued to be a place of refuge. In 1343 Clement VI. ordered the Bishops of Ancona and Osimo to cite before him within three months Gentile, Lord of Camerino, for various offences, among which was protecting the Fraticelli, impeding the inquisitors in the prosecution of their duties, and de-

---

* Wadding. ann. 1335, No. 10–11; ann. 1336, No. 1; ann. 1337, No. 1; ann. 1339, No. 1.—Raynald. ann. 1335, No. 63; ann. 1336, No. 63, 64, 66–7; ann. 1337, No. 30; ann. 1375, No. 64.—Comba, La Riforma in Italia, I. 328.—Vit. Prima Benedicti XII. ann. 1337 (Muratori S. R. I. III. II. 531).

† D'Argentré I. I. 345.—Eymeric. p. 486.

spising for several years the excommunication which they had pronounced against him. Even the inquisitors themselves, especially in Franciscan districts, were not always earnest in the work, possibly because there was little prospect of profitable confiscations to be procured from those who regarded the possession of property as a sin, and in 1346 Clement found himself obliged to reprove them sharply for their tepidity. In such districts the Fraticelli showed themselves with little concealment. When, in 1348, Cola di Rienzo fled from Rome after his first tribuneship, he betook himself to the Fraticelli of Monte Maiella; he was charmed with their holiness and poverty, entered the Order as a Tertiary, and deplored that men so exemplary should be persecuted by the pope and the Inquisition. Tuscany was full of them. It was in vain that about this period Florence adopted severe laws for their repression, placing them under the ban, empowering any one to capture them and deliver them to the Inquisition, and imposing a fine of five hundred lire on any official declining, when summoned by the inquisitors, to assist in their arrest. The very necessity of enacting such laws shows how difficult it was to stimulate the people to join the persecution. Even this appears to have been ineffectual. There is extant a letter from Giovanni delle Celle of Vallombrosa to Tommaso di Neri, a Fraticello of Florence, in which the former attacks the fatuity of the latter in making an idol of poverty; the letter was answered and led to a controversy which seems to have been conducted openly.*

Yet, trivial as was apparently the point at issue, it was impossible that men could remain contentedly under the ban of the Church without being forced to adopt principles destructive of the whole ecclesiastical organization. They could only justify themselves by holding that they were the true Church, that the papacy was heretical and had forfeited its claim of obedience, and could no longer guide the faithful to salvation. It is an interesting proof of the state of public opinion in Italy, that in spite of the thoroughly organized machinery of persecution, men who held these doctrines were able to disseminate them almost publicly and

---

* Werunsky Excerptt. ex Registt. Clem. PP. VI. pp. 23–4.—Raynald. ann. 1346, No. 70.—Comba, La Riforma, I. 326–7, 387.—Lami, Antichità Toscane, pp. 528, 595.

to make numerous proselytes. About the middle of the century they circulated throughout Italy a document written in the vernacular, " so that it can be understood by every one," giving their reasons for separating themselves from pope and prelate. It is singularly temperate in tone and logical in structure. The argument is drawn strictly from Scripture and from the utterances of the Church itself, and from even the standpoint of a canonist it is unanswerable. There are no apocalyptic hysterics, no looking forward to Antichrist or to new ages of the world, no mysticism. There is not even any reference to St. Francis, nor any claim that his Rule is inspired and inviolable. Yet none the less the whole body of the Church is declared to be heretic, and all the faithful are summoned to cut loose from it.

The reasons alleged for this are three—First, heresy ; second, simony ; third, fornication. As to the first, John XXII. is proved to be a heretic by the bulls pronouncing heretical the doctrine that Christ and the apostles possessed nothing. This is easily done by reason of the definitions of the previous popes confirmed by the Council of Vienne. The corollary of course follows that all his successors and their cardinals are heretics. As regards simony, the canons of the Decretum and the utterances of the doctors are quoted to show that it is heresy. As regards fornication, it was easy to cite the canons embodying the Hildebrandine doctrine that the sacraments of fornicating priests are not to be received. It is true that there are many priests who are not fornicators, but there are none who are not simonists—who have not given or received money for the sacraments. Even if he could be found who is innocent on all these heads, it would be necessary for him to separate himself from the rest, for, as Raymond of Pennaforte shows in his Summa, those are guilty of mortal sin and idolatry who receive the sacraments of heretics. The Fraticelli, therefore, have been obliged to withdraw from a heretical church, and they issue this manifesto to justify their course. If in any way it is erroneous, they ask to have the error pointed out ; and if it is correct, the faithful are bound to join them, because, after the facts are known, association with prelates and clergy thus heretical and excommunicate will involve in heresy all who are guilty of it.*

---

* Comba, La Riforma, I. 568–71.

All the Fraticelli, however, were not uniformly agreed upon all points. In the above document a leading argument is drawn from the assumed vitiation of the sacraments in polluted hands—a dangerous tenet, constantly recurring to plague the successors of Hildebrand—which we do not find in other utterances of the sectaries. In fact, we find them, in 1362, divided into two branches, one of which recognized as its leader Tommaso, ex-Bishop of Aquino, and held that as John XXII. and his successors were heretics, the sacrament of ordination derived from them was void, and reordination was required of all ecclesiastics entering the sect. The other, which took its name from Felipe of Majorca, was regularly organized under a general minister, and, while equally regarding the popes as heretics, recognized the ordinations of the establishment. All branches of the sect, however, drew ample store of reasons from the venality and corruption of the Church, which was doubtless their most convincing argument with the people. There is extant a letter in the vulgar tongue from a frate to two female devotees, arguing, like the more formal manifesto, that they are bound to withdraw from the communion of the heretical church. This is the beast with seven horns, which are: 1, supreme pride; 2, supreme cruelty; 3, supreme folly or wrath; 4, supreme deceit and inimitable falsehood; 5, supreme carnality or lust; 6, supreme cupidity or avarice; 7, supreme hatred of truth, or malice. The ministers of this heretic church have no shame in publicly keeping concubines, and in selling Christ for money in the sacraments. This letter further indicates the legitimate descent of the Fraticelli from the Spirituals by a quotation from Joachim to show that St. Francis is Noah, and the faithful few of his children are those who are saved with him in the Ark.*

A still closer connection may be inferred from a bull of Urban V., issued about 1365, instructing inquisitors to be active in exterminating heretics, and describing for their information the different heresies. The Fraticelli are represented as indulging in gluttony and lasciviousness under the cover of strict external sanctity, pretending to be Franciscan Tertiaries, and begging publicly or living in their own houses. It is possible, however, that his de-

---

* Tocco, Archivio Storico Napoletano, 1887, Fasc. 1.—Comba, La Riforma. I. 321-4.

scription of their holding assemblies in which they read Olivi's
" Postil on the Apocalypse" and his other works, but chiefly the account of his death, is rather borrowed from Bernard Gui's account
of the Spirituals of Languedoc, than a correct statement of the
customs of the Fraticelli of his time.*

Of the final shape which the heresy assumed we have an authoritative account from its ruthless exterminator, the Inquisitor
Giacomo della Marca. In his " Dialogue with a Fraticello," written
about 1450, there is no word about the follies of the Spirituals, or
any extraneous dogmas. The question turns wholly on the poverty of Christ and the heresy of John's definitions of the doctrine.
The Fraticelli stigmatize the orthodox as Joannistæ, and in turn
are called Michaelistæ, showing that by this time the extravagances of the Spirituals had been forgotten, and that the heretics
were the direct descendants of the schismatic Franciscans who
followed Michele da Cesena. The disorders and immorality of
the clergy still afforded them their most effective arguments in
their active missionary work. Giacomo complains that they
abused the minds of the simple by representing the priests as
simonists and concubinarians, and that the people, imbued with
this poison, lost faith in the clergy, refused to confess to them, to
attend their masses, to receive their sacraments, and to pay their
tithes. thus becoming heretics and pagans and children of the
devil, while fancying themselves children of God.†

The Fraticelli thus formed one or more separate organizations,
each of which asserted itself to be the only true Church. In the
scanty information which we possess, it is impossible to trace in
detail the history of the fragmentary parts into which they split,
and we can only say in general terms that the sect did not consist
simply of anchorites and friars, but had its regular clergy and
laity, its bishops and their supreme head or pope. known as the
Bishop of Philadelphia, that being the name assigned to the community. In 1357 this position was filled by Tommaso, the ex-
Bishop of Aquino; chance led to the discovery of such a pope in
Perugia in 1374; in 1429 we happen to know that a certain Rainaldo filled the position, and shortly after a frate named Gabriel.

---

* Martini Append. ad Mosheim de Beghardis p. 505.
† Jac. de Marchia Dial. (Baluz. et Mansi II. 595 sqq.).

There is even talk of a chief of the laity who styled himself Emperor of the Christians.*

It was in vain that successive popes ordered the Inquisition to take the most active measures for the suppression of the sect, and that occasional holocausts rewarded their exertions, as when, under Urban V. nine were burned at Viterbo, and in 1389 Frà Michele Berti de Calci suffered the same fate at Florence. This last case reveals in its details the popular sympathy which favored the labors of the Fraticelli. Frà Michele had been sent to Florence as a missionary by a congregation of the sect which met in a cavern in the Mark of Ancona. He preached in Florence and made many converts, and was about leaving the city, April 19, when he was betrayed by five female zealots, who sent for him pretending to seek conversion. His trial was short. A colleague saved his life by recantation, but Michele was firm. When brought up in judgment to be degraded from the priesthood he refused to kneel before the bishop, saying that heretics are not to be knelt to. In walking to the place of execution many of the crowd exchanged words of cheer with him, leading to considerable disturbance, and when tied to a stake in a sort of cabin which was to be set on fire, a number put their heads inside to beg him to recant. The place was several times filled with smoke to frighten him, but he was unyielding, and after his incremation there were many people, we are told, who regarded him as a saint.†

Proceedings such as this were not likely to diminish the favor with which the Fraticelli were popularly regarded. The two Sicilies continued to be thoroughly interpenetrated with the heresy. When, in 1362, Luigi di Durazzo made his abortive attempt at rebellion, he regarded the popularity of the Fraticelli as an ele-

---

* Raynald. ann. 1344, No. 8; 1357, No. 12; 1374, No. 14.—Jac. de Marchia Dial. (l. c. 599, 608-9).

It may surprise a modern infallibilist to learn that so thoroughly orthodox and learned an inquisitor as the blessed Giacomo della Marca admits that there have been heretic popes—popes who persisted and died in their heresy. He comforts himself, however, with the reflection that they have always been succeeded by Catholic pontiffs (l. c. p. 599).

† Werunsky, Excerptt. ex Registt. Clem. VI. et Innoc. VI. p. 91.— Raynald. ann. 1354, No. 31; ann. 1368, No. 16.—Wadding. ann. 1354, No. 6-7; 1368, No. 4-6.—Comba, La Riforma, I. 327, 329-37.—Cantù, Eretici d' Italia, I. 133-4.—Eymeric. p. 328.

ment of sufficient importance for him to publicly proclaim sympathy with them, to collect them around him, and have Tommaso of Aquino celebrate mass for him. Francesco Marchisio, Archdeacon of Salerno, was a Fraticello, in spite of which he was elevated to the see of Trivento in 1362, and occupied it till his death about twenty years later. In 1372 Gregory XI. was shocked to learn that in Sicily the bones of Fraticelli were venerated as the relics of saints, that chapels and churches were built in their honor, and that on their anniversaries the populace flocked thither with candles to worship them ; but it is not likely that his instructions to the inquisitors to put an end to these unseemly manifestations of mistaken piety were successful. At Perugia, in 1368, the magistrates were induced to throw many of the Fraticelli into prison, but to so little purpose that the people persisted in regarding them as the true children of St. Francis and in giving them shelter, while the Franciscans were despised on account of the laxity of their observance, the luxury of their houses, the costliness of their vestments, and the profusion of their table. They were ridiculed and insulted in the streets until they scarce dared to venture in public ; if one chanced to let the collar of his shirt show above his gown, some one would pull up the linen and ask the jeering crowd if this was the austerity of St. Francis. As a last resort, in 1374, they sent for Paoluccio of Foligno and a public disputation was arranged with the Fraticelli. Paoluccio turned the tide of popular favor by proving that obedience to the pope was of greater moment than obedience to the Rule, and the Fraticelli were driven from the town. Even then the Inquisition seems not to have dared to prosecute them.*

The proselyting efforts of the Fraticelli were by no means confined to Italy. Believing themselves the only true Church, it was their duty to carry salvation throughout the world, and there were

---

* Tocco, Archivio Storico Napoletano, 1887, Fasc. 1.—Raynald. ann. 1368, No. 16; ann. 1372, No. 36.—Wadding. ann. 1374, No. 19-23.—Pet. Rodulphii Hist. Seraph. Relig. Lib. ii. fol. 154 a.

Perugia at this period was a centre of religious excitement. A certain Piero Garigh, who seems to have been in some way connected with the Fraticelli, gave himself out as the Son of God, and dignified his disciples with the names of apostles. In the brief allusion which we have to him he is said to have obtained ten of these and to be in search of an eleventh. His fate is not recorded.—Processus contra Valdenses (Archivio Storico Italiano, 1865, No. 39, p. 50).

earnest spirits among them who were ready to dare as much as the orthodox among the infidels and barbarians. Already, in 1344, Clement VI. found himself obliged to address the archbishops, bishops, and all the faithful throughout Armenia, Persia, and the East, warning them against these emissaries of Satan, who were seeking to scatter among them the seeds of error and schism. He had no inquisitors to call upon in those regions, but he ordered the prelates to inquire after them and to punish them, authorizing them, with a singular lack of perception, to invoke, if necessary, the aid of the secular arm. The Fraticelli made at least one convert of importance, for in 1346 Clement felt himself obliged to cite for appearance within four months no less a personage than the Archbishop of Seleucia, who, infected with pseudo-minorite errors, had written in Armenian and was circulating throughout Asia a postil on St. John in which he asserted the forbidden doctrine of the poverty of Christ. In 1354 Innocent VI. heard of Fraticellian missionaries laboring among the Chazars of the Crimea, and he forthwith ordered the Bishop of Caffa to repress them with inquisitorial methods. In 1375 Gregory XI. learned that they were active in Egypt, Syria, and Asia, and he promptly ordered the Franciscan provincial of those regions to enforce on them the severity of the laws. One, named Lorenzo Carbonello, had ventured to Tunis, to infect with his heresy the Christians of that kingdom, whereupon Gregory commanded Giacomo Patani and Guillen de Ripoll, the captains of the Christian troops in the service of the Bey of Tunis, to seize him and send him in chains to the Archbishop of Naples or of Pisa. Doubtless, if the command was obeyed, it led the unthinking Moslem to thank Allah that they were not Christians.*

In Languedoc and Provence the rigorous severity with which the Spirituals had been exterminated seems to have exercised a wholesome influence in repressing the Fraticelli, but nevertheless a few cases on record shows the existence of the sect. In 1336 we hear of a number confined in the papal dungeons of Avignon— among them a papal chaplain—and that Guillaume Lombard, the judge of ecclesiastical causes, was ordered to exert against them

---

* Raynald. ann. 1344, No. 8; ann. 1346, No. 70; ann. 1354, No. 31; ann. 1375, No. 27.

the full severity of the laws. In 1354 two Tuscan Fraticelli, Giovanni da Castiglione and Francesco d' Arquata, were arrested at Montpellier for holding that John XXII. had forfeited his authority by altering the definitions of the bull *Exiit*, and that his successors were not the true Church. Innocent VI. caused them to be brought before him, but all efforts to make them recant were vain; they went tranquilly to the stake, singing *Gloria in excelsis*, and were reverenced as martyrs by a large number of their brethren. Two others, named Jean de Narbonne and Maurice had not long before met the same fate at Avignon. In northern France we hear little of the heresy. The only recorded case seems to be that of Denis Soulechat, a professor of the University of Paris, who taught in 1363 that the law of divine love does away with property, and that Christ and the apostles held none. Summoned by the Inquisitor Guillaume Rochin, he abjured before the Faculty and then appealed to the pope. At Avignon, when he endeavored to purge himself before an assembly of theologians, he only added new errors to his old ones, and was sent back to the Cardinal of Beauvais and the Sorbonne with orders to make him recant, and to punish him properly with the advice of the inquisitor. In 1368 he was forced to a public abjuration.[*]

In Spain a few cases show that the heresy extended across the Pyrenees. In Valencia, Fray Jayme Justi and the Tertiaries Guillermo Gelabert and Marti Petri, when arrested by R. de Masqueta, commissioner of the Inquisitor Leonardo de Puycerda, appealed to Clement VI., who ordered the Bishop of Valencia to release them on their giving bail not to leave the city until their case should be decided at Avignon. They must have had wealthy disciples, for security was furnished in the heavy sum of thirty thousand sols, and they were discharged from prison. The papal court was in no hurry with the case—probably it was forgotten—when, in 1353, Clement learned that the two Tertiaries were dead, and that Justi was in the habit of leaving the city and spreading his pestiferous doctrines among the people. He therefore ordered

---

[*] Raynald. ann. 1336, No. 64; ann. 1351, No. 31; ann. 1368, No. 16–7.—Archives de l'Inq. de Carcass. (Doat, XXXV. 130).—Mosheims Ketzergeschichte I. 387.—Henr. Rebdorff Annal. ann. 1353 (Freher et Struv. I. 632).—Eymeric. p. 358.—D'Argentré, I. i. 383–6.

Hugo, Bishop of Valencia, and the Inquisitor Nicolas Roselli to prosecute the case forthwith. Justi must have recanted, for he was merely imprisoned for life, while the bones of the two Tertiaries were dug up and burned. Even more obdurate was Fray Arnaldo Mutaner, who for nineteen years infected Puycerda and Urgel with the same heresy. He was contumacious and refused to appear when summoned to abjure. After consultation with Gregory XI., Berenger Darili, Bishop of Urgel, condemned him, and so did Eymerich. Pursuit apparently grew hot, and he fled to the East. The last we hear of him is in 1373, when Gregory ordered his vicar, the Franciscan Arnaud, to seize him and send him in chains to the papal court, but whether the effort was successful we have no means of knowing. A bull of Martin V. in 1426 shows the continued existence of Fraticelli in Aragon and Catalonia, and the necessity of active measures for their extirpation.*

It was probably a heresy of the same nature which, in 1442, was discovered in Durango, Biscay. The heresiarch was the Franciscan Alonso de Mella, brother of Juan, Cardinal-bishop of Zamora, and the sectaries were known as Cerceras. The story that Alonso taught indiscriminate sexual intercourse is doubtless one of the customary exaggerations. King Juan II., in the absence of the Inquisition, sent the Franciscan, Francisco de Soria, and Juan Alonso Cherino, Abbot of Alcalá la Real, to investigate the matter, with two alguazils and a sufficient force. The heretics were seized and carried, some to Valladolid and some to Santo Domingo de la Calçada, where torture was used to extract confession, and the obstinate ones were burned in considerable numbers. Fray Alonso de Mella, however, managed to escape and fled to Granada, it is said, with some of his girls; but he did not avert his fate, for he was *acañavereado* by the Moors—that is, put to a lingering death with pointed sticks. The affair must have made a profound impression on the popular mind, for even until modern times the people of Durango were reproached by their neighbors with the "*autos de Fray Alonso*," and in 1828 an overzealous alcalde, to obliterate all record of the matter, burned the

* Ripoll II. 245.—Eymeric. pp. 266-7.—Raynald. ann. 1373, No. 19; ann. 1426, No. 18.—Wadding. ann. 1371, No. 26-30.

original documents of the process, which till then had reposed quietly among the records of the parish church.*

The violent measures of John XXII., followed up by his successors, for a while effectually repressed the spiritual asceticism of the Franciscans. Yet it was impossible that impulses which were so marked a characteristic of the age should be wholly obliterated in an Order in which they had become traditional. We see this in the kindness manifested by the Franciscans to the Fraticelli when it could be done without too much risk, and we cannot doubt that there were many who aspired to imitate the founder without daring to overleap the bounds of obedience. Such men could not but look with alarm and disgust at the growing worldliness of the Order under the new dispensation of John. When the Provincial of Tuscany could lay aside five hundred florins out of the alms given to his brethren, and then lend this sum to the Hospital of S. Maria of Siena at ten per cent. per annum, although so flagrant a violation of his vows and of the canons against usury brought upon him the penalty of degradation, it required a divine visitation to impress his sin upon the minds of his fellows, and he died in 1373 in great agony and without the sacraments. Various other manfestations about the same time indicate the magnitude of the evil and the impossibility of suppressing it by human means. Under Boniface IX., Franciscans, we are told, were in the habit of seeking dispensations to enable them to hold benefices and even pluralities; and the pope decreed that any Mendicant desiring to be transferred to a non-Mendicant Order should, as a preliminary, pay a hundred gold florins to the papal camera. Under such a system there could be scarce a pretence of maintaining the holy poverty which had been the ideal of Francis and his followers.†

Yet the ardent thirst of poverty and the belief that in it lay the only assured path to salvation were too widely diffused to be repressed. Giovanni Colombini, a rich and ambitious citizen

---

* Garibay, Comp. Historial de España, Lib. xvi. c. 31.—La Puente, Epit. de la Cronica de Juan II., Lib. iv. c. i.—Pelayo, Heterodoxos Españoles, I. 546–7.—Mariana, Lib. xxi. c. 18.—Rodrigo, Inquisicion, II. 11–12.—Paramo, p. 131.

† Wadding. ann. 1383, No. 2.—Gobelinæ Personæ Cosmodrom. Æt. v. c. 84 (Meibom. Rer. German. I. 317).

of Siena had his thoughts accidentally directed to heaven. His career strikingly resembles that of Peter Waldo, save that the Church, grown wiser, utilized his zeal instead of antagonizing him. The Order of Jesuats which he founded was approved by Urban V. in 1367. It was an order of lay brethren under the Augustinian Rule, vowed to poverty and devoted to the care of the sick, not unlike that of the Cellites or Alexians of the Rhinelands.*

It was inevitable that there should be dissatisfaction among the more ascetic Franciscans, and that the more zealous of these should seek some remedy short of heresy. In 1350 Gentile of Spoleto obtained from Clement VI. authorization for some houses of stricter observance. Immediately the experience of Angelo and Liberato was repeated. The wrath of the Conventuals was excited. The innovators were accused of adopting the short and narrow gowns which had been the distinguishing mark of the dreaded Olivists. In the General Chapter of 1353, the General Farignano was urged to exterminate them by the measures which had proved so effective in Languedoc. To this he did not assent, but he set spies to work to obtain evidence against them, and soon was able to accuse them of receiving Fraticelli. They admitted the fact, but argued that this had been in the hope of converting the heretics, and when they proved obstinate they had been expelled—but they had not been reported to the Inquisition as duty required. Armed with this, Farignano represented to Innocent VI. the grave dangers of the innovation, and obtained a revocation of the papal authorization. The brethren were dispersed, Gentile and two companions were thrown into prison at Orvieto; his coadjutor, Frà Martino, a most exemplary man, who shone in miracles after death, died the next year, and the rest were reduced to obedience. After prolonged captivity Gentile was released, and died in 1362, worn out with fruitless labors to restore the discipline of the Order.†

More fortunate was his disciple, Paoluccio da Trinci, of Foligno, a simple and unlearned friar, who had obtained from his kinsman,

---

* Baluz. et Mansi IV. 566 sqq. In 1606 Paul V. allowed the Jesuats to take orders.

† Wadding. ann. 1350, No. 15; ann. 1354, No. 1, 2; ann. 1362, No. 4.—Chron. Glassberger ann. 1352, 1354, 1355.

Ugolino, Lord of Foligno, a dungeon in which to gratify his thirst for asceticism. Though he had permission for this from his superiors, he suffered much from the hostility of the laxer brethren, but his austerities gained him great popular reverence and many disciples. In 1368 the General Farignano chanced to attend a provincial chapter at Foligno, and was persuaded to ask of Ugolino a spot called Brulliano, in the mountains between Foligno and Camerino, as a hermitage for Paoluccio and his followers. After his request was granted he dreaded a schism in the Order and wished to recall it, but Ugolino held him to his purpose. The place was wild, rocky, marshy, unwholesome, infested with serpents, and almost uninhabited. Thither Paoluccio led his brethren, and they were forced to adopt the sabots or wooden shoes, which became the distinguishing foot-gear of their Order. Their reputation spread apace ; converts flocked to them ; their buildings required enlargement ; associate houses were founded in many places, and thus arose the Observantines, or Franciscans of strict observance—an event in the history of the Church only second in importance to the original foundation of the Mendicant Orders.*

When Paoluccio died, in 1390, he was already reckoned as a provincial within the Order. After an interval he was succeeded by his coadjutor, Giovanni Stronconi. In 1405 began the marvellous career of St. Bernardino of Siena, who counts as the formal founder of the Observantines. They had merely been called the Brethren of the Hermitages until the Council of Constance established them as an organization virtually independent of the Conventuals, when they took the name by which they have since been known. Everywhere their institution spread. New houses arose, or those of the Conventuals were reformed and given over to them. Thus in 1426 they were introduced into the province of Strassburg through the intervention of Matilda of Savoy, wife of the Palsgrave Louis the Bearded. Familiar in her youth with their virtues, she took occasion at Heidelberg to point out to her husband the Franciscans in their convent garden below them, amusing themselves with military exercises. It resulted in the reform of all the houses in his dominions and the introduction of the Observantine discipline, not without serious trouble. In 1453

---

* Wadding. ann. 1368, No. 10–13.

Nicholas of Cusa, as legate, forced all the houses in the diocese of
Bamberg to adopt the Observantine discipline, under threat of
forfeiting their privileges. In 1431 the holy house on Mt. Alverno, the Franciscan Mecca, was made over to them, and in 1434
the guardianship of the Holy Places in Jerusalem. In 1460 we
hear of their penetrating to distant Ireland. It is not to be supposed that the Conventuals submitted quietly to the encroachments and triumphs of the hated ascetics whom for a century and
a half they had successfully baffled and persecuted. Quarrels,
sharper and bitterer even than those with the Dominicans, were
of constant occurrence, and were beyond the power of the popes
to allay. A promising effort at reunion attempted by Capistrano
in 1430, under the auspices of Martin V., was defeated by the incurable laxity of the Conventuals, and there was nothing left for
both sides but to continue the war. In 1435 the strife rose to
such a pitch in France that Charles VII. was obliged to appeal
to the Council of Basle, which responded with a decree in favor
of the Observantines. The struggle was hopeless. The corruption of the Conventuals was so universally recognized that even
Pius II. does not hesitate to say that, though they generally excel
as theologians, virtue is the last thing about which most of them
concern themselves. In contrast with this the holiness of the new
organization won for it the veneration of the people, while the un-
flagging zeal with which it served the Holy See secured for it the
favor of the popes precisely as the Mendicant Orders had done in
the thirteenth century. At first merely a branch of the Franciscans, then placed under a virtually independent vicar-general, at
length Leo X., after vainly striving to heal the differences, gave
the Observantines a general minister and reduced the Conventuals
to a subordinate position under a general master.*

---

* Wadding. ann. 1375, No. 44; ann. 1390, No. 1–10; ann. 1403, No. 1; ann.
1405, No. 3; ann. 1415, No. 6–7; ann. 1431, No. 8; ann. 1434, No. 7; ann. 1435,
No. 12–13; ann. 1453, No. 18–26; ann. 1454, No. 22–3; ann. 1455, No. 43–7; ann.
1456, No. 129; ann. 1498, No. 7–8; ann. 1499, No. 18–20. — Chron. Glassberger
ann. 1426, 1430, 1501, 1517.—Theiner Monument. Hibern. et Scotor. No. 801, p.
425, No. 844, p. 460.—Æn. Sylvii Opp. inedd. (Atti della Accademia dei Lincei,
1883, p. 546).—Chron. Anon. (Analecta Franciscana I. 291–2).

The bitterness of the strife between the two branches of the Order is illustrated by the fact that the Franciscan Church of Palma, in Majorca, when struck

A religious revival such as this brought into service a class of men who were worthy representatives of the Peter Martyrs and Guillem Arnauds of the early Inquisition. Under their ruthless energy the Fraticelli were doomed to extinction. The troubles of the Great Schism had allowed the heretics to flourish almost unnoticed and unmolested, but after the Church had healed its dissensions at Constance and had entered upon a new and vigorous life, it set to work in earnest to eradicate them. Hardly had Martin V. returned to Italy from Constance when he issued from Mantua, November 14, 1418, a bull in which he deplores the increase of the abominable sect in many parts, and especially in the Roman province. Fortified with the protection of the temporal lords, they abuse and threaten the bishops and inquisitors who attempt to repress them. The bishops and inquisitors are therefore instructed to proceed against them vigorously, without regard to limits of jurisdiction, and to prosecute their protectors, even if the latter are of episcopal or regal dignity, which sufficiently indicates that the Fraticelli had found favor with those of highest rank in both Church and State. This accomplished little, for in a subsequent bull of 1421 Martin alludes to the continued increase of the heresy, and tries the expedient of appointing the

---

by lightning and partially ruined in 1480, remained on this account unrepaired for nearly a hundred years, until the Observantines got the better of their rivals and obtained possession of it.—Dameto, Pro y Bover, Hist. de Mallorca, II. 1064–5 (Palma, 1841). It is related that when Sixtus IV., who had been a Conventual, proposed in 1477 to subject the Observantines to their rivals, the blessed Giacomo della Marca threatened him with an evil death, and he desisted.—(Chron. Glassberger ann. 1477).

The exceeding laxity prevailing among the Conventuals is indicated by letters granted in 1421 by the Franciscan general, Antonius de Perreto, to Friar Liebhardt Forschammer, permitting him to deposit with a faithful friend all alms given to him, and to expend them on his own wants or for the benefit of the Order, at his discretion; he was also required to confess only four times a year.—(Chron. Glassberger ann. 1416). The General Chapter held at Forli in 1421 was obliged to prohibit the brethren from trading and lending money on usury, under pain of imprisonment and confiscation.—(Ib. ann. 1421). From the Chapter of Ueberlingen, held in 1426, we learn that there was a custom by which, for a sum of money paid down, Franciscan convents would enter into obligations to pay definite stipends to individual friars.—(Ib. ann. 1426). In fact, the efforts of reform at this period, stimulated by the rivalry of the Observantines, reveal how utterly oblivious the Order had become of all the prescriptions of the Rule.

Cardinals of Albano and Porto as special commissioners for its suppression. The cardinals proved as inefficient as their predecessors. In 1423 the General Council of Siena was greatly scandalized at finding that at Peniscola there was a heretic pope with his college of cardinals, apparently flourishing without an attempt at concealment, and the Gallican nation made several ineffectual efforts to induce the council to take active measures against the secular authorities under whose favor these scandals were allowed to exist. How utterly the machinery of persecution had broken down is illustrated by the case of three Fraticelli who had at this period been detected in Florence—Bartolommeo di Matteo, Giovanni di Marino of Lucca, and Bartolommeo di Pietro of Pisa. Evidently distrusting the Florentine Inquisition, which was Franciscan, Martin V. specially intrusted the matter to his legates then presiding over the Council of Siena. On the sudden dissolution of the council the legates returned to Rome, except the Dominican General, Leonardo of Florence, who went to Florence. To him, therefore, Martin wrote, April 24, 1424, empowering him to terminate the case himself, and expressly forbidding the Inquisitor of Florence from taking any part in it. In September of the same year Martin instructed Piero, Abbot of Rosacio, his rector of the Mark of Ancona, to extirpate the Fraticelli existing there, and the difficulty of the undertaking was recognized in the unwonted clemency which authorized Piero to reconcile even those who had been guilty of repeated relapses.*

Some new motive force was evidently required. There were laws in abundance for the extermination of heresy, and an elaborate organization for their enforcement, but a paralysis seemed to have fallen upon it, and all the efforts of the Holy See to make it do its duty was in vain. The problem was solved when, in 1426, Martin boldly overslaughed the Inquisition and appointed two Observantines as inquisitors, without limitation of districts and with power to appoint deputies, thus rendering them supreme over the whole of Italy. These were the men whom we have so often met before where heresy was to be combated—San Giovanni da

---

* Raynald. ann. 1418, No. 11; ann. 1421, No. 4; ann. 1424, No. 7.—Jo. de Ragusio de Init. Basil. Concil. (Mon. Conc. Gen. Sæc. XV. T. I. pp. 30–1, 40, 55).—Ripoll II. 645.

Capistrano, and the blessed Giacomo da Monteprandone, generally known as della Marca—both full of zeal and energy, who richly earned their respective canonization and beatification by lifelong devotion and by services which can scarce be overestimated. It is true that Giacomo was commissioned only as a missionary, to preach to the heretics and reconcile them, but the difference was practically undiscoverable, and when, a quarter of a century later, he fondly looked back over the exploits of his youth, he related with pride how the heretics fled from before his face, abandoned their strongholds, and left their flocks to his mercy. Their headquarters seem to have been in the Mark of Ancona, and chiefly in the dioceses of Fabriano and Jesi. There the new inquisitors boldly attacked them. There was no resistance. Such of the teachers as could do so sought safety in flight, and the fate of the rest may be guessed from the instructions of Martin in 1428 to Astorgio, Bishop of Ancona, his lieutenant in the Mark, with respect to the village of Magnalata. As it had been a receptacle of heretics, it is to be levelled with the earth, never to be rebuilt. Stubborn heretics are to be dealt with according to the law—that is, of course, to be burned, as Giacomo della Marca tells us was the case with many of them. Those who repent may be reconciled, but their leaders are to be imprisoned for life, and are to be tortured, if necessary, to force them to reveal the names of their fellows elsewhere. The simple folk who have been misled are to be scattered around in the vicinage where they can cultivate their lands, and are to be recompensed by dividing among them the property confiscated from the rest. The children of heretic parents are to be taken away and sent to a distance, where they can be brought up in the faith. Heretic books are to be diligently searched for throughout the province; and all magistrates and communities are to be warned that any favor or protection shown to heretics will be visited with forfeiture of municipal rights.*

Such measures ought to have been effective, as well as the device of Capistrano, who, after driving the Fraticelli out of Massacio and Palestrina, founded Observantine houses there to serve as citadels of the faith, but the heretics were stubborn and enduring.

---

* Wadding. ann. 1426, No. 1–4.—Raynald. ann. 1428, No. 7.—Jac. de Marchia Dial. (Baluz. et Mansi II. 597, 609).

When Eugenius IV. succeeded to the papacy he renewed Capistrano's commission in 1432 as a general inquisitor against the Fraticelli. We have no details of his activity during this period, but he was doubtless busily employed, though he was deprived of the assistance of Giacomo, who until 1440 was, as we have seen, at work among the Cathari of Bosnia and the Hussites of Hungary. The Fraticelli of Ancona were still troublesome, for, on his return from Asia in 1441, Giacomo was sent thither as special inquisitor for their suppression. When, in 1447, Nicholas V. ascended the papal throne, he made haste to renew Capistrano's commission, and in 1449 a combined attack was made on the heretics of the Mark, possibly stimulated by the capture, in his own court, of a bishop of the Fraticelli named Matteo, disguised in a Franciscan habit. Nicholas himself went to Fabriano, while Capistrano and Giacomo scoured the country. Magnalata had been rebuilt in spite of the prohibition, and it, with Migliorotta, Poggio, and Merulo, was brought back to the faith, by what means we can well guess. Giacomo boasts that the heretics gave five hundred ducats to a bravo to slay Capistrano, and on one occasion two hundred and on another one hundred and fifty to procure his own death, but the assassins in each case were touched with compunction and came in and made confession—doubtless a profitable revelation for sharpers to make, for no one acquainted with Italian society at that period can imagine that such sums would not have effected their object. The inquisitors, however, were specially protected by Heaven. Capistrano's legend relates that on one occasion the heretics waited for him in ambush. His companions passed in safety, and when he followed alone, absorbed in meditation and prayer, a sudden whirlwind, with torrents of rain, kept his assailants in their lair, and he escaped. Giacomo was similarly divinely guarded. At Matelica a heretic concealed himself in a chapel of the Virgin to assail the inquisitor as he passed, but the Virgin appeared to him with threats so terrible that he fell to the ground and lay there till the neighbors carried him to a hospital, and it was three months before he was able to seek Giacomo at Fermo and abjure.*

---

* Wadding. ann. 1426, No. 15–16; Regest. Mart. V. No. 162; ann. 1432, No. 8–9; ann. 1441, No. 37–8; ann. 1447, No. 10; ann. 1456, No. 108; ann. 1476,

The unlucky captives were brought before Nicholas at Fabriano and burned. Giacomo tells us that the stench lasted for three days and extended as far as the convent in which he was staying. He exerted himself to save the souls of those whose bodies were forfeit by reason of relapse, and succeeded in all cases but one. This hardened heretic was the treasurer of the sect, named Chiuso. He refused to recant, and would not call upon God or the Virgin or the saints for aid, but simply said "Fire will not burn me." His endurance was tested to the utmost. For three days he was burned piecemeal at intervals, but his resolution never gave way, and at last he expired impenitent, in spite of the kindly efforts to torture him to heaven.*

After this we hear little of the Fraticelli, although the sect still continued to exist for a while in secret. In 1467 Paul II. converted a number of them who were brought from Poli to Rome. Eight men and six women, with paper mitres on their heads, were exposed to the jeers of the populace on a high scaffold at the Aracœli, while the papal vicar and five bishops preached for their conversion. Their penance consisted in imprisonment in the Campidoglio, and in wearing a long robe bearing a white cross on breast and back. It was probably on this occasion that Rodrigo Sanchez, a favorite of Paul's, and subsequently Bishop of Palencia, wrote a treatise on the poverty of Christ, in which he proved that ecclesiastics led apostolic lives in the midst of their possessions. In 1471 Frà Tommaso di Scarlino was sent to Piombino and the maritime parts of Tuscany to drive out some Fraticelli who had been discovered there. This is the last allusion to them that I have met with, and thereafter they may be considered as virtually extinct. That they soon passed completely out of notice may be inferred from the fact that in 1487, when the Spanish Inquisition persecuted some Observantines, Innocent VIII. issued a general order that any Franciscans imprisoned by Dominican inquisitors should be handed over for trial to their own superiors, and that no such prosecutions should be thereafter undertaken.†

No. 24-5.—Raynald. ann. 1432, No. 24.—Jac. de Marchia Dial. (Baluz. et Mansi II. 610).

* Jac. de Marchia l. c.

† Steph. Infessuræ Diar. Urb. Rom. ann. 1467 (Eccard. Corp. Hist. II. 1893).—

The Observantine movement may be credited with the destruction of the Fraticelli, not so much by furnishing the men and the zeal required for their violent suppression as by supplying an organization in which ascetic longings could be safely gratified, and by attracting to themselves the popular veneration which had so long served as a safeguard to the heretics. When we read of Capistrano's reputation among his countrymen—how in Vicenza, in 1451, the authorities had to shut the city gates to keep out the influx of surging crowds, and when he walked the streets he had to be accompanied by a guard of Frati to keep off the people seeking to touch him with sticks or to secure a fragment of his garment as a relic ; how in Florence, in 1456, an armed guard was requisite to prevent his suffocation—we can realize the tremendous influence exercised by him and his fellows in diverting the current of public opinion to the Church which they represented. Like the Mendicants of the thirteenth century, they restored to it much of the reverence which it had forfeited, in spite of the relaxation and self-indulgence to which, if Poggio is to be believed, many of them speedily degenerated.*

Not less effective was the refuge which the Observantines afforded to those whose morbid tendencies led them to seek superhuman austerity. The Church having at last recognized the necessity of furnishing an outlet for these tendencies, as the old Fraticelli died or were burned there were none to take their place, and the sect disappears from view without leaving a trace behind it. Ascetic zeal must indeed have been intense when it could not be satiated by such a life as that of Lorenzo da Fermo, who died in 1481 at the age of one hundred and ten, after passing ninety years with the Observantines. For forty of these years he lived on Mont Alverno, wearing neither cowl nor sandals—bareheaded and barefooted in the severest weather, and with the thinnest garments. If there were natures which craved more than this, the Church had learned either to utilize or to control them. Thus was organized the Order of the Strict Observance, better known as the

---

Platinæ Vit. Pauli II. (Ed. 1574, p. 308).—Rod. Santii Hist. Hispan. P. III. c. 40 (R. Beli Rer. Hisp. Scriptt. I. 433).—Wadding. ann. 1371, No. 14.—Ripoll IV. 22.

* Barbarano de' Mironi, Hist. di Vicenza, II. 164–5.—Poggii Bracciol. Dial. contra Hypocrisim.

Recollects.   The Conde de Sotomayor, of the noblest blood of
Spain, had entered the Franciscan Order, and, becoming dissatisfied
with its laxity, obtained from Innocent VIII., in 1487, authority
to found a reformed branch, which he established in the wilds of
the Sierra Morena.   In spite of the angry opposition of both Conventuals and Observantines, it proved successful and spread permanently through France and Italy.   An irregular and unfortunate effort in the same direction was made not long after by
Matteo da Tivoli, a Franciscan whose thirst for supreme asceticism
had led him to adopt the life of a hermit, with about eighty followers, in the Roman province.   They threw off all obedience to
the Order, under the influence of Satan, who appeared to Matteo
in the guise of Christ.   He was seized and imprisoned, and commenced to doubt the reality of his mission, when another vision
confirmed him.   He succeeded in escaping with a comrade, and
lived in caves among the mountains with numerous disciples,
illuminated by God and gifted with miraculous power.   He organized his followers into an independent Order, with general, provincials, and guardians, but the Church succeeded in breaking it up
in 1495, Matteo finally returning to the Conventuals, while most
of his disciples entered the Observantines.*

In reviewing this history of the morbid aberrations of lofty
impulses, it is impossible not to recognize how much the Church
lost in vitality, and how much causeless suffering was inflicted by
the theological arrogance and obstinate perversity of John XXII.
With tact and discretion the zeal of the Fraticelli could have been
utilized, as was subsequently that of the Observantines.   The
ceaseless quarrels of the Conventuals with the latter explain the
persecutions endured by the Spirituals and the Fraticelli.   Paoluccio was fortunate in finding men high in station who were wise
enough to protect his infant organization until it had demonstrated
its usefulness and was able to defend itself, but there never was
a time, even when it was the most useful weapon in the hands of
the Holy See, when the Conventuals would not, had they been
able, have treated it as inhumanly as they had treated the followers of Angelo and Olivi and Michele da Cesena.

---

* Wadding. ann. 1481, No. 9; ann. 1487, No. 3-5; ann. 1495, No. 12.—Addis
and Arnold's Catholic Dictionary, s. v. Recollects.

CHAPTER IV.

THE identification of the cause of the Church with that of God was no new thing. Long before the formulation of laws against heresy and the organization of the Inquisition for its suppression, the advantage had been recognized of denouncing as heretics all who refused obedience to the demands of prelate and pope. In the quarrel between the empire and papacy over the question of the investitures, the Council of Lateran, in 1102, required all the bishops in attendance to subscribe a declaration anathematizing the new heresy of disregarding the papal anathema, and though the Church as yet was by no means determined on the death-penalty for ordinary heresy, it had no hesitation as to the punishment due to the imperialists who maintained the traditional rights of the empire against its new pretensions. In that same year the monk Sigebert, who was by no means a follower of the antipope Alberto, was scandalized at the savage cruelty of Paschal II. in exhorting his adherents to the slaughter of all the subjects of Henry IV. Robert the Hierosolymitan of Flanders, on his return from the first crusade, had taken up arms against Henry IV. and had signalized his devotion by depopulating the Cambresis, whereupon Paschal wrote to him with enthusiastic praises of this good work, urging him to continue it as quite as pious as his labors to recover the Holy Sepulchre, and promising remission of sins to him and to all his ruthless soldiery. Paschal himself became a heretic when, in 1111, yielding to the violence of Henry V., he conceded the imperial right of investiture of bishops and abbots, although when Bruno, Bishop of Segni and Abbot of Monte Casino, boldly proved his heresy to his face, he deprived the audacious reasoner of the abbacy and sent him back to his see. In his settlement with Henry, he had broken a consecrated host, each taking half, and had solemnly said, " Even as this body of Christ is divided, so let him be divided from the kingdom of Christ who shall attempt to violate our compact;" but the stigma of heresy was unendurable, and in 1112 he presided over the Council of Lateran, which pronounced void his oath and his bulls.   When Henry complained that he had violated his oath, he coolly replied that he had promised not to excommunicate Henry, but not that he should not be excommunicated by others.   If Paschal was not forced literally to abjure his heresy he did so constructively, and the principle was established that even a pope could not abandon a claim of which the denial had been pronounced heretical.   When, not long afterwards, the German prelates were required at their consecration to abjure all heresy, and especially the Henrician, the allusion was not to the errors of Henry of Lausanne, but to those of the emperor who had sought to limit the encroachments of the Holy See on the temporal power.*

As heresy, rightly so called, waxed and grew more and more threatening, and the struggle for its suppression increased in bitterness and took an organized shape under a formidable body of legislation, and as the application of the theory of indulgences gave to the Church an armed militia ready for mobilization without cost whenever it chose to proclaim danger to the faith, the temptation to invoke the fanaticism of Christendom for the defence or extension of its temporal interests inevitably increased in strength. In so far as such a resort can be justified, the Albigensian crusades were justified by a real antagonism of faith which foreboded a division of Christianity, and their success irresistibly led to the application of the same means to cases in which there was not the semblance of a similar excuse.   Of these one of the earliest, as well as one of the most typical, was that of the Stedingers.

The Stedingers were a mixed race who had colonized on the lower Weser the lands which their industry won from the overflow of river and sea, their territory extending southward to the neighborhood of Bremen.   A rough and semi-barbarous folk, no doubt—hardy herdsmen and fishermen, with perhaps an occasional

---

* Concil. Lateran. ann. 1102 (Harduin. VI. ii. 1861–2).—Epist. Sigebert. (Mart. Ampl. Coll. I. 587–94).—Chron. Cassinens. iv. 42, 44.   (Cf. Martene Ampl. Coll. I. 627.)—Hartzheim III. 258–65.—Martene Ampl. Coll. I. 659.

tendency to piracy in the ages which celebrated the exploits of the Vikings of Jomsburg. They were freemen under the spiritual care of the Archbishops of Bremen, who in return enjoyed their tithes. This tithe question had been immemorially a troublesome one, ever since a tincture of Christianity had overspread those regions. In the eleventh century Adam of Bremen tells us that throughout the archiepiscopate the bishops sold their benedictions and the people were not only abandoned to lust and gluttony, but refused to pay their tithes. The Stedingers were governed by judges of their own choice, administering their own laws, until, about 1187, trouble arose from the attempts of the Counts of Oldenburg to extend their authority over the redeemed marshes and islands, by building a castle or two which should keep the population in check. There were few churches, and, as the parishes were large, the matrons were accustomed to carry their daughters to mass in wagons. The garrisons were in the habit of sallying forth and seizing these women to solace their solitude, till the people arose, captured the castles, slew the garrisons, and dug a ditch across a neck of their territory, leaving only one gate for entrance. John Count of Oldenburg recovered his castles, but after his death the Stedingers reasserted their independence. Among their rights they included the non-payment of tithes, and they treated with contumely the priests sent to compel their obedience. They strengthened their defences, and their freedom from feudal and ecclesiastical tyranny attracted to them refugees from all the neighboring lands. Hartwig, Archbishop of Bremen, when on his way to the Holy Land in 1197, is said to have asked Celestin III. to preach a crusade against them as heretics, but this is evidently an error, for the Albigensian wars had not as yet suggested the employment of such methods. Matters became more embroiled when some monks who ventured to inculcate upon the peasants the duty of tithe-paying were martyred. Still worse was it when a priest, irritated at the smallness of an oblation offered at Easter by a woman of condition, in derision slipped into her mouth the coin in place of the Eucharist. Unable to swallow it, and fearing to commit sacrilege, the woman kept it in her mouth till her return home, when she ejected it in some clean linen and discovered the trick. Enraged at this insult her husband slew the priest, and thus increased the general ferment. After his return Hartwig endeavored, in 1207, to reduce the recalcitrant population, but without success, except to get some money.*

Yet the Stedingers were welcomed as fully orthodox when their aid was wanted in the struggle which raged from 1208 till 1217, between the rival archbishops of Bremen, first between Waldemar and Burchard, and then between Waldemar and Gerhardt. Ranged at first on the side of Waldemar, after the triumph of Frederic II. over Otho their defection to Gerhardt was decisive, and in 1217 the latter obtained his archiepiscopal seat, where he held his allies in high favor until his death in 1219. He was succeeded by Gerhardt II., of the House of Lippe, a warlike prelate who endeavored to overthrow the liberties of Bremen itself, and to levy tolls on all the commerce of the Weser. The Stedinger tithes were not likely to escape his attention. Other distractions, including a war with the King of Denmark and strife with the recalcitrant citizens of Bremen, prevented any immediate effort to subjugate the Stedingers, but at length his hands were free. His brother, Hermann Count of Lippe, came to his assistance with other nobles, for the independence of the Weser peasant-folk was of evil import to the neighboring feudal lords. To take advantage of the ice in those watery regions the expedition set forth in December, 1229, under the leadership of the count and the archbishop. The Stedingers resisted valiantly. On Christmas Day a battle was fought in which Count Hermann was slain and the crusaders put to flight. To celebrate the triumph the victors in derision appointed mock officials, styling one emperor, another pope, and others archbishops and bishops, and these issued letters under these titles—a sorry jest, which when duly magnified represented them as rebels against all temporal and spiritual authority.†

---

* Schumacher, Die Stedinger, Bremen, 1865, pp. 26–8.—Adam. Bremens. Gest. Pontif. Hammaburg. c. 203.—Chron. Erfordiens. ann. 1230 (Schannat Vindem. Litt. I. 93).—Chron. Rastedens. (Meibom. Rer. Germ. II. 101).—Albert. Stadens. Chron. ann. 1207 (Schilt. S. R. Germ. I. 299).—Joan. Otton. Cat. Archiepp. Bremens. ann. 1207 (Menken. S. R. Germ. II. 791).

† Albert. Stadens. Chron. ann. 1208–17, 1230.—Joan. Otton. Cat. Archiepp. Bremens. ann. 1211–20.—Anon. Saxon. Hist. Impp. ann. 1229 (Menken. III. 125).—Chron. Rastedens. (Meibom. II. 101).

There is considerable confusion among the authorities with regard to these events. I have followed the careful investigations of Schumacher, op. cit. pp. 219–23.

It was evident that some more potent means must be found to overcome the indomitable peasantry, and the device adopted was suggested by the success, in 1230, of the crusade preached by Wilbrand, Bishop of Utrecht, against the free Frisians in revenge for their slaying his predecessor Otho, a brother of Archbishop Gerhardt, and imprisoning his other brother, Dietrich, Provost of Deventer, after their victory of Coevorden. It was scarce possible not to follow this example. At a synod held in Bremen in 1230, the Stedingers were put to the ban as the vilest of heretics, who treated the Eucharist with contempt too horrible for description, who sought responses from wise-women, made waxen images, and wrought many other works of darkness.*

Doubtless there were remnants of pagan superstition in Steding, such as we shall hereafter see existing throughout many parts of Christendom, which served as a foundation for these accusations, but that in fact there were no religious principles involved, and that the questions at issue were purely political, is indicated by the praise which Frederic II., in an epistle dated June 14, 1230, bestows on the Stedingers for the aid which they had rendered to a house of the Teutonic Knights, and his exhortation that they should continue to protect it. We learn, moreover, that everywhere the peasantry openly favored them and joined them when opportunity permitted. It was simply an episode in the extension of feudalism and sacerdotalism. The scattered remains of the old Teutonic tribal independence were to be crushed, and the combined powers of Church and State were summoned to the task. How readily such accusations could be imposed on the credulity of the people we have seen from the operations of Conrad of Marburg, and the stories to which he gave currency of far-pervading secret rites of demon-worship. Yet the preliminaries of a crusade consumed time, and during 1231 and 1232 Archbishop Gerhardt had all he could do to withstand the assaults of the victorious peasants, who twice captured and destroyed the castle of Schlütter, which he had rebuilt to protect his territories from their incursions; he sought support in Rome, and in October, 1232, after ordering an investigation of the heresy by the Bishops of Lubeck, Ratzeburg, and Minden, Gregory IX. came to

---

* Emonis Chron. ann. 1227, 1230 (Matthæi Analecta III. 128, 132).—Schumacher, p. 81.

his aid with bulls addressed to the Bishops of Minden, Lubeck, and Verden, ordering them to preach the cross against the rebels. In these there is nothing said about tithes, but the Stedingers are described as heretics of the worst description, who deny God, worship demons, consult seeresses, abuse the sacrament, make wax figurines to destroy their enemies, and commit the foulest excesses on the clergy, sometimes nailing priests to the wall with arms and legs spread out, in derision of the Crucified. Gregory's long pontificate was devoted to two paramount objects—the destruction of Frederic II. and the suppression of heresy. The very name of heretic seemed to awake in him a wrath which deprived him of all reasoning powers, and he threw himself into the contest with the unhappy peasants of the Weser marshes as unreservedly as he did into that which Conrad of Marburg was contemporaneously waging with the powers of darkness in the Rhinelands. In January, 1233, he wrote to the Bishops of Paderborn, Hildesheim, Verden, Münster, and Osnabrück, ordering them to assist their brethren of Ratzeburg, Minden, and Lubeck, whom he had commissioned to preach a crusade, with full pardons, against the heretics called Stedingers, who were destroying the faithful people of those regions. An army had meanwhile been collected which accomplished nothing during the winter against the steadfast resolution of the peasants, and dispersed on the expiration of its short term of service. In a papal epistle of June 17, 1233, to the Bishops of Minden, Lubeck, and Ratzeburg, this lack of success is represented as resulting from a mistaken belief on the part of the crusaders that they were not getting the same indulgences as those granted for the Holy Land, leading them to withdraw after gaining decisive advantages. The bishops are therefore ordered to preach a new crusade in which there shall be no error as to the pardons to be earned, unless meanwhile the Stedingers shall submit to the archbishop and abandon their heresies. Already, however, another band of crusaders had been organized, which, towards the end of June, 1233, penetrated eastern Steding, on the right bank of the Weser. This district had hitherto kept aloof from the strife, and was defenceless. The crusaders devastated the land with fire and sword, slaying without distinction of age or sex, and manifesting their religious zeal by burning all the men who were captured. The crusade came to an inglorious end, however; for, encouraged by its easy success, Count Burchard of Oldenburg, its leader, was emboldened to attack the fortified lands on the west bank, when he and some two hundred crusaders were slain and the rest were glad to escape with their lives.*

Matters were evidently growing serious. The success of the Stedingers in battling for the maintenance of their independence was awakening an uneasy feeling among the populations, and the feudal nobles were no less interested than the prelates in subduing what might prove to be the nucleus of a dangerous and far-reaching revolt. The third crusade was therefore preached with additional energy over a wider circle than before, and preparations were made for an expedition in 1234 on a scale to crush all resistance. Dominicans spread like a cloud over Holland, Flanders, Brabant, Westphalia, and the Rhinelands, summoning the faithful to defend religion. In Friesland they had little success, for the population sympathized with their kindred and were rather disposed to maltreat the preachers, but elsewhere their labors were abundantly rewarded. Bulls of February 11 take under papal protection the territories of Henry Raspe of Thuringia, and Otho of Brunswick, who had assumed the cross—the latter, however, only with a view to self-protection, for he was an enemy of Archbishop Gerhardt. The heaviest contingent came from the west, under Hendrik, Duke of Brabant, consisting, it is said, of forty thousand men led by the *preux chevalier*, Florent, Count of Holland, together with Thierry, Count of Cleves, Arnoul of Oudenarde, Rasso of Gavres, Thierry of Dixmunde, Gilbert of Zotteghem, and other nobles, eager to earn salvation and preserve their feudal rights. Three hundred ships from Holland gave assurance that the maritime part of the expedition should not be lacking. Apparently warned by the disastrous outcome of his zeal in the affair of Conrad of Marburg, Gregory at the last moment seems to have felt some misgiving, and in March, 1234, sent to Bishop Guglielmo, his legate in North Germany, orders to endeavor by peaceful means to bring about the reconciliation of the peasants,

---

* Hist. Diplom. Frid. II. T. IV. p. 497.—Albert. Stadens. Chron. ann. 1232, 1234.—Raynald. ann. 1232, No. 8.—Hartzheim III. 553.—Joan. Ottonis Cat. Archiepp. Bremens. ann. 1234.—Anon. Saxon. Hist. Imperator. ann. 1229.—Chron. Cornel. Zantfliet ann. 1233.—Epistt. Select. Sæcul. XIII. T. I. No. 539 (Pertz).

but the effort came too late. In April the hosts were already assembling, and the legate did, and probably could do, nothing to avert the final blow. Overwhelming as was the force of the crusaders, the handful of peasants met it with their wonted resolution. At Altenesch, on May 27, they made their stand and resisted with stubborn valor the onslaught of Hendrik of Brabant and Florent of Holland; but, in the vast disparity of numbers, Thierry of Cleves was able to make a flank attack with fresh troops which broke their ranks, when they were slaughtered unsparingly. Six thousand were left dead upon the field, besides those drowned in the Weser in the vain attempt at flight, and we are asked to believe that the divine favor was manifested in that only seven of the crusaders perished. The land now lay defenceless before the soldiers of the Lord, who improved their victory by laying it waste with fire and sword, sparing neither age nor sex. Six centuries later, on May 27, 1834, a monument was solemnly dedicated on the field of Altenesch to the heroes who fell in desperate defence of their land and liberty.*

Bald as was the pretence for this frightful tragedy, the Church assumed all the responsibility and kept up the transparent fiction to the last. When the slaughter and devastation were over, came the solemn farce of reconciling the heretics. As the land had been so long under their control, their dead were buried indistinguishably with the remains of the orthodox, so, November 28, 1234, Gregory graciously announced that the necessity of exhumation would be waived in view of the impossibility of separating the one from the other, but that all cemeteries must be consecrated anew to overcome the pollution of the heretic bodies within them. Considerable time must have been consumed in the settlement of all details, for it is not until August, 1236, that Gregory writes to the archbishop that, as the Stedingers have abandoned their rebellion and humbly supplicated for reconciliation, he is

---

* Emonis Chron. ann. 1234 (Matthæi Analecta III. 139 sqq.).—Potthast No. 9399, 9400.—Epistt. Select. Sæcul. XIII. T. I. No. 572.—Meyeri Annal. Flandr. Lib. VIII. ann. 1233.—Chron. Cornel. Zantfliet ann. 1234.—Schumacher, pp. 116–17.—Chron. Erfordiens. ann. 1232.—Sachsische Weltchronik No. 376–8.—H.Wolteri Chron. Bremens. (Meibom. Rer. Germ. II. 58–9).—Chron. Rastedens. (Ib. II. 101).—Joan Otton. Cat. Archiepp. Bremens. ann. 1234.—Albert. Stadens. ann. 1234.—Anon. Saxon. Hist. Imperator. ann. 1229.

authorized to reconcile them on receiving proper security that they will be obedient for the future and make proper amends for the past. In this closing act of the bloody drama it is noteworthy that there is no allusion to any of the specific heresies which had been alleged as a reason for the extermination of the heretics. Perhaps the breaking of Conrad of Marburg's bubble had shown the falsity of the charges, but whether this were so or not those charges had been wholly supererogatory except as a means of exciting popular animosity. Disobedience to the Church was sufficient; resistance to its claims was heresy, punishable here and hereafter with all the penalties of the temporal and spiritual swords.*

It is not to be supposed that Gregory neglected to employ in his own interest the moral and material forces which he had thus put at the disposal of Gerhardt of Bremen. When, in 1238, he became involved in a quarrel with the Viterbians and their leader Aldobrandini, he commuted the vow of the Podestà of Spoleto to serve in Palestine into service against Viterbo, and he freely offered Holy Land indulgences to all who would enlist under his banner. In 1241 he formally declared the cause of the Church to be more important than that of Palestine, when, being in want of funds to carry on his contest with Frederic II., he ordered that crusaders be induced to commute their vows for money, while still receiving full indulgences, or else be persuaded to turn their arms against Frederic in the crusade which he had caused to be preached against him. Innocent IV. pursued the same policy when he had set up a rival emperor in the person of William of Holland, and a crusade was preached in 1248 for a special expedition to Aix-la-Chapelle, of which the capture was necessary in order to his coronation, and vows for Palestine were redeemed that the money should be handed over to him. After Frederic's death his son Conrad IV. was the object of similar measures, and all who bore arms in his favor against William of Holland were the subject of papal anathemas. To maintain the Italian interests of the

---

* Potthast No. 9777.—Hartzheim III. 554.

As the contemporary Abbot Emo of Wittewerum says, in describing the affair—" principalior causa fuit inobedientia, quæ scelere idololatriæ non est inferior" (Matthæi Analect. III. 142).

papacy, men slaughtered each other in holy wars all over Europe. The disastrous expedition to Aragon which cost Philippe le Hardi his life in 1284 was a crusade preached by order of Martin IV. to aid Charles of Anjou, and to punish Pedro III. for his conquest of Sicily after the Sicilian Vespers.*

With the systematization of the laws against heresy and the organization of the Inquisition, proceedings of this nature assume a more regular shape, especially in Italy.   It was in their character as Italian princes that the popes found the supreme utility of the Holy Office.   Frederic II. had been forced to pay for his coronation not only by the edict of persecution, but by the confirmation of the grant of the Countess Matilda.   Papal ambition thus stimulated aspired to the domination of the whole of Italy, and for this the way seemed open with the death of Frederic in 1250, followed by that of Conrad in 1254.   When the hated Suabians passed away, the unification of Italy under the triple crown seemed at hand, and Innocent IV., before his death in December, 1254, had the supreme satisfaction of lording it in Naples, the most powerful pope that the Holy See had known.   Yet the nobles and cities were as unwilling to subject themselves to the Innocents and Alexanders as to the Frederics, and the turbulent factions of Guelf and Ghibelline maintained the civil strife in every corner of central and upper Italy.   To the papal policy it was an invaluable assistance to have the power of placing in every town of importance an inquisitor whose devotion to Rome was unquestioned, whose person was inviolable, and who was authorized to compel the submissive assistance of the secular arm under terror of a prosecution for heresy in the case of slack obedience.   Such an agent could cope with podestà and bishop, and even an unruly populace rarely ventured a resort to temporary violence.   The statutes of the republics, as we have seen, were modified and moulded to adapt them to the fullest development of the new power, under the excuse of facilitating the extermination of heresy, and the Holy Office became the ultimate expression of the serviceable devotion of the Mendicant Orders to the Holy See. From this point of view we are able to appreciate the full signifi-

---

* Epistt. Selectt. Sæc. XIII. T. I. No. 720, 801.—Berger, Registres d'Innocent IV. No. 4181, 4265, 4269.—Ripoll I. 219, 225.—Vaissette, IV. 46.

cance of the terrible bulls *Ad extirpanda,* described in a previous chapter.

It was possibly with a view thus to utilize the force of both Orders that the Inquisitions of northern and central Italy were divided between them, and their respective provinces permanently assigned to each. Nor perhaps would we err in recognizing an object in the assignment to the Dominicans, who were regarded as sterner and more vigorous than their rivals, of the province of Lombardy, which not only was the hot-bed of heresy, but which retained some recollections of the ancient independence of the Ambrosian Church, and was more susceptible to imperial influences from Germany.

With the development of the laws against heresy, and the organization of special tribunals for the application of those laws, it was soon perceived that an accusation of heresy was a peculiarly easy and efficient method of attacking a political enemy. No charge was easier to bring, none so difficult to disprove—in fact, from what we have seen of the procedure of the Inquisition, there was none in which acquittal was so absolutely impossible where the tribunal was desirous of condemnation. When employed politically the accused had the naked alternative of submission or of armed resistance. No crime, moreover, according to the accepted legal doctrines of the age, carried with it a penalty so severe for a potentate who was above all other laws. Besides, the procedure of the Inquisition required that when a suspected heretic was summoned to trial, his first step was humbly to swear to stand to the mandates of the Church, and perform whatever penance it should see fit to impose in case he failed to clear himself of the suspicion. Thus an immense advantage was gained over a political enemy by merely citing him to appear, when he was obliged either to submit himself in advance to any terms that might be dictated to him, or, by refusing to appear, expose himself to condemnation for contumacy with its tremendous temporal consequences.

It mattered little what were the grounds on which a charge of heresy was based. In the intricate intrigues and factional strife which seethed and boiled in every Italian city, there could be no lack of excuse for setting the machinery of the Inquisition in motion whenever there was an object to be attained. With the organization of the Hildebrandine theocracy the heretical character of simple disobedience, which had been implied rather than expressed, came to be distinctly formulated. Thomas Aquinas did not shrink from proving that resistance to the authority of the Roman Church was heretical. By embodying in the canon law the bull *Unam Sanctam* the Church accepted the definition of Boniface VIII. that whoever resists the power lodged by God in the Church resists God, unless, like a Manichæan, he believes in two principles, which shows him to be a heretic. If the supreme spiritual power errs, it is to be judged of God alone; there is no earthly appeal. " We say, declare, define, and pronounce that it is necessary to salvation that every human creature be subjected to the Roman pontiff." Inquisitors, therefore, were fully justified in laying it down as an accepted principle of law that disobedience to any command of the Holy See was heresy; so was any attempt to deprive the Roman Church of any privilege which it saw fit to claim. As a corollary to this was the declaration that inquisitors had power to levy war against heretics and to give it the character of a crusade by granting all the indulgences offered for the succor of the Holy Land. Armed with such powers, it would be difficult to exaggerate the importance of the Inquisition as a political instrument.*

Incidental allusion has been made above to the application of these methods in the cases of Ezzelin da Romano and Uberto Pallavicino, and we have seen their efficacy even in the tumultuous lawlessness of the period as one of the factors in the ruin of those powerful chiefs. When the crusade against Ezzelin was preached in the north of Europe he was represented to the people simply as a powerful heretic who was persecuting the faith. Even more conspicuous was the application of this principle in the great

---

* Th. Aquinat. Sec. Sec. Q. 11, No. 2–3.—C. 1, Extrav. Commun. I. 8.—Zanchini Tract. de Hæret. c. ii., xxxvii.

It was probably as a derivative from the sanctity of the power of the Holy See that the Inquisition was given jurisdiction over the forgers and falsifiers of papal bulls—gentry whose industry we have seen to be one of the inevitable consequences of the autocracy of Rome. Letters under which Frà Grimaldo da Prato, Inquisitor of Tuscany in 1297, was directed to act in certain cases of the kind are printed by Amati in the Archivio Storico Italiano, No. 38, p. 6.

struggle on which all the rest depended, which in fact decided the destiny of the whole peninsula. The destruction of Manfred was an actual necessity to the success of the papal policy, and for years the Church sought throughout Europe a champion who could be allured by the promise of an earthly crown and assured salvation. In 1255 Alexander IV. authorized his legate, Rustand, Bishop of Bologna, to release Henry III. of England from his crusader's vow if he would turn his arms against Manfred, and the bribe of the Sicilian throne was offered to Henry's son, Edmund of Lancaster. When Rustand preached the crusade against Manfred and offered the same indulgences as for the Holy Land the ignorant islanders wondered greatly at learning that the same pardons could be earned for shedding Christian blood as for that of the infidel. They did not understand that Manfred was necessarily a heretic, and that, as Alexander soon afterwards declared to Rainerio Saccone, it was more important to defend the faith at home than in foreign lands. In 1264, when Alphonse of Poitiers was projecting a crusade, Urban IV. urged him to change his purpose and assail Manfred. Finally, when Charles of Anjou was induced to strive for the glittering prize, all the enginery of the Church was exerted to raise for him an army of crusaders with a lavish distribution of the treasures of salvation. The shrewd lawyer, Clement IV., seconded and justified the appeal to arms by a formal trial for heresy. Just as the crusade was bursting upon him, Clement was summoning him to present himself for trial as a suspected heretic. The term assigned to him was February 2, 1266; Manfred had more pressing cares at the moment, and contented himself with sending procurators to offer purgation for him. As he did not appear personally, Clement, on February 21, called upon the consistory to declare him condemned as a contumacious heretic, arguing that his excuse that the enemy were upon him was invalid, since he had only to give up his kingdom to avert attack. As but five days after this, on February 26, Manfred fell upon the disastrous field of Benevento, the legal proceedings had no influence on the result, yet none the less do they serve to show the spirit in which Rome administered against its political opponents the laws which it had enacted against heresy.*

---

* Th. Cantimpratens. Bonum universale, Lib. ii. c. 2.—Matt. Paris ann. 1255

III.—13

This was the virtual destruction of the imperial power in Italy.
With the Angevines on the throne of Naples and the empire nul-
lified by the Great Interregnum and its consequences, the popes
had ample opportunity to employ the penalties for heresy to gratify hatred or to extend their power.   How they used the weapon
for the one purpose is seen when Boniface VIII. quarrelled with
the Colonnas and condemned them as heretics, driving the whole
family out of Italy, tearing down their houses and destroying
their property; though after Sciarra Colonna vindicated his orthodoxy by capturing and causing the death of Boniface at Anagni,
Benedict XI. made haste to reverse the sentence, except as to confiscation.*   How the principle worked when applied to temporal
aggrandizement may be estimated from the attempt of Clement V.
to gain possession of Ferrara.   When the Marchese Azzo d' Este
died, in 1308, he left no legitimate heirs, and the Bishop of Ferrara
was Frà Guido Maltraverso, the former inquisitor who had succeeded in burning the bones of Armanno Pongilupo.   He forthwith commenced intriguing to secure the city for the Holy See,
which had some shadowy claims arising under the donations of
Charlemagne.   Clement V. eagerly grasped at the opportunity.
He pronounced the rights of the Church unquestionable, and con-
doled with the Ferrarese on their having been so long deprived of
the sweetness of clerical rule and subjected to those who devoured
them.   There were two pretenders, Azzo's brother Francesco and
his natural son Frisco.   The Ferrarese desired neither; they even

---

(p. 614).—Ripoll I. 326.—Raynald. ann. 1264, No. 14.—Arch. de l'Inq. de Carcassonne (Doat, XXXII. 27).

Clement IV. (Gui Foucoix) was regarded as one of the best lawyers of his
day, but in the severity of his application of the law against Manfred he was
not unanimously supported by the cardinals.   On February 20 he writes to
the Cardinal of S. Martino, his legate in the Mark of Ancona, for his opinion on
the question.   Manfred and Uberto Pallavicino had both been cited to appear
on trial for heresy.   Manfred had sent procurators to offer purgation, but Uberto
had disregarded the summons and was a contumacious heretic.   To the condemnation of the latter there was therefore no opposition, but some cardinals
thought that Manfred's excuse was reasonable in view of the enemy at his gates,
even though he could easily avert attack by surrender.—Clement PP. IV. Epist.
232 (Martene Thesaur. II. 279).

* C. 1, Sexto v. 3.—C. 1, Extrav. Commun. v. 4.

manifested a disregard for the blessings promised them by Clement and proclaimed a republic. Frisco sought the aid of the Venetians, while Francesco secured the support of the Church. Frisco obtained possession, but fled when Francesco advanced with the papal legate, Arnaldo di Pelagrua, who assumed the domination of the city—as a contemporary chronicler observes, Francesco had no reason to be disappointed, for ecclesiastics always act like rapacious wolves. Then, with the aid of the Venetians, Frisco regained possession, and peace was made in December, 1308. This was but the commencement of the struggle for the unhappy citizens. In 1309 Clement proclaimed a crusade against the Venetians. March 7 he issued a bull casting an interdict over Venice with confiscation of all its possessions, excommunicating the doge, the senate, and all the gentlemen of the republic, and offering Venetians to slavery throughout the world. As their ships sailed to every port, many Venetian merchants were reduced to servitude throughout Christendom. The legate assiduously preached the crusade, and all the bishops of the region assembled at Bologna with such forces as they could raise. Multitudes took the cross to gain the indulgence, Bologna alone furnishing eight thousand troops, and the legate advanced with an overwhelming army. After severe fighting the Venetians were defeated with such slaughter that the legate, to avert a pestilence, offered an indulgence to every man who would bury a dead body, and the fugitives drowned in the Po were so numerous that the water was corrupted and rendered unfit to drink. All the prisoners taken he blinded and sent to Venice, and on entering the city he hanged all the adherents of Frisco. Appointing a governor in the name of the Church, he returned to Avignon and was splendidly rewarded for his services in the cause of Christ, while Clement unctuously congratulated the Ferrarese on their return to the sweet bosom of the Church, and declared that no one could, without sighs and tears, reflect upon their miseries and afflictions under their native rulers. In spite of this the ungrateful people, chafing under the foreign domination, arose in 1310 and massacred the papalists. Then the legate returned with a Bolognese force, regained possession and hanged the rebels, with the exception of one, who bought off his life. Fresh tumults occurred, with bloody reprisals and frightful atrocities on both sides until, in 1314. Clement, wearied with his prize, made it over to Sancha, wife of Robert of Naples. The Gascon garrison excited the hatred of the people, who in 1317 invited Azzo, son of Francesco, to come to their relief. After a stubborn resistance the Gascons surrendered on promise of life, but the fury of the people would not be restrained, and they were slain to the last man. From this brief episode in the history of an Italian city we can conceive what was the influence of papal ambition stimulated by the facility with which its opponents could be condemned as heretics and armies be raised at will to defend the faith.*

John XXII. was not a pope to allow the spiritual sword to rust in the sheath, and we have seen incidentally the use which he made of the charge of heresy in his mortal combat with Louis of Bavaria. Still more characteristic were his proceedings against the Visconti of Milan. On his accession in August, 1316, his first thought was to unite Italy under his overlordship, and to keep the empire beyond the Alps, for which the contested election of Louis of Bavaria and Frederic of Austria seemed to offer full opportunity. Early in December he despatched Bernard Gui, the Inquisitor of Toulouse, and Bertrand, Franciscan Minister of Aquitaine, as nuncios to effect that purpose. Neither Guelfs nor Ghibellines were inclined to accept his views—the Ferrarese troubles, not as yet concluded, were full of pregnant warnings. Especially

---

* Barbarano de' Mironi, Hist. Eccles. di Vicenza II. 153–4.—Regest. Clement. PP. V. T. III. pp. 354 sqq.; T. IV. pp. 426 sqq., pp. 459 sqq.; T. V. p. 412. (Ed. Benedictin., Romæ, 1886–7).—Chron. Estense ann. 1309–17 (Muratori S. R. I. XV. 364–82).—Ferreti Vincentini Hist. Lib. III. (Ib. IX. 1037–47).—Cronica di Bologna, ann. 1309–10 (Ib. XVIII. 320–1).—Campi, Dell' Histor. Eccles. di Ferrara, P. III. p. 40.

Even the pious and temperate Muratori cannot restrain himself from describing Clement's bull against the Venetians as " *la piu terribile ed ingiusta Bolla che si sia mai udita*" (Annal. ann. 1309). We have seen in the case of Florence what control such measures enabled the papacy to exercise over the commercial republics of Italy. The confiscation threatened in the sentence of excommunication was no idle menace. When, in 1281, Martin IV. quarrelled with the city of Forli and excommunicated it he ordered, under pain of excommunication not removable even on the death-bed, all who owed money to the citizens to declare the debts to his representatives and pay them over, and he thus collected many thousand lire of his enemies' substance.—Chron. Parmens. ann. 1281 (Muratori S. R. I. IX. 797)

recalcitrant were the three Ghibelline chiefs of Lombardy, Matteo
Visconti, known as the Great, who ruled over the greater part of
the region and still retained the title of Imperial Vicar bestowed
on him by Henry VII., Cane della Scala, Lord of Verona, and Passerino of Mantua. They received his envoys with all due honor,
but found excuses for evading his commands. In March, 1317,
John issued a bull in which he declared that all the imperial
appointments had lapsed on the death of Henry, that until his
successor had received the papal approval all the power of the
empire vested in the Holy See, and that whoever presumed to
exercise those powers without permission was guilty of treason
to the Church. Papal imperiousness on one side and Ghibelline
stubbornness on the other rendered a rupture inevitable. It is not
our province to trace the intricate maze of diplomatic intrigue and
military activity which followed, with the balance of success pre-
ponderating decidedly in favor of the Ghibellines. April 6, 1318,
came a bull decreeing excommunication on Matteo, Cane, Passerino, and all who refused obedience. This was speedily followed by
formal monitions and citations to trial on charges of heresy, Matteo and his sons being the chief objects of persecution. It was not
difficult to find materials for these, furnished by refugees from
Milan at the papal court—Bonifacio di Farra, Lorenzo Gallini, and
others. The Visconti were accused of erring in the faith, especially
as to the resurrection, of invoking the devil, with whom they had
compacts, of protecting Guglielma; they were fautors of heretics
and impeders of the Inquisition; they had robbed churches, violated nuns, and tortured and slain priests. The Visconti remained
contumaciously absent and were duly condemned as heretics. Matteo summoned a conference of the Ghibelline chiefs at Soncino,
which treated the action of the pope as an effort to resuscitate the
failing cause of the Guelfs. A Ghibelline league was formed with
Can Grande della Scala as captain of its forces. To meet this John
called in the aid of France, appointed Philippe de Valois Imperial
Vicar, and procured a French invasion which proved bootless. Then
he sent his son or nephew, Cardinal Bertrand de Poyet as legate,
with the title of " pacifier," at the head of a crusading army raised
by a lavish distribution of indulgences. As Petrarch says, he assailed Milan as though it were an infidel city, like Memphis or
Damascus, and Poyet, whose ferocity was a proof of his paternity,

came not as an apostle, but as a robber. A devastating war ensued, with little advantage to the papalists, but the spiritual sword proved more effective than the temporal. May 26, 1321, the sentence of condemnation was solemnly promulgated in the Church of San Stefano at Bassegnano, and was repeated by the inquisitors March 14, 1322, at Valenza.*

Strange as it may seem, these proceedings appear to have had a decisive influence on public opinion. It is true that when, in the seventeenth century, Paolo Sarpi alluded to these transactions and assumed that Matteo's only crime was his adherence to Louis of Bavaria, Cardinal Albizio admitted the fact, and argued that those who adhered to a schismatic and heretic emperor, and disregarded the censures of the Church, rendered themselves suspect of heresy and became formal heretics. Yet this was not the impression at the time, and John had recognized that something more was required than such a charge of mere technical heresy. The Continuation of Nangis, which reflects with fidelity the current of popular thought, recounts the sins of Matteo and his sons, described in the papal sentence, as a new heresy arisen in Lombardy, and the papalist military operations as a righteous crusade for its suppression. Although this was naturally a French view of the matter, it was not confined to France. In Lombardy Matteo's friends were discouraged and his enemies took fresh heart. A peace party speedily formed itself in Milan, and the question was openly asked whether the whole region should be sacrificed for the sake of one man. In spite of Matteo's success in buying off Frederic of Austria, whom John had bribed with gold and promises to intervene with an army, the situation grew untenable even for his seasoned nerves. It is, perhaps, worthy of mention that Francesco Garbagnate, the old Guglielmite, association with whom was one of the proofs of heresy alleged against Matteo, was one of the efficient

---

* Preger, Die Politik des Pabstes Johann XXII., München, 1885, pp. 6–10, 21.—Petrarchi Lib. sine Titulo Epist. xviii.—Raynald. ann. 1317, No. 27; ann. 1320, No. 10–14; ann. 1322, No. 6–8, 11.—Bernard. Corio, Hist. Milanese, ann. 1318, 1320, 1321–22.

A bull of John XXII., Jan. 28, 1322, ordering the sale of indulgences to aid the crusade of Cardinal Bertrand, recites the heresy of Visconti and his refusal to obey the summons for his trial as the reason for assailing him.—Regest. Clem. PP. V., Romæ, 1885, T. I. Prolegom. p. cxcviii.

agents in procuring his downfall, for Matteo had estranged him by refusing him the captaincy of the Milanese militia. Matteo sent to the legate to beg for terms, and was told that nothing short of abdication would be listened to; he consulted the citizens and was given to understand that Milan would not expose itself to ruin for his sake. He yielded to the storm—perhaps his seventy-two years had somewhat weakened his powers of resistance —he sent for his son Galeazzo, with whom he had quarrelled, and resigned to him his power, with an expression of regret that his quarrel with the Church had made the citizens his enemies. From that time forth he devoted himself to visiting the churches. In the Chiesa Maggiore he assembled the clergy, recited the Symbol in a loud voice, crying that it had been his faith during life, and that any assertion to the contrary was false, and of this he caused a public instrument to be drawn up. Departing thence like to one crazed, he hastened to Monza to visit the Church of S. Giovanni Battista, where he was taken sick and was brought back to the Monastery of Cresconzago, and died within three days, on June 27, to be thrust into unconsecrated ground. The Church might well boast that its ban had broken the spirit of the greatest Italian of the age.*

The younger Visconti—Galeazzo, Lucchino, Marco, Giovanni, and Stefano—were not so impressionable, and rapidly concentrated the Ghibelline forces which seemed to be breaking in pieces. To give them their *coup de grâce*, the pope, December 23, 1322, ordered Aicardo, the Archbishop of Milan, and the Inquisition to proceed against the memory of Matteo. January 13, 1323, from the safe retreat of Asti, Aicardo and three inquisitors, Pace da Vedano, Giordano da Montecucho, and Honesto da Pavia, cited him for appearance on February 25, in the Church of Santa Maria at Borgo, near Alessandria, to be tried and judged, whether present or not, and this citation they affixed on the portals of Santa Maria and of the cathedral of Alessandria. On the appointed day they were there, but a military demonstration of Marco Visconti disturbed them, to the prejudice of the faith and impeding of the

---

* Sarpi, Discorso, p. 25 (Ed. Helmstadt). — Albizio, Risposto al P. Paolo Sarpi, p. 75.—Continuat. Guill. Nangiac. ann. 1317.—Bern. Corio, ann. 1322.— Regest. Joann. PP. XXII. No. 89, 93, 94, 95 (Harduin. VII. 1432).

Inquisition. Transferring themselves to the securer walls of Valenza, they heard witnesses and collected testimony, and on March 14 they condemned Matteo as a defiant and unrepentant heretic. He had imposed taxes on the churches and collected them by violence; he had forcibly installed his creatures as superiors in monasteries and his concubines in nunneries; he had imprisoned ecclesiastics and tortured them—some had died in prison and others still lingered there; he had expelled prelates and seized their lands; he had prevented the transmission of money to the papal camera, even sums collected for the Holy Land; he had intercepted and opened letters between the pope and the legates; he had attacked and slain crusaders assembled in Milan for the Holy Land; he had disregarded excommunication, thus showing that he erred in the faith as to the sacraments and the power of the keys; he had prevented the interdict laid upon Milan from being observed; he had obstructed prelates from holding synods and visiting their dioceses, thus favoring heresies and scandals; his enormous crimes show that he is an offshoot of heresy, his ancestors having been suspect and some of them burned, and he has for officials and confidants heretics, such as Francesco Garbagnate, on whom crosses had been imposed; he has expelled the Inquisition from Florence and impeded it for several years; he interposed in favor of Maifreda who was burned; he is an invoker of demons, seeking from them advice and responses; he denies the resurrection of the flesh; he has endured papal excommunication for more than three years, and when cited for examination into his faith he refused to appear. He is, therefore, condemned as a contumacious heretic, all his territories are declared confiscated, he himself deprived of all honors, station, and dignities, and liable to the penalties decreed for heresy, his person to be captured, and his children and grandchildren subjected to the customary disabilities.*

This curious farrago of accusations is worth reciting, as it shows what was regarded as heresy in an opponent of the temporal power of the papacy—that the simplest acts of self-defence against an enemy who was carrying on active war against him were gravely treated as heretical, and constituted valid reasons for inflicting all the tremendous penalties prescribed by the laws for lapses

---

* Ughelli, Italia Sacra, IV. 286–93 (Ed. 1652).

in faith. Politically, however, the portentous sentence was inoperative. Galeazzo maintained the field, and in February, 1324, inflicted a crushing defeat on the papal troops, the cardinal-legate barely escaping by flight, and his general, Raymondo di Cardona being carried a prisoner to Milan. Fresh comminations were necessary to stimulate the faithful, and March 23 John issued a bull condemning Matteo and his five sons, reciting their evil deeds for the most part in the words of the inquisitorial sentence, though the looseness of the whole incrimination is seen in the omission of the most serious charge of all—that of demon-worship—and the defence of Maifreda is replaced by a statement that Matteo had interfered to save Galeazzo, who was now stated to have been a Guglielmite. The bull concludes by offering Holy Land indulgences to all who would assail the Visconti. This was followed, April 12, by another, reciting that the sons of Matteo had been by competent judges duly convicted and sentenced for heresy, but in spite of this, Berthold of Nyffen, calling himself Imperial Vicar of Lombardy, and other representatives of Louis of Bavaria, had assisted the said heretics in resisting the faithful Catholics who had taken up arms against them. They are therefore allowed two months in which to lay down their pretended offices and submit, as they have rendered themselves excommunicate and subject to all the penalties, spiritual and temporal, of fautorship.*

It is scarce worth while to pursue further the dreary details of these forgotten quarrels, except to indicate that the case of the Visconti was in no sense exceptional, and that the same weapons were employed by John against all who crossed his ambitious schemes. The Inquisitor Accursio of Florence had proceeded in the same way against Castruccio of Lucca, as a fautor of heretics; the inquisitors of the March of Ancona had condemned Guido Malapieri, Bishop of Arezzo, and other Ghibellines for supporting Louis of Bavaria. Frà Lamberto del Cordiglio, Inquisitor of Romagnuola, was ordered to use his utmost exertions to punish those within his district. Louis of Bavaria, in his appeal of 1324, states that the same prosecutions were brought, and sentences for heresy pronounced, against Cane della Scala, Passerino, the Marquises of Montferrat, Saluces, Ceva, and others, the Genoese, the Lucchese,

---

* Raynald. ann. 1324, No. 7–12.—Martene Thesaur. II. 754–6.

and the cities of Milan, Como, Bergamo, Cremona, Vercelli, Trino, Vailate, Piacenza, Parma, Brescia, Alessandria, Tortona, Albenga, Pisa, Aretino, etc. We have a specimen of Frà Lamberto's operations in a sentence pronounced by him, February 28, 1328, against Bernardino, Count of Cona. He had already condemned for heresy Rainaldo and Oppizo d' Este, in spite of which Bernardino had visited them in Ferrara, had eaten and drunk with them, and was said to have entered into a league with them. For these offences Lamberto summoned him to stand trial before the Inquisition. He duly appeared, and admitted the visit and banquet, but denied the alliance. Lamberto proceeded to take testimony, called an assembly of experts, and in due form pronounced him a fautor of heretics, condemning him, as such, to degradation from his rank and knighthood, and incapacity to hold any honors ; his estates were confiscated to the Church, his person was to be seized and delivered to the Cardinal-legate Bertrand or to the Inquisition, and his descendants for two generations were declared incapable of holding any office or benefice. All this was for the greater glory of God, for when, in 1326, John begged the clergy of Ireland to send him money, it was, he said, for the purpose of defending the faith against the heretics of Italy. Yet the Holy See was perfectly ready, when occasion suited, to admit that this wholesale distribution of damnation was a mere prostitution of its control over the salvation of mankind. After the Visconti had been reconciled with the papacy, in 1337, Lucchino, who was anxious to have Christian burial for his father, applied to Benedict XII. to reopen the process. In February of that year, accordingly, Benedict wrote to Pace da Vedano, who had conducted the proceedings against the Visconti and against the citizens of Milan, Novara, Bergamo, Cremona, Como, Vercelli, and other places for adhering to them, and who had been rewarded with the bishopric of Trieste, requiring him to send by Pentecost all the documents concerning the trial. The affair was protracted, doubtless owing to political vicissitudes, but at length, in May, 1341, Benedict took no shame in pronouncing the whole proceedings null and void for irregularity and injustice. Still the same machinery was used against Bernabo Visconti, who was summoned by Innocent VI. to appear at Avignon on March 1, 1363, for trial as a heretic, and as he only sent a procurator, he was promptly condemned by Urban V. on March 3, and a crusade was preached against him. In 1364 he made his peace, but in 1372 the perennial quarrel broke out afresh, he was excommunicated by Gregory XI., and in January, 1373, he was summoned to stand another trial for heresy on March 28.[*]

In the same way heresy was the easiest charge to bring against Cola di Rienzo when he disregarded the papal sovereignty over Rome. When he failed to obey the summons to appear he was duly excommunicated for contumacy; the legate Giovanni, Bishop of Spoleto, held an inquisition on him, and in 1350 he was formally declared a heretic. The decision was sent to the Emperor Charles IV., who held him at that time prisoner in Prague, and who dutifully despatched him to Avignon. There, on a first examination, he was condemned to death, but he made his peace, and there appeared to be an opportunity of using him to advantage; he was therefore finally pronounced a good Christian, and was sent back to Rome with a legate.[†]

The Maffredi of Faenza afford a case very similar to that of the Visconti. In 1345 we find them in high favor with Clement VI. In 1350 they are opposing the papal policy of aggrandizement in Romagnuola. Cited to appear in answer to charges of heresy, they refuse to do so, and in July, 1352, are excommunicated for contumacy. In June, 1354, Innocent VI. recites their persistent endurance of this excommunication, and gives them until October 10 to put in an appearance. On that day he condemns them as contumacious heretics, declares them deprived of all lands and honors, and subject to the canonical and civil penalties of heresy. To execute the sentence was not so easy, but in 1356 Innocent offered Louis, King of Hungary, who had shown his zeal against the Ca-

---

[*] Martene Thesaur. II. 743–5.—Wadding. ann. 1324, No. 28; ann. 1326, No. 8; ann. 1327, No. 2.—Ripoll II. 172; VII. 60.—Regest. Clement. PP. V., Romæ, 1885, T. I. Proleg. p. ccxiii.—Theiner Monument. Hibern. et Scotor. No. 462, p. 234.—C. 4, Septimo v. 3.—Mag. Bull. Rom. I. 204.—Baluz. et Mansi III. 227.—Ughelli IV. 294–5, 314.—Raynald. ann. 1362, No. 13; ann. 1363, No. 2, 4; ann. 1372, No. 1; ann. 1373, No. 10, 12.

In spite of the decision of Benedict, Matteo and his sons, Galeazzo, Marco, and Stefano, were still unburied in 1353, when the remaining brother, Giovanni, made another effort to secure Christian sepulture for them.—Raynald. ann. 1353, No. 28.

[†] Raynald. ann. 1348, No. 13–14; ann 1350, No. 5.—Muratori Antiq. VII. 884, 928–32.

thari of Bosnia, three years' tithe of the Hungarian churches if he would put down those sons of damnation, the Maffredi, who have been sentenced as heretics, and other adversaries of the Church, including the Ordelaffi of Friuli. Frà Fortanerio, Patriarch of Grado, was also commissioned to preach a crusade against them, and succeeded in raising an army under Malatesta of Rimini. The appearance of forty thousand Hungarians in the Tarvisina frightened all Italy; the Maffredi succumbed, and in the same year Innocent ordered their absolution and reconciliation.*

It would be easy to multiply instances, but these will probably suffice to show the use made by the Church of heresy as a political agent, and of the Inquisition as a convenient instrumentality for its application. When the Great Schism arose it was natural that the same methods should be employed by the rival popes against each other. As early as 1382 we find Charles III. of Naples confiscating the property of the Bishop of Trivento, just dead, as that of a heretic because he had adhered to Clement VII. In the commission issued in 1409 by Alexander V. to Pons Feugeyron, as Inquisitor of Provence, the adherents of Gregory XII. and of Benedict XIII. are enumerated among the heretics whom he is to exterminate. It happened that Frère Étienne de Combes, Inquisi-

---

* Werunsky Excerptt. ex Registt. Clem. VI. et Innoc. VI. pp. 37, 74, 87, 101.—Wadding. ann. 1356, No. 7, 20.—Raynald. ann. 1356, No. 33.

This abuse of spiritual power for purposes of territorial aggrandizement did not escape the trenchant satire of Erasmus. He describes " the terrible thunderbolt which by a nod will send the souls of mortals to the deepest hell, and which the vicars of Christ discharge with special wrath on those who, instigated by the devil, seek to nibble at the Patrimony of Peter. It is thus they call the cities and territories and revenues for which they fight with fire and sword, spilling much Christian blood, and they believe themselves to be defending like apostles the spouse of Christ, the Church, by driving away those whom they stigmatize as her enemies, as if she could have any worse enemies than impious pontiffs."—Encom. Moriæ. Ed. Lipsiens. 1829, II. 379.

That the character of these papal wars had not been softened since the horrors described above at Ferrara, is seen in the massacre of Cesena, in 1376, when the papal legate, Robert, Cardinal of Geneva, ordered all the inhabitants put to the sword, without distinction of age or sex, after they had admitted him and his bandits into the city under his solemn oath that no injury should be inflicted on them. The number of the slain was estimated at five thousand.—Poggii. Hist. Florentin. Lib. II. ann. 1376.

tor of Toulouse, held to the party of Benedict XIII., and he retali-
ated by imprisoning a number of otherwise unimpeachable Dominicans and Franciscans, including the Provincial of Toulouse and
the Prior of Carcassonne, for which the provincial, as soon as he
had an opportunity, removed him and appointed a successor, giving rise to no little trouble.*

The manner in which the Inquisition was used as an instrument
by the contending factions in the Church is fairly illustrated by
the adventures of John Malkaw, of Prussian Strassburg (Brodnitz).
He was a secular priest and master of theology, deeply learned,
skilful in debate, singularly eloquent, and unflinching even to rash-
ness. Espousing the cause of the Roman popes against their
Avignonese rivals with all the enthusiasm of his fiery nature, he
came to the Rhinelands in 1390, where his sermons stirred the popular heart and proved an effective agency in the strife. After
some severe experiences in Mainz at the hands of the opposite faction, he undertook a pilgrimage to Rome, but tarried at Strassburg,
where he found a congenial field. The city had adhered to Urban
VI. and his successors, but the bishop, Frederic of Blankenheim,
had alienated a portion of his clergy by his oppressions. In the
quarrel he excommunicated them; they appealed to Rome and
had the excommunication set aside, whereupon he went over, with
his following, to Clement VII., the Avignonese antipope, giving
rise to inextricable confusion. The situation was exactly suited to
Malkaw's temperament; he threw himself into the turmoil, and
his fiery eloquence soon threatened to deprive the antipapalists of
their preponderance. According to his own statement he quickly
won over some sixteen thousand schismatics and neutrals, and the
nature of his appeals to the passions of the hour may be guessed
by his own report of a sermon in which he denounced Clement
VII. as less than a man, as worse than the devil, whose portion
was with Antichrist, while his followers were all condemned
schismatics and heretics; neutrals, moreover, were the worst of
men and were deprived of all sacraments. Besides this he assailed
with the same unsparing vehemence the deplorable morals of the
Strassburg clergy, both regular and secular, and in a few weeks he

---

* MSS. Chioccarello T. VIII.—Wadding. ann. 1409, No. 12.—Ripoll II. 510,
522, 566.

thus excited the bitterest hostility. A plot was made to denounce him secretly in Rome as a heretic, so that on his arrival there he might be seized by the Inquisition and burned; his wonderful learning, it was said, could only have been acquired by necromancy; he was accused of being a runaway priest, and it was proposed to arrest him as such, but the people regarded him as an inspired prophet and the project was abandoned. After four weeks of this stormy agitation he resumed his pilgrimage, stopping at Basle and Zurich for missionary work, and finally reached Rome in safety. On his return, in crossing the Pass of St. Bernard, he had the misfortune to lose his papers. News of this reached Basle, and on his arrival there the Mendicants, to whom he was peculiarly obnoxious, demanded of Bishop Imer that he should be arrested as a wanderer without license. The bishop, though belonging to the Roman obedience, yielded, but shortly dismissed him with a friendly caution to return to his home. His dauntless combativeness, however, carried him back to Strassburg, where he again began to preach under the protection of the burgomaster, John Bock. On his previous visit he had been personally threatened by the Dominican inquisitor, Böckeler—the same who in 1400 persecuted the Winkelers—and it was now determined to act with vigor. He had preached but three sermons when he was suddenly arrested, without citation, by the familiars of the inquisitor and thrown in prison, whence he was carried in chains to the episcopal castle of Benfeld and deprived of his books and paper and ink. Sundry examinations followed, in which his rare dexterity scarce enabled him to escape the ingenious efforts to entrap him. Finally, on March 31, 1391, Böckeler summoned an assembly, consisting principally of Mendicants, where he was found guilty of a series of charges, which show how easily the accusation of heresy could be used for the destruction of any man. His real offence was his attacks on the schismatics and on the corruption of the clergy, but nothing of this appears in the articles. It was assumed that he had left his diocese without the consent of his bishop, and this proved him to be a Lollard; that he discharged priestly functions without a license, showing him to be a Vaudois; because his admirers ate what he had already bitten, he was declared to belong to the Brethren of the Free Spirit; because he forbade the discussion as to whether Christ was alive when pierced with the lance, he was asserted to have taught that doctrine, and, therefore, to be a follower of Jean Pierre Olivi. All this was surely enough to warrant his burning, if he should obstinately refuse to recant, but apparently it was felt that the magistracy would decline to execute the sentence, and the assembly contented itself with referring the matter to the bishop and asking his banishment from the diocese. Nothing further is known of the trial, but as, in 1392, Malkaw is found matriculating himself in the University of Cologne, the bishop probably did as he was asked.

We lose sight of Malkaw until about 1414, when we meet him again in Cologne. He had maintained his loyalty to the Roman obedience, but that obedience had been still further fractioned between Gregory XII. and John XXIII. Malkaw's support of the former was accompanied with the same unsparing denunciation of John as he had formerly bestowed on the Avignonese antipopes. The Johannites were heretics, fit only for the stake. Cologne was as attractive a field for the audacious polemic as the Strassburg of a quarter of a century earlier. Two rival candidates for the archbishopric were vindicating their claims in a bloody civil war, one of them as a supporter of Gregory, the other of John. Malkaw was soon recognized as a man whose eloquence was highly dangerous amid an excitable population, and again the Inquisition took hold of him as a heretic. .The inquisitor, Jacob of Soest, a Dominican and professor in the university, seems to have treated him with exceptional leniency, for while the investigation was on foot he was allowed to remain in the St. Ursula quarter, on parole. He broke his word and betook himself to Bacharach, where, under the protection of the Archbishop of Trèves, and of the Palsgrave Louis III., both Gregorians, he maintained the fight with his customary vehemence, assailing the inquisitor and the Johannites, not only in sermons, but in an incessant stream of pamphlets which kept them in a state of indignant alarm. When Cardinal John of Ragusa, Gregory's legate to the Council of Constance, came to Germany, Malkaw had no difficulty in procuring from him absolution from the inquisitorial excommunication, and acquittal of the charge of heresy; and this was confirmed when on healing the schism the council, in July, 1415, declared null and void all prosecutions and sentences arising from it. Still, the wounded pride of the inquisitor and of the University

of Cologne refused to be placated, and for a year they continued
to seek from the Council the condemnation of their enemy.   Their
deputies, however, warned them that the prosecution would be
prolonged, difficult, and costly, and they finally came to the resolution that the action of the Cardinal of Ragusa should be regarded
as binding, so long as Malkaw kept away from the territory of
Cologne, but should be disregarded if he ventured to return—a
very sensible, if somewhat illogical, conclusion.   The obstinacy
with which Benedict XIII. and Clement VIII. maintained their
position after the decision of the Council of Constance prolonged
the struggle in southwestern Europe, and as late as 1428 the remnants of their adherents in Languedoc were proceeded against as
heretics by a special papal commissioner.*

When the schism was past the Inquisition could still be utilized to quell insubordination.   Thomas Connecte, a Carmelite of
Britanny, seems to have been a character somewhat akin to John
Malkaw.   In 1428 we hear of him in Flanders, Artois, Picardy,
and the neighboring provinces, preaching to crowds of fifteen or
twenty thousand souls, denouncing the prevalent vices of the time.
The *hennins*, or tall head-dresses worn by women of rank, were
the object of special vituperation, and he used to give boys certain
days of pardon for following ladies thus attired, and crying " *au
hennin*," or even slyly pulling them off.   Moved by the eloquence
of his sermons, great piles would be made of dice, tables, chess-
boards, cards, nine-pins, head-dresses, and other matters of vice
and luxury, which were duly burned.   The chief source, however,
of the immense popular favor which he enjoyed was his bitter
lashing of the corruption of all ranks of the clergy, particularly
their public concubinage, which won him great applause and
honor.   He seems to have reached the conclusion that the only
cure for this universal sin was the restoration of clerical marriage.
In 1432 he went to Rome in the train of the Venetian ambassadors, to declaim against the vices of the curia.   Usually there was
a good-natured indifference to these attacks—a toleration born of
contempt—but the moment was unpropitious.   The Hussite heresy
had commenced in similar wise, and its persistence was a warning

---

* H. Haupt, Zeitschrift für Kirchengeschichte, 1883, pp. 323 sqq.—Vaissette,
Éd. Privat, X. Pr. 2089.

not to be disregarded. Besides, at that time Eugenius IV. was engaged in a losing struggle with the Council of Basle, which was bent on reforming the curia, in obedience to the universal demand of Christendom, and Sigismund's envoys were representing to Eugenius, with more strength than courtliness, the disastrous results to be expected from his efforts to prorogue the council. Connecte might well be suspected of being an emissary of the fathers of Basle, or, if not, his eloquence at least was a dangerous element in the perturbed state of public opinion. Twice Eugenius sent for him, but he refused to come, pretending to be sick; then the papal treasurer was sent to fetch him, but on his appearing Thomas jumped out of the window and attempted to escape. He was promptly secured and carried before Eugenius, who commissioned the Cardinals of Rouen and Navarre to examine him. These found him suspect of heresy; he was duly tried and condemned as a heretic, and his inconsiderate zeal found a lasting quietus at the stake.*

There are certain points of resemblance between Thomas Connecte and Girolamo Savonarola, but the Italian was a man of far rarer intellectual and spiritual gifts than the Breton. With equal moral earnestness, his plans and aspirations were wider and of more dangerous import, and they led him into a sphere of political activity in which his fate was inevitable from the beginning.

In Italy the revival of letters, while elevating the intellectual faculties, had been accompanied with deeper degradation in both the moral and spiritual condition of society. Without removing superstition, it had rendered scepticism fashionable, and it had weakened the sanctions of religion without supplying another basis for morality. The world has probably never seen a more defiant disregard of all law, human and divine, than that displayed by both the Church and the laity during the pontificates of Sixtus IV. and Innocent VIII. and Alexander VI. Increase of culture and of wealth seemed only to afford new attractions and enlarged opportunities for luxury and vice, and from the highest to the lowest there was indulgence of unbridled appetites,

---

* Monstrelet, II. 53, 127.—Martene Ampl. Coll. VIII. 92.—Altmeyer, Précurseurs de la Réforme aux Pays-Bas, I. 237.

III.—14

with a cynical disregard even of hypocrisy. To the earnest believer it might well seem that God's wrath could not much longer
be restrained, and that calamities must be impending which would
sweep away the wicked and restore to the Church and to mankind the purity and simplicity fondly ascribed to primitive ages.
For centuries a succession of prophets—Joachim of Flora, St.
Catharine of Siena, St. Birgitta of Sweden, the Friends of God,
Tommasino of Foligno, the Monk Telesforo—had arisen with predictions which had been received with reverence, and as time
passed on and human wickedness increased, some new messenger
of God seemed necessary to recall his erring children to a sense of
the retribution in store for them if they should continue deaf to
his voice.

That Savonarola honestly believed himself called to such a
mission, no one who has impartially studied his strange career can
well doubt. His lofty sense of the evils of the time, his profound
conviction that God must interfere to work a change which was
beyond human power, his marvellous success in moving his hearers,
his habits of solitude and of profound meditation, his frequent
ecstasies with their resultant visions might well, in a mind like his,
produce such a belief, which, moreover, was one taught by the received traditions of the Church as within the possibilities of the
experience of any man. Five years before his first appearance in
Florence, a young hermit who had been devotedly serving in a
leper hospital at Volterra, came thither, preaching and predicting
the wrath to come. He had had visions of St. John and the angel
Raphael, and was burdened with a message to unwilling ears.
Such things, we are told by the diarist who happens to record
this, were occurring every day. In 1491 Rome was agitated by a
mysterious prophet who foretold dire calamities impending in the
near future. There was no lack of such earnest men, but, unlike
Savonarola, their influence and their fate were not such as to preserve their memory.*

---

* Burlamacchi, Vita di Savonarola (Baluz. et Mansi I. 533–542).—Luca Landucci., Diario Fiorentino, Firenze, 1883, p. 30.—Steph. Infessuræ Diar. (Eccard.
Corp. Hist. Med. Ævi II. 2000).

Villari shows (La Storia di Gir. Savonarola, Firenze, 1887, I. pp. viii.–xi.)
that the life which passes under the name of Burlamacchi is a *rifacimento* of an
unprinted Latin biography by a disciple of Savonarola. I take this opportunity

When, in his thirtieth year, Savonarola came to Florence, in 1481, his soul was already full of his mission as a reformer. Such opportunity as he had of expressing his convictions from the pulpit he used with earnest zeal, but he produced little effect upon a community sunk in shameless debauchery, and in the Lent of 1486 he was sent to Lombardy. For three years he preached in the Lombard cities, gradually acquiring the power of touching the hearts and consciences of men, and when he was recalled to Florence in 1489, at the instance of Lorenzo de' Medici, he was already known as a preacher of rare ability. The effect of his vigorous eloquence was enhanced by his austere and blameless life, and within a year he was made Prior of San Marco—the convent of the Observantine Dominicans, to which Order he belonged. In 1494 he succeeded in re-establishing the ancient separation of the Dominican province of Tuscany from that of Lombardy, and when he was appointed Vicar-general of the former he was rendered independent of all authority save that of the general, Giovacchino Torriani, who was well affected towards him.*

He claimed to act under the direct inspiration of God, who dictated his words and actions and revealed to him the secrets of the future. Not only was this accepted by the mass of the Florentines, but by some of the keenest and most cultured intellects of the age, such as Francesco Pico della Mirandola and Philippe de Commines. Marsilio Ficino, the Platonist, admitted it, and went further by declaring, in 1494, that only Savonarola's holiness had saved Florence for four years from the vengeance of God on its wickedness. Nardi relates that when, in 1495, Piero de' Medici was making a demonstration upon Florence, he personally heard Savonarola predict that Piero would advance to the gates and retire without accomplishing anything, which duly came to pass. Others of his prophecies were fulfilled, such as those of the deaths of Lorenzo de' Medici and Charles VIII. and the famine of 1497, and his fame spread throughout Italy, while in Florence his influence became

---

of expressing my thanks to Signore Villari, for his kindly courtesy in furnishing me with the second volume of the new edition of his classical work in advance of publication. My obligations to it will be seen in the numerous references made to it below.

* Processo Autentico (Baluz. et Mansi IV. 529, 551).—Burlamacchi (Baluz. et Mansi I. 534-5, 541-2).—Villari, op. cit. Lib. I. c. 5, 9.

dominant. Whenever he preached, from twelve to fifteen thousand persons hung upon his lips, and in the great Duomo of Santa Maria del Fiore it was necessary to build scaffolds and benches to accommodate the thronging crowds, multitudes of whom would have cast themselves into fire at a word from him. He paid special attention to children, and interested them so deeply in his work that we are told they could not be kept in bed on the mornings when he preached, but would hurry to the church in advance of their parents. In the processions which he organized sometimes five or six thousand boys would take part, and he used them most effectively in the moral reforms which he introduced in the dissolute and pleasure-loving city. The boys of Frà Girolamo were regularly organized, with officers who had their several spheres of duty assigned to them, and they became a terror to evil-doers. They entered the taverns and gambling-houses and put a stop to revelry and dicing and card-playing, and no woman dared to appear upon the streets save in fitting attire and with a modest mien. " Here are the boys of the Frate " was a cry which inspired fear in the most reckless, for any resistance to them was at the risk of life. Even the annual horse-races of Santo-Barnabo were suppressed, and it was a sign of Girolamo's waning influence when, in 1497, the Signoria ordered them resumed, saying, " Are we all to become monks ?" From the gayest and wickedest of cities Florence became the most demure, and the pious long looked back with regret to the holy time of Savonarola's rule, and thanked God that they had been allowed to see it.*

In one respect we may regret his puritanism and the zeal of his boys. For the profane mummeries of the carnival in 1498 he substituted a bonfire of objects which he deemed immodest or improper, and the voluntary contributions for this purpose were supplemented by the energy of the boys, who entered houses and palaces and carried off whatever they deemed fit for the holocaust. Precious illuminated MSS., ancient sculptures, pictures, rare tapestries, and priceless works of art thus were mingled with the gew-

---

* Landucci, op. cit. pp. 72, 88, 94, 103, 108, 109, 123-8, 154.—Memoires de Commines Liv. VIII. c. 19.—Marsilii Ficini opp. Ed. 1561, I. 963.—Nardi, Historie Fiorentine, Lib. II. (Ed. 1574, pp. 58, 60).—Perrens, Jérome Savonarole, p. 342.— Burlamacchi (loc. cit. pp. 544-6, 552-3, 556-7).

gaws and vanities of female attire, the mirrors, the musical instruments, the books of divination, astrology, and magic, which went
to make up the total. We can understand the sacrifice of copies
of Boccaccio, but Petrarch might have escaped even Savonarola's
severity of virtue. In this ruthless *auto de fé*, the value of the
objects was such that a Venetian merchant offered the Signoria
twenty thousand scudi for them, which was answered by taking
the would-be chapman's portrait and placing it on top of the pyre.
We cannot wonder that the pile had to be surrounded the night
before by armed guards to prevent the *tiepidi* from robbing it.*

Had Savonarola's lot been cast under the rigid institutions of
feudalism he would probably have exercised a more lasting influence on the moral and religious character of the age. It was his
misfortune that in a republic such as Florence the temptation to
take part in politics was irresistible. We cannot wonder that he
eagerly embraced what seemed to be an opportunity of regenerating a powerful state, through which he might not unreasonably
hope to influence all Italy, and thus effect a reform in Church and
State which would renovate Christendom. This, as he was assured
by the prophetic voice within him, would be followed by the conversion of the infidel, and the reign of Christian charity and love
would commence throughout the world.

Misled by these dazzling day-dreams, he had no scruple in
making a practical use of the almost boundless influence which he
had acquired over the populace of Florence. His teachings led to
the revolution which in 1494 expelled the Medici, and he humanely
averted the pitiless bloodshed which commonly accompanied such
movements in the Italian cities. During the Neapolitan expedition of Charles VIII., in 1494, he did much to cement the alliance
of the republic with that monarch, whom he regarded as the
instrument destined by God to bring about the reform of Italy.
In the reconstruction of the republic in the same year he had, perhaps, more to do than any one else, both in framing its structure
and dictating its laws; and when he induced the people to proclaim Jesus Christ as the King of Florence, he perhaps himself
hardly recognized how, as the mouthpiece of God, he was inevitably assuming the position of a dictator. It was not only in the

---

* Landucci, p. 163.—Burlamacchi, pp. 558-9.—Nardi, Lib. II. pp. 56-7.

pulpit that he instructed his auditors as to their duties as citizens
and gave vent to his inspiration in foretelling the result, for the
leaders of the popular party were constantly in the habit of seeking his advice and obeying his wishes. Yet, personally, for the
most part, he held himself aloof in austere retirement, and left the
management of details to two confidential agents, selected among
the friars of San Marco—Domenico da Pescia, who was somewhat hot-headed and impulsive, and Salvestro Maruffi, who was a
dreamer and somnambulist. In thus descending from the position
of a prophet of God to that of the head of a faction, popularly
known by the contemptuous name of *Piagnoni* or Mourners, he
staked his all upon the continued supremacy of that faction, and
any failure in his political schemes necessarily was fatal to the
larger and nobler plans of which they were the unstable foundation. In addition to this, his resolute adherence to the alliance
with Charles VIII. finally made his removal necessary to the success of the policy of Alexander VI. to unite all the Italian states
against the dangers of another French invasion.*

As though to render failure certain, under a rule dating from
the thirteenth century, the Signoria was changed every two
months, and thus reflected every passing gust of popular passion.
When the critical time came everything turned against him.
The alliance with France, on which he had staked his credit both
as a statesman and a prophet, resulted disastrously.   Charles VIII.
was glad at Fornovo to cut his way back to France with shattered
forces, and he never returned, in spite of the threats of God's wrath
which Savonarola repeatedly transmitted to him.   He not only
left Florence isolated to face the league of Spain, the papacy,
Venice, and Milan, but he disappointed the dearest wish of the
Florentines by violating his pledge to restore to them the stronghold of Pisa.   When the news of this reached Florence, January
1, 1496, the incensed populace held Savonarola responsible, and a
crowd around San Marco at night amused itself with loud threats
to burn "the great hog of a Frate."   Besides this was the severe
distress occasioned by the shrinking of trade and commerce in the
civic disturbances, by the large subsidies paid to Charles VIII., and

---

* Villari, Lib. ii. cap. iv. v.; T. II. App. p. ccxx.—Landucci, pp. 92–4, 112.—
Processo Autentico (Baluze et Mansi IV. 531, 554, 558).

by the drain of the Pisan war, leading to insupportable taxation
and the destruction of public credit, to all which was added the
fearful famine of 1497, followed by pestilence; such a succession
of misfortunes naturally made the unthinking masses dissatisfied
and ready for a change. The *Arrabbiati*, or faction in opposition,
were not slow to take advantage of this revulsion of feeling, and
in this they were supported by the dangerous classes and by
all those on whom the puritan reform had pressed heavily. An
association was formed, known as the Compagnacci, composed of
reckless and dissolute young nobles and their retainers, with Doffo
Spini at their head and the powerful house of Altoviti behind
them, whose primary object was Savonarola's destruction, and
who were ready to resort to desperate measures at the first favorable opportunity.*

Such opportunity could not fail to come. Had Savonarola
contented himself with simply denouncing the corruptions of the
Church and the curia he would have been allowed to exhale his
indignation in safety, as St. Birgitta, Chancellor Gerson, Cardinal
d'Ailly, Nicholas de Clemangis, and so many others among the
most venerated ecclesiastics had done. Pope and cardinal were
used to reviling, and endured it with the utmost good-nature, so
long as profitable abuses were not interfered with, but Savonarola
had made himself a political personage of importance whose influence at Florence was hostile to the policy of the Borgias. Still,
Alexander VI. treated him with good-natured indifference which
for a while almost savored of contempt. When at last his importance was recognized, an attempt was made to bribe him with
the archbishopric of Florence and the cardinalate, but the offer
was spurned with prophetic indignation—" I want no hat but that
of martyrdom, reddened with my own blood!" It was not till
July 21, 1495, after Charles VIII. had abandoned Italy and left
the Florentines to face single-handed the league of which the
papacy was the head, that any antagonism was manifested towards him, and then it assumed the form of a friendly summons to
Rome to give an account of the revelations and prophecies which
he had from God. To this he replied, July 31, excusing himself

---

* Landucci, pp. 110, 112, 122.—Villari, I. 473.—Mémoires de Commines, Liv.
VIII. ch. 19.—Processo Autentico (loc. cit. pp. 524, 541).—Perrens, p. 342.

on the ground of severe fever and dysentery; the republic, more-over, would not permit him to leave its territories for fear of his enemies, as his life had already been attempted by both poison and steel, and he never quitted his convent without a guard; besides, the unfinished reforms in the city required his presence. As soon as possible, however, he would come to Rome, and meanwhile the pope would find what he wanted in a book now printing, contain-ing his prophecies on the renovation of the Church and the de-struction of Italy, a copy of which would be submitted to the holy father as soon as ready.*

However lightly Savonarola might treat this missive, it was a warning not to be disregarded, and for a while he ceased preaching. Suddenly, on September 8, Alexander returned to the charge with a bull intrusted to the rival Franciscans of Santa Croce, in which he ordered the reunion of the Tuscan congregation with the Lombard province; Savonarola's case was submitted to the Lombard Vicar general, Sebastiano de Madiis; Domenico da Pescia and Salvestro Maruffi were required within eight days to betake themselves to Bologna, and Savonarola was commanded to cease preaching until he should present himself in Rome. To this Savonarola replied September 29, in a labored justification, objecting to Sebastiano as a prejudiced and suspected judge, and winding up with a request that the pope should point out any errors in his teaching, which he would at once revoke, and submit whatever he had spoken or written to the judgment of the Holy See. Almost immediately after this the enterprise of Piero de' Medici against Florence ren-dered it impossible for him to keep silent, and, without awaiting the papal answer, on October 11 he ascended the pulpit and ve-hemently exhorted the people to unite in resisting the tyrant. In spite of this insubordination Alexander was satisfied with Sa-vonarola's nominal submission, and on October 16 replied, merely ordering him to preach no more in public or in private until he could conveniently come to Rome, or a fitting person be sent to Florence to decide his case; if he obeyed, then all the papal briefs were suspended. To Alexander the whole affair was simply one of politics. The position of Florence under Savonarola's influence

---

* Guicciardini Lib. III. c. 6.—Burlamacchi, p. 551.—Villari, T. I. pp. civ.-cvii.
—Landucci, p. 106.

was hostile to his designs, but he did not care to push the matter further, provided he could diminish the Frate's power by silencing him.*

His voice, however, was too potent a factor in Florentine affairs for his friends in power to consent to his silence. Long and earnest efforts were made to obtain permission from the pope that he should resume his exhortations during the coming Lent, and at length the request was granted. The sermons on Amos which he then delivered were not of a character to placate the curia, for, besides lashing its vices with terrible earnestness, he took pains to indicate that there were limits to the obedience which he would render to the papal commands. These sermons produced an immense sensation, not only in Florence, but throughout Italy, and on Easter Sunday, April 3, 1496, Alexander assembled fourteen Dominican masters of theology, to whom he denounced their audacious comrade as heretical, schismatic, disobedient, and superstitious. It was admitted that he was responsible for the misfortunes of Piero de' Medici, and it was resolved, with but one dissentient voice, that means must be found to silence him.†

Notwithstanding this he continued, without interference, to preach at intervals until November 2. Even then it is a significant tribute to his power that Alexander again had recourse to indirect means to suppress him. On November 7, 1496, a papal brief was issued creating a congregation of Rome and Tuscany and placing it under a Vicar-general who was to serve for two years, and be ineligible to reappointment except after an interval. Although the first Vicar-general was Giacomo di Sicilia, a friend of Savonarola, the measure was ingeniously framed to deprive him of independence, and he might at any moment be transferred from Florence to another post. To this Savonarola replied with open defiance. In a printed "*Apologia della Congregazione di San Marco*," he declared that the two hundred and fifty friars of his convent would resist to the death, in spite of threats and excommunication, a measure which would result in the perdition of their souls. This was a declaration of open war, and on November 26

---

* Villari, I. 402–7. — Landucci, p. 120. — Diar. Johann. Burchardi (Eccard, Corp. Hist. II. 2151–9).

† Villari, I. 417, 441–5.—Landucci, pp. 125–9.—Perrens, p. 361.

he boldly resumed preaching. The series of sermons on Ezekiel, which he then commenced and continued through the Lent of 1497, shows clearly that he had abandoned all hope of reconciliation with the pope. The Church was worse than a beast, it was an abominable monster which must be purified and renovated by the servants of God, and in this work excommunication was to be welcomed. To a great extent, moreover, these sermons were political speeches, and indicate how absolutely Savonarola from the pulpit dictated the municipal affairs of Florence. The city had been reduced almost to despair in the unequal contest with Pisa, Milan, Venice, and the papacy, but the close of the year 1496 had brought some unexpected successes which seemed to justify Savonarola's exhortations to trust in God, and with the reviving hopes of the republic his credit was to some extent restored.*

Still Alexander, though his wrath was daily growing, shrank from an open rupture and trial of strength, and an effort was made to utilize against Savonarola the traditional antagonism of the Franciscans. The Observantine convent of San Miniato was made the centre of operations, and thither were sent the most renowned preachers of the Order—Domenico da Poza, Michele d' Aquis, Giovanni Tedesco, Giacopo da Brescia, and Francesco della Puglia. It is true that when, January 1, 1497, the Piagnoni, strengthened by recent successes in the field, elected Francesco Valori as Gonfaloniero di Giustizia, he endeavored to stop the Franciscans from preaching, prohibited them from begging bread and wine and necessaries, and boasted that he would starve them out, and one of them was absolutely banished from the city, but the others persevered, and Savonarola was freely denounced as an impostor from the pulpit of Santo-Spirito during Lent. Yet this had no effect upon his followers, and his audiences were larger and more enthusiastic than ever. No better success awaited a nun of S. Maria di Casignano, who came to Florence on the same errand.†

The famine was now at its height, and pestilence became threatening. The latter gave the Signoria, which was now composed of Arrabbiati, an excuse for putting a stop to this pulpit warfare, which doubtless menaced the peace of the city, and on May 3

---

* Villari, I. 489, 492–4, 496, 499, cxlii.; II. 4–6.

† Processo Autentico, pp. 533–4.—Perrens, pp. 189–90.—Landucci, pp. 144–6.

all preaching after Ascension Day (May 4) was forbidden for the reason that, with the approach of summer, crowds would facilitate the dissemination of the plague. That passions were rising beyond control was shown when, the next day, Savonarola preached his farewell sermon in the Duomo. The doors had been broken open in advance, and the pulpit was smeared with filth. The Compagnacci had almost openly made preparations to kill him; they gathered there in force, and interrupted the discourse with a tumult, during which the Frate's friends gathered around him with drawn swords and conveyed him away in safety.*

The affair made an immense sensation throughout Italy, and the sympathies of the Signoria were shown by the absence of any attempt to punish the rioters. Encouraged by this evidence of the weakness of the Piagnoni, on May 13 Alexander sent to the Franciscans a bull ordering them to publish Savonarola as excommunicate and suspect of heresy, and that no one should hold converse with him. This, owing to the fears of the papal commissioner charged with it, was not published till June 18. Before the existence of the bull was known, on May 22, Savonarola had written to Alexander an explanatory letter, in which he offered to submit himself to the judgment of the Church; but two days after the excommunication was published he replied to it with a defence in which he endeavored to prove that the sentence was invalid, and on June 25 he had the audacity to address to Alexander a letter of condolence on the murder of his son, the Duke of Gandia. Fortunately for him another revulsion in municipal politics restored his friends to power on July 1, the elections till the end of the year continued favorable, and he did not cease to receive and administer the sacraments, though, under the previous orders of the Signoria, there was no preaching. It must be borne in mind that at this period there was a spirit of insubordination abroad which regarded the papal censures with slender respect. We have seen above (Vol. II. p. 137) that in 1502 the whole clergy of France, acting under a decision of the University of Paris, openly defied an excommunication launched at them by Alexander VI. It was the same now in Florence. How little the Piagnoni recked of the excommunication is seen by a petition presented September 17 to

---

* Landucci, p. 148.—Villari, II. 18–25.

the Signoria, by the children of Florence, asking that their beloved Frate be allowed to resume preaching, and by a sermon delivered in his defence, October 1, by a Carmelite who declared that in a vision God had told him that Savonarola was a holy man, and that all his opponents would have their tongues torn out and be cast to the dogs. This was flat rebellion against the Holy See, but the only punishment inflicted on the Carmelite by the episcopal officials was a prohibition of further preaching. Meanwhile the Signoria had made earnest but vain attempts to have the excommunication removed, and Savonarola had indignantly refused an offer of the Cardinal of Siena (afterwards Pius III.) to have it withdrawn on the payment of five thousand scudi to a creditor of his. Yet, in spite of this disregard of the papal censures, Savonarola considered himself as still an obedient son of the Church. He employed the enforced leisure of this summer in writing the *Trionfo della Croce*, in which he proved that the papacy is supreme, and that whoever separates himself from the unity and doctrine of Rome separates himself from Christ.*

January, 1498, saw the introduction of a Signoria composed of his zealous partisans, who were not content that a voice so potent should be hushed. It was an ancient custom that they should go in a body and make oblations at the Duomo on Epiphany, which was the anniversary of the Church, and on that day citizens of all parties were astounded at seeing the still excommunicated Savonarola as the celebrant, and the officials humbly kiss his hand. Not content with this act of rebellion, it was arranged that he should recommence preaching. A new Signoria was to be elected for March, the people were becoming divided in their allegiance to him, and his eloquence was held to be indispensable for his own safety and for the continuance in power of the Piagnoni. Accordingly, on February 11 he again appeared in the Duomo, where the old benches and scaffolds had been replaced to accommodate the crowd. Yet many of the more timid Piagnoni abstained from listening to an excommunicate: whether just or unjust, they argued, the sentence of the Church was to be feared.†

---

* Villari, II. 25–8, 35–6, 79 ; App. xxxix.—Processo Autentico, p. 535.—Landucci, pp. 152–3, 157.

† Landucci, pp. 161–2.—Machiavelli, Frammenti istorici (Opere Ed. 1782, II. 58).

In the sermons on Exodus preached during this Lent—the last which he had the opportunity of uttering—Savonarola was more violent than ever. His position was such that he could only justify himself by proving that the papal anathema was worthless, and this he did in terms which excited the liveliest indignation in Rome. A brief was despatched to the Signoria, February 26, commanding them, under pain of interdict, to send Savonarola as a prisoner to Rome. This received no attention, but at the same time another letter was sent to the canons of the Duomo ordering them to close their church to him, and March 1 he appeared there to say that he would preach at San Marco, whither the crowded audience followed him. His fate, however, was sealed the same day by the advent to power of a government composed of a majority of Arrabbiati, with one of his bitterest enemies, Pier Popoleschi, at its head as Gonfaloniero di Giustizia. Yet he was too powerful with the people to be openly attacked, and occasion for his ruin had to be awaited.*

The first act of the new Signoria was an appeal to the pope, March 4, excusing themselves for not obeying his orders and asking for clemency towards Savonarola, whose labors had been so fruitful, and whom the people of Florence believed to be more than man. Possibly this may have been insidiously intended to kindle afresh the papal anger; at all events, Alexander's reply shows that he recognized fully the advantage of the situation. Savonarola is "that miserable worm" who in a sermon recently printed had adjured God to deliver him to hell if he should apply for absolution. The pope will waste no more time in letters; he wants no more words from them, but acts. They must either send their monstrous idol to Rome, or segregate him from all human society, if they wish to escape the interdict which will last until they submit. Yet Savonarola is not to be perpetually silenced, but, after due humiliation, his mouth shall be again opened.†

This reached Florence March 13 and excited a violent discussion. We have seen that an interdict inflicted by the pope might

---

* Landucci, p. 164.—Perrens, p. 231.—Villari, II. App. lxvi.

† Perrens, pp. 232–5, 365–72. Cf. Villari, II. 115.

The obnoxious appeal to God had really been made by Savonarola in his sermon of February 11 (Villari, II. 88).

be not merely a deprivation of spiritual privileges, but that it might comprehend segregation from the outside world and seizure of person and property wherever found, which was ruin to a commercial community. The merchants and bankers of Florence received from their Roman correspondents the most alarming accounts of the papal wrath and of his intention to expose their property to pillage. Fear took possession of the city, as rumors spread from day to day that the dreaded interdict had been proclaimed. It shows the immense influence still wielded by Savonarola that, after earnest discussions and various devices, the Signoria could only bring itself, March 17, to send to him five citizens at night to beg him to suspend preaching for the time. He had promised that, while he would not obey the pope, he would respect the wishes of the civil power, but when this request reached him he replied that he must first seek the will of Him who had ordered him to preach. The next day, from the pulpit of San Marco, he gave his answer— "Listen, for this is what the Lord saith : In asking this Frate to give up preaching it is to Me that the request is made, and not to him, for it is I who preach ; it is I who grant the request and who do not grant it. The Lord assents as regards the preaching, but not as regards your salvation." *

It was impossible to yield more awkwardly or in a manner more convincing of self-deception, and Savonarola's enemies grew correspondingly bold. The Franciscans thundered triumphantly from the pulpits at their command; the disorderly elements, wearied with the rule of righteousness, commenced to agitate for the license which they could see was soon to be theirs. Profane scoffers commenced to ridicule the Frate openly in the streets, and within a week placards were posted on the walls urging the burning of the palaces of Francesco Valori and Paolo Antonio Soderini, two of his leading supporters. The agents of the Duke of Milan were not far wrong when they exultingly wrote to him predicting the speedy downfall of the Frate, by fair means or foul.†

Just at this juncture there came to light a desperate expedient to which Savonarola had recourse. After giving Alexander fair warning, March 13, to look to his safety, for there could no longer

---

* Perrens, pp. 237, 238.—Landucci, pp. 164–66.

† Landucci, p. 166.—Villari, II. App. pp. lviii.–lxii.

be truce between them, Savonarola appealed to the sovereigns of Christendom, in letters purporting to be written under the direct command of God and in his name, calling upon the monarchs to convoke a general council for the reformation of the Church. It was diseased, from the highest to the lowest, and on account of its intolerable stench God had not permitted it to have a lawful head. Alexander VI. was not pope and was not eligible to the papacy, not only by reason of the simony through which he had bought the tiara, and the wickedness which, when exposed, would excite universal execration, but also because he was not a Christian, and not even a believer in God. All this Savonarola offered to prove by evidence and by miracles which God would execute to convince the most sceptical. This portentous epistle, with trifling variants, was to be addressed to the Kings of France, Spain, England, and Hungary, and to the emperor. A preliminary missive from Domenico Mazzinghi to Giovanni Guasconi, Florentine Ambassador in France, happened to be intercepted by the Duke of Milan, who was hostile to Savonarola, and who promptly forwarded it to the pope.[*]

Alexander's wrath can easily be conceived. It was not so much the personal accusations, which he was ready to dismiss with cynical indifference, as the effort to bring about the convocation of a council which, since those of Constance and Basle, had ever been the cry of the reformer and the terror of the papacy. In the existing discontent of Christendom it was an ever-present danger. So recently as 1482 the half-crazy Andreas, Archbishop of Krain, had set all Europe in an uproar by convoking from Basle a council on his own responsibility, and defying for six months, under the protection of the magistrates, the efforts of Sixtus IV. and the anathemas of the inquisitor, Henry Institoris, until Frederic III., after balancing awhile, had him thrown into jail. In the same year, 1482, Ferdinand and Isabella, by the threat of calling a council, brought Sixtus to renounce the claim of filling the sees of Spain with his own creatures. In 1495 a rumor was current that the emperor was about to cite the pope to a council to be held in

---

* Villari, II. 129, 132-5; App. pp. lxviii.-lxxi., clxxi. — Baluz. et Mansi I. 584-5.—Perrens. pp. 373-5.—Burlamacchi, p. 551.—In his confession of May 21, Savonarola stated that the idea of the council had only suggested itself to him three months previously (Villari, II. App. cxcii.).

Florence. Some years earlier the rebellious Cardinal Giuliano della Rovere, who had fled to France, persistently urged Charles VIII. to assemble a general council; in 1497 Charles submitted the question to the University of Paris, and the University pronounced in its favor. Wild as was Savonarola's notion that he could, single-handed, stimulate the princes to such action, it was, nevertheless, a dart aimed at the mortal spot of the papacy, and the combat thereafter was one in which no quarter could be given.*

The end, in fact, was inevitable, but it came sooner and more dramatically than the shrewdest observer could have anticipated. It is impossible, amid the conflicting statements of friends and foes, to determine with positiveness the successive steps leading to the strange *Sperimento del Fuoco* which was the proximate occasion of the catastrophe, but it probably occurred in this wise: Frà Girolamo being silenced, Domenico da Pescia took his place. Matters were clearly growing desperate, and in his indiscreet zeal Domenico offered to prove the truth of his master's cause by throwing himself from the roof of the Palazzo de' Signori, by casting himself into the river, or by entering fire. Probably this was only a rhetorical flourish without settled purpose, but the Franciscan, Francesco della Puglia, who was preaching with much effect at the Church of Santa-Croce, took it up and offered to share the ordeal with Frà Girolamo. The latter, however, refused to undertake it unless a papal legate and ambassadors from all Christian princes could be present, so that it might be made the commencement of a general reform in the Church. Frà Domenico then accepted the challenge, and on March 27 or 28 he caused to be affixed to the portal of Santa-Croce a paper in which he offered to prove, by argument or miracle, these propositions: I. The Church

* Landucci, p. 113.—Chron. Glassberger ann. 1482.—Raynald. ann. 1492, No. 25.—Pulgar, Cronica de los Reyes Catolicos, II. civ.—Comba, La Riforma in Italia, I. 491.—Nardi, Lib. II. (p. 79).

The contemporary Glassberger says of Andreas of Krain's attempt, "Nisi enim auctoritas imperatoris intervenisset maximum in ecclesia schisma subortum fuisset. Omnes enim æmuli domini papæ ad domini imperatoris consensum respiciebant pro concilio celebrando." A year's imprisonment in chains exhausted the resolution of Andreas, who executed a solemn recantation of his invectives against the Holy See. This was sent with a petition for pardon to Sixtus IV., who granted it, but before the return of the messengers the unhappy reformer hanged himself in his cell (ubi sup. ann. 1483).

of God requires renovation; II. The Church is to be scourged; III. The Church will be renovated; IV. After chastisement Flor ence will be renovated and will prosper; V. The infidel will be converted; VI. The excommunication of Frà Girolamo is void; VII. There is no sin in not observing the excommunication. Frà Francesco reasonably enough said that most of these propositions were incapable of argument, but, as a demonstration was desired, he would enter fire with Frà Domenico, although he fully expected to be burned; still, he was willing to make the sacrifice in order to liberate the Florentines from their false idol.*

Passions were fierce on both sides, and eager partisans kept the city in an uproar. To prevent an outbreak the Signoria sent for both disputants and caused them to enter into a written agreement, March 30, to undergo this strange trial. Three hundred years earlier it would have seemed reasonable enough, but the Council of Lateran, in 1215, had reprobated ordeals of all kinds, and they had been definitely marked with the ban of the Church. When it came to the point Frà Francesco said that he had no quarrel with Domenico; that if Savonarola would undergo the trial, he was ready to share it, but with any one else he would only produce a champion—and one was readily found in the person of Frà Giuliano Rondinelli, a noble Florentine of the Order. On the other side, all the friars of San Marco, nearly three hundred in number, signed the agreement pledging to submit themselves to the ordeal, and Savonarola declared that in such a cause any one could do so without risk. So great was the enthusiasm that when, on the day before the trial, he preached on the subject in San Marco, all the audience rose in mass, and offered to take Domenico's place in vindicating the truth. The conditions prescribed by the Signoria were, that if the Dominican champion perished, whether alone or with his rival, Savonarola should leave the city until officially recalled; if the Franciscan alone succumbed, then Frà Francesco should do likewise; and the same was decreed for either side that should decline the ordeal at the last moment.†

---

* Burlamacchi, p. 559.—Landucci, pp. 166-7.—Processo Autentico, pp. 535-7. —Villari, II. App. lxxi. sqq.

† Landucci, pp. 167-8.—Processo Autentico, pp. 536-8.—Villari, II. App. xci.-xciii.

III.—15

The Signoria appointed ten citizens to conduct the trial, and fixed it for April 6, but postponed it for a day in hopes of receiving from the pope a negative answer to an application for permission—a refusal which came, but came too late, possibly delayed on purpose. On April 7, accordingly, the preparations were completed. In the Piazza de' Signori a huge pile of dry wood was built the height of a man's eyes, with a central gangway through which the champions were to pass. It was plentifully supplied with gunpowder, oil, sulphur, and spirits, to insure the rapid spread of the flames, and when lighted at one end the contestants were to enter at the other, which was to be set on fire behind them, so as to cut off all retreat. An immense mass of earnest spectators filled the piazza, and every window and house-top was crowded. These were mostly partisans of Savonarola, and the Franciscans were cowed until cheered by the arrival of the Compagnacci, the young nobles fully armed on their war-horses, and each accompanied by eight or ten retainers—some five hundred in all, with Doffo Spini at their head.[*]

First came on the scene the Franciscans, anxious and terrified. Then marched in procession the Dominicans, about two hundred in number, chanting psalms. Both parties went before the Signoria, when the Franciscans, professing fear of magic arts, demanded that Domenico should change his garments. Although this was promptly acceded to, and both champions were clothed anew, considerable time was consumed in the details. The Dominicans claimed that Domenico should be allowed to carry a crucifix in his right hand and a consecrated wafer in his left. An objection being made to the crucifix he agreed to abandon it, but was unmoved by the cry of horror with which the proposition as to the host was received. Savonarola was firm. It had been revealed to Frà Salvestro that the sacrament was indispensable, and the matter was hotly disputed until the shades of evening fell, when the Signoria announced that the ordeal was abandoned, and the Franciscans withdrew, followed by the Dominicans. The crowd which had patiently waited through torrents of rain, and a storm in which the air seemed filled with howling demons, were enraged

---

* Perrens, pp. 379–81.—Burlamacchi, pp. 560, 562.—Landucci, p. 168.—Processo Autentico, pp. 540–1.

at the loss of the promised spectacle, and a heavy armed escort was necessary to convey the Dominicans in safety back to San Marco. Had the matter been one with which reason had anything to do, we might perhaps wonder that it was regarded as a triumph for the Franciscans; but Savonarola had so confidently promised a miracle, and had been so implicitly believed by his followers, that they accepted the drawn battle as a defeat, and as a confession that he could not rely on the interposition of God. Their faith in their prophet was shaken, while the exultant Compagnacci lavished abuse on him, and they had not a word to utter in his defence.*

His enemies were prompt in following up their advantage. The next day was Palm Sunday. The streets were full of triumphant Arrabbiati, and such Piagnoni as showed themselves were pursued with jeers and pelted with stones. At vespers, the Dominican Mariano de' Ughi attempted to preach in the Duomo, which was crowded, but the Compagnacci were there in force, interrupted the sermon, ordered the audience to disperse, and those who resisted were assailed and wounded. Then arose the cry, "To San Marco!" and the crowd hurried thither. Already the doors of the Dominican church had been surrounded by boys whose cries disturbed the service within, and who, when ordered to be silent, had replied with showers of stones which compelled the entrance to be closed. As the crowd surged around, the worshippers were glad to escape with their lives through the cloisters. Francesco Valori and Paolo Antonio Soderini were there in consultation with Savonarola. Soderini made good his exit from the city; Valori was seized while skirting the walls, and carried in front of his palace, which had already been attacked by the Compagnacci. Before his eyes, his wife, who was pleading with the assailants from a window, was slain with a missile, one of his children and a female servant were wounded, and the palace was sacked and burned, after which he was struck from behind and killed by his enemies of the families Tornabuoni and Ridolfi.

---

* Landucci, pp. 168-9.—Processo Autentico, p. 542.—Burlamacchi, p. 563.— Villari, II. App. pp. lxxv.-lxxx., lxxxiii.-xc.—Guicciardini, Lib. III. c. 6.

The good Florentines did not fail to point out that the sudden death of Charles VIII., on this same April 7, was a visitation upon him for having abandoned Savonarola and the republic.—Nardi, Lib. II. p. 80.

Two other houses of Savonarola's partisans were likewise pillaged and burned.*

In the midst of the uproar there came forth successive proclamations from the Signoria ordering Savonarola to quit the Florentine territories within twelve hours, and all laymen to leave the church of San Marco within one hour. Although these were followed by others threatening death to any one entering the church, they virtually legalized the riot, showing what had doubtless been the secret springs that set it in motion. The assault on San Marco then became a regular siege. Matters had for some time looked so threatening that during the past fortnight the friars had been secretly providing themselves with arms. These they and their friends used gallantly, even against the express commands of Savonarola, and a *melée* occurred in which more than a hundred on both sides were killed and wounded. At last the Signoria sent guards to capture Savonarola and his principal aids, Domenico and Salvestro, with a pledge that no harm should be done to them. Resistance ceased; the two former were found in the library, but Salvestro had hidden himself, and was not captured till the next day. The prisoners were ironed hand and foot and carried through the streets, where their guards could not protect them from kicks and buffets by the raging mob.†

The next day there was comparative quiet. The revolution in which the aristocracy had allied itself with the dangerous classes was complete. The Piagnoni were thoroughly cowed. Opprobrious epithets were freely lavished on Savonarola by the victors, and any one daring to utter a word in his defence would have been slain on the spot. To render the triumph permanent, however, it was necessary first to discredit him utterly with the people and then to despatch him. No time was lost in preparing to give a judicial appearance to the foregone conclusion. During the day a tribunal of seventeen members selected from among his special enemies, such as Doffo Spini, was nominated, which set promptly to work on April 10, although its formal commission, including power to use torture, was not made out until the

---

* Landucci, p. 170.—Processo Autentico, pp. 534, 543.—Burlamacchi, p. 564.
† Landucci, p. 171.—Processo Autentico, pp. 544, 549.—Burlamacchi, p. 564.
—Nardi, Lib. ii. p. 78.—Villari, II. 173–77; App. pp. xciv., ccxxv., ccxxxiii.

11th. Papal authority to disregard the clerical immunity of the prisoners was applied for, but the proceedings were not delayed by waiting for the answer, which, of course, was favorable, and two papal commissioners were adjoined to the tribunal. Savonarola and his companions, still ironed hand and foot, were carried to the Bargello. The official account states that he was first interrogated kindly, but as he would not confess he was threatened with torture, and this proving ineffectual he was subjected to three and a half *tratti di fune*. This was a customary form of torture, known as the strappado, which consisted in tying the prisoner's hands behind his back, then hoisting him by a rope fastened to his wrists, letting him drop from a height and arresting him with a jerk before his feet reached the floor. Sometimes heavy weights were attached to the feet to render the operation more severe. Officially it is stated that this first application was sufficient to lead him to confess freely, but the general belief at the time was that it was repeated with extreme severity.[*]

Be this as it may, Savonarola's nervous organization was too sensitive for him to endure agony which he knew would be indefinitely prolonged by those determined to effect a predestined result. He entreated to be released from the torture and promised to reveal everything. His examination lasted until April 18, but

---

[*] Landucci, pp. 171-2.—Villari, II. 178; App. p. clxv.—Processo Autentico, pp. 550-1.

Violi (Villari, II. App. cxvi.-vii.) says that the torture was repeatedly applied —on one evening no less than fourteen times from the pulley to the floor, and that his arms were so injured that he was unable to feed himself; but this must be exaggerated in view of the pious treatises which he wrote while in prison. Burlamacchi says that he was tortured repeatedly both with cord and fire (pp. 566, 568). Burchard, the papal prothonotary, states that he was tortured seven times, and Burchard was likely to know and not likely to exaggerate (Burch. Diar. *ap.* Preuves des Mémoires de Commines, Bruxelles, 1706, p. 424). The expression of Commines, who was well-informed, is "*le gesnèrent à merveilles*" (Mémoires, Lib. VIII. ch. 19). But the most emphatic evidence is that of the Signoria, who, in answer to the reproaches of Alexander at their tardiness, declare that they had to do with a man of great endurance; they had assiduously tortured him for many days with slender results, which they would suppress until they could force him to reveal all his secrets—"multa et assidua quæstione, multis diebus, per vim vix pauca extorsimus, quæ nunc celare animus erat donec omnia nobis paterent sui animi involucra" (Villari, II. 197).

even in his complying frame of mind the resultant confession required to be manipulated before it could be made public.   For this infamous piece of work a fitting instrument was at hand. Ser Ceccone was an old partisan of the Medici whose life had been saved by Savonarola's secretly giving him refuge in San Marco, and who now repaid the benefit by sacrificing his benefactor.   As a notary he was familiar with such work, and under his skilful hands the incoherent answers of Savonarola were moulded into a narrative which is the most abject of self-accusations and most compromising to all his friends.*

He is made to represent himself as being from the first a conscious impostor, whose sole object was to gain power by deceiving the people.   If his project of convoking a council had resulted in his being chosen pope he would not have refused the position, but if not he would at all events have become the foremost man in the world.   For his own purposes he had arrayed the citizens against each other and caused a rupture between the city and the Holy See, striving to erect a government on the Venetian model, with Francesco Valori as perpetual doge.   The animus of the trial is clearly revealed in the scant attention paid to his spiritual aberrations, which were the sole offences for which he could be convicted, and the immense detail devoted to his political activity, and to his relations with all obnoxious citizens whom it was desired to involve in his ruin.   Had there been any pretence of observing ordinary judicial forms, the completeness with which he was represented as abasing himself would have overreached its purpose.   In forcing him to confess that he was no prophet, and that he had always secretly believed the papal excommunication to be valid, he was relieved from the charge of persistent heresy, and he could legally be only sentenced to penance; but, as there

---

* Landucci, p. 172.—Processo Autentico, p. 550.—Perrens, pp. 267-8.—Burlamacchi, pp. 566-7.—Villari, II. 188, 193; App. cxviii.-xxi.

It is part of the Savonarola legend that Savonarola threatened Ser Ceccone with death within a year if he did not remove certain interpolations from the confession, and that the prediction was verified, Ceccone dying within the time, unhouselled, and refusing in despair the consolations of religion (Burlamacchi, p. 575.—Violi *ap.* Villari, II. App. cxxvii.).

Ceccone performed the same office for the confession of Frà Domenico (Villari, II. App. Doc. xxvii.).

was no intention of being restricted to legal rules, the first object was to discredit him with the people, after which he could be judicially murdered with impunity.*

The object was thoroughly attained. On April 19, in the great hall of the council, the confession was publicly read in the presence of all who might see fit to attend. The effect produced is well described by the honest Luca Landucci, who had been an earnest and devout, though timid, follower of Frà Girolamo, and who now grieved bitterly at the disappearance of his illusions, and at the shattering of the gorgeous day-dreams in which the disciples had nursed themselves. Deep was his anguish as he listened to the confession of one " whom we believed to be a prophet and who now confessed that he was no prophet, and that what he preached was not revealed to him by God. I was stupefied and my very soul was filled with grief to see the destruction of such an edifice, which crumbled because it was founded on a lie. I had expected to see Florence a new Jerusalem, whence should issue the laws and the splendor and the example of the holy life; to see the renovation of the Church, the conversion of the infidel, and the rejoicing of the good. I found the reverse of all this, and I swallowed the dose"—a natural enough metaphor, seeing that Landucci was an apothecary.†

Yet even with this the Signoria was not satisfied. On April 21 a new trial was ordered; Savonarola was tortured again, and further avowals of his political action were wrung from him,‡ while a general arrest was made of those who were compromised by his confessions, and those of Domenico and Salvestro, creating a terror so widespread that large numbers of his followers fled from the city. On the 27th the prisoners were taken to the Bargello and so tortured that during the whole of the afternoon their shrieks were heard by the passers-by, but nothing was wrung

---

* Processo Autentico, pp. 551–64, 567.—Villari, II. App. cxlvii. sqq.

Violi states that the confession as interpolated by Ceccone was printed and circulated by the Signoria as a justification of their action, but that it proved so unsatisfactory to the public that in a few days all copies were ordered by proclamation to be surrendered (Villari, II. App. p. cxiv.).

† Landucci, p. 173.—Burlamacchi, p. 567.

‡ This confession was never made public. Villari, who discovered the MS., has printed it, App. p. clxxv.

from them to incriminate Savonarola.   The officials in power had
but a short time for action, as their term of office ended with the
month, although by arbitrary and illegal devices they secured successors of their own party.   Their last official act, on the 30th,
was the exile of ten of the accused citizens, and the imposition on
twenty-three of various fines, amounting in all to twelve thousand
florins.*

The new government which came in power May 1 at once discharged the imprisoned citizens, but kept Savonarola and his companions.   These, as Dominicans, were not justiciable by the civil
power, but the Signoria immediately applied to Alexander for
authority to condemn and execute them.   He refused, and ordered
them to be delivered to him for judgment, as he had already done
when the news reached him of Savonarola's capture.   To this the
republic demurred, doubtless for the reason privately alleged to
the ambassador, that Savonarola was privy to too many state
secrets to be intrusted to the Roman curia ; but it suggested that
the pope might send commissioners to Florence to conduct the
proceedings in his name.   To this he assented.   In a brief of May
11 the Bishop of Vaison, the suffragan of the Archbishop of Florence, is instructed to degrade the culprits from holy orders, at the
requisition of the commissioners who had been empowered to conduct the examination and trial to final sentence.   In the selection
of these commissioners the Inquisition does not appear.   Even
had it not fallen too low in popular estimation to be intrusted
with an affair of so much moment, in Tuscany it was Franciscan,
and to have given special authority to the existing inquisitor,
Frà Francesco da Montalcino, would have been injudicious in view
of the part taken by the Franciscans in the downfall of Savonarola.
Alexander showed his customary shrewdness in selecting for the
miserable work the Dominican general, Giovacchino Torriani,
who bore the reputation of a kind-hearted and humane man.   He
was but a stalking-horse, however, for the real actor was his associate, Francesco Romolino, a clerk of Lerida, whose zeal in the
infamous business was rewarded with the cardinalate and archbishopric of Palermo.   After all, their duties were only ministerial

---

* Landucci, p. 174.—Processo Autentico, p. 563.—Villari, II. 210, 217.—Nardi,
Lib. II. p. 79.

and not judicial, for the matter had been prejudged at Rome. Romolino openly boasted, "We shall have a fine bonfire, for I bring the sentence with me." *

The commissioners reached Florence May 19, and lost no time in accomplishing their object. The only result of the papal intervention was to subject the victims to a surplusage of agony and shame. For form's sake, the papal judges could not accept the proceedings already had, but must inflict on Savonarola a third trial. Brought before Romolino on the 20th, he retracted his confession as extorted by torture, and asserted that he was an envoy of God. Under the inquisitorial formulas this retraction of confession rendered him a relapsed heretic, who could be burned without further ceremony, but his judges wanted to obtain information desired by Alexander, and again the sufferer was repeatedly subjected to the strappado, when he withdrew his retraction. Special inquiries were directed to ascertain whether the Cardinal of Naples had been privy to the design of convoking a general council, and under the stress of reiterated torture Savonarola was brought to admit this on the 21st, but on the 22d he withdrew the assertion, and the whole confession, although manipulated by the skilful hand of Ser Ceccone, was so nearly a repetition of the previous one that it was never given to the public. This mattered little, however, for the whole proceedings were a barefaced mockery of justice. From some oversight Domenico da Pescia's name had not been included in the papal commission. He was an individual of no personal importance, but some zealous Florentine warned Romolino that there might be danger in sparing him, when the commissioner carelessly replied " A *frataccio* more or less makes no difference," and his name was added to the sentence. He was an impenitent heretic, for with heroic firmness he had borne the most excruciating torture without retracting his faith in his beloved prophet.†

---

* Landucci, p. 174.—Nardi, Lib. II. p. 79.—Wadding. ann. 1496, No. 7.— Perrens, p. 399.—Processo Autentico, p. 522.—Burlamacchi, p. 568.—Brev. Hist. Ord. Prædicat. (Martene Ampl. Coll. VI. 393).

† Landucci, p. 176.—Nardi, Lib. II. pp. 80–1.—Burlamacchi, p. 568.—Violi (Villari, II. App. cxxv.).—Villari, II. 206–8, 229–33; App. clxxxiv., cxciv., cxcvii.

There was one peculiarity in this examination before Romolino which I have not seen recorded elsewhere. During the interrogatory of May 21 Savonarola

The accused were at least spared the torment of suspense. On the 22d judgment was pronounced. They were condemned as heretics and schismatics, rebels from the Church, sowers of tares and revealers of confessions, and were sentenced to be abandoned to the secular arm. To justify relaxation, it was requisite that the culprit should be a relapsed or a defiant heretic, and Savonarola was not regarded as coming under either category. He had always declared his readiness to retract anything which Rome might define as erroneous. He had confessed all that had been required of him, nor was his retraction when removed from torture treated as a relapse, for he and his companions were admitted to communion before execution, without undergoing the ceremony of abjuration, which shows that they were not considered as heretics, nor cut off from the Church. In fact, as though to complete the irregularity of the whole transaction, Savonarola himself was allowed to act as the celebrant, and to perform the sacred mysteries on the morning of the execution. All this went for nothing, however, when a Borgia was eager for revenge. On the previous evening a great pile had been built in the piazza. The next morning, May 23, the ceremony of degradation from holy orders was performed in public, after which the convicts were handed over to the secular magistrates. Was it hypocrisy or remorse that led Romolino at this moment to give to his victims, in the name of Alexander, plenary indulgence of their sins, thus restoring them to a state of primal innocence? Irregular as the whole affair had been, it was rendered still more so by the Signoria, which modified the customary penalty to hanging before the burning, and the three martyrs endured their fate in silence.*

The utmost care was taken that the bodies should be utterly consumed, after which every fragment of ashes was scrupulously gathered up and thrown into the Arno, in order to prevent the preservation of relics. Yet, at the risk of their lives, some earnest disciples secretly managed to secure a few floating coals, as well

---

was subjected to fresh torture as a preliminary to asking his confirmation of the statements just made under repeated tortures (Villari, II. App. cxcvi.).

* Landucci, pp. 176–7.—Processo Autentico, p. 546.—Villari, II. 239; App. cxcviii.—Cantù, Eretici d'Italia, I. 229.—Burlamacchi, pp. 569–70.—Nardi, Lib. II. p. 82.

as some fragments of garments, which were treasured and venerated even to recent times. Though many of the believers, like
honest Landucci, were disillusioned, many were persistent in the
faith, and for a long while lived in the daily expectation of Savonarola's advent, like a new Messiah, to work out the renovation of
Christianity and the conversion of the infidel—the realization of
the splendid promises with which he had beguiled himself and
them. So profound and lasting was the impression made by his
terrible fate that for more than two centuries, until 1703, the place
of execution was secretly strewed with flowers on the night of the
anniversary, May 23.*

The papal commissioners reaped a harvest by summoning to
Rome the followers of Savonarola, and then speculating on their
fears by selling them exemptions. Florence itself was not long
in realizing the strength of the reaction against the puritanic
methods which Savonarola had enforced. The streets again became filled with reckless desperadoes, quarrels and murders were
frequent, gambling was unchecked, and license reigned supreme.
Nardi tells us that it seemed as if decency and virtue had been
prohibited by law, and the common remark was, that since the
coming of Mahomet no such scandal had been inflicted upon the
Church of God. As Landucci says, it seemed as if hell had broken
loose. As though in very wantonness to show the Church what
were the allies whom it had sought in the effort to crush unwelcome reform, on the following Christmas eve a horse was brought
into the Duomo, and deliberately tortured to death, goats were
let loose in San Marco, and in all the churches assafœtida was
placed in the censers; nor does it seem that any punishment was
visited upon the perpetrators of these public sacrileges. The
Church had used the sceptics to gain her ends, and could not complain of the manner in which they repaid her for her assistance in
the unholy alliance.†

---

* Landucci, p. 178.—Perrens, p. 281.—Processo Autentico, p. 547.—Nardi,
Lib. II. p. 82.—Villari, II. 251.

Burlamacchi's relation (pp. 570-1) of the manner in which an arm, a hand,
and the heart of Savonarola were preserved for the veneration of the faithful,
has the evident appearance of a legend to justify the authenticity of the relics.

† Nardi, Lib. II. pp. 82-3.—Landucci, pp. 190-1.

Savonarola had built his house upon the sand, and was swept away by the waters.   Yet, in spite of his execution as a heretic, the Church has tacitly confessed its own crime by admitting that he was no heretic, but rather a saint, and the most convenient evasion of responsibility was devoutly to refer the whole matter, as Luke Wadding does, to the mysterious judgment of God.   Even Torriani and Romolino, after burning him, when they ordered, May 27, under pain of excommunication, all his writings to be de-livered up to them for examination, were unable to discover any heretical opinions, and were obliged to return them without eras-ures.   Perhaps it might have been as well to do this before con-demning him.   Paul III. declared that he would hold as a heretic any one who should assail the memory of Frà Girolamo; and Paul IV. had his works rigorously examined by a special congre-gation, which declared that they contained no heresy.   Fifteen of his sermons, denunciatory of ecclesiastical abuses, and his treatise *De Veritate Prophetica*, were placed upon the index as unfitted for general reading, *donec corrigantur*, but not as heretical. Benedict XIV., in his great work, *De Servorum Dei Beatificatione*, includes Savonarola's name in a list of the saints and men illustri-ous for sanctity.   Images of him graced with the nimbus of sanc-tity were allowed to be publicly sold, and St. Filippo Neri kept one of these constantly by him.   St. Francesco di Paola held him to be a saint.   St. Catarina Ricci used to invoke him as a saint, and considered his suffrage peculiarly efficacious; when she was canonized, her action with regard to this was brought before the consistory, and was thoroughly discussed.   Prospero Lambertini, afterwards Benedict XIV., was the *Promotor fidei*, and investi-gated the matter carefully, coming to the conclusion that this in no degree detracted from the merits of St. Catarina.   Benedict XIII. also examined the case thoroughly, and, dreading a renewal of the old controversy as to the justice of Savonarola's sentence, ordered the discussion to cease and the proceedings to continue without reference to it, which was a virtual decision in favor of the martyr's saintliness.   In S. Maria Novella and S. Marco he is pictured as a saint, and in the frescos of the Vatican Raphael in-cluded him among the doctors of the Church.   The Dominicans long cherished his memory, and were greatly disposed to regard him as a genuine prophet and uncanonized saint.   When Clement

VIII., in 1598, hoped to acquire Ferrara, he is said to have made a vow that if successful he would canonize Savonarola, and the hopes of the Dominicans grew so sanguine that they composed a litany for him in advance. In fact, in many of the Dominican convents of Italy during the sixteenth century, on the anniversary of his execution an office was sung to him as to a martyr. His marvellous career thus furnishes the exact antithesis of that of his Ferrarese compatriot, Armanno Pongilupo—the one was venerated as a saint and then burned as a heretic, the other was burned as a heretic and then venerated as a saint.*

---

* Wadding. ann. 1498, No. 23.—Landucci, p. 178.—Perrens, pp. 296–7.—Processo Autentico, pp. 524, 528.—Cantù, Eretici d'Italia, I. 234–5.—Benedicti PP. XIV. De Servorum Dei Beatificatione, Lib. III. c. xxv. §§ 17–20.—Brev. Hist. Ord. Prædic. (Martene, Ampl. Coll. VI. 394).—Reusch, Der Index der verbotenen Bücher, I. 368.

A goodly catalogue of miracles performed by Savonarola's intercession will be found piously chronicled by Burlamacchi and Bottonio (Baluz. et Mansi I. pp. 571–83).

CHAPTER V.

POLITICAL HERESY UTILIZED BY THE STATE.

It was inevitable that secular potentates should follow the example of the Church in the employment of a weapon so efficient as the charge of heresy, when they chanced to be in the position of controlling the ecclesiastical organization.

A typical illustration of this is seen when, during the anarchy which prevailed in Rome after the death of Innocent VII. in 1406, Basilio Ordelaffi incurred the enmity of the Colonnas and the Savelli, and they found that the easiest way to deal with him was through the Inquisition. Under their impulsion it seized him and two of his adherents, Matteo and Merenda. Through means procured by his daughter, Ordelaffi escaped from prison and was condemned *in contumaciam*. The others confessed—doubtless under torture—the heresies attributed to them, were handed over to the secular arm, and were duly burned. Their houses were torn down, and on their sites in time were erected two others, one of which afterwards became the dwelling of Michael Angelo and the other of Salvator Rosa.*

Secular potentates, however, had not waited till the fifteenth century to appreciate the facilities afforded by heresy and the Inquisition for the accomplishment of their objects. Already a hundred years earlier the methods of the Inquisition had suggested to Philippe le Bel the great crime of the Middle Ages—the destruction of the Order of the Temple.

When, in 1119, Hugues de Payen and Geoffroi de Saint-Adhémar with seven companions devoted themselves to the pious task of keeping the roads to Jerusalem clear of robbers, that pilgrims might traverse them in safety, and when Raymond du Puy about

---

* Ripoll II. 566.—Wadding. ann. 1409, No. 12.—Tamburini, Storia Gen. dell' Inquis. II. 437–9.

the same time organized the Poor Brethren of the Hospital of St. John, they opened a new career which was irresistibly attractive to the warlike ardor and religious enthusiasm of the age. The strange combination of monasticism and chivalry corresponded so exactly to the ideal of Christian knighthood that the Military Orders thus founded speedily were reckoned among the leading institutions of Europe. At the Council of Troyes, in 1128, a Rule, drawn up it is said by St. Bernard, was assigned to Hugues and his associates, who were known as the Poor Soldiers of the Temple. They were assigned a white habit, as a symbol of innocence, to which Eugenius III. added a red cross, and their standard, *Bauséant*, half black and half white, with its legend, "*Non nobis Domine*," soon became the rallying-point of the Christian chivalry. The Rule, based upon that of the strict Cistercian Order, was exceedingly severe. The members were bound by the three monastic vows of obedience, poverty, and chastity, and these were enforced in the statutes of the Order with the utmost rigor. The applicant for admission was required to ask permission to become the serf and slave of the "House" forever, and was warned that he henceforth surrendered his own will irrevocably. He was promised bread and water and the poor vestments of the House; and if after death gold or silver were found among his effects his body was thrust into unconsecrated ground, or, if buried, it was exhumed. Chastity was prescribed in the same unsparing fashion, and even the kiss of a mother was forbidden.*

The fame of the Order quickly filled all Europe; knights of the noblest blood, dukes and princes, renounced the world to serve Christ in its ranks, and soon in its general chapter three hundred knights were gathered, in addition to serving brethren. Their possessions spread immensely. Towns and villages and churches and manors were bestowed upon them, from which the revenues

---

* Jac. de Vitriaco Hist. Hierosol. cap. 65 (Bongars, II. 1083–4).—Rolewinck Fascic. Tempor. (Pistorii R. Germ. Scriptt. II. 546).—Regula Pauperum Commilitonum Templi c. 72 (Harduin. VI. II. 1146).—Règle et Statuts secrets des Templiers, §§ 125, 128 (Maillard de Chambure, Paris, 1840, pp. 455, 488–90, 494–5).

Since this chapter was written the Société de l'Histoire de France has issued a more correct and complete edition of the Rule and Statutes of the Templars, under the care of M. Henri de Curzon.

were sent to the Grand Master, whose official residence was Jerusalem, together with the proceeds of the collections of an organized system of beggary, their agents for which penetrated into every corner of Christendom. Scarce had the Order been organized when, in 1133, the mighty warrior, Alonso I. of Aragon, known as *el Batallador* and also as *el Emperador*, because his rule extended over Navarre and a large portion of Castile, dying without children, left his whole dominions to the Holy Sepulchre and to the Knights of the Temple and of the Hospital in undivided thirds; and though the will was not executed, the knights were promised and doubtless received compensation from his successor, Ramiro el Monje.   More practical was the liberality of Philip Augustus, in 1222, when he left the two Orders two thousand marks apiece absolutely, and the enormous sum of fifty thousand marks each on condition of keeping in service for three years three hundred knights in the Holy Land. We can understand how, in 1191, the Templars could buy the Island of Cyprus from Richard of England for twenty-five thousand silver marks, although they sold it the next year for the same price to Gui, King of Jerusalem. We can understand, also, that this enormous development began to excite apprehension and hostility. At the Council of Lateran, in 1179, there was bitter strife between the prelates and the Military Orders, resulting in a decree which required the Templars to surrender all recently acquired churches and tithes—an order which, in 1186, Urban III. defined as meaning all acquired within the ten years previous to the council.*

This indicates that already the prelates were beginning to feel jealous of the new organization. In fact, the antagonism which

---

* Jac. de Vitriaco loc. cit.—Roberti de Monte Contin. Sigeb. Gombl. (Pistorii, op. cit. I. 875).—Zurita, Añales de Aragon, Lib. I. c. 52–3.—Art de Vérifier les Dates V. 337.—Teulet, Layettes, I. 550, No. 1547.—Grandes Chroniques, IV. 86. —Gualt. Mapes de Nugis Curialium Dist. i. c. xxiii.—Hans Prutz, Malteser Urkunden, München, 1883, p. 43.

A curious illustration of the prominence which the Templars were acquiring in the social organization is afforded in 1191, when they were made conservators of the Truce of God, by which the nobles and prelates of Languedoc and Provence agreed that beasts and implements and seed employed in agriculture should be unmolested in time of war. For enforcing this the Templars were to receive a bushel of corn for every plough.—Prutz, op. cit. pp. 44–5.

we have already traced in the thirteenth century between the Mendicant Orders and the secular clergy was but the repetition of that which had long existed with respect to the Military Orders. These from the first were the especial favorites of the Holy See, whose policy it was to elevate them into a militia depending solely on Rome, thus rendering them an instrument in extending its influence and breaking down the independence of the local churches. Privileges and immunities were showered upon them; they were exempted from tolls and tithes and taxes of all kinds; their churches and houses were endowed with the right of asylum; their persons enjoyed the inviolability accorded to ecclesiastics; they were released from all feudal obligations and allegiance; they were justiciable only by Rome; bishops were forbidden to excommunicate them, and were even ordered to refer to the Roman curia all the infinite questions which arose in local quarrels. In 1255, after the misfortunes of the crusade of St. Louis, alms given to their collectors were declared to entitle the donors to Holy Land indulgences. In short, nothing was omitted by the popes that would stimulate their growth and bind them firmly to the chair of St. Peter.*

Thus it was inevitable that antagonism should spring up between the secular hierarchy and the Military Orders. The Templars were continually complaining that the prelates were endeavoring to oppress them, to impose exactions, and to regain by various devices the jurisdiction from which the popes had relieved them; their right of asylum was violated; the priests interfered with their begging collectors, and repressed and intercepted the pious legacies designed for them; the customary quarrels over burials and burial-fees were numerous, for, until the rise of the Mendicants, and even afterwards, it was a frequent thing for nobles to order their sepulture in the Temple or the Hospital. To these complaints the popes ever lent a ready ear, and the favoritism which they manifested only gave a sharper edge to the hostility of the defeated prelates. In 1264 there was a threatened rupture between the papacy and the Temple. Étienne de Sissy, Marshal of the Order and Preceptor of Apulia, refused to assist

---

* Rymer, Fœdera, I. 30.—Can. 10, 11, Extra. III. 30.—Prutz, op. cit. pp. 38, 46, 48, 49, 51, 52, 53, 56–61, 64, 76, 78–9.

in the crusade preparing against Manfred, and was removed by
Urban IV. When ordered to resign his commission he boldly
replied to Urban that no pope had ever interfered with the internal affairs of the Order, and that he would resign his office only
to the Grand Master who had conferred it. Urban excommunicated him, but the Order sustained him, being discontented because the succors levied for the Holy Land were diverted to the
papal enterprise against Manfred. The following year a new
pope, Clement IV., in removing the excommunication, bitterly reproached the Order for its ingratitude, and pointed out that only
the support of the papacy could sustain it against the hostility of
the bishops and princes, which apparently was notorious. Still
the Order held out, and in common with the Hospitallers and Cistercians, refused to pay a tithe to Charles of Anjou, in spite of
which Clement issued numerous bulls confirming and enlarging its
privileges.*

That this antagonism on the part of temporal and spiritual
potentates had ample justification there can be little doubt. If,
as we have seen, the Mendicant Orders rapidly declined from the
enthusiastic self-abnegation of Dominic and Francis, such a body
as the Templars, composed of ambitious and warlike knights, could
hardly be expected long to retain its pristine ascetic devotion.
Already, in 1152, the selfish eagerness of the Grand Master, Bernard de Tremelai, to secure the spoils of Ascalon nearly prevented
the capture of that city, and the fall of the Kingdom of Jerusalem
was hastened when, in 1172, the savage ferocity of Eudes de Saint-

---

* Prutz, op. cit. pp. 38–41, 43, 45, 47–8, 57, 64–9, 75–80.—J. Delaville le
Roulx, Documents concernant les Templiers Paris, 1882, p. 39.—Bini, Dei Tempieri in Toscana, Lucca, 1845, pp. 453–55.—Raynald. ann. 1265, No. 75–6.—Martene Thesaur. II. 111, 118.

The systematic beggary of the Templars must have been peculiarly exasperating both to the secular clergy and the Mendicants. Monsignor Bini prints a
document of 1244 in which the Preceptor of Lucca gives to Albertino di Pontre-
moli a commission to beg for the Order. Albertino employs a certain Aliotto to
do the begging from June till the following Carnival, and pays him by empowering him to beg on his own account from the Carnival to the octave of Easter
(op. cit. pp. 401–2, 439–40). For the disgraceful squabbles which arose between
the secular clergy and the Military Orders over this privileged beggary, see Faucon, Registres de Boniface VIII. No. 1,950, p. 746.

Amand, then Grand Master, prevented the conversion of the King of the Assassins and all his people. It was not without show of justification that about this time Walter Mapes attributes the misfortunes of the Christians of the East to the corruption of the Military Orders. By the end of the century we have seen from King Richard's rejoinder to Foulques de Neuilly that Templar was already synonymous with pride, and in 1207 Innocent III. took the Order to task in an epistle of violent denunciation. His apostolic ears, he said, were frequently disturbed with complaints of their excesses. Apostatizing from God and scandalizing the Church, their unbridled pride abused the enormous privileges bestowed upon them. Employing doctrines worthy of demons, they give their cross to every tramp who can pay them two or three pence a year, and then assert that these are entitled to ecclesiastical services and Christian burial, even though laboring under excommunication. Thus ensnared by the devil they ensnare the souls of the faithful. He forbears to dwell further on these and other wickednesses by which they deserve to be despoiled of their privileges, preferring to hope that they will free themselves from their turpitude. A concluding allusion to their lack of respect towards papal legates probably explains the venomous vigor of the papal attack, but the accusations which it makes touch points on which there is other conclusive evidence. Although by the statutes of the Order the purchase of admission, directly or indirectly, was simony, entailing expulsion on him who paid and degradation on the preceptor who was privy to it, there can be no doubt that many doubtful characters thus effected entrance into the Order. The papal letters and privileges so freely bestowed upon them were moreover largely abused, to the vexation and oppression of those with whom they came in contact, for, exclusively justiciable in the Roman curia, they were secure against all pleaders who could not afford that distant, doubtful, and expensive litigation. The evils thence arising were greatly intensified when the policy was adopted of forming a class of serving brethren, by whom their extensive properties were cultivated and managed without the cost of hired labor. Churls of every degree, husbandmen, shepherds, swineherds, mechanics, household servants, were thus admitted into the Order, until they constituted at least nine tenths of it, and although these were distinguished by a brown mantle in place of the white gar-

ment of the knights, and although they complained of the contempt and oppression with which they were treated by their
knightly brethren, nevertheless, in their relations with the outside world, they were full members of the Order, shrouded
with its inviolability and entitled to all its privileges, which
they were not likely by moderation to render less odious to the
community.*

Thus the knights furnished ample cause for external hostility
and internal disquiet, though there is probably no ground for the
accusation that, in 1229, they betrayed Frederic II. to the infidel, and,
in 1250, St. Louis to the Soldan of Egypt. Yet Frederic II. doubtless had ample reason for dissatisfaction with their conduct during his crusade, which he revenged by expelling them from Sicily
in 1229, and confiscating their property; and though he recalled
them soon after and assumed to restore their possessions, he retained a large portion. Still, pious liberality continued to increase
the wealth of the Order, though as the Christian possessions in the

---

* Guillel. Tyrii Hist. Lib. XVII. c. 27; xx. 31-2.—Gualt. Mapes de Nugis
Curialium Dist. I. c. xx.—Innoc. PP. III. Regest. x. 121. Cf. xv. 131.—Règle et
Statuts secrets, § 173, p. 389.—Michelet, Procès des Templiers, I. 39; II. 9, 83,
140, 186-7, 406-7 (Collection de Documents inédits, Paris, 1841-51).

When, in 1307, the Templars at Beaucaire were seized, out of sixty arrested,
five were knights, one a priest, and fifty-four were serving brethren; in June, 1310,
out of thirty-three prisoners in the Château d'Alais, there were four knights and
one priest, with twenty-eight serving brethren (Vaissette, IV. 141). In the trials
which have reached us the proportion of knights is even less. The serving brethren occasionally reached the dignity of preceptor; but how little this implies is
shown by the examination, in June, 1310, of Giovanni di Neritone, Preceptor
of Castello Villari, a serving brother, who speaks of himself as "*simplex et rus-
ticus*" (Schottmüller, Der Ausgang des Templer-Ordens, Berlin, 1887, II. 125,
130).

The pride of birth in the Order is illustrated by the rule that none could be
admitted as knights except those of knightly descent. In the Statutes a case is
cited of a knight who was received as such; those who were of his country declared that he was not the son of a knight. He was sent for from Antioch to a
chapter where this was found to be true, when the white mantle was removed
and a brown one put on him. His receptor was then in Europe, and when he
returned to Syria he was called to account. He justified himself by his having
acted under the orders of his commander of Poitou. This was found to be true;
otherwise, and but that he was a good knight (*proudons*), he would have lost the
habit (Règle, § 125, pp. 462-3).

East shrank more and more, people began to attribute the ceaseless misfortunes to the bitter jealousy and animosity existing between the rival Orders of the Temple and the Hospital, which in 1243 had broken out into open war in Palestine, to the great comfort of the infidel. A remedy was naturally sought in a union of the two Orders, together with that of the Teutonic Knights. At the Council of Lyons, in 1274, Gregory X. vainly endeavored to effect this, but the countervailing influences, including, it was said, the gold of the brethren, were too powerful. In these reproaches perhaps the Orders were held to an undeserved accountability, for while their quarrels and the general misconduct of the Latins in Palestine did much to wreck the kingdom of Jerusalem, the real responsibility lay rather with the papacy. When thousands of heretics were sent as crusaders in punishment, the glory of the service was fatally tarnished. When money raised and vows taken for the Holy Land were diverted to the purposes of the papal power in Italy, when the doctrine was publicly announced that the home interests of the Holy See were more important than the recovery of the Holy Sepulchre, the enthusiasm of Christendom against the infidel was chilled. When salvation could be gained at almost any time by a short term of service near home in the quarrels of the Church, whether on the Weser or in Lombardy, the devotion which had carried thousands to the Syrian deserts found a less rugged and a safer path to heaven. It is easy thus to understand how in the development of papal aggrandizement through the thirteenth century recruits and money were lacking to maintain against the countless hordes of Tartars the conquests of Godfrey of Bouillon. In addition to all this the Holy Land was made a penal settlement whither were sent the malefactors of Europe, rendering the Latin colony a horde of miscreants whose crimes deserved and whose disorders invited the vengeance of Heaven.*

---

* Matt. Paris. ann. 1228, 1243 (Ed. 1644, p. 240, 420).—Mansuet le Jeune, Hist. des Templiers, Paris, 1789, I. 340-1.—Prutz, op. cit. pp. 60-1.—Mag. Chron. Belgic. ann. 1274.—Faucon, Registres de Boniface VIII. No. 1691-2, 1697.—Marin. Sanuti Secret. Fidel. Lib. III. P. ix. c. 1, 2 (Bongars, II. 188-9).

The Hospital was open to the same reproaches as the Temple. In 1238 Gregory IX. vigorously assailed the Knights of St. John for their abuse of the privileges bestowed on them—their unchastity and the betrayal of the cause of

With the fall of Acre, in 1291, the Christians were driven definitely from the shores of Syria, causing intense grief and indignation throughout Europe. In that disastrous siege, brought on by the perfidy of a band of crusaders who refused to observe an existing truce, the Hospital won more glory than the Temple, although the Grand Master, Guillaume de Beaujeu, had been chosen to command the defence, and fell bravely fighting for the cross. After the surrender and massacre, his successor, the monk Gaudini, sailed for Cyprus with ten knights, the sole survivors of five hundred who had held out to the last. Again, not without reason, the cry went up that the disaster was the result of the quarrels between the Military Orders, and Nicholas IV. promptly sent letters to the kings and prelates of Christendom asking their opinions on the project of uniting them, in view of the projected crusade which was to sail on St. John's day, 1293, under Edward I. of England. At least one affirmative answer was received from the provincial council of Salzburg, but ere it reached Rome Nicholas was dead. A long interregnum, followed by the election of the hermit Pier Morrone, put an end to the project for the time, but it was again

---

God in Palestine. He even asserts that there are not a few heretics among them. —Raynald. ann. 1238, No. 31-2.

A sirvente by a Templar, evidently written soon after the fall of Acre, alludes bitterly to the sacrifice made of the Holy Land in favor of the ambition and cupidity of the Holy See—

> " Lo papa fa de perdon gran largueza
> Contr' Alamans ab Arles e Frances ;
> E sai mest nos mostram gran cobeeza,
> Quar nostras crotz van per crotz de tornes ;
> E qui vol camjar Romania
> Per la guerra de Lombardia ?
> Nostres legatz, don yeu vos dic per ver
> Qu'els vendon Dieu el perdon per aver."—

Meyer, Recueil d'anciens Textes, p. 96.

It is also to be borne in mind that indulgences were vulgarized in many other ways. When St. Francis announced to Honorius III. that Christ had sent him to obtain plenary pardons for those who should visit the Church of S. Maria di Porziuncola, the cardinals at once objected that this would nullify the indulgences for the Holy Land, and Honorius thereupon limited the Portiuncula indulgence to the twenty-four hours commencing with the vespers of August 1.—Amoni, Legenda S. Francisci, Append. c. xxxiii.

taken up by Boniface VIII., to be interrupted and laid aside, probably by his engrossing quarrel with Philippe le Bel. What was the drift of public opinion at the time is probably reflected in a tract on the recovery of the Holy Land addressed to Edward I. It is there proposed that the two Orders, whose scandalous quarrels have rendered them the object of scorn, shall be fused together and confined to their eastern possessions, which should be sufficient for their support, while their combined revenues from their western property, estimated at eight hundred thousand livres Tournois per annum, be employed to further the crusade. Evidently the idea was spreading that their wealth could be seized and used to better purpose than it was likely to be in their hands.*

Thus the Order was somewhat discredited in popular estimation when, in 1297, Jacques de Molay, whose terrible fate has cast a sombre shadow over his name through the centuries, was elected Grand Master, after a vigorous and bitter opposition by the partisans of Hugues de Peraud. A few years of earnest struggle to regain a foothold in Palestine seemed to exhaust the energy and resources of the Order, and it became quiescent in Cyprus. Its next exploit, though not official, was not of a nature to conciliate public opinion. Charles de Valois, the evil genius of his brother Philippe le Bel, and of his nephews, in 1300 married Catherine, granddaughter of Baldwin II. of Constantinople, and titular empress. In 1306 he proposed to make good his wife's claims on the imperial throne, and he found a ready instrument in Clement V., who persuaded himself that the attempt would not be a weakening of Christianity in the East, but a means of recovering Palestine, or at least of reducing the Greek Church to subjection. He therefore endeavored to unite the Italian republics and princes in this crusade against Christians. Charles II. of Naples undertook an expedition in conjunction with the Templars. A fleet was fitted out under the command of Roger, a Templar of high reputation for skill and audacity. It captured Thessalonica, but in place of actively pursuing Andronicus II., the Templars turned their

---

* Mansuet, op. cit. II. 101, 133.—De Excidio Urbis Acconis (Martene Ampl. Coll. V. 757).—Raynald. ann. 1291, No. 30, 31.—Archives Nat. de France, J. 431, No. 40.—Chron. Salisburg. ann. 1291 (Canisii et Basnage III. II. 489).—Annal. Eberhard. Altahens. (Ib. IV. 229).—De Recuperatione Terræ Sanctæ (Bongars, II. 320–1).

arms against the Latin princes of Greece, ravaged cruelly the shores of Thrace and the Morea, and returned with immense booty, having aroused enmities which were an element in their downfall.   In contrast to this the Hospitallers were acquiring fresh renown as the champions of Christ by gallantly conquering, after a four years' struggle, the island of Rhodes, in which they so long maintained the cause of Christianity in the East.   In 1306 Clement V. sent for de Molay and Guillaume de Villaret, Grand Master of the Hospitallers, to consult about a new crusade and the often discussed project of the union of the Orders.   He told them to come as secretly as possible, but while the Hospitaller, engrossed with preparations for the siege of Rhodes, excused himself, de Molay came in state, with a retinue of sixty knights, and manifested no intention of returning to his station in the East.   This well might arouse the question whether the Templars were about to abandon their sphere of duty, and if so, what were the ambitious schemes which might lead them to transfer their headquarters to France. The Teutonic knights in withdrawing from the East were carving out for themselves a kingdom amid the Pagans of northeastern Europe.   Had the Templars any similar aspirations nearer home ? *

---

* Raynald. ann. 1306, No. 3–5, 12.—Regest. Clement. PP. V. (Ed. Benedict. T. I. pp. 40–46 ; T. II. p. 55, 58, Romæ, 1885–6).—Mansuet, op. cit. II. 132.—Raynouard, Monuments historiques relatifs à la Condamnation des Chevaliers du Temple, Paris, 1813, pp. 17, 46.

The summons to the Grand Master of the Hospital is dated June 6, 1306, (Regest. Clem. PP. V. T. I. p. 190).   That to de Molay was probably issued at the same time.   From some briefs of Clement, June 13, 1306, in favor of Humbert Blanc, Preceptor of Auvergne, it would seem that the latter was engaged in some crusading enterprise (Ibid. pp. 191–2), probably in connection with the attempt of Charles of Valois.   When Hugues de Peraud, however, and other chiefs of the Order were about to sail, in November, Clement retained them (Ib. T. II. p. 5).

It has rather been the fashion with historians to assume that de Molay transferred the headquarters of the Order from Cyprus to Paris.   Yet when the papal orders for arrest reached Cyprus, on May 27, 1308, the marshal, draper, and treasurer surrendered themselves with others, showing that there had been no thought of removing the active administration of the Order.—(Dupuy, Traitez concernant l'Histoire de France, Ed. 1700, pp. 63, 132).   Raimbaut de Caron, Preceptor of Cyprus, apparently had accompanied de Molay, and was arrested with him in the Temple of Paris (Procès des Templiers, II. 374), but with this exception all the principal knights seized were only local dignitaries.

I think also that Schottmüller (Der Untergang des Templer-Ordens, Berlin,

Suspicions of the kind might not unnaturally be excited, and yet be wholly without foundation. Modern writers have exercised their ingenuity in conjecturing that there was a plot on hand for the Templars to seize the south of France and erect it into an independent kingdom. The Order had early multiplied rapidly in the provinces from the Garonne to the Rhone; it is assumed that they were deeply tinctured with Catharism, and held relations with the concealed heretics in those regions. All this is the sheerest assumption without the slightest foundation. There was not a trace of Catharism in the Order,* and we have seen how by this time the Cathari of Languedoc had been virtually exterminated, and how the land had been Gallicized by the Inquisition. Such an alliance would have been a source of weakness, not of strength, for it would have brought upon them all Europe in arms, and had there been a shred of evidence to that effect, Philippe le Bel would have made the most of it. Neither can it be assumed that they were intriguing with the discontented, orthodox population. Bernard Délicieux and the Carcassais would never have turned to the feeble Ferrand of Majorca if they could have summoned to their assistance the powerful Order of the Temple. Yet even the Order of the Temple, however great might have been its aggregate, was fatally weakened for such ambitious projects by being scattered in isolated fragments over the whole extent of Europe; and its inability to concentrate its forces for either aggression or defence was shown when it surrendered with scarce an effort at self-preservation in one country after another. Besides, it was by no means so numerous and wealthy as has been popularly supposed. The dramatic circumstances of its destruction have inflamed the imagination of all who have written about it, leading to a not unnatural exaggeration in contrasting its prosperity and its misery. An anonymous contemporary tells us that the Templars were so

---

1887, I. 66, 99; II. 38) sufficiently proves the incredibility of the story of the immense treasure brought to France by de Molay, and he further points out (I. 98) that the preservation of the archives of the Order in Malta shows that they could not have been removed to France.

* Perhaps the most detailed and authoritative contemporary account of the downfall of the Templars is that of Bernard Gui (Flor. Chronic. ap. Bouquet XXI. 716 sqq.). It is impossible to doubt that had there been anything savoring of Catharism in the Order he would have scented it out and alluded to it.

rich and powerful that they could scarce have been suppressed but
for the secret and sudden movement of Philippe le Bel. Villani,
who was also a contemporary, says that their power and wealth
were well-nigh incomputable. As time went on conceptions became magnified by distance. Trithemius assures us that it was the
richest of all the monastic Orders, not only in gold and silver, but
in its vast dominions, towns and castles in all the lands of Europe.
Modern writers have even exceeded this in their efforts to present
definite figures. Maillard de Chambure assumes that at the time
of its downfall it numbered thirty thousand knights with a revenue
of eight million livres Tournois. Wilcke estimates its income at
twenty million thalers of modern money, and asserts that in France
alone it could keep in the field an army of fifteen thousand cavaliers.
Zöckler calculates its income at fifty-four millions of francs, and
that it numbered twenty thousand knights. Even the cautious
Havemann echoes the extravagant statement that in wealth and
power it could rival all the princes of Christendom, while Schottmüller assumes that in France alone there were fifteen thousand
brethren, and over twenty thousand in the whole Order.*

The peculiar secrecy in which all the affairs of the Order were
shrouded renders such estimates purely conjectural. As to numbers, it has been overlooked that the great body of members were
serving brethren, not fighting-men—herdsmen, husbandmen, and
menials employed on the lands and in the houses of the knights,
and adding little to their effective force. When they considered it
a legitimate boast that in the one hundred and eighty years of
their active existence twenty thousand of the brethren had perished in Palestine, we can see that at no time could the roll of
knights have exceeded a few thousand at most. At the Council
of Vienne the dissolution of the Order was urged on the ground
that more than two thousand depositions of witnesses had been
taken, and as these depositions covered virtually all the prisoners

---

* Wilcke, Geschichte des Ordens der Tempelherren, II. Ausgabe, 1860, II. 51,
103–4, 183.—Chron. Anonyme (Bouquet, XXI. 149).—Villani Cron. VIII. 92.—
Mag. Chron. Belgic. (Pistor. III. 155).—Trithem. Chron. Hirsaug. ann. 1307.—
Règle et Statuts secrets, p. 64.—Real-Encyklop. XV. 305.—Havemann, Geschichte
des Ausgangs des Tempelherrenordens, Stuttgart, 1846, p. 165.—Schottmüller,
op. cit. I. 236, 695.

examined in France, England, Spain, Italy, and Germany, whose evidence could be used, it shows that the whole number can only have been insignificant in comparison with what had been generally imagined. Cyprus was the headquarters of the Order after the fall of Acre, yet at the time of the seizure there were but one hundred and eighteen members there of all ranks, and the numbers with which we meet in the trials everywhere are ludicrously out of proportion with the enormous total popularly attributed to the Order. A contemporary, of warmly papalist sympathies, expresses his grief at the penalties righteously incurred by fifteen thousand champions of Christ, which may be taken as an approximate guess at the existing number; and if among these we assume fifteen hundred knights, we shall probably be rather over than under the reality. As for the wealth of the Order, in the general effort to appropriate its possessions it was every one's interest to conceal the details of the aggregate, but we chance to have a standard which shows that the estimates of its supereminent riches are grossly exaggerated. In 1244 Matthew Paris states that it possessed throughout Christendom nine thousand manors, while the Hospitallers had nineteen thousand. Nowhere was it more prosperous than in Aquitaine, and about the year 1300, in a computation of a tithe granted to Philippe le Bel, in the province of Bordeaux, the Templars are set down at six thousand livres, the Hospitallers at the same, while the Cistercians are registered for twelve thousand. In the accounts of a royal collector in 1293 there are specified in Auvergne fourteen Temple preceptories, paying in all three hundred and ninety-two livres, while the preceptories of the Hospitallers number twenty-four, with a payment of three hundred and sixty-four livres. It will be remembered that a contemporary writer estimates the combined revenues of the two Orders at eight hundred thousand livres Tournois per annum, and of this the larger portion probably belonged to the Hospital.*

---

* Procès des Templiers, I. 144.—Raynald. ann. 1307, No. 12; ann. 1311, No. 53.—Schottmüller, op. cit. I. 465.—Ferreti Vicentini Hist. (Muratori S. R. I. IX. 1018).—Matt. Paris. ann. 1244 (p. 417).—Dom Bouquet, XXI. 545.—Chassaing, Spicilegium Brivatense, pp. 212–13.

An illustration of the exaggerations current as to the Templars is seen in the assertion, confidently made, that in Roussillon and Cerdagne the Order owned

Yet the wealth of the Order was more than sufficient to excite the cupidity of royal freebooters, and its power and privileges quite enough to arouse distrust in the mind of a less suspicious despot than Philippe le Bel. Many ingenious theories have been advanced to explain his action, but they are superfluous. In his quarrel with Boniface VIII., though the Templars were accused of secretly sending money to Rome in defiance of his prohibition, they stood by him and signed an act approving and confirming the assembly of the Louvre in June, 1303, where Boniface was formally accused of heresy, and an appeal was made to a future council to be assembled on the subject. So cordial, in fact, was the understanding between the king and the Templars that royal letters of July 10, 1303, show that the collection of all the royal revenues throughout France was intrusted to Hugues de Peraud, the Visitor of France, who had narrowly missed obtaining the Grand Mastership of the Order. In June, 1304, Philippe confirmed all their privileges, and in October he issued an Ordonnance granting them additional ones and speaking of their merits in terms of warm appreciation. They lent him, in 1299, the enormous sum of five hundred thousand livres for the dowry of his sister. As late as 1306, when Hugues de Peraud had suffered a loss of two thousand silver marks deposited with Tommaso and Vanno Mozzi, Florentine bankers, who fraudulently disappeared, Philippe promptly intervened and ordered restitution of the sum by Aimon, Abbot of S. Antoine, who had gone security for the bankers. When in his extreme financial straits he debased the coinage until a popular insurrection was excited in Paris, it was in the Temple that he took refuge, and it was the Templars that defended him against the assaults of the mob. But these very obligations were too great to be incurred by a monarch who was striving to render himself absolute, and the recollection of them could hardly fail to suggest that the Order was a dangerous factor in a kingdom where feudal

---

half the land, while an examination of its Cartulary shows that in reality it possessed but four lordships, together with fragmentary rights over rents, tithes, or villeins in seventy other places. A single abbey, that of St. Michel de Cuxa, possessed thirty lordships and similar rights in two hundred other places, and there were two other abbeys, Arles, and Cornella de Conflent, each richer than the Templars.—Allart, Bulletin de la Société Agricole, Scientifique et Littéraire des Pyrénées Orientales, T. XV. pp. 107–8.

institutions were being converted into a despotism. While it might not have strength to sever a portion of the provinces and erect an independent principality, it might at any moment become a disagreeable element in a contest with the great feudatories to whom the knights were bound by common sympathies and interests. He was engaged in reducing them to subjection by the extension of the royal jurisdiction, and the Templars were subject to no jurisdiction save that of the Holy See. They were not his subjects; they owed him no obedience or allegiance; he could not summon them to perform military service as he could his bishops, but they enjoyed the right to declare war and make peace on their own account without responsibility to any one; they were clothed in all the personal inviolability of ecclesiastics, and he possessed no means of control over them as he did with the hierarchy of the Gallican Church. They were exempt from all taxes and tolls and customs dues; their lands contributed nothing to his necessities, save when he could wring from the pope the concession of a tithe. While thus in every way independent of him, they were bound by rules of the blindest and most submissive obedience to their own superiors. The command of the Master was received as an order from God; no member could have a lock upon a bag or trunk, could bathe or let blood, could open a letter from a kinsman without permission of his commander, and any disobedience forfeited the habit and entailed imprisonment in chains, with its indelible disabilities. It is true that in 1295 there had been symptoms of turbulence in the Order, when the intervention of Boniface VIII. was required to enforce subjection to the Master, but this had passed away, and the discipline within its ranks was a religious obligation which rendered it vastly more efficient for action than the elastic allegiance of the vassal to his seigneur. Such a body of armed warriors was an anomaly in a feudal organization, and when the Templars seemed to have abandoned their military activity in the East, Philippe, in view of their wealth and numbers in France, may well have regarded them as a possible obstacle to his schemes of monarchical aggrandizement to be got rid of at the first favorable moment. At the commencement of his reign he had endeavored to put a stop to the perpetual acquisitions of both the religious Orders and the Templars, through which increasing bodies of land were falling under mainmorte, and the fruitlessness of the effort must have strengthened his convictions of its necessity. If it be asked why he attacked the Templars rather than the Hospitallers, the answer is probably to be found in the fact that the Temple was the weaker of the two, while the secrecy shrouding its ritual rendered it an object of popular suspicion.*

Walsingham asserts that Philippe's design in assailing the Templars was to procure for one of his younger sons the title of King of Jerusalem, with the Templar possessions as an appanage. Such a project was completely within the line of thought of the time, and would have resulted in precipitating Europe anew upon Syria. It may possibly have been a motive at the outset, and was gravely discussed in the Council of Vienne in favor of Philippe le Long, but it is evident that no sovereign outside of France would have permitted the Templar dominions within his territories to pass under the control of a member of the aspiring house of Capet.†

For the explanation of Philippe's action, however, we need hardly look further than to financial considerations. He was in desperate straits for money to meet the endless drain of the Flemish war. He had imposed taxes until some of his subjects were in revolt, and others were on the verge of it. He had debased the currency until he earned the name of the Counterfeiter, had found himself utterly unable to redeem his promises, and had discovered by experience that of all financial devices it was the most costly and ruinous. His resources were exhausted and his scruples were few. The stream of confiscations from Languedoc was beginning to run dry, while the sums which it had supplied to the royal treasury for more than half a century had shown the profit which was derivable from well-applied persecution of heresy. He had just car-

---

* Du Puy, Hist. du Differend, Preuves, pp. 136–7.—Baudouin, Lettres inédites de Philippe le Bel, p. 163.—Maillard de Chambure, p. 61.—Grandes Chroniques, V. 173.—Raynouard, pp. 14, 21.—Rymer, I. 30.—Regest. Clement. PP. V. T. I. p. 192 (Ed. Benedict. Romæ, 1885).—Prutz, pp. 23, 31, 38, 46, 49, 51–2, 59, 76, 78, 79, 80.—Règle et Statuts, § 29, p. 226 ; § 58, pp. 249, 254 ; § 126, pp. 463–4.—Thomas, Registres de Boniface VIII. T. I. No. 490.—Baudouin, op. cit. p. 212.

Schottmüller (Der Untergang des Templer-Ordens, Berlin, 1887, I. 65) conjectures that the loan of five hundred thousand livres to Philippe is probably a popular error arising from the intervention of the Templars as bankers in the payment of the dowry.

† D'Argentré I. i. 280.—Wilcke, op. cit. II. 304–6.

ried out a financial expedient of the same kind as his dealings with
the Templars, by arresting all the Jews of the kingdom simultane-
ously, stripping them of their property, and banishing them under
pain of death. A memorandum of questions for consideration,
still preserved in the Trésor des Chartres, shows that he expected
to benefit in the same way from the confiscation of the Templar
possessions, while, as we shall see, he overlooked the fact that
these, as ecclesiastical property, were subject to the imprescriptible
rights of the Church.*

The stories about Squin de Florian, a renegade Templar, and
Noffo Dei, a wicked Florentine, both condemned to death and con-
cocting the accusations to save themselves, are probably but the
conception of an imaginative chronicler, handed down from one
annalist to another.† Such special interposition was wholly unnecessary. The foolish secrecy in which the Templars enveloped
their proceedings was a natural stimulus of popular curiosity and
suspicion. Alone among religious Orders, the ceremonies of reception were conducted in the strictest privacy; chapters were held
at daybreak with doors closely guarded, and no participant was
allowed to speak of what was done, even to a fellow-Templar not
concerned in the chapter, under the heaviest penalty known—that
of expulsion. That this should lead to gossip and stories of rites
too repulsive and hideous to bear the light was inevitable. It was
the one damaging fact against them, and when Humbert Blanc,
Preceptor of Auvergne, was asked on his trial why such secrecy
was observed if they had nothing to conceal, he could only answer "through folly." Thus it was common report that the neophyte was subjected to the humiliation of kissing the posteriors
of his preceptor—a report which the Hospitallers took special
pleasure in circulating. That unnatural lusts should be attributed
to the Order is easily understood, for it was a prevalent vice of the
Middle Ages, and one to which monastic communities were espe-

---

* Guill. Nangiac. Contin. ann. 1306.—Vaissette, IV. 135.—Raynouard, p. 24.

† Villani, Cron. VIII. 92.—Amalr. Augerii Vit. Clem. V. (Muratori S. R. I. III.
II. 443–44).—S. Antonini Hist. (D'Argentré I. I. 281).—Trithem. Chron. Hirsaug.
ann. 1307.—Raynald. ann. 1307, No. 12. The best-informed contemporaries,
Bernard Gui, the Continuation of Nangis, Jean de S. Victor, the Grandes Chroniques, say nothing about this story.

cially subject; as recently as 1292 a horrible scandal of this kind
had led to the banishment of many professors and theologians of
the University of Paris. Darker rumors were not lacking of un-
christian practices introduced in the Order by a Grand Master
taken prisoner by the Soldan of Babylon, and procuring his release
under promise of rendering them obligatory on the members.
There was also a legend that in the early days of the Order two
Templars were riding on one horse in a battle beyond seas. The
one in front recommended himself to Christ and was sorely
wounded; the one behind recommended himself to him who best
could help, and he escaped. The latter was said to be the demon
in human shape who told his wounded comrade that if he would
believe him the Order would grow in wealth and power. The
Templar was seduced, and thence came error and unbelief into the
organization. We have seen how readily such stories obtained
credence throughout the Middle Ages, how they grew and became
embroidered with the most fantastic details. The public mind
was ripe to believe anything of the Templars; a spark only was
needed to produce a conflagration.*

---

* Règle et Statuts secrets, § 81, p. 314; § 124, p. 448.—Wilkins Concilia II.
338.—Procès des Templiers, I. 186–7, 454; II. 139, 153, 195–6, 223, 440, 445, 471.
—S. Damiani Lib. Gomorrhian.—Guillel. Nangiac. ann. 1120.—Alani de Insulis
Lib. de Planctu Naturæ.—Gualt. Mapes de Nugis Curialium I. xxiv.—Prediche
del B. Frà Giordano da Rivalto, Firenze, 1831, I. 230.—Regest. Clement. PP. V. T.
V. p. 259 (Ed. Benedictin. Romæ, 1887).—Alvar. Pelag. de Planct. Eccles. Lib. II.
Art. ii. fol. lxxxiii.—Mémoires de Jacques Du Clercq, Liv. III. ch. 42; Liv. IV.
ch. 3.—Rogeri Bacon Compend. Studii Philosophiæ cap. ii. (M. R. Series I. 412).

Unnatural crime was subject to ecclesiastical jurisdiction and the punishment
was burning alive (Très Ancien Cout. de Bretagne, Art. 112, 142 ap. Bourdot de
Richebourg, IV. 227, 232.—Statuta Criminalia Mediolani e tenebris in lucem
edita, cap. 51, Bergomi, 1594). An instance of the infliction of the penalty by
secular justice is recorded at Bourges in 1445 (Jean Chartier, Hist. de Charles
VII. Ed. Godefroy, p. 72), and another at Zurich in 1482 (V. Anshelm, Die Berner
Chronik, Bern, 1884, I. 221), though in 1451 Nicholas V. had subjected the crime
to the Inquisition (Ripoll III. 301). D'Argentré says " Hæc pœna toto regno et
vulgo statutis Italiæ indicitur per civitates, sed pene irritis legibus " (Comment.
Consuetud Duc. Britann. p. 1810). In England it was a secular crime, punishable by burning alive (Horne, Myrror of Justice, cap. IV. § 14) and in Spain by
castration and lapidation (El Fuero real de España, Lib. IV. Tit. ix. l. 2).

The gossiping experiences in Syria and Italy of Antonio Sicci da Vercelli, as

Philippe's ministers and agents—Guillaume de Nogaret, Guillaume de Plaisian, Renaud de Roye, and Enguerrand de Marigny —were quite fitted to appreciate such an opportunity to relieve the royal exchequer, nor could they be at a loss in finding testimony upon which to frame a formidable list of charges, for we have already seen how readily evidence was procured from apparently respectable witnesses convicting Boniface VIII. of crimes equally atrocious. In the present case the task was easier: the Templars could have been no exception to the general demoralization of the monastic Orders, and in their ranks there must have been many desperate adventurers, ready for any crime that would bring a profit. Expelled members there were in plenty who had been ejected for their misdeeds, and who could lose nothing by gratifying their resentments. Apostates also were there who had fled from the Order and were liable to imprisonment if caught, besides the crowd of worthless ribalds whom the royal agents could always secure when evidence for any purpose was wanted. These were quietly collected by Guillaume de Nogaret, and kept in the greatest secrecy at Corbeil under charge of the Dominican, Humbert. Heresy was, of course, the most available charge to bring. The Inquisition was there as an unfailing instrument to secure conviction. Popular rumor, no matter by whom affirmed, was sufficient to require arrest and trial, and when once on trial there were few indeed from whom the inquisitorial process could not wring conviction. When once the attempt was determined upon the result was inevitable.*

Still, the attempt could not be successful without the concurrence of Clement V., for the inquisitorial courts, both of the Holy Office and of the bishops, were under papal control, and, besides, public opinion would require that the guilt of the Order should

---

related before the papal commission in March, 1311, show the popular belief that there was a terrible secret in the Order which none of its members dared reveal (Procès, I. 644–5).

It is perhaps a coincidence that in 1307 the Teutonic Order was likewise accused of heresy by the Archbishop of Riga. Its Grand Master, Carl Beffart, was summoned by Clement, and with difficulty averted from his Order the fate of the Templars.—Wilcke, II. 118.

* Procès des Templiers, I. 36, 168.—Chron. Anonyme (Bouquet, XXI. 137).— Joann. de S. Victor. (Bouquet, XXI. 649–50).

be proved in other lands besides France. To enable Philippe to enjoy the expected confiscations in his own dominions, confiscation must be general throughout Europe, and for this the cooperation of the Holy See was essential. Clement subsequently declared that Philippe broached the subject to him in all its details before his coronation at Lyons, November 14, 1305,* but the papal bulls throughout the whole matter are so infected with mendacity that slender reliance is to be placed on their statements. Doubtless there was some discussion about the current reports defaming the Order, but Clement is probably not subject to the imputation which historians have thrown upon him, that his summons to de Molay and de Villaret in 1306 was purely a decoy. It seems to me reasonable to conclude that he sent for them in good faith, and that de Molay's own imprudence in establishing himself in France, as though for a permanence, excited at once the suspicions and cupidity of the king, and ripened into action what had previously been merely a vague conception.†

If such was the case, Philippe was not long in maturing the project, nor were his agents slow in gathering material for the accusation. In his interview with Clement at Poitiers, in the spring of 1307, he vainly demanded the condemnation of the memory of Boniface VIII., and, failing in this, he brought forward the charges against the Templars, while temporarily dropping the other matter, but with equal lack of immediate result. Clement sent for de Molay, who came to him with Raimbaud de Caron, Preceptor of Cyprus, Geoffroi de Gonneville, Preceptor of Aquitaine and Poitou, and Hugues de Peraud, Visitor of France, the principal officers of the Order then in the kingdom. The charges were communicated to them in all their foulness. Clem-

---

* Bull. *Pastoralis præeminentiæ* (Mag. Bull. Rom. Supplem. IX. 126).—Bull. *Faciens misericordiam* (Ib. p. 136).—The Itineraries of Philippe and the record of pastoral visitations by Bertrand de Goth (Clement V.) sufficiently disprove the legendary story, originating with Villani, of the conditions entered into in advance at St. Jean d'Angely between Philippe and Clement (see van Os, De Abolitione Ordinis Templariorum, Herbipoli, 1874, pp. 14–15).   None the less, however, was Clement practically subordinated to Philippe.

† Schottmüller's theory (Der Untergang des Templer-Ordens, I. 91) that Clement summoned the chiefs of the two Military Orders to arrange with them for the protection of the Holy See against Philippe appears to me destitute of all probability.

ent subsequently had the audacity to declare to all Europe that
de Molay before his arrest confessed their truth in the presence
of his subordinates and of ecclesiastics and laymen, but this is a
manifest lie. The Templars returned to Paris evidently relieved
of all anxiety, thinking that they had justified themselves completely, and de Molay, on October 12, the eve of the arrest, had
the honor to be one of the four pall-bearers at the obsequies of
Catharine, wife of Charles de Valois, evidently for the purpose of
lulling him with a sense of security. Nay, more, on August 24,
Clement had written to Philippe urging him to make peace with
England, and referring to his charges against the Templars in their
conversations at Lyons and Poitiers, and the representations on
the subject made by his agents. The charges, he says, appear to
him incredible and impossible, but as de Molay and the chief officers of the Order had complained of the reports as injurious, and
had repeatedly asked for an investigation, offering to submit to
the severest punishment if found guilty, he proposes in a few days,
on his return to Poitiers, to commence, with the advice of his cardinals, an examination into the matter, for which he asks the king
to send him the proofs.*

No impression had evidently thus far been made upon Clement,
and he was endeavoring, in so far as he dared, to shuffle the affair
aside. Philippe, however, had under his hands the machinery
requisite to attain his ends, and he felt assured that when the
Church was once committed to it, Clement would not venture to
withdraw. The Inquisitor of France, Guillaume de Paris, was his
confessor as well as papal chaplain, and could be relied upon. It
was his official duty to take cognizance of all accusations of heresy,
and to summon the secular power to his assistance, while his awful authority overrode all the special immunities and personal inviolability of the Order. As the Templars were all defamed for
heresy by credible witnesses, it was strictly according to legal form
for Frère Guillaume to summon Philippe to arrest those within
his territories and bring them before the Inquisition for trial. As

---

* Villani Chron. VIII. 91–2.—Raynald. ann. 1311, No. 26.—Ptol. Lucens. Hist.
Eccles. Lib. XXIV. (Muratori S. R. I. XI. 1228).—Contin. Guill. Nangiac. ann. 1307.
—Raynouard, pp. 18, 19.—Van Os De Abol. Ord. Templar. p. 43.—Procès des
Templiers, II. 400.— Mag. Bull. Rom. IX. 131.—Procès, I. 95.—Du Puy, Traitez
concernant l'Histoire de France, Paris, 1700, pp. 10, 117.

the enterprise was a large one, secrecy and combined operations
were requisite for its success, and Philippe, as soon as Clement's
letter had shown him that he was not to expect immediate papal
co-operation, lost no time.   He always asserted that he had acted
under requisition from the inquisitor, and excused his haste by declaring that his victims were collecting their treasures and preparing to fly.   On September 14 royal letters were sent out to the
king's representatives throughout France, ordering the simultaneous arrest, under authority from Frère Guillaume, of all members
of the Order on October 13, and the sequestration of all property.
Frère Guillaume, on September 20, addressed all inquisitors and
all Dominican priors, sub-priors, and lectors, commissioning them
to act, and reciting the crimes of the Templars, which he characterized as sufficient to move the earth and disturb the elements.
He had, he said, examined the witnesses, he had summoned the
king to lend his aid, and he cunningly added that the pope was
informed of the charges.   The royal instructions were that the
Templars when seized were to be strictly guarded in solitary confinement; they were to be brought before the inquisitorial commissioners one by one; the articles of accusation were to be read
over to them; they were to be promised pardon if they would
confess the truth and return to the Church, and be told that otherwise they were to be put to death, while torture was not to be
spared in extracting confession.   The depositions so obtained were
to be sent to the king as speedily as possible, under the seals of
the inquisitors.   All Templar property was to be sequestrated and
careful inventories be made out.   In undertaking an act which
would shock public opinion in no common fashion, it was necessary that it should be justified at once by the confessions wrung
from the prisoners, and nothing was to be spared, whether by
promises, threats, or violence, to secure the result.*

---

* Du Puy, pp. 18–19, 86.—Stemler, Contingent zur Geschichte der Templer,
Leipzig, 1783, pp. 36–50.—Pissot, Procès et Condamnation des Templiers, Paris,
1805, pp. 39–43.

Clement V., in his letters of November 21 to Edward of England, and November 22 to Robert, Duke of Calabria, describes Philippe as having acted under
the orders of the Inquisition, and as presenting the prisoners for judgment to the
Church (Rymer III. 30; MSS. Chioccarello, T. VIII.).   The Holy Office was recognized at the time as being the responsible instrumentality of the whole affair

This was all strictly in accordance with inquisitorial practice, and the result corresponded with the royal expectations. Under the able management of Guillaume de Nogaret, to whom the direction of the affair was confided, on October 13 at daybreak the arrests took place throughout the land, but few of the Templars escaping. Nogaret himself took charge of the Paris Temple, where about a hundred and forty Templars, with de Molay and his chief officials at their head, were seized, and the vast treasure of the Order fell into the king's hands. The air had been thick with presages of the impending storm, but the Templars underrated the audacity of the king and had made no preparations to avert the blow. Now they were powerless in the hands of the unsparing tribunal which could at will prove them guilty out of their own mouths, and hold them up to the scorn and detestation of mankind.*

Philippe's first care was to secure the support of public opinion and allay the excitement caused by this unexpected move. The next day, Saturday, October 14, the masters of the university and the cathedral canons were assembled in Nôtre Dame, where Guillaume de Nogaret, the Prévôt of Paris, and other royal officials made a statement of the offences which had been proved against the Templars. The following day, Sunday the 15th, the people were invited to assemble in the garden of the royal palace, where the matter was explained to them by the Dominicans and the royal spokesmen, while similar measures were adopted throughout the kingdom. On Monday, the 16th, royal letters were addressed to all the princes of Christendom announcing the discovery of the Templar heresy, and urging them to aid the king in the defence of the faith by following his example. At once

---

(Chron. Fran. Pipini c. 49 *ap.* Muratori S. R. I. IX. 749–50). The bull *Faciens misericordiam* of August 12, 1308, gives the inquisitors throughout Europe instructions to participate in the subsequent proceedings (Mag. Bull. Rom. IX. 136).

In fact, the whole matter was strictly inquisitorial business, and it is a noteworthy fact that where the Inquisition was in good working order, as in France and Italy, there was no difficulty in obtaining the requisite evidence. In Castile and Germany it failed; in England, as we shall see, nothing could be done until the Inquisition was practically established temporarily for the purpose.

* Dom Bouquet, XXI. 448. — Vaissette, IV. 139. — Chron. Anon. (Bouquet, XXI. 137, 149).—Cont. Guill. Nangiac. ann. 1307.—Joann. de S.Victor. (Bouquet, XXI. 649).—Procès des Templiers, I. 458; II. 373.

the Inquisition was set busily at work. From October 19 to November 24 Frère Guillaume and his assistants were employed in recording the confessions of a hundred and thirty-eight prisoners captured in the Temple, and so efficacious were the means employed that but three refused to admit at least some of the charges. What these methods were the records of course fail to show, for, as we have seen, the official confession was always made after removal from the torture-chamber, and the victim was required to swear that it was free and unconstrained, without fear or force, though he knew that if he retracted what he had uttered or promised to utter on the rack he would be liable to fresh torture, or to the stake as a relapsed heretic. The same scenes were enacting all over France, where the commissioners of Frère Guillaume, and sometimes Frère Guillaume himself, with the assistance of the royal officials, were engaged in the same work. In fact, the complaisant Guillaume, in default of proper material for labor so extensive, seems occasionally to have commissioned the royal deputies to act. A few of the reports of these examinations have been preserved, from Champagne, Normandy, Querci, Bigorre, Beaucaire, and Languedoc, and in these the occasional allusions to torture show that it was employed whenever necessary. In all cases, of course, it was not required, for the promise of pardon and the threat of burning would frequently suffice, in conjunction with starvation and the harshness of the prison. The rigor of the application of the inquisitorial process is shown by the numerous deaths and the occasional suicides prompted by despair to which the records bear testimony. In Paris alone, according to the testimony of Ponsard de Gisiac, thirty-six Templars perished under torture; at Sens, Jacques de Saciac said that twenty-five had died of torment and suffering, and the mortality elsewhere was notorious. When a number of the Templars subsequently repeated their confessions before the pope and cardinals in consistory, they dwelt upon the excessive tortures which they had endured, although Clement in reporting the result was careful to specify that their confessions were free and unconstrained. De Molay, of course, was not spared. He was speedily brought into a complying state of mind. Although his confession, October 24, is exceedingly brief, and only admits a portion of the errors charged, yet he was induced to sign a letter addressed to the brethren stating that he had confessed and recommending them to do the same, as having been deceived by ancient error. As soon as he and other chiefs of the Order were thus committed, the masters and students of all the faculties of the university were summoned to meet in the Temple; the wretched victims were brought before them and were required to repeat their confessions, which they did, with the addition that these errors had prevailed in the Order for thirty years and more.*

The errors charged against them were virtually five: I. That when a neophyte was received the preceptor led him behind the altar, or to the sacristy or other secret place, showed him a crucifix and made him thrice renounce the prophet and spit upon the cross. II. He was then stripped, and the preceptor kissed him thrice, on the posteriors, the navel, and the mouth. III. He was then told that unnatural lust was lawful, and it was commonly indulged in throughout the Order. IV. The cord which the Templars wore over the shirt day and night as a symbol of chastity had been consecrated by wrapping it around an idol in the form of a human head with a great beard, and this head was adored in the chapters, though only known to the Grand Master and the elders. V. The priests of the Order do not consecrate the host in celebrating mass. When, in August, 1308, Clement sent throughout Europe a series of articles for the interrogation of the accused, drawn up for him by Philippe, and varying according to different recensions from eighty-seven to one hundred and twenty-seven in number, these charges were elaborated, and varied on the basis of the immense mass of confessions which had meanwhile been obtained. The indecent kisses were represented as mutual between the receptor and the received; disbelief in the sacrament of the altar was asserted; a cat was said to appear in the chapters and to be worshipped; the Grand Master or preceptor presiding in a chapter was held to have power of absolving from all sin; all brethren

* Joann. de S. Victor (Bouquet, XXI. 649–50).—Contin. Guill. Nangiac. ann. 1307.—Chron. Anon. (Bouquet, XXI. 137).—Schottmüller, op. cit. I. 131–33.—Zurita, Añales de Aragon, Lib. v. c. 73.—Procès des Templiers, II. 6, 375, 386, 394.—Du Puy, pp. 25–6, 88–91, 101–6.—Raynouard, pp. 39–40, 164, 235–8, 240–5.—Procès des Templiers, I. 36, 69, 203, 301; II. 305–6.—Ptol. Lucens. Hist. Eccles. Lib. xxiv. (Muratori S. R. I. XI. 1230).—Trithem. Chron. Hirsaug. ann. 1307.—Chron. Anon. (Bouquet, XXI. 149).

were instructed to acquire property for the Order by fair means or foul, and all the above were declared to be fixed and absolute rules of the Order, dating from a time beyond the memory of any member. Besides these, it was reproached for the secrecy of its proceedings and neglect in the distribution of alms. Even this, however, did not satisfy the public imagination, and the most absurd exaggerations found credence, such as we have so frequently seen in the case of other heresies. The Templars were said to have admitted betraying St. Louis and the stronghold of Acre, and that they had such arrangements with the Soldan of Babylon that if a new crusade were undertaken the Christians would all be sold to him. They had conveyed away a portion of the royal treasure, to the great injury of the kingdom. The cord of chastity was magnified into a leather belt, worn next the skin, and the *mahommerie* of this girdle was so powerful that as long as it was worn no Templar could abandon his errors. Sometimes a Templar who died in this false belief was burned, and of his ashes a powder was made which confirmed the neophytes in their infidelity. When a child was born of a virgin to a Templar it was roasted, and of its fat an ointment was made wherewith to anoint the idol worshipped in the chapters, to which, according to other rumors, human sacrifices were offered. Such were the stories which passed from mouth to mouth and served to intensify popular abhorrence.[*]

It is, perhaps, necessary at this point to discuss the still mooted question as to the guilt or innocence of the Order. Disputants have from various motives been led to find among the Templars Manichæan, Gnostic, and Cabalistic errors justifying their destruction. Hammer-Purgstall boasted that he had discovered and identified no less than thirty Templar images, in spite of the fact that at the time of their sudden arrest the Inquisition, aided by the eager creatures of Philippe, was unable to lay its hands on a single one. The only thing approaching it was a metal reliquary in the form of a female head produced from the Paris Temple, which, on being opened, was found to contain a small skull preserved as a relic of the eleven thousand virgins.[†]

---

[*] Pissot, pp. 41-2.—Procès des Templiers, I. 89 sqq.—Mag. Bull. Roman. IX. 129 sqq.—Raynouard, p. 50.—Grandes Chroniques V. 188-90.—Chron. Anon. (Bouquet, XXI. 137).—Naucleri Chron. ann. 1306.

[†] Wilcke, II. 424.—Procès des Templiers, II. 218.—The flimsiness of the evi-

This fact alone would serve to dispose of the gravest of the charges, for, if the depositions of some of the accused are to be believed, these idols were kept in every commandery and were employed in every reception of a neophyte. With regard to the other accusations, not admitting thus of physical proof, it is to be observed that much has been made by modern theorists of the

---

dence which suffices to satisfy archæologists of this kind is seen in the laborious trifling of M. Mignard, who finds in a sculptured stone coffer, discovered at Essarois in 1789, all the secrets of gnostic Manichæism, and who thereupon leaps to the conclusion that the coffer must have belonged to the Templars who had a preceptory within eight or ten miles of the place, and that it served as a receptacle for the Baphometic idol (Mignard, Monographie du coffret de M. le duc de Blacas, Paris, 1852.—Suite, 1853).

It is impossible to listen without respect to Professor Hans Prutz, whose labors in the archives of Valetta I have freely quoted above, and one can only view with regret the efforts of such a man wasted in piecing together contradictory statements of tortured witnesses to evolve out of them a dualistic heresy —an amalgamation of Catharan elements with Luciferan beliefs, to which even the unlucky Stedingers contribute corroboration (Geheimlehre u. Geheimstatuten des Tempelherren-Ordens, Berlin, 1879, pp. 62, 86, 100). It ought to be sufficient to prevent such wasted labor for the future, to call attention to the fact that if there had been ardor and conviction enough in the Order to risk the organization and propagation of a new heresy, there would, unquestionably, have been at least a few martyrs, such as all other heretical sects furnished. Yet not a single Templar avowed the faith attributed to them and persisted in it. All who confessed under the stress of the prosecution eagerly abjured the errors attributed to them and asked for absolution. A single case of obstinacy would have been worth to Philippe and Clement all the other testimony, and would have been made the pivotal point of the trials, but there was not one such. All the Templars who were burned were martyrs of another sort—men who had confessed under torture, had retracted their confessions, and who preferred the stake to the disgrace of persisting in the admission extorted from them. It does not seem to occur to the ingenious framers of heretical beliefs for the Templars that they must construct a heresy whose believers will not suffer death in its defence, but will endure to be burned in scores rather than submit to the stigma of having it ascribed to them. The mere statement of the case is enough to show the fabulous character of all the theories so laboriously constructed, especially that of M. Mignard, who proves that the Templars were Cathari—heretics whose aspiration for martyrdom was peculiarly notorious.

I have not been able to consult Loiseleur's "La Doctrine Secrète des Templiers" (Orleans, 1872), but from Prutz's references to it I gather that it is grounded on the same false basis and is open to the same easy refutation. Wilcke's speculations are too perversely crude to be worth attention.

fact that the rules and statutes of the Order were reserved exclusively for its chiefs, and it has been assumed that in them were developed the secret mysteries of the heresy. Yet nothing of the kind was alleged in the proceedings; the statutes were never offered in evidence by the prosecution, although many of them must have been obtained in the sudden seizure, and this for the best of reasons. Sedulously as they were destroyed, two or three copies escaped, and these, carefully collated, have been printed. They breathe nothing but the most ascetic piety and devotion to the Church, and the numerous illustrative cases cited in them show that up to a period not long anterior to the destruction of the Order there were constant efforts made to enforce the rigid Rule framed by St. Bernard and promulgated by the Council of Troyes in 1128. Thus there is absolutely no external evidence against the Order, and the proof rests entirely upon confessions extracted by the alternative of pardon or burning, by torture, by the threat of torture, or by the indirect torture of prison and starvation, which the Inquisition, both papal and episcopal, know so well how to employ. We shall see, in the development of the affair, that when these agencies were not employed no admissions of criminality could be obtained.* No one who had studied the criminal juris-

---

* Writers unfamiliar with the judicial processes of the period are misled by the customary formula, to the effect that the confirmation of a confession is not obtained by force or fear of torture. See Raynald. ann. 1307, No. 12, and Bini, Dei Tempieri in Toscana, p. 428. Wilcke asserts positively (op. cit. II. 318) that de Molay never was tortured, which may possibly be true (Amalr. Auger. Vit. Clem. V. *ap.* Muratori III. ii. 461), but he saw his comrades around him subjected to torture, and it was a mere question of strength of nerve whether he yielded before or after the rack. Prutz even says that in England neither torture nor terrorism was employed (Geheimlehre, p. 104), which we will see below was not the case. Van Os (De Abol. Ord. Templ. pp. 107, 109) is bolder, and argues that a confession confirmed after torture is as convincing as if no torture had been used. He carefully suppresses the fact, however, that retraction was held to be relapse and entailed death by burning.

How the system worked is illustrated by the examination of the Preceptor of Cyprus, Raimbaud de Caron, before the inquisitor Guillaume, Nov. 10, 1307. When first interrogated he would only admit that he had been told in the presence of his uncle, the Bishop of Carpentras, that he would have to renounce Christ to obtain admission. He was then removed and subsequently brought back, when he remembered that at his reception he had been forced to renounce

prudence of the later Middle Ages will attach the slightest weight
to confessions obtained under such conditions. We have seen, in
the case of the Stedingers, how easy it was to create belief in the
most groundless charges. We have seen, under Conrad of Marburg, how readily the fear of death and the promise of absolution
would cause nobles of birth and station to convict themselves of
the foulest and most impossible offences. We shall see, when we
come to consider persecution for witchcraft, with what facility the
rack and strappado procured from victims of all ranks confessions
of participating in the Sabbat, and of holding personal intercourse
with demons, of charming away harvests, of conjuring hail-storms,
and of killing men and cattle with spells. Riding through the
air on a broomstick, and commerce with incubi and succubi rest
upon evidence of precisely the same character and of much greater
weight than that upon which the Templars were convicted, for
the witch was sure of burning if she confessed, and had a chance
of escaping if she could endure the torture, while the Templar was
threatened with death for obstinacy, and was promised immunity
as a reward for confession. If we accept the evidence against the
Templar we cannot reject it in the case of the witch.

As the testimony thus has no intrinsic weight, the only scientific method of analyzing the affair is to sift the whole mass of
confessions, and determine their credibility according to the internal evidence which they afford of being credible or otherwise.
Several hundred depositions have reached us, taken in France,
England, and Italy, for the most part naturally those incriminating the Order, for the assertions of innocence were usually suppressed, and the most damaging witnesses were made the most of.
These are sufficiently numerous to afford us ample material for
estimating the character of the proof on which the Order was
condemned, and to obtain from them a reasonable approximation
to the truth requires only the application of a few tests suggested
by common-sense.

There is, firstly, the extreme inherent improbability that a rich,

---

Christ and spit on the cross, and had been taught that the gratification of unnatural lust was permissible. Yet this confession, so evidently the result of torture, winds up with the customary formula that he swore it was not the result of
force or fear of prison or torture.—Procès, II. 374–5.

worldly, and ambitious body of men like the Templars should be secretly engaged in the dangerous and visionary task of laying the foundations of a new religion, which would bring them no advantage if they succeeded in supplanting Christianity, and which was certain to lead them to destruction in the infinite chances of detection. To admit this is to ascribe to them a spiritual exaltation and a readiness for martyrdom which we might expect from the asceticism of a Catharan or a Dolcinist, but not from the worldliness which was the real corroding vice of the Order. Secondly, if the Templars were thus engaged in the desperate enterprise of propagating a new faith under the eyes of the Inquisition, they would be wary in initiating strangers; they would exercise extreme caution as to the admission of members, and only reveal to them their secrets by degrees, as they found them worthy of confidence and zealously willing to incur the risk of martyrdom. Thirdly, if a new dogma were thus secretly taught as an indispensable portion of the Rule, its doctrines would be rigidly defined and its ritual be closely administered. The witnesses who confessed to initiation would all tell the same story and give the same details.

Thus evidence of the weightiest and most coherent character would be requisite to overcome the inherent improbability that the Templars could be embarked in an enterprise so insane, in place of which we have only confessions extracted by the threat or application of torture, and not a single instance of a persistent heretic maintaining the belief imputed to him. Turning to the testimony to see whether it comports with the conditions which we have named, we find that no discrimination whatever was exercised in the admission of neophytes. Not a single witness speaks of any preliminary preparation, though several intimate that they obtained entrance by making over their property to the Order.* Indeed, one of the charges was, that there was no preliminary probation, and that the neophyte at once became a professed member in full standing, which, as explained by a knight of Mas Deu, was because their services were considered to be at once required against the Saracens.† Youths and even children of tender years were admitted, although in violation of the statutes

---

* Procès, II. 188, 407.   † Ibid. II. 451.

of the Order, of ages ranging from ten or eleven years upward.* High-born knights, priding themselves on their honor, priests, laborers, husbandmen, menials of all kinds were brought in, and, if we are to believe their evidence, they were without notice obliged, by threats of death and lifelong imprisonment, to undergo the severest personal humiliation, and to perform the awful task of renouncing their Saviour and spitting on, or even more outrageously defiling, the cross which was the object of their veneration and the symbol of their faith. Such a method of propagating heresy by force in the Europe of the Inquisition, of trusting such fearful secrets to children and to unwilling men of all conditions, is so absurd that its mere assertion deprives the testimony of all claim to credence.

Equally damaging to the credibility of the evidence is the self-contradictory character of its details. It was obtained by examining the accused on a series of charges elaborately drawn up, and by requiring answers to each article in succession, so that the general features of the so-called confessions were suggested in advance. Had the charges been true there could have been little variation in the answers, but in place of a definite faith or a systematic ritual we find every possible variation that could suggest itself to witnesses striving to invent stories that should satisfy their torturers. Some say that they were taught Deism—that God in heaven alone was to be worshipped.† Others, that they were forced to renounce God.‡ The usual formula reported, however, was simply to renounce Christ, or Jesus, while others were called upon to renounce Notre Sire, or la Profeta, or Christ, the Virgin, and the Saints.§ Some professed that they could not recollect whether their renunciation had been of God or of Christ.‖ Some-

---

* Procès, I. 241, 412, 415, 602, 611; II. 7, 295, 298, 354, 359, 382, 394.—Règle, § 7, p. 211.

† Procès, I. 213, 332; II. 388, 404.—Raynouard, p. 281.—In this and the following notes I can only give a few references as examples. To do so exhaustively would be to make an analytical index of the whole voluminous mass of testimony.

‡ Procès, I. 206, 242, 302, 378, 386, etc.; II. 5, 27, etc.

§ Procès, I. 254, 417; II. 24, 62, 72, 104.—Bini, Dei Tempieri in Toscana, pp. 463, 470, 478.

‖ Procès, II. 42, 44, 59.

times we hear that instruction was given that they should not believe in Christ, that he was a false prophet, that he suffered for his own sins, but more frequently that the only reason alleged was that such was the Rule of the Order.* It was the same with the idol which has so greatly exercised the imagination of commentators. Some witnesses swore that it was produced whenever a neophyte was received, and that its adoration was a part of the ceremony; others that it was only exhibited and worshipped in the secrecy of chapters; by far the greater number, however, had never seen it or heard of it. Of those who professed to have seen it, scarce two described it alike, within the limits suggested by the articles of accusation, which spoke of it as a head. Sometimes it is black, sometimes white, sometimes with black hair, and sometimes white and black mixed, and again with a long white beard. Some witnesses saw its neck and shoulders covered with gold; one declared that it was a demon (*Maufé*) on which no one could look without trembling; another that it had for eyes carbuncles which lighted up the room; another that it had two faces; another three faces; another four legs, two behind and two before, and yet another said it was a statue with three heads. On one occasion it is a picture, on another a painting on a plaque, on another a small female figure which the preceptor draws from under his garments, and on another the statue of a boy, a cubit in height, sedulously concealed in the treasury of the preceptory. According to the testimony of one witness it degenerated into a calf. Sometimes it is called the Saviour, and sometimes Bafomet or Maguineth—corruptions of Mahomet—and is worshipped as Allah. Sometimes it is God, creating all things, causing the trees to bloom and the grass to germinate, and then again it is a friend of God who can approach him and intercede for the suppliant. Sometimes it gives responses, and sometimes it is accompanied or replaced by the devil in the form of a black or gray cat or raven, who occasionally answers the questions addressed to him, the performance winding up, like the witches' Sabbat, with the introduction of demons in the form of beautiful women.†

---

* Procès, I. 206–7, 294, 411, 426, 464, 533; II. 31, 128, 242, 366.

† Procès, I. 190, 207, 399, 502, 597; II. 193, 203, 212, 279, 300, 313, 315, 363, 364.—Du Puy, pp. 105–6.—Raynouard, pp. 246–8, 279–83, 293.—Bini, pp. 465,

Similar contradictions are observable in the evidence as to the ritual of reception. The details laid down in the Rule are accurately and uniformly described, but when the witnesses come to

---

474, 482, 487, 488.—Wilkins, Concilia, II. 358.—Schottmüller, op. cit. II. 29, 50, 68, 70, 127, 410, 411.—Vaissette, IV. 141.—Stemler, pp. 124-5.

It is in this multiform creature of the imagination that Dr. Wilcke (II. 131-2) sees alternately an image of John the Baptist and the triune Makroposopus of the Cabala.

Among the few outside witnesses who appeared before the papal commission in 1310–11, was Antonio Sicci of Vercelli, imperial and apostolic notary, who forty years before had served the Templars in Syria in that capacity, and had recently been employed in the case by the Inquisition of Paris. Among his Eastern experiences he gravely related a story current in Sidon that a lord of that city once loved desperately but fruitlessly a noble maiden of Armenia; she died, and, like Periander of Corinth, on the night of her burial he opened her tomb and gratified his passion. A mysterious voice said, " Return in nine months and you will find a head, your son!" In due time he came back and found a human head in the tomb, when the voice said, " Guard this head, for all your good-fortune will come from it!" At the time the witness heard this, Matthieu le Sauvage of Picardy was Preceptor of Sidon, who had established brotherhood with the Soldan of Babylon by each drinking the other's blood. Then a certain Julian, who had succeeded to Sidon and to the possession of the head, entered the Order and gave to it the town and all his wealth. He was subsequently expelled and entered the Hospitallers, whom he finally abandoned for the Premonstratensians (Procès, I. 645-6). This somewhat irrelevant and disconnected story so impressed the commissioners that they made Antonio reduce it to writing himself, and lost no subsequent opportunity of inquiring about the head of Sidon from all other witnesses who had been in Syria. Shortly afterwards Jean Senandi, who had lived in Sidon for five years, informed them that the Templars purchased the city, and that Julian, who had been one of its lords, entered the Order but apostatized and died in poverty. One of his ancestors was said to have loved a maiden and abused her corpse, but he had heard nothing of the head (Ib. II. 140). Pierre de Nobiliac had been for many years beyond seas, but had likewise never heard of it (Ib. 215). At length their curiosity was gratified by Hugues de Faure, who confirmed the fact that Sidon had been purchased by the Grand Master, Thomas Berard (1257–1273), and added that after the fall of Acre he had heard in Cyprus that the heiress of Maraclea, in Tripoli, had been loved by a noble who had exhumed her body and violated it, and cut off her head, a voice telling him to guard it well, for it would destroy all who looked upon it. He wrapped it up and kept it in a coffer, and in Cyprus, when he wished to destroy a town or the Greeks, he would uncover it and accomplish his purpose. Desiring to destroy Constantinople he sailed thither with it, but his old nurse, curious to know what was in the coffer so carefully preserved,

speak of the sacrilegious rites imputed to them, they flounder among almost every variation that could suggest itself to their imaginations.   Usually renunciation of God or Christ and spitting on the cross are both required, but in many cases renunciation without spitting suffices, and in as many more spitting without renunciation.* Occasionally spitting is not sufficient, but trampling is added, and even urination ; indeed some over-zealous witnesses declared that the Templars assembled yearly to perform the latter ceremony, while others, while admitting the sacrilege of their reception rites, say that the yearly adoration of the cross on Good Friday, prescribed in the Rule, was also observed with great devotion.† Generally a plain cross is described as the object of contempt, but sometimes a crucifix is used, or a painting of the crucifixion in an illuminated missal ; the cross on the preceptor's mantle is a common device, and even two straws laid crosswise on the ground suffices.   In some cases spitting thrice upon the ground was only required, without anything being said as to its being in disrespect of Christ.‡   Many witnesses declared that the sacrilege was performed in full view of the assembled brethren, others that the neophyte was taken into a dark corner, or behind the altar, or into another room carefully closed ; in one case it took place in a field, in another in a grange, in another in a cooper-shop, and in another

---

opened it, when a sudden storm burst over the ship and sank it with all on board, except a few sailors who escaped to tell the tale.   Since then no fish have been found in that part of the sea (Ib. 223–4).   Guillaume Avril had been seven years beyond seas without hearing of the head, but had been told that in the whirlpool of Setalias a head sometimes appeared, and then all the vessels there were lost (Ib. 238).   All this rubbish was sent to the Council of Vienne as part of the evidence against the Order

* Procès, I. 233, 242, 250, 414, 423, 429, 533, 536, 546, etc.

† Procès, I. 233 ; II. 219, 232, 237, 264.—Raynouard, 274–5, 279–80.—Bini, pp. 463, 497.

At the feast of the Holy Cross in May and September, and on Good Friday, the Templars all assembled, and, laying aside shoes and head-gear and swords, adored the cross, with the hymn—

> Ador te Crist et benesesc te Crist
> Qui per la sancta tua crou nos resemist.—

> (Procès, II. 474, 491, 503.)

‡ Procès, I. 233, 250, 536, 539, 541, 546, 606 ; II. 226, 232, 336, 360, 369.— Raynouard, p. 275.

in a room used for the manufacture of shoes.*   As a rule the preceptor was represented as enforcing it, but in many cases the duty was confided to one or more serving brethren, and in one instance the person officiating had his head hidden in a cowl.†   Almost universally it formed part of the ceremonies of reception, sometimes even before the vows were administered or the mantle bestowed, but generally at the conclusion, after the neophyte was fully committed, but there were occasional instances in which it was postponed until a later hour, or to the next day, or to longer intervals, extending, in one or two cases, to months and years.‡ Some witnesses declared that it formed part of all receptions; others that it had been enforced in their case, but they had never seen it or heard of it in other receptions at which they had been present.   In general they swore that they were told it was a rule of the Order, but some said that it was explained to them as a joke, and others that they were told to do it with the mouth and not with the heart.   One, indeed, deposed that he had been offered the choice between renouncing Christ, spitting on the cross, and the indecent kiss, and he selected the spitting.§   In fact, the evidence as to the enforcement of the sacrilege is hopelessly contradictory. In many cases the neophyte was excused after a slight resistance; in others he was thrust into a dark dungeon until he yielded. Egidio, Preceptor of San Gemignano of Florence, stated that he had known two recalcitrant neophytes carried in chains to Rome, where they perished in prison, and Niccolò Regino, Preceptor of Grosseto, said that recusants were slain, or sent to distant parts, like Sardinia, where they ended their days.   Geoffroi de Charney, Preceptor of Normandy, swore that he enforced it upon the first neophyte whom he received, but that he never did so afterwards, and Gui Dauphin, one of the high officers of the Order, said virtually the same thing; Gaucher de Liancourt, Preceptor of Reims, on the other hand, testified that he had required it in all cases, for

---

* Procès, I. 530, 533, 536, 539, 544, 549, 565, 572, 622; II. 24, 27, 29, 31, 120, 280, 362, 546, 579.—Schottmüller, II. 413.

† Procès, I. 386, 536, 539, 565, 572, 592.

‡ Procès, I. 413, 434, 444, 469, 504, 559, 562; II. 75, 99, 113, 123, 205.—Raynouard, p. 280.—Schottmüller, op. cit. II. 132, 410.

§ Procès, I. 407, 418, 435, 462, 572, 588; II. 27, 38, 67, 174, 185, 214.

III.—18

if he had not he would have been imprisoned for life, and Hugues de Peraud, the Visitor of France, declared that it was obligatory on him.*

It would be a work of supererogation to pursue this examination further. The same irreconcilable confusion reigns in the evidence as to the other charges—the cord of chastity, the obscene kiss, the mutilation of the canon of the mass,† the power of absolution assigned to the Grand Master, the license for unnatural crime. It might be argued, as these witnesses had been received into the Order at times varying from fifty to sixty years previous to within a few months, and at places so widely apart as Palestine and England, that these variations are explicable by local usages or by a gradually perfected belief and ritual. An investigation of the confessions shows, however, that no such explanation will suffice; there can be no grouping as to the time or place of the ceremony. Yet there can be a grouping which is of supreme significance, a grouping as to the tribunal through which the witness passed. This is often very notable among the two hundred and twenty-five who were sent to the papal commission from various parts of France, and examined in 1310 and 1311. As a rule they manifested extreme anxiety that their present depositions should accord with those which they had made when subject to inquisition by the bishops—doubtless they made them as nearly so as their memories would permit—and it is easy to see how greater or less rigor, or how concert between those confined in the same prison, had led to the concoction of stories such as would satisfy their

---

* Procès, I. 404; II. 260, 281, 284, 295, 299, 338, 354, 356, 363, 389, 390, 395, 407.—Bini, pp. 468, 488.

It is not easy to appreciate the reasoning of Michelet (Procès, II. vii.–viii.), who argues that the uniformity of denial in a series of depositions taken by the Bishop of Elne suggests concert of statement agreed upon in advance, while the variations in those who admitted guilt are an evidence of their veracity. If the Templars were innocent, denials of the charges read to them seriatim would be necessarily identical; if they were guilty, the confessions would be likewise uniform. Thus the identity of the one group and the diversity of the other both concur to disprove the accusations.

† Incontrovertible evidence that the Templar priests did not mutilate the words of consecration in the mass is furnished in the Cypriote proceedings by ecclesiastics who had long dwelt with them in the East.—Processus Cypricus (Schottmüller, II. 379, 382, 383).

judges. Thus the confessions obtained by the Ordinary of Poitiers have a character distinct from those extorted by the Bishop of Clermont, and we can classify the penitents of the Bishop of Le Mans, the Archbishop of Sens, the Archbishop of Tours, the Bishops of Amiens, Rodez, Macon, in fact of nearly all the prelates who took part in the terrible drama.*

Another feature indicating the untrustworthy character of the evidence is that large numbers of the witnesses swore that they had confessed the sacrilege committed to priests and friars of all kinds, to bishops, and even to papal penitentiaries, and had received absolution by the imposition of penance, usually of a trifling character, such as fasting on Fridays for a few months or a year.† No ordinary confessor could absolve for heresy; it was a sin reserved for the inquisitor, papal or episcopal. The most that the confessor could have done would have been to send the penitent to some one competent to grant absolution, which would only have been administered under the heaviest penance, including denunciation of the Order. To suppose, in fact, that thousands of men, during a period of fifty or a hundred years, could have been entrapped into such a heresy without its becoming matter of notoriety, is in itself so violent an assumption as to deprive the whole story of all claims upon belief.

Thus the more closely the enormous aggregate of testimony is examined the more utterly worthless it appears, and this is confirmed by the fact that nowhere could compromising evidence be obtained without the use of inquisitorial methods. Had thousands of men been unwillingly forced to abjure their faith and been terrorized into keeping the dread secret, as soon as the pressure was removed by the seizure there would have been a universal eagerness to unburden the conscience and seek reconciliation with the Church. No torture would have been requisite to obtain all the evidence required. In view, therefore, of the extreme improba-

---

* Procès, I. 230-1, 264-74, 296-307, 331-67, 477-93, 602-19, 621-41; II. 1-3, 56-85, 91-114, 122-52, 154-77, 184-91, 234-56, 263-7.

† Procès, I. 298, 305, 319, 336, 372, 401, 405, 427, 436, etc.

It is not easy to understand the prescription of Friday fasting as a penance for a Templar, for the ascetic rules of the Order already required the most rigid fasting. Meat was only allowed three days in the week, and a second Lent was kept from the Sunday before Martinmas until Christmas (Règle, §§ 15, 57).

bility of the charge, of the means employed to obtain proof for its support, and the lack of coherence in the proof so obtained, it appears to me that no judicial mind in possession of the facts can hesitate to pronounce a sentence, not merely of not proven, but of acquittal.   The theory that there were inner grades in the Order, by which those alone to be trusted were initiated in its secret doctrines, is perfectly untenable.   As there is no evidence of any kind to support it, it is a matter of mere conjecture, which is sufficiently negatived by the fact that with scarce an exception those who confessed, whether ploughmen or knights, relate the sacrilege as taking place on their admission.   If the witnesses on whom the prosecution relied are to be believed at all, the infection pervaded the whole Order.

Yet it is by no means improbable that there may have been some foundation for the popular gossip that the neophyte at his reception was forced to kiss the posteriors of his preceptor.   As we have seen, a large majority of the Order consisted of serving brethren on whom the knights looked down with infinite contempt.   Some such occasional command on the part of a reckless knight, to enforce the principle of absolute obedience, in admitting a plebeian to nominal fraternity and equality, would not have been foreign to the manners of the age.   Who can say, moreover, that men, soured with the disillusion of life within the Order, chafing under the bonds of their irrevocable vow, and perhaps released from all religious convictions amid the license of the East, may not occasionally have tested the obedience of a neophyte by bidding him to spit at the cross on the mantle that had grown hateful to him ?*   No one who recognizes the wayward perversity

---

* This would seem not unlikely if we are to believe the confession of Jean d'Aumônes, a serving brother who stated that at his reception his preceptor turned all the other brethren out of the chapel, and after some difficulty forced him to spit at the cross, after which he said "Go, fool, and confess."   This Jean at once did, to a Franciscan who imposed on him only the penance of three Friday fasts, saying that it was intended as a test of constancy in case of capture by the Saracens (Procès, I. 588–91).

Another serving brother, Pierre de Cherrut, related that after he had been forced to renounce God his preceptor smiled disdainfully at him, as though despising him (Ib. I. 531).

Equally suggestive is the story, told by the serving brother Eudes de Bures,

of human nature, or who is familiar with the condition of monasticism at the period, can deny the possibilities of such occasional performances, whether as brutal jokes or spiteful assertions of supremacy, but the only rational conclusion from the whole tremendous tragedy is that the Order was innocent of the crime for which it was punished.

While Philippe was seizing his prey, Clement, at Poitiers, was occupied in the equally lucrative work of sending collectors throughout Germany to exact a tithe of all ecclesiastical revenues for the recovery of the Holy Land. When aroused from this with the news that Philippe, under the authority of Frère Guillaume the inquisitor, had thus taken decided and irrevocable action in a matter which was still before him for consideration, his first emotion naturally was that of wounded pride and indignation, sharpened perhaps by the apprehension that he would not be able to secure his share of the spoils. He dared not publicly disavow responsibility for the act, and what would be the current of public opinion outside of France no man could divine. In this cruel dilemma he wrote to Philippe, October 27, 1307, expressing his indignation that the king should have taken action in a matter which the brief of August 24 showed to be receiving papal consideration. Carefully suppressing the fact of the intervention of the Inquisition which legally justified the whole proceeding, Clem-

---

a youth of twenty at the time, that after his reception he was taken into another room by two of the brethren and forced to renounce Christ. On his refusing at first, one of them said that in his country people renounced God a hundred times for a flea—perhaps an exaggeration, but " Je renye Dieu " was one of the commonest of expletives. When the preceptor heard him weeping he called to the tormentors to let him alone, as they would set him crazy, and he subsequently told Eudes that it was a joke (Ib. II. 100–2).

What is the real import of such incidents may be gathered from a story related by a witness during the inquest held in Cyprus, May, 1310. He had heard from a Genoese named Matteo Zaccaria, who had long been a prisoner in Cairo, that when the news of the proceedings against the Order reached the Soldan of Egypt he drew from his prisons about forty Templars captured ten years before on the island of Tortosa, and offered them wealth if they would renounce their religion. Surprised and angered by their refusal, he remanded them to their dungeons and ordered them to be deprived of food and drink, when they perished to a man rather than apostatize.—Schottmüller, op. cit. II. 160.

ent sought a further ground of complaint by reminding the king
that Templars were not under royal jurisdiction, but under that
of the Holy See, and he had committed a grave act of disobedience in seizing their persons and property, both of which must be
forthwith delivered to two cardinals sent for the purpose.   These
were Berenger de Frédole, Cardinal of SS. Nereo and Achille,
and Étienne de Suissi of S. Ciriaco, both Frenchmen and creatures
of Philippe, who had procured their elevation to the sacred college.
He seems to have had no trouble in coming to an understanding
with them, for, though the trials and tortures were pushed unre-
mittingly, another letter of Clement's, December 1, praises the
king for putting the matter in the hands of the Holy See, and one
of Philippe's of December 24 announces that he had no intention
of infringing on the rights of the Church and does not intend to
abandon his own ; he has, he says, delivered the Templars to the
cardinals, and the administration of their property shall be kept
separate from that of the crown.   Clement's susceptibilities being thus soothed, even before the trials at Paris were ended he issued, November 22, the bull *Pastoralis præeminentiæ*, addressed to
all the potentates of Europe, in which he related what Philippe
had done at the requisition of the Inquisitor of France, in order
that the Templars might be presented to the judgment of the
Church ; how the chiefs of the Order had confessed the crimes
imputed to them ; how he himself had examined one of them who
was employed about his person and had confirmed the truth of
the allegations.   Therefore he orders all the sovereigns to do likewise, retaining the prisoners and holding their property in the
name of the pope and subject to his order.   Should the Order
prove innocent the property is to be restored to it, otherwise it
is to be employed for the recovery of the Holy Land.*   This

---

* Regest. Clement. PP. V. T. II. p. 95.—Du Puy, pp. 117–18, 124, 134.—Schottmüller, I. 94.—Rymer, Fœd. III. 30.—MSS. Chioccarello T. VIII.—Mag. Bull.
Rom. IX. 126, 131.—Zurita, Lib. v. c. 73.

Apparently there was a general expectation that the Hospitallers would share
the fate of the Templars, and a disposition was manifested at once to pillage
them, for Clement felt obliged, December 21, 1307, to issue a bull confirming all
their privileges and immunities, and to send throughout Europe letters ordering
them to be protected from all encroachments (Regest. Clem. PP. V. T. III. pp.
14, 17–18, 20–1, 273 ; T. IV. p. 418).

was the irrevocable act which decided the fate of the Templars, as we shall see hereafter when we consider the action of the princes of Europe outside of France.

Philippe thus had forced Clement's hand, and Clement was fairly committed to the investigation, which in the hands of the Inquisition could only end in the destruction of the Order. Secure in his position, the king pushed on the examination of the prisoners throughout the kingdom, and the vigilance of his agents is shown in the case of two German Templars returning home, whom they arrested at Chaumont and delivered to the Inquisitor of the Three Bishoprics. One was a priest, the other a serving brother, and the inquisitor in reporting to Philippe says that he had not tortured the latter because he was very sick, but that neither had admitted that there was in the Order aught that was not pure and holy. The examinations went on during the winter of 1308, when Clement unexpectedly put a stop to them. What was his motive we can only conjecture; probably he found that Philippe's promises with regard to the Templar possessions were not likely to be fulfilled, and that an assertion of his control was necessary. Whatever his reasons, he suddenly suspended in the premises the power of all the inquisitors and bishops in France and evoked to himself the cognizance of the whole affair, alleging that the suddenness of the seizure without consulting him, although so near and so accessible, had excited in him grave suspicions, which had not been allayed by the records of the examinations submitted to him, for these were of a character rather to excite incredulity—though in November he had proclaimed to all Christendom his conviction of their truth. It shows how completely the whole judicial proceedings were inquisitional that this brought them to an immediate close, provoking Philippe to uncontrollable wrath. Angrily he wrote to Clement that he had sinned greatly: even popes, he hints, may fall into heresy; he had wronged all the prelates and inquisitors of France; he had inspired the Templars with hopes and they were retracting their confessions, especially Hugues de Peraud, who had had the honor of dining with the cardinal-deputies. Evidently some intrigue was on foot, and Clement was balancing, irresolute as to which side offered most advantage, and satisfied at least to show to Philippe that he was indispensable. Philippe at first was disposed to assert his independence and claim jurisdiction, and he applied to the University for an opinion to support his claims, but the Faculty of Theology replied, March 25, 1308, as it could not help doing: the Templars were religious and consequently exempt from secular jurisdiction; the only cognizance which a secular court could have over heresy was at the request of the Church after it had abandoned the heretic; in case of necessity the secular power could arrest a heretic, but it could only be for the purpose of delivering him to the ecclesiastical court; and finally the Templar property must be held for the purpose for which it was given to the Order.*

Philippe, thus foiled, proceeded to bring a still stronger pressure to bear on Clement. He appealed to his subservient bishops and summoned a national assembly, to meet April 15 in Tours, to deliberate with him on the subject of the Templars. Already, at the Assembly of Paris in 1302, he had called in the Tiers-État and had learned to value its support in his quarrel with Boniface, and now he again brought in the communes, thus founding the institution of the States-General. After some delay the assembly met in May. In his summons Philippe had detailed the crimes of the Templars as admitted facts which ought to arouse for their punishment not only arms and the laws, but brute cattle and the four elements. He desired his subjects to participate in the pious work, and therefore he ordered the towns to select each two deputies zealous for the faith. From a gathering collected under such impulsion it was not difficult, in spite of the secret leaning of the nobles to the proscribed Order, to procure a virtually unanimous expression of opinion that the Templars deserved death.†

With the prestige of the nation at his back, Philippe went from Tours, at the end of May, to Clement at Poitiers, accompanied by a strong deputation, including his brothers, his sons, and his coun-

---

* Du Puy, pp. 12–13, 84–5, 89, 109, 111–12, 134.—D'Achery Spicileg. II. 199.—Raynouard, p. 238, 306.

Jean de S. Victor gives the date of the declaration of the University as the Saturday after Ascension (May 25, ap. Bouquet, XXI. 651), but Du Puy describes the document as sealed with fourteen seals, and dated on Lady Day (March 25).

† Archives Administratives de Reims, T. II. pp. 65, 66.—Chassaing Spicilegium Brivatense, pp. 274–5.—Du Puy, pp. 38–9, 85, 113, 116.—Contin. Nangiac. ann. 1308.—Joann. de S. Victor. (Bouquet, XXI. 650).—Raynouard, p. 42.

cillors. Long and earnest were the disputations over the affair, Philippe urging, through his spokesman, Guillaume de Plaisian, that the Templars had been found guilty and that immediate punishment should follow; Clement reiterating his grievance that an affair of such magnitude, exclusively appertaining to the Holy See, should be carried on without his initiative. A body like the Order of the Temple had powerful friends all over Europe whose influence with the curia was great, and the papal perplexities were manifold as one side or the other preponderated; but Clement had irrevocably committed himself in the face of all Europe by his bull of November 22, and it was in reality but a question of the terms on which he would allow the affair to go on in France by removing the suspension of the powers of the Inquisition. The bargaining was sharp, but an agreement was reached. As Clement had reserved the matter for papal judgment, it was necessary that some show of investigation should be had. Seventy-two Templars were drawn from the prisons of Paris to be examined by the pope and sacred college, that they might be able to assert personal knowledge of their guilt. Clement might well shrink from confronting de Molay and the chiefs of the Order whom he was betraying, while at the same time they could not be arbitrarily omitted. They were therefore stopped at Chinon near Tours, under pretext of sickness, while the others were sent forward to Poitiers. From the 28th of June to July 1 they were solemnly examined by five cardinals friendly to Philippe deputed for the purpose. The official report of the examinations shows the care which had been exercised in the selection of those who were to perform this scene in the drama. A portion of them were spontaneous witnesses who had left, or had tried to leave, the Order. The rest, with the terrible penalty for retraction impending over them, confirmed the confessions made before the Inquisition, which in many cases had been extracted by torture. Then, July 2, they were brought before the pope in full consistory and the same scene was enacted. Thus the papal jurisdiction was recognized; Clement in his subsequent bulls could speak of his own knowledge, and could declare that the accused had confessed their errors spontaneously and without coercion, and had humbly begged for absolution and reconciliation.*

---

* Ptol. Lucens. Hist. Eccles. Lib. xxiv. (Muratori S. R. I. XI. 1229–30).—

The agreement duly executed between Clement and Philippe bore that the Templars should be delivered to the pope, but be guarded in his name by the king; that their trials should be proceeded with by the bishops in their several dioceses, to whom, at the special and earnest request of the king, the inquisitors were adjoined—but de Molay and the Preceptors of the East, of Normandy, Poitou, and Provence, were reserved for the papal judgment; the property was to be placed in the hands of commissioners named by the pope and bishops, to whom the king was secretly to add appointees of his own, but he was to pledge himself in writing that it should be employed solely for the Holy Land. Clement assumed that the fate of the Order, as an institution, was too weighty a question to be decided without the intervention of a general council, and it was decided to call one in October, 1310. The Cardinal of Palestrina was named as the papal representative in charge of the persons of the Templars—a duty which he speedily fulfilled by transferring them to the king under condition that they should be held at the disposition of the Church. Clement performed his part of the bargain by removing, July 5, the suspension of the inquisitors and bishops, and restoring their jurisdiction in the matter. Directions were sent at the same time to each of the bishops in France to associate with himself two cathedral canons, two Dominicans, and two Franciscans, and proceed with the trials of the individual Templars within his diocese, admitting inquisitors to participate at will, but taking no action against the Order as a whole; all persons were ordered, under pain of excommunication, to arrest Templars and deliver them to the inquisitors or episcopal officials, and Philippe furnished twenty copies of royal letters commanding his subjects to restore to the papal deputies all property, real and personal, of the Order.*

Joann. de S. Victor (Bouquet, XXI. 650).—Raynouard, pp. 44–5, 245–52.—Du Puy, pp. 13–14.—Schottmüller, op. cit. II. 13 sqq.—Bull. *Faciens misericordiam*, 12 Aug. 1308 (Rymer, II. 101.—Mag. Bull. Rom. IX. 136).

* Du Puy, pp. 15–17, 20, 39, 86, 107–8, 118–19, 121–22, 125.—Contin. Nangiac. ann. 1308.—Raynouard, pp. 46, 49.—Joann. de S. Victor (Bouquet, XXI. 651).—D'Achery Spicileg. II. 200.

Guillaume de Plaisian, who had been Philippe's chief instrument in these transactions, received special marks of Clement's favor by briefs dated August 5 (Regest. Clement. PP. V. T. III. pp. 216, 227).

Although Clement declared in his bulls to Europe that Philippe had manifested his disinterestedness by surrendering all the Templar property, the question was one which gave rise to a good deal of skilful fencing on both sides. It is not worth while to pursue the affair in its details, but we shall see how in the end Philippe successfully cheated his partner in the game and retained the control which he apparently gave up.[*]

The rival powers having thus come to an understanding about their victims, proceedings were resumed with fresh energy. Clement made up for his previous hesitation with ample show of zeal. De Molay and the chief officials with him were detained at Chinon until the middle of August, when the Cardinals of SS. Nereo and Achille, of S. Ciriaco and of S. Angelo, were sent thither to examine them. These reported, August 20, to Philippe, that on the 17th and following days they had interrogated the Grand Master, the Master of Cyprus, the Visitor of France, and the Preceptors of Normandy and Poitou, who had confirmed their previous confessions and had humbly asked for absolution and reconciliation, which had been duly given them, and the king is asked to pardon them. There are two things noteworthy in this which illustrate the duplicity pervading the whole affair. In the papal bulls of August 12, five days before this examination was commenced, its results are fully set forth, with the assertion that the confessions were free and spontaneous. Moreover, when, in November, 1309, this bull was read over by the papal commission to de Molay, on hearing its recital of what he was said to have confessed he was stupefied, and, crossing himself twice, said he wished to God the

---

[*] Bull. *Faciens misericordiam.*—Raynald. ann. 1309, No. 3.—Du Puy, pp. 64-5, 86-88, 127, 207-9.—Procès des Templiers I. 50-2.—Raynouard, p. 47.—Regest. Clement. PP. V. T. IV. pp. 433-4.

Clement appointed six curators in France to look after the property for the Holy See. By letters of January 5, 1309, he gave them an allowance from the Templar property of forty sous *parisis* of good money each for every night which they might have to spend away from home, at the same time cautioning them that they must not fraudulently leave their houses without necessity (Regest. T. IV. p. 439). A brief of January 28, 1310, transferring from the Bishop of Vaison to the canon, Gerard de Bussy, the custody of certain Templar houses, shows that Clement succeeded in obtaining possession of a portion (Ib. T. V. p. 56).

custom of the Saracens and Tartars were observed towards persons so perverse, for they beheaded or cut in two those who thus perverted the truth. He might have said more had not Guillaume de Plaisian, the royal agent, who pretended to be his friend, cautioned him as to the risk which he ran in thus constructively retracting his confession, and he contented himself with asking for time for consideration.*

On August 12 Clement issued a series of bulls which regulated the methods of procedure in the case, and showed that he was prepared fully to perform his part of the agreement with Philippe. The bull *Faciens misericordiam*, addressed to the prelates of Christendom, recited at great length the proceedings thus far taken against the accused, and the guilt which they had spontaneously acknowledged; it directed the bishops, in conjunction with inquisitorial commissioners appointed by the pope, to summon all Templars before them and make inquisition concerning them. After this provincial councils were to be summoned, where the guilt or innocence of the individuals was to be determined, and in all the proceedings the local inquisitors had a right to take part. The results of the inquisitions, moreover, were to be promptly transmitted to the pope. With this was enclosed a long and elaborate series of articles on which the accused were to be examined—articles drawn up in Paris by the royal officials—and the whole was ordered to be published in the vernacular in all parish churches. The bull *Regnans in cœlis*, addressed to all princes and prelates, repeated the narrative part of the other, and ended by convoking, for October 1, 1310, a general council at Vienne, to decide as to the fate of the Order, to consult as to the recovery of the Holy Land, and to take such action as might be required for the reformation of the Church. By another bull, *Faciens misericordiam*, dated August 8, a formal summons was issued to all and singular of the Templars to appear before the council, personally or by procurators, on a certain day, to answer to the charges against the Order, and the Cardinal of Palestrina, who was in charge of them, was ordered to produce de Molay and the Preceptors of France, Normandy, Poitou, Aquitaine, and Provence to receive sentence. This was the simplest requirement of judicial procedure, and the

---

* Du Puy. pp. 33–4, 133.—Bull. *Faciens misericordiam.*—Procès, I. 34–5.

manner in which it was subsequently eluded forms one of the darkest features in the whole transaction. Finally there were other bulls elaborately providing for the payment of the papal commissioners and inquisitors, and ordering the Templar possessions everywhere to be sequestrated to await the result of the trial, and to be devoted to the Holy Land in case of condemnation. Much, it was stated, had already been wickedly seized and appropriated, and all persons were summoned to make restitution, under pain of excommunication. All debtors to the Order were summoned to pay, and all persons cognizant of such debts or of stolen property were required to give information. The series of bulls was completed by one of December 30, to be read in all churches, declaring all Templars to be suspect of heresy, ordering their capture as such and delivery to the episcopal ordinaries, and forbidding all potentates and prelates from harboring them or showing them any aid or favor, under pain of excommunication and interdict. At the same time another bull was directed to all the princes of Christendom, commanding them to seize any Templars who might as yet not have been arrested.*

The prosecution of the Templars throughout Europe was thus organized. Even such distant points as Achaia, Corsica, and Sardinia were not neglected. The large number of special inquisitors to be appointed was a work of time, and the correspondence between Philippe and Clement on the subject shows that they virtually were selected by the king. In France the work of prosecution was speedily set on foot, and, after a respite of some six months, the Templars found themselves transferred from the improvised inquisitorial tribunals set on foot by Frère Guillaume to the episcopal courts as provided by Clement. In every diocese

---

* Rymer. III. 101.—Mag. Bull. Rom. IX. 134, 136.—Harduin. VII. 1283, 1289, 1321, 1353.—Schmidt, Päbstliche Urkunden und Regesten, Halle, 1886, pp. 71-2.—Raynald. ann. 1308, No. 8.—Contin. Guill. Nangiac. ann. 1308.—Raynouard, p. 50.—Regest. Clement. PP. V. T. III. pp. 281 sqq., pp. 363 sqq., 386 sqq.; T. IV. pp. 3, 276 sqq., 479-82.

The Master of England and the Master of Germany were reserved for papal judgment. The bull *Faciens misericordiam*, addressed to Germany, contained no command to assemble provincial councils (Harduin. VII. 1353).

In spite of all that had occurred, this bull seems to have taken the public by surprise outside of France. Walter of Hemingford calls it "*bullam horribilem contra Templarios*" (Chron. Ed. 1849, II. 279).

the bishops were soon busily at work.   Curiously enough, some of them doubted whether they could use torture, and applied for instructions, to which Clement answered that they were to be governed by the written law, which removed their misgivings.   The papal instructions indicate that these proceedings only concerned those Templars who had not passed through the hands of Frère Guillaume and his commissioners, but there seems to have been little distinction observed as to this.   Clement urged forward the proceedings with little regard to formality, and authorized the bishops to act outside of their respective dioceses, and without respect to the place of origin of the accused.   The sole object evidently was to extract from them satisfactory confessions, as a preparation for the provincial councils which were to be summoned for their final judgment.   Those who had already confessed were not likely to retract.   Before the papal commission in 1310, Jean de Cochiac exhibited a letter from Philippe de Vohet and Jean de Jamville, the papal and royal custodians of the prisoners, to those confined at Sens at the time the Bishop of Orleans was sent there to examine them (the archbishopric of Sens was then vacant), warning them that those who revoked the confessions made before "*los quizitor*" would be burned as relapsed.   Vohet, when summoned before the commission, admitted the seal to be his, but denied authorizing the letter, and the commission prudently abstained from pushing the investigation further.   The nervous anxiety manifested by most of those brought before the commission that their statements should accord with what they had said before the bishops, shows that they recognized the danger which they incurred.*

The treatment of those who refused to confess varied with the temper of the bishops and their adjuncts.   The records of their tribunals have mostly disappeared, and we are virtually left to gather what we can from the utterances of a few witnesses who made to the commission chance allusions to their former experiences.   Yet the proceedings before the Bishop of Clermont would show that they were not in all cases treated with undue harshness.   He had sixty-nine Templars, of whom forty confessed,

---

* Du Puy, pp. 110, 125.—Raynouard, p. 130.—Regest. Clement. PP. V. T. IV. pp. 453–55, 457–8.—Procès, I. 71–2, 128, 132, 135, 463, 511, 540, etc.

and twenty-nine refused to admit any evil in the Order. Then he assembled them and divided them into the two groups. The recusants declared that they adhered to their assertion, and that if they should subsequently confess through fear of torture, prison, or other affliction, they protested that they should not be believed, and that it should not prejudice them, nor does it appear that any constraint was afterwards put upon them. The others were asked whether they had any defence to offer, or whether they were ready for definitive sentence, when they unanimously declared that they had nothing to offer nor wished to hear their sentence, but submitted themselves to the mercy of the Church. What that mercy was we shall see hereafter. All bishops were not as mild as he of Clermont, but in the fragmentary recitals before the commission it is not always easy to distinguish the action of the episcopal tribunals from that of Frère Guillaume's inquisitors. A few instances will suffice to show how, between the two, testimony was obtained against the Order. Jean de Rompreye, a husbandman, declared that he knew nothing but good of the Order, although he had confessed otherwise before the Bishop of Orleans after being thrice tortured. Robert Vigier, a serving brother, likewise denied the accusations, though he had confessed them before the Bishop of Nevers at Paris, on account of the fierceness of the torture, under which he understood that three of his comrades, Gautier, Henri, and Chanteloup, had died. Bernard de Vado, a priest, had been tortured by fire applied to the soles of the feet to such an extent that a few days afterwards the bones of his heels dropped out, in testimony of which he exhibited the bones. Nineteen brethren from Périgord had confessed before the Bishop of Périgord through torture and starvation—one of them had been kept for six months on bread and water, without shoes or upper clothing. Guillaume d'Erré, when brought before the Bishop of Saintes, had denied all the charges, but after being put on bread and water and threatened with torture, had confessed to renouncing Christ and spitting at the cross—a confession which he now retracts. Thomas de Pamplona, under many tortures inflicted on him at St. Jean d'Angely, had confirmed the confession made by de Molay, and then, upon being put upon bread and water, had confessed before the Bishop of Saintes to spitting at the cross, all of which he now retracts. These instances might be multiplied

out of the few who had the hardihood to incur the risk of martyrdom attendant upon withdrawing their confessions.   Indeed, in
the universal terror impressed on the friendless and defenceless
wretches, we cannot condemn those who yielded, and can only ad-
mire the constancy of those who endured the torture and braved
the stake in defence of the Order.   What was the general feeling
among them was voiced by Aymon de Barbara, who had thrice
been tortured, and had for nine weeks been kept on bread and
water.   He pitifully said that he had suffered in body and soul,
but as for retracting his confession, he would not do so as long as
he was in prison.   The mental struggles which the poor creatures
endured are well illustrated by Jean de Cormèle, Preceptor of
Moissac, who when brought before the commission hesitated and
would not describe the ceremonies at his own reception, though
he declared that he had seen nothing wrong at the reception of
others.   The recollection of the tortures which he had endured in
Paris, in which he had lost four teeth, completely unnerved him,
and he begged to have time for consideration.   He was given
until the next day, and when he reappeared his resolution had
broken down.   He confessed the whole catalogue of villainies; and
when asked if he had consulted any one, denied it, but said that
he had requested a priest to say for him a mass of the Holy Ghost
that God might direct him what to do.*

These instances will illustrate the nature of the work in which
the whole episcopate of France was engaged during the remainder
of the year 1308 and through 1309 and 1310.   All this, however,
concerned merely the members of the Order as individuals.   The
fate of the Templar possessions depended upon the judgment to
be rendered on the Order as a body corporate, and for this purpose Clement had assigned for it a day on which it was to appear
by its syndics and procurators before the Council of Vienne, to
put in its defence and show cause why it should not be abolished.
Seeing that the officers and members were scattered in prison
throughout Europe, this was a manifest impossibility, and some
method was imperatively required by which they could, at least
constructively, be represented, if only to hear their sentence.

---

* Raynouard, pp. 52–3. — Procès, I. 40, 75, 230, 506–9, 511–14, 520–1, 527–8;
II. 13, 18.

Among the bulls of August 12, 1308, therefore, there was one creating a commission, with the Archbishop of Narbonne at its head, authorized to summon before it all the Templars of France, to examine them, and to report the result. Subsequent bulls of May, 1309, directed the commission to set to work, and notified Philippe concerning it. August 8, 1309, the commission assembled in the abbey of Sainte-Genevieve, and by letters addressed to all the archbishops of the kingdom cited all Templars to appear before them on the first working-day after Martinmas, and the Order itself to appear by its syndics and procurators at the Council of Vienne, to receive such sentence as God should decree. On the appointed day, November 12, the commissioners reassembled, but no Templars appeared. For a week they met daily, and daily the form was gone through of a proclamation by the apparitor that if any one wished to appear for the Order or its members the commission was ready to listen to him kindly, but without result. On examining the replies of the prelates they were found to have imperfectly fulfilled their duty. Philippe evidently regarded the whole proceeding with distrust, and was not inclined to aid it. A somewhat peremptory communication on November 18 was addressed to the Bishop of Paris, explaining that their proceedings were not against individuals, but against the whole Order; that no one was to be forced to appear, but that all who so chose must be allowed to come. This brought the bishop before them on November 22, with explanations and apologies; and a summons to Philippe de Vohet and Jean de Jamville, the papal and royal custodians of the Templars, brought those officials to promise obedience. Yet the obstacles to the performance of their task did not disappear. On the 22d they were secretly informed that some persons had come to Paris in lay garments to defend the Order, and had been thrown in prison. Thereupon they sent for Jean de Plublaveh, *prévôt* of the Châtelet, who said that by royal order he had arrested seven men said to be Templars in disguise, who had come with money to engage advocates in defence of the Order, but on torturing two of them he had found this not to be the case. The matter proved to be of little significance except as manifesting the purpose of the king to control the action of the commission.*

---

* Joann. de S. Victor (Bouquet, XXI. 654).—Procès, I. 1–31.

At length the commission succeeded in securing the presence of de Molay, of Hugues de Peraud, and of some of the brethren confined in Paris. De Molay said he was not wise and learned enough to defend the Order, but he would hold himself vile and miserable if he did not attempt it. Yet he was a prisoner and penniless; he had not four deniers to spend, and only a poor serving brother with whom to advise; he prayed to have aid and counsel, and he would do his best. The commissioners reminded him that trials for heresy were not conducted according to legal forms, that advocates were not admitted, and they cautioned him as to the risk he incurred in defending the Order after the confession which he had made. Kindly they read over to him the report of the cardinals as to his confession at Chinon; and on his manifesting indignation and astonishment, Guillaume de Plaisian, who seems to have been watching the proceedings on the part of the king, gave him, as we have already seen, another friendly caution which closed his lips. He asked for delay, and when he reappeared Guillaume de Nogaret was there to take advantage of any imprudence. From the papal letters which had been read to him he learned that the pope had reserved him and the other chiefs of the Order for special judgment, and he therefore asked to have the opportunity of appearing before the papal tribunal without delay. The shrewdness of this device thus made itself apparent. It separated the leaders from the rest; de Molay, Hugues de Peraud, and Geoffroi de Gonneville were led to hope for special consideration, and selfishly abandoned their followers. As for the brethren, their answers to the commission were substantially that of Géraud de Caux—he was a simple knight, without horse, arms, or land; he knew not how, and could not defend the Order.[*]

By this time Philippe seems to have been satisfied that no harm could come from the operations of the commission. His opposition disappeared, and he graciously lent them his assistance. November 28, a second summons was sent to the bishops threatening them with papal indignation for a continuance of their neglect, and, what was far more efficacious, it was accompanied with orders from Philippe directing his jailers to afford to the episcopal officials access to the imprisoned Templars, while the baillis were

---

[*] Procès, I. 28, 29, 41-5, 88.

instructed to send to Paris, under sure guard, all Templars desiring to defend their Order.*

February 3, 1310, was the day named in this new citation. By the 5th Templars began to pour in, nearly all eager to defend their Order. They accumulated until the commission was embarrassed how to deal with them, and finally, on March 28, five hundred and forty-six who had offered to defend were assembled in the garden of the episcopal palace, where the commissioners explained to them what was proposed, and suggested that they should nominate six or eight or ten of their number to act as procurators; they would not again have an opportunity of meeting, and the commission would proceed on the 31st, but the procurators should have access to them in their several prisons, and should agree with them as to what defence should be offered. A promiscuous crowd, whose differences of dialect rendered intercommunication impossible, abandoned by their natural leaders and thus suddenly brought together, was not fitted for deliberation on so delicate an emergency. Many hesitated about acting without orders from the Master, for all initiative on the part of subordinates was strictly forbidden by the Rule. The commissioners seem to have been sincerely desirous of getting the matter into some sort of shape, and finally, on the 31st, they ordered their notaries to visit the houses in which the Templars were confined and report their wishes and conclusions. This was a process requiring time, and the reports of the notaries after making their daily rounds are pitiful enough. The wretched prisoners floundered helplessly when called upon to resolve as to their action. Most of them declared the Order to be pure and holy, but knew not what to do in the absence of their superiors. There was a general clamor, often on bended knees, for readmission to the sacraments. Many begged to be assured that when they died they should be buried in consecrated ground; others offered to pay for a chaplain out of the miserable allowance doled to them; some asked that the allowance be increased, others that they should have clothes to cover their nakedness. They were urgent in the impossible request that they should have experts and learned men to advise with and appear for them, for they

---

* Procès, I. 47-53.

were simple and illiterate, chained in prison and unable to act; and they further begged that security should be given to witnesses, as all who had confessed were threatened with burning if they should retract.   A paper presented April 4 by those confined in the house of the Abbot of Tiron is eloquent in its suggestiveness as to their treatment, for the houses in which they were quartered had apparently taken them on speculation.   They assert the purity of the Order and their readiness to defend it as well as men can who are fettered in prison and pass the night in dark fosses.   They further complain of the insufficiency of their allowance of twelve deniers a day, for they pay three deniers each per day for their beds; for hire of kitchen, napery, and cloths, two sols six deniers per week; two sols for taking off and replacing their fetters when they appear before the commission; for washing, eighteen deniers a fortnight; wood and candles, four deniers a day, and ferriage across from Nôtre Dame, sixteen deniers.   It is evident that the poor creatures were exploited relentlessly.*

The outcome of the matter was that on April 7 nine representatives presented a paper in the name of all, declaring that without authority from the Master and Convent they could not appoint procurators, but they offer themselves one and all in defence of the Order, and ask to be present at the council or wherever it is on trial.   They declare the charges to be horrible and impossible lies fabricated by apostates and fugitives expelled for crime from the Order, confirmed by torturing those who uphold the truth, and encouraging liars with recompenses and great promises.   It is wonderful, they say, to see greater faith reposed in those corrupted thus by worldly advantage than in those who, like the martyrs of Christ, have died in torture with the palm of martyrdom, and in the living who, for conscience' sake, have suffered and daily suffer in their dungeons so many torments, tribulations, and miseries.   In the universal terror prevailing they pray that when the brethren are examined there may be present no laymen or others whom they may fear, and that security may be

---

* Procès, I. 103–51.—It must be borne in mind that the allowance was in the fearfully debased currency of Philippe le Bel.   According to a document of 1318 the livre Tournois still was to the sterling pound as 1 to 4⅓ (Olim, III. 1279).

Other Templars subsequently offered to defend the Order, making five hundred and seventy-three up to May 2.

assured them, for all who have confessed are daily threatened with burning if they retract. In reply the commissioners disavowed responsibility for their ill-usage, and promised to ask that they be humanely treated in accordance with the orders of the Cardinal of Palestrina, to whom they had been committed by the pope. The Grand Master, they added, had been urged to defend the Order, but had declined, and claimed that he was reserved for the pope.*

Having thus given the Templars a nominal opportunity for defence, the commissioners proceeded to take testimony, appointing four of the representatives, Renaud de Provins, Preceptor of Orleans, Pierre de Boulogne, procurator of the Order in the papal court, and Geoffroi de Chambonnet and Bertrand de Sartiges, knights, to be present at the swearing of the witnesses, and to do what might be requisite without constituting them formal defenders of the Order. These four on April 13 presented another paper in which, after alluding to the tortures employed to extort confessions, they stated it to be a notorious fact that to obtain testimony from Templars sealed royal letters had been given them promising them liberty and large pensions for life, and telling them that the Order was permanently abolished. This was evidently intended as a protest to pave the way for disabling the adverse witnesses, which, as we have seen, was the only defence in the inquisitorial process, and with the same object they also asked for the names of all witnesses. They did not venture to ask for a copy of the evidence, but they earnestly requested that it should be kept secret, to avert the danger that might otherwise threaten the witnesses. Subject to the interruption of the Easter solemnities, testimony, mostly adverse to the Order, continued to be taken up to May 9, from witnesses apparently carefully selected for the purpose. On Sunday, May 10, the commissioners were suddenly called together, at the request of Renaud de Provins and his colleagues, to receive the startling announcement that the provincial Council of Sens, which had been hastily assembled at Paris, proposed to prosecute all the Templars who had offered to defend the Order. Most of these had previously confessed; they had heroically taken their lives in their hands when, by asserting the purity of the Order,

---

* Procès, I. 165-72.

they had constructively revoked their confessions. The four Templars therefore appealed to the commissioners for protection, as the action of the council would fatally interfere with the work in hand; they demanded *apostoli*, and that their persons and rights and the whole Order should be placed under the guardianship of the Holy See, and time and money be allowed to prosecute the appeal. They further asked the commissioners to notify the Archbishop of Sens to take no action while the present examination was in progress, and that they be sent before him with one or two notaries to make a protest, as they can find no one who dares to draw up such an instrument for them. The commissioners were sorely perplexed and debated the matter until evening, when they recalled the Templars to say that while they heartily compassionated them they could do nothing, for the Archbishop of Sens and the council were acting under powers delegated by the pope.*

It was no part of Philippe's policy to allow the Order any opportunity to be heard. The sudden rally of nearly six hundred members, after their chiefs had been skilfully detached from them, and their preparations for defence at the approaching council promised a struggle which he proceeded to crush at the outset with his customary unscrupulous energy. The opportunity was favorable, for after long effort he had just obtained from Clement the archbishopric of Sens (of which Paris was a suffragan see) for a youthful creature of his own, Philippe de Marigny, brother of his minister Enguerrand, who took possession of the dignity only on April 5. The bull *Faciens misericordiam* had prescribed that, after the bishops had completed their inquests, provincial councils were to be called to sit in judgment on the individual brethren. In pursuance of this, the king through his archbishops was master of the situation. Provincial councils were suddenly called, that for Sens to meet at Paris, for Reims at Senlis, for Normandy at Pont de l'Arche, and for Narbonne at Carcassonne, and a demonstration was organized which should paralyze at once and forever all thought of further opposition to his will. No time was wasted in any pretence of judicial proceedings, for the canon law provided that relapsed heretics were to be condemned with-

---

* Procès, I. 173, 201–4, 259–64.

out a hearing. On the 11th the Council of Sens was opened at Paris. On the 12th, while the commissioners were engaged in taking testimony, word was brought them that fifty-four of those who had offered to defend the Order had been condemned as relapsed heretics for retracting their confessions, and were to be burned that day. Hastily they sent to the council Philippe de Vohet, the papal custodian of the Templars, and Amis, Archdeacon of Orleans, to ask for delay. Vohet, they said, and many others asserted that the Templars who died in prison declared on peril of their souls that the crimes alleged were false; Renaud de Provins and his colleagues had appealed before them from the council; if the proposed executions took place the functions of the commission would be impeded, for the witnesses that day and the day before were crazed with terror and wholly unfit to give evidence. The envoys hurried to the council-hall, where they were treated with contempt and told that it was impossible that the commission could have sent such a message. The fifty-four martyrs were piled in wagons and carried to the fields near the convent of S. Antoine, where they were slowly tortured to death with fire, refusing all offers of pardon for confession, and manifesting a constancy which, as a contemporary tells us, placed their souls in great peril of damnation, for it led the people into the error of believing them innocent. The council continued its work, and a few days later burned four more Templars, so that if there were any who still proposed to defend the Order they might recognize what would be their fate. It ordered the bones of Jean de Tourne, former treasurer of the Temple, to be exhumed and burned; those who confessed and adhered to their confessions were reconciled to the Church and liberated; those who persisted in refusing to confess were condemned to perpetual prison. This was rather more humane than the regular inquisitorial practice, but it suited the royal policy of the moment. A few weeks later, at Senlis, the Council of Reims burned nine more; at Pont de l'Arche three were burned, and a number at Carcassonne.*

---

* Fisquet, La France Pontificale, Sens, p. 68.—Procès, I. 274–5, 281.—Contin. Chron. G. de Fracheto (Bouquet, XXI. 33).—Chron. Anon. (Bouquet, XXI. 140).— Amalr. Auger. Hist. Pontif. (Eccard II. 1810).—Trithem. Chron. Hirsaug. ann. 1307.—Bern. Guidon. Flor. Chron. (Bouquet, XXI. 719).—Joann. de S. Victor

This ferocious expedient accomplished its purpose. When, on the day after the executions at Paris, May 13, the commission opened its session, the first witness, Aimery de Villiers, threw himself on his knees, pale and desperately frightened ; beating his breast and stretching forth his hands to the altar, he invoked sudden death and perdition to body and soul if he lied. He declared that all the crimes imputed to the Order were false, although he had, under torture, confessed to some of them. When he had yesterday seen his fifty-four brethren carried in wagons to be burned, and heard that they had been burned, he felt that he could not endure it and would confess to the commissioners or to any one else whatever might be required of him, even that he had slain the Lord. In conclusion he adjured the commissioners and the notaries not to reveal what he had said to his jailers, or to the royal officials, for he would be burned like the fifty-four. Then a previous witness, Jean Bertrand, came before the commission to supplicate that his deposition be kept secret on account of the danger impending over him. Seeing all this, the commission felt that during this general terror it would be wise to suspend its sittings, and it did so. It met again on the 18th to reclaim fruitlessly from the Archbishop of Sens, Renaud de Provins, who had been put on trial before the council. Pierre de Boulogne was likewise snatched away and could not be obtained again. Many of the Templars who had offered to defend the Order made haste to withdraw, and all effort to provide for it an organized hearing before the Council of Vienne was perforce abandoned. Whether Clement was privy to this high-handed interruption of the functions of his commission is perhaps doubtful, but he did nothing to rehabilitate it, and his quiescence rendered him an accomplice. He had only succeeded

---

(Bouquet, XXI. 654–55).—Contin. Guill. Nangiac. ann. 1310.—Grandes Chroniques, V. 187.—Chron. Cornel. Zantfliet ann. 1310 (Martene Ampl. Coll. V. 158).—Bessin, Concil. Rotomagens. p. iii.—Raynouard, pp. 118–20.

It was not all bishops who were ready to accept the inquisitorial doctrine that revocation of confession was equivalent to relapse. The question was discussed in the Council of Narbonne and decided in the negative.—Raynouard, p. 106.

The number of those who refused to confess was not insignificant. Some papers respecting the expenses of detention of Templars at Senlis describe sixty-five as not reconciled, who therefore cannot have confessed.—Ib. p. 107.

in betraying to a fiery death the luckless wretches whom he had tempted to come forward.*

On April 4, by the bull *Alma Mater*, Clement had postponed the Council of Vienne from October, 1310, until October, 1311, in consequence of the inquisition against the Templars requiring more time than had been expected. There was, therefore, no necessity for haste on the part of the commission, and it adjourned until November 3. Its members were long in getting together, and it did not resume its sessions until December 17. Then Guillaume de Chambonnet and Bertrand de Sartiges were brought before it, when they protested that they could not act for the Order without the aid of Renaud de Provins and Pierre de Boulogne. These, the commission informed them, had solemnly renounced the defence of the Order, had returned to their first confessions, and had been condemned to perpetual imprisonment by the Council of Sens, after which Pierre had broken jail and fled. The two knights were offered permission to be present at the swearing of the witnesses, with opportunity to file exceptions, but they declared themselves unfitted for the task and retired. Thus all pretence of affording the Order a chance to be heard was abandoned, and the subsequent proceedings of the commission became merely an *ex parte* accumulation of adverse testimony. It sat until June, industriously hearing the witnesses brought before it; but as those were selected by Philippe de Vohet and Jean de Jamville, care was evidently taken as to the character of the evidence that should reach it. Most of the witnesses, in fact, had been reconciled to the Church through confession, abjuration, and absolution, and no longer belonged to the Order which they had abandoned to its fate. Among the large number of Templars who had refused to confess, only a few, and these apparently by accident, were allowed to appear before it. There were also a few who dared to retract what they had stated before the bishops, but with these slender exceptions all the evidence was adverse to the Order. In fact, it frequently happened that witnesses were sworn who never reappeared to give their testimony, and that this was not accidental is rendered probable by the fact that Renaud de Provins was one of these. Finally, on June 5, the commission closed its labors and

* Procès, I. 275-83.

transmitted without comment to Clement its records as part of the material to guide the judgment of the assembled Church at the Council of Vienne.*

Before proceeding to the last scene of the drama at Vienne, it is necessary to consider briefly the action taken with the Templars outside of France. In England, Edward II., on October 30, 1307, replied to Philippe's announcement of October 16, to the effect that he and his council have given the most earnest attention to the matter; it has caused the greatest astonishment, and is so abominable as to be well-nigh incredible, and, to obtain further information, he had sent for his Seneschal of Agen. So strong were his convictions and so earnest his desire to protect the threatened Order that on December 4 he wrote to the Kings of Portugal, Castile, Aragon, and Naples that the accusations must proceed from cupidity and envy, and begging them to shut their ears to detraction and do nothing without deliberation, so that an Order so distinguished for purity and honor should not be molested until legitimately convicted. Not content with this, on the 10th he replied to Clement that the reputation of the Templars in England for purity and faith is such that he cannot, without further proof, believe the terrible rumors about them, and he begs the pope to resist the calumnies of envious and wicked men. In a few days, however, he received Clement's bull of November 22, and could no longer doubt the facts asserted by the head of Christendom. He hastened to obey its commands, and on the 15th elaborate orders were already prepared and sent out to all the sheriffs in England, with minute instructions to capture all the Templars on January 10, 1308, including directions as to the sequestration and disposition of their property, and this was followed on the 20th by

---

* Harduin. VII. 1334.—Procès, I. 286–7; II. 3–4, 269–73.—Raynouard, pp. 254–6.—A notarial attestation describes the voluminous record as consisting of 219 folios with forty lines to the page, equivalent to 17,520 lines.

How close a watch was kept on the witnesses is seen in the case of three, Martin de Mont Richard, Jean Durand, and Jean de Ruans, who, on March 22, asserted that they knew of no evil in the Order. Two days later they are brought back to say that they had lied through folly. When before their bishops they had confessed to renouncing and spitting, and it was true. What persuasions were applied to them during the interval no one can tell.—Procès, II. 88–96, 107–9.

similar commands to the English authorities in Ireland, Scotland, and Wales. Possibly Edward's impending voyage to Boulogne to marry Isabella, the daughter of Philippe le Bel, may have had something to do with his sudden change of purpose.*

The seizure was made accordingly, and the Templars were kept in honorable durance, not in prison, awaiting papal action; for there seems to have been no disposition on the part either of Church or State to take the initiative. The delay was long, for though commissions were issued August 12, 1308, to the papal inquisitors, Sicard de Lavaur and the Abbot of Lagny, they did not start until September, 1309, and on the 13th of that month the royal safe-conducts issued for them show their arrival in England. Then instructions were sent out to arrest all Templars not yet seized and gather them together in London, Lincoln, and York, for the examinations to be held, and the bishops of those sees were strictly charged to be present throughout. Similar orders were sent to Ireland and Scotland, where the inquisitors appointed delegates to attend to the matter. It apparently was not easy to get the officials to do their duty, for December 14 instructions were required to all the sheriffs to seize the Templars who were wandering in secular habits throughout the land, and in the following March and again in January, 1311, the Sheriff of York was scolded for allowing those in his custody to wander abroad. Popular sympathy evidently was with the inculpated brethren.†

At length, on October 20, 1309, the papal inquisitors and the Bishop of London sat in the episcopal palace to examine the Templars collected in London. Interrogated singly on all the numerous articles of accusation, they all asserted the innocence of the Order. Outside witnesses were called in who mostly declared their belief to the same effect, though some gave expression to the vague popular rumors and scandalous stories suggested by the secrecy of proceedings within the Order. The inquisitors were nonplussed. They had come to a country whose laws did not recognize the use of torture, and without it they were powerless to

---

* Rymer, Fœdera, III. 18, 34–7, 43–6.

† Regest. Clement. PP. V. T. III. pp. 316, 477.—Rymer, Fœd. III. 168–9, 173, 179–80, 182, 195, 203–4, 244.

The pay assigned to the inquisitors was three florins each *per diem*, to be assessed on the Templar property (Regest. ubi sup.).

accomplish the work for which they had been sent.   In their disgust they finally applied to the king, and on December 15 they obtained from him an order to the custodians of the prisoners to permit the inquisitors and episcopal ordinaries to do with the bodies of the Templars what they pleased, "in accordance with ecclesiastical law"—ecclesiastical law, by the hideous perversion of the times, having come to mean the worst of abuses, from which secular law still shrank.   Either the jailers or the episcopal officials interposed difficulties, for the mandate was repeated March 1, 1310, and again March 8, with instructions to report the cause if the previous one had not been obeyed.   Still no evidence worth the trouble was gained, though the examinations were prolonged through the winter and spring until May 24, when three captured fugitives were induced by means easily guessed to confess what was wanted, of which use was made to the utmost.   At length Clement grew impatient under this lack of result.   On August 6 he wrote to Edward that it was reported that he had prohibited the use of torture as contrary to the laws of the kingdom, and that the inquisitors were thus powerless to extract confessions.   No law or usage, he said, could be permitted to override the canons provided for such cases, and Edward's counsellors and officials who were guilty of thus impeding the Inquisition were liable to the penalties provided for that serious offence, while the king himself was warned to consider whether his position comported with his honor and safety, and was offered remission of his sins if he would withdraw from it—perhaps the most suggestive sale of an indulgence on record.   Similar letters at the same time were sent to all the bishops of England, who were scolded for not having already removed the impediment, as they were in duty bound to do.   Under this impulsion Edward, August 26, again ordered that the bishops and inquisitors should be allowed to employ ecclesiastical law, and this was repeated October 6 and 23, November 22, and April 28, 1311—in the last instances the word torture being used, and in all of them the king being careful to explain that what he does is through reverence for the Holy See.   August 18, 1311, similar instructions were sent to the Sheriff of York.*

---

* Wilkins, Concil. Mag. Brit. II. 329–92. — Rymer, III. 195, 202–3, 224–5, 227–32, 260, 274.—Regest. Clement. PP. V. T. V. pp. 455–7.

Thus for once the papal Inquisition found a foothold in England, but apparently its methods were too repugnant to the spirit of
the nation to be rewarded with complete success. In spite of examinations prolonged for more than eighteen months, the Templars could not be convicted. The most that could be accomplished
was, that in provincial councils held in London and York in the
spring and summer of 1311, they were brought to admit that they
were so defamed for heresy that they could not furnish the purgation required by law; they therefore asked for mercy and promised to perform what penance might be enjoined on them. Some
of them, moreover, submitted to a form of abjuration. The councils ordered them scattered among different monasteries to perform
certain penance until the Holy See should decide as to the future
of the Order. This was the final disposition of the Templars in
England. A liberal provision of fourpence a day was made for
their support, while two shillings was assigned to William de la
More, the Master of England, and on his death it was continued to
Humbert Blanc, the Preceptor of Auvergne, who, fortunately for
himself, was in England at the time of arrest, and was caught
there. This shows that they were not regarded as criminals, and
the testimony of Walsingham is that in the monasteries to which
they were assigned they comported themselves piously and righteously in every respect. In Ireland and Scotland their examinations failed to procure any proof against the Order, save the vague
conjectures and stories of outside witnesses industriously gathered
together.*

In Lorraine, as soon as news came of the seizure in France, the
Preceptor of Villencourt ordered the brethren under him to shave
and abandon their mantles, which was virtually releasing them
from the Order. Duke Thiebault followed the exterminating pol-

---

* Wilkins, II. 314, 373–83, 394–400.—Rymer, III. 295, 327, 334, 349, 472–3.—
Procès des Templiers, II. 130.—D'Argentré I. I. 280.

That the allowance for the Templars was liberal is shown by that made for
the Bishop of Glasgow when confined, in 1312, in the Castle of Porchester. His
per diem was 6*d.*, that for his valet 3*d.*, for his chaplain five farthings, and the same
for his servant (Rymer, III. 363). The wages of the janitor of the Temple in London was 2*d.*, by a charter of Edward II. in 1314 (Wilcke, II. 498).

icy of Philippe with complete success. A large number of the Templars were burned, and he managed to secure most of their property.*

In Germany our knowledge of what took place is somewhat fragmentary. The Teutonic Order afforded a career for the German chivalry, and the Templars were by no means so numerous as in France, their fate was not so dramatic, and it attracted comparatively little attention from the chroniclers. One annalist informs us that they were destroyed with the assent of the Emperor Henry on account of their collusion with the Saracens in Palestine and Egypt, and their preparation for establishing a new empire for themselves among the Christians, which shows how little impression on the popular mind was made by the assertion of their heresies. For the most part, indeed, the action taken depended upon the personal views of the princely prelates who presided over the great archbishoprics. Burchard III. of Magdeburg was the first to act. Obliged to visit the papal court in 1307 to obtain the pallium, he returned in May, 1308, with orders to seize all the Templars in his province; and as he was already hostile to them, he obeyed with alacrity. There were but four houses in his territories: on these and their occupants he laid his hands, leading to a long series of obscure quarrels, in which he incurred excommunication from the Bishop of Halberstadt, which Clement hastened to remove; by burning some of the more obstinate brethren, moreover, he involved himself in war with their kindred, in which he fared badly. As late as 1318 the Hospitallers are found complaining to John XXII. that Templars were still in possession of the greater portion of their property.†

The bull *Faciens misericordiam* of August, 1308, sent to the German prelates, reserved, with Clement's usual policy, the Grand Preceptor of Germany for papal judgment. With the exception of Magdeburg, its instructions for active measures received slack

---

* Procès, II. 267.—Calmet, Hist. Gén. de Lorraine, II. 436.

† Gassari Annal. Augstburgens. ann. 1312 (Menken. Scriptt. I. 1473).—Torquati Series Pontif. Magdeburg. ann. 1307-8 (Menken. III. 390).—Raynald. ann. 1310, No. 40.—Chron. Episc. Merseburgens. c. xxvii. § 3 (Ludewig IV. 408).—Bothonis Chron. ann. 1311 (Leibnitz III. 374).—Wilcke, II. 242, 246, 324-5.—Regest. Clement. PP. V. T. V. p. 271.—Schmidt, Päbstliche Urkunden und Regesten, Halle, 1886, p. 77.—Havemann, p. 333.

obedience. It was not to much purpose that, on December 30 of the same year, he wrote to the Duke of Austria to arrest all the Templars in his dominions, and commissioned the Ordinaries of Mainz, Trèves, Cologne, Magdeburg, Strassburg, and Constance as special inquisitors within their several dioceses, while he sent the Abbot of Crudacio as inquisitor for the rest of Germany, ordering the prelates to pay him five gold florins a day. It was not until 1310 that the great archbishops could be got to work, and then the results were disappointing. Trèves and Cologne, in fact, made over to Burchard of Magdeburg, in 1310, their authority as commissioners for the seizure of the Templar lands, and Clement confirmed this with instructions to proceed with vigor. As regards the persons of the Templars, at Trèves an inquest was held in which seventeen witnesses were heard, including three Templars, and resulting in their acquittal. At Mainz the Archbishop Peter, who had incurred Clement's displeasure by transferring to his suffragans his powers as commissioner over the Templar property, was at length forced to call a provincial council, May 11, 1310. Suddenly and unbidden there entered the Wild- and Rheingraf, Hugo of Salm, Commander of Grumbach, with twenty knights fully armed. There were fears of violence, but the archbishop asked Hugo what he had to say : the Templar asserted the innocence of the Order ; those who had been burned had steadfastly denied the charges, and their truth had been proved by the crosses on their mantles remaining unburned—a miracle popularly believed, which had much influence on public opinion. He concluded by appealing to the future pope and the whole Church, and the archbishop, to escape a tumult, admitted the protest. Clement, on hearing of these proceedings, ordered the council to be reassembled and to do its work. He was obeyed. The Wildgraf Frederic of Salm, brother of Hugo and Master of the Rhine-province, offered to undergo the red-hot iron ordeal, but it was unnecessary. Forty-nine witnesses, of whom thirty-seven were Templars, were examined, and all swore to the innocence of the Order. The twelve non-Templars, who were personages of distinction, were emphatic in their declarations in its favor. Among others, the Archpriest John testified that in a time of scarcity, when the measure of corn rose from three sols to thirty-three, the commandery at Mostaire fed a thousand persons a day. The result was a verdict of acquittal, which was so displeasing to the pope that he ordered Burchard of Magdeburg to take the matter in hand and bring it to a more satisfactory conclusion. Burchard seems to have eagerly obeyed, but the results have not reached us. Archbishop Peter continued to hope for some adjustment, and when, after the Council of Vienne, he was forced to hand over the Templar property to the Hospitallers, he required the latter to execute an agreement to return the manor of Topfstadt if the pope should restore the Order.*

In Italy the Templars were not numerous, and the pope had better control over the machinery for their destruction. In Naples the appeal of Edward II. was in vain. The Angevine dynasty was too closely allied to the papacy to hesitate, and when a copy of the bull *Pastoralis præeminentiæ*, of November 21, 1307, was addressed to Robert, Duke of Calabria, son of Charles II., there was no hesitation in obedience. Orders were speedily sent out to all the provinces under the Neapolitan crown to arrest the Templars and sequestrate their property. Philip, Duke of Achaia and Romania, the youngest son of Charles, was forthwith commanded to carry out the papal instructions in all the possessions in the Levant. January 3, 1308, the officials in Provence and Forcalquier were instructed to make the seizure January 23. The Order was numerous in those districts, but the members must have mostly fled, for only forty-eight were arrested, who are said to have been tried and executed, but a document of 1318 shows that Albert de Blacas, Preceptor of Aix and St. Maurice, who had been imprisoned in 1308, was then still enjoying the Commandery of St. Maurice, with consent of the Hospitallers. The Templar movables were divided between the pope and king, and the landed possessions were made over to the Hospital. In the kingdom of Naples itself, some fragmentary reports of the papal commission sent

---

* Harduin. VII. 1353.—Regest. Clement. PP. V. T. IV. pp. 3–4; T. V. p. 272. —Du Puy, pp. 62–3, 130–1.—Schmidt, Päbstliche Urkunden, p. 77.—Raynald. ann. 1310, No. 40.—Raynouard, pp. 127, 270.—Jo. Latomi Cat. Archiepp. Moguntt. (Menken. III. 526).—H. Mutii Chron. Lib. xxii. ann. 1311.—Wilcke, II. 243, 246, 325, 339.—Schottmüller, I. 445–6.

Even Raynaldus (ann. 1307, No. 12) alludes to the incombustibility of the Templars' crosses as an evidence in their favor.

in 1310 to obtain evidence against the Order as a whole and against the Grand Preceptor of Apulia, Oddo de Valdric, show that no obstacle was thrown in the way of the inquisitors in obtaining by the customary methods the kind of testimony desired. The same may be said of Sicily, where, as we have seen, Frederic of Aragon had admitted the Inquisition in 1304.*

In the States of the Church we have somewhat fuller accounts of the later proceedings. Although we know nothing of what was done at the time of arrest, there can be no doubt that in a territory subjected directly to Clement his bull of November 22, 1307, was strictly obeyed; that all members of the Order were seized and that appropriate means were employed to secure confessions. When the papal commission was sent to Paris to afford the Order an opportunity to prepare its defence at the Council of Vienne, similar commissions, armed with inquisitorial powers, were despatched elsewhere, and the report of Giacomo, Bishop of Sutri, and Master Pandolfo di Sabello, who were commissioned in that capacity in the Patrimony of St. Peter, although unfortunately not complete, gives us an insight into the real object which underlay the ostensible purpose of these commissions. In October, 1309, the inquisitors commenced at Rome, where no one appeared before them, although they summoned not only members of the Order, but every one who had anything to say about it. In December they went to Viterbo, where five Templars lay in prison, who declined to appear and defend the Order. In January, 1310, they proceeded to Spoleto without finding either Templars or other witnesses. In February they moved to Assisi, where they adopted the form of ordering all Templars and their fautors to be brought before them, and this they repeated in March at Gubbio, but in both places without result. In April, at Aquila, they summoned witnesses to ascertain whether the Templars had any churches in the Abruzzi, but not even the preceptor of the Hospitallers could give them any information. All the Franciscans of the place were then assembled, but they knew nothing to the discredit of the Order. A few days later, at Penna, they adopted a

---

* Mag. Bull. Rom. IX. 131–2.—Archivio di Napoli, MSS. Chioccarello, T. VIII.—Du Puy, pp. 63–4, 87, 222–6.—Raynouard, pp. 200, 279–84.—Schottmüller, II. 108 sqq.

III.—20

new formula by inviting all Templars and others who desired to defend the Order to appear before them. Here two Templars were found, who were personally summoned repeatedly, but they refused, saying that they would not defend the Order. One of them, Walter of Naples, was excused, owing to doubts as to his being a Templar, but the other, named Cecco, was brought before the inquisitors and told them of an idol kept for worship in the treasure-chamber of a preceptory in Apulia. In May, at Chieti, they succeeded in getting hold of another Templar, who confessed to renouncing Christ, idol-worship, and other of the charges. By May 23 they were back in Rome issuing citations, but again without result. The following week they were back at Viterbo, resolved to procure some evidence from the five captives imprisoned there, but the latter again sent word that none of them wished to appear before the inquisitors or to defend the Order. Five times in all they were summoned and five times they refused, but the inquisitors were not to be balked. Four of the prisoners were brought forward, and by means which can readily be guessed were induced to talk. From the 7th of June to the 19th, the inquisitors were employed in receiving their depositions as to renouncing Christ, spitting on the cross, etc., all of which was duly recorded as free and spontaneous. On July 3 the commissioners were at Albano issuing the customary summons, but on the 8th their messenger reported that he could find no Templars in Campania and Maritima; and a session at Velletri on the 16th was similarly fruitless. The next day they summoned other witnesses, but eight ecclesiastics who appeared had nothing to tell. Then at Segni they heard five witnesses without obtaining any evidence. Castel Fajole and Tivoli were equally barren, but on the 27th, at Palombara, Walter of Naples was brought to them from Penna, the doubts as to his membership of the Order having apparently been removed. Their persistence in this case was rewarded with full details of heretical practices. Here the record ends, the industrious search of nine months through these extensive territories having resulted in finding eight Templars, and obtaining seven incriminating depositions.* Even making allowance for those who may have succeeded in escaping, it shows, like the rest of the Italian proceedings, how scanty were the numbers of the Order in the Peninsula.

* Schottmüller, II. 406–19.

In the rest of Italy Clement's bull of 1307, addressed to the arch-bishops and ordering an inquest, seems to have been somewhat slack-ly obeyed. The earliest action on record is an order, in 1308, of Frà Ottone, Inquisitor of Lombardy, requiring the delivery of three Templars to the Podestà of Casale. Some further impulsion apparent-ly was requisite, and in 1309 Giovanni, Archbishop of Pisa, was ap-pointed Apostolic Nuncio in charge of the affair throughout Tus-cany, Lombardy, Dalmatia, and Istria, with a stipend of eight florins *per diem*, to be assessed on the Templar property. In Ancona the Bishop of Fano examined one Templar who con-fessed nothing, and nineteen other witnesses who furnished no in-criminating evidence, and in Romagnuola, Rainaldo, Archbishop of Ravenna, and the Bishop of Rimini interrogated two Templars at Cesena, both of whom testified to the innocence of the Order. The archbishop, who was papal inquisitor against the Templars in Lom-bardy, Tuscany, Tarvisina, and Istria, seems to have extended his inquest over part of Lombardy, though no results are recorded. Papal letters were published throughout Italy, empowering the inquisitors to look after the Templar property, of which the Arch-bishops of Bologna and Pisa were appointed administrators; it was farmed out and the proceeds remitted to Clement. Rainaldo of Ravenna sympathized with the Templars, and no very earnest efforts were to be expected of him. He called a synod at Bologna in 1309, where some show was made of taking up the subject, but no results were reached, and when, in 1310, his vicar, Bonincontro, went to Ravenna with the papal bulls, he made no secret of his favor towards the accused. At length Rainaldo was forced to action, and issued a proclamation, November 25, 1310, reciting the papal commands to hold provincial councils for the examination and judgment of the Templars, in obedience to which he summoned one to assemble at Ravenna in January, 1311, calling upon the in-quisitors to bring thither the evidence which they had obtained by the use of torture. The council was held and the matter discussed, but no conclusion was reached. Another was summoned to meet at Bologna on June 1, but was transferred to Ravenna and post-poned till June 18. To this the bishops were ordered to bring all Templars of their dioceses under strict guard, the result of which was that on June 16, seven knights were produced before the council. They were sworn and interrogated *seriatim* on all the articles as furnished by the pope, which they unanimously denied. The question was then put to the council whether they should be tortured, and it was answered in the negative, in spite of the opposition of two Dominican inquisitors present. It was decided that the case should not be referred to the pope, in view of the nearness of the Council of Vienne, but that the accused should be put upon their purgation. The next day, however, when the council met this action was reversed and there was a unanimous decision that the innocent should be acquitted and the guilty punished, reckoning among the innocent those who had confessed through fear of torture and had revoked, or who would have revoked but for fear of repetition of torture. As for the Order as a whole, the council recommended that it should be preserved if a majority of the members were innocent, and if the guilty were subjected to abjuration and punishment within the Order. In addition to the seven knights there were five brethren who were ordered to purge themselves by August 1, before Uberto, Bishop of Bologna, with seven conjurators; of these the purgations of two are extant, and doubtless all succeeded in performing the ceremony. It was no wonder that Clement was indignant at this reversal of all inquisitorial usage and ordered the burning of those who had thus relapsed—though the command was probably not obeyed, as Bishop Bini assures us that no Templars were burned in Italy. The council further, in appointing delegates to Vienne, instructed them that the Order should not be abolished unless it was found to be thoroughly corrupted. For Tuscany and Lombardy, Clement appointed as special inquisitors Giovanni, Archbishop of Pisa, Antonio, Bishop of Florence, and Pietro Giudici of Rome, a canon of Verona. These were instructed to hold the inquests, one upon the brethren individually and one upon the Order. They were troubled with no scruples as to the use of torture and, as we shall presently see, secured a certain amount of the kind of testimony desired. Venice kindly postponed the inevitable uprooting of the Order, and when it eventually took place there was no unnecessary hardship.*

---

* Regest. Clement. PP. V. T. IV. p. 301. — Bini, pp. 420-1, 424, 427-8. — Raynald. ann. 1309, No. 3.—Raynouard, pp. 273-77.—Chron. Parmens. ann. 1309 (Muratori S. R. I. IX. 880).—Du Puy, pp. 57-8.—Rubei Hist. Ravennat. Ed.

Cyprus was the headquarters of the Order. There resided the marshal, Ayme d'Osiliers, who was its chief in the absence of the Grand Master, and there was the "Convent," or governing body. It was not until May, 1308, that the papal bull commanding the arrest reached the island, and there could be no pretence of a secret and sudden seizure, for the Templars were advised of what had occurred in France. They had many enemies, for they had taken an active part in the turbulent politics of the time, and it had been by their aid that the regent, Amaury of Tyre, had been placed in power. He hastened to obey the papal commands, but with many misgivings, for the Templars at first assumed an attitude of defence. Resistance, however, was hopeless, and in a few weeks they submitted; their property was sequestrated and they were kept in honorable confinement, without being deprived of the sacraments. This continued for two years, until, in April, 1310, the Abbot of Alet and the Archpriest Tommaso of Rieti came as papal inquisitors to inquire against them individually and the Order in general, under the guidance of the Bishops of Limisso and Famagosta. The examination commenced May 1 and continued until June 5, when it came abruptly to an end, in consequence, doubtless, of the excitement caused by the murder of the Regent Amaury. All the Templars on the island, seventy-five in number, together with fifty-six other witnesses, were duly interrogated upon the long list of articles of accusation. That the Templars were unanimous in denying the charges and in asserting the purity of the Order shows that torture cannot have been employed. More convincing as to their innocence is the evidence of the other witnesses, consisting of ecclesiastics of all ranks, nobles, and burghers, many of them political enemies, who yet rendered testimony emphatically favorable. As some of them said, they knew nothing but good of the Order. All dwelt upon its liberal charities, and many described the fervor of the zeal with which the Templars discharged their religious duties. A few alluded to the popular suspicions aroused by the secrecy observed in the holding of chapters and the admission of neophytes; the Dominican Prior of Nicosia spoke

---

1589, pp. 517, 521, 522, 524, 525, 526.—Campi, Dell' Hist. Eccles. di Piacenza, P. III. p. 41.—Barbarano dei Mironi Hist. Eccles. di Vicenza, II. 157-8.—Anton, Versuch einer Geschichte der Tempelherrenordens, Leipzig, 1779, p. 139.

of the reports brought from France by his brethren after the arrest, and Simon de Sarezariis, Prior of the Hospitallers, said that he had had similar intelligence sent to him by his correspondents, but the evidence is unquestionable that in Cyprus, where they were best known, among friends and foes, and especially among those who had been in intimate relations with the Templars for long periods, there was general sympathy for the Order, and that there had been no evil attributed to it until the papal bulls had so unqualifiedly asserted its guilt.   All this, when sent to Clement, was naturally most unsatisfactory, and when the time approached for the Council of Vienne, he despatched urgent orders, in August, 1311, to have the Templars tortured so as to procure confessions.   What was the result of this we have no means of knowing.*

In Aragon, Philippe's letter of October 16, 1307, to Jayme II. was accompanied with one from the Dominican, Fray Romeo de Bruguera, asserting that he had been present at the confession made by de Molay and others.   Notwithstanding this, on November 17 Jayme, like Edward II., responded with warm praises of the Templars of the kingdom, whom he refused to arrest without absolute proof of guilt or orders from the pope.   To the latter he wrote two days later for advice and instructions, and when, on December 1, he received Clement's bull of November 22, he could hesitate no longer.   Ramon, Bishop of Valencia, and Ximenes de Luna, Bishop of Saragossa, who chanced to be with him, received orders to make in their respective dioceses diligent inquisition against the Templars, and Fray Juan Llotger, Inquisitor-general of Aragon, was instructed to extirpate the heresy.   As resistance was anticipated, royal letters were issued December 3 for the immediate arrest of all members of the Order and the sequestration of their property, and the inquisitor published edicts summoning them before him in the Dominican Convent of Valencia, to answer for their faith, and prohibiting all local officials from rendering them assistance.   Jayme also summoned a council of the prelates to meet January 6, 1308, to deliberate on the subject with the inquisitor.   A number of arrests were effected; some of the brethren shaved and

---

* Schottmüller, I. 457–69, 494; II. 147–400.—Du Puy, pp. 63, 106–7.—Raynouard, p. 285.

threw off their mantles and succeeded in hiding themselves; some endeavored to escape by sea with a quantity of treasure, but adverse storms cast them back upon the coast and they were seized. The great body of the knights, however, threw themselves into their castles. Ramon Sa Guardia, Preceptor of Mas Deu in Roussillon, was acting as lieutenant of the Commander of Aragon, and fortified himself in Miravet, while others occupied the strongholds of Ascon, Montço, Cantavieja, Vilell, Castellot, and Chalamera. On January 20, 1308, they were summoned to appear before the Council of Tarragona, but they refused, and Jayme promised the prelates that he would use the whole forces of the kingdom for their subjugation. This proved no easy task. The temporal and spiritual lords promised assistance, except the Count of Urgel, the Viscount of Rocaberti, and the Bishop of Girona; but public sympathy was with the Templars. Many noble youths embraced their cause and joined them in their castles, while the people obeyed slackly the order to take up arms against them. The knights defended themselves bravely. Castellot surrendered in November, soon after which Sa Guardia, in Miravet, rejected the royal ultimatum that they should march out with their arms and betake themselves by twos and threes to places of residence, from which they were not to wander farther than two or three bowshots, receiving a liberal allowance for their support, while the king should ask the pope to order the bishops and inquisitors to expedite the process. In response to this Sa Guardia addressed Clement a manly appeal, pointing out the services rendered to religion by the Order; that many knights captured by the Saracens languished in prison for twenty or thirty years, when by abjuring they could at once regain their liberty and be richly rewarded—seventy of their brethren were at that moment enduring such a fate. They were ready to appear in judgment before the pope, or to maintain their faith against all accusers by arms, as was customary with knights, but they had no prelates or advocates to defend them, and it was the duty of the pope to do so. A month after this Miravet was forced to surrender at discretion, and in another month all the rest, except Montço and Chalamera, which held out until near July, 1309. Clement at once took measures to get possession of the Templar property, but Jayme refused to deliver it to the papal commissioners, alleging that most of it had been derived from the crown, and that he had made heavy outlays on the sieges; the most that he would promise was that if the council should abolish the Order he would surrender the property, subject to the rights and claims of the crown. Clement seems to have sought a temporary compromise. In letters of January 5, 1309, he announces that the Templars of Aragon and Catalonia, like faithful sons of the Church, had written to him offering to surrender their persons and property to the Holy See, and to obey his commands in every way; he therefore sends his chaplain, Bertrand, Prior of Cessenon, to receive them and transfer them to the custody and care of the king, taking from him sealed letters that he holds them in the name of the Holy See. Whether Jayme assented to this arrangement as to the property does not appear, but he was not punctilious about the persons of the Templars, and on July 14 he issued orders to the viguiers to deliver them to the inquisitor and ordinaries when required. In 1310 Clement sent to Aragon, as elsewhere, special papal inquisitors to conduct the trials. They were met by the same difficulties as in England: in Aragon torture was not recognized by the law, and in 1325 we find the Cortes protesting against its use and against the inquisitorial process as infractions of the recognized liberties of the land, and the king admitting the protest and promising that such methods should not be employed except for counterfeiters, and then only in the case of strangers and vagabonds. Still the inquisitors did what they could. At their request the king, July 5, 1310, ordered his baillis to put the Templars in irons and to render their prison harsher. Then the Council of Tarragona interfered and asked that they be kept in safe but not afflictive custody, seeing that nothing had as yet proved their guilt, and their case was still undecided. In accordance with this, on October 20, the king ordered that they should be free in the castles where they were confined, giving their parole not to escape under pain of being reputed heretics. This was not the way to obtain the desired evidence, and Clement, March 18, 1311, ordered them to be tortured, and asked Jayme to lend his aid to it, seeing that the proceedings thus far had resulted only in "vehement suspicion." This cruel command was not at first obeyed. In May the Templars prayed the king to urge the Archbishop of Tarragona to have their case decided in the council then impending, and Jayme accordingly addressed the archbishop to that effect, but nothing was done, and in August he ordered them to be again put in chains and harshly imprisoned. The papal representatives were evidently growing impatient, as the time set for the Council of Vienne was approaching, and the papal demands for adverse evidence remained unsatisfied. Finally, on the eve of the assembling of the council, the king yielded to the pope. September 29 he issued an order appointing Umbert de Cap-depont, one of the royal judges, to assist at the judgment, when sentence should be rendered by the inquisitors, Pedro de Montclus and Juan Llotger, along with the Bishops of Lerida and Vich, who had been especially commissioned by the pope. We have no knowledge of the details of the investigation, but there is evidence that torture was unsparingly used, for there is a royal letter of December 3 ordering medicaments to be prepared for those of the Templars who might need them in consequence of sickness or tort-ure. At last, in March, 1312, the Archbishop of Tarragona asked to have them brought before his provincial council, then about to assemble, and the king assented, but nothing was done, probably because the Council of Vienne was still in session ; but after the dissolution of the Order had been proclaimed by Clement, and the fate of the members was relegated to the local councils, one was held, October 18, 1312, at Tarragona, which decided the question so long pending. The Templars were brought before it and rigor-ously examined. November 4 the sentence was publicly read, pronouncing an unqualified acquittal from all the errors, crimes, and impostures with which they were charged ; they were declared beyond suspicion, and no one should dare to defame them. In view of the dissolution of the Order the council was somewhat puzzled to know what to do with them, but after prolonged debate it was determined that until the pope should otherwise decree they should reside in the dioceses in which their property lay, re-ceiving proper support from their sequestrated lands. This decree was carried out, and when the property passed into the hands of the Hospitallers it was burdened with these charges. In 1319 a list of pensions thus payable by the Hospitallers would seem to show that the Templars were liberally provided for, and received what was due to them.*

---

* Allart, Bulletin de la Société des Pyrénées Orientales, 1867, Tom. XV. pp. 37–42, 67–9, 72, 76–8, 94–6.—Zurita, Añales de Aragon, Lib. v. c. 72, Lib. vi. c.

Jayme I. of Majorca was in no position to resist the pressure brought upon him by Philippe le Bel and Clement. His little kingdom consisted of the Balearic Isles, the counties of Roussillon and Cerdagne, the Seignory of Montpellier and a few other scattered possessions at the mercy of his powerful neighbor. He promptly therefore obeyed the papal bull of November 22, 1307, and by the end of the month the Templars in his dominions were all arrested. In Roussillon the only preceptory was that of Mas Deu, which was one of the strongholds of the land, and there the Templars were collected and confined to the number of twenty-five, including the Preceptor, Ramon Sa Guardia, the gallant defender of Miravet, who after his surrender was demanded by the King of Majorca and willingly joined his comrades. We know nothing of what took place on the islands beyond the fact of the arrest, but on the mainland we can follow with some exactness the course of events. Roussillon constituted the diocese of Elne, which was suffragan to the archbishopric of Narbonne. May 5, 1309, the archbishop sent to Ramon Costa, Bishop of Elne, the articles of accusation with the papal bull ordering an inquest. The good bishop seems to have been in no haste to comply, but, pleading illness, postponed the matter until January, 1310. Then, in obedience to the instructions, he summoned two Franciscans and two Dominicans, and with two of his cathedral canons he proceeded to interrogate the prisoners. It is evident that no torture was employed, for in their prolonged examinations they substantially agreed in asserting the purity and piety of the Order, and their chaplain offered in evidence their book of ritual for receptions in the vernacular, commencing, " *Quan alcum proom requer la compaya de la Mayso.*" With manly indignation they refused to believe that the Grand Master and chiefs of the Order had confessed to the truth of the charges, but if they had done so they had lied in their throats—or, as one of them phrased it, they were demons in human skin. With regard to the cord of chastity, an humble peasant serving brother explained not only that it was procured wherever they chose, but that if it chanced to break

---

61.—Regest. Clement. PP. V. T. IV. pp. 435 sqq.—La Fuente, Hist. Ecles. de España, II. 369-70.—Ptol. Lucens. Hist. Eccles. Lib. xxiv. (Muratori S. R. I. XI. 1228).—Concil. Tarraconens. ann. 1312 (Aguirre, VI. 233-4).

while ploughing it was at once temporarily replaced with one
made of reeds. The voluminous testimony was forwarded, with a
simple certificate of its accuracy, by Bishop Ramon, August 31,
1310, which shows that he was in no haste to transmit it. It could
have proved in no sense satisfactory, and there can be little doubt
that the cruel orders of Clement, in March, 1311, to procure confessions by torture were duly obeyed, for Jean de Bourgogne, sac-
ristan of Majorca, was appointed by Clement inquisitor for the
Templars in Aragon, Navarre, and Majorca, and the same methods
must unquestionably have been followed in all the kingdoms.
After the Council of Vienne there ensued a rather curious controversy between the archbishops of Tarragona and Narbonne on
the subject. The former, with the Bishop of Valencia, was papal
custodian of Templar property in Aragon, Majorca, and Navarre.
He seems thus to have imagined that he held jurisdiction over the
Templars of Roussillon, for, October 15, 1313, he declared Ramon
Sa Guardia absolved and innocent, and directed him to live with
his brethren at Mas Deu, with a pension of three hundred and
fifty livres, and the use of the gardens and orchards, the other
Templars having pensions ranging from one hundred to thirty
livres. Yet, in September, 1315, Bernard, Archbishop of Narbonne, ordered Bishop Ramon's successor Guillen to bring to the
provincial council which he had summoned all the Templars imprisoned in his diocese, together with the documents relating to
their trials, in order that their persons might be disposed of. King
Jayme I. had died in 1311, but his son and successor, Sancho, intervened, saying that Clement had placed the Templars in his
charge, and he would not surrender them without a papal order
—the papacy at that time being vacant, with little prospect of an
early election. He added that if they were to be punished it belonged to him to have them tried in his court, and to protect his
jurisdiction he appealed to the future pope and council. This was
effectual, and the Templars remained undisturbed. A statement
of pensions paid in 1319 shows that of the twenty-five examined
at Mas Deu in 1310 ten had died; the remainder, with one additional brother, were drawing pensions amounting in the aggregate
to nine hundred and fifty livres a year. On the island of Majorca
there were still nine whose total pensions were three hundred and
sixty-two livres ten sols. In 1329 there were still nine Templars

receiving pensions allotted on the Preceptory of Mas Deu, though most of them had retired to their houses, for they do not appear to have been restricted as to their place of residence.   By this time the indomitable Ramon Sa Guardia's name had disappeared. One by one they dropped off, until in 1350 there was but a single survivor, the knight Berenger dez Coll.*

In Castile no action seems to have been taken until the bull *Faciens misericordiam* of August 12, 1308, was sent to the prelates ordering them to act in conjunction with the Dominican, Eymeric de Navas, as inquisitor.   Fernando IV. then ordered the Templars arrested, and their lands placed in the hands of the bishops until the fate of the Order should be determined.   There was no alacrity, however, in pursuing the affair, for it was not until April 15, 1310, that Archbishop Gonzalo of Toledo cited the Master of Castile, Rodrigo Ybañez, and his brethren to appear before him at Toledo.   For the province of Compostella, comprising Portugal, the archbishop held a council at Medina del Campo, where thirty Templars and three other witnesses were examined, all of whom testified in favor of the Order; a priest swore that he had heard the confessions of many Templars on their deathbeds, as well as others mortally wounded by the infidel, and all were orthodox.   No better success attended inquests held by the Bishop of Lisbon at Medina Celi and Orense.   The only judicial action of which we have notice was that of the Council of Salamanca for the province of Compostella, where the Templars were unanimously acquitted, and the cruel orders to torture them issued the next year by Clement seem to have been disregarded.   After the Order was dissolved the Templars for the most part continued to lead exemplary lives.   Many retired to the mountains and ended their days as anchorites, and after death their bodies remained incorruptible, in testimony of the saintliness of their martyrdom.†

---

* Allart, op. cit. pp. 34, 42, 66, 69, 72–4, 79, 81–4, 86, 93–8, 105.—Procès, II. 424–515.—Vaissette, IV. 153.

I have met with no details as to the treatment of the Templars of Navarre; but as Louis Hutin, son of Philippe le Bel, succeeded to that kingdom in 1307, of course the French methods prevailed there, and the papal Inquisitor, Jean de Bourgogne, had full opportunity to procure testimony in what manner was most effective.

† Regest. Clement. PP. V. T. III. pp. 289, 299.—Llorente, Ch. III. Art. 2, No.

Portugal belonged ecclesiastically to the province of Compostella, and the Bishop of Lisbon, commissioned to investigate the Order, found no ground for the charges. The fate of the Templars there was exceptionally fortunate, for King Diniz, grateful for their services in his wars with the Saracens, founded a new Order, that of Jesus Christ, or de Avis, and procured its approval in 1318 from John XXII. To this safe refuge the Templars and their lands were transferred, the commander and many of the preceptors retaining their rank, and the new Order was thus merely a continuation of the old.*

The period finally set for the Council of Vienne was approaching, and thus far Clement had failed to procure any evidence of weight against the Templars beyond the boundaries of France, where bishop and inquisitor had been the tools of Philippe's remorseless energy. Clement may at the first have been Philippe's unwilling accomplice, but if so he had long since gone too far to retract. Whether, as believed by many of his contemporaries, he was sharing the spoils, is of little moment. He had committed himself personally to all Europe, in the bull of November 22, 1307, to the assertion of the Templars' guilt, and had repeated this emphatically in his subsequent utterances, with details admitting of no retraction or explanation; he, as well as they, was on trial before Christendom, and their acquittal by the council would be his conviction. He was, therefore, no judge, but an antagonist, forced by the instinct of self-preservation to destroy them, no matter through what unscrupulous methods. As the council drew near his anxiety increased, and he cast around for means to secure the testimony which should justify him by proving the heresy of the Order. We have seen how he urged Edward II. to introduce torture into the hitherto unpolluted courts of England, and how he succeeded in having the brethren of Aragon tortured in violation of the liberties of the land. These were but specimens of a series of bulls, perhaps the most disgraceful that ever proceeded from a vicegerent of God. From Cyprus to Portugal, prince and prel-

---

6, 7.—Mariana, Lib. xv. c. 10 (Ed. 1789, p. 390, note).—Raynouard, pp. 128, 265–66.—Aguirre, VI. 230.—La Fuente, Hist. Ecles. II. 368–70.

* Raynouard, pp. 204, 267.—Raynald. ann. 1317, No. 40.—Zurita, Lib. VI. c. 26.—La Fuente, II. 872.

ate were ordered to obtain confessions by torture; in some places, he said, it had been negligently and imprudently omitted, and the omission must be repaired. The canons required that in such cases those who refused to confess must be submitted to a "religious torturer" and the truth thus be forced from them. So earnest was he that he wrote to his legate in Rhodes to go to Cyprus and personally see that it was done. The result in such cases was to be sent to him as speedily as possible.*

How much of human agony these inhuman orders caused can never be known. It was not merely that those who had hitherto been spared the rack were now subjected to it, but, in the eagerness to supplement the evidence on hand, those who had already undergone torture were brought from their dungeons and again subjected to it with enhanced severity, in order to obtain from them still more extravagant admissions of guilt. Thus at Florence thirteen Templars had been duly inquisitioned in 1310, and some of them had confessed. Under the fresh papal urgency the inquisitors again assembled in September, 1311, and put them through a fresh series of examinations. Six of them yielded testimony in every way satisfactory—the adoration of idols and cats and the rest. Seven of them, however, were obstinate, and testified to the innocence of the Order. The inquisitors showed their appreciation of what Clement wanted by sending him only the six confessions. The other seven brethren, they reported, had been duly tortured, but had stated nothing that was worth the sending, as they were serving brethren or newly initiated members who, presumably, were ignorant—although elsewhere the most damaging evidence had been obtained from such brethren and utilized. Clement evidently knew his man when he selected the Archbishop of Pisa as the head of this inquisition. We happen to have another illustration of the results of Clement's urgency in preparing for the council. In the Château d'Alais the Bishop of Nîmes held thirty-three Templars who had already been examined and confessions extorted from some of them, which had mostly been retracted. Under Clement's orders for fresh tortures twenty-nine survivors of these (four having meanwhile died in prison) were brought out in August, 1311. Some of them had

---

* Raynald. ann. 1311, No. 53.—Raynouard, pp. 166-7.—Schottmüller, I. 395.

already been tortured three years before, but now all were tortured again, with the result of obtaining the kind of testimony required, including demon-worship.*

In spite of all these precautions it required the most arbitrary use of both papal and kingly influence to force from the council a reluctant assent to what was evidently regarded by Christendom as the foulest injustice. It is, perhaps, significant that the acts of the council vanished from the papal archives, and we are left to gather its proceedings from such fragmentary allusions as occur in contemporary chroniclers and from the papal bulls which record its results. Good orthodox Catholics have even denied to it the right to be considered Œcumenic, in spite of the presence of more than three hundred bishops from all the states of Europe, the presidency of a pope, and the book of canon laws which was adopted in it, no one knows how.†

The first question to be settled was Clement's demand that the Order should be condemned without a hearing. He had, as we have seen, solemnly summoned it to appear, through its chiefs and procurators, before the council, and had ordered the Cardinal of

* Bini, p. 501.—Raynouard, pp. 233-5, 303.—Vaissette, IV. 140-1.

† Hefele, Conciliengeschichte I. 66.—Franz Ehrle, Archiv f. Litt.- u. Kirchengeschichte, 1886, p. 353.—The apologetic tone in which it was felt necessary to speak of the acts of the council with regard to the Templars is well illustrated by a Vatican MS. quoted by Raynaldus, ann. 1311, No. 54.

Only fragments have reached us of the vast accumulation of documents respecting the case of the Templars. In the migrations of Clement V. doubtless some were lost (Franz Ehrle, Archiv für Litt.- u. Kirchengesch. 1885, p. 7); others in the Schism, when Benedict XIII. carried a portion of the archives to Peniscola (Schottmüller, I. 705), and others again in the transport of the papers of the curia from Avignon to Rome. When, in 1810, Napoleon ordered the papal archives transferred to Paris, where they remained until 1815, the first care of General Radet, the French Inspector-general of Rome, was to secure those concerning the trials of the Templars and of Galileo (Regest. Clement. PP. V., Romæ, 1885, T. I. Proleg. p. ccxxix.). During their stay in Paris Raynouard utilized them in the work so often quoted above, but even then only a few seem to have been accessible, and of these a portion are now not to be found in the Vatican MSS., although Schottmüller, the most recent investigator, expresses a hope that the missing ones may yet be traced (op. cit. I. 713). The number of boxes sent to Paris amounted to 3239, and the papal archivists complained that many documents were not restored. The French authorities declared that the papal agents to whom they had been delivered sold immense quantities to grocers (Reg. Clem. V. Proleg. pp. ccxciii.–ccxcviii.).

Palestrina, whom he had appointed their custodian, to present
them for that purpose; he had organized a commission expressly
to listen to those who were willing to defend it, and to arrange for
them to nominate procurators, and he had uttered no protest when
Philippe's savage violence had put an end to the attempt.   Now
the council had met and the chiefs of the Order were not brought
before it.   The subject was too delicate a one to be trusted to the
body of the council, and a picked convocation was formed of prelates selected from the nations represented—Spain, France, Italy,
Germany, Hungary, England, Ireland, and Scotland—to discuss
the matter with the pope and cardinals.   On a day in November,
while this body was listening to the reports sent in by the inquisitors, suddenly there appeared before them seven Templars offering to defend the Order in the name, they said, of fifteen hundred
or two thousand brethren, refugees who were wandering in the
mountains of the Lyonnais.   In place of hearing them, Clement
promptly cast them into prison, and when, a few days later, two
more, undeterred by the fate of their predecessors, made a similar
attempt, they were likewise incarcerated.   Clement's principal
emotion was fear for his own life from the desperation of the outcasts, leading him to take extra precautions and to advise Philippe
to do the same.   This was not calculated to make the prelates
feel less keenly the shame of what they were asked to do, for
which the only reason alleged was the injury to the Holy Land
arising from the delay to be anticipated from discussion; and when
the matter came to a vote only one Italian bishop and three
Frenchmen (the Archbishops of Sens, Reims, and Rouen, who had
burned the relapsed Templars) were found to record themselves in
favor of the infamy of condemning the Order unheard.   They
might well hesitate.   In Germany, Italy, and Spain provincial
councils had solemnly declared that they could find no evil in the
Order or its members.   In England the Templars had only confessed themselves defamed of heresy.   In France alone had there
been any general confession of guilt.   Even if individuals were
guilty, they had been condemned to appropriate penance, and there
was no warrant for destroying without a hearing so noble a member of the Church Militant as the great Order of the Temple.*

---

* Bull. *Vox in excelso* (Van Os, pp. 72–4).—Du Puy, pp. 177–8.—Ptol. Lucens.

Clement vainly used every effort to win over the Council. The most that he could do was to prolong the discussion until the middle of February, 1312, when Philippe, who had called a meeting of the Three Estates at Lyons, hard by Vienne, came thence with Charles de Valois, his three sons and a following numerous enough to impress the prelates with his power. A royal order of March 14 to the Seneschal of Toulouse to make a special levy to defray the expenses of the delegates sent by that city successively to Tours, Poitiers, Lyons, and Vienne, "on the business of the faith or of the Templars," shows how the policy, begun at Tours, of overawing the Church by pressure from the laity of the kingdom was unscrupulously pursued to the end. Active discussions followed. Philippe had dexterously brought forward again the question of the condemnation of Boniface VIII. for heresy, which he had promised, a year previous, to abandon. It was an impossibility to grant this without impugning the legitimacy of Boniface's cardinals and of Clement's election, but it served the purpose of affording an apparent concession. The combined pressure brought to bear upon the council became too strong for further resistance, and the Gordian knot was resolutely severed. In a secret consistory of cardinals and prelates held March 22, Clement presented the bull *Vox in excelso*, in which he admitted that the evidence did not canonically justify the definitive condemnation of the Order, but he argued that it had been so scandalized that no honorable men hereafter could enter it, that delay would lead to the dilapidation of its possessions with consequent damage to the Holy Land, and that, therefore, its provisional abolition by the Holy See was expedient. April 3 the second session of the council was held, in which the bull was published, and Clement apologized for it by

---

Hist. Eccles. Lib. xxiv. (Muratori S. R. I. XI. 1236).—Raynouard, p. 187.—Cf. Raynald. ann. 1311, No. 55.

If Schottmüller's assumption be correct as to the "Deminutio laboris examinantium processus contra ordinem Templi in Anglia," printed by him from a Vatican MS. (op cit. II. 78 sqq.)—that it was prepared to be laid before the commission of the Council of Vienne, it shows the unscrupulous manner in which the evidence was garbled for the purpose of misleading those who were to sit in judgment. All the favorable testimony is suppressed and the wildest gossip of women and monks is seriously presented as though it were incontrovertible.

explaining that it was necessary to propitiate his dear son, the King of France. If the popular belief was that the sentence was rendered by Philippe's command, it was not without justification. Thus, after all this cruelty and labor, the Order was abolished without being convicted. There can be little doubt that the council acquiesced willingly in this solution of the question. The individual members were thus relieved of responsibility, and they felt that the Order had been so foully dealt with that policy required injustice to be carried out to the bitter end.*

The next point to be determined was the disposition of the Templar property, which gave rise to a long and somewhat bitter debate. Various plans were proposed, but finally Clement suc-

---

* Jo. Hocsemii Gest. Episcc. Leodiens. (Chapeaville, II. 345).—Baudouin, Lettres inédites de Philippe le Bel, p. 179.—Chron. Cornel. Zantfliet ann. 1307 (Martene Ampl. Coll. V. 154).— Bull. *Vox in excelso* (Van Os, pp. 75–77).— Bern. Guidon. Flor. Chron. (Bouquet, XXI. 721).—Wilcke, II. 307.—Gürtleri Hist. Templarior. Amstel. 1703, p. 365.—Vertot, Hist. des Chev. de Malthe, Ed. 1755, Tom II. p. 136.—Contin. Guill. Nangiac. ann. 1311–12.—Martin. Polon. Contin. (Eccard. I. 1438).—Trithem. Chron. Hirsaug. ann. 1307.

When, in 1773, Clement XIV. desired to abolish the Order of Jesuits by an arbitrary exercise of papal power, he did not fail to find a precedent in the suppression of the Templars by Clement V.—as he says in his bull of July 22, 1773, "Etiamsi concilium generale Viennense, cui negotium examinandum commiserat, a formali et definitiva sententia ferenda censuerit se abstinere."—Bullar. Roman. Contin. Prati, 1847, V. 620.

The wits of the day did not allow the affair to pass unimproved. Bernard Gui cites as current at the time the Leonine verse, " Res est exempli destructa superbia Templi." Hocsemius quotes for us a chronogram by P. de Awans, possibly alluding to the treasure which Philippe gained—

> " Excidium Templi nimia pinguedine rempli
> Ad LILIVM duo C consocianda doce."

To minds of other temper there were not lacking portents to prove the anger of Heaven, whether at the crimes of the Order or at its destruction—eclipses of sun and moon, parahelia, paraselenæ, fires darting from earth to heaven, thunder in clear sky. Near Padua a mare dropped a foal with nine feet; flocks of birds of an unknown species were seen in Lombardy; throughout the Paduan territory a rainy winter was succeeded by a dry summer with hail-storms, so that the harvests were a failure. No Etruscan haruspex or Roman augur could wish for clearer omens: it reads like a page of Livy.—Albertini Mussati Hist. August. Rubr. x. xi. (Muratori S. R. I. X. 377–9).—Cf. Ptol. Lucens. Hist. Eccles. Lib. xxiv. (Ib. XI. 1233); Fr. Jordan. Chron. ann. 1314 (Muratori Antiq. XI. 789).

ceeded in procuring its transfer to the Hospitallers. It may not be true that they bribed him heavily to accomplish this, but such a belief prevailed extensively at the time, and sufficiently illustrates the estimate entertained of him by his contemporaries. May 2 the bull *Ad providam* announced that, although in view of the proceedings thus far had the Order could not legally be suppressed, it was provisionally and irrevocably abolished by apostolic ordinance; it was placed under perpetual inhibition, and any one presuming to enter it or to assume its habit incurred *ipso facto* excommunication. All the property of the Order was assumed by the Holy See, and was transferred to the Hospital of St. John of Jerusalem, saving in the kingdoms of Castile, Aragon, Majorca, and Portugal. As early as August, 1310, Jayme of Aragon had urged his brother monarchs to unite with him in defending their claims before the papal court; and though he disregarded Clement's invitation to appear in person before the council to state his reasons, the three kings took care to have their views energetically represented. Elsewhere, all who occupied and detained such property, no matter what their rank or station, were required, under pain of excommunication, to hand it over to the Hospitallers within a month after summons. This bull was sent to all princes and prelates, and the latter were instructed to enforce the surrender of the property by a vigorous use of excommunication and interdict.*

The burning question as to the property being thus settled, the less material one as to the persons of the Templars was shuffled off by referring them to their provincial councils for judgment, with the exception of the chiefs of the Order still reserved to the Holy See. All fugitives were cited to appear within a year before their bishops for examination and sentence; failure to do so incurred *ipso facto* excommunication, which if endured for another

---

* Contin. Guill. Nangiac. ann. 1312.—Raynald. ann. 1312, No. 5.—Hocsemii Gest. Episcopp. Leod. (Chapeaville, II. 346).—Chron. Fr. Pipini c. 49 (Muratori S. R. I. IX. 750).—Chron. Astens. c. 27 (Ib. XI. 194).—Chron. Cornel. Zantfliet ann. 1310 (Martene Ampl. Coll. V. 160).—Walsingham (D'Argentré I. i. 280).—Raynouard, pp. 197-8.—Bull. *Ad providam* (Rymer, III. 323.—Mag. Bull. Rom. IX. 149.—Harduin. VII. 1341-8).—Bull. *Nuper in generali* (Rymer III. 326. Mag. Bull. Rom. IX. 150).—Zurita, Lib. v. c. 99.—Allart, op. cit. pp. 71-2.—Schmidt, Päbstliche Urkunden, p. 81.

year became condemnation for heresy.   General instructions were
given that the impenitent and relapsed were to be visited with the
utmost penalties of the law.   Those who, even under torture, denied
all knowledge of error afforded a problem insoluble to the wisdom
of the council and were referred to the provincial councils to be
treated as justice and the equity of the canons required : to those
who confessed, the rigor of justice should be tempered with abun-
lant mercy.   They were to be placed in the former houses of the
Order or in monasteries, taking care that no great number should
be herded together, and be decently maintained out of the property
of the Order.   Interest in the subject, however, passed away with
the alienation of the property, and few provincial councils seem to
have been held save those of Tarragona and Narbonne already mentioned.   Many Templars rotted to death in their dungeons ; some
of the so-called "relapsed" were burned ; many wandered over
Europe as homeless vagabonds ; others maintained themselves as
best they might by manual labor.   In Naples, curiously enough,
John XXII. in 1318 ordered them to be supported by the Dominicans and Franciscans.   When some attempted to marry, John
XXII. pronounced that their vows were still binding and their
marriages void, thus admitting that their reception had been regular and not vitiated.   He likewise assumed their orthodoxy when he
permitted them to enter other Orders.   A certain number of them
did so, especially in Germany, where their fate was less bitter than
elsewhere, and where the Hospitallers welcomed them by formal
resolution of the Conference of Frankfurt-am-Mayn in 1317.   The
last Preceptor of Brandenburg, Frederic of Alvensleben, was received into the Hospital with the same preferment.   In fact, popular sympathy in Germany seems to have led to the assignment to
them of revenues of which the Hospitallers complained as an insupportable burden, and in 1318 John XXII. ordered that they
should not be so provided for as to enable them to lay up money
and live luxuriously, but should have merely a living and garments
suited to spiritual persons.*

---

* Bern. Guidon. Flor. Chron. (Bouquet, XXI. 722).—Godefroy de Paris, v.
6028-9.—Ferreti Vicentin. Hist. (Muratori S. R. I. IX. 1017).—Le Roulx, Documents, etc., p. 51.—Havemann, Geschichte des Ausgangs, p. 290.—Fr. Pipini Chron.
c. 49 (Muratori IX. 750).—Joann. de S. Victor. (Bouquet, XXI. 658).—Vaissette,

There remained to be disposed of de Molay and the other chiefs reserved by Clement for his personal judgment—a reservation which, as we have seen, by inspiring them with selfish hopes, led them to abandon their brethren. When this purpose had been accomplished Clement for a while seemed to forget them in their drear captivity. It was not till December 22, 1313, that he appointed a commission of three cardinals, Arnaud of S. Sabina, Nicholas of S. Eusebio, and Arnaldo of S. Prisca, to investigate the proceedings against them and to absolve or condemn, or to inflict penance proportionate to their offences, and to assign to them on the property of the Order such pensions as were fitting. The cardinals dallied with their duty until March 19, 1314, when, on a scaffold in front of Nôtre Dame, de Molay, Geoffroi de Charney, Master of Normandy, Hugues de Peraud, Visitor of France, and Godefroi de Gonneville, Master of Aquitaine, were brought forth from the jail in which for nearly seven years they had lain, to receive the sentence agreed upon by the cardinals, in conjunction with the Archbishop of Sens and some other prelates whom they had called in. Considering the offences which the culprits had confessed and confirmed, the penance imposed was in accordance with rule—that of perpetual imprisonment. The affair was supposed to be concluded when, to the dismay of the prelates and wonderment of the assembled crowd, de Molay and Geoffroi de Charney arose. They had been guilty, they said, not of the crimes imputed to them, but of basely betraying their Order to save their own lives. It was pure and holy; the charges were fictitious and the confessions false. Hastily the cardinals delivered them to the Prévôt of Paris, and retired to deliberate on this unexpected contingency, but they were saved all trouble. When the news was carried to Philippe he was furious. A short consultation with his council only was required. The canons pronounced that a relapsed heretic was to be burned without a hearing; the facts were notorious and no formal judgment by the papal commission need be waited for. That same day, by sunset, a pile was erected on a small island in the Seine, the Isle des Juifs, near the palace garden. There de Molay and de Charney were slowly burned to death, refusing all

---

IV. 141.—Stemler, Contingent zur Geschichte der Templer, pp. 20-1.—**Raynouard,** pp. 213-4, 233-5.—Wilcke, II. 236, 240.—Anton, Versuch, p. 142.

offers of pardon for retraction, and bearing their torment with a composure which won for them the reputation of martyrs among the people, who reverently collected their ashes as relics. It remained for a modern apologist of the Church to declare that their intrepid self-sacrifice proved them to be champions of the devil. In their death they triumphed over their persecutor and atoned for the pusillanimity with which they had abandoned those committed to their guidance. Hugues de Peraud and the Master of Aquitaine lacked courage to imitate them, accepted their penance, and perished miserably in their dungeons. Raimbaud de Caron, the Preceptor of Cyprus, had doubtless been already released by death.*

The fact that in little more than a month Clement died in torment of the loathsome disease known as lupus, and that in eight months Philippe, at the early age of forty-six, perished by an accident while hunting, necessarily gave rise to the legend that de Molay had cited them before the tribunal of God. Such stories were rife among the people, whose sense of justice had been scandalized by the whole affair. Even in distant Germany Philippe's death was spoken of as a retribution for his destruction of the Templars, and Clement was described as shedding tears of remorse on his death-bed for three great crimes, the poisoning of Henry VI. and the ruin of the Templars and Beguines. An Italian contemporary, papalist in his leanings, apologizes for introducing a story of a wandering outcast Templar carried from Naples to the presence of Clement, bearding him to his face, condemned to the stake, and from the flames summoning him and Philippe to the judgment-seat of God within the year, which was marvellously fulfilled.

---

* Raynald. ann. 1313, No. 39.—Raynouard, pp. 205–10.—Contin. Guill. Nangiac. ann. 1313.—Joann. de S. Victor. (Bouquet, XXI. 658).—Chron. Anon. (Bouquet, XXI. 143).—Godefroy de Paris v. 6033–6129.—Villani Chron. VIII. 92.— Chron. Cornel. Zantfliet ann. 1310 (Martene Ampl. Coll. V. 160). — Trithem. Chron. Hirsaug. ann. 1307.—Pauli Æmylii de Reb. Gest. Franc. Ed. 1569, p. 421. —Van Os, p. 111.

In his haste Philippe did not stop to inquire as to his rights over the Isle des Juifs. It happened that the monks of St. Germain des Près claimed *haute et basse justice* there, and they promptly complained that they were wronged by the execution, whereupon Philippe issued letters declaring that it should work no prejudice to them (Olim, II. 599).

These tales show how the popular heart was stirred and how the popular sympathies were directed.*

In fact, outside of France, where, for obvious reasons, contemporary opinion was cautious in expression, the downfall of the Templars was very largely attributed to the remorseless cupidity of Philippe and Clement. Even in France public sentiment inclined in their favor. Godefroi de Paris evidently goes as far as he dares when he says:

> " Dyversement de ce l'en parle,
> Et ou monde en est grant bataille—
> —L'en puet bien décevoir l'yglise
> Mès l'en ne puet en nule guise
> Diex décevoir. Je n'en dis plus:
> Qui voudra dira le seurplus."

It required courage animated by a lofty sense of duty when, at the height of the persecution, the Dominican, Pierre de la Palu, one of the foremost theologians of the day, voluntarily appeared before the papal commission in Paris to say that he had been present at many examinations where some of the accused confessed the charges and others denied them, and it appeared to him that the

---

* Pauli Langii Chron. Citicens. ann. 1314 (Pistorii I. 1201).—Chron. Sampetrini Erfurtens. ann. 1315 (Menken III. 325).—Naucleri Chron. ann. 1306.—Ferreti Vicentin. Hist. (Muratori S. R. I. IX. 1018).

Clement's reputation was such that this was not the only legend of the kind about his death. While yet Archbishop of Bordeaux, he had a bitter quarrel with Walter of Bruges, a holy Franciscan whom Nicholas III. had forced to accept the episcopate of Poitiers. On his elevation to the papacy he gratified his grudge by deposing Walter and ordering him to a convent. Walter made no complaint, but on his death-bed he appealed to the judgment of God, and died with a paper in his hand in which he cited the papal oppressor before the divine tribunal on a certain day. His grip on this could not be loosened, and he was buried with it. The next year Clement chanced to pass through the place; he had the tomb opened, found the body uncorrupted, and ordered the paper to be given to him. It terrified him greatly, and at the time specified he was obliged to obey the summons.—Wadding. ann. 1279, No. 13.—Chron. Glassberger ann. 1307.

Guillaume de Nogaret, who was Philippe's principal instrument, was the subject of a similar story. A Templar on his way to the stake saw him and cited him to appear within eight days, and on the eighth day he died.—Chron. Astens. c. 27 (Muratori S. R. I. XI. 194).

denials were worthy of confidence rather than the confessions.* As time wore on the conviction as to their innocence strengthened. Boccaccio took their side. St. Antonino of Florence, whose historical labors largely influenced opinion in the fifteenth century, asserted that their downfall was attributable to the craving for their wealth, and popular writers in general adopted the same view. Even Raynaldus hesitates and balances arguments on either side, and Campi assures us that in Italy, in the seventeenth century, they were regarded by many as saints and martyrs. At length, about the middle of the seventeenth century, the learned Du Puy undertook to rehabilitate the memory of Philippe le Bel in a work of which the array of documentary evidence renders it indispensable to the student. Gürtler, who followed him with a history of the Templars, is evidently unable to make up his mind. Since then

---

* Godefroi de Paris, v. 6131–45. Cf. 3876–81, 3951–2.—Procès des Templiers, II. 195.

Some of the contemporaries outside of France who attribute the affair to the greed of Philippe and Clement are—Matt. Neoburg. (Albert Argentinens.) Chron. ann. 1346 (Urstisii II. 137).—Sächsische Weltchronik, erste bairische Fortsetzung, ann. 1312 (Mon. Germ. II. 334).—Stalwegii Chron. ann. 1305 (Leibnit. III. 274). —Bothonis Chron. ann. 1311 (Leibnit. III. 374).—Chron. Comitum Schawenburg (Meibom. I. 499).—Jo. Hocsemii Gest. Episcc. Leodiens. (Chapeaville, II. 345–6).— Chron. Astens. c. 27 (Muratori S. R. I. XI. 192–4).—Istorie Pistolesi (Ib. XI. 518). —Villani Chron. VIII. 92.

Authorities who assume the guilt of the Templars are—Ferreti Vicentini Hist. (Muratori S. R. I. IX. 1017–18).—Chron. Parmens. ann. 1309 (Ib. IX. 880). —Albertin. Mussat. Hist. August. Rubr. x. (Ib. X. 377).—Chron. Guillel. Scoti (Bouquet, XXI. 205).—Hermanni Corneri Chron. ann. 1309 (Eccard. II. 971–2). The old German word Tempelhaus, signifying house of prostitution, conveys the popular sense of the license of the Order (Trithem. Chron. Hirsaug. ann. 1307).

Henri Martin assumes that the traditions of the north of France are adverse to the Templars, and that those of the south are favorable. He instances a Breton ballad in which the "Red Monks," or Templars, are represented as ferocious debauchees who carry off young women and then destroy them with the fruits of guilty intercourse. On the other hand, at Gavarnie (Bigorre), there are seven heads which are venerated as those of martyred Templars, and the popular belief is that on the night of the anniversary of the abolition of the Order a figure, armed cap-a-pie and bearing the white mantle with a red cross, appears in the cemetery and thrice cries out, "Who will defend the holy temple; who will liberate the sepulchre of the Lord?" when the seven heads answer thrice, "No one, no one! The Temple is destroyed!"—Histoire de France, T. IV. pp. 496–7 (Éd. 1855).

the question has been argued pro and con with a vehemence which promises to leave it one of the unsettled problems of history.*

Be this as it may, Philippe obtained the object of his desires. After 1307 his financial embarrassments visibly decreased. There was not only the release from the obligation of the five hundred thousand livres which he had borrowed of the Order, but its vast accumulations of treasure and of valuables of all kinds fell into his hands and were never accounted for. He collected all the debts due to it, and his successors were still busy at that work as late as 1322. The extensive banking business which the Templars had established between the East and the West doubtless rendered this feature of the confiscation exceedingly profitable, and it is safe to assume that Philippe enforced the rule that debts due by convicted heretics were not to be paid. Despite his pretence of surrendering the landed estates to the pope, he retained possession of them till his death and enjoyed their revenues. Even those in Guyenne, belonging to the English crown, he collected in spite of the protests of Edward, and he claimed the Templar castles in the English territories until Clement prevailed upon him to withdraw. The great Paris Temple, half palace, half fortress, one of the architectural wonders of the age, was retained with a grip which nothing but death could loosen. After the property had been adjudged to the Hospitallers, in May, 1312, by the Council of Vienne with Philippe's concurrence, and he had formally approved of it in August, Clement addressed him in December several letters asking his assistance in recovering what had been seized by individuals—assistance which doubtless was freely promised; but in June, 1313, we find Clement remonstrating with him over his refusal to permit Albert de Châteauneuf, Grand Preceptor of the Hospital, to administer the property either of his own Order or that of the Temple in France. In 1314 the General Chapter of the Hospital gave unlimited authority to Leonardo and Francesco de Tibertis to take possession of all the Temple property promised to the Order, and in April an *arrêt* of Parlement recites that it had been given to the Hospital at Philippe's special request, and that he had invested Leonardo de Tibertis with it; but there was

---

* Raynald. ann. 1307, No. 12.—D'Argentré I. I. 281.—Campi, Dell' Hist. Eccles. di Piacenza, P. III. p. 43, Piacenza, 1651.—Feyjoo, Cartas I. xxviii.

a reservation that it was liable for the expenses of the imprisoned Templars and for the costs incurred by the king in pushing the trials. This was a claim elastic both in amount and in the time required for settlement. Had Philippe's life been prolonged it is probable that no settlement would have been made. As it was, the Hospitallers at last, in 1317, were glad to close the affair by abandoning to Philippe le Long all claim on the income of the landed estates which the crown had held for ten years, with an arrangement as to the movables which virtually left them in the king's hands. They also assumed to pay the expenses of the imprisoned Templars, and this exposed them to every species of exaction and pillage on the part of the royal officials.*

In fact, it is the general testimony that the Hospitallers were rather impoverished than enriched by the splendid gift. There had been a universal Saturnalia of plunder. Every one, king, noble, and prelate, who could lay hands on a part of the defenceless possessions had done so, and to reclaim it required large payments either to the holder or to his suzerain. In 1286 the Margrave Otto of Brandenburg had entered the Order of the Temple and had enriched it with extensive domains. These the Margrave Waldemar seized, and did not surrender till 1322, nor was the transfer confirmed till 1350, when the Hospital was obliged to pay five hundred silver marks. In Bohemia many nobles seized and retained Templar property; the chivalrous King John is said to have kept more than twenty castles, and Templars themselves managed to hold some and bequeath them to their heirs. Religious orders were not behindhand in securing what they could out of the spoils — Dominicans, Carthusians, Augustinians, Celestinians, all are named as participators. Even the pious Robert of Naples had to be reminded by Clement that he had incurred excommunication because he had not surrendered the Templar property in Provence. In fact, he had secretly sent orders to his seneschal not to

---

* Ferreti Vicentini, loc. cit.—Raynald. ann. 1307, No. 12.—Havemann, p. 334.—Wilcke, II. 327, 329–30.—Raynouard, pp. 25–6.—Vaissette, IV. 141.—Du Puy, pp. 75, 78, 88, 125–31, 216–17.—Prutz, p. 16.—Olim, III. 580–2.

Even as late as 1337, in the accounts of the Sénéchaussée of Toulouse there is a place reserved for collections from the Templar property, although the returns in that year were nil.—Vaissette, Éd. Privat, X. Pr. 785.

For the banking business of the Templars, see Schottmüller, I. 64.

deliver it to the Archbishops of Arles and Embrun, the commissioners appointed by the pope, and before he was finally obliged to make it over he realized what he could from it. Perhaps the Hospital fared better in Cyprus than elsewhere, for when the papal nuncio, Peter, Bishop of Rhodes, published the bull, November 7, 1313, the Templar possessions seem to have been made over to it without contest. In England, even the weakness of Edward II. made a feeble attempt to keep the property. Clement had ordered him, February 25, 1309, to make it over to the papal commissioners designated for the purpose, but he seems to have paid no attention to the command. After the Council of Vienne we find him, August 12, 1312, expressing to the Prior of the Hospital his surprise that he is endeavoring under the color of papal letters to obtain possession of it, to the manifest prejudice of the dignity of the crown. Much of it had been farmed out and alienated to Edward's worthless favorites, and he resisted its surrender as long as he dared. When forced to succumb he did so in a manner as self-abasing as possible, by executing, November 24, 1313, a notarial instrument to the effect that he protested against it, and only yielded out of fear of the dangers to him and his kingdom to be apprehended from a refusal. It may be doubted whether his orders were obeyed that it should be burdened with the payment of the allowances to the surviving Templars. He succeeded, however, in getting a hundred pounds from the Hospitallers for the London Temple; and in 1317 John XXII. was obliged to intervene with an order for the restitution of lands still detained by those who had succeeded in occupying them.*

---

* Contin. Guillel. Nangiac. ann. 1312.—Villani Chron. VIII. 92.—Matt. Neoburg. (Albertin. Argentin.) Chron. ann. 1346 (Urstisii II. 137).—H. Mutii Chron. Lib. XXII. ann. 1311.—Chron. Fr. Pipini c. 49 (Muratori S. R. I. IX. 750).—Havemann, p. 338.—Vertot, II. 154.—Hocsemii Gest. Episcc. Leodiens. (Chapeaville, II. 346).—Trithem. Chron. Hirsaug. ann. 1307.—Naucleri Chron. ann. 1306.—Raynald. ann. 1312, No. 7; ann. 1313, No. 18.—Van Os, p. 81.—Wilcke, II. 340-1, 497.—Gassari Annal. Augstburg. ann. 1312 (Menken. I. 1473).—Schottmüller, I. 496; II. 427-9.—Regest. Clement. PP. V. T. IV. p. 452.—Rymer, III. 133-4, 292-4, 321, 337, 404, 409-10, 451-2, 472-3.—Le Roulx, Documents, etc., p. 50.

We happen to have a slight example of the plunder in an absolution granted February 23, 1310, by Clement to Bernard de Bayulli, canon and chancellor of the Abbey of Cornella in Roussillon, for the excommunication incurred by him for taking a horse, a mule, and sundry effects, valued in all at sixty livres Tour-

The Spanish peninsula had been excepted from the operation of the bull transferring the property to the Hospital, but subject to the further discretion of Clement.   As regards the kingdom of Majorca he exercised this discretion in 1313 by giving King Sancho II. the personal property, and ordering him to make over the real estate to the Hospital, under condition that the latter should be subject to the duties which had been performed by the Temple. Even this did not relieve the Hospitallers from the necessity of bargaining with King Sancho.   It was not until February, 1314, that the lands on the island of Majorca were surrendered to them in consideration of an annual payment of eleven thousand sols, and an allowance of twenty-two thousand five hundred sols to be made on the mesne profits to be accounted for since the donation was made.   All profits previous to that time were to remain with the crown.   No documents are extant to show what was done on the mainland, but doubtless there was a similar transaction.   In addition to this the pensions of the Templars assigned on the property were a heavy burden for many years.*

In Aragon there was less disposition to accede to the papal wishes.   Constant struggle with the Saracen had left memories of services rendered, or sharpened the sense of benefits to come from some new Order devoted wholly to national objects, which could not be expected of a body like the Hospitallers, whose primary duty was devotion to the Holy Land.   The Templars had contributed largely to all the enterprises which had enlarged the boundaries of the kingdom.   They had rendered faithful service to the monarchy in the council as well as in the field; to them was in great part attributed the rescue of Jayme I. from the hands of de Montfort, and they had been foremost in the glorious campaigns which had earned for him the title of *el Conquistador*. Pedro III. and Jayme II. had scarce had less reason for gratitude to them, and the latter, after sacrificing them, naturally desired to use their forfeited property for the establishment of a new Order from which he might expect similar advantages, but Clement's engagements with the Hospitallers were such that he turned a deaf

---

nois, from the preceptory of Gardin, in the diocese of Lerida.—Regest. Clement. PP. V. T. V. p. 41.

* Raynald. ann. 1313, No. 37.—Allart, loc. cit. pp. 87, 89.

ear to the king's repeated representations. On the accession of
John XXII., however, matters assumed a more favorable aspect,
and in 1317 Vidal de Vilanova, Jayme's envoy, procured from him
a bull authorizing the formation of the Order of Nuestra Señora
de Montesa, affiliated to the Order of Calatrava, from which its
members were to be drawn. Its duties were defined to be the
defence of the coasts and frontier of Valencia from corsairs and
Moors; the Templar property in Aragon and Catalonia was made
over to the Hospitallers, while the new Order was to have in Valencia not only the possessions of the Temple, but all those of the
Hospital, except in the city of Valencia and for half a league
around it. In 1319 the preliminaries were accomplished, and
the new Order was organized with Guillen de Eril as its Grand
Master.*

In Castile Alonso XI. retained for the crown the greater part
of the Templar lands, though, along the frontier, nobles and cities
succeeded in obtaining a portion. Some were given to the Orders
of Santiago and Calatrava, and the Hospitallers received little.
After an interval of half a century another effort was made, and
in 1366 Urban V. ordered the delivery within two months of all
the Templar property to the Hospitallers, but it is safe to assume
that the mandate was disregarded, though in 1387 Clement VII.,
the Avignonese antipope, confirmed some exchanges made of Templar property by the Hospitallers with the Orders of Santiago
and Calatrava.† Castile, as we have already seen, was always singularly independent of the papacy. In Portugal, as mentioned
above, the property was handed over as a whole to the Order of
Jesus Christ.

In the Morea, where the Templar possessions were extensive,
Clement had, as early as November 11, 1310, exercised rights of
proprietorship by ordering his administrators, the Patriarch of
Constantinople and the Archbishop of Patras, to lend to Gautier

---

* Bofarull y Brocá, Hist. de Cataluña, III. 97.—Zurita, Lib. II. c. 60; Lib. III.
c. 9; Lib. VI. c. 26. — Mariana, Ed. 1789, V. 290. — La Fuente, Hist. Ecles. II.
370–1. Ilescas (Hist. Pontifical, Lib. VI. c. 2), in the second half of the sixteenth
century, remarks that there had been fourteen Masters of Montesa and never one
married until the present one, D. Cesar de Borja, who is married.

† Mariana, V. 290. — Garibay, Compendio Historial Lib. XIII. cap. 33. — Zurita, Lib. VI. c. 26.—Le Roulx, Documents, etc., p. 52.

de Brienne, Duke of Athens, all the proceeds which they had collected, and all that they might collect for a year to come.*

Thus disappeared, virtually without a struggle, an organization
which was regarded as one of the proudest, wealthiest, and most
formidable in Europe. It is not too much to say that the very
idea of its destruction could not have suggested itself, but for the
facilities which the inquisitorial process placed in able and unscrupulous hands to accomplish any purpose of violence under the
form of law. If I have dwelt on the tragedy at a length that
may seem disproportionate, my apology is that it affords so perfect an illustration of the helplessness of the victim, no matter how
high-placed, when once the fatal charge of heresy was preferred
against him, and was pressed through the agency of the Inquisition.

The case of the learned theologian, Jean Petit, Doctor of Sorbonne, is of no great historical importance, but it is worth noting
as an example of the use made of the charge of heresy as a weapon
in political warfare, and of the elastic definition by which heresy
was brought to include offences not easily justiciable in the ordinary courts.

Under Charles VI. of France the royal power was reduced to
a shadow. His frequently recurring fits of insanity rendered him
incapable of governing, and the quarrels of ambitious princes of
the blood reduced the kingdom almost to a state of anarchy. Especially bitter was the feud between the king's brother, Louis,
Duke of Orleans, and his cousin, Jean sans Peur of Burgundy.
Yet even that age of violence was startled when, by the procure-
ment of Jean sans Peur, the Duke of Orleans, in 1407, was assassinated in the streets of Paris—a murder which remained un-
avenged until 1419, when the battle-axe of Tanneguy du Châtel
balanced the account on ·the bridge of Montereau. Even Jean
sans Peur felt the need of some apology for his bloody deed, and
he sought the assistance of Jean Petit, who read before the royal
court a thesis—the *Justificatio Ducis Burgundiæ*—to prove that
he had acted righteously and patriotically, and that he deserved

---

* Regest. Clement. PP. V. T. V. p. 235 (Romæ, 1887).

the thanks of king and people. Written in the conventional scholastic style, the tract was not a mere political pamphlet, but an argument based on premises of general principles. It is a curious coincidence that, nearly three centuries earlier, another Johannes Parvus, better known as John of Salisbury, the worthiest representative of the highest culture of his day, in a purely speculative treatise had laid down the doctrine that a tyrant was to be put to death without mercy. According to the younger Jean Petit, "Any tyrant can and ought properly to be slain by any subject or vassal, and by any means, specially by treachery, notwithstanding any oath or compact, and without awaiting judicial sentence or order." This rather portentous proposition was limited by defining the tyrant to be one who is endeavoring through cupidity, fraud, sorcery, or evil mind to deprive the king of his authority, and the subject or vassal is assumed to be one who is inspired by loyalty, and him the king should cherish and reward. It was not difficult to find Scriptural warrant for such assertion in the slaying of Zimri by Phineas, and of Holofernes by Judith; but Jean Petit ventured on debatable ground when he declared that St. Michael, without awaiting the divine command and moved only by natural love, slew Satan with eternal death, for which he was rewarded with spiritual wealth as great as he was capable of receiving.*

That this was not a mere lawyer's pleading is shown by the fact that it was written in the vernacular and exposed for sale. Doubtless Jean sans Peur circulated it extensively, and it was doubtless convincing to those who were already convinced. It might safely have been allowed to perish in the limbo of forgetfulness, but when, some six years later, the Armagnac faction obtained the upper hand, it was exhumed from the dust as a ready means of attacking the Burgundians. Jean Petit himself, by opportunely dying some years before, escaped a trial for heresy, but in November, 1313, a national council was assembled in Paris to consider nine propositions extracted from his work. Gérard, Bishop of Paris, and Frère Jean Polet, the inquisitor, summoned the masters of theology of the University to give their opinions,

---

* Johann. Saresberiens. Polycrat. VIII. 17. — D'Argentré I. II. 180–5. — Monstrelet, Chroniques, I. 39, 119.

which solemnly condemned the propositions. The council debated
the question with unwearied prolixity through twenty-eight sessions, and finally, on February 23, 1314, it adopted a sentence condemning the nine propositions to be burned as erroneous in faith
and morals, and manifestly scandalous. The sentence was duly
executed two days later on a scaffold in front of Nôtre Dame, in
presence of a vast crowd, to whom the famous doctor, Benoist
Gencien, elaborately explained the enormity of the heresy. Jean
sans Peur thereupon appealed to the Holy See from this sentence,
and John XXIII. appointed a commission of three cardinals—
Orsini, Aquileia, and Florence—to examine and report. Thus Jean
Petit had succeeded in becoming a European question, but in spite
of this a royal ordonnance on March 17 commanded all the bishops of the kingdom to burn the propositions; on March 18, the
University ordered them burned; on June 4 there was a royal
mandate to publish the condemnation; on December 4 the University came to the royal court and delivered an oration on the
subject, and on December 27 Charles VI. addressed a royal letter
to the Council of Constance asking it to join in the condemnation. Evidently the affair was exploited to the uttermost; and
when, on January 4, 1315, the long-delayed obsequies of the Duke
of Orleans were performed in Nôtre Dame, Chancellor Gerson
preached a sermon before the king and the court, the boldness of
which excited general comment. The government of the Duke
of Orleans had been better than any which had succeeded it; the
death of the Duke of Burgundy was not counselled, but his humiliation was advocated; the burning of Petit's propositions was well
done, but more remained to do, and all this Gerson was ready to
maintain before all comers.*

It was in this mood that Gerson went to Constance as head of
the French nation. In his first address to the council, March 23,
1415, he urged the condemnation of the nine propositions. The
trial of John XXIII., the condemnation of Wickliff and of communion in both elements, and the discussion over Huss for a while
monopolized the attention of the council, and no action was taken

---

* D'Argentré, I. II. 184–6. — Religieux de S. Denis, Histoire de Charles VI.
Liv. xxxiii. ch. 28. — Juvenal des Ursins, ann. 1413. — Gersoni Opp. Ed. 1494, I.
14 B, C.—Von der Hardt, T. III. Prolegom. 10–13.—Monstrelet, I. 139.

until June 15. Meanwhile Gerson found an ally in the Polish nation. John of Falckenberg had written a tract applying the arguments of Jean Petit to the slaying of Polish princes, of which the Archbishop of Gnesen had readily procured the condemnation by the University of Paris, and the Polish ambassador joined Gerson in the effort to have both put under the ban. On June 15, Andrea Lascaris, Bishop of Posen, proposed that a commission be appointed to conduct an inquisition upon new heresies. Jean Petit was not alluded to, but it was understood that his propositions were aimed at, for the only negative vote was that of Martin, Bishop of Arras, the ambassador of Jean sans Peur, who asserted that the object of the movement was to assail his master ; and he further protested against Cardinal Peter d'Ailly, who was put on the commission with Orsini, Aquileia, and Florence, as well as two representatives of the Italian nation and four each of the French, English, and German. On July 6, after rendering judgment against Huss, the council condemned as heretical and scandalous the proposition *Quilibet tyrannus,* which was virtually the first of the nine condemned in Paris. This did not satisfy the French, who wanted the judgment of the University confirmed on the whole series. During the two years and a half that the council remained assembled, Gerson was unwearied in his efforts to accomplish this object. These heresies he declared to be of more importance than those of Huss and Jerome, and bitterly he scolded the fathers for leaving the good work unfinished. Interminable was the wrangling and disputation, appeals from Charles VI. and the University on the one side, and from the Duke of Burgundy on the other. John of Falckenberg was thrown into prison, but nothing would induce the council to take further action, and the affair at last died out. It is difficult for us at the present day to understand the magnitude which it assumed in the eyes of that generation. Gerson subsequently felt himself obliged to meet the jeers of those who reproached him with having risked a question of such importance before such a body as the council, and he justified himself by alleging that he had acted under instructions from the king and the University, and the Gallican Church as represented in the province of Sens. Moreover, he argued, when the council had manifested such zeal in condemning the Wickliffite doctrines and in burning Huss and Jerome, he would have been

III.—22

rash and unjust to suppose that it would not have been equally
earnest in repressing the yet more pernicious heresies of Jean
Petit. To us the result of greatest interest was its influence on
the fate of Gerson himself. On the dissolution of the council he
was afraid to risk the enmity of the Duke of Burgundy by returning to France, and gladly accepted a refuge offered him in Austria
by Duke Ernest, which he repaid in a grateful poem. He never
ventured nearer home than Lyons, where his brother was friar of
a convent of Celestinian hermits, and where he supported himself
by teaching school till his death, July 14, 1429.*

Criticism would doubtless ere this have demonstrated the me-
teoric career of Joan of Arc to be a myth, but for the concurrent
testimony of friend and foe and the documentary evidence, which
enable us with reasonable certainty to separate its marvellous
vicissitudes from the legendary details with which they have been
obscured. For us her story has a special interest, as affording another illustration of the ease with which the inquisitorial process
was employed for political ends.

In 1429 the French monarchy seemed doomed beyond hope of
resuscitation. In the fierce dissensions which marked the reign
of the insane Charles VI. a generation had grown up in whom
adherence to faction had replaced fidelity to the throne or to the
nation; the loyalists were known not as partisans of Charles VII.,
but as Armagnacs, and the Burgundians welcomed the foreign
domination of England as preferable to that of their hereditary
sovereign. Paris, in spite of the fearful privations and losses entailed by the war, submitted cheerfully to the English through
the love it bore to their ally, the Duke of Burgundy. Joan of Arc
said that, in her native village, Domremy on the Lorraine border,
there was but one Burgundian, and his head she wished were cut
off; but Domremy and Vaucouleurs constituted the only Armagnac
spot in northeastern France, and its boys used to have frequent
fights with the Burgundian boys of Marey, from which they

---

* Von der Hardt, III. Proleg. 13; IV. 335–6, 440, 451, 718–22, 724–8, 1087–88,
1092, 1192, 1513, 1531–2. — D'Argentré, I. ii. 187–92.—Gersoni Opp. III. 56 Q–S,
57 B.

would be brought home wounded and bleeding. Such was the all-pervading bitterness of discord throughout the kingdom.*

Even the death of the brilliant Henry V., in 1423, had seemed to check in no degree the progress of the English arms. Under the able regency of his brother, the Duke of Bedford, seconded by such captains as Salisbury, Talbot, Scales, and Fastolf, the infant Henry VI. appeared destined to succeed to the throne of his grandfather, Charles VI., as provided in the treaty of Troyes. In 1424 the victory of Verneuil repeated the triumph of Agincourt. From Dauphiné alone three hundred knights were left upon the field, and but for the fidelity of the provinces won by the Albigensian crusades, Charles VII. would already have been a king without a kingdom. Driven beyond the Loire, he was known by the nickname of the Roi de Bourges. Vacillating and irresolute, dominated by unworthy favorites, he hardly knew whether to retreat farther to the south and make a final stand among the mountains of Dauphiné, or to seek a refuge in Spain or Scotland. In 1428 his last line of defence on the Loire was threatened by the leaguer of Orleans. He was powerless to raise the siege, and for five months the heroic city resisted till, reduced to despair, it sent the renowned knight, Pothon de Xaintrailles to the Duke of Burgundy to ask him to accept its allegiance. The duke was nothing loath, but the acquisition required the assent of his English ally, and Bedford scornfully refused—he would not, he said, beat the bush for another to win the bird. Two months more of weary siege elapsed: as the spring of 1429 opened, further resistance seemed useless, and for Charles there appeared nothing left but ignominious retreat and eventual exile.†

Such was the hopeless condition of the French monarchy when the enthusiasm of Joan of Arc introduced a new factor in the tangled problem, kindling anew the courage which had been extinguished by an unbroken series of defeats, arousing the sense of

---

* Journal d'un Bourgeois de Paris ann. 1431.—Epist. de Bonlavillar (Pez, Thesaur. Anecd. VI. III. 237).—Procès de Jeanne d'Arc, p. 474. (When not otherwise defined, my references to this and other documents concerning Joan are to the collection in Buchon's *Choix de Chroniques et Mémoires*, Paris, 1838.)

† Thomassin, Registre Delphinal (Buchon, p. 536, 540).—Görres, Vie de Jeanne d'Arc, Trad. Boré, Paris, 1886, p. 108.— Chronique de la Pucelle (Buchon, p. 454).

loyalty which had been lost in faction, bringing religion as a stimulus to patriotism, and replacing despair with eager confidence and
hopefulness.   It has been given to few in the world's history thus
to influence the destiny of a nation, and perhaps to none so obscure
and apparently so unfitted.*

Born January 6, 1484, in the little hamlet of Domremy, on the
border line of Lorraine, she had but completed her seventeenth
year when she confidently assumed the function of the saviour of
her native land.†   Her parents, honest peasants, had given her
such training as comported with her station ; she could, of course,
neither read nor write, but she could recite her Pater Noster, Ave
Maria, and Credo ; she had herded the kine, and was a notable
sempstress—on her trial she boasted that no maid or matron of
Rouen could teach her anything with the needle.   Thanks to her
rustic employment she was tall and strong-limbed, active and enduring.   It was said of her that she could pass six days and nights
without taking off her harness, and marvellous stories were told
of her abstinence from food while undergoing the most exhausting
labor in battle and assault.   Thus a strong physical constitution
was dominated by a still stronger and excitable nervous organization.   Her resolute self-reliance was shown when she was sought
in marriage by an honest citizen of Toul, whose suit her parents
favored.   Finding her obdurate, he had recourse, it would seem
with her parents' consent, to the law, and cited her before the
Official of Toul to fulfil the marriage promise which he alleged
she had made to him.   Notwithstanding her youth, Joan appeared
undaunted before the court, swore that she had given no pledges,
and was released from the too-ardent suitor.   At the age of thirteen she commenced to have ecstasies and visions.   The Archangel
Michael appeared to her first, and he was followed by St. Catharine and St. Margaret, whom God had specially commissioned to
watch over and guide her.   Even the Archangel Gabriel some-

---

* Though the name Joan of Arc has been naturalized in English, Jeanne's
patronymic was Darc, not D'Arc.—Vallet de Viriville, Charles du Lis, pp. xii.–
xiii.

† So close to the border was Joan's birthplace that a new delimitation of the
frontier, made in 1571, transferred to Lorraine the group of houses including the
Darc cottage, and left a neighboring group in France.—Vallet de Viriville, ubi
sup. pp. 24–5.

times came to counsel her, and she felt herself the instrument of the divine will, transmuting by a subtle psychical alchemy her own impulses into commands from on high. At length she could summon her heavenly advisers at will and obtain from them instructions in any doubtful emergency. In her trial great stress was laid upon an ancient beech-tree, near Domremy, known as the Ladies' Tree, or Fairies' Tree, from near the roots of which gushed forth a spring of miraculous healing virtue. A survival of tree and fountain worship was preserved in the annual dances and songs of the young girls of the village around the tree, and the garlands which they hung upon its boughs, but Joan, although she joined her comrades in these observances, usually reserved her garlands to decorate the shrine of the Virgin in the church hard by. Extreme religious sensibility was inseparable from such a character as hers, and almost at the first apparition of her celestial visitants she made a vow of virginity. She believed herself consecrated and set apart for some high and holy purpose, to which all earthly ties must be subordinate. When she related to her judges that her parents were almost crazed at her departure, she added that if she had had a hundred fathers and mothers she would have abandoned them to fulfil her mission. To this self-concentration, reflected in her bearing, is probably to be attributed the remark of several of her chroniclers, that no man could look upon her with a lascivious eye.*

At first her heavenly guides merely told her to conduct herself well and to frequent the church, but as she grew to understand the desperate condition of the monarchy and to share the fierce passions of the time, it was natural that these purely moral instructions should change into commands to bear from God the message of deliverance to the despairing people. In her ecstasies she felt herself to be the chosen instrument, and at length her Voices, as she habitually called them, urged her several times a week to hasten to France and to raise the siege of Orleans. To her parents she feared to reveal her mission; some unguarded revelation they must have had, for, two years before her departure,

---

* Procès, pp. 469, 470, 471, 473, 475, 476, 477, 483, 485, 487, 499.—Chron. de la Pucelle, ann. 1429, pp. 428, 435-6, 443.—L'Averdy (Académie des Inscriptions, Notices des MSS. III. 373).

her father, Jacques Darc, had dreams of her going off with the soldiers, and he told her brothers that if he thought that his dreams would come true he wished they would drown her, or he would do it himself.   Thenceforth she was closely watched, but the urgency of her celestial counsellors grew into reproaches for her tardiness, and further delay was unendurable.   Obtaining permission to visit her uncle, Denis Laxart, she persuaded him to communicate her secret to Robert de Baudricourt, who held for the king the neighboring castle of Vaucouleurs.   Her Voices had predicted that she would be twice repulsed and would succeed the third time.   It so turned out.   The good knight, who at first contemptuously advised her uncle to box her ears, at length was persuaded to ask the king's permission to send the girl to him.   She must have acquired a reputation of inspiration, for while awaiting the response the Duke of Lorraine, who was sick, sent for her and she told him that if he wished a cure he must first reconcile himself with his wife.   On the royal permission being accorded, de Baudricourt gave to her a man's dress and a sword, with a slender escort of a knight and four men, and washed his hands of the affair.*

The little party started, February 13, 1429, on their perilous ride of a hundred and fifty leagues, in the depth of winter, through the enemy's country.   That they should accomplish it without misadventure in eleven days was in itself regarded as a miracle, and as manifesting the favor of God.   On February 24 they reached Chinon, where Charles held his court, only to encounter new obstacles.   It is true that some persons of sense, as we are told, recognized in her the fulfilment of Merlin's prophecy, " *Descendet virgo dorsum sagittarii et flores virgineos obscurabit ;*" others found her foretold by the Sibyl and by the Venerable Bede ; others asked her whether there was not in her land a forest known as the Bois Chênu, for there was an ancient prediction that from the Bois Chênu there would come a wonder-working maiden—and they were delighted on learning that it lay but a league from her father's house.   Those, however, who relied on worldly wisdom shook their heads and pronounced her mission an absurdity—in fact, it was charitable to regard her as insane.   It shows, indeed, to what depth of despair the royal cause had fallen, that her pre-

---

* Procès, pp. 471, 485.—Chronique, p. 454.—L'Averdy (ubi sup. III. 301).

tensions were regarded as of sufficient importance to warrant investigation. Long were the debates. Prelates and doctors of theology, jurists and statesmen examined her for a month, and one by one they were won over by her simple earnestness, her evident conviction, and the intelligence of her replies. This was not enough, however. In Poitiers sat Charles's Parlement and a University composed of such schoolmen as had abandoned the anglicized University of Paris. Thither was Joan sent, and for three weeks more she was tormented with an endless repetition of questioning. Meanwhile her antecedents were carefully investigated, with a result in every way confirming her good repute and truthfulness. Charles was advised to ask of her a sign by which to prove that she came from God, but this she refused, saying that it was the divine command that she should give it before Orleans, and nowhere else. Finally, the official conclusion, cautiously expressed, was that in view of her honest life and conversation, and her promising a sign before Orleans, the king should not prevent her from going there, but should convey her there in safety; for to reject her without the appearance of evil would be to rebuff the Holy Ghost, and to render himself unworthy the grace and aid of God.*

---

* Procès, pp. 471, 475, 478, 482, 485.—Chronique, pp. 428, 454.—Görres, pp. 37–9.—Thomassin, pp. 537, 538.—Christine de Pisan (Buchon, p. 541).—Monstrelet, Liv. II. ch. 57.—Dynteri Chron. Duc. Brabant. Lib. VI. ch. 234.

Much has been recorded in the chronicles about the miracles with which she convinced Charles's doubts—how she recognized him at first sight, although plainly clad amid a crowd of resplendent courtiers, and how she revealed to him a secret known only to God and himself, of prayers and requests made to God in his oratory at Loches (Chronique, pp. 429, 455; Jean Chartier, Hist. de Charles VII. Ed. Godefroy, p. 19; Görres, pp. 105–9). Possibly some chance expression of hers may have caught his wandering and uncertain thoughts and made an impression upon him, but the legend of the Pucelle grew so rapidly that miracles were inevitably introduced into it at every stage. Joan herself on her trial declared that Charles and several of his councillors, including the Duc de Bourbon, saw her guardian saints and heard their voices, and that the king had notable revelations (Procès, p. 472). She also told her judges that there had been a material sign, which under their skilful cross-examination developed, from a secret revealed to him alone (p. 477), into the extraordinary story that St. Michael, accompanied by Catharine and Margaret and numerous angels, came to her lodgings and went with her to the royal palace, up the stairs and through the doors, and gave to the Archbishop of Reims, who handed it to the king, a

Two months had been wasted in these preliminaries, and it was the end of April before the determination was reached. A convoy was in preparation to throw provisions into the town, and it was resolved that Joan should accompany it. Under instructions from her Voices she had a standard prepared, representing on a white field Christ holding the world, with an angel on each side—a standard which was ever in the front of battle, which was regarded as the surest guarantee of success, and which in the end was gravely investigated as a work of sorcery. She had assigned to her a troop or guard, but does not seem to have been intrusted with any command, yet she assumed that she was taking the field as the representative of God, and must first give the enemy due notice of defiance. Accordingly, on April 18, she addressed four letters, one to Henry VI. and the others to the Regent Bedford, the captains before Orleans, and the English soldiers there, in which she demanded the surrender of the keys of all the cities held in France; she announced herself ready to make peace if they will abandon the land and make compensation for the damages inflicted, otherwise she is commissioned by God, and will drive them out with a shock of arms such as had not been seen in France for a thousand years. It is scarce to be wondered that these uncourtly epistles excited no little astonishment in the English camp. Rumors of her coming had spread; she was denounced as a sorceress, and all who placed faith in her as heretics. Talbot declared that he would burn her if she was captured, and

---

golden crown, too rich for description, such as no goldsmith on earth could make, telling him at the same time that with the aid of God and her championship he would recover all France, but that unless he set her to work his coronation would be delayed. This she averred had been seen and heard by the Archbishop of Reims and many bishops, Charles de Bourbon, the Duc d' Alençon, La Trémouille, and three hundred others, and thus she had been relieved from the annoying examinations of the clerks. When asked whether she would refer to the archbishop to vouch for the story, she replied, "Let him come here and let me speak with him; he will not dare to tell me the contrary of what I have told you"—which was a very safe offer, seeing that the trial was in Rouen, and the archbishop was the Chancellor of France (Procès, pp. 482–6, 495, 502). His testimony, however, could it have been had, would not probably have been advantageous to her, as he belonged to the party of La Trémouille, the favorite, who was persistently hostile to her.

the heralds who brought her letters were only saved from a similar fate by a determined threat of reprisals on the part of Dunois, then in command at Orleans.*

Some ten days later the convoy started under command of Gilles de Rais and the Maréchal de Sainte-Sevère. Joan had promised that it should meet with no opposition, and faith in her was greatly enhanced when her words proved true. Although it passed within one or two bow-shots of the English siege-works, and though there was considerable delay in ferrying the cattle and provisions across the Loire into the city, not an attempt at interference was made. The same occurred with a second convoy which reached Orleans May 4, to the surprise of the French and the disgust of the Parisians, who watched the affair from a distance, and were unable to understand the paralysis which seemed to have fallen on the English arms. Joan had impatiently awaited these last reinforcements, and urged immediate offensive measures against the besiegers. Without consulting her, on the same day an assault was made on one of the English works on the other side of the Loire. Her legend relates that she started up from slumber exclaiming that her people were being slaughtered, and, scarcely waiting for her armor to be adjusted, sprang on her horse and galloped to the gate leading to the scene of action. The attack had miscarried, but after her arrival on the scene not an Englishman could wound a Frenchman, and the *bastille* was carried. Hot fighting occurred on the following days. On the 6th she was wounded in the foot by a caltrop, and on the 7th in the shoulder by an arrow, but in spite of desperate resistance all the English works on the farther bank of the Loire were taken, and their garrisons slain or captured. The English loss was estimated at from six thousand to eight thousand men, while that of the French was not over one hundred. On the 8th the English abandoned the siege, marching off in such haste that they left behind them their sick and wounded, their artillery and magazines. The French, flushed with victory, were eager to attack them, but Joan forbade it—" Let them go ;

---

* Monstrelet, II. 57.—Procès, p. 478.—Thomassin, p. 538.—Chronique, pp. 430-33.

Joan's letters, when produced on her trial, were falsified—at least according to her statement.—Le Brun de Charmettes, Histoire de Jeanne d'Arc, III. 348.

it is not the will of Messire that they should be fought to-day; you will have them another time "—and by this time her moral ascendency was such that she was obeyed. So marvellous was the change in the spirit of the opposing forces, that it was a common remark that before her coming two hundred English would rout five hundred Frenchmen, but that afterwards two hundred French would chase four hundred English. Even the unfriendly Monstrelet admits that after the raising of the siege of Orleans there was no captain who so filled the mouths of men as she, though she was accompanied by knights so renowned as Dunois, La Hire, and Pothon de Xaintrailles. The Regent Bedford, in writing to the English council, could only describe it as a terrible blow from the divine hand, especially " caused of unleyefulle doubte that thei hadde of a Desciple and Lyme of the Feende called the Pucelle that used fals Enchauntements and Sorcerie." Not only, he says, were the English forces diminished in number and broken in spirit, but the enemy was encouraged to make great levies of troops.*

In the chronic exhaustion of the royal treasury it was not easy for Charles to take full advantage of this unexpected success, but the spirit of the nation was aroused and a force could be kept spasmodically in the field. D'Alençon was sent with troops to clear the Loire valley of the enemy, and took Joan with him. Suffolk had fortified himself in Jargeau, but the place was carried by assault and he was captured with all his men who were not slain. Then want of money caused a return to Tours, where Joan earnestly urged Charles to go to Reims for his coronation : she had always claimed that her mission was to deliver Orleans and to crown the king; that her time was short and that the counsel of her Voices must not be disregarded, but prudence prevailed, and it was felt that the English power in the central provinces must first be crushed. A second expedition was organized. Beaugency was besieged and taken, and on June 18 the battle of Patay gave some slight amends for Agincourt and Verneuil. After feeble resistance the English fled. Twenty-five hundred of them were left upon the

---

* Monstrelet, II. 57–61.—Thomassin, p. 538.—Chronique, pp. 430–7.—Jean Chartier, pp. 22–4.—Journal d'un Bourgeois de Paris, ann. 1429.—Rymer, X. 408.

field, and large numbers were captured, including Talbot, Scales, and others of note. Thus in little more than six weeks all the leading English captains were slain or in captivity, except Fastolf, whose flight from Patay Bedford avenged by tearing from him the Order of the Garter. Their troops were dispersed and dispirited, their prestige was gone. It was no wonder that in all this one side recognized the hand of God and the other that of the devil. Even the Norman chronicler, P. Cochon, says that the English would have abandoned France if the regent would have allowed it, and that they were so dispirited that one Frenchman would chase three of them.*

A letter written from the court of Charles VII. to the Duke of Milan three days after the triumph of Patay, recounting the marvels of the previous weeks, shows how Joan was regarded and how rapidly her legend was growing. At her birth the villagers of Domremy were joyously excited, they knew not why, and the cocks for two hours flapped their wings and uttered a song wholly different from their ordinary crowing. Her visions were described in the most exaggerated terms, as well as her personal prowess and endurance. The relief of Orleans, the capture of Jargeau, Mehun-sur-Loire, and Beaugency, and the crowning mercy of Patay were all attributed to her: hers was the initiative, the leadership, and the success; no one else is alluded to. We are told, moreover, that she was already predicting the deliverance of Charles of Orleans, a prisoner in England for fifteen years, and had sent a notice to the English to surrender him.†

It could no longer be doubted that Joan was under the direct inspiration of God, and when at Gien, on June 25, there was a consultation as to the next movement, though Charles's councillors advised him to reduce La Charité and clear the Orleannais and Berri of the enemy, it is no wonder that he yielded to Joan's urgency and gave his assent to a march to Reims. The enterprise seemed a desperate one, for it lay through a hostile country with strong cities along the road, and the royal resources were inadequate to equipping and provisioning an army or providing it with siege-

---

* Chronique, pp. 438–41.—Jean Chartier, pp. 26–7.—Chron. de P. Cochon (Éd. Vallet de Viriville, p. 456).

† Epist. P. de Bonlavillar (Pez, Thes. Anecd. VI. III. 237).

trains.   But enthusiasm was rising to fever heat, and human prudence was distrust of God.   Volunteers came pouring in as soon
as the king's intentions were noised abroad, and gentlemen too
poor to arm and mount themselves were content to serve as simple
archers and retainers.   La Trémouille, the royal favorite, thinking
his own position endangered, caused the services of multitudes to
be rejected, but for which, it was said, an army sufficient to drive
the English from France could readily have been collected.   On
went the ill-conditioned forces.   Auxerre, though not garrisoned,
refused to open its gates, but gave some provisions, and in spite
of Joan's desire to take it by assault the king went forward, induced, it was said, by La Trémouille, who had received from the
town a bribe of two thousand livres.   At Troyes there was a strong
English and Burgundian garrison ; it could not be left behind, and
the army encamped before it for five or six days, with no artillery
to breach its walls.   There was neither money nor victual, and the
only subsistence was ears of corn and beans plucked in the fields.
The situation was discouraging, and a council of war under the
impulse of the Chancellor Renaud de Chartres, Archbishop of
Reims, advised retreat.   Joan was sent for and declared that
within two days the town would surrender.   She was given the
time she asked, and at once proceeded to gather material to fill
the trenches, and to mount some small culverins.   A panic seized
the inhabitants and they demanded to surrender ; the garrison
was allowed to march out, and the city returned to its allegiance.†

When Joan entered the town she was met by a Frère Richard,
whom the people had sent to examine her and report what she
was.   The worthy friar, doubtful whether she was of heaven or
hell, approached her cautiously, sprinkling holy water and making
the sign of the cross, till she smiled and told him to come boldly
on, as she was not going to fly away.   This Frère Richard was a
noted Franciscan preacher who had recently returned from a pilgrimage to Jerusalem, and in April had made the deepest impression on Paris with his eloquence.   From April 16th to the 26th he
had preached daily to audiences of five and six thousand souls, and
had excited such a tempest of emotion that on one day a hundred

---

* Chronique, pp. 442–5.—Jean Chartier, pp. 29–31.—Jacques le Bouvier
(Godefroy, p. 378).

bonfires were built in the streets into which men threw their cards and dice and tables, and women their ornaments and frippery. Over this man Joan obtained so complete a mastery that he devoted himself to her and followed her in her campaigns, using his eloquence to convert the people, not from their sins, but from their disloyalty to Charles. When the good Parisians heard of this they resumed their cards and dice to spite him. Even a tin medal with the name of Jesus which he had given them to wear was cast aside for the red cross of Burgundy. In the passion of the hour on both sides religion was but the handmaid of partisanship.*

After this the march to Reims was a triumphant progress. Chalons-sur-Marne sent half a day's journey in advance to submit and took the oath of allegiance. At Septsaux the garrison fled and the people welcomed their king, while the Dukes of Lorraine and Bar came to join him with a heavy force. Reims was held for Burgundy by the Seigneur de Saveuse, one of the doughtiest warriors of the day, but the citizens were so frightened by the coming of the Pucelle, whose reported wonders had impressed their imaginations, that they declared for Charles, and Saveuse was obliged to fly. Charles entered the town on July 16, and was joyfully received. The next day, Sunday, July 17, he was crowned King of France. During the ceremony Joan stood by the altar with the standard : her judges on her trial seemed to imagine that she held it there for some occult influence which it was supposed to exercise, and inquired curiously as to her motive ; when she answered simply, " It had been in the strife, it had a right to be in the honor." †

Joan might well claim that her mission was accomplished. In little more than three months she had made the intending fugitive of Chinon a conquering king, to whom his flatterers gave the title of the Victorious. A few months more of such success would establish him firmly on the throne of a reunited France, and no one could doubt that success would grow more rapid if only with its own momentum. Negotiations were on foot with the Duke of Burgundy, which were expected to result in detaching

---

* Procès, p. 479.—Journal d'un Bourgeois de Paris, an 1429, 1431.
† Chronique, p. 446.—Monstrelet, II. 64.—Buchon, p. 524.—Procès, p. 494.

him from the English cause.   Joan had written to him some weeks
earlier asking him to be present at the coronation, and on the day
of the ceremony she addressed him another letter, summoning and
entreating him to return to his allegiance.   In a few days Beauvais, Senlis, Laon, Soissons, Château-Thierry, Provins, Compiègne,
and other places acknowledged Charles as king and received his
garrisons.   There was universal exultation and a contagious delirium of returning loyalty.   As he marched the peasantry would
gather with tears in their eyes to bless him, and thank God that
peace was at hand.   All men admitted that this was Joan's work.
Christine de Pisan, in a poem written about this time, compares
her to Esther, Judith, Deborah, Gideon, and Joshua, and even
Moses is not her superior.   A litany of the period contains a prayer recognizing that God had delivered France by her hand.   A
Burgundian chronicler tells us that the belief was general among
the French soldiery that she was an envoy of God who could expel the English; even after the enthusiasm of the time had passed
away Thomassin, who wrote officially in a work addressed to Louis
XI., does not hesitate to say that of all the signs of love manifested
by God to France, there has not been one so great or so marvellous
as this Pucelle—to her was due the restoration of the kingdom,
which was so low that it would have reached its end but for her
coming.   That she was regarded as an oracle of God on other subjects is seen in the application to her by the Comte d'Armagnac
to tell him which of the three popes to believe in; and her acceptance of the position is shown by her answer, that when she is relieved from the pressure of the war she will resolve his doubts by
the counsel of the King of all the world.   If on the one hand her
dizzy elevation turned her head to the extent of addressing threatening letters to the Hussites, on the other she never lost her kindly
sympathy with the poor and humble; she protected them as far as
she could from the horrors of war, comforted and supported them,
and their grateful veneration shown in kissing her hands and feet
and garments was made a crime to her by her pitiless judges.*

* Buchon, pp. 539, 545.—Bernier, Monuments inédits de France, Senlis, 1833,
p. 18.—Journal d'un Bourgeois de Paris, an 1429.—Chronique, pp. 446-7.—
Mémoires de Saint-Remy, ch. 152.—Thomassin, p. 540.—Nider Formicar. v.
viii.—Procès, p. 479.
    Christine de Pisan says of her:

With all this it does not seem that Joan had any definite rank or command in the royal armies. Christine de Pisan, it is true, speaks of her as being the recognized chief—

> " Et de nos gens preux et habiles
> Est principale chevetaine "—

but it does not appear that her position had any other warrant than the moral influence which her prodigious exploits and the belief in her divine mission afforded. Charles's gratitude gave her a handsome establishment. She was magnificently attired, noble damsels were assigned to her service, with a *maître d'hotel*, pages, and valets; she had five war-horses, with seven or more roadsters, and at the time of her capture she had in her hands ten or twelve thousand francs, which, as she told her judges, was little enough to carry on war with. Shortly after his coronation, Charles, at her request, granted to Domremy and Greux the privilege of exemption from all taxes, a favor which was respected until the Revolution; and in December, 1429, he spontaneously ennobled her family and all their posterity, giving them as arms on a field azure two *fleurs-de-lis or*, traversed by a sword, and authorizing them to bear the name of Du Lis—in all a slender return for the priceless service rendered, and affording to her judges another count in the indictment on her trial.*

" Que peut-il d'autre estre dit plus	Il tira sans estre lassez
Ne des grands faits du temps passé :	Le peuple Israël hors d'Egypte ;
Moysès en qui Dieu afflus	Par miracle ainsi repassez
Mit graces et vertus assez ;	Nous as de mal, pucelle eslite."

Buchon, p. 542.

The question which troubled Armagnac was a last struggle of the Great Schism. Benedict XIII., who had never submitted to the Council of Constance, died in 1424, when his cardinals quarrelled and elected two successors to his shadowy papacy—Clement VIII. and Benedict XIV. In 1429, the Council of Tortosa suppressed them both, but at the moment it was a subject on which Armagnac might imagine that heavenly guidance was desirable.

* Görres, pp. 241-2, 273.—Procès, p. 482.—Buchon, pp. 513-4.—Dynteri Chron. Duc. Brabant. Lib. vi. ch. 235.

In the register of taxes every year was written opposite the names of Domremy and Greux, " *Neant, la Pucelle.*" The grant of nobility to her family had the very unusual clause that it passed by the female as well as the male descendants, who were thus all exempt from taxation. As matrimonial alliances extended among the rich bourgeoisie this exemption spread so far that in 1614 the

All Europe was aroused with so portentous an apparition. It was not only statesmen and warriors that watched with astonish- ment the strange vicissitudes of the contest, but learned men and theologians were divided in opinion as to whether she was under the influence of heavenly or of infernal spirits, and were every- where disputing and writing tracts to uphold the one opinion or the other. In England, of course, there was no dissent from the popular belief which Shakespeare puts in the mouth of Talbot—

> " A witch by fear, not force, like Hannibal,
> Drives back our troops and conquers as she lists."

So general, indeed, was the terror that she excited that when, in May, 1430, it was proposed to send Henry VI. to Paris for corona- tion, both captains and soldiers in the levies appointed for his escort deserted and lay in hiding; and when, in December, after Joan lay a prisoner in Rouen Castle and the voyage was performed, the same trouble was experienced, requiring another proclama- tion to the sheriffs for the arrest of those who were daily desert- ing, to the great peril of the royal person and of the kingdom of France. Elsewhere the matter was not thus taken for granted, and was elaborately argued with all the resources of scholastic logic. Some tracts of this character attributed to Gerson have been preserved, and exhibit to us the nature of the doubts which suggested themselves to the learned of the time—whether Joan is a woman or a phantasm; whether her acts are to be considered as divine or phitonic and illusory; whether, if they are the result of supernatural causes, they come from good or evil spirits. To Joan's defenders the main difficulty was her wearing male attire and cutting her hair short—an offence which in the end proved to be the most tangible one to justify her condemnation. Even her advocates in the schools felt that in this the case was weak. It had to be admitted that the Old Law prohibits a woman from wearing man's garments, but this, it was argued, was purely juridical, and was not binding under the New Law; it had merely a moral object, to prevent indecency, and the circumstances and objects were to be considered, so that the law could not be held to pro- hibit manly and military vesture to Joan, who was both manly and

---

financial results caused its limitation to the male lines for the future (Vallet de Viriville, Charles du Lis, pp. 24, 88).

military. The cutting of her hair, prohibited by the Apostle, was justified in the same manner.*

For a few weeks after the coronation Joan was at the culmination of her career. An uninterrupted tide of success had demonstrated the reality of her divine mission. She had saved the monarchy, and no one could doubt that the invader would shortly be expelled from France. Possibly she may, as has been represented, have declared that all which God had appointed her to do had been accomplished, and that she desired to return to her parents and herd their cattle as she had been accustomed of old. In view of what followed, this was the only way to uphold the theory of divine inspiration, and such a statement inevitably formed part of her legend, whether it was true or not. In her subsequent failures, as at Paris and La Charité, Joan naturally persuaded herself that they had been undertaken against the counsel of her Voices, but all the evidence goes to prove that at the time she was as confident of success as ever. Thus a letter written from Reims on the day of coronation, evidently by a well-informed person, states that the army was to start the next day for Paris, and that the Pucelle had no doubts as to her reducing it to obedience. Nor did she really consider her mission as ended, for she had at the commencement proclaimed the liberation of Charles of Orleans as one of her objects, and on her trial she explained that she proposed either to invade England to set him free or to capture enough prisoners to force an exchange: her Voices had promised it to her, and had she not been captured she would have accomplished it in three years.†

---

* Nider Formicar v. viii.—Rymer, X. 459, 472.—Gersoni Opp. Ed. 1488, liii. T–Z.—M. de l'Averdy gives an abstract of other learned disputations on the subject of Joan (ubi sup. III. 212–17).

† Chronique, p. 447.—Buchon, p. 524.—Pez, Thesaur. Anecd. VI. III. 237.—Procès, p. 484.—L'Averdy, III. 338.

The popular explanation of Joan's career connected her good-fortune with a sword marked with five crosses on the blade, which she had miraculously discovered in the church of St. Catharine de Fierbois, and which she thenceforth carried. On the march to Reims, finding her commands disregarded as to the exclusion of prostitutes from the army, she beat some loose women with the flat of the blade and broke it. No smith could weld the fragments together; she was obliged to wear another sword, and her unvarying success disappeared.—Jean Chartier, pp. 20, 29, 42.

Be this as it may, from this time the marvellous fortune which had attended her disappears; alternations of success and defeat show that either the French had lost the first flush of confident enthusiasm, or that the English had recovered from their panic and were doggedly resolved to fight the powers of hell. Bedford managed to put a respectable force in the field, with the assistance of Cardinal Beaufort, who made over to him, it was said for a heavy bribe, four thousand crusaders whom he was leading from England to the Hussite wars. He barred the way to Paris, and three times the opposing armies, of nearly equal strength, lay face to face, but Bedford always skilfully chose a strong position which Charles dared not attack, showing that human prudence had replaced the reckless confidence of the march to Reims. We catch a glimpse of the intrigues of the factions surrounding Charles in the attempted retreat to the Loire, frustrated at Bray-sur-Seine, when the defeat of the courtiers who assailed the English guarding the passage of the river was hailed with delight by Joan, Bourbon, Alençon, and the party opposed to La Trémouille. Charles, perforce, remained in the North. Towards the end of August, Bedford, fearing an inroad on Normandy, marched thither, leaving the road to Paris open, and Charles advanced to St. Denis, which he occupied without resistance, August 25. On September 7 an attempt was made to capture Paris by surprise, with the aid of friends within the walls, and this failing, on the 8th, the feast of the Nativity of the Virgin, an assault in force was made at the Porte St. Honoré. The water in the inner moat, however, was too deep and the artillery on the walls too well served: after five or six hours of desperate fighting the assailants were disastrously repulsed with a loss of five hundred killed and one thousand wounded. As usual Joan had been at the front till she fell with an arrow through the leg, and her standard-bearer was slain by her side. Joan subsequently averred that she had had no counsel from her Voices to make this attempt, but had been over-persuaded by the eager chivalry of the army; but this is contradicted by contemporary evidence, and her letter to d'Armagnac promises him a reply when she shall have leisure in Paris, showing that she fully expected to capture the city.[*]

---

[*] Chronique, pp. 446–50.—Jean Chartier, p. 33–36.—Görres, p. 215.—Monstre-

From this time her checkered career was rather of evil fortune than of good. If at St. Pierre-les-Moustiers the old enthusiasm made the forlorn hope imagine that it ascended the breach as easily as a broad stairway, the siege of La Charité, to which it was a preliminary, proved disastrous, and again Joan averred that she had undertaken this without orders from her Voices. It was freely said that La Trémouille had sent her on the enterprise with insufficient forces and had withheld the requisite succors. During the winter she was at Lagny, where occurred a little incident which was subsequently used to confirm the charge of sorcery. A child was born apparently dead; the parents, dreading to have it buried without baptism, had it carried to the church, where it lay, to all appearance, lifeless for three days; the young girls of the town assembled in the church to pray for it, and Joan joined them. Suddenly the infant gave signs of life, gaped thrice, was hurriedly baptized, died, and was buried in consecrated ground, and Joan had the credit of working a miracle, to be turned subsequently to her disadvantage. Probably about the same time, there was trouble about a horse of the Bishop of Senlis, which Joan took for her own use. She found it worthless for her purposes and sent it back to him, and also caused him to be paid two hundred saluts d'or for it (the salut d'or was equivalent to twenty-two sols parisis), but on her trial the matter was gravely charged against her, showing how eagerly every incident in her career was scrutinized and utilized.*

As the spring of 1430 opened, the Duke of Burgundy came to the assistance of his English allies by raising a large army for the recovery of Compiègne. The activity of Joan was unabated. During Easter week, about the middle of April, we hear of her in the trenches at Melun, where her Voices announced to her that she would be a prisoner before St. John's day, but would give her no further particulars. Before the close of the month she attacked the advancing Burgundians at Pont-l'Évêque, with her old

---

let, II. 66–70.—Journal d'un Bourgeois de Paris, an 1429.—Procès, pp. 486, 490.—Mémoires de Saint-Remy, ch. 152.—Buchon, pp. 524, 539.

* Görres, pp. 292–5.—Jean Chartier, pp. 39–40.—Jean le Bouvier, p. 381.—Martial d'Auvergne, Vigiles de Charles VII.—Buchon, p. 544.—Procès, pp. 480, 488, 490.

comrade-in-arms Pothon de Xaintrailles, and was worsted. Then
she had a desperate fight with a Burgundian partisan, Franquet
d'Arras, whom she captured with all his troop; he had been a
notorious plunderer, the magistrates of Lagny claimed him for
trial, and after an investigation which lasted for fifteen days
they executed him as a robber and murderer, for which Joan was
held responsible, his death being one of the most serious charges
pressed against her. About May 1 Compiègne was invested. Its
siege was evidently to be the decisive event of the campaign,
and Joan hastened to the rescue. Before daylight on the morning of the 5th she succeeded in entering the town with reinforcements. In the afternoon of the same day a sally was resolved
upon, and Joan as usual led it, with Pothon and other captains by
her side. She fell upon the camp of a renowned knight of the
Golden Fleece named Bauldon de Noyelle, who, though taken by
surprise, made a gallant resistance. From the neighboring lines
troops hastened to his assistance, and the tide of battle swayed
back and forth. A force of a thousand Englishmen on their way
to Paris had tarried to aid Philip of Burgundy, and these were
brought up between the French and the town to take them in
the rear. Joan fell back and endeavored to bring her men off in
safety, but while covering the retreat she was unable to regain the
fortifications, and was taken prisoner by the Bâtard de Vendôme,
a follower of Jean de Luxembourg, Comte de Ligny, second in
command to the duke. There was naturally talk of treachery,
but it would seem without foundation. Pothon was likewise
captured, and it evidently was but the fortune of war.*

Great was the joy in the Burgundian camp when the news
spread that the dreaded Pucelle was a prisoner. English and
Burgundians gave themselves up to rejoicing, for, as the Burgundian Monstrelet, who was present, informs us, they valued her
capture more than five hundred fighting men, for there was no
captain or chief of whom they were so afraid. They crowded
around her quarters at Marigny, and even the Duke of Burgundy himself paid her a visit and exchanged some words with
her. At once the question arose as to her possession. She was a

---

* Procès, pp. 481, 482, 488.—Mémoires de Saint-Remy, ch. 158.—Monstrelet,
II. 84–86.—Chronique, p. 456.—Jean Chartier, p. 42.

prisoner of war, belonging to Jean de Luxembourg, and, in those days of ransoming, prisoners were valuable property. Under existing customs, Henry VI., as chief of the alliance, had the right to claim the transfer of any captured commanding general or prince on paying the captor ten thousand livres—a sort of eminent domain, for in the wars of Edward III. Bertrand du Guesclin had been held at a ransom of one hundred thousand livres, the Constable de Clisson at the same, and in 1429 it had cost the Duc d'Alençon two hundred thousand crowns to effect his liberation from the English. In the exhausted state of the English exchequer, however, even ten thousand livres was a sum not readily procurable. It was a matter of absolute necessity to the English to have her, not only to prevent her ransom by the French, but to neutralize her sorceries by condemning and executing her under the jurisdiction of the Church. To accomplish this the Inquisition was the most available instrumentality : inside the English lines Joan was publicly reported to be a sorceress, and as such was judiciable by the Inquisition, which therefore had a right to claim her for trial. Accordingly, but a few days had elapsed after her capture when Martin Billon, Vicar of the Inquisitor of France, formally demanded her surrender, and the University of Paris addressed two letters to the Duke of Burgundy urging that she should be promptly tried and punished, lest his enemies should effect her deliverance. We have seen how by this time the importance of the Inquisition in France had shrunken, and Jean de Luxembourg was by no means disposed to surrender his valuable prize without consideration. Then another device was adopted. Compiègne, where Joan was captured, was in the diocese of Beauvais. Pierre Cauchon, the Count-bishop of Beauvais, though a Frenchman of the Remois, was a bitter English partisan, whose unscrupulous cruelty at a later period excited the cordial detestation even of his own faction. He had been driven from his see the previous year by the returning loyalty of its people under the impulse given by Joan, and may be assumed to have looked upon her with no loving eye. He was told to claim her for trial under his episcopal jurisdiction, but even he shrank from the odious business, and refused unless it could be proved that it was his duty. Possibly the promise of the reversion of the bishopric of Lisieux, with which he was subsequently rewarded, may have assisted in convincing him, while the authority of the University of Paris was invoked to quiet his scruples. July 14, the University addressed letters to Jean de Luxembourg reminding him that his oath of knighthood required him to defend the honor of God and the Catholic faith, and the holy Church. Through Joan, idolatries, errors, false doctrines, and evils innumerable had spread through France, and the matter admitted of no delay. The Inquisition had earnestly demanded her for trial, and Jean was urgently begged to surrender her to the Bishop of Beauvais, who had likewise claimed her; all inquisitor-prelates are judges of the faith, and all Christians of every degree are bound to obey them under the heavy penalties of the law, while obedience will acquire for him the divine grace and love, and will aid in the exaltation of the faith. When furnished with this, Pierre Cauchon lost no time. He left Paris at once with a notary and a representative of the University, and on the 16th presented it to the Duke of Bur gundy in the camp before Compiègne, together with a summons of his own addressed to the Duke, Jean de Luxembourg, and the Bâtard de Vendôme, demanding the surrender of Joan for tria before him on charges of sorcery, idolatry, invocation of the devil and other matters involving the faith—trial which he is ready to hold, with the assistance of the inquisitor and of doctors of theo logy, for the exaltation of the faith and the edification of those who have been misled by her. He further offered a ransom o six thousand livres and a pension to the Bâtard de Vendôme o two or three hundred livres, and if this was not enough the sun would be increased to ten thousand livres, although Joan was no so great a person as the king would have a right to claim on giv ing that amount; if required, security would be furnished for the payment. These letters the duke transferred to Jean de Luxem bourg, who after some discussion agreed to sell her for the stipu lated sum. He would not trust his allies, however, even with security, and refused to deliver his prisoner until the money was paid. Bedford was obliged to convene the states of Normandy and levy a special tax to raise it, and it was not till October 20 that Jean received his price and transferred his captive.[*]

---

* Monstrelet, II. 86.—Jean Chartier, p. 25.—Journal d'un Bourgeois de Paris an 1435.—L'Averdy (ubi sup. III. 8).—Chronique et Procès, pp. 462–4.

During all this long delay Charles, to his eternal dishonor, made no effort to save the woman to whom he owed his crown. While her prolonged trial was under way he did not even appeal to Eugenius IV. or to the Council of Basle to evoke the case to their tribunal, an appeal which would hardly have been rejected in a matter of so much interest. It is true that her recent labors had not been so brilliantly successful as those of the earlier period : he may have recognized that after all she was but human ; or he may have satisfied his conscience with the reflection that if she were an envoy of God, God might be trusted to extricate her. Besides, the party of peace in his court, headed by La Trémouille, the favorite, had no desire to see the heroine at large again, and the weak and self-indulgent monarch abandoned her to her fate as, twenty years later, he abandoned Jacques Cœur.

Meanwhile Joan had been carried, strictly guarded to prevent her escape by magic arts, from Marigny to the Castle of Beaulieu, and thence to the Castle of Beaurevoir. In the latter prison she excited the interest of the Dame de Beaurevoir, and of the Demoiselle de Luxembourg, aunt of Jean. The latter earnestly remonstrated with her nephew when she learned that he was treating with the English, and both ladies endeavored to persuade Joan to adopt female habiliments. They must have impressed her with their kindness, for she subsequently declared that she would have made the change for them rather than for any other ladies in France. Her restless energy chafed at the long captivity, and twice she made attempts to escape. Once she succeeded in shutting her guards up in her cell, and would have got off but that her jailer saw her and secured her. Again, when she heard that she was to be surrendered to the English, she despairingly threw herself from her lofty tower into the ditch, careless whether it would kill her or not. Her Voices had forbidden the attempt, but she said that she had rather die than fall into English hands—and this was subsequently charged against her as an attempted suicide and a crime. She was picked up for dead, but she was reserved for a harsher fate and speedily recovered. She might well regret the recovery when she was carried to Rouen, loaded with chains and confined in a narrow cell where brutal guards watched her day and night. It is even said that an iron cage was made, into which she was thrust with fetters on wrist, waist, and ankles. She had been delivered to the Church, not to the secular authorities; she was entitled to be kept in an ecclesiastical prison, but the English had paid for her and would listen to no reclamations. Warwick had charge of her and would trust her to no one.*

Pierre Cauchon still was in no haste to commence the iniquitous work which he had undertaken. After a month had passed, Paris grew excited at the delay. The city, so ardently Anglicized, had a special grudge against Joan, not only on account of believing that she had promised her soldiers on the day of assault to allow them to sack the city and put the inhabitants to the sword, but because they were exposed to the greatest privations by the virtual blockade resulting from the extension of the royal domination caused by her successes. This feeling found expression in the University, which from the first pursued her with unrelenting ferocity. Not content with having intervened to procure her surrender to the English, it addressed letters, November 21, to Pierre Cauchon, reproaching him with his tardiness in commencing the process, and to the King of England, asking that the trial be held in Paris, where there are so many learned and excellent doctors. Still Cauchon hesitated. Doubtless when he came to consider the evidence on which he would have to act he recognized, as irresponsible partisans could not, how flimsy it was, and he was busy in obtaining information as to all the points in her career—for the interrogatories showed a marvellous familiarity with everything that could possibly be wrested against her. Besides, there were indispensable preliminaries to be observed. His jurisdiction arose from her capture in his diocese, but he was an exile from it, and was expected to try her not only in another diocese, but in another province. The archbishopric of Rouen was vacant, and he adopted the expedient of requesting of the chapter permission to hold an ecclesiastical court within their jurisdiction. The request was granted, and he selected an assembly of experts to sit with him as assessors. A number came willingly from the University, whose expenses were paid by the English government, but it was more difficult to find accomplices among the local prelates and doctors. In one of the early sessions, Nicholas de Houppeland

---

* Monstrelet, II. 86.—Chronique, p. 462.—Procès, pp. 478, 480-1, 486, 487, 488, 489.—Le Brun de Charmettes, Histoire de Jeanne d'Arc, III. 182-3.

plainly told Cauchon that neither he nor the rest, belonging to the party hostile to Joan, could sit as judges, especially as she had already been examined by the Archbishop of Reims, who was the metropolitan of Beauvais. For this Nicholas was imprisoned in the Castle of Rouen, and was threatened with banishment to England and with drowning, but his friends eventually procured his liberation. Undoubtedly every man who sat on the tribunal had the conviction that any leaning to the accused would expose him to English vengeance, and it was found necessary to impose a fine on any one who should absent himself from a single session. Eventually a respectable body of fifty or sixty theologians and jurists was got together, including such men as the Abbots of Fécamp, Jumièges, Ste. Catharine, Cormeilles, and Préaux, the Prior of Longueville, the archdeacon and treasurer of Rouen, and other men of recognized position. On January 3, 1431, royal letters-patent were issued ordering Joan to be delivered to Pierre Cauchon whenever she was wanted for examination, and all officials to aid him when called upon. As though she were already convicted, the letters recited the heresies and evil deeds of the culprit, and significantly concluded with a clause that if she was acquitted she was not to be liberated, but to be returned to the custody of the king. Yet it was not until the 9th that Cauchon assembled his experts, at that time eight in number, and laid before them what had been already done. They decided that the informations were insufficient and that a further inquest was necessary, and they also protested ineffectually against Joan's detention in a state prison. Measures were at once taken to make the investigations required. Nicholas Bailly was despatched to obtain the details of Joan's childhood, and as he brought back only favorable details Cauchon suppressed his report and refused to reimburse his expenses. The inquisitorial method of making the accused betray herself was adopted. One of the assessors, Nicholas l'Oyseleur, disguised himself as a layman and was introduced into her cell, pretending to be a Lorrainer imprisoned for his loyalty. He gained her confidence, and she grew into the habit of talking to him without reserve. Then Warwick and Cauchon with two notaries ensconced themselves in an adjoining cell of which the partition wall had been pierced, while l'Oyseleur led her on to talk about her visions; but the scheme failed, for one of the notaries, unfamiliar with inquisitorial practice, pronounced the whole proceeding to be unlawful, and courageously refused to act. Then Jean Estivet, the prosecutor and canon of Beauvais, tried the same expedient, but without success.*

It was not until February 19 that the articles of accusation were ready for submission to the assessors, and then a new difficulty arose. Thus far the tribunal had contained no representative of the Inquisition, and this was recognized as a fatal defect. Frère Jean Graveran was Inquisitor of France, and had appointed Frère Jean le Maître, in 1424, as his vicar or deputy for Rouen. Le Maître seems to have had no stomach for the work, and to have kept aloof, but he was not to be let off, and at the meeting of February 19 it was resolved to summon him, in the presence of two notaries, to take part in the proceedings and to hear read the accusation and the depositions of witnesses. Threats are said to have been freely employed, and his repugnance was overcome. Another session was held in the afternoon, at which he appeared, and on being summoned to act professed himself willing to do so, if the commission which he held was sufficient authorization. The scruple which he alleged was ingenious. He was Inquisitor of Rouen, but Cauchon was bishop in a different province, and, as he was exercising jurisdiction belonging to Beauvais in the " borrowed territory," le Maître doubted his powers to take part in it. It was not till the 22d that his doubts were overcome, and, while awaiting enlarged powers from Graveran, he consented to assist, for the discharge of his conscience and to prevent the whole proceedings from being null and void, which by common consent seems to have been assumed would be the case if carried on without the participation of the Inquisition. It was not until

---

* Journal d'un Bourgeois de Paris, an 1429.—Le Brun de Charmettes, III. 201–7, 210–12, 215, 224–6.—Procès, pp. 465–7, 477.—L'Averdy, pp. 391, 475, 499.

At least one of the assessors, Thomas de Courcelles, was a man of the highest character and of distinguished learning. Immediately after the trial of Joan he played a distinguished part at the Council of Basle, in opposing the claims of the papacy. Æneas Sylvius says of him, " Inter sacrarum literarum doctores insignis, quo nemo plura ex decretis sacri concilii dictavit, vir juxta doctrinam mirabilis et amabilis, sed modesta quadam verecundia semper intuens terram " (Æn. Sylv. Comment. de Gestis Concil. Basil. Lib. I. p. 7, Ed. 1571).—He died in 1469 as Dean of Nôtre Dame (Le Brun, III. 235).

March 12 that he received a special commission from Graveran, who declined to come personally, after which he presided in conjunction with Cauchon ; sentence was rendered in their joint names, and he was duly paid by the English for his services.*

At length, on February 21, Jean Estivet, the prosecutor, demanded that the prisoner be produced and examined. Before she was introduced Cauchon explained that she had earnestly begged the privilege of hearing mass, but, in view of the crimes whereof she was accused and her wearing male attire, he had refused. This prejudgment of the case was acquiesced in, and Joan was brought in with fetters on her legs. Of this cruelty she complained bitterly. Even the Templars, as we have seen, had their irons removed before examination, but Joan was only nominally in the hands of the court, and Cauchon accepted the responsibility for the outrage by telling her that it was because she had repeatedly tried to escape, to which she replied that she had a right to do so, as she had never given her parole. Then Cauchon called up the English guard who accompanied her and went through the farce of swearing them to watch her strictly—apparently for the futile purpose of asserting some control over them.†

It would be superfluous to follow in detail the examinations to which she was subjected during the next three months, with an intermission from April 18 to May 11 on account of sickness which nearly proved mortal. The untaught peasant girl, enfeebled by the miseries of her cruel prison, and subjected day after day to the shrewd and searching cross-questions of the trained and subtle intellects of her carefully selected judges, never lost her presence of mind or clearness of intellect. Ingenious pitfalls were constructed for her, which she evaded almost by instinct. Questions puzzling to a theologian of the schools were showered upon her ; half a dozen eager disputants would assail her at once and would interrupt her replies ; the disorder at times was so great that the notaries finally declared themselves unable to make an intelligent record. Her responses would be carefully scrutinized, and she would be recalled in the afternoon, the same ground would be gone over in a differ-

---

* Ripoll III. 8.—Procès, pp. 467-8, 470, 509.—Le Brun de Charmettes, III. 188, 192, 219, 407-8.—L'Averdy, p. 391.

† Procès, pp. 468-9.

ent manner, and her pursuers would again be foiled.   In the whole series of interrogatories she manifested a marvellous combination of frank simplicity, shrewdness, presence of mind, and firmness that would do honor to a veteran diplomat.   She utterly refused to take an unconditional oath to answer the questions put to her, saying, frankly, " I do not know what you will ask me; perhaps it may be about things which I will not tell you : " she agreed to reply to all questions about her faith and matters bearing upon her trial, but to nothing else.   When Cauchon's eagerness overstepped the limit she would turn on him and warn him, " You call yourself my judge : I know not if you are, but take care not to judge wrongfully, for you expose yourself to great danger, and I warn you, so that if our Lord chastises you I shall have done my duty."   When asked whether St. Michael was naked when he visited her, she retorted, " Do you think the Lord has not wherewith to clothe his angels ?"   When describing a conversation with St. Catharine about the result of the siege of Compiègne, some chance expression led her examiner to imagine that he could entrap her, and he interrupted with the question whether she had said, " Will God so wickedly let the good folks of Compiègne perish ?" but she composedly corrected him by repeating, " What! will God let these good folks of Compiègne perish, who have been and are so loyal to their lord ?"   She could hardly have known that an attempt to escape from an ecclesiastical court was a sin of the deepest dye, and yet when tested with the cunning question whether she would now escape if opportunity offered, she replied that if the door was opened she would walk out; she would try it only to see if the Lord so willed it.   When an insidious offer was made to her to have a great procession to entreat God to bring her to the proper frame of mind, she quietly replied that she wished all good Catholics would pray for her.   When threatened with torture, and told that the executioner was at hand to administer it, she simply said, " If you extort avowals from me by pain I will maintain that they are the result of violence."   Thus alternating the horrors of her dungeon with the clamors of the examination-room, where perhaps a dozen eager questioners would bait her at once, she never faltered through all those weary weeks.*

---

* Procès, pp. 468, 472, 473, 476, 486, 487, 489, 501.—L'Averdy, pp. 107, 395.

In this she was sustained by the state of habitual spiritual exaltation resulting from the daily and nightly visions with which she was favored, and the unalterable conviction that she was the chosen of the Lord, under whose inspiration she acted and whose will she was prepared to endure with resignation. In her prison her ecstatic raptures seem to have become more frequent than ever. Her heavenly visitants came at her call, and solved her difficulties. Frequently she refused to answer questions until she could consult her Voices and learn whether she was permitted to reveal what was wanted, and then, at a subsequent hearing, she would say that she had received permission. The responses evidently sometimes varied with her moods. She would be told that she would be delivered with triumph, and then again be urged not to mind her martyrdom, for she would reach paradise. When she reported this she was cunningly asked if she felt assured of salvation, and on her saying that she was as certain of heaven as if she was already there, she was led on with a question whether she held that she could not commit mortal sin. Instinctively she drew back from the dangerous ground—"I know nothing about it; I depend on the Lord." *

Finally, on one important point her judges succeeded in entrapping her. She was warned that if she had done anything contrary to the faith she must submit herself to the determination of the Church. To her the Church was represented by Cauchon and his tribunal; to submit to them would be to pronounce her whole life a lie, her intercourse with saints and angels an invocation of demons, herself a sorceress worthy of the stake, and only to escape it through the infinite mercy of her persecutors. She offered to submit to God and the saints, but this, she was told, was the Church triumphant in heaven, and she must submit to the Church militant on earth, else she was a heretic, to be inevitably abandoned to the secular arm for burning. Taking advantage of her ignorance, the matter was pressed upon her in the most absolute form. When asked if she would submit to the pope she could only say, "Take me to him and I will answer to him." At last she was brought to admit that she would submit to the Church, provided it did not command what was impossible; but, when asked to de-

* Procès, p. 487.

fine the impossible, it was to abandon doing what the Lord had commanded, and to revoke what she had asserted as to the truth of her visions. This she would submit only to God.*

The examinations up to March 27 had been merely preparatory. On that day the formal trial commenced by reading to Joan a long series of articles of accusation based upon the information obtained. A lively debate ensued among the experts, but at last it was decided that she must answer them *seriatim* and on the spot, which she did with her wonted clearness and intrepidity, declining the offer of counsel, which Cauchon proposed to select for her. Sundry further interrogatories followed; then her sickness delayed the proceedings, and on May 12, twelve members of the tribunal assembled in Pierre Cauchon's house to determine whether she should be subjected to torture. Fortunately for the reputation of her judges this infamy was spared her. One of them voted in favor of torture to see whether she could be forced to submit to the Church; another, the spy, Nicholas l'Oyseleur, humanely urged it as a useful medicine for her; nine were of opinion either that it was not yet required, or that the case was clear enough without it; Cauchon himself apparently did not vote. Meanwhile a secret

---

* Procès, pp. 489, 491, 494, 495, 499, 500, 501.

When, in 1456, the memory of Joan was rehabilitated, and the sentence condemning her was pronounced null and void, it was of course necessary to show that she had not refused to submit to the Church. Evidence was furnished to prove that Nicholas l'Oyseleur, in whom she continued to have confidence, secretly advised her that she was lost if she submitted herself to the Church; but that Jean de la Fontaine, another of the assessors, visited her in prison with two Dominicans, Isambard de la Pierre and Martin l'Advenu, and explained to her that at the Council of Basle, then sitting, there were as many of her friends as of enemies, and at the next hearing, on March 30, Frère Isambard de la Pierre openly repeated the suggestion, in consequence of which she offered to submit to it, and also demanded to be taken to the pope, all of which Cauchon forbade to be inserted in the record, and but for the active intervention of Jean le Maître, the inquisitor, all three would have incurred grave peril of death (L'Averdy, pp. 476-7.—Le Brun de Charmettes, IV. 8-13.—Buchon, pp. 518-19). The rehabilitation proceedings are quite as suspect as those of the trial; every one then was anxious to make a record for himself and to prove that Joan had been foully dealt with. As late as the nineteenth interrogatory, on March 27, 1431, Jean de la Fontaine was one of those who voted in favor of the most rigorous dealings with Joan (Procès, p. 495).

junto, selected by Cauchon, had reduced the articles of accusation to twelve, which, though grossly at variance with the truth, were assumed to have been fully proved or confessed, and these formed the basis of the subsequent deliberations and sentence. We have seen, in the case of Marguerite la Porete, that the Inquisition of Paris, in place of calling an assembly of experts, submitted to the canonists of the University a written statement of what was assumed to be proved, and that the opinion rendered on this, although conditioned on its being a true presentation of the case, was equivalent to a verdict. This precedent was followed in the present case. Copies of the articles were addressed to fifty-eight learned experts, in addition to the Chapter of Rouen and the University of Paris, and their opinions were requested by a certain day. Of all those appealed to, the University was by far the most important, and a special mission was despatched to it bearing letters from the royal council and the Bishop of Beauvais. In view of the tendencies of the University this might seem a superfluous precaution, and its adoption shows how slender was the foundation on which the whole prosecution was based. The University went through an elaborate form of deliberation, and caused the faculties of theology and law to draw up its decision, which was adopted May 14 and sent to Rouen.*

On May 19 the assessors were assembled to hear the report from the University, after which their opinions were taken. Some were in favor of immediate abandonment to the secular arm, which would have been strictly in accordance with the regular inquisitorial proceedings, but probably the violent assumption that the articles represented truthfully Joan's admissions was too much for some of the assessors, and the milder suggestion prevailed that Joan should have another hearing, in which the articles should be read to her, with the decision of the University, and that the verdict should depend upon what she should then say. Accordingly, on May 23, she was again brought before the tribunal for the purpose. A brief abstract of the document read to her will show, from the triviality of many of the charges and the guilt ascribed to them, how conviction was predetermined. The University, as

---

* Procès, pp. 496-8, 502.—L'Averdy, pp. 33, 50.—Le Brun de Charmettes, IV. 62-3, 94-5.

usual, had guarded itself by conditioning its decision on the basis of the articles being fully proved, but no notice was taken of this, and Joan was addressed as though she had confessed to the articles and had been solemnly condemned.

I. The visions of angels and saints.—These are pronounced superstitious and proceeding from evil and diabolical spirits.

II. The sign given to Charles of the crown brought to him by St. Michael.—After noting her contradictions, the story is declared a lie, and a presumptuous, seductory, and pernicious thing, derogatory to the dignity of the angelic Church.

III. Recognizing saints and angels by their teaching and the comfort they bring, and believing in them as firmly as in the faith of Christ.—Her reasons have been insufficient, and her belief rash; comparing faith in them to faith in Christ is an error of faith.

IV. Predictions of future events and recognition of persons not seen before through the Voices.—This is superstition and divination, presumptuous assertion, and vain boasting.

V. Wearing men's clothes and short hair, taking the sacrament while in them, and asserting that it is by command of God.—This is blaspheming God, despising his sacraments, transgressing the divine law, holy writ, and canonical ordinances, wherefore, "thou savorest ill in the faith, thou boastest vainly and art suspect of idolatry, and thou condemnest thyself in not being willing to wear thy sex's garments and in following the customs of the heathen and Saracen."

VI. Putting Jesus, Maria, and the sign of the cross on her letters, and threatening that if they were not obeyed that she would show in battle who had the best right.—"Thou art murderous and cruel, seeking effusion of human blood, seditious, provoking to tyranny, and blaspheming God, his commandments and revelations."

VII. Rendering her father and mother almost crazy by leaving them; also promising Charles to restore his kingdom, and all by command of God.—"Thou hast been wicked to thy parents, transgressing the commandment of God to honor them. Thou hast been scandalous, blaspheming God, erring in the faith, and hast made a rash and presumptuous promise to thy king."

VIII. Leaping from the tower of Beaurevoir into the ditch and preferring death to falling into the hands of the English, after the

Voices had forbidden it.—This was pusillanimity, tending to desperation and suicide; and in saying that God had forgiven it, "thou savorest ill as to human free-will."

IX. Saying that St. Catharine and St. Margaret had promised her paradise if she preserved her virginity, feeling assured of it, and asserting that if she were in mortal sin they would not visit her.—"Thou savorest ill as to the Christian faith."

X. Saying that St. Catharine and St. Margaret spoke French and not English because they were not of the English faction, and that, after knowing that these Voices were for Charles, she had not loved the Burgundians.—This is a rash blasphemy against those saints and a transgression of the divine command to love thy neighbor.

XI. Reverencing the celestial visitants and believing them to come from God without consulting any churchman; feeling as certain of it as of Christ and the Passion; and refusing to reveal the sign made to Charles without the command of God.—"Thou art an idolater, an invoker of devils, erring in the faith, and hast rashly made an illicit oath."

XII. Refusing to obey the mandate of the Church if contrary to the pretended command of God, and rejecting the judgment of the Church on earth.—"Thou art schismatic, believing wrongly as to the truth and authority of the Church, and up to the present time thou errest perniciously in the faith of God." *

Maître Pierre Maurice, who read to her this extraordinary document, proceeded to address her with an odious assumption of kindness as "*Jehanne ma chere amie,*" urging her earnestly and argumentatively to submit herself to the judgment of the Church, without which her soul was sure of damnation, and he had shrewd fears for her body. She answered firmly that if the fire was lighted and the executioner ready to cast her in the flames she would not vary from what she had already said. Nothing remained but to cite her for the next day to receive her final sentence.†

---

* Procès, pp. 503–5.—L'Averdy, pp. 56–97.

† Le Brun de Charmettes, IV. 102–4, 106.—Procès, p. 506.

In considering the verdict of the University and the Inquisition it must be borne in mind that visions of the Saviour, the Virgin, and the Saints were almost every-day occurrences, and were recognized and respected by the Church. The

On the 24th preparations for an *auto de fé* were completed in
the cemetery of St. Ouen. The pile was ready for lighting, and
on two scaffolds were assembled the Cardinal of Beaufort and
other dignitaries, while on a third were Pierre Cauchon, Jean le
Maître, Joan, and Maître Guillaume Erard, who preached the customary sermon. In his eloquence he exclaimed that Charles VII.
had been proved a schismatic heretic, when Joan interrupted him,
"Speak of me, but not of the king; he is a good Christian!" She
maintained her courage until the sentence of relaxation was partly read, when she yielded to the incessant persuasion mingled with
threats and promises to which she had been exposed since the
previous night, and she signified her readiness to submit. A
formula of abjuration was read to her, and after some discussion
she allowed her hand to be guided in scratching the sign of the
cross, which represented her signature. Then another sentence,
prepared in advance, was pronounced, imposing on her, as a matter of course, the customary penance of perpetual imprisonment
on bread and water. Vainly she begged for an ecclesiastical
prison. Had Cauchon wished it he was powerless, and he ordered
the guards to conduct her back whence she came.*

The English were naturally furious on finding that they had
overreached themselves. They could have tried Joan summarily
in a secular court for sorcery and burned her out of hand, but to

---

spiritual excitability of the Middle Ages brought the supernatural world into
close relations with the material. For a choice collection of such stories see the
Dialogues of Cæsarius of Heisterbach. As a technical point of ecclesiastical law,
moreover, Joan's visions had already been examined and approved by the prelates and doctors at Chinon and Poitiers, including Pierre Cauchon's metropolitan,
Renaud, Archbishop of Reims.

* Procès, pp. 508–9.—Journal d'un Bourgeois de Paris, an 1431.—Le Brun
de Charmettes, IV. 110–41.

There are two forms of abjuration recorded as subscribed by Joan; one brief
and simple, the other elaborate (Procès, p. 508; Le Brun de Charmettes, IV.
135–7). Cauchon has been accused of duplicity in reading to her the shorter
one and substituting the other for her signature. She subsequently complained
that she had never promised to abandon her male attire—a promise which
was contained in the longer but not in the shorter one. Much has been made
of this, but without reason. The short abjuration is an unconditional admission
of her errors, a revocation and submission to the Church, and was as binding
and effective as the other.

obtain possession of her they had been obliged to call in the ecclesiastical authorities and the Inquisition, and they were too little familiar with trials for heresy to recognize that inquisitorial
proceedings were based on the assumption of seeking the salvation
of the soul and not the destruction of the body. When they saw
how the affair was going a great commotion arose at what they
inevitably regarded as a mockery. Joan's death was a political
necessity, and their victim was eluding them though in their grasp.
In spite of the servility which the ecclesiastics had shown, they
were threatened with drawn swords and were glad to leave the
cemetery of St. Ouen in safety.*

In the afternoon Jean le Maître and some of the assessors visited her in her cell, representing the mercy of the Church and the
gratitude with which she should receive her sentence, and warning
her to abandon her revelations and follies, for if she relapsed she
could have no hope. She was humbled, and when urged to wear
female apparel she assented. It was brought and she put it on;
her male garments were placed in a bag and left in her cell.†

What followed will never be accurately known. The reports
are untrustworthy and contradictory—mere surmises, doubtless—
and the secret lies buried in the dungeon of Rouen Castle. The
brutal guards, enraged at her escape from the flames, no doubt
abused her shamefully; perhaps, as reported, they beat her,
dragged her by the hair, and offered violence to her, till at last
she felt that her man's dress was her only safety. Perhaps, as
other stories go, her Voices reproached her for her weakness, and
she deliberately resumed it. Perhaps, also, Warwick, resolved to
make her commit an act of relapse, had her female garments removed at night, so that she had no choice but to resume her male
apparel. The fact that it was left within her reach and not conveyed away shows at least that there was a desire to tempt her to
resume it. Be this as it may, after wearing her woman's dress
for two or three days word was brought to her judges that she
had relapsed and abandoned it. On May 28 they hastened to her
prison to verify the fact. The incoherence of her replies to their
examination shows how she was breaking down under the fearful

---

* Le Brun de Charmettes, IV. 141.

† Procès, pp. 508-9.—Le Brun de Charmettes, IV. 147.

stress to which she had been subjected. First she merely said that she had taken the dress; then that it was more suitable since she was to be with men; nobody had compelled her, but she denied that she had sworn not to resume it. Then she said that she had taken it because faith had not been kept with her—she had been promised that she should hear mass and receive the sacrament, and be released from her chains; she would rather die than be kept in fetters—could she hear mass and be relieved of her irons she would do all that the Church required. She had heard the Voices since her abjuration, and had been told that she had incurred damnation by revoking to save her life, for she had only revoked through dread of the fire. The Voices are of St. Catharine and St. Margaret, and come from God: she had never revoked that, or, if she had, it was contrary to truth. She had rather die than endure the torture of her captivity, but if her judges wish she will resume the woman's dress; as for the rest she knows nothing more.*

These rambling contradictions, these hopeless ejaculations of remorse and despair, so different from her former intrepid self-confidence, show that the jailers had understood their work, and that body and soul had endured more than they could bear. It was enough for the judges; she was a self-confessed relapsed, with whom the Church could have nothing more to do except to declare her abandoned to the secular arm without further hearing. Accordingly, the next day, May 29, Cauchon assembled such of his assessors as were at hand, reported to them how she had relapsed by resuming male apparel and declaring, through the suggestion of the devil, that her Voices had returned. There could be no question as to her deserts. She was a relapsed, and the only discussion was on the purely formal question, whether her abjuration should be read over to her before her judges abandoned her to the secular arm. A majority of the assessors were in favor of this, but Cauchon and le Maître disregarded the recommendation.†

At dawn on the following day, May 30, Frère Martin l'Advenu and some other ecclesiastics were sent to her prison to inform her

---

* Procès, p. 508.—Le Brun de Charmettes, IV 166-70.—L'Averdy, p. 506.

† Procès, p. 509.—Le Brun de Charmettes, IV. 175-8.

of her burning that morning. She was overcome with terror, threw herself on the ground, tore her hair and uttered piercing shrieks, declaring, as she grew calmer, that it would not have happened had she been placed in an ecclesiastical prison, which was an admission that only the brutality of her dungeon had led her to revoke her abjuration. She confessed to l'Advenu and asked for the sacrament. He was puzzled and sent for instructions to Cauchon, who gave permission, and it was brought to her with all due solemnity. It has been mistakenly argued that this was an admission of her innocence, but the sacrament was never to be denied to a relapsed who asked for it at the last moment, the mere asking, preceded by confession, being an evidence of contrition and desire for reunion to the Church.*

The platform for the sermon and the pile for the execution had been erected in the Viel Marché. Thither she was conveyed amid a surging crowd which blocked the streets. It is related that on the way Nicholas l'Oyseleur, the wretched spy, pierced the crowd and the guards and leaped upon the tumbril to entreat her forgiveness, but before she could grant it the English dragged him off and would have slain him had not Warwick rescued him and sent him out of Rouen to save his life. On the platform Nicholas Midi preached his sermon, the sentence of relaxation was read, and Joan was handed over to the secular authorities. Cauchon, le Maître, and the rest left the platform, and the Bailli of Rouen took her and briefly ordered her to be carried to the place of execution and burned. It has been assumed that there was an informality in not having her sentenced by a secular court, but this, as we have seen, was unnecessary, especially in the case of a relapsed. On her head was placed a high paper crown inscribed " Heretic, Relapsed, Apostate, Idolator," and she was carried to the stake. One account states that her shrieks and lamentations moved the crowd to tears of pity; another that she was resigned and composed, and that her last utterance was a prayer. When her clothes

---

* Le Brun de Charmettes, IV. 180–4.—L'Averdy, p. 488, 493 sqq.

A week after Joan's execution a statement was drawn up by seven of those present in her cell to the effect that she acknowledged that her Voices had deceived her and begged pardon of the English and Burgundians for the evil she had done them, but this is evidently manufactured evidence, and does not even bear a notarial attestation.—Le Brun de Charmettes, IV. 220–5.

were burned off the blazing fagots were dragged aside, that the
crowd might see, from her blackened corpse, that she really was
a woman, and when their curiosity was satisfied the incineration
was completed, the ashes being thrown into the Seine.*

It only remained for those who had taken part in the tragedy
to justify themselves by blackening the character of their victim
and circulating false reports as to the proceedings. That the
judges felt that, in spite of sheltering themselves behind the University of Paris, they had incurred dangerous responsibility is shown
by their obtaining royal letters shielding them from accountability for what they had done, the king pledging himself to constitute
himself a party in any prosecution which might be brought against
them before a general council or the pope. That the regency felt
that justification was needed in the face of Europe is seen in the
letters which were sent to the sovereigns and the bishops in the
name of Henry VI., explaining how Joan had exercised inhuman
cruelties until the divine power had in pity to the suffering people
caused her capture; how, though she could have been punished by
the secular courts for her crimes, she had been handed to the
Church, which had treated her kindly and benignantly, and on her
confession had mercifully imposed on her the penance of imprisonment; how her pride had burst forth in pestilential flames, and she
had relapsed into her errors and madness; how she had then been
abandoned to the secular arm, and, finding her end approaching,
had confessed that the spirits which she invoked were false and
lying, and that she was deceived and mocked by them, and how
she had finally been burned in sight of the people. This official
lying was outdone by the reports which were industriously circu-

---

* Le Brun de Charmettes, IV. 188–210.—Procès, pp. 509–10.—Journal d'un
Bourgeois de Paris, an 1431.

When the excitement which led to Joan's condemnation passed away, and
she was found to have been a useless victim, there was an effort made to shift the
responsibility from the ecclesiastical to the secular authorities: it was claimed
that there had been an irregularity in her execution without a formal judgment
in the lay court. Two years afterwards, Louis de Luxembourg, then Archbishop
of Rouen, and Guillaume Duval, vicar of the inquisitor, condemned for heresy
a certain Georges Solenfant, and in delivering him to the Bailli of Rouen they
gave instructions that he should not be put to death, as Joan had been, without
a definitive judgment, in consequence of which there was a form of sentencing
him.—L'Averdy, p. 498.

lated about her and her trial. The honest Bourgeois of Paris, in entering her execution in his journal, details the offences for which she was condemned, mixing up with the real articles others showing the exaggerations which were industriously circulated. According to him she habitually rode armed with a great staff with which she cruelly beat her people when they displeased her, and in many places she pitilessly slew men and women who disobeyed her; once, when violence was offered her, she leaped from the top of a lofty tower without injury, and boasted that, if she chose, she could bring thunder and other marvels. He admits, however, that even in Rouen there were many who held her to be martyred for her lawful lord.* It evidently was felt that in her dreadful death she had fitly crowned her career, and that sympathy for her fate was continuing her work by arousing popular sentiment, for, more than a month later, on July 4, an effort was made to counteract it by a sermon preached in Paris by a Dominican inquisitor— probably our friend Jean le Maître himself. At great length he expatiated on her deeds of wickedness, and the mercy which had been shown her. She had confessed that from the age of fourteen she had dressed like a man, and her parents would have killed her could they have done so without wounding their consciences. She had therefore left them, accompanied by the devil, and had thenceforth lived by the homicide of Christians, full of fire and blood, till she was burned. She recanted and abjured, and would have had as penance four years' prison on bread and water, but she did not suffer this a single day, for she had herself served in prison like a lady. The devil appeared to her with two demons, fearing greatly that he would lose her, and said to her, "Wicked creature, who through fear hast abandoned thy dress, be not afraid, for we will protect thee from all." Then at once she disrobed and dressed herself in her male attire, which she had thrust in the straw of her bed, and she so trusted in Satan that she said she repented of hav-

---

* Journal d'un Bourgeois de Paris, an 1431.—August 8, 1431, a monk named Jean de la Pierre was brought before Cauchon and le Maître charged with having spoken ill of the trial of Joan. This was a perilous offence when the Inquisition was concerned. He asked pardon on his knees, and excused himself on the ground that it was at table after taking too much wine. He was mercifully treated by imprisonment on bread and water in the Dominican convent until the following Easter.—L'Averdy, p. 141.

ing abandoned it. Then, seeing that she was obstinate, the masters of the University delivered her to the secular arm to be burned, and when she saw herself in this strait she called on the devils, but after she was judged she could not bring them by any invocation. She then thought better of it, but it was too late. The reverend orator added that there were four of them, of whom we have caught three, this Pucelle, and Péronne and her companion, and one who is with the Armagnacs, named Catharine de la Rochelle, who says that when the host is consecrated she sees wonders of the highest secrets of the Lord.*

This last allusion is to certain imitators of Joan. The impression which she produced on the popular mind inevitably led to imitation, whether through imposture or genuine belief. The Péronne referred to was an old woman of Britanny who, with a companion, was captured at Corbeil, in March, 1430, and brought to Paris. She not only asserted that Joan was inspired, but swore that God often appeared to her in human form, with a white robe and vermilion cape, ordering her to assist Joan, and she admitted having received the sacrament twice in one day—Frère Richard being the person who had given it to her at Jargeau. The two were tried by the University; the younger woman recanted, but Péronne was obstinate, and was burned September 3. Catharine de la Rochelle was another of the *protegées* of the impressionable Frère Richard, who was much provoked with Joan for refusing to countenance her. She came to Joan at Jargeau and again at Montfaucon in Berri, saying that every night there appeared to her a white woman clad in cloth-of-gold, telling her that the king would give her horses and trumpets, and she would go through the cities proclaiming that all who had money or treasure should bring it forth to pay Joan's men, and if they concealed it she would discover all that was hidden. Joan's practical sense was not to be allured by this proposition. She told Catharine to go home to her husband and children, and on asking counsel of her Voices was told that it was all folly and falsehood. Still, she wrote to the king on the subject and accepted Catharine's offer to exhibit to her the nightly visitant. The first night Joan fell

---

* Le Brun de Charmettes, IV. 238-40.—L'Averdy, p. 269.—Monstrelet, II. 105.—Journal d'un Bourgeois de Paris, an 1431.

asleep and was told on waking that the apparition had shown itself during her slumber. Then she took a precautionary sleep during the day, and lay awake all night without seeing the white lady. Catharine was probably an impostor rather than an enthusiast, and seems to have escaped the Inquisition.*

During Joan's imprisonment her place for a time was taken by a peasant, variously known as Pastourel or Guillaume le Berger, who professed to have had divine revelations ordering him to take up arms in aid of the royal cause. He demonstrated the truth of his mission by exhibiting stigmata on hands, side, and feet, like St. Francis, and commanded wide belief. Pothon de Xaintrailles, Joan's old companion-in-arms, placed confidence in him and carried him along in his adventurous forays. Guillaume's career, however, was short. He accompanied an expedition into Normandy under the lead of the Maréchal de Boussac and Pothon, which was surprised and scattered by Warwick. Pothon and the shepherd were both captured and carried in triumph to Rouen. Experience of inquisitorial delays in the case of Joan probably caused the English to prefer more summary methods, and the unlucky prophet was tossed into the Seine and drowned without a trial. His sphere of influence had been too limited to render him worth making a conspicuous example.†

Thus Joan passed away, but the spirit which she had aroused was beyond the reach of bishop or inquisitor. Her judicial murder was a useless crime. The Treaty of Arras, in 1435, withdrew Burgundy from the English alliance, and one by one the conquests of Henry V. were wrenched from the feeble grasp of his son. When, in 1449, Charles VII. obtained possession of Rouen he ordered an inquest on the spot into the circumstances of her trial, for it ill comported with the dignity of a King of France to owe his throne to a witch condemned and burned by the Church. The time had not come, however, when a sentence of the Inquisition could be set aside by secular authority, and the attempt was abandoned.

---

* Journal d'un Bourgeois de Paris, an 1430. — Nider Formicar. v. viii. — Procès, p. 480.

† Monstrelet, II. 101.—Journal d'un Bourgeois, an 1431.—Mémoires de Saint-Remy ch. 172.—Abrégé de l'Hist. de Charles VII. (Godefroy, p. 334).

In 1452 another effort was made by Archbishop d'Estouteville of Rouen, but though he was a cardinal and a papal legate, and though he adjoined in the matter Jean Brehal, Inquisitor of France, he could do nothing beyond taking some testimony.   The papal intervention was held to be necessary for the revision of a case of heresy decided by the Inquisition, and to obtain this the mother and the two brothers of Joan appealed to Rome as sufferers from the sentence.   At length, in 1455, Calixtus III. appointed as commissioners to hear and judge their complaints the Archbishop of Rouen, the Bishops of Paris and Coutances, and the Inquisitor Jean Brehal.   Isabelle Darc and her sons appeared as plaintiffs against Cauchon and le Maître, and the proceedings were carried on at their expense.   Cauchon was dead and le Maître in hiding— concealed probably by his Dominican brethren, for no trace of him could be found.   Although the University of Paris does not appear in the case, every precaution was taken to preserve its honor by emphasizing at every stage the fraudulent character of the twelve articles submitted to its decision, and in the final judgment special care was taken to characterize them as false and to order them to be judicially torn to pieces, though it may well be doubted whether they were any more deceptive than innumerable reports made habitually by inquisitors to their assemblies of experts.   Finally, on July 7, 1456, judgment was rendered in favor of the complainants, who were declared to have incurred no infamy; the whole process was pronounced to be null and void; the decision was ordered to be published in Rouen and all other cities of the kingdom; solemn processions were to be made to the place of her abjuration and that of her execution, and on the latter a cross was to be erected in perpetual memory of her martyrdom. In its restored form it still remains there as a memorial of the utility of the Inquisition as an instrument of statecraft.*

---

* Le Brun de Charmettes, Liv. xv.

CHAPTER VI.

SORCERY AND OCCULT ARTS.

FEW things are so indestructible as a superstitious belief once fairly implanted in human credulity. It passes from one race to another and is handed down through countless generations; it adapts itself successively to every form of religious faith; persecution may stifle its outward manifestation, but it continues to be cherished in secret, perhaps the more earnestly that it is unlawful. Religion may succeed religion, but the change only multiplies the methods by which man seeks to supplement his impotence by obtaining control over supernatural powers, and to guard his weakness by lifting the veil of the future. The sacred rites of the superseded faith become the forbidden magic of its successor. Its gods become evil spirits, as the Devas or deities of the Veda became the Daevas or demons of the Avesta; as the bull-worship of the early Hebrews became idolatry under the prophets, and as the gods of Greece and Rome were malignant devils to the Christian Fathers.

Europe thus was the unhappy inheritor of an accumulated mass of superstitions which colored the life and controlled the actions of every man. They were vivified with a peculiar intensity by the powerful conception of the Mazdean Ahriman—the embodiment of the destructive forces of nature and the evil passions of man—which, transfused through Judaism and adorned with the imaginings of the Haggadah, became a fixed article of the creed as the fallen prince of angels, Satan, who drew with him in rebellion half of the infinite angelic hosts, and thenceforth devoted powers inferior only to those of God himself to the spiritual and material perdition of mankind. Omnipresent, and well-nigh omnipotent and omniscient, Satan and his demons were ever and everywhere at work to obtain, by cunning arts, control over the souls of men, to cross their purposes, and to vex their bodies. The food of these beings was the suffering of the damned, and human salvation their most exquisite torment. To effect their objects human agents were indispensable, and Satan was always ready to impart a portion of his power, or to consign a subordinate demon, to any one who would serve him. Thus a dualistic system sprang up, less hopeful and inspiring than that of Zarathustra Spitama, which in its vivid realization of the ever-present and ever-acting Evil Principle, cast a sombre shadow over the kindly teachings of Christ. Some even held that human affairs were governed by demons, and this belief grew sufficiently prevalent to induce Chrysostom to undertake its refutation. He admitted that they were inspired with a fierce and irreconcilable hatred for man, with whom they carried on an immortal war, but he argued that the evil of the world was the just punishment inflicted by God.*

Man thus lived surrounded by an infinite world of spirits, good and bad, whose sole object was his salvation or his perdition, and who were ever on the watch to save him or to lure him to destruction. Thus was solved the eternal problem of the origin of evil, which has perplexed the human soul since it first began to think, and thus grew up a demonology of immense detail which formed part of the articles of faith. Almost every race has shared in such belief, whether the evil spirits were of supernatural origin, as with the Mazdeans and Assyrians, or whether, as with the Buddhists and Egyptians, they were the souls of the damned seeking to gratify their vindictiveness. Although Greece and Rome had no such distinctive class, yet had they peopled the world with a countless number of genii and inferior supernatural beings, who were accepted by Christianity and placed at the service of Satan. As theology grew to be a science in which every detail of the dealings of God with man was defined with the most rigid precision, it became necessary to determine the nature and functions of the spirit world with exactitude, and the ardent intellects which framed the vast structure of orthodoxy did not shrink from the

---

* Minuc. Felicis Octavius (Mag. Bib. Pat. Ed. 1618, III. 7, 8).—Tertull. de Idololat. x.—Lactant. Divin. Instit. ii. 9.—Augustin. de vera Relig. c. 13, c. 40 No. 75; De Genesi ad Litt. xi. 13, 17, 22, 27; Sermon. Append. No. 278 (Edit. Benedict.).—Gregor. PP. I. Moral. in Job iv. 13, 17, 32.—Chrysostom. de Imbecillitate Diaboli Homil. i. No. 6.

task. The numberless references to the character and attributes of demons in patristic literature show how large a space the subject occupied in the thoughts of men and the confidence which was felt in the accuracy of knowledge concerning it.[*]

Origen informs us that every man is surrounded by countless spirits eager to help or harm him. His virtues and good deeds are attributable to good angels; his sins and crimes are the work of demons of pride and lust and wrath, and of all passions and vices. Powerful as these are, however, the human soul is still superior to them and can destroy their capacity for evil; if a holy man baffles the spirit of lust who has tempted him, the conquered demon is cast into outer darkness or into the abyss, and loses his potency forever. This was received throughout the Middle Ages as orthodox doctrine. Gregory the Great tells us how the nun of a convent, walking in the garden, ate a lettuce-leaf without making the cautionary sign of the cross, and was immediately possessed of a demon. St. Equitius tortured the spirit with his exorcisms till the unhappy imp exclaimed, "What have I done? I was sitting on the leaf and she ate me;" but Equitius would listen to no excuse and forced him to depart. Cæsarius of Heisterbach relates a vast number of cases proving the perpetual interference of demons with human affairs, though he asserts as a well-known fact that Satan drew with him only one tenth of the hosts of heaven, and he proceeds to show, on the authority of Gregory the Great, that at the Day of Judgment the saved will be nine times as numerous as the devils, and of course the damned greatly more in excess; yet at the death-bed of a monk of Hemmenrode fifteen thousand demons gathered together, and at that of a Benedictine abbess more assembled than there are leaves in the forest of Kottinhold. Thomas of Cantimpré, though less profuse in his illustrative examples, is equally emphatic in showing that man is surrounded with evil spirits, who lose no opportunity to tempt, to seduce, to mislead, and to vex him. The blessed Reichhelm, Abbot of Schöngau, about 1270, had received from God the gift of being

---

[*] Minuc. Felic. loc. cit.—Tertull. Apol. adv. Gentes c. 22.—Lactant. Divin. Instit. v. 22.—Testam. XII. Patriarch. I. 2–3.—Augustin. de Divin. Dæmon. c. 3, 4, 5, 6; de Civ. Dei xv. 23, xxi. 10; Enarrat. in Psalm. 61, 63.—Isidor. Hispalens. Lib. de Ord. Creatur. c. 8.

able to discern the aerial bodies of these creatures, and often saw them as a thick dust, or as motes in a sunbeam, or as thickly falling rain.   He describes their numbers as so great that the atmosphere is merely a crowd of them; all material sounds, water falling, stones clashing, winds blowing, are their voices.   Sometimes they would materialize as a woman to tempt him, or as a huge cat or a bear to terrify him, but their efforts were mostly directed to diverting the thoughts from pious duties and contemplations, and to inciting to evil passions, which they could well do, as an innumerable army was assigned to each individual man.   These enemies of man were ever on the watch to take advantage of every unguarded thought or act.   Sprenger tells us that if an impatient husband says to a pregnant wife, "Devil take you," the child will be subject to Satan; such children, he says, are often seen; five nurses will not satisfy the appetite of one, and yet they are miserably emaciated, while their weight is great.   Thus man was at all times exposed to the assaults of supernatural enemies, striving to lead him to sin, to torture his body with disease, or to afflict him with material damage.   We cannot understand the motives and acts of our forefathers unless we take into consideration the mental condition engendered by the consciousness of this daily and hourly personal conflict with Satan.*

It is true that all demons were not equally malignant.   The converted Barbarians of Europe could not wholly give up their belief in helpful spirits, and as Christianity classed them all as devils, it was necessary to find an explanation by suggesting that their characters varied with the amount of pride and envy of God which they entertained before the fall.   Those who merely followed their companions and have repented are not always mali-

---

* Origen. sup. Jesu Nave Homil. xv. 5, 6.—Ivon. Carnotens. Decret. xi. 106. —Pselli de Operat. Dæmon. Dial.—Gregor. PP. I. Dial. i. 4.—Cæsar. Heisterb. Dial. Dist. iv., v., xi. 17, xii. 5.—B. Richalmi Lib. de Insid. Dæmon. (Pez Thesaur. Anecd. I. ii. 376).—S. Hildegardæ Epist. 67 (Martene Ampl. Coll. II. 1100). —Mall. Maleficar. P. ii. Q. 1, c. 3.

It was not every one who, like St. Francis, when demons were threatening to torment him, could coolly welcome them, saying that his body was his worst enemy, and that they were free to do with it whatever Christ would permit—a view of the case which so abashed them that they incontinently departed.— Amoni, Legenda S. Francisci, Append. c. liii.

cious. Cæsarius tells us of one who faithfully served a knight for a long while, saved him from his enemies, and cured his wife of a mortal illness by fetching from Arabia lion's milk with which to anoint her. This aroused the knight's suspicions, and the demon confessed, explaining that it was a great consolation to him to be with the children of men. Fearing to retain such a servitor, the knight dismissed him, offering half of his possessions as a reward, but the demon would accept only five sous, and these he returned, asking the knight to purchase with them a bell and hang it on a certain desolate church, that the faithful might be called to divine service on Sundays. Froissart's picturesque narrative is well known of the demon Orton, who served the Sieur de Corasse out of pure love, bringing to him every night tidings of events from all parts of the world, and finally abandoning him in consequence of his imprudent demand to see his nocturnal visitor. Froissart himself was at Ortais in 1385, when the Count of Foix miraculously had news of the disastrous battle of Aljubarotta in Portugal the day after it occurred, and the courtiers explained that he heard of it through the Sieur de Corasse. Thus, for good or for evil, the barriers which divided the material from the spiritual world were slight, and intercourse between them was too frequent to excite incredulity.*

It was inevitable that this facility of intercourse should encourage belief in the Incubi and Succubi who play so large a part in mediæval sorcery, for such a belief has belonged to superstition in all ages. The Akkads had their Gelal and Kiel-Gelal, the Assyrians their Lil and Lilit, and the Gauls their Dusii, lustful spirits of either sex who gratified their passions with men and women, while the Welsh legends of the Middle Ages show the continuance of the belief among the Celtic tribes. The Egyptians drew a distinction and admitted of Incubi but not of Succubi. The Jews accepted the text concerning the sons of God and daughters of men (Gen. vi. 1) as proving that fruitful intercourse could occur between spiritual and human beings, and they had their legends of the evil spirit Lilith, the first wife of Adam, who bore to him the innumerable multitude of demons. The anthropomorphic mythology and hero-worship of Greece consisted of little else, and the

---

* Cæsar. Heisterb. III. 26, v. 9, 10, 35, 36.—Froissart, III. 22.

name of Satyr has passed into a proverb.   The simpler and purer
Latin pantheon had yet its Sylvans and Fauns, who, as St. Augustin tells us, "are commonly called Incubi."   The medical faculty
in vain explained the belief by Ephialtes or nightmare, and recommended for it belladonna rather than exorcisms.   Though St.
Augustin, who did so much to transmit pagan superstitions to succeeding ages, hesitates to believe in the possibility of such powers
on the part of aerial spirits, even he dares not deny it, and though
Chrysostom ridiculed it, other authorities accepted it as a matter
of course.   Thus it came to be received as a truth which few
thought of disputing.   In 1249 an incubus child was born on the
Welsh marches, which in half a year had a full set of teeth and the
stature of a youth of seventeen, while the mother wasted away and
died.   The belief grew still more definite as perfected processes of
trial enabled judges to extort from their victims whatever confessions they desired, such as that of Angèle de la Barthe, who, in the
Toulousain in 1275, admitted that she had habitual intercourse
with Satan, to whom, seven years before, at the age of fifty-three,
she had borne a son—a monster with a wolf's head and a serpent's
tail, which she fed for two years on the flesh of year-old babies
whom she stole by night, after which it disappeared; or those of
the witches of Arras, in 1460, who were brought to confess that
their demon lovers wore the shapes of hares, or foxes, or bulls.
Innocent VIII. asserts the existence of such connections in the
most positive manner, and Silvester Prierias declares that to
deny it is both unorthodox and unphilosophical, and could only
be prompted by sheer wantonness.*

Liaisons of this kind would be entered into with demons, and

---

* Fr. Lenormant, La Magie chez les Chaldéens, p. 36.—Plutarch. vit. Numæ,
IV.—Joseph. Antiq. Jud. I. 3.—Augustin. de Civ. Dei III. 5; xv. 23.—Gualt.
Mapes de Nugis Curialium Dist. II. c. xi., xii., xiii.—Paul. Æginet. Instit. Med.
III. 15.—Chrysost. Homil. in Genesim XXII., No. 2.—Clem. Alexand. Stromat.
Libb. III., v. (Ed. Sylburg. pp. 450, 550).—Tertull. Apol. adv. Gentes, c. xxii.; De
Carne Christi c. vi., xiv.—Hincmar. de Divort. Lothar. Interrog. xv.—Guibert.
Noviogent. de Vita sua Lib. III. c. 19.—Cæsar. Heisterb. III. 8, 11, 13.—Gervas.
Tilberien. Otia Imp. Decis. III. c. 86.—Matt. Paris. ann. 1249 (p. 514).—Chron.
Bardin. (Vaissette, IV. Pr. 5).—Mémoires de Jacques Du Clercq, Liv. IV. c. 8.—
Innoc. PP. VIII. Bull. Summis desiderantes, 2 Dec. 1484.—Silv. Prieriat. de Stri-
gimagar. Lib. I. c. 2; Lib. II. c. 3.

would be maintained with the utmost fidelity on both sides for thirty or forty years; and the connection thus established was proof against all the ordinary arts of the exorciser. Alvaro Pelayo relates that in a nunnery under his direction it prevailed among the nuns, and he was utterly powerless to put a stop to it. In fact, it was peculiarly frequent in such pious establishments. As a special crime it grew to have a special name, and was known among canonists and casuists as Demoniality; and Sprenger, whose authority in such matters is supreme, assures us that to its attractiveness was due the alarming development of witchcraft in the fifteenth century. The few who, like Ulric Molitoris, while admitting the existence of Incubi, denied to them the power of procreation, were silenced by the authority of Thomas Aquinas, who explained how, by acting alternately as Succubus and Incubus, the demon could accomplish the object, and by the indubitable facts that the Huns were sprung from demons, and that an island in Egypt, or, as some said, Cyprus, was peopled wholly by descendants of Incubi, to say nothing of the popular legend which attributed such paternity to the prophet and enchanter, Merlin. Into the physiological speculations by which these possibilities were proved, it is not worth our while to enter. There is nothing fouler in all literature than the stories and illustrative examples by which these theories were supported.*

As Satan's principal object in his warfare with God was to seduce human souls from their divine allegiance, he was ever ready with whatever temptation seemed most likely to effect his purpose. Some were to be won by physical indulgence such as that just alluded to; others by conferring on them powers enabling them apparently to forecast the future, to discover hidden things, to gratify enmity, and to acquire wealth, whether through forbidden

---

* Gianfrancesco Pico della Mirandola, La Strega, Milano, 1864, p. 80.—Thomæ Cantimpratens. Bonum universale, Lib. ii. c. 55.—Alvar. Pelag. de Planct. Eccles. Lib. ii. Art. xlv. No. 102.—Prieriatis de Strigimagar. ii. iii., xi.—Sinistrari de Dæmonialitate No. 1-3.—Mall. Maleficar. P. ii. Q. i. c. 4-8; P. ii. Q. ii. c. 1.— Ulric. Molitor. Dial. de Python. Mulieribus Conclus. v.—Th. Aquin. Summ. i. li. Art. iii. No. 6.—Nider Formicar. Lib. v. c. ix., x.—Guill. Arvern. Episc. Paris. de Universo (Wright, Proceedings against Dame Alice Kyteler, Camden Soc. p. xxxviii.).—Villemarqué, Myrdhinn, ou l'Enchanteur Merlin, p. 11.—Alonso de Spina, Fortalicium Fidei, Ed. 1494, fol. 282.

arts or by the services of a familiar demon subject to their orders.
As the neophyte in receiving baptism renounced the devil, his
pomps and his angels,* it was necessary for the Christian who
desired the aid of Satan to renounce God. Moreover, as Satan
when he tempted Christ offered him the kingdoms of the earth in
return for adoration—"If thou therefore wilt worship me all shall
be thine" (Luke IV. 7)—there naturally arose the idea that to obtain this aid it was necessary to render allegiance to the princes
of hell. Thence came the idea, so fruitful in the development of
sorcery, of compacts with Satan by which sorcerers became his
slaves, binding themselves to do all the evil they could encompass
and to win over as many converts as they could to follow their
example. Thus the sorcerer or witch was an enemy of all the
human race as well as of God, the most efficient agent of hell in
its sempiternal conflict with heaven. His destruction, by any
method, was therefore the plainest duty of man.

This was the perfected theory of sorcery and witchcraft by
which the gentile superstitions inherited and adopted from all
sides were fitted into the Christian dispensation and formed part
of its accepted creed. From the earliest periods of which records
have reached us there have been practitioners of magic who were
credited with the ability of controlling the spirit world, of divining the future, and of interfering with the ordinary operations of
nature. When this was accomplished by the ritual of an established religion it was praiseworthy, like the augural and oracular
divination of classic times, or the exorcism of spirits, the excommunication of caterpillars, and the miraculous cures wrought by
relics or pilgrimages to noted shrines. When it worked through
the invocation of hostile deities, or of a religion which had been
superseded, it was blameworthy and forbidden. The Yatudhana,
or sorcerer of the Vedas, doubtless sought his ends through the
invocation of the Rakshasas and other dethroned divinities of the
conquered Dasyu. His powers were virtually the same as those
of the mediæval sorcerer: with his *yatu*, or magic, he could encompass the death of his enemies or destroy their harvests and
their herds; his *kritya*, or charmed images and other objects, had
an evil influence which could only be overcome by discovering

---

* Tertull. de Corona c. iii.

and removing them, exactly as we find it in the Europe of the fifteenth century; while the counter-charms and imprecations employed against him show that there was virtually no difference between sacred and prohibited magic.* The same lesson is taught by
Hebrew tradition, which admitted that wonders could be wrought
by the *Elohim acherim,* or "other gods," as instanced in the contest
between Moses and the Chakamim, or wise men of Egypt. The
Talmudists inform us that when he changed his rod into a serpent
Pharaoh laughed at him for parading such tricks in a land full of
magicians, and sent for some little children who readily performed
the same feat, but the failure of Jannes and Jambres to cope with
him when he came to the plague of the lice was because their art
would not extend to the imitation of things smaller than a barley-
corn. The connection between their magic and the worship of
false gods is seen in the legend that it was Jannes and Jambres
who fabricated for Aaron the golden calf. A similar indication is
seen in the Samaritan tradition that the falling away of the Hebrews from the ancient faith was explicable by the magic arts of
Eli and Samuel, who studied them in the books of Balaam, gaining thereby wealth and power, and seducing the people from the
worship of Jehovah.†

How great was the impression produced on the surrounding
nations by the powers of the Egyptian Chakamim is shown by
the later Jews, who, familiar as they were with the mysteries of
the Magi and Chaldeans, yet declared that of the ten portions of
magic bestowed upon the earth, nine had fallen to the lot of Egypt.
That kingdom therefore furnishes naturally enough the oldest
record of a trial for sorcery, occurring about 1300 B.C., showing that
the use of magic was not regarded as criminal of itself, but only
when employed by an unauthorized person for wrongful ends.

---

* Rig Veda V. VIII. iv. 15, 16, 24 (Ludwig's Rig Veda, Prag, 1876–8, II. 379,
III. 345).—Atharva Veda II. 27, III. 6, IV. 18, v. 14, VI. 37, 75 (Grill, Hundert
Lieder des Atharva Veda, Tübingen, 1879).

† Polano, Selections from the Talmud, pp. 174, 176.—Augustin. de Trinitate
Lib. III. c. 8, 9.—Targum of Palestine on Exod. i.; vii. 11; Numb. xxii. 22.—Fa-
bricii Cod. Pseudepig. Vet. Testam. I. 813 ; II. 106.—Chron. Samaritan. xli., xliii.

Curiously enough, the fame as magicians of Moses and of his opponents was
preserved together. Pliny (N. H. xxx. 2) attributes the founding of what he
calls the second school of magic to "Moses and Jannes and Lotapes."

The proceedings in the case recite that a certain Penhaiben, a farm superintendent of cattle, when passing by chance the Khen, or hall in the royal palace where the rolls of mystic lore were kept, was seized with a desire to obtain access to their secrets for his personal advantage. Procuring the assistance of a worker in stone named Atirma, he penetrated into the sacred recesses of the Khen and secured a book of dangerous formulas belonging to his master, Rameses III. Mastering their use, he soon was able to perform all the feats of the doctors of mysteries. He composed charms which, when carried into the royal palace, corrupted the concubines of the Pharaoh; he caused hatred between men, fascinated or tormented them, paralyzed their limbs, and in short, as the report of the tribunal states, " He sought and found the real way to execute all the abominations and all the wickedness that his heart conceived, and he performed them, with other great crimes, the horror of every god and goddess. Consequently he has endured the great punishment, even unto death, which the divine writings say that he merited." *

Hebrew belief, which necessarily served as a standard for orthodox Christianity, drew from these various sources an ample store of magic practitioners. There was the *At*, or charmer; the *Asshaph, Kasshaph, Mekassheph*, the enchanter or sorcerer; the *Kosem*, or diviner; the *Ob, Shoel Ob, Baal Ob*, the consulter with evil spirits, or necromancer (the Witch of Endor was a *Baalath Ob*); the *Chober Chaber*, or worker with spells and ligatures; the *Doresh el Hammathim*, or consulter with the dead; the *Meonen*, or augur, divining by the drift of clouds or voices of birds—the "observer of times" of the A. V.; the *Menachesh*, or augur by enchantments; the *Jiddoni*, or wizard; the *Chakam*, or sage; the *Chartom*, or hierogrammatist; the *Mahgim*, or mutterers of spells; and in later times there were the *Istaginen*, or astrologer; the *Charori*, or soothsayer; the *Magush, Amgosh*, or enchanter; the *Raten*, or magus; the *Negida*, or necromancer; and the *Pithom*, inspired by evil spirits. There was here an ample field in which Christian superstition could go astray.

Greece contributed her share, although of strictly Goetic magic

---

* Talmud Babli, Kiddushin, fol. 49 *b* (Wagenseilii Sota, pp. 502–3). — Thonissen, Droit Criminel des Anciens, II. 222 sqq.

—the invocation of malignant spirits or the use of illicit means
for wrongful ends—there was little need, in a religion of which
the deities, great and small, were subject to all the weaknesses of
humanity, were ready at any moment to inflict on man the direst
calamities to gratify their love or their spleen or their caprice, and
could be purchased by a prayer or a sacrifice to exercise their omnipotence irrespective of justice or morality. In such a religion
the priest exercises the functions which in purer faiths are relegated to the sorcerer. Yet it is only necessary to mention the
names of Zetheus and Amphion, of Orpheus and Pythagoras, of
Epimenides, Empedocles, and Apollonius of Tyana to show that
both tradition and history taught the existence and power of
thaumaturgy and theurgy.* This theurgy was developed to its
fullest extent in the marvels related of the Neo-Platonists, thus
directly influencing Christian thought, which necessarily ascribed
its miracles to the invocations of demons.† Yet by the side of all
this there was no lack of Goetic magic, such as the legends attribute to the Cretan Dactyls or Curetes, to the Telchines, to Medea,
and to Circe.‡ This is said to have received a powerful impetus
in the Medic wars, when the Magian Osthanes, who accompanied
Xerxes, scattered the seeds of his unholy lore throughout Greece.
Plato speaks with the strongest reprobation of the venal sorcerers
who hire themselves at slender wages to those desirous of destroying enemies with magic arts and incantations, ligatures, and
the figurines, or waxen images, which have always been one of
the favorite resources of malignant magic, and which in Greece
wrought their evil work by being set up in the cross-roads, or affixed to the door of the victim or to the tomb of his ancestors.
Philtres, or love-potions, which would excite or arrest love at will

---

* Hesiod. Frag. 202.—Pherecyd. Frag. 102, 102*a*.—Pausan. VI. xx.; IX. xviii.,
xxx.—Apollodor. I. ix. 25.—Plut. de Defectu. Orac. 13; de Pythiæ Orac. 12.—
Diog. Laert. VIII. ii. 4; viii. 20.—Iambl. Vit. Pythag. 134–5, 222.—Philost. Vit.
Apollon. passim.—Æl. Lamprid. Alex. Sever. xxix.—Flav. Vopisc. Aurelian.
xxiv.—Cedren. Hist. Compend. sub Claud. et Domit.

† Porphyr. de Abstinent. II. 41, 52–3.—Marini Vit. Procli 23, 26–8.—Damas-
cii Vit. Isidori 107, 116, 126.—Porphyr. Vit. Plotini 10, 11.

‡ Apollon. Rhod. Argonaut. I. 1128–31.—Pherecyd. Frag. 7.—Diod. Sicul. v.
55–6.—Ovid. Metam. VII. 365–7.—Suidas s. v. Τελχῖνες.—Strabon. X.—Odyss. x.
211–396.

were among their ordinary resources.   Even the triform Hecate
was subject to their spells; they could arrest the course of nature
and bring the moon to earth.   The fearful rites which superstition
attributed to these sorcerers are indicated in one of the charges
brought against Apollonius of Tyana when tried before Domitian
—that of sacrificing a child.*

In Rome the gods of the nether world furnished a link between
the sacred ceremonies of the priest and the incantations of the
sorcerer, for while they were objects of worship to the pious, they
were also the customary sources of the magician's power.   Lucan's
terrible witch, Erichtho, is a favorite with Erebus; she wanders
among tombs from which she draws their shades; she works her
spells with funeral-torches and with the bones and ashes of the
dead; her incantations are Stygian; gluing her lips to those of a
dying man, she sends her dire messages to the under-world.   Horace's Canidia and Sagana seek their power at the same source, and
the description of their hideous doings bears a curious resemblance
to much that sixteen centuries later occupied the attention of half
the courts in Christendom.   It is the same throughout all the allusions to Latin sorcery—the deities invoked are infernal, and the
rites are celebrated at night.†   The identity of the means employed with those of modern sorcery is perfect.   When Germanicus
Cæsar, the idol of the empire, was doomed by the secret jealousy
of Tiberius; when his subordinate in command of the East, Cneius
Piso, was commissioned to make way with him, and Germanicus
was stricken with mortal illness, it reads like a passage in Gril-
landus or Delrio to see that his friends, suspecting Piso's enmity,
dug from the ground and the walls of his house the objects placed
there to effect his destruction—fragments of human bodies, half-
burned ashes smeared with corruption, leaden plates inscribed
with his name, charms, and other accursed things, by which, says
Tacitus, it is believed that souls may be dedicated to the infernal
gods.   The ordinary feats of the witch could be more easily per-

_____

* Plin. N. H. xxx. ii.—Platon. de Repub. ii.; de Legg. i.; ix. (Ed. Astius, IV.
80; VI. 68, 348–50).—Luciani Philopseud. 14.—Philost. Vit. Apollon. viii. 5.

† Ovid. Fastor. ii. 571–82.—Lucan. Pharsal. vi. 507–28, 534–7, 567–9, 766.—
Appul. de Magia Orat. pp. 37, 62–4 (Ed. Bipont.).—Horat. Sat. i. viii.; Epod. v.
—Petron. Arb. Satyr.—Pauli Sentt. Receptt. v. xxxiii. 15.

formed. A simple incantation would blight the harvest or dry
the running fountain, would destroy the acorn on the oak and the
ripening fruit on the bough. The figurine, or waxen image, of the
person to be assailed, familiar to Hindu, Egyptian, and Greek
sorcery, assumes in Rome the shape in which we find it in the
Middle Ages. Sometimes the name of the victim was traced on it
in letters of red wax. If a mortal disease was to be induced in
any organ, a needle was thrust in the corresponding part of the
image; or if he was to waste away in an incurable malady, it was
melted with incantations at a fire. The victim could moreover be
transformed into a beast—a feat which St. Augustin endeavors to
explain by dæmonic delusion.* It is observable that the terrible
magician is almost always an old woman—the *saga*, *strix*, or *volatica*
—the wise-woman or nocturnal bird or night-flyer—corresponding precisely with the hag who in mediæval Europe almost monopolized sorcery. But the male sorcerer, like his modern de-
scendant, had the power of transforming himself into a wolf, and
was thus the prototype of the wer-wolves, or *loups-garoux*, who
form so picturesque a feature in the history of witchcraft.†

The philtres, charms, and ligatures for exciting desire or pre-
venting its fruition, or for arousing hatred, which meet us at
every step in modern sorcery, were equally prevalent in that of
Rome. The virtual insanity of Caligula was attributed to powerful drugs administered to him in a love-potion by Cæsonia, whom
he married after the death of his sister and concubine Drusilla,
and so firm was the conviction of this that when he was assassinated she was likewise put to death for having thus brought the
greatest calamities on the republic. That such a man as Marcus
Aurelius could be supposed to have caused his wife Faustina to
bathe in the blood of the luckless gladiator who was the object of
her affections before seeking his own embraces, while doubtless invented to account for the character of his son Commodus, shows
the profound belief accorded to such arts. Appuleius found this
to his cost when he was tried for his life on the charge of having

---

* Tacit. Annal. II. 69; III. 13.—Sueton. Calig. 3.—Ovid. Amor. III. vii. 29–34;
Heroid. VI. 90–2.—Horat. Sat. I. viii. 29–32, 42–3.—August. de Civ. Dei XVIII. 18.

† Festus s. v. Strigæ.—Virg. Eclog. VIII. 97.—August. de Civ. Dei XVIII. 17.
—Paul Æginet. Instit. Medic. III. 16.—Gervas. Tilberiens. Otia Imperial. Decis.
III. c. 120.—Cf. Volsunga Saga V., VIII.

by incantations and sorcery secured the affections of his bride
Pudentilla, a woman of mature age who had been fourteen years
a widow. Had the court, like those of the Middle Ages, enjoyed
the infallible resource of torture, he would readily have been forced
to confession, with the attendant death-penalty; but as there was
no charge of treason involved, he was free to disculpate himself
by evidence and argument, and he escaped.*

The severest penalties of the law, in fact, were traditionally
directed against all practitioners of magic. The surviving fragments of the Decemviral legislation show that this dated from an
early period of the republic. With the spread of the Roman conquests, the introduction of Orientalized Hellenism was followed by
the magic of the East, more imposing than the homelier native
practices, arousing the liveliest fear and indignation. In 184 B. C.
the praetor L. Naevius was detained for four months from proceeding to his province of Sardinia, by the duty assigned to him of
prosecuting cases of sorcery. A large portion of these were scattered through the suburbicarian regions; the culprits had a short
shrift, and he manifested a diligence which Pierre Cella or Bernard
de Caux might envy, if the account be true that he condemned no
less than two thousand sorcerers. Under the empire decrees against
magicians, astrologers, and diviners were frequent, and from the
manner in which accusations of sorcery were brought against
prominent personages the charge would seem to have been then,
as it proved in the fourteenth and fifteenth centuries, one of those
convenient ones, easy to make and hard to disprove, which are
welcome in personal and political intrigue. Nero persecuted
magic with such severity that he included philosophers among
magicians, and the cloak or distinctive garment of the philosopher
was sufficient to bring its wearer before the tribunals. Musonius
the Babylonian, who ranked next to Apollonius of Tyana in wisdom and power, was incarcerated, and would have perished as intended but for the exceptional robustness which enabled him to
endure the rigors of his prison. Caracalla went even further and

---

* Propert. IV. v. 18.—Virg. Æneid. IV. 512-16.—Plin. N. H. VIII. 56.—Livii
XXXIX. 11.—Joseph. Antiq. Jud. XIX. 12.—Tibull. I. viii. 5-6.—Ovid. Amor. III.
vii. 27-35.—Petron. Arb. Sat.—Jul. Capitolin. Marc. Aurel. 19.—Appul. de Magia Orat.

punished those who merely wore on their necks amulets for the cure
of tertian and quartan fevers. The darker practices of magic were
repressed with relentless rigor. To perform or procure the performance of impious nocturnal rites with the object of bewitching
any one was punished with the severest penalties known to the
Roman law—crucifixion or the beasts. For immolating a man or
offering human blood in sacrifices the penalty was simple death or
the beasts, according to the station of the offender. Accomplices
in magic practices were subjected to crucifixion or the beasts,
while magicians themselves were burned alive. The knowledge
of the art was forbidden as well as its exercise; all books of
magic were to be burned, and their owners subjected to deportation or capital punishment, according to their rank. When the
cross became the emblem of salvation, it of course passed out of
use as an instrument of punishment; with the abolition of the
arena the beasts were no longer available; but the fagot and
stake remained, and for long centuries continued to be the punishment for more or less harmless impostors.*

With the triumph of Christianity the circle of forbidden practices was enormously enlarged. A new sacred magic was introduced which superseded and condemned as sorcery and demon-
worship a vast array of observances and beliefs, which had become
an integral and almost ineradicable part of popular life. The
struggle between the rival thaumaturgies is indicated already in
Tertullian's complaint, that when in droughts the Christians by
prayers and mortifications had extorted rain from God, the credit
was given to the sacrifices offered to Jove; he challenges the
pagans to bring before their own tribunals a demoniac, when a
Christian will force the possessing spirit to confess himself a
demon. The triumph of the new system was typified in the
encounter between St. Peter and Simon Magus, when the flight
through the air of the heathen theurgist was arrested by the
prayers of the Christian, and he fell with a disastrous crash, breaking a hip-bone and both heels. If, as conjectured by some modern

---

* Legg. XII. Tabul. Tab. viii.—Senecæ Quæst. Natural. Lib. IV. c. 7.—Plin.
N. H. XXVIII. 4.—Liv. XXXIX. 41.—Tacit. Annal. II. 32; IV. 22, 52; XVI. 28-31.
—Philost. Vit. Apollon. IV. 35.—Spartian. Anton. Caracall. 5.—Lib. XLVII. Dig.
viii. 14.—Pauli Sententt. Receptt. v. xxiii. 14-18.

critics, Simon Magus is the Petrine designation of St. Paul, the partisans of the latter were not behindhand in recounting the triumph of their leader over the older thaumaturgists, for when he wrought wonders at Ephesus and the Jewish conjurers were put to shame, then "many of them also which used curious arts brought their books together and burned them before all men; and they counted the price of them, and found it fifty thousand pieces of silver." *

Still more convincing was the incident which occurred to Marcus Aurelius in the Marcomannic war when, in the territory of the Quadi, he was cut off from water, so that his army was perishing from thirst. Though he had persecuted the Christians, he had recourse to the intervention of Christ, when a sudden tempest supplied the Romans abundantly with water, while the lightning slew the Teutons and dispersed them, so that they were readily slaughtered. When, finally, the new faith and the old met in their death-grapple, Eusebius describes Constantine as preparing for the struggle by calling around him his most holy priests and marching under the shade of the sacred Labarum. Licinius on his side collected diviners and Egyptian prophets and magicians. They offered sacrifices and endeavored to learn the result from their deities. Oracles everywhere promised victory; the sacrificial auguries were favorable; the interpreters of dreams announced success. On the eve of the first battle Licinius assembled his chief captains in a sacred grove where there were many idols, and explained to them that this was to be the decisive test between the gods of their ancestors and the unknown deity of the barbarians—if they were vanquished it would show that their gods were dethroned. In the ensuing combat the cross bore down everything before it; the enemy fled when it appeared, and Constantine seeing this sent the Labarum as an amulet of victory, wherever his troops were sore bestead, and at once the battle would be restored. Defeat only hardened the heart of Licinius, and again he had recourse to his magicians. Constantine, on the other hand, arranged an oratory in his camp, to which before battle he would retire to pray with the men of God, and then sallying forth would give the signal for

---

* Tertull. Apol. 23, 40.—Constitt. Apostol. vi. 9.—Arnob. adv. Gentes ii. 12. —Hippol. Refut. omn. Hæres. Lib. vi.—Acts xix. 19.

attack, when his troops would slay all who dared to stand before them. So complete became the trust enjoined in the efficacy of the invocation of God, that enthusiasts denounced it as unworthy a Christian to rely upon human prudence and sagacity in trouble. St. Nilus tells us that in cases of sickness recourse is to be had to prayer, rather than to physicians and physic; and St. Augustin, in his recital of miraculous cures beyond the reach of science to effect, evidently regards the appeal to God and the saints as far more trustworthy than all the resources of the medical art.*

It was inevitable that the triumphant theurgy should set to work with remorseless vigor to extirpate its fallen rival, as soon as it could fully control the powers of the State. It was not so much the worship and propitiation of the pagan gods that was first attacked, as the thousand methods of divination and devices to avert evil which had become ingrained in daily life—oracles and auguries and portents and omens and soothsaying. Their efficacy was the work of Satan to deceive and seduce mankind, and their use was the direct or indirect invocation of demons. To attempt to foretell the future in any way was sorcery, and all sorcery was the work of the devil; and it was the same with the amulets and charms, the observance of lucky and unlucky days, and the innumerable trivial superstitions which amused the popu-

---

* Pauli Diac. Hist. Miscell. x., xi.—Euseb. Vit. Constant. ii. 4–7, 11–12.—S. Nili Capita parænetica No. 61.—S. August. de Civ. Dei xxii. 8. Cf. Evodii de Mirac. S. Stephani.

The Labarum of Constantine was the Greek cross with four equal arms, a symbol frequently seen on Chaldean and Assyrian cylinders. Oppert attaches to it the root לבר, thus explaining the word Labarum, the derivation of which has never been understood (Oppert et Menant, Documents juridiques de l'Assyrie, Paris, 1877, p. 209). The fetichism connected with the cross probably took its rise from the Labarum. Maxentius, we are told, was an ardent adept in magic, and relied upon it for success against Constantine, who was much alarmed until reassured by the vision of the cross and its starry inscription, "*In hoc vince*" (Euseb. H. E. ix. 9; Vit. Const. i. 28–31, 36.—Pauli Diac. Hist. Miscell. Lib. xi.—Zonaræ Annal. T. iii.). The melting of pagan superstitions into Christian is illustrated by the incident that when Constantine routed Maxentius at the Milvian Bridge he was preceded in battle by an armed cavalier bearing a cross, and at Adrianople two youths were seen who slaughtered the troops of Licinius (Zonaræ Annal. T. iii.). The Christian annalists had no difficulty in identifying with angels of God those whom Pagan writers would designate as Castores.

lar imagination. Zeal for the repression of every species of magic
was not only stimulated by the conviction that it was an essential
part of the conflict with a personal Satan, but by obedience to the
commands of God in the Mosaic law. The awful words, "Thou
shalt not suffer a witch (*Mekasshepha*) to live" have rung through
the centuries, and have served as a justification for probably more
judicial slaughter than any other sentence in the history of human
jurisprudence. Rabbinical Judaism enforced this relentlessly in
spite of the kindliness of the rabbis and their extreme indisposition to shed human blood. One of the first reforms of the Pharisees on coming into power after the persecution of Alexander
Jannai was the abrogation of the Mosaic penal code in favor of
milder laws. The leader in the revolution was Simon ben Shetach,
who in organizing the Sanhedrin refused the presidency and conferred it on Judah ben Tabbai. The latter chanced to condemn a
man for false witness on the testimony of a single person, though
the law required two, when Simon reproached him as blood-guilty,
and he resigned. Yet this man, so scrupulous about taking life,
had no hesitation in hanging at Ascalon eighty witches in a single
day. According to the Mishna, the Pithom and the Jiddoni are
to be stoned, and false diviners and those who read the future in
the name of idols are to be hanged, while the Talmud adds that
he who learns a single word from a Magus is to be put to death.
Christianity thus derived from Judaism the complete assurance
that in ruthlessly exterminating all thaumaturgy save that of
its own priesthood it was obeying the unquestioned command of
God.*

The machinery of the Church was therefore early set to work
to exhort and persuade the faithful against a sin so unpardonable and apparently so ineradicable; and as soon as it gathered
its prelates together in councils it commenced to legislate for the
suppression of such practices.† When it grew powerful enough to

---

* Cohen, Les Pharisiens, I. 311.—Lightfooti Horæ Hebraicæ, Matt. xxiv. 24.—
Mishna, Sanhedrin, vii. 7; x. 16.—Talmud Babli, Shabbath, 75 *a* (Buxtorfi Lexicon, p. 1170).

† Minuc. Felic. Octavius (Bib. Mag. Pat. III. 7–8).—Tertull. Apol. 35; de
Anima 57.—Acta SS. Justin. et Cyprian. (Martene Thesaur. II. 1629).—Constitt.
Apostol. II. 66.—Lactant. Divin. Inst. ii. 17.—Concil. Ancyræns. ann. 314 c. 24
—C. Laodicens. ann. 320 c. 36.—C. Eliberitan. circa 324 c. 6.

influence the head of the State it procured a series of cruel edicts which doubtless were effective in destroying the remains of tolerated paganism as well as in suppressing the special practices so offensive in the eyes of the orthodox. It was not difficult to commence with the time-honored practices of divination, for, although these had formed part of the machinery of State, yet when the State was centred in the person of its master, any inquiry into the future of public affairs was an inquiry into the fortune and fate of the monarch, and no crime was more jealously repressed and more promptly punished than this. Even so warm an admirer of ancestral institutions as Cato the Elder had long before warned his paterfamilias to forbid his *villicus*, or farm-steward, to consult any haruspex or augur. These gentry had a way of breeding trouble, and it boded no good to the master when the slaves were over-curious and too well-informed. In the same spirit Tiberius prohibited the secret consultation of haruspices. Constantine was thus serving a double purpose when, as early as 319, he threatened with burning the haruspex who ventured to cross another's threshold, even on pretext of friendship; the man who called him in was punished with confiscation and deportation, and the informer was rewarded. Priest and augur were only to celebrate their rites in public. Even this was withdrawn by Constantius in 357; any consultation with diviners was punishable with death, and the practitioners themselves, whether of magic or augury, or the expounding of dreams, when on trial were deprived of exemption from torture and could be subjected to the rack or the hooks to extort confession.* Under this Constantius organized an active persecution throughout the East, in which numbers were put to death upon the slightest pretext; passing among the tombs at night was evidence of necromancy, and hanging a charm around the neck for the cure of a quartan was proof of forbidden arts. The witch-trials of modern times were prefigured and anticipated. Under Julian there was a reaction, and in 364 Valentinian and Valens proclaimed freedom of belief; in 371 they included in this the old religious divination, while capital punishment was restricted

---

* Cato. Rei Rust. 5.—Sueton. Tiber. 63.—Lib. ix. Cod. Theod. xvi. 1–6.

For the care with which the Romans suppressed unauthorized soothsaying see Livy, xxxix. 16, and Pauli Sententt. Receptt. v. xxi. 1, 2, 3.

to magic arts, but the persecution in the East under Valens in 374, following the conspiracy of Theodore, obliterated all distinction. Commencing with those accused of magic, it extended to all who were noted for letters or philosophy. Terror reigned throughout the East; all who had libraries burned them. The prisons were insufficient to contain the prisoners, and in some towns it was said that fewer were left than were taken. Many were put to death, and the rest were stripped of their property. In the West, under Valentinian, persecution was not so sweeping, but the laws were enforced, at least in Rome, with sufficient energy to reduce greatly the number of sorcerers; and a law of Honorius, in 409, by its reference to the bishops, shows that the Church was beginning to participate with the State in the supervision over such offenders.* Yet that even the faithful could not be restrained from indulging in these forbidden practices is seen in the earnest exhortations addressed to them by their teachers, and the elaborate repetition of proofs that all such exhibitions of supernatural power were the work of demons.†

The Eastern Empire maintained its severity of legislation and continued with more or less success to repress the inextinguishable thirst for forbidden arts. From some transactions under Manuel and Andronicus Comnenus in the latter half of the twelfth century we learn that blinding was a usual punishment for such offences, that the classical forms of augury had disappeared to be replaced by necromantic formulas, and that such accusations were a convenient method of disposing of enemies.‡

---

* Ammian. Marcellin. XIX. xii. 14; XXVI. iii.; XXIX. i. 5–14, ii. 1–5.—Zozimi IV. 14.—Lib. IX. Cod. Theod. xvi. 7–12.

Yet favoritism led Valens to pardon Pollentianus, a military tribune, who confessed that, for the purpose of ascertaining the destiny of the imperial crown, he had ripped open a living woman and extracted her unborn babe to perform a hideous rite of necromancy (Am. Marcell. XXIX. ii. 17). In the later Roman augury, contaminated with Eastern rites, omens of the highest significance were found in the entrails of human victims, especially in those of the fœtus (Æl. Lamprid. Elagabal. 8.—Euseb. H. E. VII. 10, VIII. 14.—Paul. Diac. Hist. Miscell. XI.).

† Augustin. de Civ. Dei x. 9; XXI. 6; de Genesi ad Litteram XI.; de Divinat. Dæmon. v.; de Doctr. Christ. II. 20–4; Serm. 278.—Concil. Carthag. IV. ann. 398, c. 89.—Dracont. de Deo II. 324–7.—Leon. PP. I. Serm. XXVII. c. 3.

‡ Lib. IX. Cod. xviii. 2–6.—Basilicon Lib. LX. Tit. xxxix. 3, 28–32.—Photii

In the West the Barbarian domination introduced a new element. The Ostrogoths, who occupied Italy under Theodoric, were, it is true, so much Romanized that, although Arians, they adopted and enforced the laws against magic. Divination was classed with paganism and was capitally punished. About the year 500 we hear of a persecution which drove all the sorcerers from Rome, and Basilius, the chief thaumaturge among them, although he escaped at the time, was burned on venturing to return. When Italy fell back into the hands of the Eastern Empire the prosecution of these offences seems to have been committed to the Church as a part of its ever-widening sphere of influence and jurisdiction.*

The Wisigoths who took possession of Aquitaine and Spain, although less civilized than their Eastern brethren, were profoundly influenced by Roman legislation, and their princes issued repeated enactments to discourage the forbidden arts. It is significant of the Barbarian tenderness for human life, however, that the penalties were greatly less than those of the savage Roman edicts. A law of Recared declares magicians and diviners and those who consult them to be incapable of bearing testimony; one of Egiza places these crimes in the class for which a slave could be tortured against his accused master; and several edicts of Chindaswind provide, for those who invoke demons or bring hail upon vineyards, or use ligatures or charms to injure men or cattle or harvests, scourging with two hundred lashes, shaving, and carrying around for exhibition in the vicinage, to be followed by imprisonment. Those who consult diviners about the health of the king or of others are threatened with scourging and enslavement to the fisc, including confiscation, if their children are accomplices; judges who have recourse to divination for guidance in doubtful cases are subjected to the same penalties, while the simple observation of auguries is visited with fifty lashes. These provisions, which were mostly carried with little change into the Fuero Juzgo, remained the law of the Spanish Peninsula until the Middle Ages

---

Nomocanon. Tit. ix. cap. 25.—Nicet. Choniat. Man. Comnen. Lib. iv.; Andron. Lib. ii.

* Edict. Theodorici c. 108.—Gregor. PP. I. Dial. Lib. i. c. 4.—Cassiodor. Variar. iv. 22, 23, ix. 18.—Gregor. PP. I. Epist. xi. 53.

were well advanced. They show how impossible it had been to eradicate the old superstitions, and that the pagan observances and auguries still flourished among all classes, which is confirmed by the denunciations of the Spanish councils and ecclesiastical writers. They have a further significance as presenting a middle term between the severity of Rome and the laxity of the other Barbarian tribes.*

These latter were ruder and less amenable to Roman influences. In their conversion the Church rendered an immense service to humanity, and it did not dare to interfere too rudely with the customs and prejudices of its unruly neophytes; in fact, it harmonized its own with them as far as it could, and became considerably modified in consequence. This process is well symbolized in the instructions of Gregory the Great to Augustin, his missionary to England, to convert the pagan temples into churches by sprinkling them with holy water, so that converts might grow accustomed to their new faith by worshipping in the wonted places, while the sacrifices to demons were to be replaced by processions in honor of some saint or martyr, when oxen were to be slaughtered, not to propitiate idols, but in praise of God, to be eaten by the faithful. In this assimilation of Christianity to paganism it is not surprising that Redwald, King of East Anglia, after his conversion set up in his temple two altars, at one of which he worshipped the true God and at the other offered sacrifices to demons.† The similar adoption by Christian magic of elements from that which it supplanted is well illustrated by the hymn, or rather incantation, known as the Lorica of St. Patrick, in which the forces of nature and the Deity are both summoned as by an enchanter to the assistance of the thaumaturge. A MS. of the seventh century assures us that "Every person who sings it every day with all his attention on God shall not have demons appearing to his face. It will be a safeguard to him against sudden death. It will be a protection to him against every poison and envy. It will be an armor to his soul after his death. Patrick sang this at

---

* Ll. Wisigoth. II. iv. 1; VI. i. 4; VI. ii. 1, 3, 4, 5.—Fuero Juzgo II. iv. 1; VI. ii. 1, 3, 5.—Concil. Bracarens. II. ann. 572 c. 71.—Conc. Toletan. IV. ann. 633 c. 28.—Isidor. Hispalens. Etymol. VIII. 9; de Ord. Creatur. viii.—S. Pirmiani de Libb. Canon. Scarapsus.

† Haddan and Stubbs, Concil. III. 37.—Bedæ H. E. II. 15.

the time that the snares were set for him by Loegaire, so that it appeared to those who were lying in ambush that they were wild deer and a fawn after them." *

The Barbarians brought with them their own superstitions, whether transmitted from the prehistoric Aryan home, or acquired in the course of their wanderings, and they readily added to these such as they found among their new subjects, whether they were under the ban of the Church or not. They had parted from their brethren before the religious revolution caused by Zoroaster's dualistic conception of Hormazd and Ahriman, and their religions have no trace of a personification of the Evil Principle. Loki, its nearest representative, was rather tricky than incorrigible. It is true that there were evil beings, such as the Hrimthursar, Trolls,

---

* Haddan and Stubbs, II. 320–3. Three stanzas of the eleven of which the hymn consists will show its character as an incantation:

1.

I bind to myself to-day
The strong power of an invocation of the Trinity,
The faith of the Trinity in Unity,
The Creator of the elements.

4.

I bind to myself to-day
The power of Heaven,
The light of the Sun,
The whiteness of Snow,
The force of Fire,
The flashing of Lightning,
The velocity of Wind,
The stability of the Earth,
The hardness of Rocks.

6.

I have set around me all these powers,
Against every hostile savage power,
Directed against my body and my soul,
Against the incantations of false prophets,
Against the black laws of heathenism,
Against the false laws of heresy,
Against the deceits of idolatry,
Against the spells of women and smiths and druids,
Against all knowledge which blinds the soul of man.

or Jotuns, the Jotun-dragon Fafnir, the wolf Fenrir, Beowulf's
Grendal and others, but they were none of them analogous to the
Mazdean Ahriman or the Christian Satan, and when the Teutonic
races adopted the latter they came to represent him, as Grimm well
points out, rather as the blundering Jotun than as the arch-enemy.
To how late a period the ancestral conceptions of the spirit-world
prevailed in Germany may be seen in the answers of the learned
Abbot John of Trittenheim to the questions of Maximilian I.*

The Teutonic tribes had little to learn from the conquered
peoples in the wide circle of the magic arts, for in no race, probably, has the supernatural formed a larger portion of daily life,
or claimed greater power over both the natural and the spiritual
worlds. Divination in all its forms was universally practised.
Gifted beings known as *menn forspair* could predict the future
either by second sight, or by incantations, or by expounding
dreams. Still more dreaded and respected was the Vala or
prophetess, who was worshipped as superhuman and regarded
as in some way an embodiment of the subordinate Norns or
Fates, as in the case of Veleda, Aurinia, and others who, as Tacitus assures us, were regarded as goddesses, in accordance with the
German custom of thus venerating their fatidical women; and in
the Volüspa the Vala communes on equal terms with Odin himself.† For those not thus specially gifted there was ample store
of means to forecast the future. The most ordinary method was
by necromancy, either by placing under the tongue of a corpse a
piece of wood carved with appropriate runes, or by raising the
shades of the dead precisely as the Witch of Endor did with
Samuel, or as was practised in Rome.‡ The lot was also used extensively, whether to ascertain the divine will, like the Hebrew
Urim and Thummim, or to ascertain the future with a bundle of
sticks, apparently almost identical with the Chinese trigrams and
hexagrams.§ As in Greece and Rome, sacrifices were often offered

---

* Grimm's Teutonic Mythol., Stallybrass's Transl. III. 1028.—Trithem. Lib.
Quæst. Q. VI.

† Volsunga Saga, XXIV., XXV., XXXII. — Gripispa.—Keyser's Religion of the
Northmen, Pennock's Transl. pp. 191, 285–7.—Tacit. Histor. IV. 61, 65; German.
viii.—Volüspa, 2, 21, 22.

‡ Saxo. Grammat. Lib. I.—Havamal, 159.—Grougaldr, 1.—Vegtamskvida, 9.

§ Cæsar. de Bell. Gall. I. 53.—Remberti Vit. S. Anscharii c. 16, 23, 24, 27.—

to the gods in expectation of a response ; auguries were drawn from the flight of birds as carefully as by the Roman augurs, while the sacred chickens were replaced with white horses conse-. crated to the gods, whose motions and actions when harnessed to the sacred chariot were carefully observed.* Saving the Etruscan *haruspicium* and the omens derived from sacrificial victims, Hellenic and Italiote divination had little to distinguish it from that of the Teutons.

As regards magic, scarce any limit can be set to the power of the sorcerer. In no literature do his marvels fill a larger space, nor are the feats of wizard or witch received with more unquestioning faith than in what remains to us of the sagas of the North. Especially were the lands around the Baltic regarded as the peculiar home and nursery of sorcerers, whither people from every land, even from distant Greece and Spain, resorted for instruction or for special aid. In Adam of Bremen's "Churland" every house was full of diviners and necromancers, while the people of northern Norway could tell what every man in the world was doing, and could perform with ease all the evil deeds ascribed to witches in Holy Writ. Both Saxo Grammaticus and Snorri Sturlason, in their widely differing Euhemeristic accounts of the origin of the Æsir, or gods, agree that the founders of the Northern kingdom owed their deification solely to the magic skill which led their subjects and descendants to venerate them as divine.†

Tacit. German. x.—Ammian. Marcellin. xxxi. 2.—Carolomanni Capit. ii. ad Liptinas.—Carol. Mag. Capit. de Partibus Saxon. c. 23.

* Tacit. German. ix., x.

† Adam. Bremens. iv. 16, 31.—Saxon. Grammat. Lib. i.—Ynglinga Saga, 6, 7 (Laing's Heimskringla).

The Finns were not behind their neighbors in the powers attributed to spells and incantations. In the Kalevala, Louhi, the sorceress of the North, steals the sun and moon, which had come down from heaven to listen to Wainamoinen's singing, and hides them in a mountain, but is compelled to let them out again through dread of counter-spells. The powers of magic song are fairly summarized in the final contest between Wainamoinen and Youkahainen :

> "Bravely sang the ancient minstrel,
> Till the flinty rocks and ledges
> Heard the trumpet tone and trembled,
> And the copper-bearing mountains

Norse magic was roughly classified into that which was legitimate, or *galder*, and that which was wicked, or *seid*. To the former belonged the infinite powers of runes, whether sung as incantations or carved as talismans and amulets. Their invention was attributed to the ancient Hrimthursar or Jotuns, and it was his profound knowledge of this magic lore which enabled Odin to achieve his supremacy. Runes it was that kept the sun upon his course and maintained the order of nature. All runes were mingled together in the sacred drink of the Æsir, whence were derived their supernatural attributes, and some have been allowed

----

Shook along their deep foundations,
Flinty rocks flew straight asunder,
Falling cliffs afar were scattered,
All the solid earth resounded,
And the ocean billows answered.
　　And, alas! for Youkahainen,
Lo! his sledge so fairly fashioned,
Floats, a waif upon the ocean.
Lo! his pearl-enamelled birch-rod
Lies, a weed upon the margin.
Lo! his steed of shining forehead
Stands, a statue in the torrent,
And his hame is but a fir-bough
And his collar naught but corn-straw.
　　Still the minstrel sings unceasing,
And, alas! for Youkahainen,
Sings his sword from out his scabbard,
Hangs it in the sky before him
As it were a gleam of lightning;
Sings his bow, so gayly blazoned,
Into driftwood on the ocean;
Sings his finely feathered arrows
Into swift and screaming eagles;
Sings his dog, with crooked muzzle,
Into stone-dog squatting near him;
Into sea-flowers sings his gauntlets,
And his vizor into vapor,
And himself, the sorry fellow,
Ever deeper in his torture,
In the quicksand to the shoulder,
To his hip in mud and water."

—*Porter's Selections from the Kalevala*, pp. 84–5.

to reach man, which were carefully classified and studied.* As an adjunct of these was the *seidstaf*, or wand, so indispensable to the magician of all races. The Icelandic Vala Thordis had one of these known as Hangnud, which would deprive of memory him whom it touched on the right cheek and restore it with a touch on the left cheek. Philtres and love-potions, causing irresistible desire or indifference or hatred, were among the ordinary resources of Norse magic. Pricking with the sleep-thorn produced magic sleep for an indefinite time. Magicians could also throw themselves into a deep trance, while the spirit wandered abroad in some other form: women who were accustomed to do this were called *hamleypur*, and if the *ham*, or assumed form, were injured, the hurt would be found on the real body—a belief common to almost all races.† The adept, moreover, could assume any form at will, as in the historical case of the wizard who in the shape of a whale swam to Iceland as a spy for Harold Gormsson of Denmark, when the latter was planning an expedition thither; or two persons could exchange appearances, as Signy did with a witch-wife, or Sigurd with Gunnar, when Brynhild was deceived into marrying

---

* Havamal, 142, 150–63.—Harbarsdliod, 20. — Sigrdrifumal, 6–13, 15–18.—Skirnismal, 36.—Rigsmal, 40, 41.—Grougaldr, 6–14.

† Harbardsliod, 20. — Skirnismal, 26–34.—Keyser, op. cit. pp. 270, 293.—Hyndluliod, 43.—Lays of Sigurd and Brynhild.—Gudrunarkvida, II. 21.—Sigrdrifumal, 4.

At the close of the fifteenth century, Sprenger relates (Mall. Maleficar. P. II. Q. i. c. 9) as a recent occurrence in a town in the diocese of Strassburg, that a laborer cutting wood in a forest was attacked by three enormous cats, which after a fierce encounter he succeeded in beating off with a stick. An hour afterwards he was arrested and cast in a dungeon on the charge of brutally beating three ladies of the best families in the town, who were so injured as to be confined to their beds, and it was not without considerable difficulty that he proved his case and was discharged under strict injunctions of secrecy. Gervais of Tilbury, early in the thirteenth century, had already referred to such occurrences as an established fact (Otia Imp. Decis. III. c. 93).

The same belief was current among the Slavs. Prior to the conversion of Bohemia, in a civil war under Necla, a youth summoned to battle had a witch stepmother who predicted defeat, but counselled him, if he wished to escape, to kill the first enemy he met, cut off his ears and put them in his pocket. He obeyed and returned home in safety, but found his dearly beloved bride dead, with a sword-thrust in the bosom and both ears off—which he had in his pocket.—Æn. Sylv. Hist. Bohem. c. 10.

the latter.* Enchanted swords that nothing could resist, enchanted coats that nothing could penetrate, caps of darkness
which, like the Greek helm of Pluto, rendered the wearer invisible, are of frequent occurrence in Norse legendary history.†

All this was more or less lawful magic, while the impious sorcery known as *seid* or *trolldom* was based on a knowledge of the
evil secrets of nature or the invocation of malignant spirits, such
as the Jotuns and their troll-wives. *Seid* is apparently derived
from *sjoda*, to seethe or boil, indicating that its spells were
wrought by boiling in a caldron the ingredients of the witches'
hell-broth, as we see it done in Macbeth. It was deemed infamous, unworthy of men, and was mostly left to women, known
as *seid konur*, or seid wives, and as "riders of the night." In the
oldest text of the Salic law, which shows no trace of Christian influence, the only allusion to sorcery is a fine imposed for calling a
woman a witch, or for stigmatizing a man as one who carries the
caldron for a witch.‡ Scarce any limit was assigned to the power
of these sorcerers. One of their most ordinary feats was the raising and allaying of tempests, and to such perfection was this
brought that storm and calm could be enclosed in bags for use by
the possessor, like those which Æolus gave to Ulysses. As Christianity spread, this power gave rise to trials of strength between
the old and the new religion, such as we have seen when Constantine overcame Licinius. St. Olaf's first expedition to Finland
barely escaped destruction from a dreadful tempest excited by the
Finnish sorcerers. Olaf Tryggvesson was more fortunate in one
of his missionary raids, when he defeated Raud the Strong and
drove him to his fastness on Godo Island in the Salten Fiord—a
piece of water whose fierce tidal currents were more dreaded than
the Maelström itself. Repeated attempts to follow him were vain,
for, no matter how fair was the weather outside, inside Raud maintained a storm in which no ship could live. At length Olaf invoked the aid of Bishop Sigurd, who promised to test whether

---

* Olaf Tryggvesson's Saga, 37 (Laing's Heimskringla).—Volsunga Saga, VII.,
XXVII.—Sigurdtharkvida Fafnisbana I. 37, 38.

† Olaf Haraldsson's Saga, 204, 240 (Laing's Heimskringla).—Volsunga Saga,
III. 15.—Keyser, op. cit. p. 294.

‡ Havamal, 157.—Harbardsliod, 20.—L. Salic. Tit. lxiv. (First Text of Pardessus).

God would vouchsafe to overcome the devil. Tapers and vestments and holy water and sacred texts were too much for the evil spirits; the king's ships sailed into the fiord with smooth water around them, though everywhere else the waves ran high enough to hide the mountains: Raud was captured, and, as he obstinately refused baptism, Olaf put him to the most cruel death that his ingenuity could devise.*

The sorcerer also had endless power of creating illusions. A beleaguered wizard could cause a flock of sheep to appear like a band of warriors hastening to his assistance. Yet this would appear superfluous, since by his glances alone he could convulse nature and cause instant death. Gunhild, who married King Eric Blood-Axe, says of the two Lap sorcerers who taught her magic: "When they are angry the very earth turns away in terror and whatever living thing they look upon falls dead." When she betrayed them to Eric she cast them into a deep sleep and drew seal-skin bags over their heads, so that Eric and his men could despatch them in safety. Similarly when Olaf Pa surprised Stigandi asleep he drew a skin over the wizard's head. There chanced to be a small hole in it through which Stigandi's glance fell upon the grassy slope of an opposite mountain, whereupon the spot was torn up with a whirlwind and living herb never grew there again.†

One of the most terrifying powers of the witch was her fearful cannibalism, a belief which the Teutons shared with the Romans. This is referred to in some of the texts of the Salic law and in the legislation of Charlemagne, and the unlimited extent of popular credulity with regard to it is seen in an adventure of Thorodd, an envoy of St. Olaf, who saw a witch-wife tear eleven men to pieces, throw them on the fire, and commence devouring them, when she was driven off.‡

---

* Grougaldr.—Olaf Haraldsson's Saga, 8.—Olaf Tryggvesson's Saga, 85–7. (Laing's Heimskringla).

† Keyser, op. cit. pp. 268, 271–2.—Harald Harfaager's Saga, 34 (Laing's Heimskringla).—All this is nearly equalled by the powers attributed in 1437 by Eugenius IV. to the witches of his time, who by a simple word or touch or sign could regulate the weather or bewitch whom they pleased (Raynald. ann. 1437, No. 27).

‡ L. Salic. Text. Herold, Tit. lxvii (also in the third text of Pardessus, and the L. Emendata Tit. lxvii., but not in the others).—Capit. Carol. Mag. de Partibus

The *trolla-thing*, or nocturnal gathering of witches, where they danced and sang and prepared their unholy brewage in the caldron, was a customary observance of these wise-women, especially on the first of May (St. Walpurgis' Night), which was the great festival of pagandom.* We shall see hereafter the portentous growth of this, which developed into the Witches' Sabbat. It is a feature common to the superstition of many races, the origin of which cannot be definitely assigned to any.

That the practice of this impious sorcery was deemed infamous is clear from the provision of the Salic law, already alluded to, imposing a fine of eighty-nine sols for calling a free woman a witch without being able to prove it. Yet the mere addiction to it in pagan times was not a penal offence, and penalties were only inflicted for injuries thus committed on person or property. In extreme cases, where death was encompassed, there seems to have been a popular punishment of lapidation, which was the fate incurred, after due sentence, by three noted sorcerers, Katla and Kotkel and Grima. The codified laws of the barbarians, however, never prescribed the death penalty, fines being the universal retribution for crime, and in a later text of the Salic law two hundred sols is designated for the witch who eats a man. Yet individual cases can be found of persecution, such as that by Harald Harfaager, whose early experience had inspired him with intense hatred of the art. One of his sons, Rögnvald Rettilbein, received from him the government of Hadeland, where he learned sorcery and became a great adept; so when Vitgeir, a noted wizard of Hordeland, was ordered by Harald to abandon his evil ways he retorted:

> "The danger surely is not great,
> From wizard born of mean estate,
> When Harald's son in Hadeland,
> King Rögnvald, to the art lays hand."

Rögnvald's wrong-doing being thus betrayed, Harald lost no time in despatching Eric Blood-Axe, his son by another wife, who promptly burned his half-brother in a house, along with eighty

---

Saxoniæ ann. 794, c. vi.—Olaf Haraldsson's Saga, 151 (Laing's Heimskringla). **Cf.** Horace (Ars Poet.), "Neu pransæ Lamiæ vivum puerum extrahat alvo."

* Grimm, op. cit. III. 1044, 1050–1.

other sorcerers—a piece of practical justice which we are told met with general popular applause.*

Such were the beliefs and practices of the races with which the Church had to do in its efforts to obliterate paganism and sorcery. There was little difference between the provinces which had belonged to the empire and the regions over which Christianity began for the first time to spread, for in the former the conquerors and the conquered were imbued, as we have just seen, with superstitions nearly akin. The exchange of imperial for barbarian rule worked the same result as to sorcery as that related in a former chapter with regard to the persecution of heresy, though it must be borne in mind that, while heresy almost disappeared in the intellectual hebetude of the times, sorcery grew ever more vigorous. Its suppression was practically abandoned. As mentioned above, the earliest text of the Salic law provides no general penalty for it. In subsequent recensions, besides the fine imposed for cannibalism, some MSS. have clauses imposing fines for bewitching with ligatures and killing men with incantations—in the latter case, with the alternative of burning alive—but even these disappear in the *Lex Emendata* of Charlemagne, possibly in consequence of the legislation of the Capitularies described below. The Ripuarian code only treats murder by sorcery like any other homicide, to be compounded for by the ordinary wer-gild, or blood-money, and for injuries thus inflicted it provides a fine of one hundred sols, to be avoided by compurgation with six conjurators. The other codes are absolutely silent on the subject.†

As under the Frankish rule laws were personal and not territorial, the Gallo-Roman population was still governed by the Roman law, but evidently there was no attempt made to enforce it. Gregory of Tours relates for us several miracles to prove the superiority of the Christian magic of relics and invocation of saints over the popular magic of the conjurer, which indicate that the

---

* L. Salic. First Text, Tit. lxiv. § 2 ; Text. Herold. Tit. lxvii. ; Third Text, Tit. lxiv.—Blackwell's Mallet, Bohn's Ed. p. 524.—Keyser, op. cit. pp. 266-7.—Harald Harfaager's Saga, 25, 36 (Laing's Heimskringla).

† L. Salic. Text. Herold. Tit. xxii. ; MS. Guelferbit. Tit. xix.—L. Ripuar. Tit. lxxxiii.

first impulse of the people in case of accident or sudden sickness was to send for the nearest *ariolus*, or practitioner of forbidden arts, and that the profession was exercised openly and without fear of punishment, in spite of repeated condemnations by the councils of the period. How little such persons had to fear is seen in the case of a woman of Verdun, who professed to be a soothsayer and to discover stolen goods. She was so successful that she drove a thriving trade, purchased her freedom of her master, and accumulated a store of money. At length she was brought before Bishop Ageric, who only treated her for demoniacal possession with exorcisms and inunctions of holy oil, and finally discharged her.*

Occasionally, of course, cases occurred in which the unrestrained passions of the Merovingians wreaked savage cruelty on those who had incurred their ill-will, but these were exceptional and outside of the law. When Fredegonda lost two children by pestilence, her stepson Clovis was accused of causing it by sorcery. The woman designated as his accomplice was tortured until she confessed, and was burned, although she retracted her confession, after which Chilperic delivered his son Clovis to Fredegonda, who caused him to be assassinated. When, subsequently, another son, Thierry,

---

* Greg. Turon. de Mirac. Lib. ii. c. 45 ; de Mirac. S. Martini Lib. i. c. 26.— Concil. Venetic. ann. 465 c. 16.—Concil. Agathens. ann. 506 c. 42, 68.—C. Aurelianens. I. ann. 511 c. 30.—C. Autissiodor. ann. 578 c. 4.—C. Narbonnens. ann. 589 c. 14.—C. Remens. ann. 630 c. 14.—C. Rotomagens. ann. 650 c. 4.—Greg. Turon. Hist. Francor. vii. 44.

The hostility of Christian magic to its rivals extended even to rational medicine. Gregory of Tours develops the teaching of St. Nilus by giving examples to show that it was a sin to have recourse to natural remedies, such as bloodletting, instead of trusting wholly to the intercession of saints.—Hist. Franc. v. 6 ; de Mirac. S. Martini ii. 60.

It was in vain for the Church to proscribe goetic magic while it fostered the beliefs on which the superstition was based by encouraging the practice of sacred magic. For example, there was little use in endeavoring to suppress amulets and charms while the faithful were taught to carry the Agnus Dei, or figure of a lamb stamped in wax remaining from the paschal candles, and consecrated by the pope. In forbidding the decoration and sale of these in 1471, Paul II. expatiates on their efficacy in preserving from fire and shipwreck, in averting tempests and lightning and hail, and in assisting women in childbirth.—Raynald. ann. 1471, No. 58.

died in 584, Mummolus, the royal favorite, whom Fredegonda disliked, was accused of having caused it by incantations. Thereupon she seized some women of Paris, and by scourging and torture forced them to confess themselves sorceresses who had caused numerous deaths, including that of Thierry, whose soul was accepted in place of that of Mummolus. Some of these poor wretches were simply put to death, others she burned, and others she broke on the wheel. Chilperic then caused Mummolus to be tortured by suspension with his arms tied behind his back, but he only confessed to having obtained from the women philtres and ointments to secure the favor of the king and queen. Unluckily he said to the executioner on being taken down, " Tell the king that I feel no ill from what has been done." On hearing this Chilperic exclaimed, " Is he really a sorcerer that this does not hurt him ?" and had him stretched on a rack and scourged with leathern thongs till the executioners were exhausted. Mummolus finally begged his life of Fredegonda, but was stripped of his possessions and sent in a wagon to his native city, Bordeaux, where he died on his arrival. Cases like this throw light on the beliefs of the period, but not upon its judicial routine.*

The Lombards in Italy fell to a greater degree under Roman influence, and towards the close of their domination adopted general laws of some severity against the practice of sorcery, irrespective of the injury committed. The sorcerer was to be sold as a slave beyond the province, and the price received was divided between the judge and other officials, according to their respective merits in the prosecution : if through bribes or pity the judge refused to condemn, he was mulcted in his whole wer-gild, or the amount of his blood-money, and half as much if he neglected to discover a sorcerer who was found out by another. The penalty for consulting a sorcerer, or for not informing on him, or for performing incantations, was half the wer-gild of the offender. At the same time the grosser superstitions were rejected, and Rotharis forbade putting sorceresses to death, under the popular belief that they could devour men internally.†

In the long anarchy which accompanied the fall of the Mero-

---

* Greg. Turon. Hist. Franc. v. 40 ; vii. 35.

† L. Langobard. ii. xxxviii. l. 2 (Liutprand).—i. ii. 9 (Rotharis).

vingians, all respect for the Church, its precepts and observances, was well-nigh lost throughout the Frankish kingdoms. One of the incidents of reconstruction, as the Carlovingian dynasty slowly emerged, and as St. Boniface, under papal authority, sought to restore the Church, was the suppression of Bishop Adalbert, who taught the invocation of the angels Uriel, Raguel, Tubuel, Inias, Tubuas, Sabaoc, and Simiel. Adalbert was venerated as a saint, and the clippings of his nails and hair were treasured as relics. Repeated condemnations at home had no effect on this false worship of angels, and Pope Zachary held, in 745, a synod in Rome which declared it to be a worship of demons, as the only angels whose names are known are Michael, Gabriel, and Raphael. Yet this superstition took so firm a hold upon the people that it was long before it could be eradicated; indeed, it seems to be alluded to, even in the middle of the tenth century, by Atto of Vercelli.* When such was the condition of the Church, no suppression of sorcery was to be looked for.

Among the instructions to Boniface and his fellow-missionaries was the eradication of all pagan observances, including divination, sorcery, and cognate superstitions. As the Church became reorganized, councils were held in 742 and 743, in which Church and State united in prohibiting them, although only a moderate fine was threatened, but the ecclesiastical jurisdiction over such offences was established by ordering the bishops to make yearly visitations of their sees to suppress paganism and the forbidden arts. Boniface, however, complained to Zachary that when the Frank or German visited Rome he saw there, openly practised, the things which they were laboriously endeavoring to suppress at home. The first of January was celebrated with pagan dances; women wore amulets and ligatures, and publicly offered them for sale. The pope could only reply that these things had long ago been prohibited, but as they had broken out afresh he had forbidden them again—but we may be assured without success.†

---

* Concil. Suessionens. ann. 744.—Zachar. PP. Epist. 9, 10.—Bonifacii Epist. lvii. — Synod. Roman. ann. 745 (Bonifacii Opp. III. 10). — Carol. Mag. Capit. Aquisgr. ann. 789 c. 16.—Capit. Herardi Archiep. Turon. ann. 838 c. 3 (Baluz. Capitular. I. 677).—Atton. Vercell. Capitular. c. 48.

† Gregor. PP. II. Capit. data legatis in Bavariam, c. 8, 9.—Concil. German. L

In the Carlovingian reconstruction which followed, efforts were made to suppress all superstitious arts, and they were treated with gradually increasing severity, but still with comparative lenity. The most vigorous legislation was an edict of Charlemagne in 805, which confides the matter to the Church, and orders the archpriest of each diocese to investigate all who were accused of divination or sorcery, apparently permitting moderate torture to obtain confession, and keeping the culprits in prison until they amend. In his efforts to christianize Saxony, on the one hand Charlemagne punished with death all who burned witches and ate them, under the belief so widely spread that they ate men, and on the other hand all soothsayers and sorcerers were made over to the Church as slaves. During this period, moreover, and for a couple of centuries following, the parallel legislation of the Church, inflicting spiritual penalties, was singularly mild, although the different penitentials vary so much that it is impossible to deduce any system from them. That which passes under the name of Theodore of Canterbury, and was of general authority, only prescribes a penance of twoscore days or a year for sorcery, or, if the offender is an ecclesiastic, three years, but it orders seven years for placing a child on a roof or in an oven to cure it of fever, and Ecbert of York indicates five years for the same practice. There evidently was no settled rule, but the most systematic code is that of Gaerbald, who was Bishop of Liége about the year 800. He orders all offenders to be brought before him for trial, and enacts seven years' penance and liberal almsgiving for committing homicide by means of sorcery, seven years without almsgiving for rendering the victim insane, five years and almsgiving for consulting diviners or practising augury from birds, seven years for sorcerers who bring on tempests, three years and almsgiving for honoring sorcerers, one year for sorcery to excite love, provided it did not result in death, but if the offender was a monk, the penalty was increased to five years. Another penitential of the period prescribes twoscore days or a year for divination or diabolical incantations, but seven years if a woman threatens another with sorcery, to be reduced to four if she is poor. In 829 the Council of

---

(Caroloman. Capit. I., Baluz. I. 104–5).—Concil. Liptinens ann. 743 (Caroloman. Capit. II., Baluz. I. 106–8).—Bonifac. Epistt. 49, 63.—Zachar. PP. Epist. II. c. 6.

Paris attributes the misfortunes of the empire to the prevalence of crime, and especially of sorcery; it quotes the savage provisions of the Mosaic law, and enumerates at considerable length the evil deeds of the offenders—how men are rendered insane by philtres and love-potions, how tempests and hail are induced, how harvests and milk and fruits are transferred from their lawful owners, and how the future is predicted, but it indicates no penalties, and only asks the secular rulers to punish these crimes sharply. Similarly Erard, Archbishop of Tours, in 838 uttered a general prohibition, but only threatened public penance without indicating details. All that we can gather from this confused legislation, from the collections known as the Capitularies, and from the speculations and arguments of Rabanus Maurus and Hincmar of Reims, is that every species of divination and sorcery, Roman and Teutonic, was rife; that it was held to derive its power directly from Satan; that the Church was wholly unable to deal with it; that secular legislation threatened only moderate penalties, and that these were for the most part wholly unenforced.*

Yet, outside of the organized machinery of the Church and State, there was a rough popular justice—a sort of Lynch law—which handled individual offenders with scant ceremony. A chance allusion about this period to Gerberga, who was drowned by the Emperor Lothair in the river Arar, "as is customary with sorcerers," indicates that much was going on not provided for in the Capitularies. The same is seen in a curious statement by St. Agobard, Archbishop of Lyons, who waged such ineffectual battle with many of the superstitions of the time. One of these, as we have seen, was that tempests could be caused by sorcery—a belief which the Church at first pronounced heretical because it inferred

---

* Carol. Mag. Capit. Aquisgr. ann. 789 c. 18, 63; Capit. II. ann. 806 c. 25; Capit. de Partibus Saxon. ann. 789 c. 6, 23.—S. Gregor. PP. III. De Crimin. et Remed. 16.—Theodori Pœnitent. Lib. I. c. xv. (Haddan and Stubbs, III. 190).—Egberti Pœnitent. VIII. 1 (Ib. p. 424).—Burchardi Decret. x. 8, 24, 28, 31.—Ghaerbaldi Instruct. Pastoral. c. x.; Judic. Sacerdotal. c. x., xi., xx., xxiv., xxv., xxxi., xxxvi. (Martene Ampl. Coll. VII. 25–33).—Libell. de Remed. Peccat. c. 9 (Ib. p. 44).—Concil. Paris. ann. 829 Lib. III. c. 2 (Harduin. IV. 1352).—Herardi Turon. Capit. iii. ann. 838 (Baluz. I. 1285).—Capitul. I. 21, 63; v. 69; VI. 215; Addit. II. c. 21.—Rabani Mauri de Magicis Artibus.—Hincmar. de Divort. Lothar. Interrog. xv.

the Manichæan dualistic theory, which placed the visible world under the control of Satan, but which it finally accepted as orthodox, and Thomas Aquinas proved that, with the permission of God, demons could bring about perturbations of the air. Agobard tells us that the belief in his province was universal, among all ranks, that there was a region named Magonia, whence ships came in the clouds and carried back thither the harvests destroyed by hail, the Tempestarii, as these sorcerers were called, being paid by the Magonians for bringing on the storms. Whenever the rumbling of thunder was heard it was a customary remark that a sorcerer's wind was coming. These Tempestarii carried on their nefarious trade in secrecy, but there was a recognized class of practitioners who professed to be able to neutralize them, and were regularly paid for doing so with a portion of the crops, which came to be known as the "canonical portion," and men who paid no tithes and gave nothing in charity were regular in contributing to these impostors. On one occasion three men and a woman were seized, charged with being Magonians who had fallen from one of their aerial ships. A meeting of the people was summoned, before whom the prisoners were brought in chains, and they were promptly condemned to be stoned to death, when Agobard himself came to the rescue, and after prolonged argument succeeded in procuring their liberation. A similar instance of extra-judicial action was seen when a destructive murrain invaded the herds, and the story spread that it was caused by Grimoald, Duke of Benevento, who, out of enmity to Charlemagne, sent emissaries to scatter a magic powder on the mountains and fields and streams. As Agobard says, every inhabitant of Benevento, with three wagons apiece, could not have sprinkled a territory so extensive as that affected, but nevertheless large numbers of wretches were captured and put to death on the charge of being concerned in the matter. When he adds that it was marvellous that these persons confessed their pretended crime, and could not be prevented from bearing false witness against themselves, either by scourging, torture, or the fear of death, we learn the means adopted to secure conviction ; and in this early and irregular instance of the use of torture we see a foreshadowing of the time when all the extravagant absurdities of the Witches' Sabbat were, by the same efficacious methods, eagerly confessed, and the confessions persisted in to the stake. We see also what an atmosphere of superstitious terror pervaded the life of Europe.*

Carlovingian civilization was but a brief episode in the darkness of those dreary centuries. In the disorder which accompanied the breaking-up of the empire, the organization of feudalism, and the founding of the European monarchies, although the Church was quietly attributing to itself the functions and the jurisdiction on which were based its subsequent claims of theocratic supremacy, it took no efficient steps to destroy the kingdom of Satan, though his agents the diviners and sorcerers were as numerous as ever. The Council of Pavia in 850 merely prescribed penance during life for sorceresses who undertook to provoke love and hatred, leading to the death of many victims. There may have been an occasional explosion of popular cruelty, such as indicated by the brief mention in a doubtful MS. of the burning of a number of sorcerers in Saxony in 914, but in fact the Church came almost virtually to tolerate them. About the middle of the tenth century Bishop Atto of Vercelli felt it necessary to revive and publish anew a forgotten canon of the Fourth Council of Toledo, which threatened with degradation and perpetual penance in a monastery any bishop, priest, deacon, or other ecclesiastic who should consult magicians or sorcerers or augurs. Atto, however, was a puritan, who endeavored to resist the general demoralization of the age. How little repugnance was felt for the forbidden arts is seen in the fact that the reputation for necromantic skill gained in Spain did not prevent the election of Gerbert of Aurillac to the archiepiscopal sees of Reims and Ravenna, and finally to the papacy itself; while as late as 1170 we have seen an

---

* Nithardi Hist. Lib. I. c. 5, ann. 834.—Concil. Bracarens. I. ann. 563 c. 8.—Burchard. Decret. x. 8.—Ivon. Decret. XI. 36.—Bernardi Comens. de Strigiis c. 14.—Ghaerbald. Judic. Sacerd. 20.—Herard. Turon. capit. iii.—Conc. Paris. ann. 829 Lib. III. c. 2.—S. Agobardi Lib. de Grandine c. 1, 2, 15, 16.

Even as late as the eleventh century Bishop Burchard prescribes penance for believing that sorcerers can affect the weather or influence the human mind to affection or hatred (Decret. XIX. 5). In less than two centuries and a half Thomas of Cantimpré shows that it was perfectly orthodox to assert that tempests were caused by demons (Bonum universale, Lib. II. c. 56).—It could scarce be otherwise when we consider the complete control over the weather attributed to sorcerers in Norse magic, and the adoption of the heathen superstitions by mediæval Christianity.

archbishop of Besançon have recourse to an ecclesiastic skilled in necromancy to aid him in detecting some heretics.*

In fact, the Church occupied an inconsistent attitude. Occasionally it took the enlightened view that these beliefs were groundless superstitions. An Irish council of the ninth century anathematizes any Christian who believes in the existence of witches, and forces him to recant before admitting him to reconciliation. Similarly, in 1080, Gregory VII. in writing to Harold the Simple of Denmark, strongly reproves the custom of attributing to priests and women all tempests, sickness, and other bodily misfortunes: these are the judgments of God, and to wreak vengeance for them on the innocent is only to provoke still more the divine wrath. More generally, however, the Church admitted their truth and sought, though with little energy, to repress them with spiritual censures. This halting position is well illustrated by the canons of Burchard, Bishop of Worms, in the early part of the eleventh century, where sometimes it is the belief in the existence of sorcery that is penanced, and sometimes it is the practice of the art. If confessors, moreover, followed Burchard's instructions and interrogated their penitents in detail as to the various magic processes which they might have performed, it could only result in disseminating a knowledge of those wicked arts in a most suggestive way. At the same time Burchard, like the other canonists, Regino of Pruhm and Ivo of Chartres, gave an ample store of prohibitory canons drawn from the early councils and the writings of the fathers, showing that the reality of sorcery was freely admitted as well as the duty of the Church to combat it. So implicit was

---

* Concil. Ticinens. ann. 850 c. 25.—Annal. Corbeiens. ann. 914 (Leibnit. S. R. Brunsvic. II. 299).—Atton. Vercell. Capit. c. 48.—Sigebert. Gemblacens. ann. 995.—Alberic. Trium Font. ann. 998, 999, 1002.—Cæsar. Heisterbach. Dist. v. c. 18.

For the acquirements of Gerbert of Aurillac see Richeri Hist. Lib. ii. c. xliii. sqq. A man capable of making, in the tenth century, a sphere to represent the earth, with the Arctic Circle and Tropic of Cancer traced on it, might well pass for a magician, although the sphericity of the earth was no secret to the Arabic philosophers (Avicenna de Cœlo et Mundo c. x.). How durable was Gerbert's unsavory reputation is seen in the retention of the stories concerning him by the mediæval historians down to the time of Platina (Ptol. Lucens. Hist. Eccles. Lib. XVIII. c. vi.-viii.—Platinæ Vit. Pontif. s. v. Silvest. II.).

the belief in magic powers that the Church conceded the dissolution of the indissoluble sacrament of matrimony when the consummation of marriage was prevented by the arts of the sorcerer,
and exorcisms and prayers and almsgiving and other ecclesiastical
remedies proved powerless for three years to overcome the power
of Satan. Guibert of Nogent relates, with pardonable pride, that
although this occurred when his father and mother were married,
through the malice of a stepmother, yet his mother resisted all
persuasion to avail herself of a divorce, although the impediment
continued for seven years, and the spell was broken at last, not
by priestly ministrations, but by an ancient wise-woman. Such
a cause was alleged when Philip Augustus abandoned his bride,
Ingeburga of Denmark, on their marriage-day, and Bishop Durand,
in his *Speculum Juris*, tells us that these cases were of daily occurrence. Even so enlightened a man as John of Salisbury airs his
learning in describing all the varieties of magic, and is careful to
define that if sorcerers kill men with the violence of their spells
it is through the permission of God; while Peter of Blois, if he
shows himself superior to the vulgar belief in omens, admits the
potency of Satanic suggestiveness in the darker forms of magic.*

With this universal belief in sorcery and in its diabolic origin,
there seems to have been no thought of enforcing the severity of
the laws. About 1030, Poppo, Archbishop of Trèves, sent to a
nun a piece of his cloak of which to make him a pair of shoes to
be worn in saying mass. She bewitched them so that when he

---

* Synod. Patricii c. 16 (Haddan and Stubbs, II. 329).—Gregor. PP. VII. Re-
gist. VII. 21.—Reginon. de Discip. Eccles. II. 347 sqq.—Burchardi Decret. Lib.
x., Lib. XIX. c. 5.—Ivon. Decreti P. XI.—Ivon. Panorm. VI. 117; VIII. 61 sqq.—P.
II. Decret. caus. XXXIII. Q. 1, c. 4. — Mall. Maleficar. P. I. Q. 8. — Guibert. Noviogent. de Vita sua I. 12.—Rigord. de Gest. Phil. Aug. ann. 1193.—Durandi
Specul. Juris Lib. IV., Partic. iv., Rubr. de Frigidis, etc.—Johann. Saresberiens.
Polycrat. II. 9–12.—Pet. Blesens. Epist. 65.

The belief in "ligatures" is one of the oldest and most universal of superstitions. Herodotus (II. 181) relates that Amasis who reigned in Egypt about
the middle of the sixth century B. C., found himself thus afflicted when he married the Cyrenean princess Ladice. Notwithstanding the political importance of
maintaining the alliance cemented by the marriage, he accused her of employing sorcery and threatened her with death. In her extremity she made a vow
in the temple of Venus to send a statue of the goddess to Cyrene. Her prayer
was heard and her life was saved.

put them on he found himself dying of love for her. He resisted the desire and gave the shoes to one of his chief ecclesiastics, who experienced the same effect. The experiment was tried with like result on all the principal clergy of the cathedral, and when the evidence was overwhelming the fair offender was condemned simply to expulsion from the convent, while Poppo himself expiated his transient passion by a pilgrimage to the Holy Land. It was felt, however, that the discipline of the nunnery must be dangerously lax, and the other nuns were given the option of adopting a stricter rule or of dispersion. They chose the latter, and were replaced with a body of monks. When, in 1074, a revolt in Cologne forced the archbishop to fly, it is related among the excesses of the triumphant rebels that they threw from the walls and killed a woman defamed for having crazed a number of men by magic arts. That was regarded as a crime which three centuries later would have been a manifestation of praiseworthy zeal. About the same time a council in Bohemia warns the faithful not to have recourse in their troubles to sorcerers; but it only prescribes confession and repentance and to abstain from a repetition of the offence.*

Still, the accusation of sorcery was felt to be damaging, and as it was easy to bring and hard to disprove, it was bandied about somewhat recklessly. It was not enough for Berenger of Tours to be compelled to abjure his notions concerning transubstantiation, but he was stigmatized as the most expert of necromancers. In the bitter strife of Gregory VII. with the empire, when, in 1080, the Synod of Brescia deposed him and elected Wiberto of Ravenna as antipope, one of the reasons alleged against him was that he was a manifest necromancer—an art which he was supposed to have learned in Toledo. The manner in which partisanship availed itself of this method of attack is curiously illustrated by the opposing accounts given of Liutgarda, niece of Egilbert, Archbishop of Trèves, at this period. He was a resolute imperialist, and accepted his pallium from Wiberto, after which he made Liutgarda abbess of a convent in his diocese. The account of his episcopate is written by a contemporary; one MS., which is

---

* Gest. Treviror. Archiep. c. 19.—Lambert. Hersfeld. Annal. ann. 1074.—Höfler, Prager Concilien, p. xvi.

doubtless the genuine one, describes her as a cultured and exemplary woman, who ruled her nunnery in the service of God for forty years, leaving a happy memory behind her; another MS. of the same chronicle calls her a blasphemous witch and sorceress, under whose government the convent was almost ruined. After the Church had triumphed over the empire, it is easy to understand why such an interpolation should have been made.*

While thus the ancient laws against sorcery were practically falling into desuetude on the Continent, the legislation of the Anglo-Saxons shows that in England *lyblac* or witchcraft was the object of greater solicitude. About the year 900 the laws of Edward and Guthrum class witches and diviners with perjurers, murderers, and strumpets, who are ordered to be driven from the land, with the alternatives of reforming, of being executed, or of paying heavy fines—a provision which was repeatedly re-enacted by succeeding monarchs to the time of Cnut. Athelstan soon after decreed that when death was caused by *lyblac*, and the perpetrator confessed it, he should pay with his life; if he denied, he underwent the triple ordeal: failing in this he was imprisoned for four months, after which his kinsmen could release him on paying the wer-gild of the slain, the heavy fine of one hundred and twenty shillings to the king, and giving security for his good behavior. Towards the middle of the tenth century, Edward the Elder denounced perpetual excommunication for *lyblac* unless the offender repented. In the compilation known as the Laws of Henry I. murder by sorcery forfeited the privilege of redemption by paying wer-gild, and the perpetrator was handed over to the kinsmen of the slain, to be dealt with at their pleasure. For minor injuries thus caused, redemption was allowed as in other cases. When the accused denied, he was tried before the bishop, thus subjecting this offence to ecclesiastical jurisdiction. This severity seems to have changed with the Norman Conquest, for William the Conqueror, when besieging the Island of Ely, by advice of Ivo Taillebois placed at the head of his army a sorceress whose incantations were expected to paralyze the resistance of the defenders. Unluckily for the scheme, Hereward of Burgh made a flank attack on the

---

* Chron. Turon. ann. 1061.—Chron. Halberstadiens. (Leibnit. S. R. Brunsv. II. 127-8).—Gest. Treviror. c. 38 (Martene Ampl. Coll. IV. 181-2).

invaders, and, setting fire to the reeds, burned the sorceress and all who were with her.*

When Olaf Tryggvesson, early in the eleventh century, endeavored to christianize Norway, he recognized the sorcerers as the most formidable enemies of the faith, and handled them unsparingly. At a Thing, or assembly, in Viken, he proclaimed that he would banish all who could be proved to deal with spirits or in witchcraft, and this he followed up with proceedings somewhat rigorous. He ransacked the district and had all the sorcerers brought together; he gave them a great feast with plenty of liquor, and when they were drunk he had the house fired, so that none escaped save Eyvind Kellda, a grandson of Harald Harfaager, and a peculiarly obnoxious wizard, who climbed through the smoke-hole in the roof. In the spring Olaf celebrated Easter on Kormt Island, when thither came Eyvind in a long ship fully manned with sorcerers. Landing, they put on caps of darkness, which rendered them invisible, and surrounded themselves with a thick mist, but when they came to Augvaldsness, where King Olaf lay, it became clear day and they were stricken with blindness, so that they wandered helplessly around till the king's men seized them and brought them before him. He had them bound and placed on a rock which was bare only at low water, and Snorri Sturlason says that in his time it was still known as the Skerry of Shrieks. Another pious act related of Olaf illustrates both the methods requisite to spread the gospel among the rugged heroes of Norway and one of the explanations given by the Christians of the powers of sorcerers. Olaf captured Eyvind Kinnrif, a noted sorcerer, and sought to convert him, but in vain. Then a pan of fire was placed upon his belly, which he stoically endured until he burst asunder before asking its removal. Regarding this tardy request as a sign of yielding, Olaf asked him "Eyvind, wilt thou now believe in Christ?" "No," replied Eyvind, "I can take no baptism, for I am an evil spirit placed in a man's body by Lapland sorcery, because in no other way could my father and mother

---

* Laws of Edward and Guthrum, 11.—Laws of Ethelred, v. 7.—Cnut Secular. 4 (Ed. Kolderup Rosenvinge p. 36).—Athelstan's Dooms, I. 6.—Laws of Edward the Elder, 6.—Ll. Henrici lxxi. § 1.—Ingulph's Chron. Contin. (Bohn's Edition, p. 258).

have a child," and with that he died.   Yet in the earliest Icelandic
code, the Grágás, compiled probably in 1118, there is no mention
of sorcery, which seems to have been left to the spiritual courts;
while in the contemporary ecclesiastical body of law the punishment of magic arts is only three years' exile, unless injury or death
to man or beast has been wrought, when it is perpetual.   In either
case the accused is entitled to trial before twelve good men and
true.*

Elsewhere thoughout Europe, by the end of the twelfth century, the repression of sorcery seems to have been well-nigh abandoned by both secular and ecclesiastical authorities.   This was
not because its practice had been either given up or rendered lawful.   In 1149 we find Abbot Wibald of Corvey accusing Walter,
one of his monks, of using diabolical incantations.   The cause
which led Alexander III., in 1181, to monopolize for the Holy See
the canonization of saints was that the monks of the Norman
abbey of Gristan were addicted to magic, and by its means endeavored to gain the reputation of working miracles; during the
absence in England of the abbot, the prior one day got drunk at
dinner and struck with a table-knife two of his monks, who retali-
ated by beating him to death, and he perished unhouselled, yet by
evil arts the monks succeeded in inducing the people to adore him
as a saint until Bishop Arnoul of Lisieux reported the truth to
Alexander.   So easily were such offences condoned that in the case
of a priest who, to recover something stolen from his church, employed a magician and looked into an astrolabe, Alexander only
ordered the punishment of a year's suspension, and this decision
was embodied by Gregory IX. in the canon law as a precedent to
be followed.   This method of divination involved the invocation
of spirits, and was wholly unlawful, yet it was employed without
scruple.   John of Salisbury, who died in 1181, relates that when
he was a boy he was given to a priest to be taught the psalms.
His instructor mingled with his sacred functions the practice of catoptromancy, and once made use of his pupil and an older scholar

---

* Olaf Tryggvesson's Saga, 69, 70, 83 (Laing's Heimskringla).—Kristinrettr
Thorlaks oc Ketils, c. xvi.

For the intimate connection between sorcery and malignant spirits, see Finn
Magnusen's Priscæ Vet. Boreal. Mythologiæ Lexicon, s. v. Tröll, pp. 474 sqq.

to look into the polished basin, after due conjurations and the use of the holy chrism. John could see nothing, and was relieved from further service of the kind, but his comrade discerned shadowy forms and thus was a more useful subject. Thus the forbidden arts flourished with but slender repression, and in this period of virtual toleration they worked little evil, save perhaps an occasional case of poisoning in a love-potion.*

It might be expected that this toleration would cease as the human mind awakened and in its gropings began to cultivate with increased assiduity the occult sciences, in the endeavor to penetrate the secrets of nature; as scholastic theology developed itself into a system which sought to frame a theory of the universe; as the revived study of the Roman law brought again into view the imperial edicts against sorcery, and as the spiritual courts became effectively organized for their enforcement. Yet the development of persecution was wonderfully slow. The Church had a real and a dangerous enemy to combat in the threatening growth of heresy, and had little thought to bestow on a matter which did not endanger the power and privileges of the hierarchy. An occasional council, like those of Rouen in 1189 and of Paris in 1212, denounced the practitioners of magic, but there was no defined penalty, and only excommunication was threatened against them. Yet there was a popular idea that, like heresy, burning was the appropriate punishment, as in the case, about the same period, of a young cleric of Soest named Hermann, who, when vainly tempted by an unchaste woman, was accused by her of magic arts, was condemned and burned. In the flames he sang the Ave Maria until silenced by a blazing stick thrust into his mouth by a kinsman of the accuser; but his innocence shone

---

* Wibaldi Epist. 157 (Martene Ampl. Coll. II. 352).—Baron. Annal. ann. 1181, No. 6–10.—C. 1 Extra. xlv. 3.—C. 2 Extra. v. 21.—Johan. Saresberiens. Polycrat. c. xxviii.

Catoptromancy was a practice duly handed down from classical times. Didius Julianus, during his short reign, found time to obtain foreknowledge of his own downfall and the succession of Septimius Severus, by means of a boy who with bandaged eyes looked into a mirror after proper spells had been muttered over him (Æl. Spartiani Did. Julian. 7), and Hippolytus of Porto gives us in full detail the ingenious frauds by which this and similar feats were accomplished (Refut. omn. Hæres. iv. 15, 28–40).

forth in the miracles wrought at his grave, and a chapel was built over it which stood as a warning against such inconsiderate zeal.*

Cæsarius of Heisterbach, to whom we owe this incident, has an ample store of marvels which show that superstition was as active as ever, that men were eager to gain what advantage they could from intercourse with Satan, and that such practices were virtually unrepressed. He tells of a certain ecclesiastic named Philip, a celebrated necromancer, dead only a few years previous, apparently without trouble from Church or State. A knight named Henry of Falkenstein, who disbelieved in demons, applied to him to satisfy his doubts. Philip obligingly drew a circle with a sword at a cross-roads and muttered his spells, when, with a tumult like rushing waters and roaring tempests, the demon came, taller than the trees, black, and of a most fearful aspect. The knight kept within the charmed circle and escaped immediate ill, but lost his color, and remained pallid during the few years in which he survived. A priest undertook the same experience, but became frightened and allowed himself to be dragged out of the circle; he was so injured that he died on the third day, whereupon Waleran of Luxembourg piously confiscated his house, showing that immunity was not always to be reckoned on.†

Compacts with Satan were also not infrequent. The heretics burned at Besançon in 1180 were found to have such compacts inscribed on little rolls of parchment under the skin of their armpits. It would be difficult to find any historical fact of the period apparently resting on better authority than the story of Everwach, who was still living as a monk of St. Nicholas at Stalum when Cæsarius described his adventures as related by eye-witnesses. He had been steward of Theodoric, Bishop of Utrecht, whom he served faithfully. Accused of malversation, he found some of his accounts missing, and in despair he invoked the devil, saying, "Lord, if thou wilt help me in my necessity I will do homage to thee and serve thee in all things." The devil appeared,

---

* Concil. Rotomagens. ann. 1189 c. 29 (Bessin, Concil. Rotomagens. I. 97).—Concil. Paris. ann. 1212 P. v. (Martene Ampl. Coll. VII. 105).—Cæsar. Heisterb. IV. 99.

† Cæsar. Heisterb. v. 2, 3.

and Everwach accepted his conditions of renouncing Christ and the Virgin and paying him homage, after which the accounts were proved without difficulty. Thenceforth Everwach was in the habit of openly saying, "Those who serve God are wretched and poor, but they who believe in the devil are prosperous," and he devoted himself to the study of magic arts. It shows how lax was the discipline of the time, when, in his zeal for Satan, he bitterly opposed Master Oliver, the Scholasticus of Cologne, who preached the cross in Utrecht, and on being reproved sought to slay him, being only prevented by a sickness of which he died. He was plunged into hell and subjected to the indescribable torments of the damned, but the Lord pitied him, and he returned to life on the bier at his own funeral. Thenceforth he was a changed man. In company with Bishop Otto of Utrecht he made the pilgrimage to the Holy Sepulchre, inflicting on himself all manner of austerities, and on his return gave his property to the Church and entered the convent at Stalum. There is another story, of a spendthrift young knight near Liége, who, after squandering his fortune, was induced by one of his peasants to appeal to Satan. On the promise of wealth and honors he renounced allegiance to God and rendered regular feudal homage to Satan; the latter, however, required him to also renounce the Virgin, and this he refused to do, wherefore, on his repenting, he was pardoned at her intercession.*

These instances, which could readily be multiplied, will suffice to show the tendency of popular thought and belief at this period. It is true that Roger Bacon, who was in so many things far in advance of the age, argued that much of magic was simply fraud and delusion; that it is an error to suppose that man can summon and

---

* Cæsar. Heisterb. II. 12; v. 18; XII. 23.

In spite of their lifelike contemporary details, these stories are evidently founded on that of Theophilus of Cilicia, which had so great a currency during the Middle Ages. He was archdeacon until dismissed by his bishop, when in despair he had recourse to Satan, to whom he gave a written compact pledging himself to endure the pains of hell throughout eternity. He was forthwith restored to his position and enjoyed high consideration until, overwhelmed with remorse, he appealed to the Virgin. By assiduous penitence he won her aid, and she caused the compact to be returned to him.—Hroswithæ de Lapsu et Convers. Theophili.

dismiss malignant spirits at will, and that it is much simpler to pray directly to God because demons can influence human affairs only through God's permission. Even Bacon, however, in asserting the uselessness of charms and spells, gives as his reason that their efficacy depended on their being made under certain aspects of the heavens, the determination of which was very difficult and uncertain. Bacon's partial incredulity only indicates the universality of the belief in less scientific minds, and, in view of the activity assigned to Satan in seeking human agents and servitors, and the ease with which men could evoke him and bind themselves to him, the supineness of the Church with regard to such offences is remarkable. The terrible excitement aroused by the persecution of the Stedingers and of Conrad of Marburg's Luciferans must indubitably have given a stimulus to the belief in demonic agencies. Thomas of Cantimpré tells us that he had from Conrad, the Dominican provincial, as happening to one of Conrad of Marburg's Luciferans, the well-known story that the heretic, endeavoring to convert a friar, conducted him to a vast palace where the Virgin sat enthroned in ineffable splendor surrounded by innumerable saints; but the friar, who had provided himself with a pyx containing a consecrated host, presented it to the Virgin with a demand that she should adore her Son, when the whole array vanished in darkness. Yet this excitement left behind it a reaction which rather created indisposition to further persecution. Pierre de Colmieu, afterwards Cardinal of Albano, when Archbishop of Rouen, in 1235, included invoking and sacrificing to demons and the use of the sacraments in sorcery only among the cases reserved to the bishops for granting absolution; and the cursory allusion to the subject by Bishop Durand in his *Speculum Juris* shows that, for at least a half-century later, the subject attracted little attention in the ecclesiastical courts. A synod of Anjou, in 1294, declares that according to the canons priests should expel from their parishes all diviners, soothsayers, sorcerers, and the like, and laments that they were permitted to increase and multiply without hindrance, to remedy which all who know of such persons are ordered to report them to the episcopal court, in order that their horrible malignity may be restrained.[*]

---

* Rogeri Bacon Epist. de Secretis Operibus Artis c. i., ii. (M. R. Series, pp

Still more remarkable is the indifference of secular jurists and lawgivers during the thirteenth century, when the jurisprudence of Europe was developing and assuming definite shape. In England there is a strong contrast with the Anglo-Saxon period in the silence respecting sorcery in Glanvill, Bracton, the Fleta, and Britton. The latter, in describing the circuits of the sheriffs, gives an elaborate enumeration of the offences about which they are to make inquisition, including renegades and misbelievers, but omitting sorcery, and the same omission is observable in the minute instructions given by Edward I. to the sheriffs in the Statute of Ruddlan in 1283, although Peter, Bishop of Exeter, in his instructions to confessors in 1287, mentions sorcerers and demon-worshippers among the criminals to whom they are to assign penance. It is true that Horn's *Myrror of Justice* classes sorcery and heresy together as *majestas*, or treason to the King of Heaven, and we may assume that both were liable to the same penalty, though neither were actively prosecuted. It is the same with the mediæval laws of Scotland as collected by Skene. The *Iter Camerarii* embodies detailed instructions for the inquests to be held by the royal chamberlain in his circuits, but in the long list of crimes and misdemeanors requiring investigation there is no allusion to sorcery or divination.*

It is nearly the same in French jurisprudence. The *Conseil* of Pierre de Fontaines and the so-called *Établissements* of St. Louis contain no references to sorcery. The *Livres de Jostice et de Plet*, though based on the Roman law, makes no mention of it in its long list of crimes and penalties, although incidentally an imperial law is said to apply to those who slay by poisons or enchantments. Beaumanoir, however, though he seems only to know of sorcery employed to excite love, tells us that it is wholly under ecclesiastical jurisdiction; its practitioners err in the faith, and thus are justiciable by the Church, which summons them to abandon their errors, and in case of refusal condemns them as misbelievers. Then secular justice lays hold of them and inflicts death if it ap-

---

523–7).—Th. Cantimprat. Bonum universal. Lib. II. c. 56.—Præcept. Antiq. Rotomag. c. 109 (Bessin, Concil. Rotomagens. II. 67, 76).—Durandi Specul. Juris Lib. IV. Partic. IV. Rubr. de Sortilegiis.—Synod. Andegavens. ann. 1294 c. 2 (D'Achery, I. 737).

* Britton, ch. 29.—Owen's Laws and Institutes of Wales, II. 910–2.—P. Exon.

pears that their sorcery may bring death on man or woman, while
if there is no danger of this, it imprisons them until they recant.
Thus sorcery is heresy cognizable by the Church only, and punishable when abjured only by penitence; yet, when the obstinate sorcerer is handed over to the secular arm, in place of being burned like a
Waldensian refusing to swear, the character of his heresy is weighed
by the secular court, and if its intent be not homicide he is simply
imprisoned until he recants, showing that sorcery was treated as
the least dangerous form of heresy. Beaumanoir's assertion of
ecclesiastical jurisdiction is confirmed by a contemporaneous decision of the Parlement of Paris in 1282, in the case of some
women arrested as sorceresses in Senlis and tried by the maire
and jurats. The Bishop of Senlis claimed them, as their offence
pertained to his court; the magistrates asserted their jurisdiction,
especially as there had been cutting of skin and effusion of blood,
and the Parlement, after due deliberation, ordered the women delivered to the spiritual court. Yet, though this was the law at the
time, it did not long remain so. Under the ancestral systems of
criminal practice, when conviction or acquittal in doubtful cases
depended on the ordeal or the judicial duel or on compurgation,
the secular courts were poorly equipped for determining guilt in
a crime so obscure, and they naturally abandoned it to the encroachments of the spiritual tribunals. As the use of torture, however, gradually spread, the lay officials became quite as competent
as the ecclesiastical to wring confession and conviction from the
accused, and they speedily arrogated to themselves the cognizance
of such cases. At the South, where the Inquisition had familiarized
them with the use of torture at an earlier period, we already, in
1274 and 1275, hear of an inquest held and of wizards and witches
put to death by the royal officials in Toulouse. In the North,
the trials of the Templars accustomed the public mind to the use
of torture, and demonstrated its efficiency, so that the lay courts
speedily came to have no hesitation in exercising jurisdiction
over sorcery. In 1314 Petronille de Valette was executed in Paris
as a sorceress. She had implicated Pierre, a merchant of Poitiers,
and his nephew Perrot. They were forthwith put to the ban and

---

Summula exigendi Confess. (Harduin VII. 1126).—Myrror of Justice c. i. § 4; c.
ii. § 22; c. iii. § 14.—Regiam Majest. Scotiæ, Edinburgi, 1609, fol. 163–7.

their property sequestrated, but at the place of execution Petronille had exculpated them, declaring them innocent on the peril of her soul. They hastened to Paris and purged themselves, and the Parlement, May 8, 1314, ordered the Seneschal of Poitou to withdraw the proceedings and release the property. Sorcery was now beginning to be energetically suppressed, and henceforth we shall see it occupy the peculiar position of a crime justiciable by both the ecclesiastical and secular courts.*

Spain had been exposed to a peculiarly active infection. The fatalistic belief of the Saracens naturally predisposed them to the arts of divination ; they cultivated the occult sciences more zealously than any other race, and they were regarded throughout Europe as the most skilled teachers and practitioners of sorcery. In the school of Cordoba there were two professors of astrology, three of necromancy, pyromancy, and geomancy, and one of the *Ars Notoria*, all of whom lectured daily. Arabic bibliographers enumerate seven thousand seven hundred writers on the interpretation of dreams, and as many more who won distinction as expounders of goetic magic. Intercourse with the Saracens naturally stimulated among the Christians the thirst for forbidden knowledge, and as the Christian boundaries advanced, there was left in the conquered territories a large subject population allowed to retain its religion, and propagate the beliefs which had so irresistible an attraction. It was in vain that, in 845, Ramiro I. of Asturias burned a large number of sorcerers, including many Jewish astrologers. Such exhibitions of severity were spasmodic, while the denunciation of superstitions in the councils occasionally held indicate the continued prevalence of the evil without the application of an effective remedy. Queen Urraca of Castile, in the early part of the twelfth century, describes her former husband, Alonso el Batallador of Aragon, as wholly given to divination and the augury of birds, and about 1220, Pedro Muñoz, Archbishop of Santiago, was so defamed for necromancy that by order of Honorius III. he was relegated to the hermitage of San Lorenzo. The ancient Wisigothic Law, or Fuero Juzgo, was for a time almost lost sight of in the innumerable local *fueros* which sprang up, until in

---

* Livres de Jostice et de Plet, pp. 177–83, 284 (Dig. XLVIII. viii. 3., Marcianus).—Beaumanoir, Coutumes du Beauvoisis, Cap. XI. §§ 25, 26.—Olim, II. 205, 619.—Vaissette, IV. 17–18; Chron. Bardin, Ib. IV. Pr. 5.

the eleventh century it was rehabilitated by Fernando I. of Castile. In Aragon, Jayme I., el Conquistador, in the thirteenth century, when recasting the Fuero of Aragon and granting the Fuero of Valencia, introduced penalties for sorcery similar to those of the Fuero Juzgo.* Thus the Wisigothic legislation was practically in force until, about 1260, Alonzo the Wise, of Castile, issued his code known as the *Siete Partidas*, in which all branches of magic are treated as completely under the secular power and in a fashion singularly rationalistic. There is no allusion to heresy or to any spiritual offence involved in occult science, which is to be rewarded or punished as it is employed for good or evil. Astrology is one of the seven liberal arts; its conclusions are drawn from the courses of the stars as expounded by Ptolemy and other sages; when an astrologer is applied to for the recovery of lost or stolen goods, and designates where they are to be found, the party aggrieved has no recourse against him for the dishonor inflicted, because he has only answered in accordance with the rules of his art. But if he is a deceiver, who pretends to know that whereof he is ignorant, the complainant can have him punished as a common sorcerer. These sorcerers and diviners who pretend to reveal the future and the unknown by augury, or lots, or hydromancy, or crystallomancy, or by the head of a dead man, or the palm of a virgin, are deceivers. So are necromancers who work by the invocation of evil spirits, which is displeasing to God and injurious to man. Philtres and love-potions and figurines, to inspire desire or aversion, are also condemned as often causing death and permanent infirmity, and all these practitioners and cheats are to be put to death when duly convicted, while those who shelter them are to be banished. But those who use incantations for a good purpose, such as casting out devils from the possessed, or removing ligatures between married folk, or for dissolving a hail-cloud or fog which threatens the harvests, or for destroying locusts or caterpillars, are not to be punished, but rather to be rewarded.†

---

* José Amador de los Rios (Revista de España, T. XVII. pp. 382, 384-5, 388, 392-3; T. XVIII. p. 6).—Concil Legionens. ann. 1012 c. 19; C. Compostellan. ann. 1031 c. 6; C. Coyacens. ann. 1050 c. 4; C. Compostellan. ann. 1056 c. 6 (Aguirre, IV. 388, 396, 405, 414).—Histor. Compostellan. Lib. I. c. lxiv.—Pelayo, Heterodoxos Españoles, I. 590.

† Partidas, P. VII. Tit. ix. l. 17; Tit. xxiii. ll. 1, 2, 3.

Italy affords us the earliest example of mediæval legislation on the subject. In the first half of the twelfth century the Norman king of the two Sicilies, Roger, threatened punishment for compounding a love-potion, even though no injury resulted from it. The next recorded measure is found in the earliest known statutes of Venice, by the Doge Orlo Malipieri in 1181, which contain provisions for the punishment of poisoning and sorcery. Frederic II. was accused by his ecclesiastical adversaries of surrounding himself with Saracenic astrologers and diviners, whom he employed as counsellors, and who practised for his benefit all the forbidden arts of augury by the flight of birds and the entrails of victims, but though Frederic shared the universal belief of his age in keeping in his service a corps of astrologers with Master Theodore at their head, and was addicted to the science of physiognomy, he was too nearly a sceptic to have faith in vulgar sorcery. His reputation merely shared the fate of that of his *protégé*, Michael Scot, who translated for him philosophical treatises of Averrhoes and Avicenna. In his collection of laws known as the Sicilian Constitutions, he retained indeed the law of King Roger just alluded to, and added to it a provision that those who administer love-potions, or noxious, illicit, or exorcised food for such purposes, shall be put to death if the recipient loses his life or senses, while if no harm ensues they shall suffer confiscation and a year's imprisonment, but this was merely a concession to current necessities, and he was careful to accompany it with a declaration that the influencing of love or hatred by meat or drink was a fable, and he took no note in his code of any other form of magic. In the Latin kingdoms of the East the Assises de Jerusalem and the Assises d'Antioch are silent on the subject, unless it may be deemed to be comprised in a general clause in the former, declaring that all malefactors and all bad men and bad women shall be put to death. Yet, that sorcery was punished throughout Italy, and was regarded as subject to the secular tribunals, is shown by an expression in the bull *Ad extirpanda* of Innocent IV. in 1252, ordering all potentates in public assembly to put heretics to the ban as though they were sorcerers.*

* Constitt. Sicular. III. xlii. 1–3.—Cechetti, La Republica di Venizia e la Corte di Roma I. 15.—Chron. Senoniens. Lib. IV. c. 4 (D'Achery II. 631).—

In German legislation the *Treuga Henrici*, about 1224, contains the earliest reference to sorcery, classing it with heresy and leaving the punishment to the discretion of the judge; but the Kayser-Recht, the Sachsische Weichbild, and the Richstich Landrecht contain no allusion to it. In the Sachsenspiegel it is curtly included with heresy and poisoning as punishable with burning, and there is the same provision in the Schwabenspiegel, while in a later recension of the latter the subject is developed by providing that whoever, man or woman, practises sorcery or invokes the devil by words or otherwise, shall be burned or exposed to a harsher death at the discretion of the judge, for he has renounced Christ and given himself to Satan. In this it is evident that the spiritual offence is alone kept in view, without regard to evil attempted or performed, and it would further seem that the matter was within the competence of the secular courts. The earliest legislation of the Prussian marches, about 1310, specifies for sorcerers the loss of an ear, branding on the cheek, exile, or heavy fines, but says nothing of capital punishment. Among the Norsemen the temper of legislation on the subject is to be found in the *Jarnsida*, compiled in 1258 by Hako Hakonsen for his Icelandic subjects, and the almost identical *Leges Gulathingenses*, issued by

---

Huillard-Bréholles, Introd. pp. DXXV., DXXX.—Assises de Jerusalem, Baisse Court c. 271 (Ed. Kausler, Stuttgart, 1839).—Mag. Bull. Rom. I. 91.

Frederic's reputation is indicated in the lines—

> " Amisit astrologos et magos et vates.
> Beelzebub et Astaroth, proprios penates
> Tenebrarum consulens per quos potestates
> Spreverat Ecclesiam et mundi magnates."
>
> (Huillard-Bréholles, l. c.).

And Michael Scot, to succeeding generations, was not the philosopher, but the magician—

> " Michele Scotto fu, che veramente
> Delle magiche frode seppe il giuoco "—(INFERNO, XX.)

whose wonders are commemorated in the " Lay of the Last Minstrel "—

> " In these fair climes it was my lot
> To meet the wondrous Michael Scott,
> A wizard of such dreaded fame
> That when in Salamanca's cave
> Him listed his magic wand to wave,
> The bells would ring in Nôtre Dame."

his son, Magnus Hakonsen, in 1274, which for five hundred years remained the common law of Norway. Magic, divination, and the evocation of the dead are unpardonable crimes, punished with death and confiscation; but the accused can purge himself with twelve compurgators, according to the Jarnsida, and with six, according to the code of Gula, thus showing that the crime was subject to the secular courts.*

In Sweden there is no allusion to sorcery in the laws compiled early in the thirteenth century by Andreas, Archbishop of Lunden; but in those issued by King Christopher in 1441, attempts on life by poison or sorcery are punished with the wheel for men and lapidation for women, and are tried by the *Nämd*—a sort of permanent jury of twelve men selected in each district as judges. In Denmark the laws in force until the sixteenth century were singularly mild. The accused had the right of defence with selected compurgators; the punishment for a first offence was infamy and withdrawal of the sacraments; for relapse, imprisonment, and finally death for persistent offending. In Sleswick the ancient code of the thirteenth century makes no provision for sorcery, nor does that of the free Frisians in the fourteenth. That this leniency was not the result of outgrowing the ancient superstitions we learn from Olaus Magnus, who characterizes the whole Northern regions as literally the seat of Satan.† In all this confused and varying legislation we can trace a distinct tendency to increased severity after the thirteenth century.

The slight attention paid in the thirteenth century by the Church to a crime so abhorrent as sorcery is proved by the fact

---

* Treuga Henrici, No. 21 (Böhlau, Nove Constit. Dom. Alberti, Weimar, 1858, p. 78). — Sachsenspiegel Lib. II. c. 13.— Schwabenspiegel, c. CXVI. § 12 (Ed. Senckenberg); Cod. Uffenbach. c. CCLXXI. § 6.—Lilienthal, Die Hexenprocesse der beiden Städten Braunsberg, Königsberg, 1861, p. 70.—Iarnsida, Mannhelge c. vi., xxv. (Ed. Hafniæ, 1847, pp. 22, 46).—Ll. Gulathingens. Mannhelge-Bolkr, c. iv., xxv. (Ed. Hafniæ, 1817, pp. 137, 197).

† Leges Scaniæ Provin. Andreæ Sunonis Archiep. Lunden. (Thorsen, Skanske Lov, Kjobenhavn, 1853).—Raguald. Ingermund. Ll. Suecor. Lib. x. c. 5 (Stockholmiæ, 1614).—Canut. Episc. Vibergens. Exposit. Legum Juciæ Lib. III. c. lxix. (Hafniæ, 1508).—Ancher, Farrago Legum Antiq. Daniæ (Hafniæ, 1776).—Leges Opstalbomicæ ann. 1323 (Gaertner Saxonum Leges Tres, Lipsiæ, 1730).—Olai Magni de Gent. Septentrion. Lib. III. c. 22.

that when the Inquisition was organized it was for a considerable time restrained from jurisdiction over this class of offences. In 1248 the Council of Valence, while prescribing to inquisitors the course to be pursued with heretics, directs sorcerers to be delivered to the bishops, to be imprisoned or otherwise punished. In various councils, moreover, during the next sixty years the matter is alluded to, showing that it was constantly becoming an object of increased solicitude, but the penalty threatened is only excommunication. In that of Trèves, for instance, in 1310, which is very full in its description of the forbidden arts, all parish priests are ordered to prohibit them; but the penalty proposed for disobedience is only withdrawal of the sacraments, to be followed, in case of continued obduracy, by excommunication and other remedies of the law administered by the Ordinaries; thus manifesting a leniency almost inexplicable. That the Church, indeed, was disposed to be more rational than the people, is visible in a case occurring in 1279 at Ruffach, in Alsace, when a Dominican nun was accused of having baptized a waxen image after the fashion of those who desired either to destroy an enemy or to win a lover. The peasants carried her to a field and would have burned her, had she not been rescued by the friars.*

Yet, as the Inquisition perfected its organization and grew conscious of its strength, it naturally sought to extend its sphere of activity, and in 1257 the question was put to Alexander IV. whether it ought not to take cognizance of divination and sorcery. In his bull, *Quod super nonnullis*, which was repeatedly reissued by his successors, Alexander replied that inquisitors are not to be diverted from their duties by other occupations, and are to leave such offenders to their regular judges, unless there is manifest heresy involved, and this rule, at the end of the century, was embodied in the canon law by Boniface VIII. The Inquisition being

---

* Concil. Valentin. ann. 1248 c. 12 (Harduin. VII. 427). — C. Cenomanens. ann. 1248 (Martene Ampl. Coll. VII. 1377).—C. Mogunt. ann. 1261 c. 30 (Hartzeim III. 604).—C. Nugaroliens. ann. 1290 c. 4 (Hard. VII. 1161).—C. Baiocens. ann. 1300 c. 63 (Ib. VII. 1234). — C. Treverens. ann. 1310 c. 79–84 (Martene Thesaur. IV. 257–8).—C. Palentin. ann. 1322 c. 24 (Hard. VII. 1480).—C. Salmanticens. ann. 1335 c. 15 (Ib. VII. 1973–4).—Annal. Domin. Colmariens. ann. 1279 (Urstisii II. 16).

thus in possession of a portion of the field, rapidly extended its jurisdiction. There was no limitation expressed when the pious Alfonse of Toulouse and his wife Jeanne, in 1270, at Aigues-mortes, when starting on the crusade of Tunis, issued letters-patent conceding that their servants and household should be answerable to the Inquisition for abjuration of the faith, heresy, magic, sorcery, and perjury. It is doubtless to this extension of the inquisitorial jurisdiction that we may attribute the increasing rigor which henceforth marked the persecution of sorcery.*

Alexander's definition, it is true, had left open for discussion a tolerably wide and intricate class of questions as to the degree of heresy involved in the occult arts, but in time these came all to be decided "in favor of the faith." It was not simply the worship of demons and making pacts with Satan that were recognized as heretical by the subtle casuistry of the inquisitors. A figurine to be effective required to be baptized, and this argued an heretical notion as to the sacrament of baptism, and the same was the case as to the sacrament of the altar in the various superstitious uses to which the Eucharist was put. Scarce any of the arts of the diviner in forecasting the future or in tracing stolen articles could be exercised without what the inquisitors assumed to be at least a tacit invocation of demons. For this, in fact, they had the authority of John of Salisbury, who, as early as the twelfth century, argued that all divination is an invocation of demons; for if the operator offers no other sacrifice, he sacrifices his body in performing the operation. This refinement was not reduced to practice, but in time the ingenious dilemma was invented that a man who invoked a demon, thinking it to be no sin, was a manifest heretic; if he knew it to be a sin he was not a heretic, but was to be classed with heretics, while to expect a demon to tell the truth is the act of a heretic. To ask of a demon, even without adoration, that which depends upon the will of God, or of man, or upon the future, indicated heretical notions as to the power of demons. In short, as Sylvester Prierias says, it is not necessary to inquire into the motives of those who invoke demons—they are all heretics, real or presumptive. Love-potions and philtres, by a similar system of

* Raynald. ann. 1258. No. 23.—Potthast. No. 17745, 18396.—Eymeric. p. 133.
—C. 8, § 4, Sexto v. 2.—Chron. Bardin. ann. 1270 (Vaissette, IV. Pr. 5).

exegesis, were heretical, and so were spells and charms to cure disease, the gathering of herbs while kneeling, face to the east, and repeating the Paternoster, and all the other devices which fraud and superstition had imposed on popular credulity. Alchemy was one of the *sept ars demonials*, for the aid of Satan was necessary to the transmutation of metals, and the Philosopher's Stone was only to be obtained by spells and charms; although Roger Bacon, in his zeal for practical science, assumes that both objects could be obtained by purely natural means, and that human life could be prolonged for several centuries.* In 1328 the Inquisition of Carcassonne condemned the Art of St. George, through which buried treasure was sought by spreading oil on a finger-nail with certain conjurations, and making a young child look upon it and tell what he saw. Then there was the Notory Art, communicated by God to Solomon, and transmitted through Apollonius of Tyana, which taught the power of the Names and Words of God, and operated through prayers and formulas consisting of unknown polysyllables, by which all knowledge, memory, eloquence, and virtue can be obtained in the space of a month—a harmless delusion enough, which Roger Bacon pronounces to be one of the figments of the magicians, but Thomas Aquinas and Ciruelo prove that it operates

---

* Archives de l'Inq. de Carc. (Doat, XXVII. 7).—Bern. Guidon. Practica, P. III. c. 42, 43.—Th. Aquin. Summ. Sec. Sec. xc. 2; xcv. 4.—Johann. Saresberiens. Polycrat. c. xxviii.—Bern. Basin de Artibus Magiæ, conclus. iii.-ix.—Prieriat. de Strigimagar. Lib. III. c. 1.—Eymeric. pp. 342, 443.—Alonso de Spina, Fortalic. Fidei, fol. 51, 284.—Revelat. S. Brigittæ Lib. VII. c. 28.—Archidiac. Gloss. super c. *accusatus* § *sane* (Eymeric. 202).—Rogeri Bacon Op. Tert. c. xii.; Epist. de Secret. Operibus Artis c. vi., vii., ix.-xi.

When, in 1473, some Carmelites of Bologna asserted that it was not heretical to obtain responses from demons, Sixtus IV. promptly ordered an investigation, and directed the results to be transmitted to him under seal.—Pegnæ Append. ad Eymeric. p. 82.

Bernardo di Como draws the nice distinction that it is not heretical to invoke the devil to obtain the illicit love of a woman, for the function of Satan is that of a tempter.—Bernardi Comens. Lucerna Inquisit. s. v. *Dæmones*, No. 2.

In 1471 the arts of printing and alchemy were coupled together as reprehensible by the Observantine Franciscans, and their practice was forbidden under pain of disgrace and removal. Friar John Neyseeser disobeyed this rule, and "apostatized" to the Conventual branch of the Order, which was less rigid.—Chron. Glassberger ann. 1471.

solely through the devil. A monk was seized in Paris in 1323 for possessing a book on the subject; his book was burned, and he probably escaped with abjuration and penance.*

The most prominent and most puzzling to the lawgiver of all the occult arts was astrology. This was a purely Eastern science— the product of the Chaldean plains and of the Nile valley, unknown to any of the primitive Aryan races, from Hindostan to Scandinavia. When the dominion of Rome spread beyond the confines of Italy it was not the least of the Orientalizing influences which so profoundly modified the original Roman character; and after a struggle it established itself so firmly that in great measure it superseded the indigenous auguries and haruspicium, and by the early days of the empire some knowledge of the influences of the stars formed an ordinary portion of liberal education. The same motives which led to the prohibition of haruspicium—that the death of the emperor was the subject most eagerly inquired into —caused the Chaldeans or astrologers to be the objects of repeated savage edicts, issued even by monarchs who themselves were addicted to consulting them, but it was in vain. Human credulity was too profitable a field to remain uncultivated, and, as Tacitus says, astrologers would always be prohibited and always retained. Although the complexity of the science was such that it could be grasped in its details only by minds exceptionally constituted, through lifelong application, it was brought in homely fashion within the reach of all by restricting it to the observation of the moon, and applying the results by means of the diagram and tables known as the Petosiris, a description of which, attributed to the Venerable Bede, shows how the superstitions of pagandom were transmitted to the Northern races, and were eagerly accepted in spite of the arguments of St. Augustin to prove the nullity of the influence ascribed to the heavenly bodies.†

---

* Doat, XXVII. 7; XXX. 185.—Rogeri Bacon Epist. de Secretis operibus Artis c. iii.—Th. Aquin. Summ. Sec. Sec. xcvi. i.—Ciruelo, Reprovacion de las Superstitiones, P. iii. c. 1.—Grandes Chroniques V. 272.—Guill. Nangiac. Contin. ann. 1323.—Savonarola contra l' Astrologia, Vinegia, 1536, fol. 33.—Ars Notoria, *ap.* Cornel. Agrippæ Opp. Ed. Lugduni, I. 606.—The Notory Art of Solomon, translated by Robert Turner, London, 1657.

† Tacit. Annal. ii. 28–32; iii. 22; xii. 14, 52, 68; Histor. ii. 62.—Zonaræ T. ii. (pp. 185, 192).—Sueton. Vitell. 14. — Tertull. de Idololat. ix.—Lib. ix. Cod.

We have seen astrology classed as one of the liberal arts by
Alonso the Wise of Castile, and the implicit belief universally accorded to it throughout the Middle Ages caused it to be so generally employed that its condemnation was difficult.   I have alluded
above to the confidence reposed by Frederic II. in the science,
and to the Dominican astrologer who accompanied the Archbishop
of Ravenna when as papal legate he led the crusade against Ezzelin da Romano.   Ezzelin himself kept around him a crowd of
astrologers, and was led to his last disastrous enterprise by their
mistaken counsel.   So thoroughly accepted were its principles
that when, in 1305, the College of Cardinals wrote to Clement V.
to urge his coming to Rome, they reminded him that every planet
is most powerful in its own house.   Savonarola assures us that at
the end of the fifteenth century those who could afford to keep
astrologers regulated every action by their advice: if the question
were to mount on horseback or to go on board ship, to lay the
foundation of a house or to put on a new garment, the astrologer
stood by with his astrolabe in hand to announce the auspicious
moment—in fact, he says that the Church itself was governed by
astrology, for every prelate had his astrologer, whose advice he
dared not disregard.   It is observable that astrology is not included, as a forbidden practice, in the inquisitorial formulas of
interrogation during the thirteenth and fourteenth centuries.   No
books on astrology seem to be enumerated in the condemnation
pronounced in 1290 by the Inquisitor and Bishop of Paris and the
Archbishop of Sens, aided by the Masters of the University, on all
books of divination and magic — treatises on necromancy, geomancy, pyromancy, hydromancy, and chiromancy, the book of
the Ten Rings of Venus, the books of the Greek and German
Babylon, the book of the Four Mirrors, the book of the Images
of Tobias ben Tricat, the book of the Images of Ptolemy, the
book of Hermes the Magician to Aristotle, which they say Aros,
or Gabriel, had from God, containing horrible incantations and
detestable suffumigations.   Astrology does not appear for condemnation in the Articles of the University of Paris in 1398,
and the great learning of the irreproachable Cardinal Peter
d'Ailly was employed in diffusing belief in its truths.   On the

xviii. 2.—Prudent. contra Symmach. ii. 449-57.—Bedæ opp. Ed. Migne I. 963-
66.—Augustin. de Civ. Dei Lib. v. c. 1-7.

other hand, as early as the twelfth century John of Salisbury, while asserting that the power of the stars was grossly exaggerated, declares that astrology was forbidden and punished by the Church, that it deprived man of free-will by inculcating fatalism, and that it tended to idolatry by transferring omnipotence from the Creator to his creations. He adds that he had known many astrologers, but none on whom the hand of God did not inflict divine vengeance. These views became virtually the accepted doctrine of the Church as expounded by Thomas Aquinas in the distinction that when astrology was used to predict natural events, such as drought or rain, it was lawful; when employed to divine the future acts of men dependent on free-will, it involved the operation of demons, and was unlawful. Zanghino says that though it is one of the seven liberal arts and not prohibited by law, yet it has a tendency to idolatry, and is condemned by the canonists. There was, in fact, much in both the theories and practice of astrologers which trenched nearly upon heresy, not only through demoniac invocations, but because it was impossible that astrology could be cultivated without denying human free-will and tacitly admitting fatalism. The very basis of the so-called science lay in the influence which the signs and planets exercised on the fortunes and characters of men at the hour of birth, and no ingenious dialectics could explain away its practical denial of supervision to God and of responsibility to man. Even Roger Bacon failed in this. He fully accepted the belief that the stars were the cause of human events, that the character of every man was shaped by the aspect of the heavens at his birth, and that the past and future could be read by tables which he repeatedly and vainly sought to construct, yet he was illogical enough to think that he could guard against it by nominally reserving human free-will.* All astrologers thus practised their profession under liabil-

---

* Rolandini Chron. Lib. xii. c. 2 (Murat. S. R. I. VIII. 344).—Monach. Patavin. Chron. (Ib. VIII. 705).—Raynald. ann. 1305, No. 7.—Savonarola contra l' Astrologia, fol. 25.—Villari, Storia di Savonarola, Ed. 1887, I. 197–8.—MS. Bib. Nat., fonds latin, No. 14930, fol. 229–30.—Doat, XXXVII. 258.—Bern. Guidon. Pract. P. v.—Johann. Saresberiens. Polycrat. ii. xix., xx., xxv., xxvi.—Th. Aquin. Summ. Sec. Sec. xcv.—Zanchini Tract. de Hæret. c. xxii.—D'Argentré, I. i. 263; ii. 154. —Eymeric. p. 317.—Manilii Astron. Lib. iv.—Rogeri Bacon Op. Tert. c. xi.(M. R. Series I. 35–6. Cf. 559–61).

ity of being at any moment called to account by the Inquisition.
That this did not occur more often may be attributed to the fact
that all classes, in Church and State, from the lowest to the highest,
believed in astrology and protected astrologers, and some special
inducement or unusual indiscretion was required to set in motion
the machinery of prosecution.

We can thus understand the case of the celebrated Peter of
Abano or Apono, irrespective of his reputation as the greatest
magician of his age, earned for him among the vulgar by his marvellous learning and his unsurpassed skill in medicine. We have
no details of the accusations brought against him by the Inquisition, but we may reasonably assume that there was little difficulty
in finding ample ground for condemnation. In his *Conciliator
Differentium*, written in 1303, he not only proved that astrology
was a necessary part of medicine, but his estimate of the power
of the stars practically eliminated God from the government of
the world. The Deluge took place when the world was subject
to Mars, in consequence of the conjunction of the planets in Pisces;
it was under the lead of the moon when occurred the confusion of
tongues, the destruction of Sodom and Gomorrah, and the exodus
from Egypt. Even worse was his Averrhoistic indifference to religion manifested in the statement that the conjunction of Saturn
and Jupiter in the head of Aries, which occurs every nine hundred
and sixty years, causes changes in the monarchies and religions of
the world, as appears in the advent of Nebuchadnezzar, Moses,
Alexander the Great, Christ, and Mahomet—a speculation of which
the infidelity is even worse than the chronology.* It is not surprising that the Inquisition took hold of one whose great name
was popularizing such doctrines in the University of Padua, especially as there was a large fortune to be confiscated. We are
told that he at first escaped its clutches, but this probably was

---

* P. de Abano Conciliator Different. Philos. Diff. ix., x. (Ed. Venet. 1494, fol.
14–15.). Cf. Albumasar de Magnis Conjunctionibus Tract III. Diff. i. (Aug. Vindel. 1489).

The *Conciliator* was a work of immense reputation. The preface of the edition of 1494 speaks of three or four previous printed editions, and there were
repeated later ones up to 1596. Curiously enough, it was never included in the
Roman and Spanish Indexes, though it appears in that of Lisbon of 1624 (Reusch,
der Index der verbotenen Bücher, I. 35).

only through confession and abjuration, so that when he was prosecuted a second time it was for relapse.   That he would have
been burned there can be little doubt, had he not evaded the stake
by opportunely dying in 1316, before the termination of his trial,
for he was posthumously condemned: according to one account
his bones were burned; according to another his faithful mistress
Marietta conveyed them secretly away, and an effigy was committed to the flames in his place.   If Benvenuto da Imola is to be
believed, he lost his faith in the stars on his death-bed, for he said
to his friends that he had devoted his days to three noble sciences,
of which philosophy had made him subtle, medicine had made him
rich, and astrology had made him a liar.   His name passed into
history as that of the most expert of necromancers, concerning
whom no marvels were too wild to find belief.   It mattered little
that Padua erected a statue to him as to one of her greatest sons,
and that Frederic, Duke of Urbino, paid him the same tribute.
Like Solomon and Hermes and Ptolemy, so long as magic flourished his name served as an attractive frontispiece to various treatises on incantations and the occult sciences.*

Very similar, but even more illustrative, is the case of Cecco
d'Ascoli.   He early distinguished himself as a student of the liberal arts, and devoted himself to astrology, in which he was
reckoned the foremost man of his time.   His vanity led him to
proclaim himself the profoundest adept since Ptolemy, and his
caustic and biting humor made him abundance of enemies.   Regarding astrology as a science, he inevitably brought it within
Aquinas's definition of heresy.   In his conception the stars ruled
everything.   A man born under a certain aspect of the heavens
was doomed to be rich or poor, lucky or unlucky, virtuous or
vicious, unless God should interfere specially to turn aside the
course of nature.   Cecco boasted that he could read the thoughts

---

* Bayle, s. v. Apone.—G. Naudé, Apologie pour les Grands Hommes, Ch. xiv.
—Muratori Antiq. Ital. III. 374-5.

For the printed works attributed to Peter of Abano, see Grässe, " Bibliotheca
Magica et Pneumatica," Leipzig, 1843.   The one by which he is best known is
the " Heptameron seu Elementa Magiæ," a treatise on the invocation of demons,
printed with the works of Cornelius Agrippa.   This version, however, is incomplete.   A fuller and better one is among the MSS. of the Bibliothèque Nationale,
fonds latin, No. 17870.

of a man or tell what he carried in his closed hand by knowing his nativity and comparing it with the position of the stars at the moment, for no one could help doing or thinking what the stars at the time rendered inevitable. All this was incompatible with free-will, it limited the intervention of God, it relieved man from responsibility for his acts, and it thus was manifestly heretical. So his numerous predictions, which we are told were verified, as to the fortunes of Louis of Bavaria, of Castruccio Castrucani, of Charles of Calabria, eldest son of Robert of Naples, won him great applause in that stirring time, yet, as they were not revealed by the divine spirit of prophecy, but were foreseen by astrologic skill, they implied the forbidden theory of fatalism. Cecco became official astrologer to Charles of Calabria, but his confidence in his science and his savage independence unfitted him for a court. On the birth of a princess (presumably the notorious Joanna I.), he pronounced that the stars in the ascendant would render her not only inclined, but absolutely constrained, to sell her honor. The unwelcome truth cost him his place, and he betook himself to Bologna, where he publicly taught his science. Unluckily for him, he developed his theories in commentaries on the *Sphœra* of Sacrobosco.* Villani tells us that in this he taught how, by incantations under certain constellations, malignant spirits could be constrained to perform marvels, but this manifestly is only popular rumor; such practices were wholly inconsistent with his conceptions, and there is no allusion to them in the inquisitorial proceedings. Cecco's audacity, however, rendered the book amply offensive to pious ears. To illustrate his views he cast the horoscope of Christ, and showed how Libra, ascending in the tenth degree, rendered his crucifixion inevitable; as Capricorn was at

---

* The *Sphœra* of Sacrobosco is a remarkably lucid and scientific statement of all that was known, in the thirteenth century, about the earth in its cosmical relations. Although it accepts, of course, the current theory of the nine spheres, it indulges in no astrological reveries as to the influence of the signs and planets on human destiny. It remained for centuries a work of the highest authority, and so lately as 1604, sixty years after the death of Copernicus, and on the eve of the development of the new astronomy by Galileo, it was translated, with a copious commentary, by a professor of mathematics in the University of Siena, Francesco Pifferi, whose astrological credulity offers a curious contrast to the severe simplicity of the original.

the angle of the earth, he was necessarily born in a stable; as
Scorpio was in the second degree, he was poor; while Mercury in
his own house in the ninth section of the heavens rendered his
wisdom profound. In the same way he proved that Antichrist
would come two thousand years after Christ, as a great soldier
nobly attended, and not surrounded by cowards as was Christ.
This was almost a challenge to the Inquisition, and Frà Lamberto
del Cordiglio, the Bolognese inquisitor, was not slow to take it up.
Cecco was forced to abjure, December 16, 1324, and was mercifully
treated. He was condemned to surrender all his books of astrology and forbidden to teach the science in Bologna, publicly or
privately; he was deprived of his Master's degree and subjected
to certain salutary penance of fasting and prayer, together with a
fine of seventy-five lire, which latter may possibly explain the
lightness of the rest of the sentence. The most serious feature of
the affair for him was that now he was a penitent heretic who
could expect no further mercy; it behooved him to walk warily,
for in case of fresh offence he would be a relapsed, doomed inevitably to the stake. Cecco's temperament, however, was not one
to brook such constraint. He came to Florence, then under the
rule of Charles of Calabria, and resumed the practice of his art.
He circulated copies of his forbidden work, which he claimed had
been corrected by the Bolognese inquisitor, but which contained
the same erroneous doctrines; he advanced them anew in his
philosophical poem, *L'Acerba*, and he employed them in the responses given to his numerous clients. In May, 1327, when all
Italy was excited at the coming of Louis of Bavaria, he predicted
that Louis would enter Rome and be crowned, he announced the
time and manner of his death, and gave advice, which was followed,
not to attack him when he passed by Florence. Perhaps all this
might have escaped animadversion but for the personal enmity
and jealousy of Charles of Calabria's chancellor, the Bishop of
Aversa, and of Dino del Garbo, a renowned doctor of philosophy,
esteemed the best physician in Italy. Be this as it may, in July,
1327, Frà Accursio, the Inquisitor of Florence, arrested him.
There was ample evidence that he had continued to teach and act
on the fatalistic theories which were subversive of free-will, but
the Inquisition as usual required a confession, and torture was
freely used to obtain it. A copy of the sentence and abjuration

of 1324 was furnished by the Inquisitor of Bologna, and there was no question as to his relapse. From the beginning the end was inevitable, but there was a mockery of opportunity for defence allowed him, and it was not until December 15 that sentence was pronounced. In accordance with rule, the Bishop of Florence sent a delegate to act with the inquisitor, and an assembly of high dignitaries and experts was assembled to participate, including the Cardinal-legate of Tuscany, the Bishop of Aretino, and Cecco's enemy, the chancellor of Duke Charles. He was abandoned to the secular arm and delivered to Charles's vicar, Jacopo da Brescia. All his books and astrological writings were further ordered to be surrendered within twenty-four hours to the bishop or inquisitor. Cecco was forthwith conducted to the place of execution beyond the walls. Tradition relates that he had learned by his art that he should die between Africa and " Campo Fiore," and so sure was he of this that on the way to the stake he mocked and ridiculed his guards; but when the pile was about to be lighted he asked whether there was any place named Africa in the vicinage, and was told that that was the name of a neighboring brook flowing from Fiesole to the Arno. Then he recognized that Florence was the Field of Flowers and that he had been miserably deceived.*

Astrology continued to hold its doubtful position with a growing tendency to its condemnation. There were few who could take the common-sense view of Petrarch, that astrologers might be useful if they confined themselves to predicting eclipses and storms, and heat and cold, but that when they talked about the fate of men, known only to God, they simply proved themselves to be liars. Eymerich tells us that if a man was suspected of necromancy and was found to be an astrologer it went far to prove him a necromancer, for the two were almost always conjoined. Gerard Groot denounced astrology as a science hostile to God and aiming to supersede his laws. In Spain, in the middle of the fourteenth

---

* Villani x. 40, 41.—Lami, Antichità Toscane, pp. 593-4.—Raynald. ann. 1327, No. 46.—Cantù, Eretici d' Italia, I. 149-52.

I owe many of the above details to a sketch of Cecco's life in a Florentine MS. which I judge from the handwriting to be of the seventeenth century, and of which the anonymous author appears to be well informed; also, to a MS. copy of the elaborate sentence, much more full than the fragments given by Lami and Cantù.

century, both Pedro the Cruel of Castile and Pedro IV. of Aragon kept many astrologers whom they constantly consulted, but in 1387 Juan I. of Castile included astrology among other forms of divination subject to the penalties of the Partidas. Yet it continued to number its votaries among high dignitaries of both State and Church. The only shade on the lustre of Cardinal Peter d'Ailly's reputation was his earnest devotion to the science, and it would have gone hard with him had justice been meted out to him as to Cecco d'Ascoli, for it was impossible for the astrologer to avoid fatalism. It was a curiously erroneous prediction of his, uttered in 1414, that, in consequence of the retrogression of Jupiter in the first house, the Council of Constance would result in the destruction of religion, and peace in the Church would not be obtained; that, in fact, the Great Schism was probably the prelude to the coming of Antichrist. More fortunate was the computation by which he arrived at the date of 1789 as that which would witness great perturbations if the world should so long endure. The tolerance which spared Cardinal d'Ailly did not proceed from any change in the theory of the Church as to the heresy of interfering with the doctrine of free-will. Alonso de Spina points out that the astrological belief that men born under certain stars cannot avoid sinning is manifestly heretical. None the less so was the teaching that when the moon and Jupiter were in conjunction in the head of the Dragon any one praying to God could obtain whatever he wanted, as Peter of Abano found when he used this fortunate moment to secure stores of knowledge beyond the capacity of the unassisted human mind. Sprenger, the highest authority on demonology, held that in astrology there was a tacit pact with the demon.*   All this shows that in the increasing hostility to occult arts astrology had gradually come under the ban, and the disputed question as to its position was finally brought to

---

* Petrarchi de Rebus Senilibus Lib. III. Epist. 1.—Eymeric. p. 443.—Acquoy, Gerardi Magni Epistt. pp. 111–19.—Amador de los Rios (Revista de España, T. XVIII. p. 9).—Novisima Recopilacion, Lib. XII. Tit. iv. l. 1.—Concord. Astron. Veritatis et Narrat. Histor. c. lix., lx. (August. Vindel. 1490).—Fortalic. Fidei Lib. II. Consid. vi.—Savonarola contra l' Astrol. fol. 26.—Bayle, s. v. Apone.— Malleus Malef. P. I. Q. xvi.

The supreme power of the conjunction of Jupiter and the moon above alluded to is probably based on Albumasar de Magnis Conjunctionibus Tract. III. Diff. 2.

a decision, at least for France, by the case of Simon Pharees, in 1494. He had been condemned by the archiepiscopal court of Lyons for practising astrology, and was punished with the light penance of Friday fasting for a year, with the threat of perpetual imprisonment for relapse, and his books and astrolabe had been detained. He had the audacity to appeal to the Parlement, which referred his books to the University. The report of the latter was that his books ought to be burned, even as others had recently been to the value of fifty thousand deniers. All astrology pretending to be prophetic, or ascribing supernatural virtue to rings, charms, etc., fabricated under certain constellations, was denounced as false, vain, superstitious, and condemned by both civil and canon law, as well as the use of the astrolabe for finding things lost or divining the future, and the Parlement was urged to check the rapid spread of this art invented by Satan. The Parlement accordingly pronounced a judgment handing over the unlucky Simon to the Bishop and Inquisitor of Paris, to be punished for his relapse. Astrology, which is described as practised openly everywhere, is condemned. All persons are prohibited from consulting astrologers or diviners about the future, or about things lost or found; all printers are forbidden to print books on the subject, and are ordered to deliver whatever copies they may have to their bishops, and all bishops are instructed to prosecute astrologers. This was a very emphatic condemnation, but, in the existing condition of human intelligence, it could do little to check the insatiable thirst for impossible knowledge. Yet there were some superior minds which rejected the superstition. The elder Pico della Mirandola and Savonarola were of these, and Erasmus ridiculed it in the Encomium Moriæ.*

The question of oneiroscopy, or divination by dreams, was a puzzling one. On the one hand there was the formal prohibition of the Deuteronomist (xviii. 10), which in the Vulgate included

---

* D'Argentré I. ii. 325–31.—Erasmi Encom. Moriæ, Ed. Lipsiens. 1829, III. 360.

The superstitions concerning comets scarce come within our present scope. They will be found ably discussed by Andrew D. White in the Papers of the American Historical Association, 1887. We are told by a contemporary that Henry IV. lost his life in 1610 through neglect of the warning sent him by the learned Doctor Geronymo Oller, priest and astrologer of Barcelona, based upon the portents of a comet which appeared in 1607.—(Guadalajara y Xavierr, Ex pulsion de los Moriscos, Pampeluna, 1613, fol. 107).

the observer of dreams in its denunciations; on the other there
were the examples of Joseph and Daniel, and the formal assertion
of Job "when deep sleep falleth upon man, in slumberings upon
the bed, then he openeth the ears of men and sealeth their instruction" (Job xxxiii. 15, 16). In the twelfth century the expounding
of dreams was a recognized profession which does not seem to
have been forbidden. John of Salisbury endeavors to prove that
no reliance is to be placed on them; Joseph and Daniel were inspired, and short of inspiration no divination from dreams is to be
trusted. This, at least, was a more sensible and practical solution
than the conclusion reached by Thomas Aquinas that divination
from dreams produced by natural causes or divine revelation is
licit, but if the dreams proceed from dæmonic influence it is illicit.
Tertullian had long before ascribed to the pagans the power of
sending prophetic dreams through the agency of demons, but unfortunately, no one could furnish a criterion to distinguish between
the several classes of visions, and as a rule the dream-expounders
were regarded as harmless.*

There was another class of cases which puzzled the casuists,
for the bounds which divided sacred from goetic magic were very
vague. There was a practice of celebrating mortuary masses in
the name of a living man, under the belief that it would kill him.
As early as 694 the seventeenth Council of Toledo prohibits this,
under pain of degradation for the officiating priest and perpetual
exile for him and for his employer; and in the middle of the
fifteenth century the learned Lope Barrientos, Bishop of Cuenca,
condemns it unreservedly. Yet a MS. of uncertain date, printed
by Wright, while pronouncing it sin if done through private malice,
for which the officiating priest should be deposed unless he purge
himself with due penance, states that for a public object it is not
a sin, because it manifests humility in placating God. Somewhat
similar was a question which arose during a quarrel between
Henry, Bishop of Cambrai, and his chapter in 1500. As a mode
of revenge the dean, provost, and canons suspended divine service,
for which they were excommunicated by the Archbishop of Reims.
Under this pressure they resumed their holy functions, but varied
them by introducing in the canon of the mass a sort of impreca-

---

* Johann. Saresberiens. Polycrat. c. xiv.–xvii.—Th. Aquin. Summ. Sec. Sec.
xcv. 6.—Tertull. Apol. 23.

tory litany, composed of comminatory fragments from the psalms
and prophets, recited by the officiating priest with his back to the
altar, while the responses were given by the boys in the choir. The
frightened bishop appealed to the University of Paris, which, after
many months' deliberation, gravely decided that the position of the
priest and the responses of the boys rendered the services suspect of
incantation; that imprecatory services are to be dreaded by those
who give cause for them; that they are not lightly to be used, especially against a bishop who is ready for settlement in the courts, and
that they ought not to be employed even against a contumacious
bishop except in case of necessity arising from extreme peril.*

When, towards the close of the thirteenth century, the Inquisition succeeded in including sorcery within its jurisdiction, its organizing faculty speedily laid down rules and formulas for the
guidance of its members which aided largely in shaping the uncertain jurisprudence of the period and gave a decided impulse to
the persecution of those who practised the forbidden arts. A
manual of practice, which probably bears date about the year
1280, contains a form for the interrogation of the accused covering all the details of sorcery as known at the time. This served
as the foundation on which still more elaborate formulas were
constructed by Bernard Gui and others. If space permitted, a re-
production of these would present a tolerably complete picture of
current superstitions, but I can only pause to call attention to one
feature in them. The earliest draught contains no allusion to the
nocturnal excursions of the "good women" whence the Witches'
Sabbat was derived, while the later ones introduce an interrogation concerning it, showing that during the interval it was attracting increased attention. It is further noteworthy that none of the
formulas embrace questions concerning practices of vulgar witchcraft, which in the fifteenth and succeeding centuries, as we shall
see, furnished nearly the whole basis of prosecutions for sorcery.†

---

* Concil. Toletan. XVII. ann. 694, c. v.—Amador de los Rios (Revista de España, T. XVIII. p. 19).—Wright, Proceedings against Dame Alice Kyteler, pp.
xxxii.-xxxiii.—D'Argentré, I. II. 344-5.

† MSS. Bib. Nat., fonds latin, No. 14930 fol. 229-30.—Doat, XXXVII. 258.—
Vaissette, III. Pr. 374.—Bern. Guidon. Pract. P. v.

Molinier (Études sur quelques MSS. des Bibliothèques d'Italie, Paris, 1887,

When sorcery thus came under the jurisdiction of the Inquisition it came simply as heresy, and the whole theory of its treatment was altered. The Inquisition was concerned exclusively with belief; acts were of interest to it merely as evidence of the beliefs which they inferred, and all heresies were equal in guilt, whether they consisted in affirming the poverty of Christ or led to demon-worship, pacts with Satan, and attempts on human life. The sorcerer might, therefore, well prefer to fall into the hands of the Inquisition rather than to be judged by the secular tribunals, for in the former case he had the benefit of the invariable rules observed in dealings with heresy. By confession and abjuration he could always be admitted to penance and escape the stake, which was the customary secular punishment; while, having no convictions such as animated the Cathari and Waldenses, it cost his conscience nothing to make the necessary recantation. In the inquisitorial records, in so far as they have reached us, we meet with no cases of hardened and obdurate demon-worshippers. Inquisitorial methods could always secure confession, and the inquisitorial manuals give us examples of the carefully drawn formulas of abjuration administered and forms for the sentences to be pronounced. It may perhaps be questioned whether the fiery torture of the stake were not preferable to the inquisitorial mercy which confined its penitents to imprisonment for life in chains and on bread and water; but few men have resolution to prefer a speedy termination to their sufferings, and there was always the hope that exemplary conduct in prison might earn a mitigation of the penalty. It was probably in consequence of this apparent lenity that Philippe le Bel, in 1303, forbade the Inquisition to take cognizance of usury, sorcery, and other offences of the Jews; and we shall see hereafter that when it was forced to summon all its energies in the epidemics of witchcraft, it was obliged to abandon the rule and find excuses for delivering its repentant victims to the stake.*

About this time Zanghino gives us the current Italian ecclesiastical view of the subject. In his detailed description of the various species of magic, vulgar witchcraft finds no place, showing

---

pp. 35, 45) mentions the occurrence of similar formulas in the other manuals of the period.

* Bern. Guidon. Pract. P. iii. 42, 43; P. v. vii. 12.--Doat, XXVII. 150.

that it was unknown in Italy as in France.   All such matters are under episcopal jurisdiction, and the Inquisition cannot meddle with them unless they savor of manifest heresy.   But it is heretical to assert that the future can be foretold by such means, as this belongs to God alone; to receive responses from demons is heretical, or to make them offerings, or to worship sun, moon, or stars, planets or the elements, or to believe that anything is to be obtained except from God, or that anything can be done without the command of God, or that anything is proper and lawful which is disapproved by the Church.   All this falls within the jurisdiction of the Inquisition, and it will be seen that the meshes of the net were small enough to let little escape.   The penalties of death and confiscation, to be inflicted by the secular judge, doubtless refer to the impenitent and relapsed, as the cases which savored of heresy were punished as heresy by the inquisitor.   Magic which did not thus savor of manifest heresy was subject to the episcopal courts, and was punishable by declaring the offender in mortal sin and debarred from communion; he and those who employed him were infamous; he was to be warned to abstain, with excommunication and other penalties, at the episcopal discretion, in case of disobedience.   Yet the secular power by no means abandoned its jurisdiction over sorcery, which continued to be subject to the lay as well as to the ecclesiastical courts.   The time, moreover, had not come for the pitiless extermination of all who dabbled in forbidden arts. By the Milanese law of the period the punishment of the sorcerer was left to the discretion of the judge, who could inflict either corporal or pecuniary penalties proportioned to the gravity of the offence.*

Sorcery was one of the aberrations certain to respond to persecution by more abundant development.   So long as its reality was acknowledged and its professors were punished, not as sharpers, but as the possessors of evil powers of unknown extent, the more public attention was drawn to it the more it flourished.   As soon as the Inquisition had systematized its suppression, we begin to find it occupy a larger and larger share of public attention.   In 1303 one of the charges brought against Boniface VIII., in the Assem-

---

* Zanchini Tract. de Hæret. c. xxii.—Statuta Criminalia Mediolani e tenebris in lucem edita c. 63 (Bergami, 1594).

bly of the Louvre, was that he had a familiar demon who kept
him informed of everything, and that he was a sorcerer who consulted diviners and soothsayers.   About the same time the Bishop
of Coventry and Lichfield, treasurer of Edward I., was accused of
murder, simony, and adultery, to which was added that he consulted the devil, to whom he had rendered homage and kissed on
the posteriors.   King Edward intervened energetically in his behalf, and an inquisition ordered upon him by Boniface reported
that the common fame existing against him proceeded from his
enemies, so that he was allowed to purge himself with thirty-seven
compurgators.   In 1308 the Sire d'Ulmet was brought to Paris on
the charge of endeavoring to kill his wife by sorcery, and the
women whom he had employed were burned or buried alive.   We
have seen how nearly akin to these accusations were the charges
brought against the Templars, and the success of that attempt
was suggestive as to the effectiveness of the methods employed.
When, after the death of Philippe le Bel, Charles of Valois was resolutely bent on the destruction of Enguerrand de Marigny, and the
long proceedings which he instituted threatened to prove fruitless,
it was opportunely discovered that Enguerrand had instigated his
wife and sister to employ a man and woman to make certain wax-
en images which should cause Charles, the young King Louis Hutin, the Count of Saint-Pol, and other personages to wither and die.
As soon as Charles reported this to Louis, the king withdrew his
protection and the end was speedy.   April 26, 1315, Enguerrand
was brought before a selected council of nobles at Vincennes and
was condemned to be hanged, a sentence which was carried out
on the 30th; the sorcerer was hanged with him and the sorceress
was burned, the images being exhibited to the people from the
gallows at Montfaucon, which Enguerrand himself had built, while
the Dame de Marigny and her sister, the Dame de Chantelou, were
condemned to imprisonment.   Thus Enguerrand perished by the
methods which he and his brother, the Archbishop of Sens, had
used against the Templars, and the further moral of the story is
seen in the remorse of Charles of Valois, ten years later, when he
lay on his death-bed and sent almoners through the streets of
Paris to distribute money among the poor, crying, " Pray for the
soul of Messire Enguerrand de Marigny, and of Messire Charles de
Valois!"   One of the accusations against Bernard Délicieux was

that he had attempted the life of Benedict XI. by magic arts, and although this failed of proof, he confessed under torture that a book of necromancy found in his chest belonged to him, and that certain marginal notes in it were in his own handwriting. In this he could not have been alone among his brethren, for in the general chapter of the Franciscans in 1312 a statute was adopted forbidding, under penalty of excommunication and prison, any member of the Order from possessing such books, and dabbling in alchemy, necromancy, divination, incantation, or the invocation of demons.*

The growing importance of sorcery in popular belief received a powerful impetus from John XXII., who in so many ways exercised on his age an influence so deplorable. As one of the most learned theologians of the day, he had full convictions of the reality of all the marvels claimed for magic, and his own experience led him to entertain a lively dread of them. The circumstances of his election were such as to render probable the existence of conspiracies for his removal, and he lent a ready ear to suggestions concerning them. His barbarity towards the unfortunate Hugues, Bishop of Cahors, has been already alluded to, and before the first year of his reign was out he had another group of criminals to dispose of. In 1317 we find him issuing a commission to Gaillard, Bishop of Reggio, and several assessors to try a barber-surgeon named Jean d'Amant and sundry clerks of the Sacred Palace on the charge of attempting his life. Under the

---

* Differend de Boniface VIII. et de Ph. le Bel, Preuves, 103.—Rymer, Fœd. II. 931-4.—Joann. S. Victor. Vit. Clement. V. (Muratori S. R. I. III. II. 457).— Grandes Chroniques V. 217-20, 291.—Guill. Nangiac. Contin. ann. 1315, 1325.— MSS. Bib. Nat., fonds latin, No. 4270 fol. 37-8, 144-5.

Enguerrand de Marigny had been all-powerful under Philippe le Bel, controlling the papal as well as the royal court, and his marvellous rise from obscurity led to the popular impression that he must be a skilful necromancer—

> "Ce fu cil qui fist cardonnaux,
> Et si le pape tint en ses las,
> Qui de petits clers fist prélats—
> —Si orent mainte gent créance
> Que ce par art de nigromance
> Fait, qu'en ce monde faisoit."—
> Godefroi de Paris, v. 6620-9.

persuasive influence of torture they confessed that they had at
first intended to use poison, but finding no opportunity for this
they had recourse to figurines, in the fabrication of which they
were skilled. They had made them under the invocation of demons; they could confine demons in rings and thus learn the secrets of the past and of the future; they could induce sickness, cause
death, or prolong life by incantations, charms, and spells consisting simply of words. Of course they were condemned and executed, and John set to work vigorously to extirpate the abhorred
race of sorcerers to which he had so nearly fallen a victim. We
hear of proceedings against Robert, Bishop of Aix, accused of
having practised magic arts at Bologna; and John, regarding
the East as the source whence this execrable science spread over
Christendom, sought to attack it in its home. In 1318 he ordered
the Dominican provincial in the Levant to appoint special inquisitors for the purpose in all places subject to the Latin rite, and
he called upon the Doge of Venice, the Prince of Achaia, and the
Latin barons to lend their effective aid. He even wrote to the
Patriarch of Constantinople and the Oriental archbishops, urging
them to assist in the good work. Not satisfied with the implied
jurisdiction conferred on the Inquisition by Alexander IV., in
1320 he had letters sent out by the Cardinal of S. Sabina formally
conferring it fully on inquisitors and urging them to exercise it
actively. Subsequent bulls stimulated still further the growing
dread of magic by expressing his grief at the constant increase of
the infection which was spreading throughout Christendom, and
by ordering sorcerers to be publicly anathematized and punished
as heretics and all books of magic lore to be burned. When he
warned all baptized Christians not to enter into compacts with
hell, or to imprison demons in rings or mirrors so as to penetrate
the secrets of the future, and threatened all guilty of such practices that, if they did not reform within eight days, they should
be subject to the penalties of heresy, he took the most effective
means to render the trade of the sorcerer profitable and to increase the number of his dupes. Apparently he became dissatisfied with the response to these appeals, for in 1330 he deplored
the continued existence of demon-worship and its affiliated errors;
he ordered the prelates and inquisitors to speedily bring to conclusion all cases on hand and send the papers under seal to him

for decision, and the inquisitors were commanded to undertake no new cases without a special papal mandate. Whatever may have been the motive of this last prohibition, it was not allowed to take effect in France. We have seen how the royal power about this time was commencing to exercise control over the Inquisition, and we shall see how, at the close of his life, John XXII. was ac cused of heresy as to the Beatific Vision, and was roundly threatened by Philippe de Valois. It was probably an incident of this quarrel that led the king, in 1334, to assume that the jurisdiction of the Inquisition over idolators, sorcerers, and heretics had been conferred by the crown, and to order his seneschals to see that no one should interfere with them in its exercise. This royal rescript seems to have been forgotten with the circumstances which called it forth, for in 1374 the Inquisitor of France applied to Gregory XI. to ask whether he should take cognizance of sorcery, and Gregory replied with instructions to prosecute such cases vigorously.*

The necessary result of all this bustling legislation was to strengthen the popular confidence in sorcery and to multiply its practice. In Bernard Gui's book of sentences rendered in the Inquisition of Toulouse from 1309 to 1323, there are no cases of sorcery, but we meet with several, tried in 1320 and 1321 in the episcopal Inquisition of Pamiers, and the fragmentary records of Carcassonne in 1328 and 1329 show quite a number of convictions. Inquisitors, moreover, commenced to insert a clause renouncing sorcery in all abjurations administered to repentant heretics, so that in case they should become addicted to it they could be promptly burned for relapse.†

Under the influence of this efficient advertisement the trade of the sorcerer flourished. In 1323 a remarkable case attracted much attention in Paris. The dogs of some shepherds, passing a cross-roads near Chateau-Landon, commenced scratching at a certain spot and could not be driven off. The men's suspicions were aroused, and they informed the authorities, who, on digging, found

---

* Raynald. ann. 1317, No. 52–4; ann. 1318, No. 57; ann. 1320, No. 51; ann. 1327, No. 45.—Mag. Bull. Roman. I. 205.—Ripoll II. 192.—Arch. des Frères Prêcheurs de Toulouse (Doat, XXXIV. 181).—Arch. de l'Inq. de Carc. (Doat, XXXV. 89).—Vaissette, IV. Pr. 23.—Raynald. ann. 1374, No. 13.

† Molinier, Études de quelques MSS. des Bibliothèques d'Italie, Paris, 1887, pp. 102–3.—Doat, XXVII. 7 sqq., 140, 156, 177, 192; XXVIII. 161.

a box in which was imprisoned a black cat, with some bread moistened with chrism, blessed oil, and holy water, two small tubes being arranged to reach the surface and supply the animal with air. All the carpenters in the village were summoned, and one identified the box, which he had made for a certain Jean Prevost. Torture promptly brought a confession inculpating the Cistercian abbot of Sarcelles, some canons, a sorcerer named Jean de Persant, and an apostate Cistercian monk, his disciple. The abbot, it seems, had lost a sum of money, and had employed the sorcerer to recover it and find the thief. The cat was to remain three days in the box, to be then killed, and its skin cut into strips, with which a circle was to be made. In this circle a man standing with the remains of the cat's food thrust into his rectum was to invoke the demon Berich, who would make the desired revelation. The Inquisitor of Paris and the episcopal Ordinary promptly tried the guilty parties. Prevost opportunely died, but his remains were burned with his accomplice de Persant, while the ecclesiastics escaped with degradation and perpetual imprisonment. It is evident that de Persant was not allowed the benefit of abjuration, while the Cistercians were exposed to a penalty more severe than those imposed by the rules of their Order. These had been defined in the general chapter of 1290 to be merely incapacity for promotion, or for taking any part in the proceedings of the body, the lowest seat in choir and refectory, and Friday fasting on bread and water until released by the general chapter. The intervening quarter of a century had, however, wrought a most significant change in the attitude of the Church towards this class of offences.*

The monastic orders evidently contributed their full share to this class of criminals. We happen to have the sentence, in 1329, by Henri de Chamay, of a Carmelite named Pierre Recordi, which illustrates the effectiveness of inquisitorial methods in obtaining avowals. The trial lasted for several years, and though the accused tergiversated and retracted repeatedly, his endurance finally gave way. He adhered at last to the confession that on five occasions, to obtain possession of women, he had made wax figurines with invocations of demons, mixing with them the blood

---

* Guill. Nangiac. Contin. ann. 1323.—Grandes Chroniques V. 269-73.—Statut Ord. Cisterc. ann. 1290 c. 2 (Martene Thesaur. IV. 1485).

of toads and his own blood and saliva, as a sacrifice to Satan. He would then place the image under the threshold of the woman, and if she did not yield to him she would be tormented by a demon. In three cases this had succeeded; in the other two it would have done so, had he not been suddenly sent by his superiors to another station. On one occasion he pricked an image in the belly, when it bled. After the images had done their work he would cast them into the river and sacrifice a butterfly to the demon, whose presence would be manifested by a breath of air. He was condemned to perpetual imprisonment on bread and water, with chains on hands and feet, in the Carmelite convent of Toulouse; out of respect to the Order he was not subjected to the ceremony of degradation, and the sentence was rendered privately in the episcopal palace of Pamiers. One peculiar feature of the sentence is the apprehension expressed lest the officials of the convent should allow him to escape.*

The trade of the magician received a further advertisement in the story current at this time about Frederic of Austria. When, after his defeat at Mühldorf in 1322, by Louis of Bavaria, he lay a prisoner in the stronghold of Trausnitz, his brother Leopold sought the services of an expert necromancer, who promised to release the captive through the aid of the devil. In response to his invocation, Satan came in the guise of a pilgrim, and readily promised to bring Frederic to them if he would agree to follow him; but when he appeared to Frederic and told him to get into a bag which he carried around his neck and he would bring him to his brother in safety, Frederic asked him who he was. "Never mind who I am," he replied: "Will you leave your prison, as I tell you?" Then a great fear fell upon Frederic; he crossed himself and the devil disappeared.†

Even to distant Ireland the persecution of sorcery was brought in 1325 by that zealous Franciscan, Richard Ledrede, Bishop of Ossory. The Lady Alice Kyteler of Kilkenny had had four husbands, and their testamentary dispositions not suiting her children by the last three, the most efficient means of breaking their wills was to accuse her of having killed them by sorcery, after bewitch-

---

* Archives de l'Inq. de Carcassonne (Doat, XXVII. 150).

† Matt. Neoburg. (Alb. Argentorat.) ann. 1323 (Urstisii II. 123).—Chronik des Jacob v. Königshofen (Chroniken der deutschen Städte, VII. 467).

ing them to leave their property to her and to her eldest son, William Outlaw. Bishop Ledrede proceeded vigorously to make inquisition, but Lady Alice and William were allied to the leading officials in Ireland, who threw every difficulty in the way, and, as the canons against heresy were unknown in the island, he had an arduous task, being himself at one time arrested and thrown into prison. A less indomitable spirit would have succumbed, but he triumphed at last, though Lady Alice herself escaped his clutches and was conveyed to England. The trials of her assumed accomplices would seem to have been conducted without much respect to form, but with ample energy. Torture being unknown in English law, the bishop might have failed in eliciting confession had he not found an effective, if illegal, substitute in the whip. Petronilla, for instance, one of Lady Alice's women, after being scourged six times could endure no longer the endless increase of agony, and confessed all that was wanted of her. She admitted that she was a skilful sorceress, but inferior to her mistress, who was equal to any in England, or any in the world. She told how, at Lady Alice's command, she had sacrificed cocks in the cross-roads to a demon named Robert Artisson, her mistress's incubus or lover, and how they made from the brains of an unbaptized child, with herbs and worms, in the skull of a robber who had been beheaded, powders and charms to afflict the bodies of the faithful, to excite love and hatred, and to make the faces of certain women appear horned in the eyes of particular individuals. She had been the intermediary between her mistress and the demon; on one occasion he had come to Lady Alice's chamber with two others, black as Ethiopians, when followed love-scenes of which the disgusting details may be spared. The case is interesting as developing a transition state of belief between the earlier magic and the later witchcraft; and it illustrates one of the most important points in the criminal jurisprudence of the succeeding centuries, which explains the unquestioning belief universally entertained as to the marvels of sorcery. Torture administered with unlimited repetition not only brought the patient into a condition in which he would confess whatever was required of him, but the impression produced was such that he would not risk its renewal by retraction even at the last. It was so with this poor creature, who persisted to the end with this tissue of absurdities, and

who was burned impenitent.   Some others involved in the accusation likewise perished at the stake, while some were permitted
to abjure and were punished with crosses—probably the only occasion in which this penance was administered in the British Isles.*

While Bishop Ledrede was busy at this good work a trial occurred in England which illustrates the difference in efficiency
between the ecclesiastical methods of trial by torture and those of
the common law.   Twenty-eight persons were accused of employing John of Nottingham and his assistant, Richard Marshall of
Leicester, to make wax figures for the destruction of Edward II.,
the two Despensers, and the Prior of Coventry, with two of his
officials who had tyrannized over the people and had been sustained by the royal favorites.   Richard Marshall turned accuser,
and the evidence was complete.   The enormous sums of twenty
pounds to Master John and fifteen pounds to Richard had been
promised, and they had been furnished with seven pounds of wax
and two ells of canvas.   From September 27, 1324, until June 2,
1325, the two magicians labored at their work.   They made seven
images, the extra one being experimental, to be tried on Richard
de Sowe.   On April 27 they commenced operating with this by
thrusting a piece of lead into its forehead, when at once Richard de
Sowe lost his reason and cried in misery until May 20, when the
lead was transferred to his breast, and he died May 23.   The accused pleaded not guilty and put themselves on the country.   An
ordinary jury trial followed, with the result that they were all
acquitted.   A similar case came to light at Toulouse in June, 1326,
when some sorcerers were discovered who had undertaken to
make way with King Charles le Bel by means of figurines.   They
were promptly despatched to Paris, and the matter was taken in
hand by the secular court of the Châtelet.   It had all the resources of torture at its command, and its speedy and vigorous
justice undoubtedly soon consigned them to the stake, although
Pierre de Vic, a favored nephew of John XXII., who had been
inculpated in their confessions, was pronounced innocent.   It was
probably not long after this that a similar attempt was made on the
life of John XXII., though the culprits escaped until 1337, when

---

* Wright's Contemporary Narrative of the Proceedings against Dame Alice
Kyteler, Camden Soc., 1843.

they were tried and executed by Benedict XII. To shield themselves they implicated the Bishop of Béziers as their instigator.*

Yet organized persecution seems to have died away with the withdrawal of sorcery from the jurisdiction of the Inquisition by John XXII. in 1330, while the stimulus which his proclamations had given to the trade of the magician continued to extend it and render it profitable. The tendency of popular thought is shown by the attribution, in some places, of the Black Death to the incantations as well as to the poisons of the Jews. Such an expedient as that of the Council of Chartres in 1366, which ordered sorcerers to be excommunicated in mass every Sunday in all parish churches, would only serve to impress the popular mind with the reality and importance of their powers. During this period the study and practice of magic arts were pursued with avidity, and in many cases almost without concealment. Miguel de Urrea, who was Bishop of Tarazona from 1309 to 1316, was honored with the title of *el Nigromantico*, and his portrait in the archiepiscopal palace of Tarragona bears an inscription describing him as a most skilful necromancer, who even deluded the devil with his own arts. Gerard Groot himself, claimed by the Brethren of the Common Life as their revered founder, was in his youth an earnest student of the occult sciences, but during an illness he solemnly abandoned them before a priest and burned his books. Many years later he turned his knowledge to account by exposing a certain John Heyden, who had long practised on the credulity of the people of Amsterdam and its vicinity. On his coming to Deventer, Groot examined him and found him ignorant of necromancy and its allied arts, and concluded that he operated through a compact with Satan. Not willing to incur the irregularity of shedding blood, Groot contented himself with driving him away, and then, on learning that he had settled at Harderwick, wrote to the brethren there giving them an account of him; but the whole affair shows that such persons could count on practical toleration unless some zealot chose to set the laws in motion. The extent to which this toleration was carried, and the limitless credulity to which the popular mind had been trained are shown in the ac-

---

* Wright, op. cit. pp. xxiii.–xxix.—Vaissette, IV. Pr. 173.—Raynald. ann. 1337, No. 30.

counts given by grave historians of the feats of Zyto, the favorite magician of the Emperor Wenceslas, who, in spite of the repeated condemnation of magic by the Councils of Prague during the latter half of the century, reckoned among his evil qualities a fondness for forbidden arts. When, in 1389, he married Sophia, daughter of the Elector of Bavaria, the latter, knowing his proclivities, brought to Prague a wagon-load of skilful conjurers and jugglers. While the chief of these was giving an exhibition of his marvels Zyto quietly walked up to him, opened his mouth, and swallowed him entire, spitting out his muddy boots, and then evacuated him into a vessel of water and exhibited him dripping to the admiring crowd. At the royal banquets Zyto would bother the guests by changing their hands into the hoofs of horses or oxen so that they could not handle their food; if something attracted them to look out of the window he would adorn them with branching antlers, so that they could not withdraw their heads, while he would leisurely eat their delicacies and drink their wine. On one occasion he changed a handful of corn into a drove of fat hogs which he sold to a baker, with a caution not to let them go to the river, but the purchaser disregarded the warning and they suddenly became grains of corn floating on the water. Of course such a character could not end well, and Zyto, when his time came, was carried off by his demon. Not only are all these marvels recorded as unquestionable facts by the Bohemian chroniclers, but they are conscientiously copied by the papal historian Raynaldus.*

Although Gregory XI., in 1374, had authorized the Inquisition to prosecute in all cases of sorcery, in France the Parlement included the subject within its policy of encroachment upon the ecclesiastical jurisdiction. In 1390 an occurrence at Laon, where a secular official named Poulaillier arrested a number of sorcerers, gave it occasion to intervene. As Bodin says, at that time Satan

---

* Lilienthal, Die Hexenprocesse der beiden Städte Braunsberg, p. 113.—Concil. Carnotens. ann. 1366 c. 11 (Martene Ampl. Coll. VII. 1368).—Florez, España Sagrada, XLIX. 188.—Acquoy, Gerardi Magni Epistt. pp. 107–11.—Concil. Pragens. ann. 1355 c. 61 (Hartzheim, IV. 400).—Statuta brevia Arnesti ann. 1353 (Höfler, Prager Concilien, p. 2).—Concil. Pragens. ann. 1381 c. 7 (Ib. p. 28).—Statut. Synod. Pragens. ann. 1407, No. 6 (Ib. p. 59).—Dubrav. Hist. Bohem. Lib. XXIII.—Raynald. ann. 1400, No. 14.

managed to have it believed that the stories of sorcery were false, so the Parlement stopped the proceedings, and thus having its attention drawn to the matter, decreed that in future cognizance of such offences should be confined to the secular tribunals, to the exclusion of the spiritual courts.* Secular judges, however, were ready to treat these cases with abundant sharpness. A case occurring at the Paris Châtelet in 1390 has much interest as affording us an insight into the details of procedure, and as illustrating the efficacy of torture in securing conviction. Except as regards the use of this expedient, now universal in all criminal cases, we see that the process is much fairer to the accused than that of the Inquisition, and we observe once more the ineffaceable impression produced by torture, which leads the despairing victim to adhere to the self-condemnation conducting him inevitably to the stake. Marion l'Estalée was a young *fille de folle vie*, madly in love with a man named Hainsselin Planiete, who deserted her, and, about July 1, 1390, married a woman named Agnesot. Eager to prevent this, if her confession is to be believed, she had applied to an old procuress named Margot de la Barre, for a philtre to fix his wandering affection, and when this failed Margot made for her two enchanted chaplets of herbs, which she threw where the bride and groom would tread on them during the festivities of the wedding-day, assured that this would prevent the consummation of the marriage. The plot was unsuccessful, but Hainsselin and Agnesot fell sick, leading to the arrest of the two women.

On July 30 Margot was examined and denied all complicity. She was promptly tortured on *le petit et le grand tresteau*—which I conjecture to mean, the former, pouring water down the throat till the stomach was distended and then forcing it out by paddling the belly; the latter, the rack. This reduplicated torture produced no confession, and she was remanded for further hearing. August 17 Marion was taken in hand, when she denied, and was similarly tortured without result. On the 3d she was again examined and denied, and on being again ordered to the torture, she appealed to the Parlement; the appeal was promptly heard and rejected, and she was tortured as before, then taken to the kitchen and warmed, after which she was tortured a third time, but to no effect. On

---

* Bodini de Magor. Demonoman. Lib. iv. c. 1.

the 4th she was brought in and refused to confess, but the indefinite repetition of torment without prospect of cessation had produced its effect on body and mind; the torture had been pitiless,
for she is subsequently alluded to as much crippled and weakened
by it, and when she was again bound on the *tresteau*, and the executioner was about to commence his work, she yielded and agreed
to confess.   On being unbound she detailed the whole story, and in
the afternoon, on being brought in again, she confirmed it " *sans
aucune force ou constrainte.*"   Then Margot was introduced, and
Marion repeated her confession, which Margot denied and offered
the wager of battle, of which no notice was taken.   Margot then
asserted her ability to prove an alibi on the day when she was said
to have made the chaplets.   The parties whom she named as witnesses were looked up for her and brought in the next day, when
the evidence proved rather incriminating than otherwise.   Marion
was then made to repeat her confession, and not till then was
Margot tortured a second time, but still without result.   On the
6th Marion was again made to repeat her confession, after which
Margot was brought in and bound to the *tresteau*.   Marion's
youthful vigor had enabled her to endure the torture thrice.
Margot's age had diminished her power of resistance, and the two
applications sufficed.   Her resolution gave way, and before the
torture commenced she promised to confess.   Her story agreed
with that of Marion, except in some embellishments, which serve
to show how thoroughly untrustworthy were all such confessions,
of which the sole object was to satisfy the merciless ministers of
justice.   When she enchanted the chaplets she invoked the demon
by thrice repeating "*Ennemi je te conjures au nom du Père, du
Fils et du Saint Esperit que tu viegnes a moy icy ;*" then an "ennemi," or demon, promptly appeared, like those she had seen in
the Passion-play, and after she had instructed him to enter into
the bodies of Hainsselin and Agnesot he flew out of the window in
a whirlwind, making a great noise and throwing her into mortal
fear.   The evidence was thus complete, and there would seem to
be nothing left but prompt sentence, yet the tribunal manifested
commendable desire to avoid precipitate judgment.   Assessors and
experts were called in.   On August 7, 8, and 9 Marion was thrice
made to repeat her confession, and Margot twice.   On the latter day
a consultation was held, and the decision was unanimous against

Margot, who was pilloried and burned the same day; but three of the experts thought that the pillory and banishment would suffice for Marion. Her case was postponed till the 23d, when another consultation was held; opinions remained unaltered, and as the majority was in favor of condemnation the *prévôt* condemned her, and she was burned the next day. Both the victims may have been innocent, and the whole story may have been invented to avoid the repetition of the intolerable torture; but, inevitable as was the result under the conditions of the trial, the judges manifested every disposition to deal fairly with the unfortunates in their hands, and could entertain no possible doubt as to the reality of the offence and of the apparition of the demon as described by Margot.* It is necessary to bear this in mind when estimating the conduct of the judges and inquisitors who sent thousands of unfortunates to the stake in the next two centuries, for offences which to a modern mind are purely chimerical, for, according to the jurisprudence of the age, no evidence could be more absolute than that on which rested the cruelly punished absurdities of witchcraft.

Simultaneous with this case was the burning of a sorceress named Jeanette Neuve or Revergade, August 6, 1390, in Velay. Although she was tried and executed by the court of the Abbey of Saint-Chaffre, this was in its capacity as *haut-justicier*, and not as a spiritual tribunal. A century later we should have found the case embroidered with full accounts of the Sabbat and of demon-worship, but the time had not yet arrived for this. Jeanette was a poor wandering crone who had come to Chadron, within the abbatial jurisdiction, and earned a livelihood by curing diseases with charms, to which she usually added the prescription of a pilgrimage to some shrine of local renown. She must have gained reputation as a wise-woman, for the Sire de Burzet, quarrelling with his wife and desiring reconciliation, came to her for a philtre. She gave him a potion of which he died, and her fate was sealed.†

About this period may be dated a fresh impulse given to the belief in sorcery, whose continued growth during the fifteenth and sixteenth centuries was destined to produce results so deplorable,

---

* Registre Criminel du Châtelet de Paris, I. 332–63 (Paris, 1861).
† Chassaing, Spicilegium Brivatense, pp. 438–46.

and to present one of the most curious problems in the history of
human error.   The first indication of this new development is
found in the action of the University of Paris.   September 19,
1398, the theological faculty held a general congregation in the
Church of St. Mathurin, and adopted a series of twenty-eight
articles which thenceforth became a standard for all demonologists, and were regarded as an unanswerable argument to sceptics
who questioned the reality of the wickedness of the arts of magic.
The preamble recites that action was necessary in view of the
active emergence of ancient errors which threatened to infect society; the old evils, which had been well-nigh forgotten, were
reviving with renewed vigor, and some positive definition was required to guard the faithful from the snares of the enemy.   The
University then proceeded to declare that there was an implied
contract with Satan in every superstitious observance, of which
the expected result was not reasonably to be anticipated from
God and from Nature, and it condemned as erroneous the assertion that it was permissible to invoke the aid of demons or to seek
their friendship, or to enter into compacts with them, or to imprison them in stones, rings, mirrors, and images, or to use sorcery
for good purposes or for the cure of sorcery, or that God could be
induced by magic arts to compel demons to obey invocations, or
that the celebration of masses or other good works used in some
forms of thaumaturgy was permissible, or that the prophets and
saints of old performed their miracles by these means which were
taught by God, or that by certain magic arts we can attain to the
sight of the divine essence.   These latter clauses point to a dangerous tendency of coalescence between the arts of the sorcerer
and of the theurgist, and indicate that in the higher magic of the
day there was a claim to be considered as penetrating to the ineffable mysteries which surrounded the throne of God ; in fact,
these adepts declared that their arts were lawful, and they sought
to prove their origin in God by pointing out that good flowed
from them, and that the wishes and prophecies of those using
them were fulfilled.   All this the University condemned, and while
on the one hand it denied that images of lead or gold or wax, when
baptized, exorcised, and consecrated on certain days, possessed the
powers ascribed to them in the books of magic, on the other hand
it was equally emphatic in animadverting on the incredulity of

those who denied that sorcery, incantations, and the invocation of demons possessed the powers claimed for them by sorcerers.*

Like all other efforts to repress sorcery, this of course only served to give it fresh significance and importance. The declaration that it was erroneous to doubt the reality of sorcery and its effects became a favorite argument of the demonologists. Gerson declared that to call in question the existence and activity of demons was not only impious and heretical, but destructive to all human and political society. Sprenger concludes that the denial of the existence of witchcraft is not in itself heresy, as it may proceed from ignorance, but such ignorance in an ecclesiastic is in itself highly culpable; such denial is sufficient to justify vehement suspicion of heresy, calling for prosecution, and we have seen what was the significance of "vehement suspicion" in inquisitorial practice.†

With popular credulity thus stimulated, the insanity of Charles VI. afforded a tempting opportunity for charlatans to market their wares. In 1397 the Maréchal de Sancerre sent to Paris from Guyenne two Augustinian hermits who had great reputation for skill in the occult sciences, and who promised relief. They pronounced the royal patient a victim of sorcery, and after some incantations he recovered his senses, but it proved only a lucid interval, and in a week he relapsed. This they charged upon the royal barber and a porter of the Duke of Orleans, who were arrested, but nothing could be proved against them, and they were discharged. For months the two impostors led a joyous life with ample fees, but at last they were compelled to name the author of the sorceries, and this time they had the audacity to pitch upon the king's brother, Louis of Orleans himself. This grew serious, and on being threatened with torture they confessed themselves sorcerers, apostates, and invokers of demons. They were accordingly tried, condemned, degraded from the priesthood, and mercifully beheaded and quartered. Undeterred by this example, in 1403 a priest named Ives Gilemme, who boasted that he had three

---

* D'Argentré I. II. 154. Cf. Bodin. de Magor. Demonoman.—Murner Tract. de Python. Contractu.—Basin de Artibus Magiæ.—Pegnæ Comment. in Eymeric. p. 346.

† Gersoni Tract. de Error. circa Artem Magicam (Opp. Ed. 1494, xxi. G–H).— Mall. Maleficar. P. I. Q. 1, 8.

demons in his service, with some other invokers of demons, the Demoiselle Marie de Blansy, Perrin Hemery, a locksmith, and Guillaume Floret, a clerk, offered to cure the king, and were given a trial. They asked to have twelve men loaded with iron chains placed at their disposal; these they surrounded with an enclosure, and, after telling them not to be afraid, proceeded with all the invocations they could muster, but accomplished no results. They excused their failure by alleging that the men had crossed themselves, but this availed them nothing. Floret confessed to the Prévôt of Paris that the whole affair was a deception, and on March 24, 1404, they were all duly burned. It was probably this case which induced Cardinal Louis of Bourbon, in his provincial synod of Langres, in 1404, to prohibit strictly all sorcery and divination, and to warn his flock to place no trust in such arts, as their practitioners were mostly deceivers whose only object was to trick them out of their money. Priests, moreover, were strictly ordered, as had already been done by the Council of Soissons the year before, to report to the episcopal ordinaries all cases coming to their knowledge and all persons defamed for such practices. Had this policy been carried out, of treating sorcerers as sharpers, and of instituting an episcopal police to replace the Inquisition, at this time rapidly falling into desuetude, it might have averted the evils which followed, but the well-meant effort of Cardinal Louis was followed by no results. The belief in sorcery continued to strengthen, and when Jean Petit undertook to justify Jean sans Peur for the assassination of the Duke of Orleans, it was almost a matter of course that he should accuse the murdered prince of encompassing the king's insanity by magic, of which the most minute details were given, including the names of the two demons, Hynars and Astramein, whose assistance had been successfully invoked.[*]

In England, sorcery, as we have seen, had thus far attracted

---

[*] Religieux de S. Denis, Hist. de Charles VI., Liv. xvii. ch. i., Liv. xviii. ch. 8.—Juvenal des Ursins, Hist. de Charles VI. ann. 1403.—Raynald. ann. 1404, No. 22–3.—Concil. Suessionens. ann. 1403 c. 7.—Monstrelet, I. 39 (Ed. Buchon, 1843, pp. 80–3).—Chron. de P. Cochon (Ed. Vallet de Viriville, p. 385).

Valentine of Milan, wife of Louis of Orleans, and her father, Galeazzo Visconti, had the reputation of being addicted to magic and of being privy to the attempt on the life of the king (ubi sup.).

little attention. Even as late as 1372 a man was arrested in South-
wark with the head and face of a corpse in his possession, and a
book of magic was found in his trunk. Tried before the Inquisition he would infallibly have confessed under torture a series of
misdeeds and have ended at the stake; but he was brought before
Sir J. Knyvet, in the King's Bench. No indictment even was
found against him; he was simply sworn not to practise sorcery
and was discharged, but the head and book were burned at Tot-
hill at his expense. To the fair and open character of English law
is doubtless to be attributed the comparative exemption of the
island from the terror of sorcery, but when, at last, persecuting
excitement arose in the Lollard troubles, the Church used its influence with the new Lancastrian dynasty to suppress the emissaries
of Satan. In 1407 Henry IV. issued letters to his bishops reciting
that sorcerers, magicians, conjurers, necromancers, and diviners
abounded in their dioceses, perverting the people and perpetrating
things horrible and detestable. The bishops, therefore, were commissioned to imprison all such malefactors, either with or without
trial, until they should recant their errors or the king's pleasure
could be learned respecting them. The placing of the matter thus
in the hands of the Church, and depriving the accused of all legal
safeguards, is most significant as a recognition that the ordinary
forms of English law were not to be depended upon in such cases,
and that public opinion as yet was too unformed for juries to be
trusted. Under the regency the royal council seems to have
assumed jurisdiction over the matter. In 1432 a Dominican of
Worcester, Thomas Northfield, suspected of sorcery, was summoned before it with all his books of magic. A few days later
it heard the celebrated Witch of Eye, Margery Jourdemayne, with
the Dominican John Ashewell and John Virby, a clerk, who had
been confined at Windsor under charge of sorcery, but they were
discharged on giving bonds for good behavior. The Witch of Eye
did not fare so well when, in 1441, she was implicated in the accusation brought against the Duchess of Gloucester, of making and
melting a wax figurine of Henry VI. The duchess confessed and
escaped with the penance of walking bareheaded thrice through
the streets with wax tapers of two pounds each, and offering them
at the shrines of St. Paul's, Christ Church, and St. Michael's in
Cornhill, after which she was imprisoned and finally banished to

Chester. Her secretary, Roger, was hanged, drawn, and quartered, and Margery was burned—the whole affair being political. A similar endeavor to take political advantage of the belief in sorcery occurred in 1464, in connection with the marriage of Edward IV. and Elizabeth Woodville, when his constancy to her was attributed to the magic arts of her mother, Jacquette, widow of the Regent Bedford in first marriage. Jacquette did not wait to be attacked, but turned upon her accusers, Thomas Wake and John Daunger, who had talked about her using leaden images of the king and queen, and had shown one of them broken in two and wired together. They disclaimed responsibility, and endeavored to shift the burden each on the other; but in 1483 Richard III. did not fail to make the most of the matter, and in the act for the settlement of the crown described Edward's "pretensed marriage" as brought about by "sorcerie and witchcraft committed by the said Elizabeth and her moder, Jacquette duchesse of Bedford." Thus England was gradually prepared to share in the horrors of the witchcraft delusions.*

Perhaps the most remarkable trial for sorcery on record is that of the Maréchal de Rais, in 1440, which has long ranked as a *cause célébre*, although it is only of late that the publication of the records has enabled it to be properly understood. The popular belief at the time is indicated by Monstrelet, who tells us that the marshal was accustomed to put to death pregnant women and children in order with their blood to write the conjurations which secured him wealth and honors; Jean Chartier alludes to his putting children to death and performing strange things contrary to the faith to attain his ends, and in the next century Gaguin speaks of his slaying children in order with their blood to divine the future.† Curious as is the case in many aspects, perhaps its chief interest lies in the psychological study which it affords as an illustration of the extreme development of the current ecclesiastical teaching with regard to the remission of sins.

In the France of the fifteenth century there was no career more

---

* Wright, Dame Kyteler, pp. ix., xv.–xx.—Rymer, Fœd. VIII. 427; X. 505; XI. 851.

† Monstrelet, II. 248.—Jean Chartier, Hist. de Charles VII. ann. 1440 (Ed. Godefroy, p. 106).—Rob. Gaguin. Hist. Franc. Lib. x. c. 3.

promising than that of Gilles de Rais. Born in 1404 of the noble stock of Montmorency and Craon, grandson of the renowned knight, Brumor de Laval, grandnephew of du Guesclin, of kindred with the Constable Clisson, and allied with all that was illustrious in the west of France, his barony of Rais rendered him the head of the baronage of Britanny. His territorial possessions were ample, and when, while still a youth, he married the great heiress, Catharine de Thouars, he might count himself among the wealthiest nobles of France. His bride is said to have brought him one hundred thousand livres in gold and movables, and his revenue was reckoned at fifty thousand. At the age of sixteen he won the esteem of his suzerain, Jean V., Duke of Britanny, by his courage and skill in the campaign which ended the ancient rivalry between the houses of de Montfort and de Penthièvre. At twenty-two, following the duke's brother, the Constable Artus de Richemont, he entered the desperate service of Charles VII., with a troop maintained at his own expense, and he distinguished himself in the seemingly hopeless resistance to the English arms. When Joan of Arc appeared he was charged with the special duty of watching over her personal safety, and, from the relief of Orleans to the repulse at the gates of Paris, he was ever at her side. In the coronation ceremonies at Reims he received, though but twenty-five years old, the high dignity of Marshal of France, and in the September following he was honored with permission to add to his arms a border of the royal fleurs-de-lis. There was no dignity beneath the crown to which his ambition might not aspire, for he maintained himself so skilfully between the opposing factions of the constable and of the royal favorite, La Trémouille, that when the latter fell, in 1433, his credit at the court was unimpaired.*

He was, moreover, a man of unusual culture. His restless curiosity and thirst for knowledge led him to accumulate books at a time when it was rare for knights to be able to sign their names. Chance has preserved to us the titles of St. Augustin's "City of God," "Valerius Maximus," Ovid's "Metamorphoses" and "Suetonius," as fragments of his library; and on his trial one of the reasons he gave for liking an Italian necromancer was the choice

---

* Bossard et Maulde, Gilles de Rais, dit Barbe-bleue, Paris, 1886, pp. 16, 43, 49–51, 53, 57, Pr. p. clvii.

Latinity of his speech. He delighted in rich bindings and illumi-
nations. On one occasion he is described, but a few months before
his arrest, as engaged in his study in ornamenting with enamels the
cover of a book of ceremonies for his chapel. Of music and the
drama he was also passionately fond. In these pursuits he was a
fit comrade for the good King René, as in the field he was the
mate of Dunois and La Hire.*

Yet the life which promised so much in camp and court was
blighted by the fatal errors of his training. The death of his
father while he was a child of eleven left him to the care of a weak
and indulgent grandfather, Jean de Craon, whose authority he
soon shook off. His fiery nature ran riot, and he grew up devoured with the wildest ambition, abandoned to sensual excesses
of every kind, and with passions unrestrained and untamable.
When on trial he repeatedly addressed the wondering crowd, urging all parents to train their children rigidly in the ways of virtue,
for it was his unbridled youth that had led him to crime and a
shameful death.†

Although, in the charges preferred against him, his aberrations are said to have commenced in 1426, he himself asserted
that the fatal plunge was not made until 1432, after the death of
his grandfather. About that time he began to withdraw from
active life, and after 1433 he is no longer heard of in the field,
although the war of liberation offered its prizes as abundantly as
ever.‡

Then commenced a strange and unexampled dual existence.
To the outward world he was the magnificent seigneur, intent
only on display and frivolity. His immeasurable ambition, diverted from its natural career, found unworthy gratification in
making the vulgar stare with his gorgeous splendor. He affected
a state almost royal. A military household of over two hundred
horsemen accompanied him wherever he went. He founded a
chapter of canons, with service and choir fit for a cathedral, and
this was his private chapel, likewise attached to his person, costing him immense sums, including portable organs carried on the

---

* Bossard et Maulde, Gilles de Rais, dit Barbe-bleue, Paris, 1886, Pr. pp. liii.,
lxxvii., clii.

† Ibid. p. 21; Pr. pp. xlix., lviii.

‡ Ib. pp. 48–51; Pr. pp. xxi.–xxvi., xlvi., xlix.

shoulders of six stout serving-men. Not less extravagant was his
passion for theatrical displays. The drama of the age, though rude,
was costly, and when he exhibited freely to the multitude spec-
tacular performances, there were immense structures to be built
and hundreds of actors to be clad in cloths of gold and silver, silks
and velvets, and handsome armor, the whole followed by public
banquets to the spectators, in which rich viands were served in
profusion and rare wines and hippocras flowed like water. These
were only items in his expenditure; his purse and table were open
to all and his artistic tastes were gratified without regard to cost.
In one visit to Orleans, where his retinue filled every inn in the
city, he was said to have squandered eighty thousand gold crowns
between March and August, 1435. This ruinous prodigality was
accompanied with the utmost disorder in his affairs. It was beneath the dignity of a great seigneur to attend to business, and all
details were abandoned to the crowd of pimps and parasites and
flatterers attracted by his lavish recklessness, among whom the
principal were Roger de Briqueville and Gilles de Sillé. Gold
must be raised at any price; his revenues were farmed out in advance, the produce of field and forest and salt-works was disposed
of at low prices, and he soon began to sell his estates at less than
their value, usually reserving a right of redemption within six
years. In a short time he is estimated to have consumed from
this source alone not less than two hundred thousand crowns.
Already, in 1435 or 1436, his family became alarmed at his mad
career; they appealed to Charles VII., who issued letters, in accordance with a legal custom of the time, interdicting him from
alienating lands and revenues, and all persons from contracting
with him. This was published with sound of trump in Orleans,
Angers, Blois, Machecoul, and elsewhere outside of Britanny.
Within the duchy, Jean V. prohibited its publication. Notwithstanding his surname of le Bon and le Sage, he was a greedy and
unscrupulous prince, who, as one of the chief purchasers of the
marshal's estates, was interested in the ruin of his subject. He
continued to secure profitable bargains, subject always to the right
of redemption, and manifested for his dupe the greatest friendship,
appointing him lieutenant-general of the duchy, and entering into
a brotherhood of arms with him, while privately mocking and
ridiculing him as a fool. As a last resort, Gilles's younger brother,

René de la Suze, and his cousin, the Admiral de Loheac, captured and garrisoned the castles of Champtocé and Machecoul, but in 1437 and 1438 Gilles retook them, with the aid of the duke, to whom he had sold the former.*

Such was the external life of Gilles de Rais, to all appearance that of a liberal, pious noble, whose worst foible was thoughtless extravagance. Beneath the surface, however, lay an existence of crime more repulsive than anything chronicled by Tacitus or Suetonius. There are some subjects so foul that one shrinks from the barest allusion to them, and of such are the deeds of Gilles de Rais. For the sake of human nature one might hope that the charges which brought him to the gallows and stake were invented by those who plotted his ruin, but an attentive examination of the evidence brings conviction that amid manifest exaggeration there was substantial foundation of fact. Ordinary indulgence having palled upon the senses of the youthful voluptuary, about the year 1432 he abandoned himself to unnatural lusts, selecting as his victims children, whom he promptly slew to secure their silence. At first their bodies were thrown into *oubliettes* at the bottom of towers in his ordinary places of residence. When Champtocé was about to be surrendered to the duke, the bones of about forty children were hastily gathered together and carried off; when René de la Suze was advancing on Machecoul, the same number were extracted from their hiding-place and burned. Scared by this narrow escape from detection, Gilles subsequently had the bodies burned at once in the fireplace of his chamber and the ashes scattered in the moats. So depraved became his appetites that he found his chief enjoyment in the death agonies of his victims, over whose sufferings he gloated as he skilfully mangled them and protracted their torture. When dead he would criticise their beauties with his confidential servitors, would compare one with another, and would kiss with rapture the heads which pleased him most. Not Caligula, when, to gain fresh appetite for his revels, he caused criminals to be tortured by the side of his banquet-table, or Nero, when enjoying the human torches

---

* Bossard et Maulde, Gilles de Rais, dit Barbe-bleue, Paris, 1886, pp. 61–66, 72–3, 78–81, 92–116, 173, 269; Pr. pp. cliv.–clv., clvii., clix.—Très-Ancien Coutume de Bretagne c. 83 (Bourdot de Richebourg, IV. 220).—D'Argentré, Comment. in Consuetud. Britann. pp. 1647–55.

illuminating his unearthly orgies, found such delirium of delight in inflicting and in watching human agony.*

While such were his recreations, his serious pursuit was the search for the philosopher's stone—the Universal Elixir which should place unlimited wealth and power in his hands. To this end his agents were on the watch to bring him skilled professors in the art, and he served as the dupe of a succession of charlatans, whose promises kept him ever in the hope that he was on the point of attaining the fulfilment of his desires. He never ceased to believe that once, at his castle of Tiffauges, the operation was about to be crowned with success, when the sudden arrival of the Dauphin Louis forced him to destroy his furnaces; for though, as we have seen, alchemy was not positively included in the prohibited arts, its practice was ground for suspicion, and Louis, even in his youth, was not one to whom he could afford to confide so dangerous a secret. This confident hope explains the recklessness of his expenditures and his careless alienations, in which he retained a right of redemption, for any morrow might see him placed beyond the need of reckoning with his creditors. Yet, as already stated, although alchemy assumed to be a science, in practice it was almost universally coupled with necromancy, and few alchemists pretended to be able to achieve results without the assistance of demons, whose invocation became a necessary department of their art. So it was with those employed by Gilles de Rais, and no more instructive chapter in the history of the frauds of magic can be found than in his confession and that of his chief magician, Francesco Prelati. The latter had a familiar demon named Barron, whom he never had any difficulty in evoking when alone, but who would never show himself when Gilles was present, and in the naïve accounts which the pair give of their attempts and failures, one cannot help admiring the quick-witted ingenuity of the Italian and the facile credulity of the baron. On one occasion, in answer to Prelati's earnest prayer for gold, the tantalizing demon spread countless ingots around the room, but forbade his touching them for some days. When this was reported to Gilles he naturally desired to feast his eyes upon the treasure, and Prelati conducted him to the chamber. On opening the door, however, he

---

* Bossard et Maulde, Pr. pp. lxxxiv.–xcii., xcv.–xcix.

cried out that he saw a great green serpent as large as a dog coiled up on the floor, and both took to their heels.   Then Gilles armed himself with a crucifix containing a particle of the true cross, and insisted on returning, but Prelati warned him that such expedients only increased the danger, and he desisted.   Finally the malicious demon changed the gold into tinsel, which, when handled, turned into a tawny dust.   It was in vain that Gilles gave to Prelati compacts signed with his blood, pledging himself to obedience in return for the three gifts of knowledge, wealth, and power; Barron would have none of them.   The demon was offended with Gilles for not keeping a promise to make some offering to him; if a small request were made it should be a trifle, such as a pullet or a dove; if something greater it must be the member of a child. Children's bodies were not scarce where Gilles resided, and he speedily placed in a glass vessel a child's hand, heart, eyes, and blood, and gave them to Prelati to offer.   Still the demon was obdurate, and Prelati, as he said, buried the rejected offering in consecrated ground.   Gilles has had the reputation of sacrificing unnumbered children in his necromantic operations, but this is the only case elicited on his trial, and the number of times it is brought into the evidence shows the immense importance attached to it by the prosecution.*

It was impossible that a career such as this could continue for eight years without exciting suspicion.   Though for the most part Gilles selected his victims from among the beggars who crowded his castle gates, attracted by his ostentatious charities—children for whom there was no one to make inquiry—yet he had his agents out through the land enticing from parents the offspring whom they would see no more.   Two women, Etiennette Blanchu and Perrine Martin, better known as La Meffraye, were the most successful of these purveyors, and it came to be noticed that when he was in Nantes the children who frequented the gates of his Hôtel de la Suze were apt to disappear unaccountably.   His confidential servants, Henri Griart, known as Henriet, and Étienne Corillaut, nicknamed Poitou, when they saw a handsome youth would engage him as a page without concealment, ride off with

---

* Bossard et Maulde, Pr. pp. xxvi., xxxiv., xlvii.–lii., lv.–lvi., lxii.–lxxii., lxxxviii., xcviii., ci., cxvii.—Monstrelet, II. 248.

him, and he would be heard of no more. It is rather curious, indeed, how tardily suspicion was aroused, for up to within a year or two of the end there were mothers who had no hesitation in confiding their children to the terrible baron. At his castles of Tiffauges and Machecoul there was little disguise. He was *haut-justicier* in his lands: between him and his villeins there was, as de Fontaines says, no judge but God; they could not fly, for they were attached to the glebe, and they could only rest silent in dread suspense as to where the next bolt would fall. Even as far off as St. Jean-d'Angely, Machecoul had the name of a place where children were eaten, and at Tiffauges they said that for one child that disappeared at Machecoul there were seven at Tiffauges. Yet so far was the truth from being guessed that the story ran among the peasantry that Michel de Sillé, when a prisoner with the English, had been obliged to promise, as part of his ransom, twenty-four boys to serve as pages, and that when the tale was complete the disappearances would cease. Still suspicion grew. One of the marshal's confidants, though not fully initiated in his secrets, a priest named Eustache Blanchet, grew alarmed and ran away from Tiffauges, taking up his residence at Mortagne-sur-Sèvre. Here he learned from Jean Mercier, castellan of La Roche-sur-Yon, that in Nantes and Clisson and elsewhere it was public rumor that Gilles killed numbers of children, in order with their blood to write a necromantic book which, when completed, would enable him to capture any castle and prevent any one from withstanding him. This grew to be the popular belief, as recorded by Monstrelet, and so impressed was Blanchet's imagination with it that, after his return to Tiffauges, at Easter, 1440, just before the catastrophe, when Gilles invited him and another priest into his study to exhibit to them his ornamentation of the binding of the ceremonial book of his chapel, some sheets of paper written in red, lying on the desk, convinced him that the popular report was true. In this little scene, the contrast between the peaceful artistic labors of the marshal and the dread conjurations supposed to be written with his own hand in innocent blood, is a type of his strange career.*

What was the number of his victims can never be known.

---

* Bossard et Maulde, Pr. pp. lxxv., lxxvii., lxxxviii.–xcii., xcv.–xcix., cxvii.–cxl.

With the exaggeration customary in such cases some writers have estimated them at seven hundred or eight hundred. In his confession Gilles said that the number was great, but he kept no count. In the civil process against him it is stated at over two hundred, but in the articles of accusation in the ecclesiastical court, which were elaborately drawn up after obtaining all possible testimony, the figure is given as one hundred and forty, more or less, and this is probably a full estimate.*

Yet, strange as were the crimes of Gilles de Rais, even stranger was his profound conviction that he had in no way so incurred the wrath of God that the Church could not readily insure his salvation at the cost of some of the customary penances. He was solicitous about his soul in a fashion very uncommon with demonworshippers, and in all his projected and rejected compacts with Satan he was careful to insert a clause that he should not suffer in body or soul. He was regular in the observances of religion. On the Easter previous to his arrest a witness describes him as going behind the altar with a priest for confession, and then taking the communion with the rest of the parishioners, and when these latter, uneasy at their companionship with so great a lord, desired to rise he bade them stay, and all remained together until the Eucharist was administered to all. When he founded his chapter of canons and dedicated it to the Holy Innocents, there might seem to be a grim pleasantry in his choice of patron saints, yet there can be no doubt that he felt that he was thus atoning for the massacre of the innocents which he himself was constantly perpetrating. More than once he had a transient emotion of repentance; he took vows to abandon his guilty life, and by a pilgrimage to the Holy Sepulchre to obtain pardon for the evil he had wrought—pardon which he never seems to have doubted could be thus easily won, and reasonably enough, in view of the plenary indulgences which were so lavishly distributed and sold. After making his public confession, when he could have no further hope on earth, he turned to the crowded audience and exhorted them to hold fast to the Church and to pay her the highest honor. He had always, he said, kept his heart and his affections on the Church, but for which, in view of his crimes, he believed that Satan would have strangled

---

* Bossard et Maulde, pp. 212–13 ; Pr. pp. xxiv., l.

him and carried him off, body and soul. This trust in the saving power of the Church gave him the absolute confidence in his salvation which is not the least noteworthy feature in his strange character. When, after he and Francesco Prelati had corroborated each other's confessions, and they were about to part, he embraced and kissed his necromancer with sobs and tears, saying, "*Adieu, Francoys, mon amy;* we shall see each other no more in this world: I pray God to give you patience and knowledge: be certain that if you have patience and hope in God we shall meet each other in the great joy of paradise. Pray God for me, and I will pray for you." There was none of the agonizing doubt that racked the tender conscientiousness of the Friends of God, no mental struggle, but the calm assurance, born of implicit belief in the teachings of the Church, that a man might lead a life of unimaginable crime and at any moment purchase his salvation.*

How long Gilles might have continued his devastating career it would be hard to guess, had it not suited the interest of Duke Jean and of his chancellor, Jean de Malestroit, Bishop of Nantes, to bring him to the stake. Both of them had been purchasers of his squandered estates, and might wish to free themselves from the equity of redemption, and both might hope to gain from the confiscation of what remained to him. To assail so redoubtable a baron was, however, a task not lightly to be undertaken: the Church must be the leader, for the civil power dared not risk arousing the susceptibilities of the whole baronage of the duchy. Gilles's impetuous temper furnished them the excuse.

The marshal had sold the castle and fief of Saint-Etienne de Malemort to Geoffroi le Ferron, treasurer of the duke—possibly a cover for the duke himself — and had delivered seizin to Jean le Ferron, brother of the purchaser, a man who had received the tonsure and wore the habit of a clerk, thus entitling him to clerical immunity, even though he performed no clerical functions. Some cause of quarrel subsequently arose, which Gilles proceeded to settle in the arbitrary fashion customary at the time. On Pentecost, 1440, he led a troop of some sixty horsemen to Saint-Étienne, left them in ambush near the castle, and with a few followers went to the church where Jean was at his devotions. Mass

---

* Bossard et Maulde, Pr. pp. xxvii.–xxviii., xlvi., xlvii., lii., lv., lviii., lxxii., lxxx.

was about concluded when the intruders rushed in with brand-
ished weapons, and Gilles addressed Jean: "Ha, scoundrel, thou
hast beaten my men and committed extortions on them; come out
or I will kill thee!" It was with difficulty that the frightened
clerk could be reassured. He was dragged to the gate of the
castle and forced to order its surrender, when Gilles garrisoned it
and carried him off, finally imprisoning him in Tiffauges, chained
hand and foot.*

The offence was one for which the customs of Britanny provided a remedy in the civil courts, but the duke zealously took up
the cause of his treasurer and summarily ordered his lieutenant-
general to surrender the castle and the prisoners under a penalty
of fifty thousand crowns. Indignant at this unlooked-for intervention, Gilles maltreated the messengers of the duke, who promptly raised a force and recaptured the place in dispute. Tiffauges,
where the prisoners lay, was in Poitou, beyond his jurisdiction,
but his brother, the Constable de Richemont, besieged it, and Gilles
was forced to liberate them. Having thus submitted, he ventured
in July to visit the duke at Josselin: he had some doubts as to his
reception, but Prelati consulted his demon and announced that he
could go in safety. He was graciously received, and imagined
that the storm had blown over. So safe did he feel that while at
Josselin he continued his atrocities, putting to death several children and causing Prelati to evoke his demon.†

While the powers of the State thus hesitated to attack the
criminal, the Church was busily preparing his downfall. He had
been guilty of sacrilege in the violence committed in the church
of Saint-Étienne, and he had violated its immunities in the person of Jean le Ferron. Yet, in that cruel age, when war spared
neither church nor cloister, these were offences too frequent to
justify his ruin, and in the earlier stages of the proceedings they
are not even alluded to. On July 30 Jean de Malestroit, in whose
bishopric of Nantes the barony of Rais was situated, issued privately a declaration reciting that in a recent visitation he and his
commissioners had found that Gilles was publicly defamed for

---

* Bossard et Maulde, pp. 231-5; Pr. pp. xxix., cii.-cxvi., cliv.

† Très Anc. Cout. de Bretagne c. 62 (Bourdot de Richebourg IV. 216).—Bossard
et Maulde, pp. 235-6; Pr. pp. liii., lxxi.

murdering many children, after gratifying his lust on them, of invoking the demon with horrid rites, of entering into compacts with him, and of other enormities. Though in a general way synodal witnesses were quoted in substantiation of these charges, only eight witnesses were personally named, seven of them women, all residents of Nantes, whose subsequent testimony shows us that they had lost children, whose disappearance they thought they could connect with Gilles. The object of this paper was doubtless to loosen the tongues of those to whom it might be shown, but whatever diligence was used in gathering evidence was fruitless, for when the trial opened, two months later, but two additional witnesses had been procured, of the same indecisive kind as the previous ones. The only charge they made was the abduction of children, and this was in no sense a crime within the competence of the ecclesiastical court. Evidently the awful secrets of Tiffauges and Machecoul had not leaked out. It was necessary to hazard something, to strike boldly, and when Gilles and his retainers were in the hands of justice its methods could be relied upon to procure from them evidence sufficient for their own conviction.*

The blow fell September 13, when the bishop issued a citation summoning Gilles to appear for trial before him on the 19th. The recital of his misdeeds in the previous letter was repeated, with the significant addition of " other crimes and offences savoring of heresy." This was served upon him personally the next day, and he made no resistance. Some rumor of what was impending must have been in the air, for his two chief instigators and confidants, Gilles de Sillé and Roger de Briqueville, saved themselves by flight. The rest of his nearest servitors and procurers, male and female, were seized, including Prelati, and carried to Nantes. On the 19th he had a private hearing before the bishop. The prosecuting officer, Guillaume Capeillon, cunningly preferred certain charges of heresy against him, when he fell into the trap and boldly offered to purge himself before the bishop or any other ecclesiastical judge. He was taken at his word, and the 28th was fixed for his appearance before the bishop and the vice-inquisitor of Nantes, Jean Blouyn.†

---

* Bossard et Maulde, Pr. pp. i., ii., vi.–ix.

† Ibid. Pr. pp. iii.–iv., v.—Jean Chartier Hist. de Charles VII. ann. 1440 (Ed. Godefroy, p. 106).

The records are imperfect, and tell us nothing of what was done with the followers of Gilles, but we may be sure that during this interval the methods of the inquisitorial process were not spared to extract information from them, and that it was spread among the people to create public opinion, for already, by the 28th, some of the sorrowing parents who came forward to confirm their previous complaints assert that since La Meffraye had been in the secular prison they had been told that she said their children had been delivered to Gilles. At this hearing of the 28th only these ten witnesses were heard, with their vague conjectures as to the loss of their offspring. Gilles was not present, and apparently the result of the torture of his servants had not yet been satisfactory, for further proceedings were adjourned till October 8.*

In the succeeding hearings the rule of secrecy seems to have been abandoned. There evidently was extreme anxiety to create popular opinion against the prisoner, for the court-room in the Tour Neuve was crowded. On October 8 proceedings opened with the frantic cries of the bereaved parents clamoring for justice against him who had despoiled them and had committed a black catalogue of crimes, which shows that since their last appearance their ignorance had been carefully enlightened. Like the chorus of a Greek tragedy, the same dramatic use was made of them on the 11th, after which, as the object was presumably accomplished, they disappear.†

At the hearing of the 8th the articles of accusation were presented orally by the prosecutor. Gilles thereupon appealed from the court, but as his appeal was verbal it was promptly set aside, though no offer was made to him of counsel, or even of a notary to reduce it to writing. If anything could move us to commiseration for such a criminal it would be the mockery of justice in a trial where, alone and unaided, he was called upon to defend his life without preparation or the means of defence. He doubtless was guilty, but if he had been innocent the result would have been the same. Yet the trial was not carried on "*simpliciter et de plano*" according to the forms of the Inquisition. There was a semblance of a *litis contestatio*. The prosecutor took the *juramentum de calumnia*, to tell the truth and avoid deceit, and

---

* Bossard et Maulde, Pr. pp. vi.–ix.   † Ibid. pp. ix., xii.

demanded that Gilles should do the same, as prescribed by legal form, but the latter obstinately refused, though summoned four times and threatened with excommunication. The only notice he would take of the proceedings was to denounce all the charges as false.*

It was worse at the hearing of the 13th, when the accusations had been reduced to writing in a formidable series of forty-nine articles. When the bishop and inquisitor asked him what he had to say in defence, Gilles haughtily retorted that they were not his judges; he had appealed from them and would make no reply to the charges. Then, giving rein to his temper, he stigmatized them as simoniacs and scoundrels, before whom it was degradation for him to appear; he would rather be hanged by the neck than acknowledge them as his judges; he wondered that Pierre de l'Hôpital, president or chief judicial officer of Brittany, who was present, would allow ecclesiastics to meddle with such crimes as were alleged against him. In spite of his reclamations the indictment was read, when he simply denounced it as a pack of lies and refused to answer formally. Then, after repeated warnings, the bishop and inquisitor pronounced him contumacious and excommunicated him. He again appealed, but the appeal was rejected as frivolous, and he was given forty-eight hours in which to frame a defence.†

The charges formed a long and most elaborate paper, showing by its detail of individual cases that by this time Gilles's servitors must have been induced to make full confessions. For the first time there appear in it the sacrilege and violation of clerical immunity committed at Saint-Étienne, and the charge of child-murder only figures as an accessory to the other crimes to which it was connected. Everything, however, that could be alleged against him was gathered together, even to inordinate eating and drinking, which were assumed to have led to his other excesses. His transient fits of repentance and vows of amendment were utilized ingeniously to prove that he was a relapsed heretic and thus deprived of all chance of escape. In the conclusion the prosecutor apportioned the charges between the two jurisdictions. The bishop and inquisitor conjointly were prayed to declare him

---

* Bossard et Maulde, Pr. pp. xi–xii.   † Ibid. Pr. pp. xiii.–xiv.

III.—30*

guilty of heretical apostasy and the invocation of demons, while the bishop alone was to pronounce sentence on his unnatural crimes and sacrilege, the Inquisition having no cognizance of these offences. It is worthy of note that there is no allusion to alchemy; apparently it was not regarded as an unlawful pursuit.*

It is not easy to understand what followed. When two days later, on the 15th, Gilles was brought into court he was a changed man. We have no means of knowing what influences had meanwhile been brought to bear upon him, but the only probable explanation would seem to be that he recognized from the details of the charges that his servants had been forced to betray him, that further resistance would only subject him to torture, and, in his earnest care for the salvation of his soul, that submission to the Church and endurance of the inevitable was the only path to heaven. Still, he could not at once summon resolution to incur the humiliation of a detailed public confession. While he humbly admitted the bishop and inquisitor to be his judges, and on bended knee, with tears and sighs, craved their pardon for the insults which he had showered upon them, and begged for absolution from the excommunication incurred by contumacy; while he took with the prosecutor the *juramentum de calumnia;* while in general terms he acknowledged that he had no objection to make to the charges and confessed the crimes alleged against him, yet when he was required to answer to the articles *seriatim* he at once denied that he had invoked, or caused to be invoked, any malignant spirits; he had, it is true, dabbled in alchemy, but he freely offered himself to be burned if the witnesses to be produced, whose testimony he was willing to accept in advance, should prove that he had invoked demons or entered into pacts with them and offered them sacrifices. All the rest of the charges he specifically denied, but he invited the prosecutor to produce what witnesses he chose, and he (Gilles) would admit their evidence to be conclusive. Although in all this there is a contradiction which casts doubt upon the frankness of the official record, it may perhaps be explained by vacillation not improbable in his terrible position. He did not shrink, however, when his servants and agents, Henriet, Poitou, Prelati, Blanchet, and his two procuresses were brought forward and sworn in his

* Bossard et Maulde, Pr. pp. xvii.–xxx.

presence; he declined the offer of the bishop and inquisitor to frame the interrogatories for their examination, and he declared that he would stand to their depositions and make no exceptions to them or to their evidence. It was the same when, on the 15th and 19th, additional witnesses were sworn in his presence. The examinations of these witnesses, however, were made by notaries in private. The depositions made by Henriet and Poitou, which have been preserved to us, are hideous catalogues of the foulest crimes, minute in their specifications, though the identity between them in trifles, where omissions or discrepancies would be natural, strongly suggests manipulation either of witnesses or of records. That of Prelati is equally full in its details of necromancy, and raises at once the question, not easily answered, why the necromancer, who had richly earned the stake, seems to have escaped all punishment; and the same may be said as to Blanchet, La Meffraye and her colleague, and some others of those involved. It is worthy of note, that in these confessions or depositions the customary formula that they are made without fear, force, or favor is conspicuous by its absence.*

At the hearing of October 20 Gilles was again asked if he had anything to propose, and he replied in the negative. He waived all delay as to the publication of the evidence against him, and when the depositions of his accomplices were read he said he had no exceptions to make to them; in fact, that the publication was unnecessary in view of what he had already said, and what he intended to confess. One would think that this was quite sufficient, for his guilt was thus proved and admitted, but the infernal curiosity of the jurisprudence of the time was never satisfied until it had wrung from the accused a detailed and formal confession. The prosecutor, therefore, earnestly demanded of the bishop and inquisitor that Gilles should be tortured, in order, as he said, to develop the truth more fully. They consulted with the experts and decided that torture should be applied.†

The proud man had hoped to be spared the humiliation of a detailed confession, but this was not to be allowed. On the next

---

* Bossard et Maulde, Pr. pp. xxxii.–xxxvi., xxxvii.–xxxviii., lxiv.–lxxii., lxxiii.–lxxxi., lxxxii.–xcii., xciii.–ci.

† Ibid. Pr. pp. xli.–xlii.

day, October 21, the bishop and inquisitor ordered him to be brought in and tortured. Everything was in readiness for it, when he humbly begged them to defer it until the next day, and that meanwhile he would make up his mind so as to satisfy them and render it unnecessary. He further asked that they should commission the Bishop of Saint-Brieuc and Pierre de l'Hôpital to hear his confession in a place apart from the torture. This last prayer they granted, but they would only give him a respite until two o'clock, with the promise of a further postponement until the next day, in case he confessed meanwhile. When the confession made that afternoon, under these circumstances, is officially declared to have been made "freely and willingly and without coercion of any kind," it affords another example of the value of these customary formulas.*

Before the commissioners he made no difficulty of accusing himself of all the crimes wherewith he stood charged. Pierre de l'Hôpital found the recital hard of credence, and pressed him vigorously to disclose the motive which had led to their commission. He was not satisfied with Gilles's declaration that it was simply to gratify his passions, till he exclaimed, "Truly, there was no other cause, object, or intention than I have said. I have told you greater things than that—enough to put ten thousand men to death." The president pressed the matter no further, but sent for Prelati, when the two accomplices freely confirmed each other's statements, and they parted in tears with the affectionate farewell already alluded to.†

There was no further talk of torture. Gilles was now fairly embarked in his new course. Apparently resolved to win heaven by contrition and by the assistance of the Church, this extraordinary man presents, during the remainder of the trial, a spectacle which is probably without an example. When, on the next day, October 22, he was brought before his judges, the proud and haughty baron desired that his confession should be read in public, so that his humiliation should aid in winning pardon from God. Not content with this, he supplemented his confession with abundant details of his atrocities, as though seeking to make to God an acceptable oblation of his pride. Finally, after exhorting those

---

* Bossard et Maulde, Pr. pp. xliii.-xlv.   † Ibid. Pr. pp. xlv.-xlvii.

present to honor and obey the Church, he begged with abundant tears their prayers, and entreated pardon of the parents whose children he had murdered.*

On the 25th he was brought up for sentence. After the bishop and inquisitor had duly consulted their assembly of experts, two sentences were read. The first, in the name of both judges, condemned him as guilty of heretical apostasy and horrid invocation of demons, for which he had incurred excommunication and other penalties of the law, and for which he should be punished according to the canonical sanctions. The second sentence, rendered by the bishop alone, in the same form, condemned him for unnatural crime, for sacrilege, and for violating the immunities of the Church. In neither sentence was there any punishment indicated. He was not pronounced relapsed, and therefore could not be abandoned to the secular arm, and it was apparently deemed superfluous to enjoin on him any penance, as a prosecution had been going on *pari passu* in the secular court, of which the result was not in doubt. The ecclesiastical court had dropped the accusation of murder, after it had served its purpose in exciting popular odium, and had left it to the civil authorities to which it belonged. In fact, the whole elaborate proceedings were a nullity, except so far as they served as a shield for the civil process, and as a basis for confiscating his estates.†

After the reading of the sentences he was asked if he wished reincorporation in the Church. He replied that he had not known what heresy was, nor that he had lapsed into it, but as the Church had declared him guilty, he begged on his knees, with sighs and groans, to be reincorporated. When this ceremony was accomplished he asked for absolution, which was granted. It shows the deceptive nature of the whole proceedings, and how little the bishop and inquisitor thought of anything but the secret object to be attained, that although Gilles was condemned for heresy, he was absolved without subjection to the indispensable ceremony of abjuration, and his request for a confessor was promptly met by the appointment of Jean Juvenal, a Carmelite of Ploermel.‡

---

* Bossard et Maulde, Pr. pp. xlviii.–lviii.　　　† Ibid. Pr. pp. lxiii.–lxiv.
‡ Bossard et Maulde, Pr. pp. lx.–lxi.

From the Tour Neuve, where the ecclesiastical court held its sittings, Gilles was at once hurried before the secular tribunal in the Bouffay. It had commenced its inquest on September 18, and had been busily employed in collecting evidence concerning the child-murders, besides which, its presiding judge, Pierre de l'Hôpital, had been present at much of the ecclesiastical trial, and had personally received Gilles's confession. It was thus fully prepared to act, and indeed had already condemned Henriet and Poitou to be hanged and burned. When Gilles was brought in and arraigned he immediately confessed. Pierre urged him to confess in full, and thus obtain alleviation of the penalty due to his sins, and he freely complied. Then the president took the opinions of his assessors, who all voted in favor of death, although there was some difference as to the form. Finally Pierre announced that he had incurred the "*peines pecunielles*," which were to be levied on his goods and lands "with moderation of justice." As for his crimes, for these he was to be hanged and burned, and that he might have opportunity to crave mercy of God, the time was fixed for one o'clock the next day. Gilles thanked him for the designation of the hour, adding that as he and his servants, Henriet and Poitou, had committed the crimes together, he asked that they might be executed together, so that he who was the cause of their guilt might admonish them, and show them the example of a good death, and by the grace of our Lord be the cause of their salvation. If, he said, they did not see him die they might think that he escaped, and thus be cast into despair. Not only was this request granted, but he was told that he might select the place of his burial, when he chose the Carmelite church, the sepulchre of the dukes, and of all that was most illustrious in Brittany. As a last prayer, he begged that the bishop and clergy might be requested to walk in procession prior to his execution the next day, to pray God to keep him and his servants in firm belief of salvation. This was granted, and the morning saw the extraordinary spectacle of the clergy, followed by the whole population of Nantes, who had been clamoring for his death, marching through the streets and singing and praying for his salvation.*

On the way to execution Gilles devoted himself to comforting

* Bossard et Maulde, p. 333; Pr. pp. cxli.–cxliv.

the servants whom he had brought to a shameful death, assuring
them that as soon as their souls should leave their bodies they
would all meet in paradise.   The men were as contrite and as sure
of salvation as their master, declaring that they welcomed death
in their unbounded trust in God.   They were all mounted on
stands over piles of wood, with halters around their necks attached
to the gallows.   The stands were pushed aside, and as they swung
the fagots were lighted.   Henriet and Poitou were allowed to
burn to ashes, but when Gilles's halter was burned through and his
body fell, the ladies of his kindred rushed forward and plucked it
from the flames.   It was honored with a magnificent funeral, and
it is said that some of the bones were kept by his family as relics
of his repentance.*

Under the Breton laws execution for crime entailed confiscation of movables to the seigneur justicier, but not of the landed
estates.   Condemnation for heresy, as we have seen, everywhere
carried with it indiscriminate confiscation and inflicted disabilities
for two generations.   Gilles was convicted as a heretic, but the
secular sentence is obscure on the subject of confiscation, and in
the intricate and prolonged litigation which arose over his inheritance it is difficult to determine to what extent confiscation was
enforced.   Some twenty years later the "Mémoire des Héritiers"
argues that death had expiated his crimes and removed all cause
of confiscation, which would seem to indicate that it had taken
place.   Certain it is that, to assist the Duke of Brittany, René of
Anjou in 1450 confiscated Champtocé and Ingrandes, which were
under his jurisdiction, and ceded them to the duke to confirm his
title.   Charles VII., on the other side, had already decreed confiscation in order to help the heirs.†

No disabilities were inflicted upon the descendants, and the
house was still regarded as eligible to the noblest alliances.   After
a year of widowhood, Catharine de Thouars married Jean de Vendôme, Vidame of Chartres, and in 1442 Gilles's daughter, Marie, espoused Prégent de Coétivy, Admiral of France and one of the
most powerful men in the royal court.   He must have considered
the match most desirable, for he submitted to hard conditions in

---

* Bossard et Maulde, pp. 337–41.

† Très-Anc. Cout. de Bretagne c. 118 (Bourdot de Richebourg, IV. 228).—
Bossard et Maulde, pp. 357, 377.

the marriage contract.   He resolutely set to work to recover the
alienated or confiscated lands, and succeeded in gaining possession
of some of the finest estates, including Champtocé and Ingrandes,
though his death at the siege of Cherbourg, in 1450, prevented his
enjoying them.   Marie not long after was remarried with André
de Laval, Marshal and Admiral of France, who caused her rights
to be respected, but on her death without issue in 1457 the inheritance passed to Gilles's brother, René de la Suze.   The interminable
litigation revived and continued until after his death in 1474.   He
left but one daughter, who had been married to the Prince de
Déols in 1446; they had but one son, André de Chauvigny, who
died without issue in 1502, when the race became extinct.   The
barony of Rais lapsed into the house of Tournemine, and at length
passed into that of Gondy, to become celebrated in the seventeenth
century through the Cardinal de Retz.*

Admitting as we must the guilt of Gilles de Rais, all this
throws an uncomfortable doubt over the sincerity of his trial and
conviction, and this is not lessened by the fate of his accomplices.
Only Henriet and Poitou appear to have suffered; there is no
trace of the death-penalty inflicted on any of the rest, though their
criminality was sufficient for the most condign punishment, and
the facility with which self-incriminating evidence was obtainable
by the use of torture rendered unknown the device of purchasing
testimony with pardon.   Gilles de Sillé, who was regarded as the
worst of the marshal's instigators, disappeared and was heard of
no more.   Next to him ranked Roger de Briqueville.   It is somewhat mysterious that the family seem to have regarded this man
with favor.   Marie de Rais cherished his children with tender
care.   In 1446 he obtained from Charles VII. letters of remission
rehabilitating him, which he certainly could not have procured
had not Prégent de Coétivy favored him, and the latter, in a letter
to his brother Oliver, in 1449, desires to be remembered to Roger.†

If the student feels that there is an impenetrable mystery
shrouding the truth in this remarkable case, the Breton peasant
was troubled with no such doubts.   To him Gilles remained the
embodiment of cruelty and ferocity.   I am not sufficiently versed
in folk-lore to express an opinion whether M. Bossard is correct in

---

* Bossard et Maulde, pp. 370–82.   † Ibid. pp. 380; Pr. pp. cxlv.–cxlvi.

maintaining that Gilles is the original of Bluebeard, the monster
of the nursery-tale rendered universally popular in the version of
Charles Perrault. Yet, even without admitting that the story is of
Breton origin, there would seem to be no doubt that in Brittany,
La Vendée, Anjou, and Poitou, where the terrible baron had his
chosen seats of residence, he is known by the name of Bluebeard,
and the legend—possibly an older one—of cruelty to seven wives,
has been attached to him who had but one, and who left that one
a widow. Tradition relates how the demon changed to a brilliant
blue the magnificent red beard that was his pride; and everywhere,
at Tiffauges, at Champtocé, at Machecoul, for the peasant, Bluebeard is the lord of the castle where Gilles ruled over their forefathers. Even yet, when the dreaded ruins are approached at dusk,
the wayfarer crosses himself and holds his breath. In one ballad
the name of Bluebeard and of the Baron de Rais are interchanged
as identical, and Jean de Malestroit, Bishop of Nantes, is the champion who delivers the terrorized people from their oppressor.[*]

Another phase of the popular belief in magic is illustrated in
Don Enrique de Aragon, commonly known as the Marquis of Vil-
lena. Born in 1384, uniting the royal blood of both Castile and
Aragon, his grandfather, the Duke of Gandia and Constable of
Castile, destined him for a military life, and forbade his instruction
in aught but knightly accomplishments. The child's keen thirst
for knowledge, however, overcame all obstacles, and he became
a marvel of learning for his unlettered companions. He spoke
numerous languages, he was gifted as a poet, and he became a
voluminous historian. The occult arts formed too prominent a
portion of the learning of the day for him to neglect them, and
he became noted for his skill in divination, and for interpreting
dreams, sneezes, and portents—things, we are told, not befitting a
royal prince or a good Catholic, wherefore he was held in slight
esteem by the kings of his time, and in little reverence by the
fierce chivalry of Spain. In fact, he is spoken of in terms of undis-
guised contempt, as one who with all his acquirements knew little
that was worth knowing, and who was unfit for knighthood and
for worldly affairs, even for regulating his own household; that he

* Bossard et Maulde, pp. 406, 408, 412.

was short and fat, and unduly fond of women and of eating. His astrological learning was ridiculed in the saying that he knew much of heaven and little of earth. He left his wife and gave up his earldom of Tineo in order to obtain the mastership of the Order of Calatrava, but the king soon deprived him of it, and thus, in the words of the chronicler, he lost both. After his death, at the age of fifty, in 1434, the King Juan II. ordered all his books to be examined by Fray Lope de Barrientos, afterwards Bishop of Cuenca, a professor of Salamanca and tutor of the Infante Enrique. A portion of them Fray Lope burned publicly on the plaza of the Dominican convent of Madrid, where the marquis lay buried. He kept the rest—probably to aid him in the books on the occult sciences which he wrote at command of the king.

Don Enrique evidently was a man of culture despised by a barbarous age which could see in his varied accomplishments only the magic skill so suggestive to the popular imagination. He was no vulgar magician. In his commentary on the Æneid he speaks of magic as a forbidden science, of whose forty different varieties he gives a curious classification. The only one of his writings that has reached us on a topic of the kind is a treatise on the evil eye. In common with his age he regards this as an admitted fact, but he attributes it to natural causes; and in the long and learned catalogue of remedies employed by different races from ancient times, he counsels abstinence from those which savor of superstition and are forbidden by the Church. Had he seriously devoted himself to the occult sciences he would scarce have written his "Art of Carving," which was printed in 1766. In this work he not only gives the most minute directions for carving all manner of flesh, fowls, fish, and fruits, but gravely proposes that there shall be a school for training youth of gentle blood in this indispensable accomplishment, with privileges and honors to reward the most efficient graduates.

Yet of this unworldly scholar, neglected and despised during life, popular exaggeration speedily made a magician of wondrous power. His legend grew until there was nothing too wild to be attributed to him. He caused himself to be cut up and packed in a flask with certain conjurations, so as to become immortal; he rendered himself invisible with the herb Andromeda; he turned the sun blood-red with the stone heliotrope; he brought rain and tempest with a copper vessel; he divined the future with the stone chelonites; he gave his shadow to the devil in the cave of San Cebrian. Every feat of magic was attributed to him; he became the inexhaustible theme of playwright and story-teller, and to the present day he is the favorite magician of the Spanish stage. From this example it is easy to trace the evolution of the myths of Michael Scot, Roger Bacon, Albertus Magnus, Pietro d' Abano, Dr. Faustus, and other popular necromantic heroes.*

---

* La Puente Epit. de la Chronica del Rey don Juan II. Lib. III. c. 23; Lib. v. c. 27 (Fernan Perez de Guzman).—Monteiro, Hist. da Santa Inquisição, P. I. Lib. II. c. 40.—Paramo, p. 131.—La Fuente, Hist. Gen. de España, IX. 60.—Pelayo, Heterodoxos Españoles I. 582, 608–11.—Amador de los Rios, Revista de España, T. XVIII. pp. 15–16.

CHAPTER VII.

WITCHCRAFT.

WHILE, as we have seen, princes and warriors were toying with the dangerous mysteries of the occult sciences, influencing the destinies of states, there had been for half a century a gradually increasing development of sorcery in a different direction among the despised peasantry, which, before it ran its course, worked far greater evils than any which had thus far sprung from the same source, and left an ineffaceable stain upon the civilization and intelligence of Europe. There is no very precise line of demarcation to be drawn between the more pretentious magic and the vulgar details of witchcraft; they find their origin in the same beliefs and fade into each other by imperceptible gradations, and yet, historically speaking, the witchcraft with which we now have to deal is a manifestation of which the commencement cannot be distinctly traced backward much beyond the fifteenth century. Its practitioners were not learned clerks or shrewd swindlers, but ignorant peasants, for the most part women, who professed to have skill to help or to ban, or who were credited by their neighbors with such power, and were feared and hated accordingly. Of such we hear little during the darkest portion of the Middle Ages, but with the dawn of modern culture they confront us as a strange phenomenon, of which the proximate cause is exceedingly obscure. Probably it may be traced to the effort of the theologians to prove that all superstitious practices were heretical in implying a tacit pact with Satan, as declared by the University of Paris. Thus the innocent devices of the wise-women in culling simples, or in muttering charms, came to be regarded as implying demon-worship. When this conception once came to be firmly implanted in the minds of judges and inquisitors, it was inevitable that with the rack they should extort from their victims confessions in accordance with their expectations. Every new trial would add fresh embellishments to this, until at last there was built up a stupendous mass of facts which demonologists endeavored to reduce to a science for the guidance of the tribunals.

That such was the origin of the new witchcraft is rendered still more probable by the fact that its distinguishing feature was the worship of Satan in the Sabbat, or assemblage, held mostly at night, to which men and women were transported through the air, either spontaneously or astride of a stick or stool, or mounted on a demon in the shape of a goat, a dog, or some other animal, and where hellish rites were celebrated and indiscriminate license prevailed. Divested of the devil-worship now first introduced, such assemblages have formed part of the belief of all races. In Hindu superstition the witches, through the use of mystic spells, flew naked through the night to the places of meeting, where they danced, or to a cemetery, where they gorged themselves with human flesh or revived the dead to satiate their lust. The Hebrew witch flew to the Sabbat with her hair loosened, as when it was bound she was unable to exercise her full power. Among the Norsemen we have seen the *trolla-thing*, or assemblage of witches, for their unholy purposes.* In the Middle Ages the first allusion which we meet concerning it occurs in a fragment, not later than the ninth century, in which it is treated as a diabolical illusion— "Some wicked women, reverting to Satan, and seduced by the illusions and phantasms of demons, believe and profess that they ride at night with Diana on certain beasts; with an innumerable multitude of women, passing over immense distances, obeying her commands as their mistress, and evoked by her on certain nights. It were well if they alone perished in their infidelity and did not draw so many along with them. For innumerable multitudes, deceived by this false opinion, believe all this to be true, and thus relapse into pagan errors. Therefore, priests everywhere should preach that they know this to be false, and that such phantasms are sent by the Evil Spirit, who deludes them in dreams. Who is there who is not led out of himself in dreams, seeing much in sleeping that he never saw waking? And who is such a fool that he believes that to happen in the body which is only done in the

---

* Weber, Indische Skizzen, p. 112.—Wagenseilii Comment. ad Mishna, Sootah, I. 5.—Grimm's Teuton. Mythol. III. 1044.

spirit? It is to be taught to all that he who believes such things
has lost his faith, and he who has not the true faith is not of God,
but the devil." In some way this utterance came to be attributed
to a Council of Anquira, which could never be identified; it was
adopted by the canonists and embodied in the successive collections of Regino, Burchard, Ivo, and Gratian—the latter giving it
the stamp of unquestioned authority—and it became known among
the doctors as the *Cap. Episcopi*. The selection of Diana as the
presiding genius of these illusory assemblages carries the belief
back to classical times, when Diana, as the moon, was naturally a
night-flyer, and was one of the manifestations of the triform Hecate, the favorite patroness of sorcerers. Under the Barbarians,
however, her functions were changed. In the sixth century we
hear of "the demon whom the peasants call Diana," who vexed a
girl and inflicted on her visible stripes, until expelled by St. Cæsarius of Arles. Diana was the *dæmonium meridianum*, and the name
is used by John XXII. as synonymous with succubus. In some inexplicable way Bishop Burchard, in the eleventh century, when
copying the text, came to add to Diana Herodias, who remained
in the subsequent recensions, but Burchard in another passage sub-
stitutes as the leader Holda, the Teutonic deity of various aspect,
sometimes beneficent to housewives and sometimes a member of
Wuotan's Furious Host. In a tract attributed to St. Augustin,
but probably ascribable to Hugues de S. Victor, in the twelfth
century, the companion of Diana is Minerva, and in some conciliar
canons of a later date there appears another being known as Ben-
zozia, or Bizazia; but John of Salisbury, who alludes to the belief
as an illustration of the illusions of dreams, speaks only of Herodias
as presiding over the feasts for which these midnight assemblages
were held. We also meet with Holda, in her beneficent capacity
as the mistress of the revels, under the name of the Domina Abun-
dia or Dame Habonde. She was the chief of the *dominæ noc-
turnæ*, who frequented houses at night and were thought to bring
abundance of temporal goods. In the year 1211 Gervais of Tilbury
shows the growth of this belief in his account of the *lamiæ* or
mascæ, who flew by night and entered houses, performing mis-
chievous pranks rather than malignant crimes, and he prudently
avoids deciding whether this is an illusion or not. He also had
personal knowledge of women who flew by night in crowds with

these *lamiæ*, when any one who incautiously pronounced the name of Christ was precipitated to the earth. Half a century later Jean de Meung tells us that those who ride with Dame Habonde claim that they number a third of the population, and when the Inquisition undertook the suppression of sorcery, in its formula of interrogatories, as we have seen in the preceding chapter, there was a question as to the night-riding of the good women.[*]

Thus the Church, in its efforts to suppress these relics of pagandom, preferred to regard the nocturnal assemblages as a fiction, and denounced as heretical the belief in the reality of the delusion. This, as part of the canon law, remained unalterable, but alongside of it grew up, with the development of heresy, tales of secret conventicles, somewhat similar in character, in which the sectaries worshipped the demon in the form of a cat or other beast, and celebrated their impious and impure rites. Stories such as this are told of the Cathari punished at Orleans in 1017, and of their successors in later times ; and the Universal Doctor, Alain de Lille, even derives the name of Cathari from their kissing Lucifer under

---

[*] Frag. Capitular. c. 13 (Baluz. II. 365). — Reginon. de Eccles. Discip. II. 364.—Burchard. Decret. XI. 1, XIX. 5.—Ivon. Decret. XI. 30.—Gratian. Decret. II. XXVII. v. 12.—Servius in Virgil. Æneid. IV. 511, VI. 118.—Vit. S. Cæsar. Arelat. Lib. II. c. 2. — Raynald. ann. 1317, No. 53. — Grimm's Teut. Mythol. I. 268 sqq.—Finn Magnusen Boreal. Mythol. Lexicon, pp. 7, 71, 567.—Lib. de Spiritu et Anima c. 28.—Augerii Cenomanens. Statut. (Du Cange s. v. *Diana*).—Conc. Trevirens. ann. 1310 c. 81 (Martene Thesaur. IV. 257).—Conc. Ambianens. cap. iii. No. 8 (Martene Ampl. Coll. VII. 1241).—Johann. Saresberiens. Polycrat. II. xvii. — Grimm's Teut. Mythol. III. 1055–7. — Wright's Dame Kyteler, pp. iv., xxxvi.—Gervas. Tilberiens. Otia Imp. Decis. III. c. 86, 93.—Jean de Meung says—

"Maintes gens par lor folie   Li tiers enfant de nacion
  Cuident estre par nuict estrées   Sunt de ceste condicion."
  Errant avecques Dame Habonde;   (Roman de la Rose, 18624.—Wright,
  Et dient que par tout le monde   loc. cit.)..

A story in Jac. de Voragine's life of St. Germain l'Auxerrois illustrates the genesis of the belief concerning the Dame Habonde and her troop, who assisted in household work. On visiting a certain house St. Germain found that the supper-table was set by "the good women who walk by night." He remained up and saw a crowd of demons, in the shape of men and women, who came to set it ; he commanded them to stay, and woke the family, who recognized in the intruders their neighbors, but the latter, on investigation, were found in their beds, and the demons confessed that the likenesses were assumed for the purpose of deception.—Jac. de Vorag. s. v. *S. Germanus.*

the tail in the shape of a cat.* How the investigators of heresy
came to look for such assemblages as a matter of course, and led
the accused to embellish them until they assumed nearly the development of the subsequent Witches' Sabbat, is seen in the confessions of Conrad of Marburg's Luciferans, and in some of those
of the Templars.

Yet the belief in the night-riders with Diana and Herodias
continued, until the latter part of the fifteenth century, to be denounced as a heresy, and any one who persisted in retaining it
after learning the truth was declared to be an infidel and worse
than a pagan.† It was too thoroughly implanted, however, in
ancestral popular superstition to be eradicated. In the middle of
the thirteenth century the orthodox Dominican, Thomas of Cantimpré, speaks of the demons who, like Diana, transport men from
one region to another and delude them into worshipping mortals
as gods. Others, he says, carry away women, replacing them
with insensible images, who are sometimes buried as though dead.
Thus, when the peasant wise-women came to be examined as to
their dealings with Satan, they could hardly help, under intolerable
torture, from satisfying their examiners with accounts of their
nocturnal flights. Between judge and victim it was easy to build
up a coherent story, combining the ancient popular belief with the
heretical conventicles, and the time soon came when the confession
of a witch was regarded as incomplete without an account of her
attendance at the Sabbat, which was the final test of her abandonment to Satan. These stories became so universal and so complete in all their details that they could not be rejected without
discrediting the whole structure of witchcraft. The theory of
illusion was manifestly untenable, and demonologists and inquisitors were sadly at a loss to reconcile the incontrovertible facts
with the denunciations by the Church of such beliefs as heresy. A
warm controversy arose. Some held to the old doctrine that the

* Pauli Carnot. Vet. Agano. Lib. vi. c. 3.—Adhemari Cabannens. ann. 1022.
—Gualteri Mapes de Nugis Curialium Dist. i. c. 30.—Alani de Insulis contra
Hæret. Lib. i. c. 63.

† Concil. Trevirens. ann. 1310 c. 81 (Martene Thes. IV. 257).— Concil. Ambianens. c. 1410 cap. iii. No. 8 (Martene Ampl. Coll. VII. 1241).—Eymeric. p.
341.—Alonso de Spina, Fortalic. Fidei, fol. 284.—Albertini Repertor. Inquisit.
s. v. Xorguinæ.

devil cannot transport a human body or make it pass through a disproportionate opening, but they endeavored to explain the admitted facts by enlarging on his powers of creating illusions. The witch consecrated herself to him with words and with anointing, when he would take her figure or phantasm and lead it where she wished, while her body remained insensible and covered with a diabolical shadow, rendering it invisible; when the object had been accomplished, he brought back the phantasm, reunited it to the body, and removed the shadow. The question turned upon the ability of the devil to carry off human beings, and this was hotly debated. A case adduced by Albertus Magnus, in a disputation on the subject before the Bishop of Paris, and recorded by Thomas of Cantimpré, in which the daughter of the Count of Schwalenberg was regularly carried away every night for several hours, gave immense satisfaction to the adherents of the new doctrine, and eventually an ample store of more modern instances was accumulated to confirm Satan in his enlarged privileges.*

In 1458 the Inquisitor Nicholas Jaquerius hit upon the true solution of the difficulty by arguing that the existing sect of witches was wholly different from the heretics alluded to in the *Cap. Episcopi*, and adduced in evidence of their bodily presence in the Sabbat numberless cases which had come before him in his official capacity, including one of a man who, as a child, fifty-five years before, had been carried thither by his mother in company with an infant brother, and presented to Satan wearing the form of a goat, who with his hoofs had imprinted on them an indelible mark—the *stigma diabolicum*. Jaquerius, however, adds, reasonably enough, that even if the affair is an illusion, it is none the less heretical, as the followers of Diana and Herodias are necessarily

---

* Thom. Cantimprat. Bonum universal. Lib. II. c. 56.—Alonso de Spina, Fortalic. Fidei, fol. 284.—Bern. Basin de Artibus Magicis.—Ulric. Molitor. de Python. Mulierib. Conclus. IV.—Th. Cantimprat. ubi sup.—Mall. Maleficar. P. ii. Q. i. c. 3.—Prieriat. de Strigimag. Lib. i. c. xiv., Lib. ii. c. 1.

Friar Thomas gives circumstantial contemporary instances occurring in Flanders, where women were carried away and their images were on the point of burial, when the deception was accidentally discovered, and the images, on being cut open, were found to consist of rotten wood covered with skin. He admits his inability to explain these cases, and says that on consulting Albertus Magnus about them the latter evaded a positive answer (Bonum universale, ubi sup.).

heretics in their waking hours.   These speculations of Jaquerius attracted little attention at the time.   Thirty years later, Sprenger,
who did so much to formulate belief and organize persecution,
found the *Cap. Episcopi* a constant stumbling-block in his path,
as sceptics were apt to argue that, if the Sabbat was an illusion,
all witchcraft was illusory.   He endeavored, therefore, to argue it
away, assuming that, while the devil undoubtedly possessed the
power of transportation, the presence of the witch frequently was
only mental.   In such case she lay down on the left side and invoked the devil, when a whitish vapor would issue from her mouth,
and she saw all that occurred.   If she went personally, and had a
husband, an accommodating demon would assume her shape and
take her place to conceal her absence.   Gianfrancesco Pico della
Mirandola takes the same ground, that presence at the Sabbat was
sometimes real and sometimes imaginary ; the place of assemblage
was beyond the river Jordan, and transportation thither took place
instantaneously.   He avoids the definition of the *Cap. Episcopi* by
assuming that the Decretum of Gratian had not the authority of
law, and was corrupt in many places.   The Inquisitor Bernardo di
Como, about 1500, in addition to these arguments, had triumphantly adduced the fact that numerous persons had been burned
for attending the Sabbat, which could not have been done without
the assent of the pope, and this was sufficient proof that the heresy
was real, for the Church punishes only manifest crimes.*

About this time the learned jurist, Gianfrancesco Ponzinibio,
wrote a tract on the subject of witchcraft in which he upheld the
doctrine of the *Cap. Episcopi* and boldly applied it to all magic
and sorcery, which he treated as delusions.   With a vast array of
authorities he proved his case ; he exposed the baldness of the
pretence that existing witches belonged to a different sect ; he
argued that their confessions are not to be received, as they confess what is illusory and impossible, and that their evidence as to
their associates is to be rejected, as they are deluded and can only
delude others.   Lawyers, he added, ought to take part in trials
before the Inquisition, as they are trained to deal with criminal

---

* Fr. Nich. Jaquerii Flagellum Hæret. Fascinar. c. vii., xxviii.—Mall. Malef.
P. i. Q. i. c. 10 ; P. ii. Q. i. c. 3, 9.—G. F. Pico della Mirandola, La Strega,
Milano, 1864, pp. 61, 73.—Bernardi Comensis de Strigiis c. 3-6.

cases. This aroused the learned theologian, Silvestro Mozzolino of Prierio, Master of the Sacred Palace and subsequently Dominican General, who, in 1521, responded in a voluminous treatise devoted to the disputed canon. As the utterance of the Council of Anquira, presumably confirmed by the Holy See, he does not dare to deny its authority, but he adopts the same reasoning as Jaquerius, and laboriously argues that the heretics to whom it refers had disappeared, that the existing witches are a new sect, originating in 1404, and that the definitions of the canon are, therefore, obsolete and inapplicable to existing circumstances. To deny the bodily presence of witches at the Sabbat, he says, is to discredit the infinite number of cases tried by the Inquisition, and consequently to discredit the laws themselves.* He was followed by his successor in the mastership of the Sacred Palace, Bartolomeo de Spina, who devoted three tracts to the annihilation of Ponzinibio. The latter had suggested, logically enough, though maliciously, that as the *Cap. Episcopi* had defined as a heresy the belief that witches are corporally carried to the Sabbat, inquisitors in administering abjuration to their penitents ought to make them abjure this heresy among others. The absurd position in which this placed the Inquisition aroused Spina's indignation to the utmost. "O wonderful presumption! O detestable insanity!" he exclaimed. "Only heretics abjure, only heresies are abjured before inquisitors. Is then that belief a heresy which inquisitors defend, and according to which they judge the enemies of the faith to be worthy of extreme damnation?—that opinion which illustrious theologians and canonists prove to be true and catholic? O the extreme stolidity of the man! Must, then, all theologians and judges, the inquisitors themselves, of all Italy, France, Germany, and Spain, holding this opinion abjure before the Inquisition?"—and he concludes by calling upon the Inquisition to proceed against Ponzinibio as vehemently suspect of heresy, as a fautor and defender of heretics, and

---

* Ponzinib. de Lamiis c. 49, 50, 52–3, 61–3, 65–6.—Prieriat. de Strigimagar. Lib. II. c. 1.

Paramo (De Orig. Offic. S. Inq. p. 296) also adopts the date of 1404 as that of the origin of the sect of witches. This is probably founded on confusing Innocent VIII., who commenced to reign in 1484, with Innocent VII., who began in 1404. In the former's bull *Summis desiderantes*, dated in his first regnal year, he speaks of witches as a new sect, and Prierias refers this to 1404.

as an impeder of the Holy Office.*   This sufficiently shows that
the new beliefs had completely conquered the old.   The question
had passed beyond the range of reason and argument, and everywhere throughout Europe the Witches' Sabbat was accepted as an
established fact, which it was dangerous to dispute.   Jurists and
canonists might amuse themselves with debating it theoretically;
practically it had become the veriest commonplace of the courts,
both secular and ecclesiastical.

That the details of the Sabbat varied but little throughout Europe is doubtless to be ascribed to the leading questions habitually
put by judges, and to the desire of the tortured culprits to satisfy
their examiners, yet this consentaneity at the time was an irrefragable proof of truth.   The first step of the witch was to secure
a consecrated wafer by pretending to receive communion, and carrying the sacrament home.   On this was fed a toad, which was
then burned, and the ashes were mixed with the blood of an infant,
unbaptized if possible, powdered bone of a man who had been
hanged, and certain herbs.   With this mixture the witch anointed
the palms of her hands, or her wrist, and a stick or stool which
she placed between her legs, and she was at once transported to
the place of meeting.   As a variant of this the ride was sometimes made on a demon in the shape of a horse, or goat, or dog.
The assembly might be held anywhere, but there were certain
spots specially resorted to—in Germany the Brocken, in Italy
an oak-tree near Benevento, and there was, besides, the unknown
place beyond the Jordan.   At all these they gathered in thousands.   Thursday night was the one generally selected.   They
feasted at tables loaded with meat and wine which rose from the
earth at the command of the presiding demon, and they paid homage to the devil, who was present, usually in the form of a goat,
dog, or ape.   To him they offered themselves, body and soul, and
kissed him under the tail, holding a lighted candle.   They trampled and spat upon the cross and turned up their backs to heaven
in derision of God.   The devil preached to them, sometimes commencing with a parody of the mass; he told them that they had
no souls and that there was no future life; they were not to go
to church or confession, or to use holy water, or, if they did so to

---

* Ponzinib. de Lamiis c. 65.—Bart. Spinei de Strigibus, p. 175, Romæ, 1575.

avoid suspicion, they must say "By leave of our Master," and they were to bring him as many converts as they could, and work all possible evil to their neighbors. There was usually a dance, which was unlike any seen at honest gatherings. At Como and Brescia a number of children from eight to twelve years of age, who had frequented the Sabbat, and had been reconverted by the inquisitors, gave exhibitions in which their skill showed that they had not been taught by human art. The woman was held behind her partner and they danced backwards, and when they paid reverence to the presiding demon they bent themselves backwards, lifting a foot in the air forwards. The rites ended with indiscriminate intercourse, obliging demons serving as incubi or succubi as required. The reality of all this did not depend alone upon the confessions of the accused, for there was a well-known case occurring about the year 1450, when the Inquisitor of Como, Bartolomeo de Homate, the podestà Lorenzo da Concorezzo, and the notary Giovanni da Fossato, either out of curiosity or because they doubted the witches whom they were trying, went to a place of assembly at Mendrisio and witnessed the scene from a hiding-place. The presiding demon pretended not to know their presence, and in due course dismissed the assembly, but suddenly recalled his followers and set them on the officials, who were so beaten that they died within fifteen days.*

All this was, of course, well fitted to excite the horror of the faithful and stimulate the zeal of the inquisitor, but it was only the pastime of the witch, and the reward given to her by her master for her labors and her allegiance. Her serious occupation was in works of evil. She was abandoned, body and soul, to Satan, and was the instrument which he used to effect his malignant purposes. The demonologists argued that the witch was as necessary to the demon as the demon to the witch, and that neither could operate without the other. She was not like the magicians and sorcerers, who merely earned their livelihood by selling their services, sometimes for good purposes and sometimes for bad, but she was a being wholly evil, delighting in the exercise of her powers

---

* Mémoires de Jacques du Clercq, Liv. iv. ch. 4.—Chron. Cornel. Zantfliet ann. 1460 (Martene Ampl. Coll. V. 502).—Bernardi Comensis de Strigiis c. 3.—Prieriat. de Strigimag. Lib. i. c. 2, 14; Lib. ii. c. 1, 4.

for the destruction of her neighbors, and constantly exhorted to activity by her master. Those powers, moreover, were sufficient to justify the terror in which she was held by the people. Sprenger divides witches into three classes, those who can injure and not cure, those who can cure and not injure, and those who can do both, and the worst are those who unite these faculties, for the more they insult and offend God, the greater power of evil he gives them. They kill and eat children, or devote them to the devil if unbaptized. They cause abortion by merely laying a hand upon a woman, or dry up her milk if she is nursing. By twirling a moistened broom, or casting flints behind them towards the east, or boiling hogs' bristles in a pot, or stirring a pool with a finger, they raise tempests and hail-storms which devastate whole regions; they bring the plagues of locusts and caterpillars which devour the harvests; they render men impotent and women barren, and cause horses to become suddenly mad under their riders. They can make hidden things known and predict the future, bring about love or hatred at will, cause mortal sickness, slay men with lightning, or even with their looks alone, or turn them into beasts. We have the unquestioned authority of Eugenius IV. that by a simple word or touch or sign they can bewitch whom they please, cause or cure sickness, and regulate the weather. Sometimes they scattered over the fields powders which destroyed the cattle. They constantly entered houses at night, and, sprinkling a powder on the pillows of the parents which rendered them insensible, would touch the children with fingers smeared with a poisonous unguent causing death in a few days; or they would thrust needles under the nails of an infant and suck the blood, which was partly swallowed and partly spit into a vessel to serve in the confection of their infernal ointments; or the child would be put upon the fire and its fat be collected for the same purpose. Witches, moreover, could transform themselves into cats and other beasts, and Bernardo di Como gravely cites the case of the companions of Ulysses, as adduced by St. Augustin, to prove the reality of such illusions. Ludicrous as all this may seem, every one of these details has served as the basis of charges under which countless human beings have perished in the flames.*

---

* Mall. Maleficar. P. II. Q. i. c. 2, 4, 11, 15; Q. ii. c. 4.—Prieriat. de Strigimag.

One very peculiar power ascribed to witches was that of banqueting in the Sabbat on infants and cattle, and then restoring them to life. We have seen the belief in early times, and among races far apart, that sorceresses could gnaw and eat men internally, which probably arose from painful gastric maladies ascribed to sorcery. In the genesis of the Sabbat this took the shape, as described by Bishop Burchard in the eleventh century, that in the nocturnal meetings under the guidance of Holda men would be slain without weapons, their flesh cooked and eaten, and then they would be brought to life again, with straw or a piece of wood substituted for their hearts. The Church was not as yet ready to accept these marvels, and Burchard penances belief in them with fasting on bread and water for seven Lents. In the next century John of Salisbury ascribes to the illusion of dreams the popular superstition that lamiæ tore children to pieces, devoured them, and returned them to their cradles; and about 1240 Guillaume d'Auvergne speaks of the superstition spread by old women of the "ladies of the night" or "good women" who appear to tear children to pieces, or to cook them on the fire. Of course this formed part of the perfected stories of the Sabbat. In some witch-trials in the Tyrol, in 1506, there are frequent allusions to children and domestic animals carried to the feast and devoured, and though they remained alive, they were doomed to die soon afterwards. The witches of the Canavese confessed that their practice was to select fat cattle from a neighboring farmer, slaughter and eat them, and then, collecting the bones and hides, resuscitate them with the simple formula "*Sorge, Ranzola.*" In one case a farmer of Levone, named Perino Pasquale, killed a sick ox and skinned it, and, naturally enough, himself died within a week, as well as his dog, which lapped some of the blood; and the occurrence, according to custom, was subsequently explained by a witch on trial, who confessed that the ox was one which had thus been eaten and

---

Lib. II. c. 7, 9. — Ulric. Molitor. de Python. Mulierib. — Ripoll III. 193. — Pico della Mirandola, La Strega, pp. 84–5. — Bernardi Comens. de Strigiis c. 7.

It is the universal testimony of the demonologists that vastly more women than men were thus involved in the toils of the Devil. To explain this, Sprenger indulges in a most bitter tirade against women, and piously thanks God for preserving the male sex from such wickedness (Mall. Malef. P. I. Q. vii.).

resuscitated, when the assembled witches resolved that whoever killed it, and the first who should eat of it, should perish. Such feats as these, it is true, gave the opponents of witchcraft the advantage of arguing that they attributed to Satan the power of God in resuscitating and recreating the dead, and the demonologists, thus hard pushed, were obliged to admit that this portion of the Sabbat was illusory, but they triumphantly added that this only proved the empire of Satan over his dupes.*

The killing of unbaptized children was one of the special duties imposed by Satan on his servants, which the theologians explained by the fact that they were thus damned for original sin, and, therefore, the Day of Judgment was postponed, as the number of the elect requisite before the destruction of the world is thus more tardily completed. At a little town near Basle a witch who was burned confessed that while acting as midwife she had killed more than forty infants by thrusting a needle into the superior fontanelle. Another, of the diocese of Strassburg, had thus disposed of innumerable children, when she was detected by accidentally letting fall the arm of a new-born child while passing the gate of a town in which she had been performing her functions. Witch midwives, when they abstained from this, were in the habit of dedicating to Satan the babes whom they delivered. It was doubtful whether the infants were thus in reality surrendered to Satan, but at least they were subjected to his influence, and likely to grow up witches. This, and dedication by witch mothers, explain the fact that girls even of eight and ten years of age were

---

* Burchardi Decret. xix. 5.—Johann. Saresberiens. Polycrat. ii. xvii.—Grimm, Teut. Mythol. III. 1059.—Rapp, Die Hexenprocesse und ihre Gegner aus Tyrol, Innsbruck, 1874, p. 146.—P. Vayra, Le Streghe nel Canavese (Curiosità di Storia Subalpina, 1874, pp. 229, 234-5). —Bernardi Comensis de Strigiis c. 8.

A development of this belief is seen in the feat, referred to in the preceding chapter, of Zyto, the magician of the Emperor Wenceslas, who swallowed a rival conjurer and discharged him alive in a vessel of water.

Yet concurrently with this the belief existed in the absolute eating of children. Peter of Berne told Nider that in his district thirteen were thus despatched in a short time, and he learned from a captured witch that they were killed in their cradles with incantations, dug up after burial, and boiled in a caldron. The magic unguent was made out of the flesh, while the soup had the power of winning over to the sect of Devil-worshippers whoever partook of it.— Nider Formicar. Lib. v. c. iii.

able to bewitch people and to raise tempests of hail and rain. In Swabia a case occurred of one who, at the age of eight, innocently revealed her power to her father, in consequence of which her mother, who had thus dedicated her, was burned. The witch midwives were so numerous that there was scarce a hamlet without them.*

There was apparently no limit to the evil wrought by Satan through the instrumentality of those who had thus surrendered themselves to him. Sprenger relates that one of his colleagues on a tour of duty reached a town almost depopulated on account of pestilence. Hearing a report that a woman lately buried was swallowing her winding-sheet, and that the mortality would not cease until she had accomplished the deglutition, he caused the grave to be opened and the sheet was found half swallowed. The mayor of the town drew his sword and cut off the head of the corpse and threw it out of the grave, when the pest ceased at once. An inquisition was held and the woman was found to have long been a witch. Sprenger might well deplore the threatened devastation of Christendom arising from the neglect of the authorities to suppress these crimes with due severity.†

To understand the credulity which accepted these marvels as the most portentous and dreadful of realities, it must be borne in mind that they were not the wild inventions of the demonologists, but were facts substantiated by evidence irrefragable according to the system of jurisprudence. Torture by this time had long been used universally in criminal trials when necessary; no jurist conceived that the truth could be elicited in doubtful cases without it. The criminal whom endless repetition of torment had reduced to stolid despair naturally sought to make his confession square with the requirements of his judge; the confession once made he was doomed, and knew that retraction, in place of saving him, would only bring a renewal and prolongation of his sufferings. He therefore adhered to his confession, and when it was read to him in public at his condemnation he admitted its truth.‡ In many cases,

---

* Mall. Malef. P. II. Q. i. c. 13; P. III. Q. xxxiv.
† Mall. Malef. P. I. Q. xii., xv.
‡ In England, where torture was illegal, the growth of witchcraft was much slower. When the craze came an efficient substitute for torture was found in

moreover, torture and prolonged imprisonment in the foulest of dungeons doubtless produced partial derangement, leading to belief that he had committed the acts so persistently imputed to him. In either case, desire to obtain the last sacrament, which was essential to salvation and which was only administered to contrite and repentant sinners, would induce him to maintain to the last the truth of his confession. No proof more unquestionable than this could be had of any of the events of life, and belief in the figments of witchcraft was therefore unhesitating. To doubt, moreover, if not heresy, was cause for vehement suspicion. The Church lent its overpowering authority to enforce belief on the souls of men. The malignant powers of the witch were repeatedly set forth in the bulls of successive popes for the implicit credence of the faithful, and the University of Cologne, in 1487, when expressing its approval of the *Malleus Maleficarum* of Sprenger, warned every one that to argue against the reality of witchcraft was to incur the guilt of impeding the Inquisition.*

What rendered the powers of the witch peculiarly dreadful was the deplorable fact that the Church had no remedy for the evils which she so recklessly wrought. It is true that the sign of the cross, and holy water, and blessed oil, and palms, and candles, and wax and salt, and the strict observance of religious rites were in some sense a safeguard and a preventive. A witch confessed that she had been employed to kill a certain man, but when she invoked the devil for the purpose he replied that he could not do it, as the intended victim kept himself protected by the sign of the cross, and that the utmost injury that could be inflicted on him was the destruction of one eleventh of his harvests; and another one stated that on their nocturnal rounds to destroy children they were unable to enter houses in which were kept palms and blessed bread or crosses of palms or olive, or to injure those who habitually protected themselves with the sign of the cross. But it was acknowledged that, when once the spell had been cast, the victim

---

"pricking" or thrusting long needles in every part of the victim's body in search of the insensible spot which was a characteristic of the witch.

* Ripoll III. 193.—Pegnæ Append. ad Eymeric. pp. 83, 84, 85, 99, 105.—Approbat. Univ. Coloniens. in Mall. Malef.

For an official selection of papal bulls on the subject see Lib. Sept. Decret. Lib. v. Tit. xii.

could find no relief on earth or in heaven—human means were useless, and exorcism and the invocation of saints were powerless except in demoniacal possession. The only cure was from the devil through other witches. Curative sorcery had long been a subject of debate in theologic ethics, but it had been formally condemned as inadmissible. It not only was a pact, tacit or expressed, with Satan, but it was ascertained that one of his leading objects in urging his acolytes to injure their neighbors was to force the sufferer in despair to have recourse to sorcery and thus be drawn into evil ways. This was illustrated by a case, celebrated among demonographers, of a German bishop who, in Rome, fell madly in love with a young girl and induced her to accompany him home. During the journey she undertook to kill him by sorcery, that she might make off with the jewels with which he had loaded her, and he was nightly attacked with a burning pain in his chest which resisted all the resources of his physicians. His life was despaired of, when recourse was had to an old woman who recognized the source of his affection and told him he could only be saved by the same methods, involving the death of the bewitcher. His conscience would not allow him to assent to this without permission; he applied to Pope Nicholas V., who kindly granted him a dispensation, and then he ordered the old woman to do what she proposed. That night he was perfectly well, and word was brought him that his young paramour was dying. He went to console her, but she naturally received him with maledictions, and died devoting her soul to Satan. As Bodin admiringly remarks, the devil was cunning enough to make a pope, a bishop, and a witch all obey him, and all become accomplices in a homicide.*

Thus a very profitable trade sprang up in counteracting witchcraft, and many witches confined themselves to this branch of the profession, although they were as liable as their adversaries to condemnation for compact with the devil, for it was an incontrovertible fact that they could only relieve a sufferer by transferring

---

* Bernardi Comens. de Strigiis c. 14.— Mall. Maleficar. P. II. Q. i., ii.—P. Vayra, Le Streghe nel Canavese, op. cit. p. 230.—Artic. Univers. Paris. No. 5.— Concil. Lingonens. ann. 1403 c. 4.—Prieriat. de Strigimag. Lib. II. c. 10.—Bodini Magor. Dæmonoman. p. 288.

his disease to some one else or by performing some equivalent evil act. Sprenger tells us that they were to be found every German mile or two. At Reichshofen was one whose business was so large that the lord of the place levied a toll of a penny on every one who came to her for relief, and used to boast of the large revenue which he derived from this source. A man named Hengst, at Eningen, near Constance, had more applicants than any shrine of the Virgin—even than that at Aix—and in winter, when the high-ways were blocked with snow, those which led to his house were trampled smooth by the crowds of his patients.*

When once the belief was fairly started in the existence of beings possessed of the powers which I have described, and actu-ated by motives purely malignant, it was destined to inevitable extension under the stimulus afforded by persecution. Every mis-fortune and every accident that occurred in a hamlet would be attributed to witchcraft. Suspicion would gradually attach to some ill-tempered crone, and she would be seized, for inquisitors held that a single careless threat, such as "You will be sorry for this," if followed by a piece of ill-luck, was sufficient to justify arrest and trial.† All the neighbors would flock in as accusers— this one had lost a cow, that one's vintage had been ruined by hail, another's garden-patch had been ravaged by caterpillars, one mother had suffered an abortion, another's milk had suddenly dried, another had lost a promising child, two lovers had quar-relled, a man had fallen from an apple-tree and had broken his neck—and under the persuasive influence of starvation or of the rack the unfortunate woman would invent some story to account for each occurrence, would name her accomplices in each, and tell whom she had met in the Sabbats, which she attended regularly. No one can read the evidence adduced at a witch-trial, or the con-fessions of the accused, without seeing how every accident and every misfortune and every case of sickness or death which had occurred in the vicinage for years was thus explained, and how the circle of suspicion widened so that every conviction brought new victims ; burnings multiplied, and the terrified community was ready to believe that a half or more of its members were slaves of

---

* Prieriat. Lib. III. c. 3.—Mall. Malef. P. II. Q. ii.
† Bernard. Comens. de Strigiis c. 14.

Satan, and that it would never be free from their malignant vengeance until they should all be exterminated.   For more than two centuries this craze was perpetually breaking out in one part of Europe after another, carefully nursed and stimulated by popes and inquisitors like Innocent VIII. and Leo X., Sprenger and Institoris, Bernard of Como and Bishop Binsfeld, and the amount of human misery thence arising is simply incomputable.

Fortunately on one side there was a limitation upon the otherwise illimitable powers of the witch.   The contrast was so absurd between the faculties attributed to her and her utter inability to protect herself against those who tortured and burned her with impunity, that some explanation of the inconsistency was requisite.   The demonologists therefore invented the comforting theory that through the goodness of God the witch instantaneously lost her power as soon as the hand of an officer of justice was laid upon her.   But for this, indeed, it might have been difficult to find men hardy enough to seize, imprison, try, and execute these delegates of Satan, whose slightest ill-will was so dangerous. Judges and their officials thus were encouraged to perform their functions and were told that they need dread no reprisals.   It was true that, like all theories framed to meet artificial conditions, this one was not always reconcilable to the facts.   The strange fortitude with which the culprits occasionally endured the severest and most prolonged tortures, so far from being a proof of innocence, was regarded as showing that even in the hands of justice the devil was sometimes able to protect his servants by endowing them with what was called the gift of taciturnity, and the ingenuity of the inquisitors was taxed to the utmost to overcome his wiles.   When this was once admitted it was difficult to deny that he could assist them in other ways, and it was recommended to the officers charged with the arrest that when they seized a witch they should on no account allow her to enter her chamber, lest she should secure some charm that would enable her to endure the torture.   Such charms might be secreted about her person, or under the skin, or even in accessible cavities of the body, so the first thing to be done was to shave the prisoner from head to foot and subject her to the most indecent examination.   It was on record that in Ratisbon some heretics condemned to be burned remained unhurt in the flames; vainly were they submerged in the river and roasted again. A three days' fast was ordered for the whole city, when it was revealed that they had charms concealed in a certain spot under the skin, and after the removal of these there was no further trouble in reducing them to ashes. Charms could also be used from a distance. At Innsbruck a witch boasted that if she had a single thread of a prisoner's garment she could cause him to endure torture to the death without confessing. Some inquisitors, to break the spell of taciturnity, were wont to try sacred magic by administering to the prisoner, on an empty stomach, after invoking the Trinity, three drinks of holy water in which blessed wax had been melted. In one case the most excruciating torture, continued through two whole days, failed to elicit confession, but the third day chanced to be the feast of the Virgin, and during the celebration of the holy rites the devil lost the power with which he had thus far sustained the prisoner, who revealed a plot to make way with the implacable judge, Peter of Berne, by means of sorcery. These were simple devices; a more elaborate one was to take a strip of paper of the length of the body of Christ, and write on it the seven words uttered on the cross; on a holy day, at the hour of mass, this was to be bound around the waist of the witch with relics, she was to be made to drink holy water, and be at once placed on the rack. When all these efforts failed it was a mooted question whether the Church in her extremity could have recourse to the devil by calling in other magicians to break the spell, and Prierias succeeds by ingenious casuistry in proving that she could. One precaution, held indispensable by some experienced practitioners, was that the witch on arrest was to be placed immediately in a basket and thus be carried to prison, without allowing her feet to touch the earth, for if she were permitted to do so she could slay her captors with lightning and escape.*

There was another comfortable theory that those who exercised public functions for the suppression of witchcraft were not subject to the influence of witches or demons. Sprenger tells us that he and his colleagues had been many times assailed by devils in the shape of monkeys, dogs, and goats, but by the aid of God they

---

* Mall. Maleficar. P. II. Q. i.; P. II. Q. viii.; P. III. Q. xv.—Prieriat. Lib. II. c. 9; Lib. III. c. 3.—Nider Formicar. Lib. v. c. 7.

had always been able to overcome the enemy. Yet there were exceptions to this, as we have seen in the case of the unlucky inquisitor and podestà of Como; and the lenity of some judges was explained by the fact that the witch was sometimes able so to affect their minds that they were unable to convict. This steeled the heart of the conscientious inquisitor, who repressed all sentiments of compassion in the belief that they were prompted by Satan. The witch was specially able to exert this power over her judge when she looked upon him before he saw her, and it was a wise precaution to make her enter the court backwards, so that the judge had the advantage of the first glance. He and his assistants were also advised to be very careful not to let a witch touch them, especially on the wrist or other joint, and to wear around the neck a bag containing salt exorcised on Palm Sunday, with consecrated herbs enclosed in blessed wax, besides constantly protecting themselves with the sign of the cross. It was doubtless through neglect of these salutary precautions that at a witch-burning in the Black Forest, as the executioner was lifting the convict on the pile she blew in his face, saying, "I will reward you," whereupon a horrible leprosy broke out which spread over his body, and in a few days he was dead. Occasionally, moreover, the familiar demon of the witch, in the shape of a raven, would accompany her to the place of execution and prevent the wood from burning until he was driven off.*

To combat an evil so widespread and all-pervading required the combined exertions of Church and State. The secular and episcopal courts both had undoubted jurisdiction over it; the action of John XXII., in 1330, may have caused some question as to the Inquisition, but if so it was settled in 1374, when the Inquisitor of France was proceeding against some sorcerers and his competence was disputed, and Gregory XI., to whom the matter was referred, instructed him to prosecute them with the full severity of the laws. Commissions issued in 1409 and 1418 to Pons Feugeyron, Inquisitor of Provence, enumerate sorcerers, conjurers, and invokers of demons among those whom he is to suppress. As the growth of witchcraft became more alarming, Eugenius

---

* Mall. Malef. P. ii. Q. i.; Q. i. c. 4, 11; P. iii. Q. xv.—Prieriat. Lib. iii. c. 2.—Jahn, Hexenwesen und Zauberei in Pommern, Breslau, 1886, p. 8.

IV., in 1437, stimulated the inquisitors everywhere to greater activity against it, and these instructions were repeated in 1445. In 1451 Nicholas V. even enlarged the powers of Hugues le Noir, Inquisitor of France, by granting him jurisdiction over divination, even when it did not savor of heresy. There was occasional clashing, of course, between the episcopal officials and the inquisitors, but the rule seems to have been generally observed that either could proceed separately, while the Clementine regulation should be observed which prescribed their co-operation in the use of torture and punitive imprisonment and when rendering final sentence. The bishops, moreover, assumed that their assent was necessary to the action of the secular courts. In the case of Guillaume Edeline, condemned to perpetual imprisonment at Evreux in 1453, when the sentence was read by the episcopal official the bishop added "We retain our power of pardon," but the inquisitor at once entered a formal protest that the prisoner should not be released without the consent of the Inquisition.[*]

Yet in France at this period the royal jurisdiction, as embodied in the Parlement, was, as we have seen in a former chapter, successfully exerting its superiority over both bishops and inquisitors. A curious case occurring in 1460 illustrates both this and the superstitions current at the time. A priest of the diocese of Soissons named Yves Favins brought a suit for tithes against a husbandman named Jean Rogier, who held of the Hospitallers. These, like the Templars, were exempt from tithes; Favins lost his case, was condemned in the expenses, which were heavy, and was eager for revenge. A poor woman of the village who had come from Merville in Hainault, had quarrelled with the wife of Rogier over the price of some spinning, and to her Yves had recourse. She gave him a great toad which she kept in a pot, and told him to baptize it and feed it on a consecrated wáfer, which he did, giving it the name of John. The woman then killed it and made of it a "*sorceron*," which her daughter took to Rogier's house under pretence of demanding the money in dispute, and cast it under the table at which Rogier, his wife, and his son were dining. They

---

[*] Raynald. ann. 1374, No. 13; ann. 1437, No. 27.—Ripoll II. 566–7; III. 193, 301.—Prieriat. Lib. III. c. 1.—Mall. Maleficar. P. II. Q. i. c. 16; P. III. Q. i.—Anon. Carthus. de Relig. Orig. c. xxvi. (Martene Ampl. Coll. VI. 59).

all died within three days; suspicion was aroused, and the two women were arrested and confessed. The mother was burned, but the daughter obtained a respite on the plea of pregnancy, escaped from jail and fled to Hainault, but was brought back and was carried on appeal to Paris. Yves was rich and well-connected. He was arrested and confined in the prison of the Bishop of Paris, but he obtained counsel and appealed to the Parlement; the Parlement allowed the appeal, tried him, and acquitted him.*

All secular tribunals were not as enlightened as the Parlement of Paris, but there seems to have been at least sometimes an effort to administer even-handed justice. About this time a case occurred at Constance in which an accuser formally inscribed himself against a peasant whom he had met riding on a wolf, and had immediately become crippled. He applied to the peasant, who cured him, but observing that the wizard bewitched others, he felt it his duty to prosecute him. The case was exhaustively argued before the magistrates, for the prosecution and the defence, by two eloquent advocates, Conrad Schatz and Ulric Blaser. Torture was not used, but the accused was condemned and burned on the testimony of witnesses.†

In the ecclesiastical tribunals offenders had not the same chance. We have seen in a former chapter how skilfully the inquisitorial process was framed to secure conviction, and when, after a prolonged period of comparative inactivity, the Inquisition was aroused to renewed exertion in combating the legions of Satan, it sharpened its rusted weapons to a yet keener edge. The old hesitation about pronouncing a sentence of acquittal was no longer entertained, for though the accused might be dismissed with a verdict of not proven, the inquisitor was formally instructed never to declare him innocent. Yet few there were upon whom even this doubtful clemency was exercised, for all the resources of

---

* Mémoires de Jacques du Clercq, Liv. IV. ch. xxiii.

The constant recurrence of the toad in all the operations of witchcraft opens a suggestive question in zoölogical mythology. Space will not admit its discussion here, but I may mention, as a proof of the antiquity of the superstitions connected with the animal, that in Mazdeism the toad was one of the special creations of Ahriman, and was devoted to his service. It was a toad which he set to destroying the Gokard, or Tree of all plants, and which will always be endeavoring to do so until the resurrection (Bundehesh, ch. xviii.).

† Ulric. Molitoris de Python. Mulierib. c. iv.

fraud and force, of guile and torment, were exhausted to secure
conviction with even less reserve than of old.   Engaged in a personal combat with Satan, the inquisitor was convinced in advance
of the guilt of those brought before him as defamed for sorcery,
and the ancient expedients were refined upon and improved.
Formerly endurance of torture might be regarded as an evidence
of innocence, now it was only an additional proof of guilt, for it
showed that Satan was endeavoring to save his servitor, and the
duty to defeat him was plain, even though, as Sprenger tells us
was frequently the case, the witch would allow herself to be torn
in pieces before she would confess.   Though, as formerly, torture
could not be repeated, it could be "continued" indefinitely, with
prolonged periods of intervening imprisonment in dungeons of
which the squalor was purposely heightened to exhaust the mental and physical forces of the victim.   It is true that confession
was not absolutely requisite, for when the evidence was sufficient
the accused could be convicted without it, but it was held that
common justice required that the criminal should avow his guilt,
and therefore the use of torture was universal when confession
could not be otherwise secured.   Yet in view of the satanic gift
of taciturnity it was desirable to avoid recourse to it, and therefore promises of pardon, not indefinitely veiled under a juggle of
words as of old, but positive and specifying a moderate penance
or exile, were to be freely made.   If the fraud was successful, the
inquisitor could let the sentence be pronounced by some one else,
or allow a decent interval to elapse before himself sending his
deluded victim to the stake.   All the other devices to entrap or
seduce the prisoner to confession which we have seen employed
by the older inquisitors were also still recommended.   One new
and infallible sign was the inability of the witch to shed tears
during torture and before the judges, though she could do so
freely elsewhere.   In such a case the inquisitor was instructed to
adjure her to weep by the loving tears shed for the world by Christ
on the cross, but the more she was adjured, we are told, the drier
she would become.   Still, with the usual logic of the demonologist,
if she did weep it was a device of the devil and was not to be reckoned in her favor.*

---

* Prieriat. Lib. III. c. 3.—Mall. Maleficar. P. II. Q. vii., xvi. ; P. III. Q. xiii., xiv.

The most significant change, however, between the old procedure and the new regarded the death-penalty. We have seen that with the heretic the object was held to be the salvation of his soul, and, except in case of relapse, he could always purchase life by recantation, at the expense of lifelong imprisonment, with the prospect that in time submission might win him release. At what period the rule changed with respect to witches is uncertain. When convicted by the secular courts they were invariably burned, and the Inquisition came to adopt the same practice. In 1445 the Council of Rouen still treats them with singular mildness. Invokers of demons were to be publicly preached with mitres on their heads, when, if they abjured, the bishop was empowered to release them after performance of appropriate penance; after this, if they relapsed, clerks were to be perpetually imprisoned, and laymen abandoned to the secular arm, while for minor superstitions and incantations a month's prison and fasting were sufficient, with heavier penance for relapse. In 1448 the Council of Lisieux contented itself with ordering priests on all Sundays and festivals to denounce as excommunicate all usurers, sorcerers, and diviners. In 1453 Guillaume Edeline escaped with abjuration and prison. In 1458 Jaquerius laboriously argues that the witch is not to be treated like other heretics, to be spared if she recants, showing that the change was still a novelty, requiring justification. In 1484 Sprenger says positively that while the recanting heretic is to be imprisoned, the sorcerer, even if penitent, is to be put to death, indicating that by this time there was no longer any question on the subject. There was, as usual, a pretence of shifting the responsibility of this upon the secular authorities, for Sprenger adds that the most the ecclesiastical judge can do is to absolve the penitent and converted witch from the *ipso facto* excommunication under which she lies and let her go, to be apprehended by the lay courts and be burned for the evil which she has wrought. Silvester Prierias shows us how transparent was this juggle, when he instructs the inquisitor that if the witch confesses and is penitent she is to be received to mercy and not be delivered to the secular arm: she is to abjure, is absolved and sentenced to perpetual imprisonment in a black dress; the dress is put on her and she is led to the church-door—but not to prison. The Inquisition takes no further concern about her; if the secular court is content, well and good—if

not, it does as it pleases. What the inquisitors would have said if
it pleased the secular authorities to let the witch go free may be
judged by the maledictions of Sprenger on the incredulous laity
who disbelieved in the reality of witchcraft, and through whose
supineness the secular arm had allowed the cursed sect to so increase that its extirpation appeared impossible.* Still more instructive, as we shall see hereafter, was the indignation of Leo X.
when the Signory of Venice refused to burn the witches of Brescia condemned by the Inquisition.

Equally frivolous was the pretence that the punishment of
burning was merely for the injuries wrought by the witch, for we
shall see that in the case of the Vaudois of Arras the convicts
were burned as a matter of course, although attendance upon the
Sabbat was the only crime with which most of the sufferers were
charged, and that they were delivered for the purpose by the ecclesiastical court to the magistrates, and even burned without such
formality. Besides, Sprenger tells us that in the case of prominent and influential witches the death-penalty was frequently commuted to perpetual imprisonment on bread and water, as a reward
for betraying their accomplices, which shows that the fate of the
accused in reality rested with the inquisitor. Still, there appears
to have been, in at least one case, a simulacrum of judgment by
the secular court which I have rarely met where heretics were concerned. November 5, 1474, at Levone, in Piedmont, Francesca
Viloni and Antonia d' Alberto were condemned by the acting
inquisitor Francesco Chiabaudi. The sentence orders their delivery to the secular arm with a protest that no corporal punishment was thereby indicated, directly or indirectly, although the
goods of the convicts were declared confiscated. The same day
the assistant inquisitor, Frà Lorenzo Butini, delivered them to the
podestà, Bartolomeo Pasquale, with the protest, to protect himself
from "irregularity," that he did not intend to indicate for them
any corporal punishment or to consent to it. The podestà allowed
two days to elapse and then held, November 7, a solemn court to

---

* Concil. Rotomagens. ann. 1445 c. 6 (Bessin Concil. Rotomagens. I. 184).—
C. Lexoviens. ann. 1448 c. 9 (Ibid. II. 482).—Nic. Jaquerii Flagellum Hæret.
Fascinar. c. 27.—Mall. Malef. P. ɪ. Q. xiv.; P. ɪɪ. Q. i. c. 3, 16.—Prieriat. de
Strigimag. Lib. ɪɪɪ. c. 3.

which the population was summoned by blast of trumpet. The convicts were brought before him, when his *consultore*, or legal adviser, Lorenzo di Front, addressed him to the effect that the women had been condemned by the Inquisition for witchcraft, heresy, and apostasy, and that, according to the laws, he must sentence them to the legal punishment of burning alive, which he incontinently did. It evidently was the merest formality, and possibly, as the death of two of the podestà's children had been attributed to one of the witches, he may have wished to magnify his share in the retribution.*

As of old, practically the sole defence of the accused lay in disabling the witnesses for enmity, and judges were reminded that the enmity must be of the most violent nature, for, with the wonted happy facility of assuming guilt in advance, they were told that there was almost always some enmity involved, since witches were odious to everybody. At the same time all the old methods of reducing this slender chance to a minimum were followed, supplemented with such as additional experience had suggested. The names of the witnesses were generally suppressed, but if they were communicated they were so arranged as to mislead, and in advance effort was made to debar the accused from disabling the most damaging ones by enticing her to deny all knowledge of them or to declare them to be her friends. If she insisted on seeing the evidence, it might be given to her after interpolating in it extraneous matters and accusations to lead her astray.†

Appeals were always to be refused if possible. Outside of France the only one that could be made was to Rome for refusing counsel, for improper torture, and other unjust proceeding; and then, as we have seen, the inquisitor could either refuse "apostoli" or grant either reverential or negative ones. If conscious of injustice and aware that an appeal was coming, he could elude it by appointing some one to sit in his place. The danger of appeals was small, however, for if the accused insisted on having counsel she was not allowed to select him. The inquisitor appointed him; he was bound not to assume the defence if he knew it to be un-

---

* Mall. Maleficar. P. II. Q. xiv.—P. Vayra, Le Streghe nel Canavese, op. cit. pp. 218–21, 232.

† Prieriat. Lib. III. c. 3.—Mall. Maleficar. P. III. Q. xii.

just; he was not allowed to know the names of the witnesses, and his functions were restricted to advising his client either to confess or to disable the witnesses. If he made difficulties and delays and interjected appeals he was subject to excommunication as a fautor of heresy, and was worse than the witches themselves—of all of which he was to be duly warned when accepting the case.*

The consequences of neglecting these salutary precautions are seen in two trials in 1474, at Rivara in Piedmont. A number of witches had been burned, and as usual they had implicated others. The matter had been conducted by Francesco Chiabaudi, a canon regular, commissioned by both the Bishop of Turin and Michele de' Valenti, the Inquisitor of Lombardy. Inexperienced and unskilled, he had appointed Tommaso Balardi, parish priest of Rivara, to make the preliminary informations in five fresh accusations. The evidence, as usual, was overwhelming; Balardi arrested the culprits and gave them ten days to show cause why they should not be tortured. At the same time, with incredible ignorance of his duties, he allowed them to select defenders, when they chose their husbands or brothers or sons. In the case of three, these defenders did nothing and the trials were conducted as usual, though the fragmentary documents remaining do not acquaint us with the result. The other two, Guglielmina Ferreri and Margherita Cortina, were more fortunate. They seem to have been rich peasants, and their families retained three able lawyers for their defence. When these were once admitted before the tribunal the prosecution went to pieces. Chiabaudi, unacquainted with the privileges of the inquisitorial process, was wholly unable to control them. He allowed them to enter protests against the initial informations for irregularity, and even permitted them, against all precedent, to introduce witnesses for the defence. They had the audacity to summon Balardi himself, and made him testify that the accused were regular in all religious observances; after which they poured in evidence that the so-called witches were eminently pious and charitable women, and that the rumors against them had only arisen a couple of years before, on the burning of three sisters who were said to have named them in their confessions. Chiabaudi sought refuge in appointing An-

---

* Mall. Maleficar. P. III. Q. x., xi., xxxv.—Prieriat. Lib. III. c. 3.

tonio Valo, a local legal luminary, as procurator-fiscal, or prosecutor, an official unknown to the Inquisition of the period, whom the counsel for the accused speedily drove out of court. With each hearing they grew more aggressive. They boldly quoted the Digest and the rules of law and justice as though such things had not been expressly prohibited in inquisitorial trials. Finally they told Chiabaudi that he was himself suspect; that as a canon he had no right to leave his convent for such business, and that all his acts were null. The whole prosecution, they said, was merely an attempt to extort money and to divide the plunder of the accused, and they appealed to the episcopal vicar of Turin, with a threat, if necessary, to obtain the intervention of the Duke of Savoy himself. Chiabaudi yielded to the storm which he had imprudently allowed to gather strength, and in February, 1375, he permitted the transfer of the case to the episcopal court of Turin. Whether the unfortunate women fared better there will, doubtless, never be known, but the case shows the wisdom of the precautions adopted by the regular inquisitors of selecting counsel themselves and threatening them with excommunication if they defended their clients. It is interesting, moreover, as probably the only inquisitorial trial on record, save that of Gilles de Rais, in which the forbidden *litis contestatio* was carried out.[*]

A much more typical and illustrative case, of which we happen to have the details, is that of the "Vaudois,"[†] or witches of Arras, showing how witchcraft panics were developed and what could be accomplished by inquisitorial methods, even under the supreme jurisdiction of the Parlement of Paris. In 1459, while a general chapter of the Dominican Order was in session at Langres, there chanced to be burned there as a witch a hermit named Robinet de Vaulx. He was forced to name all whom he had seen in the Sabbat, and among them was a young *femme de folle vie* of Douai, named Deniselle, and a resident of Arras, advanced in years, named Jean la Vitte—a painter and poet, who had written many

---

* P. Vayra, Le Streghe nel Canavese, op. cit. pp. 658–715.

† It will be remembered (Vol. II. p. 158) that by this time in France, Vaudois and Vaudoisie had become the designation of all deviations from faith, and was especially applied to sorcery. Hence is derived the word Voodooism, descriptive of the negro sorcery of the French colonies, transmitted to the United States through Louisiana.

beautiful ballads in honor of the Virgin, and who was a general favorite, though, as he was popularly known as the Abbé-de-peu-de-sens, he was probably not a very sedate character.* Pierre le Brousart, the Inquisitor of Arras, was present at the chapter, and on his return he lost no time in looking after the accused. Deniselle was soon arrested and thrown into the episcopal prison; Jean, Bishop of Arras, whom we have seen promoted to the cardinalate for his services in procuring the repeal of the Pragmatic Sanction, was then in Rome; his suffragan was a Dominican, Jean, titular Bishop of Beirut, formerly a papal penitentiary, and his vicars were Pierre du Hamel, Jean Thibault, Jean Pochon, and Mathieu du Hamel. These took up the matter warmly and were earnestly supported by Jacques du Boys, a doctor of laws and dean of the chapter, who thrust himself into the affair and pushed it with relentless vigor. After repeated torture, Deniselle confessed to have attended the Sabbat and named various persons seen there, among them Jean la Vitte. He had already been compromised by Robinet, and had gone into hiding, but the inquisitor hunted him up at Abbeville, arrested him, and brought him to Arras, when he was no sooner in prison than in despair he tried to cut out his tongue with a pocket-knife, so as to prevent himself from confessing. He did not succeed, but though he was long unable to speak, this did not save him from torture, for he could use the pen and was obliged to write out his confession. Forced to name all whom he had seen in the Sabbat, he implicated a large number, including nobles, ecclesiastics, and common folk. Six more arrests were made among the latter, including several women of the town; the affair threatened to spread farther than had at first been expected; the vicars grew timid and concluded to dis-

---

* There was some debate whether the evidence of a witch as to those whom she had seen in the Sabbat was to be received, but it was settled in favor of the faith by the unanswerable argument that otherwise the principal means of detecting witches would be lost. If the accused alleged that the devil had caused an apparition resembling him to be present, he was to be required to prove the fact, which was not easy (Jaquerii Flagell. Hæret. Fascinar. c. 26).—Bernardo di Como (de Strigiis, c. 13, 14) says that the mere accusation of being seen in the Sabbat is not sufficient to justify arrest, as the individual may be personated by a demon, but it has to be reinforced by " conjectures and presumptions," which, of course, were never lacking.

charge all the prisoners. Then Jacques du Boys and the Bishop of Beirut constituted themselves formal complainants ; the latter, moreover, went to Péronne and brought to Arras the Comte d'Estampes, Captain-general of Picardy for Philippe le Bon of Burgundy, who ordered the vicars to do their duty under threats of prosecuting them.

Four women of the last batch of prisoners confessed under torture and implicated a large number of others. The vicars, uncertain as to their duty, sent the confessions to two notable clerks, Gilles Carlier, dean, and Gregoire Nicolai, official, of Cambrai, who replied that if the accused were not relapsed and if they would recant they were not to be put to death, provided they had not committed murder and abused the Eucharist. Here we recognize a transition period between the old practice with heretics and the new with sorcerers, but du Boys and the Bishop of Beirut were fully imbued with the new notions, and insisted that all should be burned. They declared that whoever disputed this was himself a sorcerer, that any one who should presume to aid or counsel the prisoners should share their fate. The welfare of Christendom was concerned, a full third of nominal Christians were secretly sorcerers, including many bishops, cardinals, and grand masters, and that if they could assemble under a leader it would be difficult to estimate the destruction which they could inflict on religion and society. Possibly one of these worthies may be credited with the authorship of a tract upon the subject, a copy of which, formerly belonging to Philippe le Bon, is now in the Royal Library of Brussels. The anonymous writer, who describes himself as a priest, speaks of "Vauderie" as something new and unheard of, more execrable than all the detestable errors of paganism since the beginning of the world. He calls on the prelates to arise and purge Christendom of these abominable sectaries, and to excite the people by denouncing their most damnable crimes, but his most burning eloquence is addressed to the princes. Not without significance is the sword borne before them, for it is to remind them that they are ministers and officers of God, whose duty it is to order unsparing vengeance on these criminals. If the sectaries are allowed to multiply the most fearful results are to be expected, and the King of Darkness is already rejoicing at the prospect. Wars and enmities will come ; strife and sedition will rage in the fields, in the cities, and in the kingdoms. In mutual slaughter men will fall dead in heaps. Children will rise against their elders and the villeins will assail the nobles. It was not only religion, but the whole social order, which was threatened by a few strumpets and the Abbé-de-peu-de-sens.*

Like the agent of Conrad Tors in the days of Conrad of Marburg, the Bishop of Beirut boasted that he could recognize a Vaudois or sorcerer at sight. In conjunction with du Boys he procured another arrest, and induced the Comte d'Estampes to order the vicars to hasten their proceedings. Under this pressure, an assembly of all the principal ecclesiastics of Arras, with some jurists, was held on May 9, 1460, to consider the evidence. The deliberation was short, and the accused were condemned. The next day, on a scaffold in front of the episcopal palace, and in presence of a crowd which had gathered from twelve leagues around, the convicts were brought forward, together with the body of one of them, Jean le Febvre, who had been found hanging in his cell. Mitres were placed on their heads, with pictures representing them as worshipping the devil. The inquisitor preached the sermon, and read the description of the Sabbat and of their visits to it, and then asked them individually if it was true, to which they all assented. Then he read the sentence abandoning them to the secular arm, their property to be confiscated, the real estate to the seigneur and the movables to the bishop, and they were delivered to their several jurisdictions, Deniselle being handed over to the authorities of Douai who were present to receive her, and the rest to those of Arras. At once they began with shrieks to assert that they had been cruelly deceived—that they had been promised that if they would confess they would be discharged with a pilgrimage of ten or twelve leagues, and had been threatened with burning for persistence in denial. With one voice they declared that they had never been to the "Vauderie," that their confessions had been extorted under stress of torture and false promises and blandishments, and until they were silenced by the flames they begged the people to pray for them, and their friends to have masses sung in their behalf. The last words heard from

---

* MSS. Bib. Roy. de Bruxelles, No. 11209.

the Abbé-de-peu-de-sens, were "*Jesus autem transiens per medium illorum.*" Gilles Flameng, an advocate who had been active
in the whole proceeding, was the especial object of their reproaches; they reviled him as a traitor who had been particularly earnest in the false promises which had lured them to destruction.

Appetite grew by what it fed on. This execution was followed
immediately by the arrest, on the requisition of the inquisitor, of
thirteen persons, including six public women, who had been implicated by the confessions. The managers of the business, however,
seemed to tire of the pursuit of such worthless game, and grew bold
enough to strike higher. On June 22 Arras was startled by the
arrest of Jean Tacquet, an eschevin and one of the richest citizens;
on the next day by that of Pierre des Carieulx, equally wealthy
and esteemed the best accountant in Artois; and on the next by
that of the Chevalier Payen de Beauffort, a septuagenary and
the head of one of the most ancient and richest houses in the
province, who had manifested his piety by founding three convents.
He had been warned that his name was on the list of accused, but
had declared that if he were a thousand leagues away he would
return to meet the charge, and in fact he had come to the city
for the purpose. In his hôtel of la Chevrette his children and
friends had entreated him to depart if he felt himself guilty, when
with the most solemn oaths he asserted his innocence. His arrest
had not been ventured upon without the consent of Philippe le
Bon, secured by Philippe de Saveuse; the Comte d'Estampes had
come to Arras to insure it, and refused to see him when he begged
an interview. This was followed, July 7, by an *auto de fé* of seven
of those arrested on May 9; five of these were burned, and, like
their predecessors, asserted that their confessions had been wrung
from them by torture, and died begging the prayers of all good
Christians. Two were sentenced to imprisonment for definite
terms, the reason alleged being that they had not revoked after
their first confession—a highly irregular proceeding of which the
object was to facilitate further convictions.

The affair was now beginning to attract general attention and
animadversion. Philippe le Bon was disturbed, for he heard that
at Paris and elsewhere it was reported that he was seizing the
rich men of his dominions to confiscate their property. Accord-

ingly he sent to Arras, as supervisors, his confessor, a Dominican and titular Bishop of Selimbria, together with the Chevalier Baudoin de Noyelles, Governor of Péronne, while the Comte d'Estampes deputed his secretary, Jean Forme, together with Philippe de Saveuse, the Seigneur de Crèvecœur, who was bailly of Amiens, and his lieutenant, Guillaume de Berri. The first effort of these new-comers seems to have been to share in the spoils. On July 16 Baudoin de Noyelles arrested Antoine Sacquespée, an eschevin and one of the richest of the citizens, who had been urged to fly, but who, like de Beauffort, had declared that he would come a thousand leagues to face the accusation. The next day another eschevin, Jean Josset, was seized, and a sergent-de-ville named Henriet Royville, while three whose arrest was pending fled, two of them being wealthy men, Martin Cornille, and Willaume le Febvre, whom the Comte d'Estampes pursued as far as Paris without success. A panic terror by this time pervaded the community; no one knew when his turn would come, and men scarce dared to leave the city for fear they would be accused of flying through conscious guilt, while citizens who were absent were unwelcome guests everywhere, and could scarce find lodgings. Similarly, strangers would not venture to visit the city. Arras was a prosperous seat of manufactures, and its industries suffered enormously. Its merchants lost their credit; creditors importunately demanded settlement, for the risk of confiscation hung over every man, and we have seen how the rights of creditors in such cases were extinguished. The vicars endeavored to soothe the general alarm and distress by a proclamation that no one need fear arrest who was innocent, for none were arrested unless eight or ten witnesses swore to seeing them at the Sabbat—though it was afterwards found that many were seized on the evidence of only one or two.

At length, at the expense of the prisoners, the inquisitor, with the vicars and Gilles Flameng, was sent to the Duke of Burgundy at Brussels, to lay before him the evidence of the trials. The duke called a great assembly of clerks, including the doctors of Louvain, who gravely debated the matter. Some held, with the *Cap. Episcopi*, that it was all a delusion, others that it was a reality. No conclusion was reached, and the duke finally sent his herald, Toison d'Or (Lefebvre, Seigneur de Saint-Remy) in whom he had great confidence, back with the vicars, to be present at all examinations. They reached Arras August 14, after which there were no further arrests, although innumerable names were on the lists of accused. The prisoners were less inhumanly treated, and but four of the pending trials were pushed to a conclusion. Reports of these were sent to Brussels for the duke's consideration, and they were brought back, October 12, by the president of the ducal chamber, Adrien Collin, in whose presence the accused were again examined. Finally, on October 22, the customary assembly was held, immediately followed by the *auto de fé*, where the sermon was preached by the Inquisitor of Cambrai, and the sentences were read by the Inquisitor of Arras, and by Michael du Hamel, one of the vicars. The four convicts had different fates.

The Chevalier de Beauffort, it was recited, had confessed that he had thrice been to the Sabbat—twice on foot and once by flying on an anointed staff. He had refused to give his soul to Satan, but had given him four of his hairs. The inquisitor asked him if this was true, and he replied in the affirmative, begging for mercy. The inquisitor then announced that, as he had confessed without torture, and had never retracted, he should not be mitred and burned but be scourged (a penance inflicted by the inquisitor on the spot, but without removing the penitent's clothes), be imprisoned for seven years, and pay a long list of fines for pious purposes, amounting in all to eight thousand two hundred livres, including one thousand five hundred to the Inquisition. But besides these fines, thus publicly announced, he was obliged to pay four thousand to the Duke of Burgundy, two thousand to the Comte d'Estampes, one thousand to the Seigneur de Crèvecœur, and one hundred to his lieutenant, Guillaume de Berry.*

The next was the rich eschevin, Jean Tacquet. He admitted that he had been to the Sabbat ten times or more. He had endeavored to withdraw his allegiance from Satan, who had forced him to continue it by beating him cruelly with a bull's pizzle. He was now condemned to scourging, administered as in the case of

---

* This was, doubtless, in commutation for confiscation, and reveals the object of the whole affair. To estimate the magnitude of the fines, it may be mentioned that de Beauffort's annual revenue was estimated at five hundred livres. The richest citizens of Arras who were arrested were said to be worth from four hundred to five hundred livres a year.

de Beauffort, to ten years' prison, and to fines amounting to one thousand four hundred livres, of which two hundred went to the Inquisition; but, as in de Beauffort's case, there were secret contributions exacted from him.

The third was Pierre du Carieulx, another rich citizen. His sentence recited that he had been to the Sabbat innumerable times; holding a lighted candle he had kissed, under the tail, the devil in the shape of a monkey; he had given him his soul in a compact written with his own blood; he had thrice given to the Abbé-de-peu-de-sens consecrated wafers received at Easter, out of which, with the bones of men hanged, which he had picked up under the gallows, and the blood of young children, of whom he had slain four, he had helped to make the infernal ointment and certain powders, with which they injured men and beasts. When asked to confirm this he denied it, saying that it had been forced from him by torture; and he would have added much more, but he was silenced. Abandoned to secular justice, the eschevins demanded him as their bourgeois, and on their paying his prison expenses he was delivered to them. They allowed him to talk in the town-hall, when he disculpated all whom he had accused, of whom he said there were many present, eschevins and others, adding that, under torture, he had accused every one he knew, and if he had known more he would have included them. He was burned the same day.

The fourth was Huguet Aubry, a man of uncommon force and resolution. In spite of the severest and most prolonged torture, he had confessed nothing. He had been accused by nine witnesses, and he was now asked if he would confess under promise of mercy; but he repeated that he knew nothing of Vauderie, and had never been to the Sabbat. Then the inquisitor told him that he had broken jail and been recaptured, which rendered him guilty. He threw himself on his knees and begged for mercy, but was condemned to prison, on bread and water, for twenty years; a most irregular sentence, which could never have been rendered under the perfected system of procedure, for the evidence against him was strong, and his constancy under torture only proved that Satan had endowed him with the gift of taciturnity.

This was the last of the persecution. There had been only thirty-four arrests and twelve burnings; which, in the flourishing times of witchcraft, would have been a trifle, but the novelty of the occurrence in Picardy, the character of the victims, and the subsequent proceedings in the Parlement attracted to it a disproportionate attention. That it came to so early a termination is possibly attributable to the fact that Philippe de Saveuse had directed the torture of the women not only to convict de Beauffort, but to incriminate the Seigneurs de Croy and others, from avaricious and perhaps political motives. The de Croy were at this time all-powerful at the ducal court, and doubtless used their interest to arrest the ecclesiastical machinery which was strong enough to crush even them. It has every appearance of a repetition of the old story of Conrad of Marburg.

Whatever the cause, the inquisitor and the vicars now put a stop to the prosecutions, without calling in the Bishop of Beirut, Jacques du Boys, de Saveuse, and others, who urged them to proceed with the good work. In vain the latter talked of the imminent dangers impending over Christendom from the innumerable multitude of sorcerers, many of whom held high station in the Church and in the courts of princes. Vainly even the last card was played, and the superstitious were frightened by rumors that Antichrist was born, and that the sorcerers would support him.*

One by one the accused were discharged, as they were able to raise money to pay the expenses of their prison and of the Inquisition, which was a condition of liberation in all cases except those of utter poverty. Some had to undergo the formality of purging themselves with compurgators. Antoine Sacquespée, for instance,

---

* The belief in the imminent advent of Antichrist was as strong in the fifteenth century as in its predecessors. In 1445 the University of Paris was astonished by a young Spaniard, about twenty years of age, who came there and overcame the most learned schoolmen and theologians in disputation. He appeared equally at home in all branches of learning, including medicine and law; he was matchless with the sword, and played ravishingly on all instruments of music. After confounding Paris, he went to the Duke of Burgundy, at Ghent, and thence passed into Germany. The doctors of the University pondered over the apparition, and finally concluded that he was Antichrist, who, it was well known, would possess all arts and sciences by the secret aid of Satan, and would be a good Christian until he attained the age of twenty-eight (Chron. de Mathieu de Coussy, ch. VIII.). The wonderful stranger was Fernando de Cordoba, who settled in the papal court, and wrote several books, which have been forgotten. See Nich. Anton. Biblioth. Hispan. Lib. x. cap. xiii. No. 734-9.

who had been tortured without confession, had to furnish seven,
and was not allowed to escape without surrendering a portion of
his substance.   Others had light penance, like Jennon d'Amiens,
a woman who had confessed after being several times tortured, and
was now only required to make a five-league pilgrimage to Nôtre
Dame d'Esquerchin.   This was an admission that the whole affair
was a fraud; and even more remarkable was the case of a *fille de
joie* named Belotte, who had been repeatedly tortured, and had
confessed.   She would have been burned with the other women
on May 9, but it happened, accidentally or otherwise, that her
mitre was not ready, and her execution was postponed, and now
she was only banished from the diocese, and ordered to make a
pilgrimage to Nôtre Dame de Boulogne.   Of the whole number
arrested nine had the constancy to endure torture—in most cases
long and severe—without confession.

As the terror passed away the feelings of the people expressed
themselves sportively in some verses scattered through the streets,
lampooning the principal actors in the tragedy.   The stanza devoted to Pierre le Brousart runs thus:

> "Then the inquisitor, with his white hood,
>   His shining nose and his repulsive mazzard,
> Among the foremost in the game has stood
>   To torture these poor folk as witch or wizard.
> But he knows only what he has been told,
>   For his sole thought throughout has been to hold
>   And keep their goods and chattels at all hazard.
> But he has failed in this, and been cajoled."

The vicars and their advocates and the assembly of experts are
all held guilty, and the verses conclude by threatening them:

> "But you shall all be punished in a mass,
>   And we shall learn who caused the wondrous tale
> Of Vaudois in our city of Arras."*

---

* The Chronicler of Arras tells us that at this time there was no enforcement
of the laws in Arras; every one did as he pleased, and no one was punished but
the friendless.   His statement is borne out by the cases of homicide and other
crimes which he relates, and of which no notice was taken (Mém. de Jacques du
Clercq, Liv. IV. ch. 22, 24, 40, 41).   Yet vigorous search was made for the author
of this pasquinade, and Jacotin Maupetit was arrested by an usher-at-arms of the
duke on the charge of writing it.   He adroitly slipped out of his doublet, and
sought asylum in three successive churches, finally succeeding in getting to Paris,

The prophecy was not wholly unverified. Fortunately there was in France a Parlement which had succeeded in establishing its jurisdiction over both the great vassals and the Inquisition, and the relations between the courts of Paris and Brussels were such as to render it nothing loath to interfere. De Beauffort, before his examination, had made an appeal to this supreme tribunal, which had been disregarded and suppressed, but his son Philippe had carried to Paris the tale of the wrongs committed on his father. The Parlement moved slowly, but on January 16, 1461, Philippe came back with an usher commissioned to bring de Beauffort before it after investigating the case. This official took testimony, and on the 25th, accompanied by de Beauffort's four sons and thirty well-armed men, he presented himself before the vicars. Frightened by this formidable demonstration, they refused to see him; but he went to the episcopal palace, took the keys of the prison by force, and carried de Beauffort to the Conciergerie in Paris, after serving notice on the vicars to answer before the Parlement on February 25. The matter was now fairly in train for a legal investigation in which both sides could be heard. The convicts who had been condemned to imprisonment were set at liberty and carried to Paris, where their evidence confirmed that of de Beauffort. The conspirators were grievously alarmed. Jacques du Boys, the dean, who had been the prime mover, became insane about the time set for the hearing; and though he recovered his senses, his limbs failed him; he took to his bed, where bed-sores ate great holes in his flesh, and he died in about a year, some persons attributing to sorcery and others to divine vengeance what evidently was mental trouble, causing temporary insanity followed by paresis. The Bishop of Beirut was thrown in prison, charged with having set the affair on foot, but he managed to escape, by miracle as he asserted; he made a pilgrimage to Compostella, and on his return secured the position of confessor to Queen Marie, dowager of Charles VII., where he was safe. Other conspicuous actors in the tragedy left Arras to escape the hatred of their fellow-citizens. Meanwhile the legal proceedings

---

where he constituted himself a prisoner of the Parlement, and returned to Arras free, to find that, meanwhile, his property had been confiscated and sold. (Ibid. ch. 24.)

dragged on with the interminable delays for which the Parlement was notorious, enhanced on this occasion by the political vicissitudes of the period, and the final decision was not rendered until 1491, thirty years after its commencement, when all the sufferers had passed off the scene except the indomitable Huguet Aubry, who was still alive to enjoy a rehabilitation celebrated in a manner as imposing as possible. On July 18 the decree was published from a scaffold erected on the spot where the sentences had been pronounced. The magistrates had been ordered to proclaim a holiday, and to offer prizes for the best *folie moralisée* and *pure folie*, and to send notice to all the neighboring towns, so that a crowd of eight or nine thousand persons was collected. After a sermon of two hours and a half, preached by the celebrated Geoffroi Broussart, subsequently chancellor of the University, the decree was read, condemning the Duke of Burgundy to pay the costs, and the processes and sentences to be torn and destroyed as unjust and abusive; ordering the accused and condemned to be restored to their good name and fame, all confiscations and payments to be refunded, while the vicars were to pay twelve hundred livres each, Gilles Flameng one thousand, de Saveuse five hundred, and others smaller sums, amounting in all to six thousand five hundred; out of which fifteen hundred were to be applied to founding a daily mass for the souls of those executed, and erecting a cross on the spot where they had been burned. The cruel and unusual tortures made use of in the trials were, moreover, prohibited for the future in all secular and ecclesiastical tribunals. It was probably the only case on record in which an inquisitor stood as a defendant in a lay court to answer for his official action. One cannot help reflecting that, if the Council of Vienne had done its duty as fearlessly as the Parlement, the affair of the Templars, so similar in many of its features, might have had a similar termination; and the contrast between this and the rehabilitation proceedings in the case of Joan of Arc shows how the Inquisition had fallen during the interval.*

---

* The details of this case have, fortunately, been preserved for us in the Mémoires de Jacques du Clercq, Livre IV., with the decree of Parlement in the appendix. Mathieu de Coussy (Chronique ch. 129) and Cornelius Zantfliet (Martene, Ampl. Coll. V. 501) also give brief accounts. Some details omitted by

Besides the general significance of this transaction in the history of witchcraft and of its persecution, there are several points worthy of attention in their bearing on the practical application of the methods of procedure described above. In the first place, it is evident throughout that no counsel were allowed to the accused. Then, the combined episcopal and inquisitorial court permitted no appeals, even to the Parlement, whose supreme jurisdiction was unquestioned. Not only was the attempt of de Beauffort to interject such an appeal contemptuously suppressed, but when Willaume le Febvre, who had fled to Paris and constituted himself a prisoner there to answer all charges, sent his son Willemet with a notary to serve an appeal, the service was rightly regarded as involving considerable risk. After watching their opportunity, Willemet and the notary served the notice on one of the vicars at church, then leaped on their horses and made all speed for Paris, but the vicars instantly despatched well-mounted horsemen, who overtook them at Montdidier and brought them back. They were clapped in jail, along with a number of friends and kinsmen who had been privy to their intention without betraying it, and were not released until they agreed to withdraw the appeal. Thus, an appeal was treated as an offence justifying vigorous measures. It is more difficult to understand the contemptuous indifference with which a papal bull was treated. Martin Cornille, the other fugitive, had pursued a different policy. He carried with him an ample store of money, part of which he invested in a bull from Pius II. transferring the whole matter to Gilles Charlier and Grégoire Nicolai of Cambrai, and two of the Arras vicars. This was brought to Arras in August, 1460, by the Dean of Soignies, after which we hear nothing more of it, though it may have contributed to cool the ardor of those who were expecting to profit by the prosecutions.*

The means employed to obtain confession show that Sprenger only recorded the usage of the period in advising recourse to whatever fraud or force might prove necessary. Promises of immunity

---

du Clercq are to be found in the learned sketch of Duverger, " La Vauderie dans les États de Philippe le Bon," Arras, 1885, which, it is to be hoped, will be followed by the more elaborate work promised by the author.

* Du Clercq, Liv. IV. ch. 10· 11.

or of trifling penance were lavished on those whom it was intended to burn if they yielded to the blandishment, and these were supplemented with threats of burning as the punishment of taciturnity. De Beauffort's confession without torture excited general astonishment until it was known that, on his arrest, after he had sworn to his innocence, Jacques du Boys entreated him to confess, even kneeling before him and praying him to do so, assuring him that if he refused he could not be saved from the stake, and that all his property would be confiscated, to the beggaring of his children, while, if he would confess, he should be released within four days without public humiliation or exposure; and when de Beauffort argued that this would be committing perjury, du Boys told him not to mind that, as he should have absolution. Those whose constancy was proof against such persuasiveness were tortured without stint or mercy. The women were frightfully scourged. Huguet Aubry was kept in prison for eleven months, during which, at intervals, he was tortured fifteen times, and when the ingenuity of the executioners failed in devising more exquisite forms of torment, he was threatened with drowning and thrown into the river, and then with hanging and suspended from a tree with his eyes duly bandaged. Le petit Henriot's resolution was tried with seven months' incarceration, during which he was also tortured fifteen times, fire being applied to the soles of his feet until he was crippled for life. Others are mentioned whose endurance was equally tried, and we hear of such strange devices as pouring oil and vinegar down the throat, and other expedients not recognized by law.*

With regard to the death-penalty, it is to be observed that none of these were cases of relapse, and under the old inquisitorial practice they would all have been entitled to the penance of imprisonment. Their burning had not even the pretext of being punishment for injuries inflicted on their neighbors, for, with the exception of Pierre du Carieulx, the only offence assigned to them was attendance at the Sabbat. At the same time there was no resort to the juggle suggested by later authorities, of assigning penance, and then not inquiring what the secular power might see fit to do. The condemned were formally delivered to the

---

* Du Clercq, Liv. IV. ch. 14, 15, 28; Append. II.

magistrates to be burned, and though at the first *auto* a death-sentence was pronounced by the eschevins, at the second even this formality was omitted, and the victims were dragged directly from the place of sentence to that of execution.*

One specially notable feature of the whole affair was the utter incredulity everywhere excited. Just as the crimes imputed to the Templars found credence nowhere out of France, so, outside of Arras, we are told not one person in a thousand believed in the truth of the charges. This was fortunate, for the victims naturally included in their lists of associates many residents of other places, and the conflagration might readily have spread over the whole country, had it found agents like Pierre le Brousart, who carried the spark from Langres to Arras. On the strength of revelations in the confessions several persons were arrested in Amiens, but the bishop, who was a learned clerk and had long resided in Rome, promptly released them and declared that he would dismiss all brought before him, for he did not believe in the possibility of such offences. At Tournay others were seized, and the matter was warmly debated, with the result that they were set free, although Jean Taincture, a most notable clerk, wrote an elaborate treatise to prove their guilt. It was the same with the accused who managed to fly. Martin Cornille was caught in Burgundy and brought before the Archbishop of Besançon, who acquitted him on the strength of informations made in Arras. Willaume le Febvre surrendered himself to the Bishop of Paris; the Inquisitor of Paris came to Arras to get the evidence concerning him, and the vicars furnished the confessions of those who had implicated him. The result was that the tribunal, consisting of the Archbishop of Reims, the Bishop of Paris, the Inquisitor of France, and sundry doctors of theology, not only acquitted him, but authorized him to prosecute the vicars for reparation of his honor, and for expenses and damages.† Evidently up to this time the excitement con-

---

* Du Clercq, Liv. IV. ch. 4, 8.

† Du Clercq, Liv. IV. ch. 6, 11, 14, 28.—A copy of Jean Taincture's tract is in the Bib. Roy. de Bruxelles, MSS. No. 2296.—About this time Jeannin, a peasant of Inchy, was executed at Cambrai, and at Lille Catharine Patée was condemned as a witch, but escaped with banishment, and the same was the case with Marguerite d'Escornay at Nivelles. One unfortunate, Noel Ferri of Amiens, became insane on the subject, and after wandering over the land, accused himself at

cerning witchcraft was to a great extent artificial—the creation
of a comparatively few credulous ecclesiastics and judges: the mass
of educated clerks and jurists were disposed to hold fast to the definition of the *Cap. Episcopi*, and to regard it as a delusion. Had
the Church resolutely repressed the growing superstition, in place
of stimulating it with all the authority of the Holy See, infinite
bloodshed and misery might have been spared to Christendom.

The development of the witchcraft epidemic, in fact, had not
been rapid. The earliest detailed account which we have of it
is that of Nider, in his *Formicarius*, written in 1337. Although
Nider himself seems to have sometimes acted as inquisitor, he tells
us that his information is principally derived from the experience
of Peter of Berne, a secular judge, who had burned large numbers
of witches of both sexes, and had driven many more from the
Bernese territory, which they had infested for about sixty years.
This would place the origin of witchcraft in that region towards
the close of the fourteenth century, and Silvester Prierias, as we
have seen, attributes it to the first years of the fifteenth. Bernardo di Como, writing about 1510, assigns to it a somewhat earlier
origin, for he says the records of the Inquisition of Como showed
that it had existed for a hundred and fifty years. It is quite likely,
indeed, that the gradual development of witchcraft from ordinary
sorcery commenced about the middle of the fourteenth century.
The great jurist Bartolo, who died in 1357, when acting as judge
at Novara, tried and condemned a woman who confessed to having adored the devil, trampled on the cross, and killed children by
touching and fascinating them. This approach to the later witchcraft was so novel to him that he appealed to the theologians to
explain it. In this there seems no reference to the distinctive
feature of the Sabbat, but the popular beliefs concerning Holda
and Dame Habonde and their troop were rife, and the coalescence
of the various superstitions was only a question of time. As early
as 1353 an allusion to the witches' dance occurs in a trial at Toulouse. Thus the stories grew, under the skilful handling of such

Mantes of belonging to the accursed sect. He was burned August 26, 1460.
His wife, whom he had implicated, escaped sharing his fate by an appeal to
the Parlement.—Duverger, La Vauderie dans les États de Philippe le Bon,
pp. 52–3, 84.

judges as Peter of Berne, until they assumed the detailed and definite shape that we find in Nider. The latter also acknowledges his obligation to the Inquisitor of Autun, which would indicate that witchcraft was prevalent in Burgundy at a comparatively early period. In 1424 we hear of a witch named Finicella burned in Rome for causing the death of many persons and bewitching many more. According to Peter of Berne, the evil originated with a certain Scavius, who openly boasted of his powers, and always escaped by transforming himself into a mouse, until he was assassinated through a window near which he incautiously sat. His principal disciple was Poppo, who taught Staedelin; the latter fell into the hands of Peter, and, after four vigorous applications of torture, confessed all the secrets of the diabolical sect. The details given are virtually those described above, showing that the subsequent inquisitors who drew their inspiration from Nider were skilled in their work and knew how to extract confessions in accordance with their preconceived notions. There are a few unimportant variants, of course; infants, as already stated, when killed, were boiled down, the soup being used to procure converts by its magic power, while the solid portion was worked up into ointment required for the unholy rites. Apparently, moreover, the theory had not yet established itself that the witch was powerless against officers of public justice, for the latter were held to incur great dangers in the performance of their functions. It was only by the most careful observance of religious duties and the constant use of the sign of the cross that Peter of Berne escaped, and even he once, at the castle of Blankenburg, nearly lost his life when, going up a lofty staircase at night in such haste that he forgot to cross himself, he was precipitated violently to the bottom—manifestly the effect of sorcery, as he subsequently learned by torturing a prisoner.*

Although, in 1452, a witch tried at Provins declared that in all France and Burgundy the total number of witches did not exceed

---

* Nider Formicar. Lib. v. c. 3, 4, 7.—Grimm's Teutonic Mythol. III. 1066.—Soldan, Geschichte der Hexenprocesse, Stuttgart, 1843, p. 186.—Bernardi Comensis de Strigiis c. 4.—Steph. Infessuræ Diar. Urb. Romæ ann. 1424 (Eccard. Corp. Hist. II. 1874–5).

Peter of Berne's efforts to purify his territory were fruitless, for we hear of witches burned in 1482 at Murten, Canton Berne (Valerius Anshelm, Berner-Chronik, Bern, 1884, I. 224).

sixty, no believer contented himself with figures so moderate.   In 1453 we hear of an epidemic of witchcraft in Normandy, where the witches were popularly known as Scobaces, from *scoba*, a broom, in allusion to their favorite mode of equitation to the Sabbat. The same year occurred the case of Guillaume Edeline, which excited wide astonishment from the character of the culprit, who was a noted doctor of theology and Prior of St. Germain-en-Laye. Madly in love with a noble lady, he sought the aid of sorcery. He doubtless fell victim to some sharper, for on his person was found a compact with Satan, formally drawn up with reciprocal obligations, one of which was that in his sermons he should assert the falsity of the stories told of sorcerers, and this, we are told, greatly increased their number, for the judges were restrained from prosecuting them.   Another condition was that he should present himself before Satan whenever required.   The methods of his examination must have been sharp, for he confessed that he performed this obligation by striding a broomstick, when he would be at once transported to the Sabbat, where he performed the customary homage of kissing the devil, in the form of a white sheep, under the tail.   Prosecuted before Guillaume de Floques, Bishop of Evreux, he persuaded the University of Caen to defend him ; but the bishop procuring the support of the University of Paris, he was forced to confess and was convicted.   It shows the uncertainty of procedure as yet that he was not burned, but was allowed to abjure, and was penanced with perpetual imprisonment on bread and water.   At the *auto de fé* the inquisitor dwelt upon his former high position and the edification of his teaching, when the unfortunate man burst into tears and begged mercy of God.   He was thrown into a *basse-fosse* at Evreux, where he lingered for four years, showing every sign of contrition, and at last he was found dead in his cell in the attitude of prayer.   The epidemic was spreading, for in 1446 several witches were burned in Heidelberg by the inquisitor, and in 1447 another, who passed as their teacher; but there was as yet no uniform practice in such cases, for in this same year, 1447, at Braunsberg, a woman convicted of sorcery was only banished to a distance of two (German) miles, and three securities were required for her in the sum of ten marks.[*]

---

[*] Duverger, La Vauderie dans les États de Philippe le Bon, p. 22.—Anon.

It was probably about this time that the inquisitors of Toulouse were busy with burning the numerous witches of Dauphiné and Gascony, as related by Alonso de Spina, who admired on the walls of the Toulousan Inquisition pictures painted from their confessions, representing the Sabbat, with the votaries adoring, with lighted candles, Satan in the form of a goat. The allusions of Bernardo di Como show that at the same period persecution was busy in Como. In 1456 we hear of two burned at Cologne. They had caused a frost so intense in the month of May that all vegetation was blasted, without hope of recovery. The steward of the archbishop asked one of them to give him an example of her art, when she took a cup of water, and muttering spells over it for the space of a couple of Paternosters, it froze so solidly that the ice could not be broken with a dagger. In this case, at least, the hand of justice had not weakened her power, though why she allowed herself to be burned is not recorded. In 1459 Pius II. called the attention of the Abbot of Tréguier to somewhat similar practices in Britanny, and gave him papal authority for their suppression, showing how vain had been the zeal of Duke Artus III., of whom, at his death in 1457, it was eulogistically declared that he had burned more sorcerers in France, Britanny, and Poitou than any man of his time.*

These incidents will show the growth and spread of the belief throughout Europe, and it must be borne in mind that they are but the indications of much that never attracted public attention or came to be recorded in history. A chance allusion, in a pleading of 1455, shows what was working under the surface in probably every corner of Christendom. In the parish of Torcy (Normandy) there had been for forty years a belief that a family of laborers—Huguenin de la Meu and his dead father before him, and Jeanne his wife—were all sorcerers who killed or sickened many men and beasts. An appeal to the Inquisition would doubtless have ex-

---

Carthus. de Relig. Orig. c. 25-6 (Martene Ampl. Coll. VI. 57-9).—Jean Chartier, Hist. de Charles VII. ann. 1453.—Mémoires de Jacques du Clercq, Liv. III. ch. 11.—D'Argentré, I. II. 251.—Soldan, Gesch. der Hexenprocesse, p. 198.—Lilienthal, Die Hexenprocesse der beiden Städte Braunsberg, p. 70.

* Alonso de Spina, Fortalic. Fidei, fol. 284.—Bernardi Comens. de Strigiis c. 3.—Chron. Cornel. Zantfliet, ann. 1456 (Martene Ampl. Coll. V. 491).—Raynald. ann. 1459, No. 30.—Guill. Gruel, Chroniques d'Artus III. (Ed. Buchon, p. 405).

tracted from them confessions of the Sabbat and devil-worship, with lists of accomplices leading to a widespread epidemic, but the simple peasants found a speedier remedy in beating Huguenin and his wife, when the person or animal whom they had bewitched would recover. A certain André suspected them of causing the death of some of his cattle, and Jeanne said to his wife, Alayre, "Your husband has done ill in saying that I killed his cattle, and he will find it so before long." That same day Alayre fell sick and was not expected to survive the night. To cure her André went next morning to Jeanne, and threatened that if she did not restore Alayre he would beat her so that she would never be well again—and Alayre recovered the next day.*

This shows the material which existed everywhere for development into organized persecution when properly handled by the Inquisition, and the *Flagellum Hæreticorum Fascinariorum* of the Inquisitor, Nicholaus Jaquerius, in 1458, indicates that the Holy Office was beginning to appreciate the necessity of organizing its efforts for systematic work. Perhaps the untoward result of the affair at Arras may have retarded this somewhat by the over-zeal and unscrupulous greed of its manipulators, but if there was a reaction it was limited, both in extent and duration. All the accumulated beliefs in the occult powers of demonic agencies inherited from so many creeds and races still flourished in their integrity. In the existing wretchedness of the peasantry throughout the length and breadth of Europe, recklessness as to the present and hopelessness as to the future led thousands to wish that they could, by transferring their allegiance to Satan, find some momentary relief from the sordid miseries of life. The tales of the sensual delights of the Sabbat, where exquisite meats and drink were furnished in abundance, had an irresistible allurement for those who could scantily reckon on a morsel of black bread, or a turnip or a few beans, to keep starvation at bay. Sprenger, as already stated, tells us that the attraction of intercourse with incubi and succubi was a principal cause of luring souls to ruin. The devastating wars, with bands of écorcheurs and condottieri pillaging everywhere with savage cruelty, reduced whole populations to despair, and those who fancied themselves abandoned by God might well

---

* Du Cange, s. v. *Sortiarius.*

turn to Satan for help. According to Sprenger, a prolific source of witches was the seduction of young girls who when refused marriage had nothing more to hope for, and sought to avenge themselves on society by acquiring at least the power of evil.* Not only thus was there on the part of many a desire to enter the abhorred sect of Satan-worshippers, which the Church declared to be so numerous and powerful, but doubtless not a few performed the ceremonies to effect it, when perhaps some evil wish which chanced to be realized would convince them that Satan had really accepted their allegiance, and granted them the power which they sought. Certain minds might, in moments of high-wrought exaltation, even imagine that they had obtained admission to the foul mysteries whose reality was rapidly becoming an article of orthodox belief. Others again, in weakness and poverty, found that the reputation of possessing the power of evil was a protection and a support, and they encouraged rather than repressed the credulity of their neighbors. To these must be added the multitudes who derived a source of gain from curing the sorcery which the Church was confessedly unable to relieve, and there was ample material in the despised and lower stratum of society for the innumerable army of witches conjured up by the heated imaginations of the demonographers.

Unfortunately the Church, in its alarm at the development of this new heresy, stimulated it to the utmost in the endeavor to repress it. Every inquisitor whom it commissioned to suppress witchcraft was an active missionary who scattered the seeds of the belief ever more widely. We have seen what a brood of witches Pierre le Brousart hatched at Arras out of the single one burned at Langres, and how Chiabaudi succeeded in infecting the valleys of the Canavese. It mattered little in the end that le Brousart overreached himself and that Chiabaudi was outwrangled. The minds of the people became more and more familiarized with the idea that witches were everywhere around them, and that every misfortune and accident was the result of their malignity. Every man was thus assiduously taught, when he lost an ox or a child, or a harvest, or was suddenly prostrated with illness, to suspect his neighbors and look for evidence to confirm his suspicions, so that

---

* Mall. Malef. P. i. Q. i. c. 1.

wherever an inquisitor passed he was overwhelmed with accusations against all who could be imagined to be guilty, from children of tender years to superannuated crones. When Girolamo Visconti was sent to Como he speedily raised such a storm of witchcraft that in 1485 he burned no less than forty-one unfortunates in the little district of Wormserbad in the Grisons—an exploit repeatedly referred to by Sprenger with honest professional pride.*

A special impulse was given to this development when Innocent VIII., December 5, 1484, issued his Bull *Summis desiderantes,* in which he bewailed the deplorable fact that all the Teutonic lands were filled with men and women who exercised upon the faithful all the malignant power which we have seen ascribed to witchcraft, and of which he enumerates the details with awe-inspiring amplification. Henry Institoris and Jacob Sprenger had for some time been performing the office of inquisitors in those regions, but their commissions did not specially mention sorcery as included in their jurisdiction, wherefore their efforts were impeded by overwise clerks and laymen who used this as an excuse for protecting the guilty. Innocent therefore gives them full authority in the premises and orders the Bishop of Strassburg to coerce all who obstruct or interfere with them, calling in, if necessary, the aid of the secular arm. After this, to question the reality of witchcraft was to question the utterance of the Vicar of Christ, and to aid any one accused was to impede the Inquisition. Armed with these powers the two inquisitors, full of zeal, traversed the land, leaving behind them a track of blood and fire, and awakening in all hearts the cruel dread inspired by the absolute belief thus inculcated in all the horrors of witchcraft. In the little town of Ravenspurg alone they boast that they burned forty-eight in five years.†

It is true that they were not everywhere so successful. In the

---

* Mall. Malef. P. I. Q. xi.; P. II. Q. i. c. 4, 12; P. III. Q. 15.

† Mall. Malef. P. II. Q. i. c. 4.

Innocent's bull was not confined to Germany alone, but was operative everywhere. In an Italian inquisitorial manual of the period it is included in a collection of bulls "*contra hereticam pravitatem,*" which also contains a letter on the subject from the future Emperor Maximilian, dated Brussels, November 6, 1486.—Molinier, Études sur quelques MSS. des Bibliothèques d'Italie, Paris, 1887, p. 72.

Tyrol the Bishop of Brixen published Innocent's bull July 23, 1485, and on September 21 he issued to the inquisitor Henry Institoris a commission granting him full episcopal jurisdiction, but recommending him to associate with him a secular official of the suzerain, Sigismund of Austria. The latter, however, ordered the bishop to appoint a commissioner, and he named Sigismund Samer, pastor of Axams near Innsbruck. The pair commenced operations October 14, but their career, though vigorous, was short and inglorious. It chanced that some of the archduke's courtiers desired to separate him from his wife, Catharine of Saxony, and spread reports that she had endeavored to poison him; and they followed this up by placing in an oven a worthless woman who personated an imprisoned demon and denounced a number of people. Institoris at once seized the accused and applied torture without stint. Then the bishop interposed, and by the middle of November ordered him to leave the diocese and betake himself to his convent, the sooner the better. Institoris, however, was loath to abandon his duty, and drew upon himself a sharper reproof on Ash Wednesday, 1486; he was told that he had nought to do there, that the bishop would attend to all that was necessary through the exercise of the ordinary jurisdiction, and he was warned that if he persisted in remaining he was in danger of assassination from the husbands or kinsmen of the women whom he was persecuting. He finally withdrew to Germany, richly rewarded for his labor by Sigismund, and from his account of the matter it is easy to see that all the sick and withered of Innsbruck had flocked to him with complaints of their neighbors so detailed that he was justified in regarding the place as thoroughly infected. The next year the Tyrolese Landtag complained to the archduke that recently many persons, on baseless denunciations, had been imprisoned, tortured, and disgracefully treated, and we can readily understand the complaint of the *Malleus Maleficarum* that Innsbruck abounded in witches of the most dangerous character, who could bewitch their judges and could not be forced to confess. Still, the seeds of superstition were scattered to fructify in due time. Although in the Tyrolese criminal ordinance issued by Maximilian I., in 1499, there is no allusion to sorcery and witchcraft, yet in 1506 we find the craze fully developed. Some records which have been preserved show trials before secular judges with juries of twelve men,

in which the unfortunate women accused, after due torture, confess all the customary horrors.*

One result of this campaign of Institoris in the Tyrol was that
it left Sigismund of Austria in a condition of perplexity as to the
reality of witchcraft. His judges had apparently been inexperienced in such matters, the confessions of the accused had varied
greatly, and the inquisition had been cut short before they could
be forced to consentaneous avowals. To satisfy his mind, in 1487,
he consulted on the subject two learned doctors of the law, Ulric
Molitoris and Conrad Stürtzel, and the result was published at
Constance in 1489 by Ulric, in the form of a discussion between
the three. Sigismund is represented as urging the natural argument that the results obtained by witchcraft were so wofully inadequate to the powers ascribed to it as to cast doubt upon the
reality of those powers—if they were real, a conqueror would only
have, like William the Manzer at Ely, to put a witch at the head
of his army to overcome all opposition. Against this view the
customary texts and citations were alleged, and the conclusions
reached represent very fairly the moderate opinions of the conserv-
atives, who had not as yet yielded fully to the witchcraft craze,
but who shrank from a rationalistic denial of that which had
been handed down by the wisdom of ages. These are summed
up in eight propositions: 1. Satan cannot himself, or by means
of human instruments, disturb the elements, or injure men and
animals, or render them impotent, but God sometimes permits
him to do so to a certain determinate extent. 2. He cannot
exceed this designated limit. 3. By permission of God he can
sometimes cause illusions by which men appear to be transformed.
4. The night-riding and assemblages of the Sabbat are illusions.
5. Incubi and succubi are incapable of procreation. 6. God alone
knows the future and the thoughts of men; the devil can only
conjecture and use his knowledge of the stars. 7. Nevertheless
witches, by worshipping and sacrificing to Satan, are real heretics
and apostates. 8. Finally, they should therefore be put to death.
In this cautious endeavor to harmonize the old school and the new,
the witch thus gained nothing; everything was conceded that had

---

* Rapp, Die Hexenprocesse und ihre Gegner aus Tirol, pp. 5–8, 12–13, 143
sqq.—Mall. Maleficar. P. II. Q. 1, c. 12; P. III. Q. 15.

a practical bearing on the tribunals, and it was a mere matter of speculation whether the Sabbat was a dream or a reality, and whether the evil she wrought was the result of a special or a general concession of power by God to Satan. Thus the work of Molitoris is important as showing how feeble were the barriers which intelligent and fair-minded men could erect against the prevailing tendencies so sedulously fostered by popes and inquisitors.*

The fine-drawn distinctions of such men were quickly brushed aside by the aggressive self-confidence of the inquisitors. Even more potent than the personal activity of Sprenger was the legacy which he left behind him in the work which he proudly entitled the *Malleus Maleficarum*, or Hammer of Witches, the most portentous monument of superstition which the world has produced. All his vast experience and wide erudition are brought to the task of proving the reality of witchcraft and the extent of its evils, and, further, of instructing the inquisitor how to elude the wiles of Satan and to punish his devotees. He was no vulgar witch-finder, but a man trained in all the learning of the schools. He apparently was not inhumane. In many places he manifests a laudable desire to give the accused the benefit of whatever pleas they might rightfully put forward, but he is so fully convinced of the gigantic character of the evils to be combated, he so thoroughly believes that his tribunal is engaged in a contest with Satan for human souls, that he eagerly justifies every artifice and every cruelty that could be suggested to outwit the adversary, on whom fair play would be thrown away. Like Conrad of Marburg and Capistrano, he was a man of the most dangerous type, an honest fanatic. His work is, moreover, an inexhaustible storehouse of marvels to which successive generations resorted whenever evi-

---

* Molitoris Dial. de Pythonicis Mulieribus c. 1, 10.

The absurd contrast between the illimitable powers ascribed to the witch and her personal wretchedness was explained under torture by the victims as the result of the faithlessness of Satan, who desired to keep them in poverty. When steeped in misery he would appear to them and allure them into his service by the most attractive promises, but when he had attained his end those promises were never kept. Gold given to them would always disappear before it could be used. As one of the Tyrolese witches in 1506 declared, "The devil is a Schalk (knave)." (Rapp, Die Hexenprocesse und ihre Gegner aus Tirol, p. 147.)

dence was needed to prove any special manifestation of the power
or malignity of the witch.   Told as the results of his own experience or that of his colleagues, with the utmost good faith, they
carried conviction with them.   In fact, but for the delusive character of human testimony in such matters, the evidence would
seem to be overwhelming.   Statements of disinterested eye-witnesses, complaints of sufferers, confessions of the guilty, even after
condemnation, and at the stake, when there was no hope save of
pardon of their sins by God, are innumerable, and so detailed and
connected together that the most fertile imagination would seem
inadequate to their invention.   Besides, the work is so logical in
form, according to the fashion of the time, and so firmly based on
scholastic theology and canon law, that we cannot wonder at the
position accorded to it for more than a century of a leading authority on a subject of the highest practical importance.   Quoted
implicitly by all succeeding writers, it did more than all other
agencies, save the papal bulls, to stimulate and perfect the persecution, and consequently the extension of witchcraft.*

Thus the Inquisition in its decrepitude had a temporary re-
sumption of activity, before the Reformation came to renew its
vigor in a different shape.   Yet it was not everywhere allowed to
work its will upon this new class of heretics.   In France edicts of
1490 and 1493 treat them as subject exclusively to the secular
courts, unless the offenders happen to be justiciable by the ecclesiastical tribunals, and no allusion whatever is made to the Inquisition.   At the same time the growing sharpness of persecution is
seen in provisions which subject those who consult necromancers
and sorcerers to the same penalties as the practitioners themselves,
and threaten judges who are negligent in arresting them with loss

---

* Diefenbach, the latest writer on witchcraft (Die Hexenwahn, Mainz, 1886),
sees clearly enough that the witch-madness was the result of the means adopted
for the suppression of witchcraft, but in his eagerness to relieve the Church from
the responsibility he attributes its origin to the *Carolina*, or criminal code of
Charles V., issued in 1531, and expressly asserts that ecclesiastical law had nothing to do with it (p. 176).   Other recent writers ascribe the horrors of the witch-
process to the bull of Innocent VIII., and the *Malleus Maleficarum* (Ib. pp.
222–6).   We have been able to trace, however, the definite development of the
madness and the means adopted for its cure from the beliefs and the practice of
preceding ages.   It was, as we have seen, a process of purely natural evolution
from the principles which the Church had succeeded in establishing.

of office, perpetual disability, and heavy arbitrary fines. It was doubtless owing to this exclusion of spiritual jurisdiction over sorcery that the spread of witchcraft in France was slower than in Germany and Italy.*

Cornelius Agrippa, whose learned treatises on the occult sciences trench so nearly on forbidden ground, when he held the position of Town Orator and Advocate of Metz, had the hardihood, in 1519, to save from the clutches of the inquisitor, Nicholas Savin, an unfortunate woman accused of witchcraft. The only evidence against her was that her mother had been burned as a witch. Savin quoted the "*Malleus Maleficarum*" to show that if she were not the offspring of an incubus she must undoubtedly have been devoted to Satan at her birth. In conjunction with the episcopal official, John Leonard, he had her cruelly tortured, and she was then exposed to starvation in her prison. When Agrippa offered to defend her he was turned out of court and threatened with prosecution as a fautor of heresy, and her husband was refused access to the place of trial, lest he should interject an appeal. Leonard chanced to fall mortally sick, and, touched with remorse on his death-bed, he executed an instrument declaring his conviction of her innocence and asked the chapter to set her at liberty; but Savin demanded that she should be further tortured and then burned. Agrippa, however, labored so effectually with Leonard's successor and with the chapter that the woman was discharged; but his disinterested zeal cost him his office, and he was obliged to leave Metz. Relieved of his presence, the inquisitor speedily found another witch, whom he burned after forcing her by torture to confess all the horrors of the Sabbat and customary evil deeds wrought through the power of Satan. Encouraged by this, he organized a search for others, doubtless based on the confessions of the victim, and imprisoned a number, while others fled, and there would have been a pitiless massacre had not Roger Brennon, parish priest of St. Cross, openly opposed him and vanquished him in disputation, whereupon the jail doors were thrown open and the fugitives returned.†

---

* Fontanon, Edicts et Ordonnances, IV. 237.—Isambert, XI. 190, 253.

† Cornel. Agrippa de Occult. Philos. Lib. I. c. 40; Lib. III. c. 33; Epistt. II. 38, 39, 40, 59; De Vanitate Scientiarum c. xcvi.

The most decided rebuff, however, which the Inquisition experienced in its new sphere of activity was administered by Venice. I have had occasion more than once to allude to the controversy between the Signory and the Holy See over the witches of Brescia, when the Republic definitely refused to execute the sentences of the inquisitors. To understand the full significance of its action, it is to be observed that for two generations the Church had been energetically cultivating witchcraft throughout Lombardy by unceasingly urging its persecution and breaking down all resistance on the part of the intelligent laity, until it had succeeded in rendering upper Italy a perfect hot-bed of the heresy. In 1457 Calixtus III. ordered his nuncio, Bernardo di Bosco, to use active measures in repressing its growth in Brescia, Bergamo, and the vicinage. Thirty years later Frà Girolamo Visconti found an abundant field for his labor in Como, the result of which he communicated to the world in his *Lamiarum Tractatus*, and Sprenger assures us that a whole book would be required to record the cases, in Brescia alone, of women who had become witches through despair in consequence of seduction, although the episcopal court had shown the most praiseworthy vigor in suppressing them. In 1494 we find Alexander VI. stimulating the Lombard inquisitor, Frà Angelo da Verona, to greater activity, assuring him that witches were numerous in Lombardy and inflicted great damage on men, harvests, and cattle. When at Cremona, in the early years of the sixteenth century, the inquisitor, Giorgio di Casale, endeavored to exterminate the numberless witches flourishing there, and was interfered with by certain clerks and laymen, who asserted that he was exceeding his jurisdiction, Julius II., following the example of Innocent VIII. in the case of Sprenger, promptly came to the rescue by defining his powers, and offering to all who would aid him in the good work indulgences such as were given to crusaders—provisions which, in 1523, were extended to the Inquisitor of Como by Adrian VI. The result of all this careful stimulation is seen in the description of the Lombard witches by Gianfrancesco Pico, and in the alarming report by Silvester Prierias that they were extending down the Apennines and boasting that they would outnumber the faithful. The spread of popular belief is illustrated in the remark of Politian, that when he was a child he had great dread of the witches whom his grandmother used to tell him lie in wait in the woods to swallow little boys.*

Venice had always been careful to preserve the secular jurisdiction over sorcery. A resolution of the great council in 1410 allows the Inquisition to act in such cases when they involve heresy or the abuse of sacraments, but if injury had resulted to individuals the spiritual offence alone was cognizable by the Inquisition, while the resultant crimes were justiciable by the lay court; and when, in 1422, some Franciscans were charged with sacrificing to demons, the Council of Ten committed the affair to a councillor, a capo, an inquisitor, and an advocate. Brescia was a spot peculiarly infected with witchcraft. As early as 1455 the inquisitor, Frà Antonio, called upon the Senate for aid to exterminate it, which was presumably afforded, but when a fresh persecution arose in 1486 the podestà refused to execute the inquisitorial sentences, and the Signoria supported him, calling forth, as we have seen, the vigorous protest of Innocent VIII. Under the stimulus of persecution the evil increased with terrible rapidity. In 1510 we hear of seventy women and seventy men burned at Brescia; in 1514 of three hundred at Como. In such an epidemic every victim was a new source of infection, and the land was threatened with depopulation. In the madness of the hour it was currently reported that on the plain of Tonale, near Brescia, the customary gathering at the Sabbat exceeded twenty-five thousand souls; and in 1518 the Senate was officially informed that the inquisitor had burned seventy witches of the Valcamonica, that he had as many in his prisons, and that those suspected or accused amounted to about five thousand, or one fourth of the inhabitants of the valleys. It was time to interfere, and the Signoria interposed effectually, leading to violent remonstrances from Rome. Leo X. issued, February 15, 1521, his fiery bull, *Honestis*, ordering the inquisitors to use freely the excommunication and the interdict, if their sentences on the witches were not executed without examination or revision, showing how transparent were the subterfuges adopted to throw

---

* Raynald. ann. 1457, No. 90.—P. Vayra, Le Streghe nel Canavese, op. cit. p. 250.—Mall. Maleficar. P. II. Q. i. c. 1, 12.—Ripoll IV. 190.—Pegnæ Append. ad Eymeric. p. 105.—G. F. Pico, La Strega, p. 17.—Prieriat. de Strigimag. Lib. II. c. 1, 5.—Ang. Politian. Lamia. Colon. 1518.

upon the secular courts the responsibility of putting to death those who were not relapsed. On March 21 the imperturbable Council of Ten quietly responded by laying down regulations for all trials, including the cases in question, of which the sentences were treated as invalid, and all bail heretofore taken was to be discharged. The examinations were to be made without the use of torture by one or two bishops, an inquisitor, and two doctors of Brescia, all selected for probity and intelligence. The result was to be read in the court of the podestà, with the participation of the two *rettori*, or governors, and four more doctors. The accused were to be asked if they ratified their statements, and were to be liable to torture if they modified them. When all this was done with due circumspection, judgment was to be rendered in accordance with the counsel of all the above-named experts, and under no other circumstances was a sentence to be executed. In this way the Signoria hoped that the errors said to have been committed would be avoided for the future. Moreover, the papal legate was to be admonished to see that the expenses of the Inquisition were moderate and free from extortion, and was to find expedients to prevent greed for money from causing the condemnation of the innocent, as was said to have often been the case. He should also depute proper persons to investigate the extortions and other evil acts of the inquisitors, which had excited general complaint, and he should summarily punish the perpetrators to serve as an example. He was further requested to consider that these poor people of Valcamonica were simple folk of the densest ignorance, much more in need of good preachers than of persecutors, especially as they were so numerous.*

In an age of superstition this utterance of the Council of Ten stands forth as a monument of considerate wisdom and calm common-sense. Had its enlightened spirit been allowed to guide the counsels of popes and princes, Europe would have been spared the most disgraceful page in the annals of civilization. The lesson of cruel fear so sedulously inculcated on the nations was thoroughly learned. Hideous as are the details of the persecution of witchcraft which we have been considering up to the fifteenth century,

---

* G. de Castro, Il Mondo Secreto, IX. 128, 133, 135-6.—Mag. Bull. Rom. I. 440, 617.—Archiv. di Venezia, Misti, Concil. X. Vol. 44, p. 7.

they were but the prelude to the blind and senseless orgies of destruction which disgraced the next century and a half. Christendom seemed to have grown delirious, and Satan might well smile at the tribute to his power seen in the endless smoke of the holocausts which bore witness to his triumph over the Almighty. Protestant and Catholic rivalled each other in the madness of the hour. Witches were burned no longer in ones and twos, but in scores and hundreds. A bishop of Geneva is said to have burned five hundred within three months, a bishop of Bamburg six hundred, a bishop of Würzburg nine hundred. Eight hundred were condemned, apparently in one body, by the Senate of Savoy. So completely had the intervention of Satan, through the instrumentality of his worshippers, become a part of the unconscious process of thought, that any unusual operation of nature was attributed to them as a matter of course. The spring of 1586 was tardy in the Rhinelands and the cold was prolonged until June : this could only be the result of witchcraft, and the Archbishop of Trèves burned at Pfalz a hundred and eighteen women and two men, from whom confessions had been extorted that their incantations had prolonged the winter. It was well that he acted thus promptly, for on their way to the place of execution they stated that had they been allowed three days more they would have brought cold so intense that no green thing could have survived, and that all fields and vineyards would have been cursed with barrenness. The Inquisition evidently had worthy pupils, but it did not relax its own efforts. Paramo boasts that in a century and a half from the commencement of the sect, in 1404, the Holy Office had burned at least thirty thousand witches who, if they had been left unpunished, would easily have brought the whole world to destruction.*
Could any Manichæan offer more practical evidence that Satan was lord of the visible universe ?

---

* Michelet, La Sorcière, Liv. II. ch. iii.—P. Vayra, op. cit. p. 255.—Annal. Novesiens. ann. 1586 (Martene Ampl. Coll. IV. 717).—Paramo de Orig. Off. S. Inquis. p. 296.

CHAPTER VIII.

INTELLECT AND FAITH.

THE only heresies which really troubled the Church were those which obtained currency among the people unassisted by the ingenious quodlibets of dialecticians. Possibly there may be an exception to this in the theories of the Brethren of the Free Spirit, which apparently owed their origin to the speculations of Amaury of Bène and David of Dinant; but, as a whole, the Cathari and the Waldenses, the Spirituals and the Fraticelli, even the Hussites, had little or nothing in common with the fine-spun cobwebs of the schoolmen. For a heresy to take root and bear fruit, it must be able to inspire the zeal of martyrdom; and for this it must spring from the heart, and not from the brain. We have seen how, during centuries, multitudes were ready to face death in its most awful form rather than abandon beliefs in which were entwined their sentiments and feelings and their hopes of the hereafter; but history records few cases, from Abelard to Master Eckart and Galileo, in which intellectual conceptions, however firmly entertained, were strong enough to lead to the sacrifice. It is sentiment rather than reason which renders heretics dangerous; and all the pride of intellect was insufficient to nerve the scholar to maintain his thesis with the unfaltering resolution which enabled the peasant to approach the stake singing hymns and joyfully welcoming the flames which were to bear him to salvation.

The schools, consequently, have little to show us in the shape of contests between free thought and authority pushed to the point of invoking the methods of the Inquisition. Yet the latter, by the system which it rendered practicable of enforcing uniformity of belief, exercised too potent an influence on the mental development of Europe for us to pass over this phase of its activity without some brief review.

There were two tendencies at work to provoke collisions between the schoolmen and the inquisitors. The ardor of persecution, which rendered the purity of the faith the highest aim of the Christian and the most imperative care of the ruler, secular and spiritual, created an exaggerated standard of orthodoxy, which regarded the minutest point of theology as equally important with the fundamental doctrines of religion. We have already seen instances of this in the questions as to the poverty of Christ, as to whether he was dead when lanced on the cross, and as to whether the blood which he shed in the Passion remained on earth or ascended to heaven; and Stephen Palecz, at the Council of Constance, proved dialectically that a doctrine in which one point in a thousand was erroneous was thereby rendered heretical throughout. Moreover, erroneous belief was not necessary, for the Christian must be firm in the faith, and doubt itself was heresy.*

The other tendency was the insane thirst which inflamed the minds of the schoolmen for determining and defining, with absolute precision, every detail of the universe and of the invisible world. So far as this gratified itself within the lines of orthodoxy laid down by an infallible Church it resulted in building up the most complex and stupendous body of theology that human wit has ever elaborated. The *Sentences* of Peter Lombard grew into the *Summa* of Thomas Aquinas, an elaborate structure to be grasped and retained only by minds of peculiar powers after severe and special training. When this was once defined and accepted as orthodox, theology and philosophy became the most dangerous of sciences, while the perverse ingenuity of the schoolmen, revelling in the subtleties of dialectics, was perpetually rearguing doubtful points, raising new questions, and introducing new refinements in matters already too subtle for the comprehension of the ordinary intellect. The inquirer who disturbs the dust now happily covering the records of these forgotten wrangles can only feel regret that such wonderful intellectual acuteness and energy should have been so wofully wasted when, if rightly applied, it might have advanced by so many centuries the progress of humanity.

The story of Roger Bacon, the *Doctor Mirabilis*, is fairly illustrative of the tendencies of the time. That gigantic intellect

---

* Von der Hardt I. XVI. 829. — Bernardi Comens. Lucerna Inquisit. s. v. *Dubius.*

bruised itself perpetually against the narrow bars erected around it by an age presumptuous in its learned ignorance. Once a transient gleam of light broke in upon the darkness of its environment, when Gui Foucoix was elevated to the papacy, and, as Clement IV., commanded the Englishman to communicate to him the discoveries of which he had vaguely heard. It is touching to see the eagerness with which the unappreciated scholar labored to make the most of this unexpected opportunity; how he impoverished his friends to raise the money requisite to pay the scribes who should set forth in a fair copy the tumultuous train of thought in which he sought to embody the whole store of human knowledge, and how, within the compass of little more than a single year, he thus accomplished the enormous task of writing the *Opus Majus*, the *Opus Minus*, and the *Opus Tertium*. Unfortunately, Clement was more concerned at the moment with the fortunes of Charles of Anjou than with the passing fancy which had led him to call upon the scholar; in little more than two years he was dead, and it is doubtful whether he even repaid the sums expended in gratifying his wishes.*

It was inevitable that Bacon should succumb in the unequal struggle at once with the ignorance and the learning of his age. His labors and his utterances were a protest against the whole existing system of thought and teaching. The schoolmen evolved the universe from their internal consciousness, and then wrangled incessantly over subtleties suggested by the barbarous jargon of their dialectics. It was the same with theology, which had usurped the place of religion. Peter Lombard was greater than all the prophets and evangelists taken together. As Bacon tells us, the study of Scripture was neglected for that of the Sentences, in which lay the whole glory of the theologian. He who taught the Sentences could select his own hour for teaching, and had accommodations provided for him. He who taught the Scriptures had to beg for a time in which to be heard, and had no assistance. The former could dispute, and was held to be a master; the latter was condemned to silence in the debates of the schools. It is impossible, he adds, that the Word of God can be understood, on account of the abuse of the Sentences; and whoso seeks in Script-

---

* R. Bacon Opp., M. R. Series, J. S. Brewer's Preface, p. xlv.

ure to elucidate questions is stigmatized as whimsical, and is not listened to. Worse than all, the text of the Vulgate is horribly corrupt, and where not corrupt it is doubtful, owing to the ignorance of would-be correctors and their presumption, for every one deemed himself able to correct the text, though he would not venture to alter a word in a poet. First of moderns, Bacon discerned the importance of etymology and of comparative philology, and he exposed unsparingly the wretched blunders customary among the so-called learned, who only succeeded in leading their pupils into error. Bacon's methods were strictly scientific. He wanted facts, actual facts, as a basis for all reasoning, whether on dogma or physical and mental experiences. To him all study of nature or of man was empirical; to know first, and then to reason. Mathematics was first in the order of sciences; then metaphysics; and to him metaphysics was not a barren effort to frame a system on postulates assumed at caprice and built up on dialectical sophisms, but a solid series of deductions from ascertained observations, for, according to Avicenna, "the conclusions of other sciences are the principles of metaphysics." *

The vast labors of the earnest life of a great genius were lost to a world too conceited of its petty vanities to recognize how far he was in advance of it. It was enamored of words; he dealt in things: the actual was rejected for the unsubstantial, and an intellectual revolution of priceless value to mankind was stifled in its inception. It was as though Caliban should chain Prospero and cast him into the ocean. How completely Bacon was unappreciated by an age unable to understand him and his antagonism towards its methods is evidenced by the scarcity of manuscripts of his works, the fragmentary condition of some of them, and the utter disappearance of others. "It is easier," says Leland, "to collect the leaves of the Sibyl than the titles of the works of Roger Bacon." The same evidence is furnished by the absence of detail as to his life no less than by the vulgar stories of his proficiency in magic arts. Even the tragic incident of his imprisonment by his Franciscan superiors and the prohibition to pursue his studies is so obscure that it is told in contradictory fashion, and its truth has been not

---

* Op. Minus, M. R. Series I. 326–30. — Compend. Studii Philosoph. VII.— Brewer, Preface, p. li.

unreasonably denied. According to one account he was accused of unorthodox speculations, in 1278, to Geronimo d'Ascoli, General of the Order; his opinions were condemned, the brethren were ordered scrupulously to avoid them, and he himself was cast into prison, doubtless because he did not submit as serenely as Olivi to Geronimo's sentence. He must have had followers and sympathizers, for Geronimo is said to have prevented their complaints by promptly applying to Nicholas III. for a confirmation of the judgment. How long his imprisonment lasted is not known, though there is a tradition that he perished in jail, either through sickness or the ill-treatment which we have seen was freely visited by the Franciscans on their erring brethren. Another statement attributes his incarceration to the ascetic Raymond Gaufridi, who was General of the Order from 1289 to 1295. In either case it would not be difficult to explain the cause of his disgrace. In the fierce passions of the schools, one who antagonized so completely the prevailing currents of thought, and who exposed so mercilessly the ignorance of the learned, could not fail to excite bitter enmities. The daring scholar who preferred Scripture to the Sentences, and pronounced the text of the Vulgate to be corrupt, must have given ample opportunity for accusations of heresy in a time when dogma had become so intricate, and mortal heresy might lurk in the minutest aberration. The politic Geronimo might readily listen to enemies so numerous and powerful as those whom Bacon must have provoked. The ascetic Raymond, whose aim was to bring back the Order to its primitive rudeness and simplicity, would regard Bacon's labors with the same aversion as that manifested by the early Spirituals to Crescenzio Grizzi's learning. It was a standing complaint with his section of the Order that Paris had destroyed Assisi. As Jacopone da Todi sang:

> "Tal' è, qual' è, tal' è,
> Non religione c' è.
> Mal vedemmo Parigi
> Che n' a destrutto Assisi,"

and the Spiritual General might well like to strike a blow at the greatest scholar of the Order.*

---

* Brewer, Pref. p. xcviii.—Wadding. ann. 1278, No. 26; ann. 1284, No. 12.—

While Bacon suffered because he antagonized the thought of his time, there was much of scholastic bitterness which escaped animadversion because it was the development of the tendencies of the age, and the schoolmen were allowed to indulge in endless wrangling for the most part without censure. The great quarrel between the Nominalists and the Realists occupies too large a space in the intellectual history of Europe to be wholly passed over, although its relation to our immediate subject is not intimate enough to justify detailed consideration.

In the developed theory of the Realists, genera and species— the distinctive attributes of individual beings, or the conceptions of those attributes—are real entities, if not the only realities. Individuals are ephemeral existences which pass away; the only things which survive are those which are universal and common to all. In man this is humanity, but humanity again is but a portion of a larger existence, the animate, and the animate is but a transitory form of an Infinite Being, which is All and nothing in particular. This is the sole Immutable. These conceptions took their origin in the Periphyseos of John Scot Erigena in the ninth century, whose reaction against the prevailing anthropomorphism led him to sublimated views of the Divine Being, which trenched closely on Pantheism. The heresy latent in his work lay undiscovered until developed by the Amaurians, when the book, after nearly four centuries, was condemned by Honorius III., in 1225.*

Nominalism, on the other hand, regarded the individual as the primal substance; universals are only abstractions or mental conceptions of qualities common to individuals, with no more of reality than the sounds which express them. Even as Realism in the hands of daring thinkers led to Pantheism, so, step by step, Nominalism could be brought to recognize the originality of the individual and finally to Atomism.†

The two antagonistic schools were first clearly defined in the beginning of the twelfth century, with Roscelin, the teacher of

---

Wood's Life of Bacon (Brewer, pp. xciv.-xcv.).—C. Müller, Die Anfänge des Minoritenordens, pp. 104-5.

* Tocco, L'Heresia nel Medio Evo, p. 2.—J. Scoti Erigenæ de Divis. Naturæ I. 14; IV. 5.—Alberic. Trium Font. ann. 1225.

† Tocco, p. 4.

Abelard, as the leader of the Nominalists, and William of Champeaux at the head of the Realists. Discussion continued in the schools with constantly increasing bitterness, though neither side dared to push their own views to their ultimate conclusions. Realism in a modified form achieved a triumph with the immense authority of Albertus Magnus and Thomas Aquinas. Duns Scotus was a Realist, though he differed with Aquinas on the problem of individuation, and the Realists became divided into the opposing factions of Thomists and Scotists. While they were thus weakened with dissension, William of Ockham revived Nominalism, and it became bolder than ever. The perennial hostility between the Dominicans and Franciscans tended to range the two Orders under the opposing banners, while Ockham's defence of Louis of Bavaria in his quarrel with the papacy served to impress upon the new school of Nominalists his views upon the relations between Church and State.*

The schools continued to resound with the clangor of disputation, occasionally growing so hot that blows supplied the deficiency of words, and even murder is said to have not been wanting. Under Peter d'Ailly and John Gerson the University of Paris was Nominalist. With the English domination the Realists triumphed and expelled their adversaries, who were unable to return until the restoration of the French monarchy. In 1465 there arose in the University of Louvain a strife which lasted for ten years over some propositions of Pierre de la Rive on fate and divine foreknowledge, in which the rival sects took sides. The University of Paris was drawn in; the Nominalists triumphed in condemning de la Rive, and the Realists took their revenge by procuring from Louis XI. an edict prohibiting the teaching of Nominalist doctrines in the University and in all the schools of the kingdom; all Nominalist books were boxed up and sealed until 1481, when Louis was persuaded to recall his edict, and the university rejoiced to regain her liberty. One tragic incident in the long quarrel has been already alluded to in the trial of John of Wesel which led to his death in prison, and it illustrates how readily scholastic ardor assumed that in gratifying its vindictiveness it was vindicating the faith. The contemporary reporter of the trial assumes that the persecution

---

* Johann. Saresberiens. Metalog. II. 17.—Tocco, 26, 39, 40, 57.

was caused by the antagonism of the Dominican Realists to the Nominalism of the victim, and he deplores the rage which led the Thomists to regard every one who denied the existence of universals as though guilty of the sin against the Holy Ghost, and as a traitor to God, to the Christian religion, to justice, and to the State.*

The annals of the schools are full of cases which show how the recklessness of disputatious logic led to subtleties most perilous in minute details of theology, and also how sensitive were the conservators of the faith as to anything that might be construed by perverse ingenuity as savoring of heresy. Duns Scotus did not escape, nor Thomas Bradwardine; William of Ockham and Buridan were enveloped in a common condemnation by the University of Paris, of which the latter had been rector. The boundaries between philosophy and the theology which sought to define everything in the visible and invisible world were impossible of definition, and it was a standing grievance that the philosophers were perpetually intruding on the domains of the theologians. When their daring speculations were unorthodox they sought to shelter themselves behind the assertion that according to the methods of philosophy the Catholic religion was erroneous and false, but that it was true as a matter of faith, and that they believed it accordingly. This only made matters worse, for, as the authorities pointed out, it assumed that there were two opposite truths, contradicting each other. It was not merely that orthodox sensitiveness was called upon to condemn, as was done in 1447 by the University of Louvain, such vain sophisms as the assertion that it is possible to conceive of a line a foot long which shall yet have neither beginning nor end, and that a whole may be in England while all its parts are in Rome; or those of Jean Fabre, condemned by the University of Paris in 1463, that any part of a man is a man, that one man is infinite men, that no man is ever corrupted, though sometimes a man is corrupted—propositions in which lurked the possibilities of heretical development—or the apparently yet more innocent grammatical obtuseness which recognized no difference between the phrases "the pot boils" and "pot, thou boilest"—an obtuseness which Erasmus tells us was regarded as an infallible

---

* Bruckeri Instit. Hist. Philos. Ed. 1756, p. 530.—D'Argentré I. II. 258–84, 298, 302–4.—Baluz. et Mansi, II. 293–6.—Isambert, X. 664–72.

sign of infidelity. Philosophers were not satisfied unless they could prove by logic the profoundest and holiest mysteries of theology, and, however zealous they were in the faith, the intrusion of reason into the theological preserves was not only resented as an interference, but was rightfully regarded with alarm at its possible consequences. When the Arab philosophers were disputing as to the nature and operation of the Divine Knowledge, the calm wisdom of Maimonides interposed, saying, "To endeavor to understand the Divine Knowledge is as though we endeavored to be God himself, so that our perception should be as his. . . . It is absolutely impossible for us to attain this kind of perception. If we could explain it to ourselves we should possess the intelligence which gives this kind of perception." Ambitious schoolmen, however, as well as orthodox theological doctors, refused to admit that the finite cannot grasp the infinite, and their pride of reason awakened, not unnaturally, the jealousy of those who considered it their exclusive privilege to guard the Holy of Holies and to explain the will of God to men. This feeling finds expression as early as 1201 in the story told of the learned doctor, Simon de Tournay, who proved by ingenious arguments the mystery of the Trinity, and then, elated by the applause of his hearers, boasted that if he were disposed to be malignant, he could disprove it with yet stronger ones, whereupon he was immediately stricken with paralysis and idiocy. The self-restraint of such men was a slender reliance, and yet slenderer was the chance that the interposition of Heaven would always furnish so salutary a warning.*

The audacity of these rash intruders upon the sacred precincts increased immeasurably with the introduction of the works of Averrhoes in the second quarter of the thirteenth century, constituting a real danger of the perversion of Christian thought. In the hands of the Arab commentators the theism of Aristotle became a transcendental materialism, carried to its furthest expression by the latest of them, Ibn Roschd or Averrhoes, who died in 1198. In his system matter has existed from the beginning, and

---

* D'Argentré I. ɪ. 275, 285–90, 323–30, 337–40; I. ɪɪ. 249, 255.—R. Lullii Lamentatio Philosophiæ (Opp. Ed. 1651, p. 112).—Erasmi Encom. Moriæ (Ed. Lipsiens. 1828, p. 365).—Maimonides, Guide des Égarés P. ɪɪɪ. ch. xxi. (Trad. Munk, III. 155).—Matt. Paris ann. 1201 (Ed. 1644, p. 144).

the theory of creation is impossible. The universe consists of a hierarchy of principles, eternal, primordial, and autonomous, vaguely connected with a superior unity. One of these is the Active Intellect, manifesting itself incessantly and constituting the permanent consciousness of humanity. This is the only form of immortality. As the soul of man is a fragment of a collective whole, temporarily detached to animate the body, at death it is reabsorbed into the Active Intellect of the universe. Consequently there are no future rewards or punishments, no feelings, memory, sensibility, love, or hatred. The perishable body has the power of reproducing itself and thus enjoys a material immortality in its descendants, but it is only collective humanity that is immortal.* To those whose conceptions of paradise and the resurrection were as material as the Swarga of the Brahman or the Kama Loka heavens of the Buddhist, such collective and insensible immortality, like the Moksha and Nirvana, was virtually equivalent to annihilation, and the Averrhoists were universally stigmatized as materialists.

Such theories as these necessarily induced the loftiest indifferentism as to religious formulas, although a wholesome dread of the rising Moslem fanaticism, from which Averrhoes had not escaped scathless, rendered him cautious as to assailing the established faith. "The special religion of philosophers," he says, "is to study what exists, for the most sublime worship of God is the contemplation of his works, which leads us to a knowledge of him in all his reality. In the eye of God this is the noblest of actions, while the vilest is to accuse of error and presumption him who pays to divinity this worship, nobler than all other worship; who adores God by this religion, the best of all religions." At the same time the received religions are an excellent instrument of morality. He who inspires among a people doubts as to the national religion is a heretic, to be punished as such by the established penalties. The wise man will utter no word against the national religion, and will especially avoid speaking of God in a manner equivocal to the vulgar. When several religions confront each other, one should select the noblest. Thus all religions are of human origin, and the choice between them is a matter of opinion or policy—but policy, if nothing else, must have prevented

---

* Renan, Averrhoès et l'Averrhoïsme, 3e Éd. 1866, pp. 152–3, 156–60, 168.

Averrhoes from uttering the phrase commonly attributed to him
—" The Christian faith is impossible; that of Judaism is a religion
of children, that of Islam, a religion of hogs." *

Still less credible is the popular assertion which assigns to him
the famous speech referring to Moses, Christ, and Mahomet as the
three impostors who had deluded the human race. This saying
became a convenient formula with which the Church horrified the
faithful by attributing it successively to those whom it desired to
discredit. Thomas of Cantimpré fathered it upon Simon de Tournay, whose paralytic stroke in 1201 he ascribed to this impiety.
Gregory IX., when in 1239 he arraigned Frederic II. before the
face of Europe, did not hesitate to assert that he was the author
of this utterance, which Frederic made haste to deny in the most
solemn manner. A certain renegade Dominican named Thomas
Scot, who was condemned and imprisoned in Portugal, was said
to have been guilty of this blasphemy among others, and the
phrase drifted through the centuries until there was a current belief that an impious book existed under the title *De Tribus Im-
postoribus*, the authorship of which was attributed variously to
Petrus de Vineis, Boccaccio, Poggio, Machiavelli, Erasmus, Servetus, Bernardino Ochino, Rabelais, Pietro Aretino, Étienne Dolet,
Francesco Pucci, Muret, Vanini, and Milton. Queen Christina of
Sweden vainly caused all the libraries of Europe to be searched
for it, but it remained invisible until, in the eighteenth century, various scribblers put forth volumes to gratify the popular curiosity.†

Yet to Frederic II. may be attributed the introduction of
Averrhoism in central Europe. In Spain it was so prevalent that
about 1260 Alonso X. describes heresies as consisting of two principal divisions, of which the worst was that which denies the immortality of the soul and future rewards and punishments, and in

---

* Renan, pp. 22, 29–36, 167–9, 297.

† Th. Cantimpr. Bon. Univers. Lib. II. c. 47.— Matt. Paris ann. 1238. — Hist.
Diplom. Frid. II. T. V. pp. 339, 349.—Pelayo, Heterodoxos Españoles, I. 507–8,
782–3.

One of these supposititious *Traité des Trois Imposteurs*, published at Yver-
don in 1768, is written from a pantheistic standpoint, and not without a certain
measure of learning. Although it quotes Descartes, there is a somewhat clumsy
attempt to represent it as a translation of a tract sent by Frederic II. to Otho of
Bavaria.

1291 we find the Council of Tarragona ordering the punishment
of those who disbelieved in a future existence. It was from Toledo that Michael Scot came with translations of Aristotle and
Averrhoes, and was warmly welcomed at the court of Frederic,
whose insatiable thirst for knowledge and whose slender reverence
for formulas led him to grasp eagerly at these unexpected sources
of philosophy. It was probably these translations which formed
the body of Aristotelism distributed by him to the universities of
Italy. Hermannus Alemannus continued Michael's work at Toledo and brought versions of other books to Manfred, who inherited
his father's tastes, so that by the middle of the century the principal labors of Averrhoes were accessible to scholars.*

The infection spread with rapidity almost incredible. Already,
in 1243, Guillaume d'Auvergne, Bishop of Paris, and the Masters
of the University condemned a series of scholastic errors, not indeed distinctively Averrhoist, but manifesting in their bold independence the influence which the Arab philosophy was beginning
to exercise. In 1247 the papal legate Otto, Bishop of Frascati,
condemned Jean de Brescain for certain heretical speculations
concerning light and matter; he was banished from Paris and forbidden to teach, or dispute, or to live where there was a college.
At the same time a certain Master Raymond who had been imprisoned for his erroneous views was found to be contumacious
and was ordered back to prison, while, for the future, logicians
were forbidden to argue theologically and theologians logically,
as they were growing accustomed to do. This accomplished little,
and as little was effected by Albertus Magnus and Thomas Aquinas, who employed their keenest dialectics to check the spread of
these dangerous opinions. Bonaventura likewise denounced the
audacious philosophy which denied immortality and asserted the
unity of intellect and the eternity of matter, showing that Dominicans and Franciscans could co-operate against a common enemy.
In 1270, Étienne Tempier, Bishop of Paris, was called upon to condemn a series of thirteen errors, distinctively Averrhoist, which
found defenders among the schools, to the effect that the intellect
of all men is the same and is one in number; that human will is

---

* Partidas, P. vii. Tit. xxvi. l. 1.—Concil. Tarraconens. ann. 1291 c. 8 (Martene
Ampliss. Coll. VII. 294).—Renan, pp. 205–16.

controlled by necessity; that the world is eternal and there never
was a first man; that the soul is corrupted with the corruption of
the body and does not suffer from corporeal fire; that God does
not know individual things, he knows nothing but himself, and
cannot give immortality and incorruptibility to that which is mortal and corruptible.*

This availed as little as the previous effort. In 1277 it was
deemed necessary to invoke the authority of John XXI., under
which Bishop Tempier condemned a list of two hundred and nineteen errors, mostly the same as the previous ones, or deductions
drawn from them, tending to systematize materialism and fatalism. The daring progress made by free-thought is shown by the
sharply defined antagonism proclaimed between philosophy and
theology: The philosopher must deny the creation of the world
because he relies upon natural causes alone, but the believer may
assert it because he relies upon supernatural causes; the utterances
of the theologians are based upon fables, and theology is a study
unworthy the pursuing, for philosophers are the only sages and
the Christian law impedes the progress of learning: prayer, of
course, is unnecessary, and sepulture is not worth consideration by
the wise man, but confession may be practised to save appearances.
The Averrhoist theory of the universe and the celestial spheres was
fully expressed, as well as the controlling influences of the stars
upon human will and fortunes, for which, as we have seen, Peter of
Abano and Cecco d'Ascoli subsequently suffered. In addition we
have the speculation that with every cycle of thirty-six thousand
years the celestial bodies returned to the same relative positions,
producing a repetition of the same series of events.†

About the same time Robert Kilwarby, Archbishop of Canterbury, together with the Masters of Oxford, condemned some errors
evidently originating from the same source, but not asserting materialism in a manner so absolute, and this condemnation was confirmed in 1284 by Archbishop Peckham, but the only punishment
threatened was deposition for a Master, and for a Bachelor expulsion with disability for promotion. These articles were combined

---

* Matt. Paris ann. 1243 (p. 415). — S. Bonaventuræ Serm. de decem Præceptis
II. (Opp. Venet. 1584, II. 617).—D'Argentré I. i. 158-9, 186-88.

† D'Argentré I. i. 177-83.

with those of Bishop Tempier, and together the collection had wide currency, as shown by the number of MSS. containing it. That the opinions thus condemned continued to be regarded as a source of real danger to the Church is manifested by the articles being customarily printed during the fifteenth and sixteenth centuries at the end of the fourth book of the *Sentences*, and also in an edition each of Thomas Aquinas, Duns Scotus, and Bonaventura.*

Yet after the death of Bishop Tempier these articles aroused considerable complaint as interfering with freedom of discussion, and they became the object of no little debate. In fact, in so long a list of errors, many of them scarce apprehensible save by the scholastic mind, it was almost impossible to avoid trenching upon positions held to be orthodox in a theology of which the complexity had grown beyond the grasp of finite intelligence and finite memory. Considerable trouble was occasioned by the fact that some of the articles assailed positions held by Thomas Aquinas himself; others were attacked by William of Ockham and Jean de Poilly. How perilous, indeed, was the position of the theological expert in the war of dialectics is seen in the case of the *Doctor Fundatissimus*, Egidio Colonna, better known as Egidio da Roma. There was no more earnest and active opponent of Averrhoism, and his list of its errors long continued to be the basis of its condemnation. Yet he translated a commentary on Aristotle, and in 1285 he was accused in Paris of entertaining some of the errors condemned in 1277. After considerable discussion the matter was carried before the Holy See, and Honorius IV. referred him back to the University of Paris for sentence. He made his peace so effectually that Philippe le Bel, whose tutor he had been, presented him to the great archbishopric of Bourges.†

At the close of the thirteenth and the commencement of the fourteenth century the principal figure in the contest with Averrhoes is Raymond Lully—aptly styled by Renan the hero of the crusade against it—but the career of Lullism was so remarkable that it must be considered independently hereafter. All efforts failed to suppress a philosophy which offered such attractions to the rising energies of the human intellect. An avowed school of

---

* D'Argentré I. i. 185, 212–13, 234.

† D'Argentré I. i. 214–15, 235–6.—Renan, pp. 467–70.—Eymeric. pp. 238, 241.

Averrhoists arose, whose tenets, introduced in the University of
Padua seemingly by Peter of Abano, reigned there supreme until
the seventeenth century.   The University of Bologna likewise
adopted them.   Jean de Jandun, the collaborator of Marsilio of
Padua, was a modified Averrhoist, as were Walter Burleigh, Buridan, and the Ockhamists.   John of Baconthorpe, who died in 1346
as General of the Carmelites, rejoiced in the title of Prince of
Averrhoists, and through him the philosophy became traditional
in the Order.   These men might conceal to themselves the dangerous irreligion which lurked under their cherished theories, but
when these spread among the people, divested of the subtle dialectics of the schools, they developed into frank materialism.   Dante's
description of the portion of hell where

> " Suo cimitero da questa parte hanno
>   Con Epicuro tutti i suoi seguaci
>   Che l'anima col corpo morta fanno " (INFERNO, X.)

manifests by its occupants that Averrhoism in its crudest form
was openly professed by men high in station ; and some proceedings
of the Inquisitions of Carcassonne and Pamiers in the first quarter
of the fourteenth century indicate that even in the lower strata of
society such opinions were not uncommon.   The indignation of
Petrarch shows us how fashionable and how outspoken by the
middle of the century this indifferentism had become in the Venetian provinces, where men did not hesitate to ridicule Christ and
to regard Averrhoes as the fountain of wisdom.   In Florence the
tradition of the same philosophic contempt for dogma is indicated
by Boccaccio's story of the Three Rings, wherein Melchisedech the
Jew, by an ingenious parable, conveys to Saladin the conclusion
that all three religions are on the same plane, with equal claims
for reverence.   In Spain, although philosophy was little cultivated, Moorish tradition seems to have kept Averrhoism alive.   The
revolted nobles who, in 1464, presented their complaints to King
Enrique IV., declare him suspect in the faith because he keeps
about his person enemies of Catholicism, and others who, while
nominally Christians, boast of their disbelief in the immortality of
the soul.*

---

* Renan, pp. 318–20, 322, 325, 339, 342, 345–6. — Molinier, Études sur quelques
MSS. des Bibliothèques d'Italie, p. 103.—Petrarchi Lib. sine Titulo Epist. XVIII.

Averrhoism had thus fairly conquered a position for itself, and it is one of the inscrutable problems why the Inquisition, so unrelenting in its suppression of minor aberrations, should have conceded impunity to speculations which not only sapped the foundations of Christian faith, but by plain implication denied all the doctrines on which were based the wealth and power of the hierarchy. Even the University of Paris, so vigilant in its guard over orthodoxy, seems during the remainder of the fourteenth century to have abstained from condemning Averrhoism and its deductions, although there were numerous decisions against minute errors of scholastic theology. Yet to Gerson Averrhoes was still the most insolent adversary of the faith; he was the man who had condemned all religions as bad, but that of the Christians as worst of all, for they daily ate their God; and, in the allegorical paintings of Orcagna, Traini, Taddeo Gaddi, and their successors, Averrhoes commonly figures as the impersonation of rebellious unbelief.*

It was not till 1512 that Averrhoism had its first recorded victim since Peter of Abano, in the person of Hermann of Ryswick, who, in 1499, had been condemned for teaching its materialistic doctrines—that matter is uncreated and has existed with God from the beginning, that the soul dies with the body, and that angels, whether good or bad, are not created by God. He abjured and was sentenced to perpetual imprisonment, but escaped and persisted in propagating his errors. When again apprehended, in 1512, the inquisitor at The Hague had no hesitation in handing him over as a relapsed to the secular arm, and he was duly burned.†

In northern Europe, where scholastic theology was engaged in mortal combat with Humanism, rigor like this is to be looked for, but the case was different in Italy. There letters had long before got the better of faith. The infection of culture and philosophy, of elegant paganism, pervaded all the more elevated ranks of society. A succession of cultured popes, who were temporal princes rather than vicars of Christ, and who prided themselves on the patronage of scholars, could turn aside from the affairs of state to

---

Ejusd. contra Medicum Lib. II. (Ed. Basil. 1581, p. 1098).—Decamerone, Giorn. I. Nov. 3.—Marina, Théorie des Cortès, Trad. Fleury. Paris, 1822, II, 515.

* Gerson. sup. Magnificat. Tract. IX. (Ed. 1489, 89f, 91f).—Renan, p. 314.

† D'Argentré I. II. 342.—Alph. de Castro adv. Hæreses, Lib. II. s. v. *Angelus*.

stimulate the burning of miserable witches, but not to condemn
the errors of the philosophers who adorned their courts. If Rome
was to remain the mistress of the world under the New Learning,
she could not afford to be relentless in repressing the aspirations
and speculations of scholars and philosophers.* The battle had
been fought and lost over Lorenzo Valla. It is true that his destructive criticism of the Donation of Constantine was written at
Naples about 1440, when Alfonso I. was in conflict with Eugenius
IV. Yet, as he not only swept away the foundations of the temporal power, but argued that the papacy should be deprived of it,
the impunity which he enjoyed is a remarkable proof of the freedom of speech permitted at the period. His troubles arose from
a different cause, and even these he would probably have escaped
but for the quarrelsome humor of the man, and his unsparing ridicule of the horrible jargon of the schools and even of the earlier
Humanists. He made enemies enough to conspire for his ruin at
the court of Naples, where Alfonso had studied Latin under his
teaching, and he soon gave occasion for their attack. Becoming
involved in a contest with an ignorant priest who asserted that
the Symbol was the production of the Apostles, the discussion
spread to the authenticity of the communications between Christ
and King Abgar of Edessa. Valla posted a list of the propositions assailed, and hired a hall in which to defend them against
all comers, when his enemies procured from the king a prohibition
of disputation. Valla then posted on the hall-door a triumphant
distich:

> "Rex pacis miserans sternendas Marte phalanges,
> Victoris cupidum continuit gladium."

Then the Inquisition interposed, but Alfonso exercised the royal
Neapolitan prerogative of putting a stop to the prosecution, Valla

---

* For a luminous presentation of the influence of Humanism on the policy of
the Church in the fifteenth century, see Creighton's History of the Popes, II. 333
sqq. It was one of the complaints of Savonarola that learning and culture had
supplanted religion in the minds of those to whom the destinies of Christianity
were confided until they had become infidels—" Vattene a Roma e per tutto il
Cristianesimo; nelle case de' gran prelati e de' gran maestri non s' attende se non
a poesie e ad arte oratoria. . . . Essi hanno introdotto fra noi le feste del diavolo;
essi non credono a Dio, e si fanno beffe dei misteri della nostra religione " (Villari, Storia di Savonarola, Ed. 1887, I. 197, 199).

being only forced to make a general declaration that he believed as Holy Mother Church believed—the sincerity of which appeared when, attacked on a point of dialectics, he defended himself by saying: "In this, too, I believe as Mother Church believes, though Mother Church knows nothing about it." When, in 1443, Alfonso and Eugenius were reconciled, Valla sought to go to Rome, but was unable to do so; but when the monkish Eugenius was succeeded by the humanist Nicholas V., the way was opened. Nicholas not only welcomed him, but gave him a position among the papal secretaries and rewarded his translation of Thucydides with a gift of five hundred ducats. Calixtus III. provided him with a prebend in the pope's own church of St. John Lateran, and here he was honorably buried. So little reverence, indeed, existed at the time for the most sacred subjects that Æneas Sylvius relates with admiration, as an illustration of Alfonso's keenness, that when he had been wearied with a sermon by Frà Antonio, a Sicilian Dominican, on some questions concerning the Eucharist, he put to the preacher the following puzzle: A man enclosed a consecrated host in a vase of gold; a month later, on opening it, he found only a worm; the worm could not have been formed from the pure gold, nor from the accidents which were there, without the subject; it was therefore produced from the body of Christ; but from the substance of God nothing but God can proceed, therefore the worm was God. In such a spiritual atmosphere it was in vain that Lorenzo's enemy Poggio, whom he had mercilessly ridiculed and abused, urged that his errors as to the nature of God and the vow of chastity should be reproved by fire rather than by argument. His commentary on the New Testament, in which he corrected the errors of the Vulgate by the aid of the Greek text, although subsequently put in the index by Paul IV. in 1559, was not condemned at the time. Nicholas V. saw it, Bessarion contributed to it, Nicholas of Cusa begged a copy of it, and Erasmus, in 1505, published it with enthusiastic encomiums, under the patronage of Christopher Fischer, papal prothonotary. We have seen from Bacon how hopelessly corrupt the text of the Vulgate had become; Valla's attempt to purify it was warmly contested, but in his controversy over it with Poggio he won the victory, and the right to do so was thenceforth conceded.*

---

* Laurent. Vallæ in Donat. Constant. Declam. (Fasciculus Rer. Expetendar. I.

After this, scholarship, however heretical, had little to fear in Italy; and the toleration thus extended to the most daring speculations offers abundant food for thought, when we remember that at this very time the Franciscans and Dominicans were turbulently endeavoring to burn each other over the infinitesimal question as to whether the blood of Christ shed in the Passion remained on earth or not. It is true that in 1459 the Lombard inquisitor, Jacopo da Brescia, condemned to degradation and perpetual imprisonment Doctor Zanino da Solcia, Canon of Bergamo, who entertained some crazy theories that the end of the world was approaching, and that God had created another world populated by human beings, so that Adam was not the first man, together with some Averrhoistic tenets that it was the power of the stars, and not love for humanity that led Christ to the cross, and that Christ, Moses, and Mahomet governed mankind at their pleasure; but

---

132, Ed. 1690).—Bayle, s. v. *Valle.*—Raynald. ann. 1446, No. 9.—Paramo de Orig. Offic. S. Inq. p. 297.—Wagenmann, Real-Encykl. VIII. 492–3.—Creighton's Hist. of the Popes, II. 340.—Æn. Sylv. Comment. in Dict. et Fact. Alfonsi Regis Lib. I. —Erasmi Epistt. Lib. IV. Ep. 7; Lib. VII. Ep. 3. — Reusch, Der Index der Verbotenen Bücher, I. 227.

The immediate conviction wrought by Valla's criticism of the Donation of Constantine is shown in Æneas Sylvius's defence of the temporal power, where he abandons Constantine entirely, basing the territorial claims of the Holy See on the gifts of Charlemagne, and its authority over kings on the power of the keys and the headship granted to Peter (Æn. Sylvii Opp. inedd. pp. 571–81). Yet the Church soon rallied and renewed its claims. Arnaldo Albertino, Inquisitor of Valencia, in alluding to the Donation of Constantine, says, in 1533, that Lorenzo Valla endeavored to dispute its truth, but that every one else is united in maintaining it, so that to deny it is to come near heresy (Arn. Albertini Repetitio nova, Valentiæ, 1534, col. 32–3). Curiously enough, he adds that it is asserted in the bull *Unam Sanctam,* which is not the case (I. Extrav. Commun. Lib. I. Tit. viii.). In fact, Boniface VIII. founded his claims on Christ, and a reference to Constantine would only weaken them.

Valla's bitter and captious criticisms provoked sundry epigrams after his death.

"Nunc postquam manes defunctus Valla petivit,
    Non audet Pluto verba Latina loqui.
Jupiter hunc cæli dignatus parte fuisset,
    Censorem linguæ sed timet esse suæ."

"Ohe ut Valla silet solitus qui parcere nulli est!
    Si quæris quid agat nunc quoque mordet humum."—(Bayle, l. c.).

Pius II., in confirming the sentence, moderated it with the evident purpose in due time of remedying the over-zeal of the inquisitor. He also interfered when the Inquisition had condemned a high official of Udine for virtually denying immortality by asserting that the blood is the soul: the sentence was set aside, and the offender was offered the easy opportunity of escaping punishment as a heretic by publicly declaring this to be an error. Pius, however, showed his orthodoxy by reproving the laxity of Eugenius IV. in the case of Braccio da Montone, the condottiere lord of Perugia, an avowed infidel, whose body, on his death in 1424 at the siege of Aquila, was brought to Rome and thrust into unconsecrated ground until Eugenius had it translated and honorably buried in the cathedral of Perugia. A more typical case is that of Gismondo Malatesta, Lord of Rimini. He was a man of high culture, and an ardent adept of the new philosophy, who manifested his zeal by bringing from the Peloponnesus and burying with a laudatory inscription, in the cathedral of Rimini, Gemistus Plethon, the half-pagan founder of a new philosophical religion. All this might have escaped animadversion had not his ambition led him to extend his dominions at the expense of papal territory. In the quarrel which ensued his heterodoxy served as a convenient object of attack, and in 1461 Pius II. condemned him as a heretic who denied the immortality of the soul, and in default of his body burned his effigy before a Roman crowd. So little effect had this that the Venetians maintained their alliance with Gismondo, and the Bishop of Treviso incurred imminent risk of losing his see by reason of publishing the sentence. More efficacious was a crusade, in 1463, under the Cardinal of Theane and Federigo d' Urbino, when Gismondo was stripped of nearly all his possessions and was forced to sue for peace. His heresy then was so little regarded that he was allowed to abjure by deputy, and was reconciled under the trifling penance of Friday fasting on bread and water.*

In fact, as Gregory of Heimburg bitterly declares, it was safer to discuss the power of God than that of the popes. This was very clearly demonstrated in the persecution of the "Academy"

---

* Raynald. ann. 1459, No. 31; ann. 1461, No. 9, 10.—Æn. Sylvii Opp. inedd. pp. 453, 506-7, 524, 653.—B. Platinæ Vit. Pauli III.—Creighton, Hist. of the Popes, II. 440; III. 39.

by Paul II. Pius II. had formed in the curia a college of sixty "abbreviators" for the expedition of papal briefs, which became for the most part a refuge for needy men of letters. Platina, the papal biographer, who was one of them, tells us that it was customary among both philosophers and theologians to dispute about the soul, the existence of God, the separated essences, and other matters, and he seeks to palliate the evil repute thence arising by saying that people confounded search for the truth with heretical doubt. The people probably had ample cause for scandal in such debates among papal officials, which was not diminished when Pomponio Leto founded in honor of Plato an academy of the leading Humanists, who bestowed on their leader the title of Pontifex Maximus, offered sacrifices on the anniversary of the foundation of Rome, and discarded their baptismal names in favor of classical ones. Pomponio himself would study nothing later than the golden age of Roman literature, thus dismissing with contempt the Scriptures and the Fathers, and he daily knelt before an altar dedicated to Romulus. All this might have passed unrepressed had these classical zealots borne with philosophy the withdrawal of papal patronage. One of the early acts of Paul II., in his effort to reform abuses, was the suppression of the College of Abbreviators in consequence of ugly rumors as to the venality and extortion of its members. The men of letters, many of whom had purchased their positions, were indignant at this deprivation of their means of livelihood. Platina was hardy enough to ask the pope to have their rights decided by the Auditors of the Rota, and was refused with abundant emphasis. He then had the incredible audacity to write to Paul threatening him with an appeal to the princes of Christendom to call a council on the subject. After Constance and Basle, the word council was not one to be safely uttered within earshot of a pope; Platina was promptly arrested on a charge of high-treason and thrown into jail, where he lay in chains, without fire, during four winter months, until released on the intercession of Cardinal Gonzaga. All this was not likely to create harmony between Paul and the Humanists; we can readily imagine that epigrams and satires on the pope were freely circulated and that the breach grew wider, but the men of letters, if allowed to remain hungry, were not molested until, early in 1468, Paul was informed that the members of the Academy were conspiring against him.   That a crazy admiration of antiquity should culminate in an effort to restore the liberty of Rome was not improbable, and the situation in Italy was such as to render an effort of the kind abundantly capable of causing trouble.   Paul was thoroughly alarmed, and at once imprisoned the suspected conspirators.   The unlucky Platina, who was one of them, has given us an account of the relentless tortures to which, for two days, about twenty of them were subjected, while Pomponio, who chanced to be in Venice, was dragged to Rome like another Jugurtha.   No criminating evidence of treason was discovered, but they were kept in durance for a year, and, in order to find some justification for the affair, which had excited much comment, they were accused of heresy, of disputing about the immortality of the soul, and of venerating Plato.   It proves how leniently such aberrations were regarded that they were finally acquitted of all heresy and discharged; and that although Paul abolished the Academy, prohibiting even the mention of its name, his successor, Sixtus IV., as a patron of letters, permitted its re-establishment and appointed Platina librarian of the Vatican library which he founded.*

The tolerance thus extended to the paganism of the enthusiastic votaries of the New Learning produced a curious development of religious sentiment among them as insidiously dangerous to the faith, except in its lack of popular attractiveness, as the dogmas so ruthlessly exterminated by Peter Martyr and François Borel. Marsilio Ficino, the Platonist, evidently regarded himself, and was regarded, as a champion of Christianity and a most deserving son of the Church, and yet he kept a lamp lighted in honor of Plato, whom he repeatedly declared to be a Greek-speaking Moses.   He brought all religions upon the same level.   The worship of the pagan gods of antiquity was a worship of the true God, and not, as the Church held, an adoration of demons.   He found Para-

---

* Gregor. Heymburg. Confut. Primatus Papæ (Fascic. Rer. Expetend. II. 117). —B. Platinæ Vit. Pauli II.—Cantù, I. 186–7, 198.

Creighton (Hist. of the Popes, III. 276 sqq.) has printed from a Cambridge MS. a curious correspondence between Pomponio, while imprisoned in the Castle of Sant' Angelo, and his jailer, Rodrigo de Arevalo, afterwards Bishop of Zamora. It shows how fragile was the philosophy of the Platonists when exposed to real privations.

dise in the Elysian Fields, and Purgatory in Hades. Zoroaster, Orpheus, Hermes Trismegistus, Socrates, Plato, and Virgil were prophets on whose evidence he relies to prove the divinity of Christ. The Crito confirms the Evangel and contains the foundation of religion. Even the Neo-Platonists, Plotinus and Proclus, and Iamblichus, are shown to have been supporters of the faith which they so earnestly combated while alive. For teachings far less dangerous than this hundreds of men had been forced to the alternative of recantation or the stake, but Marsilio was honored as a light of his age. It is true that he avoided the errors of Averrhoism, but as these were likewise tolerated his impunity is not to be ascribed to this. While admitting the importance of astrology, he held that the stars have no power of themselves; they can merely indicate, and their indication of the future by their regular revolutions shows that affairs are not abandoned to chance, but are ruled by Providence. So, while human character is affected by the position of the stars at the hour of birth, it is much more the result of heredity and training. Perhaps the most curious illustration which Marsilio gives us of the confusion and upturning of religious ideas in the Renaissance is a letter addressed to Eberhard, Count of Wirtemberg, in which he seriously proves that the sun is not to be worshipped as God. In one respect he was more orthodox than most of his brethren of the New Learning, for he believed in the immortality of the soul, and maintained it in a laborious treatise, but he could not convince his favorite pupil, Michele Mercato, and made with him a compact that the one dying first should return, if there was a future life, and inform the other. One morning Mercato was awakened by the trampling of a horse and a voice calling to him: on rushing to the window the horseman shouted, "Mercato, it is true!". Marsilio had that moment died.*

An exception to this prevalent tolerance is commonly said to

---

* Marsil. Ficin. Epistt. Libb. VIII., XI., XII. (Opp. Ed. 1561, I. 866–7, 931, 946, 962–3); De Christ. Relig. c. 11, 13, 22, 24, 26 (I. 15, 18, 25, 29); De Vita Cœlitus comparanda Lib. III. c. 1, 2 (I. 532–33); In Platonem (II. 1390); In Plotinum c. 6, 7, 12, 15 (II. 1620–22, 1633, 1636).—Cantù, I. 179.

Yet we find him attributing a fever and diarrhœa to the influence of Saturn in the house of Cancer, for Saturn had been in his geniture from the beginning; and his cure he ascribes to a vow made to the Virgin.—Epistt. Opp. I. 644, 733.

be found in the case of Matteo Palmiere of Pisa, reported to have been burned in 1483 for maintaining in his poem, the *Città di Vita*, that the souls of men are the angels who stood neutral in the revolt of Satan. In reality, however, although the Inquisition disapproved his book, the author was not persecuted; he was honorably buried in Florence, and his portrait by Sandro Botticelli was placed over the altar of San Pietro Maggiore.*

That it was not, however, always safe to presume on this favor shown to humanism is evident by the case of Giovanni Pico della Mirandola, the wonder of his age, who in 1487, when but twenty-four years old, published a series of nine hundred propositions which he offered to defend in Rome against all comers, paying the expenses of scholars who might travel for the purpose from distant lands. The list was virtually *de omni scibili*, comprising everything recognized as knowable in theology, philosophy, and science, even including the mysteries of the East. It was doubtless the pretentiousness of the young scholar which provoked enmity leading to animadversion on his orthodoxy, and it was not difficult in so vast an array of conclusions to find some thirteen which savored of heresy. To us it might appear a truism to say that belief is independent of volition; we might hesitate to affirm positively whether Christ descended into hell personally or only effectively; we might even agree with him that mortal sin, limited and finite, is not to be visited with chastisement unlimited and infinite; and we might hesitate to embark with him in investigating too narrowly the mysteries of transubstantiation; but these speculative assumptions of the self-sufficient thinker were condemned as heretical by the theologians appointed for their examination by Innocent VIII., who quietly remarked: "This youth wishes to end badly, and be burned some of these days, and then be infamous forever like many another." Pico was urged to resist and raise a schism, but nothing was further from his thoughts. His few remaining years were passed in the assiduous study of Scripture; he designed, after completing certain works in hand, to wander barefoot over Europe preaching Christ; then, changing his purpose, he intended to enter the Dominican Order, but his projects were cut short, at the age of thirty-two, by the fever

---

* D'Argentré I. ii. 250.—Cantù, I. 182, iii. 699–700.

which carried him off, gratified in his last hours with a vision of the Virgin. Such a man was an easy victim; the voluminous apology which he wrote to explain his errors availed him nothing, and he was compelled to make a full submission, which earned from Alexander VI., in 1493, not long before Pico's death, a bull declaring his orthodoxy and forbidding the Inquisition to trouble him.[*]

In curious contrast to this exceptional rigor was the toleration manifested towards the Averrhoists. It is true that Leo X., in the Council of Lateran, December 21, 1513, procured the confirmation of a bull in which he deplored the spread of the doctrine of the mortality of the soul and of there being but one soul common to mankind. He also condemned the opinions which maintained the eternity of the earth and that the soul has not the form of the body, and in prohibiting their teaching in the schools he especially alluded to the ingenious device adopted by professors of arguing against them so equivocally as to lead to the conviction of their truth. In 1518, moreover, when commissioning Master Leonardo Crivelli as Inquisitor-general of Lombardy, he calls his appointee's special attention to those who seek to know more than it is well to know, and who think ill of the Holy See; these he is to repress with the free use of torture, incarceration, and other penalties, and to pay over their confiscated property to the papal camera, no matter of what condition or dignity they might be. Yet debates on points of Averrhoistic philosophy were the favorite amusement of the semi-pagan philosophers who gathered in Leo's court, and who deemed that all that was necessary to preserve them from the Inquisition was to present arguments on both sides, pronounce the questions insoluble to human reason, and conclude with a hypocritical submission to the Church. Such was the device of Pomponazio (1473–1525), under whom Averrhoism became more popular than ever, although he ridiculed Averrhoes and called himself an Alexandrian, from Alexander of Aphrodisias, the Aristotelian commentator, from whom Averrhoes had derived much. Pomponazio invented the dilemma, " If the three religions are false, all men are deceived: if only one is true, the majority of men are

---

* J. Pic. Mirand. Vita, Conclusiones, Apologia, Alexand. PP. VI. Bull. *Omnium Catholicor.* (Opp. Basil. 1572). Cf. Cantù, I. 185.

deceived." He argued, "If there is a will superior to mine, why
should I be responsible for my acts and deeds? Now a will, a
superior order exists, therefore all that happens must be in accordance with a preordained cause : whether I do right or wrong there
is neither merit nor sin." In his treatise *De Incantationibus* he
argued away all miracles. The bones of a dog would effect cures
as readily as the relics of a saint if the patient's imagination entertained the same belief in them. Like Peter of Abano, moreover,
he held that everything is according to the order of nature; revolutions of empires and religions follow the course of the stars;
thaumaturgists are but skilful physicists who foresee the occult
influences at work and profit by the suspension of ordinary laws
to found new religions; when the influences cease, miracles cease,
religions decay, and incredulity would triumph if renewed con-
junctions of the planets did not cause fresh prodigies and new
thaumaturgists. All this was far worse than anything for which
Cecco d'Ascoli suffered, but Pomponazio escaped his fate by cautiously excepting the Christian faith.[*]

In fact, the only work which gave him serious trouble was his
treatise *De Immortalitate Animæ*, written after the Lateran denunciation, in 1516, which Prierias informs us ought rather to
have been entitled "*De Mortalitate*." In this it is true that he
rejects the Averrhoist theory of a universal intelligence as unworthy of refutation through its monstrous and unintelligible fatuity;

---

[*] Concil. Lateran. V. Sess. VIII. (Harduin. IX. 1719).—Ripoll IV. 373.—Renan,
pp. 53, 363.—P. Pomponatii Tract. de Immort. Animæ c. xiv.—Cantù, I. 179-81.
—Bayle, s. v. *Pomponace*, Note D.

The device by which philosophers escaped responsibility for their philosophy
is illustrated by the concluding words of Agostino Nifo's treatise *De Cœlo et
Mundo*, in 1514 : "In qua omnibus pateat me omnia esse locutum ut phylosophum :
quæ vero viderentur Sanctæ Romanæ Ecclesiæ dissonare illico revocamus,
asserentes ea incuria nostra proficisci non autem a malitia, quare nostras has
interprætationes omnes et quascunque alias in quibusvis libris editis Sanctæ
Romanæ Ecclesiæ submittimus."

And so Marsilio Ficino—"Nos autem in omnibus quæ scribimus eatenus
affirmari a nobis aliisque volumus quatenus Christianorum theologorum concilio videatur"—De Immort. Animæ, Lib. XVIII. c. 5.

Pomponazio winds up his treatise on the immortality of the soul with
"Hæc itaque sunt quæ mihi in hac materia dicenda videntur. Semper tamen in
hoc et in aliis subjiciendo sedi Apostolicæ"—De Immort. Animæ c. xv.

but, after stating the various arguments for and against immortality, with an evident bearing towards the latter, he sums up by declaring the problem to be "neutral," like that of the eternity of the earth; there are no natural reasons proving the soul either to be immortal or mortal, but God and Scripture assert immortality, and therefore reasons proving mortality must be false. He evidently seeks to indicate that immortality is a matter of faith, and not of reason; and he even goes so far as to attribute much of the popular belief in departed spirits and in visions to the frauds of corrupt priests, examples of which he says were not uncommon at the time. The thin veil thus cast over its infidelity did not save the book in Venice, where the patriarch had it publicly burned, and wrote to Cardinal Bembo to have it condemned in Rome. Bembo read it with gusto, pronounced it conformable with the faith, and gave it to the Master of the Sacred Palace, who reached the same opinion. The latter's successor in office, however, Prierias, was less indulgent. In his treatise on witches (1521) he declares that the example of the Venetians ought to be everywhere followed, while his elaborate argumentation to prove the immortality of the soul, and that the souls of brutes are not the same as those of men, shows how widespread were irreligious opinions, and how freely the questions were debated at the time. This is further illustrated in the confession of Eugenio Tarralba before the Spanish Inquisition in 1528, when he testified that as a youth he had studied in Rome, where his three masters, Mariana, Avanselo, and Maguera, all taught him that the soul was mortal, and he was unable to answer their arguments.*

Pomponazio did not remain unanswered. In 1492 Agostino Nifo, professor at Padua, in his work *De Intellectu et Dæmonibus*, had contended for the Averrhoist theory of the unity of intelligence; a single intellect pervades the universe, and modifies all things at its will. He had already had trouble with the Dominicans, and this gave them the advantage; it would have fared ill with him had not Pietro Barozzi, the enlightened Bishop of Padua, saved him, and induced him to modify his teachings. Despite his philosophy, he was a skilful courtier, and became a favor-

---

* P. Pomponatii Tract. de Immort. Animæ c. iv., viii., xiv., xiv.—Prieriat. de Strigimagar. Lib. I. c. iv., v.—Llorente, Hist. de l'Inq. d'Espagne, ch. xv. Art. ii. No. 4.

ite with Leo X., who made him count of the palace, and paid
him to prove against Pomponazio that Aristotle maintained the
immortality of the soul. He became the accepted interpreter of
Averrhoes throughout Italy, and his mitigated Averrhoism remained the doctrine taught at Padua during the remainder of
the century.*

It was impossible that the ministers of the Church should escape the contagion of this fashionable infidelity, however little, in
their worldly self-seeking, they might trouble themselves about
the theories of Averrhoism. In his sermons on Ezekiel, in the
Lent of 1497, Savonarola describes the priests of the period as
slaying the souls of their flocks by their wicked example; their
worship, he says, is to spend the night with strumpets and the
day in singing in the choir; the altar is their shop; they openly
assert that the world is not ruled by the providence of God, but
that everything is the result of chance, and that Christ is not in the
Eucharist.† It was no wonder, then, that the more thoughtful of
the laity, conscious of the evils of the dominant faith, and yet
powerless, under the watchful eye of the Inquisition, to apply a
corrective short of indifferentism or practical atheism; striving
helplessly for something better than they saw around them, and
yet unable to release the primal principles of Christianity from the
incrustations of scholastic theology, should find their only refuge
in these philosophical speculations which virtually reduced Christianity to nothingness. Had not the Reformation come, the culture of Europe would inevitably have been atheistic, or devoted
to sublimated deism, scarce distinguishable from atheism. The
Church would permit no dissidence within its pale, and yet was
singularly tolerant of these aberrations of the fashionable Humanism. It persecuted the Fraticelli who dared to uphold the poverty
of Christ, yet it allowed the paganism of the revived Hellenism to
be disseminated almost without interference. Occasionally some
zealous Dominican, eager to defend the inspired doctrines of the
Angelic Doctor, would threaten trouble, and would burn a too
daring book, but the author could readily find protectors high in
the Church, some Barozzi or Bembo, who conjured the storm.

---

* Renan, pp. 367–72.—Cantù, I. 183.

† Villari, Frà Girolamo Savonarola, Ed. 1887, T. II. p. 3.

The Reformation served a double purpose in checking this tendency to dangerous speculation. It destroyed the hard-and-fast lines of the rigid scholastic theology, and gave to active intellects a wide field for discussion within the limits of the Christian faith. The assaults of Luther and Melanchthon and Calvin were not to be met with the dialectics of the schools, but with a freer and wider scope of reasoning. The worn-out debates over Aristotle and Alexander and Averrhoes, over Nominalism and Realism, were replaced with new systems of Scriptural exegesis and an earnest inquiry into man's place in the universe and his relations to his fellows and to his God. Then the counter-Reformation aroused a zeal which could no longer tolerate the philosophical quodlibets leading to speculations adverse to the received faith. Servetus and Giordano Bruno belong to a period beyond our present limits, but their fate shows how little either Protestant or Catholic, in the fierce strife which enkindled such uncompromising ardor, were disposed to listen to philosophical discussions upon religious beliefs.

Before leaving this branch of our subject we must recur to the curious episode of the career of Raymond Lully, the *Doctor Illuminatus*, of whom Padre Feyjoo truly says, "Raymond Lully, looked upon from every side, is a very problematical object. Some make him a saint, others a heretic; some a most learned man, others an ignoramus; some regard him as illuminated, others as hallucinated; some attribute to him a knowledge of the transmutation of metals, others deny it; finally, some applaud his *Ars Magna*, others depreciate it." *

This enigmatical being was born in Palma, the capital of Majorca, January 25, 1235. Sprung from a noble family, he was bred in the royal court, where he rose to the post of seneschal. He married and had children, but followed a gay and dissolute career until, like Peter Waldo and Jacopone da Todi, he was suddenly converted by an experience of the nothingness of life. He was madly in love with Leonor del Castello, and his reckless temper manifested itself by pursuing her on horseback into the church of Santa Eulalia during a Sunday service, to the great scandal of priest and congregation. To rid herself of such importunate pur-

---

* Cartas de D. Fr. Feyjoo, Carta xxii. (T. I. p. 180).

suit, Leonor, with consent of her husband, exhibited to him her bosom, which was ravaged by a foul and mortal cancer. The shock brought to him so profound a recognition of the vanity of earthly things that he renounced the world and distributed his wealth in charity, after making provision for his family; and the same indomitable ardor which had rendered him extravagant in his pleasures sustained him to the end in his new vocation. Thenceforth he devoted his life to the rescue of the Holy Sepulchre, to the conversion of the Jews and Saracens, and to the framing of a system which should demonstrate rationally the truth of the Christian faith, and thus overcome the Averrhoism in which he recognized its most dangerous adversary.*

Ten years or more were spent in preparation for this new career. We hear of a pilgrimage to Compostella in 1266, and of his retirement to the Monte de Randa, near Palma, in 1275. He was so ignorant of letters that he was not even acquainted with Latin, the key to all the knowledge of the age. This he studied, and also Arabic, from a Saracen slave purchased for the purpose, and the earnest labors of an indefatigable mind can account for the enormous stores of learning which he subsequently displayed; so wonderful that to his followers they appeared necessarily the result of inspiration. In his retreat on Monte de Randa, where he conceived his *Ars Universalis*, he is said to have had repeated visions of Christ and the Virgin, which illuminated his mind; and the mastic-tree under which he habitually wrote bore testimony to the miracle, in its leaves inscribed with Latin, Greek, Chaldee, and Arabic characters. It continued to put forth such leaves. In the seventeenth century Vicente Mut vouches for the fact, and says he has some of them, while Wadding tells us that in his time they were carried to Rome, where they excited much wonder. When his work was completed an angel in the guise of a shepherd appeared, who kissed the book many times, and predicted that it would prove an invincible weapon for the faith.†

Emerging from his retreat, for forty years he led a wandering

---

* Historia General de Mallorca, III. 40–2 (Palma, 1841).—Pelayo, Heterodoxos Españoles, I. 514–15.—Nic. Anton. Bibl. Hispan. Lib. IX. c. iii. No. 73.

† Mariana, Hist. de España, Lib. XV. c. 4.—Hist. Gen. de Mallorca, I. 601, III. 44–6.—Nic. Anton. l. c. No. 74.—Wadding. ann. 1275, No. 12.

life of incessant activity, now stimulating popes and kings to renewed crusades, or to found colleges of the Oriental tongues to
aid in missionary labors, now pouring forth volume after volume
with incredible fecundity, now disputing and teaching against
Averrhoism at Montpellier, Paris, and elsewhere, and now venturing himself among the infidel to spread among them the light of
Christianity.   In any one of these fields of action his labors would
seem enough to exhaust the energies of an ordinary man.   While
on his way, in 1311, to the Council of Vienne, with projects for
founding schools of Oriental tongues, for uniting in one all the
military Orders, for a holy war against the infidel, for suppressing
Averrhoism, and for teaching his art in all universities, he summed
up his life : " I was married and a father, sufficiently rich, worldly,
and licentious.   For the honor of God, for the public weal, and
for the advancement of the faith I abandoned all.   I learned
Arabic, and I have been repeatedly among the Saracens to preach
to them, where I have been beaten and imprisoned.   For forty-five
years I have labored to excite the rulers of the Church and the
princes of Christendom for the public good.   Now I am old, I am
poor, and I still have the same purpose, which, with the help of
God, I will retain till I die."   At Vienne his only success was in
obtaining a decree founding schools of Hebrew, Arabic, and Chaldee in the papal court and in the Universities of Paris, Oxford,
Bologna, and Salamanca.   Thence he went, for the second time,
to Algiers, where, at Bugia, he made many converts, until thrown
into prison and starved ; then he was released and ordered out of
the country, but continued proselyting.   With wonderful forbearance the Moors contented themselves with placing him on board
a ship bound for Genoa, and warning him not to return.   Ship-
wrecked in sight of land, he saved his life by swimming, but lost
his books.   Determined to win the palm of martydom, in August,
1314, he again embarked at Palma for Bugia.   Promptly recognized, he was thrown into jail, beaten, and starved ; but in prison he
continued to preach to his fellow-captives, until the Moors, finding
him unconquerable, took him out, June 30, 1315, and stoned him.
Some Genoese merchants about to sail carried his yet breathing
body on board their ship and laid their course for Genoa, but to
their surprise found themselves at the entrance of the port of
Palma.   In vain they endeavored to leave the spot till, recognizing

the will of Heaven, they carried the body ashore. Immediately it shone in miracles, and the cult of the martyr began. In 1448 a splendid chapel was erected in his honor in the church of the Franciscans, of which Order he was a Tertiary, and another one was dedicated to him in the beginning of the seventeenth century. In 1487 his bones were deposited in a richly carved alabaster urn, standing in a niche in the church-wall over an elaborate sepulchral monument, where they still remain.*

Slender were the results achieved at the moment by the self-devotion of this noble and indefatigable intellect. Averrhoism continued to gain strength, the Christian princes could not be stimulated to a new crusade, the conversion of Jew and infidel made no progress, and the only reward of labor so strenuous and so prolonged were Oriental schools established in Majorca and Sicily, and the foundation of others commanded by the Council of Vienne. Yet the prodigious literary activity of Lully left behind him a mass of writings destined to exercise no little influence on succeeding generations. He was perhaps the most voluminous author on record. Juan Llobet, who in the middle of the fifteenth century taught the Art of Lully in the University of Palma, had read five hundred of his books; some authors assert that their total number reached a thousand, others three thousand. Many have been lost, many spurious ones have been attributed to him, and the bibliography of his works is hopelessly confused; but Nicolas Antonio, after careful sifting, gives the titles of three hundred and twenty-one which may safely be ascribed to him. Of these there are sixty-one on the art of learning and general subjects, four on grammar and rhetoric, fifteen on logic, twenty-one on philosophy, five on metaphysics, thirteen on various sciences—astrology, geometry, politics, war, the quadrature of the circle, and the art of knowing God through grace—seven on medicine, four on law, sixty-two on spiritual contemplation and other religious subjects, six on homiletics, thirteen on Antichrist, the acquisition of the Holy Land, and other miscellaneous subjects, forty-six controversial works against Saracens, Jews, Greeks, and Averrhoists, and sixty-four on theology, embracing the most abstruse points,

---

* Wadding. ann. 1293, No. 3; ann. 1215, No. 2, 5.—C. 1 Clement. v. 1.—Nic. Anton. l. c. No. 76.—Hist. Gen. de Mallorca, II. 1058-9, 1063; III. 64-5, 72.

and religious poetry.   The great collective edition of his works
printed in Mainz from 1721 to 1742 forms ten folios.   Like all
other great scholars of his day, his name was a convenient one to
affix to books on alchemy and magic, but all such are supposititious.
His reputation as an alchemist is seen in the tradition that in England he made six million gold florins, and gave them to the king
to stimulate him to a crusade, but his own opinion of alchemy is
expressed in a passage of his *Ars Magna:* "Each element has its
own peculiarities so that one species cannot be transmuted to another, wherefore the alchemists grieve and have occasion to weep,"
and in other equally outspoken expressions.*

For our purpose we need consider but one phase of his marvellous productiveness.   In the solitude of Monte de Randa he conceived the Art which passes by his name—a method in which, by
diagrams and symbols, the sublimest truths of theology and philosophy can be deduced and memorized.   Of this the *Ars Brevis*
is a compend, while the *Ars Magna* describes it in greater detail
and proceeds to build upon it a system of the universe.   As the
product of a man untinctured with culture till after the age of
thirty it is a wonderful performance, revealing a familiar acquaintance with all the secrets of the material and spiritual worlds, the
powers, attributes, motives, and purposes of God and his creatures
logically deduced, which the Lullists might well hold to be inspired.   This Art he himself taught at Montpellier and Paris, and
in 1309 forty members of the latter University joined in a cordial
recommendation of it as useful and necessary for the defence of
the faith.   At home it had great and enduring vogue.   Favored
by successive monarchs, it was taught in the Universities of Aragon and Valencia.   In the middle of the fifteenth century the
Estudio Lulliano was founded at Palma, subsquently enlarged into
the Universidad Lulliana, where the tradition of his teaching was
preserved almost to our own days.   Cardinal Ximenes was its
great admirer; Angelo Politiano says that to it he owed his ability to dispute on any subject; Jean Lefèvre d'Etaples prized it

---

* Nic. Anton. l. c. No. 87–154.—Hist. Gen. de Mall. III. 68, 70, 96–8.—R.
Lullii Art. Mag. P. ix. c. 52 (Opp. Ed. Argentorati, 1651, p. 438).

For an account of Lully's poetical works, see Chabaneau (Vaissette, Éd.
Privat, x. 379).

highly, as likewise did other men of note. On the other hand, it was condemned by Gerson and its use forbidden in the University of Paris; it was ill thought of by Cornelius Agrippa and Jerome Cardan; and Mariana tells us that in his time many considered it useless and even harmful, while others praised it as a gift from heaven to remedy ignorance, and in 1586 its use was prohibited in the University of Valencia.*

In this and in many of his other works Lully's object was to prove by logical processes of thought the truths of Christianity and the positions of theology. We have already seen how the Church recognized the risk involved in this and forbade it, and Lully felt that he was treading on dangerous ground. He therefore lost no opportunity of declaring that faith is superior to reason, and that they were mistaken who held that faith proved by reason lost its merit. Devoting his life to combating Averrhoism and converting the infidel, he had felt that Christianity could only be spread by argument—that to convert men he had to convince them. Without this the work must stop, and he urged that the heathen might logically complain of God if it were impossible to convince their reason of the truth.† It was the same effort as that made two centuries later by Savonarola in his *Crucis Triumphus*, to combat the incredulity of the later Averrhoists and of the Renaissance.

The result showed the danger which lurked in his single-minded efforts. As his reputation spread and his disciples multiplied, Nicholas Eymerich, the Inquisitor of Aragon, to whom I have so often had occasion to refer, undertook to condemn his memory. Perhaps among the Lullists there were men whose zeal outran their discretion. Eymerich speaks of one, named Pedro Rosell, whose errors are a curious echo of the Joachites and Olivists, for he taught that, as the doctrine of the Old Testament was attributable to the Father and that of the New to the Son, so was that of Lully to the Holy Ghost, and that in the time of Antichrist

---

* Hist. Gen. de Mall. III. 71, 78.—Pelayo, I. 530, 535, 537, 539.—Nic. Anton. l. c. No. 82.—Gersoni Epist. ad. Bart. Carthus; Ejusd. De Exam. Doctr. P. II. Consid. 1.—Corn. Agrippæ de Vanitate Scient. c. 9.—Hieron. Cardan. de Subtil. Rer. Lib. xv.—Mariana, Lib. xv. c. 4.

† Pelayo, I. 519-23.—R. Lullii Lamentat. Philosoph.

all theologians would apostatize, when the Lullists would convert
the world, and all theology but that of their master would disappear. Perhaps also, Eymerich, as a Dominican, was eager to
attack one in whom the Franciscans gloried as one of their greatest sons. Doubtless, too, there is truth in the assertion of the Lullists that their defence of the Immaculate Conception rendered
Eymerich desirous of suppressing them. Be this as it may, in a
mass of writings embracing every conceivable detail of doctrine
and faith, set forth with logical precision, it was not difficult for
an expert to find points liable to characterization as errors. A
royal privilege for the teaching of Lullism, issued by Pedro IV.
in 1369, shows that already opposition had been aroused, and in
1371 Eymerich went to Avignon, where he obtained from Gregory XI. an order for the examination of Lully's writings. On his
return the king peremptorily forbade the publication of the papal
mandate, but the irrepressible inquisitor in 1374 sent twenty of the
inculpated books to Gregory, and in 1376 he had the satisfaction
of exhibiting a bull reciting that these works had been carefully
investigated by the Cardinal of Ostia and twenty theologians, who
had found in them two hundred (or, according to Eymerich, five
hundred) errors manifestly heretical. As the rest of Lully's writings must presumably be erroneous, the Archbishop of Tarragona
was ordered to cause all of them to be surrendered and sent to
Rome for examination. Then King Pedro again interposed, and
asked the pope to have any further proceedings carried on in Barcelona, as Lully's works were mostly in Catalan, and could best be
understood there.*

Eymerich triumphed for a time, and in his *Directorium In-
quisitorum* he gives full rein to his hatred. Lully, he says, was
taught his doctrine by the devil, but, to avoid prolixity, he enumerates only a hundred of the five hundred errors condemned by
Gregory. Some of these trench on mystic illuminism, others are
merely extravagant modes of putting ordinary propositions. For
the most part they hinge on the assertion, condemned in the ninety-
sixth error, " that all points of faith and the sacraments and the
power of the pope can be and are proved by reasoning, neces-

---

* Pelayo, I. 499, 528.—Hist. Gen. de Mall. III. 85.—D'Argentré I. I. 256–7,
259—Pegnæ Append. ad Eymeric. pp. 67–8.—Bofarull, Documentos, VI. 360.

sary, demonstrative, and evident;" for they consist of efforts to define logically the mysteries of faith in a manner of which conceptions so subtle are incapable. Two or three, however, are manifestly heretical—that faith can err, but not reason, that it is wrong to slay heretics, and that the mass of mankind will be saved, even Jews and Saracens who are not in mortal sin. The Lullists had not been disposed to submit quietly. Eymerich describes them as numerous and impudent, and guilty of the error of holding that Gregory erred grossly in condemning their master, whose doctrine had been divinely revealed and excelled all other doctrine, even that of St. Augustin; that it is not to be gained by study, but by the inspiration of the Holy Ghost, in thirty, forty, fifty, or sixty hours; that modern theologians know nothing of true theology, for, on account of their sins, God has transferred all knowledge to the Lullists, who are to constitute the Church in the times of Antichrist.*

There was in all this evidently the material which only needed nursing and provocation to develop into a new and formidable heresy under inquisitorial methods. Fortunately the king and a large part of the population were in sympathy with the Lullists; the Great Schism broke out in 1378, and Don Pedro acknowledged neither Urban VI. nor Clement VII. The kingdom was thus virtually independent; the Lullists boldly claimed that the bull of Gregory XI. had been forged by Eymerich; in 1385 an investigation was held which resulted in driving him from Aragon, when he was succeeded by his enemy, Bernardo Ermengaudi, who was devoted to the king, and who hastened to make a formal declaration that in Lully's *Philosophia Amoris* there were not to be found the errors attributed to it by Eymerich. The banishment of the latter, however, did not long continue. He returned and resumed his office, which he exercised with unsparing rigor against the Lullists. This excited considerable commotion. In 1391 the city of Valencia sent to the pope Doctor Jayme de Xiva to com-

---

* Eymeric. Direct. pp. 255–61.

Pegna says (p. 262) that in the MSS. of Eymerich's work the list of errors is fewer than in the printed text, and this is confirmed by Father Denifle (Archiv. für Litt.- u. K. 1885, p. 143). Apparently the Dominicans of the fifteenth century, when they printed the *Directorium*, interpolated errors to aid them in the controversy over Lully.

plain of Eymerich's enormous crimes, and to supplicate his removal.   The envoy stopped at Barcelona to solicit the co-operation of that powerful community, and the town council, after listening to him, resolved that if the action of Valencia was general
and not special, they would make " one arm and one heart " with
their sister city ; and, moreover, they begged the pope to command some prelate of the kingdom to examine and declare, under
papal authority, whether the articles attributed to Lully had been
justly or unjustly condemned by Eymerich.*

The popular effervescence grew so strong that in 1393 Eymerich was again banished by Juan I. He ended his life in exile,
maintaining to the end the enormity of Lully's heresy and the
genuineness of Gregory's bull.   Antonio Riera, a Lullist who was
active in the matter, he denounced as a heretic who foretold that
before the end of the century all divine service would cease, that
churches would be used as stables, and the laws of Christian, Jew,
and Saracen would be converted into one; but which of these
three it would be he could not tell.   Meanwhile, in 1395, the Holy
See granted the prayer of the Lullists for an examination, and the
Cardinal of San Sesto was sent as special commissioner for the
purpose.   Gregory's registers for 1376 were carefully examined,
and the archivists testified that no record of the bull in question
could be found.   Still the question would not remain settled, for
the honor of the Dominican Order and the Inquisition was at
stake, and again, in 1419, another investigation was held.   The
papal legate, Cardinal Alamanni, deputed Bernardo, Bishop of
Città di Castello, to examine the matter definitely.   His sentence
pronounced the bull to be evidently false, and all action taken under it to be null and void, but expressed no opinion on the writings of Lully, which he reserved for the decision of the Holy See.
From that time forth the genuineness of the bull remained a matter hotly contested.   Father Bremond prints it as authentic, and
declares that after a dispassionate examination he is convinced
that it is so; that the original autograph is preserved in the archives at Gerona, and he quotes Bzovius to the effect that the
Lullists themselves admit that it is in the archives of Barcelona,
Tarragona, and Valencia, whose bishops would not have admitted

---

* D'Argentré I. i. 258, 260.—Hist. Gen. de Mall. III. 82-4.—Pelayo, I. 784-5.

it if false; but Bzovius was a Dominican whose bitterness on the subject is seen in his stigmatizing Lully as a vagabond swindler. Certain it is that in the prolonged and ardent contest which raged over the question of Lully's orthodoxy in the papal court, the Dominicans, with successive popes on their side, were never able to produce the original nor offer any evidence of its authenticity.*

In Aragon the decision of 1419 was regarded as settling the question. Royal letters in favor of Lullism were issued by Alonso V. in 1415 and 1449, by Ferdinand the Catholic in 1483 and 1503, by Charles V. in 1526, and by Philip II. in 1597; the latter monarch, indeed, had great relish for Lully's writings, some of which he habitually carried with him on his journeys to read on the way, and in the library of the Escorial many copies of them were found annotated with his own hand. This royal favor was needed in the curious controversy which followed. Lully's name had passed into the received catalogues of heretics, and as late as 1608 it was included in the list published by the Doctor of Sorbonne, Gabriel du Préau. Paul IV., in 1559, put it in the first papal *Index Expurgatorius*. When this came to be published in Spain, Bishop Jayme Cassador and the inquisitors suspended it and referred the matter to the *consejo de la suprema*, which ordered the entry to be *borrado*, or expunged. At the Council of Trent, Doctor Juan Villeta, acting for Spain, presented a petition in favor of Lully, which was considered in a special congregation, September 1, 1563, and a unanimous decision was reached, confirming all the condemnations passed on Eymerich for falsehood, and ordering the Index of Paul IV. to be expurgated by striking out all that related to Lully. This was a secret determination of the council, and was not allowed to appear in the published acts. It settled the matter for a time, but the question was revived in 1578, when Francisco Pegna reprinted Eymerich's book with the special sanction of Gregory XIII., bringing anew before the world the bull of Gregory XI. and the errors condemned in Lully's writings. Gregory XIII. ordered Pegna to examine the papal registers for the contested bull. Those in Rome were found imperfect, and the missing portions were sent for from Avignon, but the most

---

* Hist. Gen. de Mall. III. 59, 83–6.—Pelayo, I. 498, 787–88.—D'Argentré I. l. 259–61.—Nic. Anton. l. c. No. 78.—Ripoll II. 290.

diligent search failed to find the desired document, though it was alleged that two volumes of the year 1386 could not be found. Battle was now fairly joined between the partisans of Eymerich and those of Lully.   In 1583 the Congregation of the Index determined to include Lully among the prohibited writers, but again Spanish influence was strong enough to prevent it.   Under Sixtus V. there was another attempt, but Juan Arce de Herrera, in the name of Philip II., presented an *Apologia* to the Congregation of the Index, and again the danger was conjured.   When the Index of Clement VIII. was in preparation the question was again taken up, June 3, 1594, and rejected out of respect for Spain; at the request of the Spanish ambassador the pope was asked to order a complete set of Lully's works to be sent to Rome for examination, that the matter might be definitely settled; but this was not done, and in March, 1595, it was announced that his name was omitted from the Index.   In 1611 Philip III. revived the controversy by applying to Paul V. for the canonization of Lully and the expurgation of Eymerich's *Directorium ;* a request which was repeated by Philip IV.   After a confused controversy, it was determined that certain articles admittedly extracted from his books were dangerous, audacious, and savoring of heresy, and some of them manifestly erroneous and heretical.   At a sitting, under the presidency of the pope himself, held August 29, 1619, it was resolved to send this censure to the Spanish nuncio, with instructions to inform the king and the inquisitors that Lully's books were forbidden.   Then came an appeal from the kingdom of Majorca begging that the books might be corrected, to which Paul replied, August 6, 1620, imposing silence; and on August 30 Cardinal Bellarmine drew up for the Inquisition a final report that Lully's doctrine was forbidden until corrected, adding his belief that correction was impossible, but that the condemnation was thus phrased so as to mitigate its severity.   Thus Lully was branded by the Holy See as a heretic, but, out of respect for the Spanish court, the sentence was never published : the matter was supposed by the public to be undecided, and the worship of him as a saint continued uninterruptedly.   Raynaldus, in fact, writing in 1658, states that the question is still *sub judice.*   About the same time certain Jesuits took up his cause against the Dominicans, and in 1662 a translation of his "Triumph of Love" appeared in Paris, on the title of which he was qualified as "Saint Raymond Lully, Martyr and Hermit." The Dominican ire was aroused: appeal was made to the Congregation of Rites, which reported that Lully was included in the Franciscan martyrology under March 29, but that he must not be qualified as a saint, and that a careful examination should be made of his works, to prohibit them if necessary—a recommendation which was never carried out. Yet when, in 1688, Doctor Pedro Bennazar issued at Palma a book in praise of Lully, it was condemned by the Inquisition in 1690; and a compendium of his theology, by Sebastian Krenzer in 1755, was put on the Index, although this was not done with the numerous controversial writings which continued to appear, nor with the great edition of his works published from 1721 to 1742, in the title of which he was qualified as *Beatus*. Benedict XIV., in his work *De Servorum Dei Beatificatione*, after carefully weighing the authorities on both sides, says that his claims to sanctity are to be suspended until the decision of the Holy See. That decision was postponed for a century. In 1847 Pius IX. approved an office of "the holy Raymond Lully" for Majorca, where he had been immemorially worshipped; the office reciting that so fully was he imbued with the divine wisdom that he who had previously been uncultured was enabled to discourse most excellently on divine things. In 1858, moreover, Pius permitted the whole Franciscan Order to celebrate his feast on November 27. Yet the Dominicans had not forgotten their old rancor, for in 1857 there appeared in a Roman journal, published under the approbation of the Master of the Sacred Palace, an argument to prove that the alleged bull of Gregory XI. is still in force, and consequently that Lully's books are forbidden, although they do not appear in the Index. This case and that of Savonarola serve to indicate how dangerously nebulous are the boundaries between heresy and sanctity.*

---

* Hist. Gen. de Mall. III. 65–6, 92, 94–5.—Gabrieli Prateoli Elenchus Hæret. Colon. 1608, p. 423.—D'Argentré I. ɪ. 259, 261.—Reusch, Der Index der verbotenen Bücher, I. 27–33.—Benedict. PP. XIV. De Servorum Dei Beatif. Lib. I. c. xl. § 4.—Raynald. ann. 1372, No. 35.

In 1533 Arnaldo Albertino, Inquisitor of Valencia, complained bitterly of the injustice which ranked as a heretic such a man as Lully, who was inspired by

The example of Raymond Lully illustrates the pitfalls which surrounded the footsteps of all who ventured on the dangerous path of theology. That science assumed to know and define all the secrets of the universe, and yet it was constantly growing, as ingenious or daring thinkers would suggest new theories or frame new deductions from data already settled. Hosts of these were condemned; the annals of an intellectual centre like the University of Paris are crowded with sentences pronounced against novel points of faith and their unlucky authors. Occasionally, however, some new dogma would arise, would be vehemently debated, would refuse to be suppressed, and would finally triumph after a more or less prolonged struggle, and would then take its place among the eternal verities which it was heresy to call in question. This curious process of dogmatic evolution in an infallible Church is too instructive not to be illustrated with one or two examples.

It might seem a question beyond the grasp of finite intelligence to determine whether the souls of the blessed are wafted to heaven and at once enjoy the ineffable bliss of beholding the Divine Essence, or whether they have to await the resurrection and the Day of Judgment. This was not a mere theoretical question, however, but had a very practical aspect, for in the existing anthropomorphism of belief, it might well be thought that the efficacy of the intercession of saints depended on their admission to the presence of God, and the guardians of every shrine boasting of a relic relied for their revenues on the popular confidence that its saint was able to make personal appeals for the fulfilment of his worshippers' prayers. The desired conclusion was only reached by gradual steps. The subject was one which had not escaped the attention of the early Fathers, and St. Augustin assumes that the full fruition of the Vision of God can only be enjoyed by the soul after it has been clothed in the resurrected body. Among the errors condemned in 1243 by Guillaume d'Auvergne and the University of Paris were two, one of which held that the Divine Essence is not and will not be seen by either

---

God and was rather to be worshipped as a saint.—Albertini Repetitio nova, Valentia, 1534, col. 406.

The publication of a complete critical edition of Lully's works has recently been commenced at Padua by D. Jerón. Roselló, under the patronage of the Archduke Ludwig Salvator of Austria.

angels or glorified souls; the other, that while angels dwell in the empyrean heaven, human souls, even including the Virgin, will never advance beyond the aqueous heaven. The decision of the bishop and University was cautious as regards the Divine Vision, which was only asserted in the future and not in the present tense, both as regards angels and human souls, but there was no hesitation in declaring that all occupied the same heaven. Thomas Aquinas argues the question with an elaborateness which shows both its importance and its inherent difficulty, but he ventures no further than to prove that the Blessed will, after the resurrection, enjoy the sight of God, face to face. It must be borne in mind that the prevalent expectation in each successive generation that the coming of Antichrist and the second advent were not far off, rendered of less importance the exact time at which the Beatific Vision would be bestowed, while the development of mystic theology tended to bring into ever more intimate relations the intercourse between the soul and its Creator. Bonaventura does not hesitate to treat as an accepted fact that the souls of the just will see God, and he asserts that some of them are already in heaven, while others wait confidently in their graves for the appointed time. The final step seems to have been taken soon after this by the celebrated Dominican theologian, Master Dietrich of Friburg, who wrote a tract to prove that the Blessed are immediately admitted to the Beatific Vision, a fact revealed to him by one of his penitents who, by order of God to solve his doubts, appeared to him ten days after death and assured him that she was in sight of the Trinity.*

Yet the doctrine was not formally accepted by the Church, and the mystical tendencies of the time rendered dangerous a too rapid progress in this direction. The Illuminism of the Brethren of the Free Spirit was a contagious evil, and the Council of Vienne in 1312 refrained from an expression of opinion on the subject, except to condemn the error of the Beghards, that man does not

---

* S. Augustin, De Genesi ad litteram Lib. xii. c. 35, 36; De Civ. Dei Lib. xxii. c. 29. Cf. De Doctr. Christ. Lib. i. c. 31; Epistt. cxviii. § 14, clxix. § 3 (Ed. Benedict.).—Matt. Paris ann. 1243 (p. 415).—Th. Aquinat. Sum. Suppl. Q. xcii. —S. Bonavent. Breviloq. vii. 5, 7; Centiloq. iii. 50; Pharetræ iv. 50.—W. Preger, Zeitschrift für die histor. Theol. 1869, pp. 41–2.

need the light of glory to elevate him to the sight of God—thus
only by implication admitting that with the light of glory the
soul is fitted to enjoy the Beatific Vision.   When and how the
dogma spread that the souls of the just are admitted at once to
the presence of God does not appear, but it seems to have become
generally accepted without any definite expression of approbation by the Holy See.   In October, 1326, John XXII. treats as
a heresy to be extirpated among the Greeks the belief that the
saints will not enter paradise until the Day of Judgment, but
not long afterwards he changed his mind, and his pride in his
theological skill and learning would not let him rest until he had
forced Christendom to change with him.   He expressed his doubts
as to the truth of the new dogma and indicated an intention of
openly condemning it.   His temper rendered opposition perilous,
and none of the cardinals and doctors of the papal court dared
to discuss it with him until, in 1331, an English Dominican, Thomas
Walleys, in a sermon preached before him, boldly maintained the
popular opinion and invoked the divine malediction on all who
asserted the contrary.   John's wrath burst forth.   Walleys was
seized and tried by the Inquisition, cast into jail and almost starved
to death, when Philippe de Valois intervened and procured his
liberation.   Having thus silenced his opponents, John proceeded
to declare his opinions publicly.   In the Advent of 1331 he
preached several sermons in which he asserted that the saints in
heaven will not have distinct vision of the Divine Essence before
the Resurrection of the body and the Day of Judgment, until
which time they will only see the humanity of Christ.   "I know,"
he said, "that some persons murmur because we hold this opinion,
but I cannot do otherwise." *

   It shows the peculiar condition of the human mind engendered
by the persecution of heresy that this was a political event of the
gravest importance.   We have seen how much stress was laid, in
the quarrel between the empire and papacy, upon John's innova-

---

* C. 3, Clem. v. iii.—Ripoll II. 172.—Wadding. ann. 1331, No. 5.—Paul Lang.
Chron. Citicens. (Pistor, I. 1207, 1210).—Gob. Person. Cosmodr. Æt. vi. c. 71.—
D'Argentré I. i. 315 sqq.—P. de Herenthals Vit. Joann. XXII. ann. 1333 (Mura-
tori S. R. I. III. ii. 501).—Guill. Nangiac. Contin. ann. 1331.—Villani, X. 226.—
Chron. Glassberger ann. 1331.

tion on the accepted belief as to Christ's poverty, and the manner in which his resolute purpose had carried that dogma against all opposition. On this occasion he was the conservator of the previously received faith of the Church, but the political conjuncture was against him. Not only was Louis of Bavaria consolidating the empire in resistance to the aggressiveness of the papacy, but France, the main support of the Avignonese popes, was indisposed. Philippe de Valois had been offended by the rejection of his excessive demands in compensation of fulfilling his vows of a new crusade, and had been alienated by John's yielding to the schemes of John of Bohemia, who was endeavoring to secure the imperial territories in Italy. Both monarchs took active steps to turn to the fullest account the papal heresy. It was a received principle that, as a dead man was no longer a man, so a pope detected in heresy was no longer a pope, seeing that he had *ipso facto* forfeited his office. Nothing better could serve the purpose of Louis of Bavaria and his junto of exiled Franciscans. Under the advice of Michele da Cesena he took steps to call a German national council, for which Bonagrazia drew up a summons based upon the papal heresy, and the plan was approved by Cardinal Orsini and his dissatisfied brethren. This came to nought, however, through the still greater promptness of Philippe de Valois to avail himself of the situation. He made the celebrated William Durand, Bishop of Mende, write a treatise in opposition to the papal views, and protected him when John sought to punish him. He assembled the University of Paris, which, January 3, 1333, pronounced emphatically in favor of the Beatific Vision, and addressed to the pope a letter asserting it without equivocation. Gerard Odo, the time-serving Franciscan General, was despatched, ostensibly to make peace between England and Scotland, but instructed to dally in Paris and endeavor to win over public opinion. He ventured to preach in favor of John's conservative views, but only succeeded in arousing a storm before which he was forced to bow and humbly to declare that his argument was only controversial and not assertive. Philippe took the boldest and most aggressive position. He wrote to John that to deny the Beatific Vision was not only to destroy belief in the intercession of the Virgin and saints, but to invalidate all the pardons and indulgences granted by the Church, and so firmly was

III.—38

he convinced of its truth that he would take steps to burn all who denied it, including the pope himself. Even Robert of Naples joined in remonstrance. Haughty and obstinate as John had proved himself, he could not resist single-handed the indignation of all Europe, and he yielded. He purchased peace by political concessions, and wrote humbly to Philippe and Robert that he had never positively denied the Beatific Vision, but had treated it simply as an open question, subject to discussion. Even this was not enough. All his ambitious schemes had broken down. In Germany, Louis of Bavaria was posing as the defender of the faith. In France, even the weak Philippe de Valois had resumed his ascendency over Avignon. In Italy, John's son, Cardinal Bertrand, had been forced to fly, and Lombardy had freed itself. For the wretched old man there was nothing left but to recant and die. He had convoked a consistory for December 2, 1234, to choose a successor to Louis of Bavaria, but before daybreak he was seized with a fatal flux which stretched him hopeless on his bed. Towards evening of the next day he assembled the cardinals and exhorted them to select a worthy successor to the chair of St. Peter, when his kindred urged him to save his soul and the reputation of the Church by withdrawing from his opinions as to the Beatific Vision. The secrets of that awful death-bed have never been revealed, but after he passed away on the 5th, a bull was promulgated over his name in which he professed his belief as to the Divine Vision, and, if he had in that or anything else held opinions in conflict with those of the Church, he revoked all that he might have said or done, and submitted himself to its judgment. Humiliating as was this, Michele da Cesena pronounced it insufficient, as he made no formal confession of error and recantation, whence it was to be inferred that he died a contumacious heretic. Even Paris was not satisfied, although conclusions were not expressed so openly.*

---

* W. Preger, Die Politik des Pabstes Johann XXII. pp. 14, 66, 69.—Alphons. de Spina Fortalic. Fidei Lib. II. Consid. xii.—Vitodurani Chron. (Eccard. Corp. Hist. I. 1806–7).—Martene Thesaur. I. 1383.—D'Argentré I. I. 316–17, 319–22.— Isambert, Anc. Loix Franç. IV. 387.—Guillel. Nangiac. Contin. ann. 1333.—Raynald. ann. 1334, No. 27, 37, etc.—Wadding. ann. 1334, No. 14.—Villani, XI. 19.— Baluz. et Mansi, III. 350.—Grandes Chroniques, ann. 1334 (V. 97).

Benedict XII., who was elected December 20, was a zealous defender of the faith who had manifested his determination to extirpate all forms of heresy when, as Bishop of Pamiers, he had personally conducted for years a very active episcopal Inquisition in co-operation with the labors of Jean de Beaune and Bernard Gui. Such a man was not likely to underrate the importance of his predecessor's error, and in fact he lost no time in correcting it. On the 22d a significant threat to Gerard Odo to beware, for he would tolerate no heresy, was a notice to all who had yielded to John's imperiousness. On February 2, 1335, he preached a sermon on the text, "Behold, the bridegroom cometh," in which he clearly enunciated the doctrine that the saints have a distinct vision of the Divine Essence. Two days later he summoned before the consistory all who had given in their adhesion to the opinion of John and demanded a statement of their motives, by way, we may presume, of admitting them back into the fold as easily as possible. A twelvemonth later, January 29, 1336, he held a public consistory in which he published decisively that the saints enjoy the Beatific Vision, and decreed that all holding the contrary opinion should be punished as heretics. Benedict had earned the reputation of a ruthless upholder of orthodoxy and persecutor of dissent, and no victims were necessary to enforce the reception of the new article of faith. So thoroughly was it received that it passed into the formulas of the Inquisition as one of the points on which all suspected heretics were interrogated; and when, at the Council of Florence, in 1439, a nominal union was patched up with the Greek Church, one of the articles enunciated for the acceptance of the latter asserts that souls which after baptism incur no sin, or after sinning have been duly purged, are received at once into heaven and enjoy the sight of the Triune God. Thus a new dogma was adopted by the Church in spite of the opposition of one of the most arbitrary and headstrong of the successors of St. Peter.*

---

* Molinier, Études sur quelques MSS. des Bibliothèques d'Italie, p. 116.— Chron. Glassberger ann. 1334.—Benedict. XII. Vit. Tert. ann. 1335–6 (Muratori S. R. I. III. II. 539–41).—Ejusd. Vit. Prim. ann. 1338 (Ibid. p. 534).—Eymeric. p. 421.—Concil. Florent. ann. 1439 P. II. Union. Decret. (Harduin. IX. 986).

A remark of Æneas Sylvius in 1453 shows that, notwithstanding these au-

An even more instructive instance of the development of theological doctrine is to be found in the history of the dogma of the Immaculate Conception of the Virgin.   Up to the twelfth century it was not questioned that the Virgin was conceived and born in sin, and doctors like St. Anselm found their only difficulty in explaining how Christ could be born sinless from a sinner.   With the growth of Mariolatry, however, there came a popular tendency to regard the Virgin as free from all human corruption, and towards the middle of the twelfth century the church of Lyons ventured to place on the calendar a new feast in honor of the Conception of the Virgin, arguing that as the Nativity was feasted as holy, the Conception, which was a condition precedent to the Nativity, was likewise holy and to be celebrated.   St. Bernard, the great conservative of his day, at once set himself to suppress the new doctrine.   He wrote earnestly to the canons of Lyons, showing them that their argument applied equally to the nativity and conception of all the ancestors of the Virgin by the male and female lines ; he begged them to introduce no novelties in the Church, but to hold with the Fathers ; he argued that the only immaculate conception was that of Christ, who was conceived of the Holy Ghost, and proved that Mary, who was sprung of the union between man and woman, must necessarily have been conceived in original sin.   He admitted that she was born sanctified, whence the Church properly celebrated the Nativity, but this sanctification was operated in the womb of St. Anne, even as the Lord had said to Jeremiah, "Before thou camest out of the womb I sanctified thee" (Jer. i. 5).   It illustrates the recklessness of theological controversy to find St. Bernard subsequently quoted as sustaining the Immaculate Conception.   Peter Lombard, the great Master of Sentences, was not willing to concede even as much as St. Bernard, and quotes John of Damascus to show that the Virgin was not cleansed of original sin until she accepted the duty of bearing Christ.   To this view of the question Innocent III. lent the authority of his great name by asserting it in the most positive manner.[*]

thoritative definitions, the old belief still lingered that the glory of the saints was postponed till the Day of Judgment (Opp. inedd.—Atti della Accad. dei Lincei, 1883, p. 567).

   [*] S. Anselmi Cur Deus Homo Lib. ii. c. xvi.; Ejusd. Lib. de Conceptu Virginali.

These irresistible authorities settled the question for a while as one of dogma, but the notion had attractiveness to the people, and in the constant development of Mariolatry anything which tended to strengthen her position as a subordinate deity and intercessor found favor with the extensive class to whom her cult was a source of revenue. There is something inexpressibly attractive in the mediæval conception of the Virgin, and the extension of her worship was inevitable. God was a being too infinitely high and awful to be approached; the Holy Ghost was an abstraction not to be grasped by the vulgar mind; Christ, in spite of his infinite love and self-sacrifice, was invoked too often as a judge and persecutor to be regarded as wholly merciful; but the Virgin was the embodiment of unalloyed maternal tenderness, whose sufferings for her divine Son had only rendered her more eagerly beneficent in her desire to aid and save the race for which he had died. She was human, yet divine; in her humanity she shared the feelings of her kind, and whatever exalted her divinity rendered her more helpful, without withdrawing her from the sympathy of men. "The Virgin," says Peter of Blois, "is the sole mediator between man and Christ. We were sinners and feared to appeal to the Father, for he is terrible, but we have the Virgin, in whom there is nothing terrible, for in her is the plenitude of grace and the purity of human life;" and he goes on to virtually prove her divinity by showing that if the Son is consubstantial with the Father, the Virgin is consubstantial with the Son. In fact, he exclaims, "if Mary were taken from heaven there would be to mankind nothing but the blackness of darkness." God, says St. Bonaventura, could have made a greater earth and a greater heaven, but he exhausted his power in creating Mary. Yet Bonaventura, as a doctor of the Church, was careful to limit her sinlessness to sin arising with herself, and not to include the absence of inherited sin. She was sanctified, not immaculately conceived.*

—S. Bernardi Epist. 174, ad Canon. Lugdun. — D'Argentré I. ii. 60. — Pet. Lombardi Sententt. Lib. iii. Dist. iii. Q. 1. — Innoc. PP. III. Sermo xii. in Purif. S. Mariæ.

* Pet. Blesens. Sermo xii., xxxiii., xxxviii.—S. Bonavent. Speculi Beatæ Virginis c. i., ii., viii., ix.—The mediæval conception of the Virgin, as the intercessor

In spite of St. Bernard's remonstrance, the celebration of the Feast of the Conception gradually spread. Thomas Aquinas tells us that it was observed in many churches, though not in that of Rome, and that it was not forbidden, but he warns us against the inference that because a feast is holy therefore the conception of Mary was holy. In fact, he denies the possibility of her immaculate conception, though he admits her sanctification at some period which cannot be defined. This settled the question for the Dominicans, whose reverence for their Angelic Doctor rendered it impossible for them to swerve from his teachings. For a while, strange to say, the Franciscans agreed with their rivals. There is a tradition that Duns Scotus, in 1304, defended the new doctrine against the Dominicans in the University of Paris, and that in 1333 the University declared in its favor by a solemn decree, but this story only makes its appearance about 1480 in Bernardinus de Bustis, and there is no trace in the records of any such action, while Duns Scotus only said that it was possible to God, and that God alone knew the truth. There were few more zealous Franciscans than Alvaro Pelayo, penitentiary to John XXII., and he, in refuting the illuminism of the Beghards, makes use of the Virgin's conception in sin as an admitted fact which he employs as an argument; and he adds that this is the universal opinion of the received authorities, such as Bernard, Aquinas, Bonaventura, and Richard de Saint Victor, although some modern theologians, abandoning the teachings of the Church, have controverted it through a false devotion to the Virgin, whom they thus seek to assimilate to God and Christ. Yet as, about this very time, the Church of Narbonne commenced, in 1327, to celebrate the Feast of the Conception, and in 1328 the Council of London ordered its observance in all the churches of the Province of Canterbury, we see how rapidly the new dogma was spreading.*

---

between God and man and the source of all good, is expressed by Fazio degli Uberti—

"Tu sola mitigasti la discordia
Che fu tra Dio e l' uomo; e tu cagione
Sei d' ogni bene che quaggiù si esordia."

* Thom. Aquin. Summ. I. ii. Q. 81, Art. 4; III. Q. 14, Art. 4, Q. 27. — D'Argentré I. I. 275. — Alvar. Pelag. de Planctu Eccles. Lib. II. Art. 52. — Chron. de Saint-

As it was impossible for the Dominicans to change their position, it was inevitable that in time the Franciscans should range themselves under the opposite banner. The clash between them first came in 1387, when the struggle was carried on with all the ferocity of the *odium theologicum.* Juan de Monçon, a Dominican professor in the University of Paris, taught that the Virgin was conceived in sin. This aroused great uproar, and he fled to Avignon from impending condemnation. Then, at Rouen, another Dominican preached similar doctrine, and, as we are told, was generally ridiculed. The University sent to Avignon a deputation headed by Pierre d'Ailly, who claimed that they procured the condemnation of Juan, but he escaped to his native Aragon, while the Dominicans of Paris declared that the papal decision had been in their favor. If the chronicler is to be believed, they preached on the conception of the Virgin in the grossest terms and indulged in the most bestial descriptions, till the fury of the University knew no bounds. The Dominicans were expelled from all positions in the Sorbonne, and the Avignonese Clement VII. was too dependent upon France to refuse a bull proclaiming as heretics Juan and all who held with him. Charles VI. was persuaded not only to force the Dominicans of Paris to celebrate every year the Feast of the Conception, but to order the arrest of all within the kingdom who denied the Immaculate Conception, that they might be brought to Paris and obliged to recant before the University. It was not until 1403 that the Dominicans were readmitted to the Sorbonne, to the disgust of the other Mendicants, who had greatly profited by their exile. It was natural that where the Dominicans had authority they should indulge in reprisals. The Lullists were ardent defenders of the Immaculate Conception, which accounts in part for the hostility which they incurred.*

Just (Vaissette, Éd. Privat, VIII. 225).—Concil. Londin. ann. 1328 c. 2 (Harduin. VII. 1538).

The epitaph of Duns Scotus gives him the credit of defending the Immaculate Conception.

> " Concepta est virgo primi sine labe parentis
> Hic tulit—"   (Mosheim de Beghardis, p. 234.)

* Religieux de S. Denis, Hist. de Charles VI. vii. 5 ; viii. 2, 14 ; xxiii. 5.—Pelayo, Heterodoxos Españoles, I. 536.

The University of Paris was the stronghold of the new doctrine, and as its activity and influence were greatly curtailed by the disturbances which preceded the invasion of Henry V. and by the English domination, we hear little of the question until the restoration of the French monarchy. The belief, however, had continued to spread. In 1438 the clergy and magistrates of Madrid, on the occasion of a pestilence, made a vow thereafter to observe the Feast of the Conception. The next year the Council of Basle, which had long been discussing the matter in a desultory fashion, came to a decision in favor of the Immaculate Conception, forbade all assertions to the contrary, and ordered the feast to be everywhere celebrated on December 8, with due indulgences for attendance. As the council, however, had previously deposed Eugenius IV., its utterances were not received as the inspiration of the Holy Ghost, and the doctrine, though strengthened, was not accepted by the Church. In fact, the rival Council of Florence, in 1441, in its decree of union with the Jacobines, although it spoke of Christ assuming his humanity in the immaculate womb of the Virgin, showed that this was but a figure of speech, by declaring as a point of faith that no one born of man and woman has ever escaped the domination of Satan except through the merits of Christ.*

A new article could not be introduced without creating a new heresy. Here was one on which the Church was divided, and the adherents on each side denounced the other as heretics and persecuted them as far as they dared where they had the power. In this the Dominicans were decidedly at a disadvantage, as their antagonists had greatly the preponderance and were daily growing in strength. In 1457 the Council of Avignon, presided over by a papal legate, the Cardinal de Foix, who was a Franciscan, confirmed the decree of Basle, and ordered under pain of excommunication that no one should teach to the contrary. The same year the University of Paris was informed that a Dominican in Britanny was preaching the old doctrine. Immediately it held an assembly, wrote to the Duke of Britanny asking that the friar, if

* Wadding. Addit. ad T. V. No. 16 (T. VII. p. 491); ann. 1439, No. 47-8.—Concil. Basil. Sess. xxxvi. (Harduin. IX. 1160).—Concil. Florent. Decr. pro Jacobinis (Harduin. IX. 1024-5).

guilty, should be punished as a heretic, and declared its intention of formulating an article on the dogma.*

Thus far the popes had skilfully eluded compromising themselves on the subject. In the quarrels between the Mendicant Orders they could not afford to alienate either, and we have seen how, in the wrangle over the blood of Christ, they avoided entanglements and managed to let the dispute die out. The present debate was far too bitter and too extended for them to escape being drawn in, and they endeavored to follow the same line of policy as before. In 1474 Vincenzo Bandello, a Dominican, who was subsequently general of the Order, provoked a fierce discussion on the subject in Lombardy by a book on the Conception. The strife continued for two years with so many scandals that in 1477 Sixtus IV. evoked the matter before him, when it was hotly debated by Bandello for the Dominicans, or "*Maculistæ*," and Francesco, General of the Franciscans, in defence of the Immaculate Conception. The only result seems to have been that Sixtus issued a bull ordering the Feast of the Conception to be celebrated in all the churches, with the grant of appropriate indulgences. This was a decided defeat for the Dominicans, who found it excessively galling to celebrate the feast, and thus admit before the people that they were wrong. They endeavored to elude it in some places by qualifying it as the Feast of the Sanctification of the Virgin, but this was not permitted, and they were forced to submit. In 1481, at Mantua, Frà Bernardino da Feltre was formally accused of heresy before the episcopal court for preaching the Immaculate Conception, but defended himself successfully; and the next year, at Ferrara, the Franciscans and Dominicans preached so fiercely on the subject, and denounced each other as heretics so bitterly, that popular tumults were excited. To quiet matters Ercole d'Este caused a disputation to be held before him, which proved fruitless, and Sixtus IV. was again obliged to intervene. After listening to both sides he issued another bull, in which he excommunicated all who asserted that the feast was in honor of the Sanctification of the Virgin, and also all who on either side should denounce the other as heretics.†

---

* Concil. Avenionens. ann. 1457 (Harduin. IX. 1388).—D'Argentré I. ii. 252.

† Wadding. ann. 1477, No. 1; ann. 1479, No. 17-18.—C. 1, 2, Extrav. Commun. III. xii.

As a means of evading a decision without exasperating either Order this policy was successful, but as a measure of peace it was an utter failure. Renewed disturbances forced Alexander VI. to confirm the bull of Sixtus IV., with a clause calling upon the secular arm to keep the peace, if necessary ; but in France the University of Paris wholly disregarded the prescriptions of both popes and treated as heretics all who denied the Immaculate Conception. In 1495, on the Feast of the Conception, December 8, a Franciscan named Jean Grillot so far forgot his fealty to his Order as to deny the dogma in preaching in Saint-Germain l'Auxerrois. He was immediately laid hold of and so energetically handled that by the 25th of the same month he made public recantation in the same church. This put the University on its mettle, and on March 3, 1496, it adopted a statute, signed by a hundred and twelve doctors in theology, affirming the doctrine and ordering that in future no one should be admitted into its body without taking an oath to maintain it, when if he proved recreant he should be expelled, degraded from all honors, and treated as a heathen and a publican. This example was followed by the Universities of Cologne, Tübingen, Mainz, and other places, arraying nearly all the learned bodies against the Dominicans, and training the vast majority of future theologians in the doctrine. Most of the cardinals and prelates everywhere gave in their adhesion ; kings and princes joined them ; the Carmelites took the same side, and the Dominicans were left almost alone to fight the unequal battle. When in 1501, at Heidelberg, the Dominicans offered a disputation on the subject which the Franciscans eagerly accepted, the aspect of public opinion grew so threatening that they were obliged to get the palsgrave and magistrates to forbid it.*

So sensitive did the supporters of the Immaculate Conception become that a Dominican preaching on December 8 had needs be wary in the allusions to the Virgin which were unavoidable on that day of his humiliation. At Dieppe, on the feast of 1496, Jean de Ver, a Dominican, made use of expressions which were thought to oppose the dogma indirectly ; he was at once brought to account and forced to confess publicly, and swear that in future

---

* D'Argentré I. II. 331-5, 342-3.—Trithem. Chron. Hirsaug. ann. 1498.—Wadding. ann. 1500, No. 29.—Chron. Glassberger ann. 1501.

he would uphold it. On the next anniversary Frère Jean Aloutier argued that the Virgin had never sinned even venially, although St. John Chrysostom said that she had done so out of vain-glory on her wedding-day. This was regarded as a covert attack, and Frère Jean was disciplined, though not publicly. Soon afterwards another Dominican, Jean Morselle, in a sermon, said it was a problem whether Eve or the Virgin was the fairer; it was apocryphal whether Christ went to meet the Virgin when she was raised to paradise; and that it was not an article of faith that she was assumed to heaven, body and soul, and that to doubt it was not mortal sin. All this sounds innocent enough as to matters incapable of positive assertion, but Frère Jean was compelled publicly to declare the first article to be suspect of heresy, the second to be false, and the third to be heretical. It is only this hyperæsthesia of doctrinal sensibility that will explain the rigorous measures taken with Piero da Lucca, a canon of St. Augustin, who, in 1504, at Mantua, in a sermon, said that Christ was not conceived in the womb of the Virgin, but in her heart, of three drops of her purest blood. At once he was seized by the Inquisition, condemned as a heretic, and came near being burned. A controversy arose which greatly scandalized the faithful. Baptista of Mantua wrote a book to prove the true place of Christ's conception. Julius II. evoked the matter to Rome and committed it to the cardinals of Porto and San Vitale, who called together an assembly of learned theologians. After due deliberation, in 1511 these condemned the new theory as heretical, and the purity of the faith was preserved.*

The position of the Dominicans was growing desperate. Christendom was uniting against them. Only the steady refusal of the papacy to pronounce definitely on the question saved them from the adoption of a new article of faith which Aquinas had proved to be false. Aquinas was their tower of strength, whom the received tradition of the Order held to be inspired. It never occurred to them, as to his modern commentators, to prove that he did not mean what he said, and, in default of this, to yield on the point of the Immaculate Conception was to admit his fallibility.

---

* Trithem. Chron. Hirsaug. ann. 1497.—D'Argentré I. II. 336–40, 347.—Ripoll IV. 267.–Bernardi Comens. Lucerna Inquis. s. v. *Hæresis*, No. 23.

The alternative was a cruel one, but they had no choice. They could only hope to secure the neutrality of the papacy and to prolong the hopeless fight against the growing strength of the new doctrine, which their banded enemies propagated with all the enthusiasm of approaching victory. The perplexity of the position was all the more keenly felt, as they claimed the Virgin as the peculiar patroness of their Order; the devotion of the Rosary, in her special honor, was a purely Dominican institution. They who had always worshipped her with the most extravagant devotion were forced to become her apparent detractors, and were everywhere stigmatized as "*maculistæ*." Would she not condescend to save her devotees from the cruel dilemma into which they had fallen?

Suddenly, in 1507, the rumor spread that in Berne the Virgin had interposed to save her servants. In a convent of Observantine Dominicans she had repeatedly appeared to a holy friar and revealed to him her vexation at the guilt of the Franciscans in teaching the Immaculate Conception. After conception she had been three hours in original sin before sanctification; the teaching of St. Thomas was true and divinely inspired; Alexander Hales, Duns Scotus, and many other Franciscans were in purgatory for asserting the contrary. Julius II. would settle the question and would institute in honor of the truth a greater feast than that of December 8. To help towards this consummation the Virgin gave the friar a cross tinged with her son's blood, three of the tears which he had shed over Jerusalem, the cloths in which he was wrapped in the flight to Egypt, and a vial of the blood which he had shed for man, together with a letter to Julius II. in which he was promised glory equal to that of St. Thomas Aquinas in return for what was expected of him, and this letter, duly authenticated by the seals of the Dominican priors of Berne, Basle, and Nürnberg, was sent to the pope. The reports of these divine appearances produced an immense sensation; countless multitudes assembled in the Dominican Church to look upon the friar thus favored, and he performed feats of fasting, prayer, and scourging, which increased the reputation for sanctity acquired by the visitations. After a trance he appeared with the stigmata of Christ; the church was arranged to enable him in his devotions to represent the various acts of the Passion, and an immense crowd looked on with awestruck admiration. Then an image of the Virgin wept, and it was explained that her grief arose from the disregard of her warnings of what would befall the city unless it ceased to receive a pension from France, unless it expelled the Franciscans, and unless it ceased to believe in the Immaculate Conception.

People flocked from all the region around, and the fame of the miraculous apparitions spread, when the magistrates of Berne were surprised by Letser, the favored recipient of the visitations, taking refuge with them, and begging protection from his superiors, who were torturing and endeavoring to poison him. An investigation developed the whole plot. Wigand Wirt, Master of the Observantine Dominicans, and professor of theology, had had, in 1501, a quarrel with a parish priest in Frankfort, in which they abused each other from their respective pulpits. In a sermon the priest thanked God that he did not belong to an Order which had slain the Emperor Henry VII. with a poisoned host, and which denied the Immaculate Conception. Wirt, who was present, shouted to him that he was a liar and a heretic. An uproar followed, in which the Order sustained Wirt and appealed to Julius II., who appointed a commission. The result was adverse to Wirt, who left Frankfort filled with wrath, and published a savage attack upon his adversaries, which the Archbishop of Mainz caused to be publicly burned, while all his suffragans prohibited its circulation. Greatly excited, the Dominicans, in a chapter held at Wimpffen, resolved to prove by miracle the falsity of the Immaculate Conception. Frankfort was at first selected as the theatre, but was abandoned through fear of the archbishop; then Nürnberg, but the number of learned men there was an obstacle; and Berne was finally chosen as a city populous and powerful, but simple and unlearned. The officials of the Dominican convent there, John Vetter the prior, Francis Ulchi the sub-prior, Stephen Bolshorst the lector, and Henry Steinecker the procurator, undertook to carry out the design, and selected as an instrument a tailor of Zurzach, John Letser, who had been recently admitted to the Order. To suit the taste of the age, it was proved on the trial that they had commenced by invoking the assistance of the devil and had signed compacts with him in their blood, but their own ingenuity was sufficient for what followed, though we are told that when they produced the stigmata on Letser they first rendered him insensible with a magic potion formed of blood from the navel of a new-born Jew and nineteen hairs from his eyelashes. The victim was carefully prepared by a series of apparitions, commencing with an ordinary ghost and ending with the Virgin. According to his own account he believed in the visions till one day entering Bolshorst's room suddenly he found him in female attire like that of the Virgin, preparing for making an appearance. By threats and promises he had been prevailed upon to continue the imposture a while longer, till, fearing for his life, he escaped and told his tale.

Letser was sent to the Bishop of Lausanne, who heard his story and authorized the magistrates of Berne to act. The four Dominicans were confined separately in chains, and envoys were sent to Rome, where, only after the greatest difficulty, they obtained audience of the pope. A papal commission was sent, but with insufficient powers, and prolonged delays were experienced in procuring another, but finally it came, having at its head Achilles afterwards Cardinal of San Sesto, one of the most learned jurists of the age. Torture was freely used on both Letser and the accused, and full confessions were obtained. These were so damaging that the commissioners desired to keep them secret even from the magistrates, and when the latter were dissatisfied it was determined that they should be shown to a select committee of eight under pledge of secrecy, and that, to satisfy the people, only certain articles sufficient to justify burning should be publicly read. These were four, viz., renouncing God, painting and reddening the host, falsely representing the weeping Virgin, and counterfeiting the stigmata. The four culprits were abandoned to the secular arm, and eight days afterwards, as Nicholas Glassberger piously hopes, they were sent to heaven through fire, for they were burned in a meadow beyond the Arar, their ashes being thrown into the river to prevent their being reverenced as relics—not without reason, for the Order promptly pronounced them to be martyrs. It is worthy of note that in the published sentence the Immaculate Conception was kept wholly out of sight. In the existing tension between the Mendicant Orders the papal representatives evidently deemed it wise to keep this question in the background. Paulus Langius tells us that the story made an immense sensation, and that the "*maculistæ*" endeavored in vain to suppress it, and circulated all manner of distorted and false accounts of it. Julius II., so far from obeying the visions of Letser, confirmed in 1511 the religious order of the Immaculate Conception founded at Toledo in 1484 by the zeal of Beatriz de Silva.*

Wigand Wirt did not wholly escape, though he does not seem to have been directly implicated in the fraud. The Observantine Franciscans prosecuted him before the Holy See for his savage tract against his adversaries. The case was heard by two successive commissions of cardinals, until, October 25, 1512, Wirt abandoned the defence and was sentenced to make the most humiliating of retractions. In public he revoked, abolished, repudiated, and extirpated his book as scandalous, insulting, defamatory, useless, and prejudicial; he confessed that in it he had injured theological doctrine and wounded the fraternal charity of many, including the venerable Franciscans, and the honor and fame of Conrad Henselin, Thomas Wolff, Sebastian Brandt, and Jacob of Schlettstadt (Wimpheling); and he declared his belief that those who upheld the doctrine of the Immaculate Conception did not err. Moreover, under penalty of perpetual imprisonment, he promised, within four months after November 1, to repeat his recantation publicly in Heidelberg, after giving three days' notice to the Franciscan convent there; he begged pardon of all whom he had injured, and he obligated himself to undergo perpetual imprisonment if he should in any way, directly or indirectly, repeat the offence. The Dominican general who took part in the sentence, commanded all priors and prelates of the Order to confine him for life, wherever he might be found, in case of non-fulfil-

---

* I have followed a contemporary account of this curious affair—"De Quatuor Hæresiarchis in civitate Bernensi nuper combustis, A.D. 1509," 4to, *sine nota* (Strassburg, 1509), attributed to Thomas Murner. It accords sufficiently with the briefer reports of Trithemius (Chron. Hirsaug. ann. 1509) and Sebastian Brandt (Pauli Langii Chron. Citicens. ann. 1509), and that of the Chron. Glassberger ann. 1501, 1506, 1507, 1509.—Garibay, Compendio Historial de España, Lib. xx. cap. 13.

The Bernese community was piously devoted to the Virgin. In 1489 a certain Nicholas Rotelfinger was inconsiderate enough to declare that she helped the wicked as well as the good. For this he was obliged to stand a whole day in an iron collar and to make oath that he would personally seek the pope and bring home a written absolution.—Valerius Anshelm, Berner-Chronik, Bern, 1884, I. 355.

ment of his pledges. In due course, on Ash-Wednesday, February 24, 1513, in the church of the Holy Spirit of Heidelberg, when the concourse of the faithful was greatest, Wirt appeared and repeated the humiliating retraction. So bitter was the trial that he could not repress an ejaculation that it was hard to endure. The Franciscans had a notary present who recorded officially the whole proceeding, which was forthwith printed and spread abroad so as to publish far and wide the degradation of the unlucky disputant.*

Despite the fate of the martyrs of Berne the Dominicans still held out gallantly against the constantly increasing preponderance of their antagonists. I have before me a little tract, evidently printed by a Dominican about this time as a manual for disputants, in which the opinions of two hundred and sixteen doctors of the Church are collected in proof of the conception of the Virgin in original sin. It presents a formidable array of all the greatest names in the Church, including many popes; and the compiler doubtless felt peculiar pleasure in grouping together the most revered authorities of the Franciscan Order—St. Antony of Padua, Alexander Hales, St. Bonaventura, Richard Middleton, Duns Scotus, William of Ockham, Nicholas de Lyra, Jacopone da Todi, Alvaro Pelayo, Bartolomeo di Pisa, and others. In spite of this preponderance of authority the Dominicans had a hard struggle in the Council of Trent, but they possessed strength enough, after a keen discussion, to have the question left open, with a simple confirmation of the temporizing bull of Sixtus IV. Still the controversy went on, as heated as ever, causing tumults and scandals, which the Church deplored but could not cure. In 1570 Paul IV. endeavored to suppress them by suppressing public discussion. He renewed the bull of Sixtus IV., pointed out that the Council of Trent permitted every one to enjoy his own opinion, and he allowed learned men to debate it in universities and chapters until it should be decided by the Holy See. All public disputation or assertion on either side in sermons or addresses was, however, forbidden under pain of *ipso facto* deprivation and perpetual disability. This endeavor to preserve the peace of the Church was as futile as its predecessors. In 1616 Paul V. deplored that, in spite of the salutary provisions existing on the subject, quarrels

---

* Revocatio fratris Vuygandi Vuirt (apud Trebotes, *sine anno*).

and scandals continued and threatened to grow more dangerous. He therefore added to the existing penalties perpetual disability for preaching or teaching, and ordered the bishops and inquisitors everywhere to punish severely all contraventions of these regulations. Yet the scale continued to incline against the Dominicans. A twelvemonth later, in August, 1617, Paul, in a general congregation of the Roman Inquisition, issued another constitution, in which he extended these penalties to all who in public should assert the Virgin to have been conceived in original sin. He did not reprove the opinion, but left it as before, and ordered those who asserted publicly the Immaculate Conception to do so simply, without assailing the other side, and, as before, bishops and inquisitors were instructed to punish all infractions. In 1622 Gregory XV. went a step further in suppressing the perpetual discord by a further extension of the penalties to all who in private asserted the Virgin's conception in sin; but at the same time he forbade the use of the word "immaculate" in the office of the Feast of the Conception. The Dominicans grew restive under this gagging, and in a couple of months procured a relaxation of the prohibition in so far as to allow them privately with each other to maintain and defend their opinion. These bulls brought considerable business to the Inquisition, for disputatious ardor could not be restrained. A contemporary manual informs us that in spite of the prohibition of discussion it still continued, and that offenders on both sides were sent to Rome for judgment by the supreme tribunal, care being taken, as far as possible, not to have Dominican witnesses when the offender was Franciscan, and *vice versa.* In spite of this the Dominican, Thomas Gage, who wandered through the Spanish colonies about 1630, speaks of holding public discussions on the subject in Guatemala, in which he maintained the Thomist doctrine against the Franciscan, Scotist, and Jesuit opinions.*

---

* De Beatæ Virginis Conceptione Ducentorum et sexdecim Doctorum vera, tuta, et tenenda Sententia (*sine nota, sed c.* 1500).—Concil. Trident. Sess. v. Decr. de Orig. Peccat. § 5.—Pauli PP. IV. Bull. *Super speculum* (Mag. Bull. Rom. II. 343).—Pauli PP. V. Bull. *Regis pacifici* (Ibid. p. 392).—Ejusd. Constit. *Sanctissimus* (Ib. p. 400).—Gregor. PP. XV. Constit. *Sanctissimus* (Ib. p. 477).—Ejusd. Bull. *Eximii* (Ib. p. 478).—Prattica del Modo da procedersi nelle Cause del S. Offitio, cap. xix. (MSS. Bib. Reg. Monachens. Cod. Ital. 598.— MSS. Bib. Nat., fonds italien, 139).—Gage, New Survey of the West Indies, London, 1677, p. 266.

So minutely was the question reasoned out that it became heresy to assert that one would undergo death in defence of the doctrine of the Immaculate Conception. In 1571 Alonso de Castro, although a Franciscan, uses this as an illustration that it is heretical thus to declare adhesion to a point which is not an article of faith. In the heated controversy everywhere raging ardent polemics showed their zeal by offering to stake their existence upon it, and the question became a practical one for the Inquisition to deal with. A vow or oath to defend the doctrine was declared to be valid, but in 1619 the inquisitors of Portugal, with the assent of Paul V., condemned as heretical the opinion that one who should die in defence of the Immaculate Conception would be a martyr. As the Inquisition was largely in Dominican hands, it doubtless was used .effectually to persecute the too zealous assertors of the doctrine, and to this probably is attributable the rule that in all such cases the denunciation should be sent to the supreme Inquisition in Rome and its decision be awaited, thus tying the hands of the local inquisitors. From Carena's remarks, it is evident that these cases were not infrequent and that they gave much trouble.*

The Jesuits threw the immense weight of their influence in favor of the Immaculate Conception, and in time it became not

---

* Alph. de Castro de justa Hæret. Punitione Lib. I. c. viii. Dub. 4.—Carenæ Tract. de Modo procedendi Tit. XVII. § 9.

Yet in Spain the intense popular devotion to the Virgin rendered the Inquisition very sensitive in its reverence for her. In 1642 an inquisitor, Diego de Narbona, in his *Annales Tractatus Juris* alluded to an assertion of Clement of Alexandria (Stromata, Lib. VII.) that some persons believed that after the Nativity the Virgin was inspected by the midwife to prove her virginity. Although he condemned the statement as most indecent and dishonoring to the Virgin, his work was denounced to the Inquisition of Granada, which referred it to the Inquisitor-general. Narbona in vain endeavored to defend himself. It was shown that in the Index Expurgatorius of 1640 the passage of Clement, as well as those in all other authors alluding to it, had been ordered to be *borrado*, or expunged, so that the very memory of so scandalous a tale might be lost. Narbona alleged in his defence a passage in Padre Basilio Ponce de Leon, but the Inquisition showed that this had likewise been *borrado*, and, as every one who possessed a copy of a book containing a prohibited passage was bound to blot it out and render it illegible, he was culpable in not having done so.—MSS. Bibl. Bodleian. Arch S. 130.

uncommon among them, at least in certain places, to take the heretical vow to defend it with life and blood. In 1715 Muratori, under the cautious pseudonym of Lamindus Pritanius, published a book attacking this practice. This drew forth a reply, in 1729, from the Jesuit Francesco Burgi, which Muratori answered under the name of Antonius Lampridius. A lively controversy arose which lasted for a quarter of a century or more, and Muratori's second book was in 1765 placed on the Spanish Index. Benedict XIV., in his great work *De Beatificatione,* says that the Church inclines to the doctrine of the Immaculate Conception, but has not yet made it an article of faith, and he even leaves the question undecided whether one who dies in its defence is to be reckoned as a martyr. Yet when, in 1840, Bishop Peter A. Baines, the Apostolic Vicar in England, spoke inconsiderately on the subject in a pastoral letter, he was sharply reproved and obliged to sign a pledge that on the first fitting occasion he would publicly declare his adhesion to whatever the Holy See might define on the subject. The decision was not long in coming. In 1849 Pius IX. consulted all the bishops as to the expediency of proclaiming the Immaculate Conception as a dogma of the Church. Those of Italy, Spain, and Portugal, about four hundred and ninety in number, were almost unanimously in its favor, while many in other lands hesitated and deprecated such action. The latter were not heeded; December 8, 1854, Pius issued a solemn definition declaring it to be an article of faith, and thus, after a gallant struggle, protracted through five centuries with unyielding tenacity, the Dominicans were finally defeated, and could only console themselves with ingenious glosses on Thomas Aquinas to prove that he had never really denied the doctrine.*

It is interesting thus to trace the evolution of dogma, even though the result cannot be regarded as a finality. In the insatiable desire to define every secret of the invisible world every decision is only a stepping-stone to a new discussion. The next point is to ascertain how the Immaculate Conception took place, and this has already been mooted. In 1876 a condemnation was pronounced on Joseph de Félicité (Vercruysse?) among whose

---

* Reusch, Der Index der verbotenen Bücher, II. 843, 986.—Addis and Arnold's Catholic Dictionary s. v. *Immaculate.*

errors was the assertion that Mary was conceived by the operation of the Holy Ghost, without the intervention of St. Joachim.*
Yet who can say that in the centuries to come this dogma may
not also win its place, and the Virgin thus be elevated to an
equality with her Son?

One function of the Inquisition remains to be considered—the
censorship of the press—although its full activity in this direction
belongs to a period beyond our present limits. We have seen
how Bernard Gui burned Talmuds by the wagon-load, and the
special training of the inquisitors would seem to point them out
as the most available conservators of the faith from the dangerous
abuse of the pen. Yet it was long before any definite system was
adopted. The universities were almost the only centres of intellectual activity, and they usually exercised a watchful care over
the aberrations of their members. When some work of importance was to be condemned the authority of the Holy See was
frequently invoked, as in the case of Erigena's *Periphyseos, the
Everlasting Gospel,* William of St. Amour's assault upon the Mendicants, and Marsilio of Padua's *Defensor Pacis.* On the other
hand, as we have seen, in 1316 the episcopal vicar of Tarragona
had no hesitation in assembling some monks and friars and condemning a number of Arnaldo de Vilanova's writings, and about
the same time the inquisitors of Bologna took similar action with
respect to Cecco d'Ascoli's commentary on the *Sphæra* of Sacrobosco. Yet no thought seems to have occurred of using the Inquisition for this purpose as a general agency with power of immediate decision, before Charles IV. endeavored to establish the Holy
Office in Germany. The heresy of the Brethren of the Free Spirit
was largely propagated by means of popular books of devotion;
to check this and the forbidden use by the laity of translations of
Scripture in the vernacular, the emperor, in 1369, empowered the
inquisitors and their successors to seize and burn all such books,
and to employ the customary inquisitorial censures to overcome
resistance. All the subjects of the empire, secular and clerical,
from the highest to the lowest, were ordered to lend their aid,
under pain of the imperial displeasure. In 1376 Gregory XI. fol-

---

* Reusch, op. cit. II. 989.

lowed this with a bull in which he deplored the dissemination of heretical books in Germany, and directed the inquisitors to examine all suspected writings, condemning those found to contain errors, after which it became an offence punishable by the Inquisition to copy, possess, buy, or sell them. No trace remains of any results of these regulations, but they are interesting as the first organized literary censorship. About the same period Eymerich was engaged in condemning the works of Raymond Lully, of Raymond of Tarraga, and others, but he seems always to have referred the matter to the Holy See and to have acted only under special papal authority. When, as we have seen, Archbishop Zbinco burned Wickliff's writings in Prague, a papal commission decided that his act was not justified, and their final condemnation was pronounced by the Council of Rome in 1413.*

With the gradual revival of letters books assumed more and more importance as a means of disseminating thought, and this increased rapidly after the invention of printing. It became a recognized rule with the Inquisition that he into whose hands an heretical book might fall and who did not burn it at once or deliver it within eight days to his bishop or inquisitor was held vehemently suspect of heresy. The translation of any part of Scripture into the vernacular was also forbidden. It was not, however, until 1501 that any organized censorship of the press seems to have been thought of, and even then Germany was the only land where the issue of dangerous and heretical books was considered to require it. All printers were ordered in future, under pain of excommunication and of fines applicable to the apostolic chamber, to present to the archbishop of the province or to his ordinary all books before publication, and only to issue those for which a license should be granted after examination, the prelates being commanded on their consciences to make no charge for such license. All existing books in stock, moreover, were to be subject to similar inspection, and of such as should be found to contain errors all copies accessible were to be delivered up for burning.†

It shows to what a state of contempt the German Inquisition

---

* Mosheim de Beghardis, pp. 368, 378.—Eymeric. pp. 311–16.

† Albertini Repertor. Inquis. s. vv. *Libri, Scriptura.*—Raynald. ann. 1501, No. 36.

had fallen, that in this comprehensive measure to restrict the license of the press it seems not to have been even thought of as an instrumentality, and that dependence was placed on the episcopal organization alone. The archbishops, however, were as usual too much engrossed in the temporal concerns of their princely provinces to pay attention to such details, and there is apparently no result to be traced from the effort. The evil continued to increase, and in 1515, at the Council of Lateran, Leo X. endeavored to check it by general regulations still more rigid in a bull which was unanimously approved, except by Alexis, Bishop of Amalfi, who said that he concurred in it as to new books, but not as to old ones. After an allusion to the benefits conferred by the art of printing, the bull proceeded to recite that numerous complaints reached the Holy See that printers in many places printed and sold books translated from the Greek, Hebrew, Arabic, and Chaldee, as well as in Latin and the vernaculars, containing errors in faith and pernicious dogmas, and also libels on persons of dignity, whence many scandals had arisen and more were threatened. Therefore forever thereafter no one should be allowed to print any book or writing without a previous examination, to be testified by manual subscription, by the papal vicar and master of the sacred palace in Rome, and in other cities and dioceses by the Inquisition, and the bishop or an expert appointed by him. For neglect of this the punishment was excommunication, the loss of the edition, which was to be burned, a fine of a hundred ducats to the fabric of St. Peters, and suspension from business for a year. Persistent contumacy was further threatened with such penalty as should serve as a warning deterrent to others.* The precaution came too late.

---

* Concil. Lateran. V. Sess. IX. (Harduin. IX. 1779–81).

These rules were probably enforced only where there was an Inquisition in working order. In the edition of Nifo's work, *De Cœlo et Mundo*, printed at Naples in 1517, there is an *imprimatur* by Antonio Caietano, prior of the Dominican convent, reciting the conciliar decree, and stating that in the absence of the inquisitor he had been deputed by the Vicar of Naples to examine the work, in which he found no evil.

In the Venice editions of Joachim of Flora, printed in 1516 and 1517, there is not only the permission of the inquisitor and of the Patriarch of Venice, but also that of the Council of Ten, showing that the press was subjected to no little impediment.

In the contemporaneous Lyons edition of Alvaro Pelayo's *De Planctu Ecclesiæ*

Except with regard to witches, the machinery of persecution was too thoroughly disorganized to curb the rising tide of human intelligence which speedily swept away all such flimsy barriers. We have seen how prolonged and unsatisfactory was the attempt to silence Reuchlin. The printing-press multiplied indefinitely the satires of Erasmus and Ulric Hutten, and when Luther appeared it scattered far and wide among the people his vigorous attacks on the existing system. It required time and the exigencies of the counter-reformation to perfect a plan by which, in the lands of the Roman obedience, the faithful could be preserved from the insidious poison flowing from the fountain of the printing-press.

(1517), however, there is no *imprimatur*, and evidently there was no censorship, and the same is the case in such German books of the period as I have had an opportunity of examining.

CHAPTER IX.

HAVING thus considered with some fulness what the Inquisition accomplished, directly and indirectly, it only remains for us to glance at what it did not do.

The relations of the Greek Church to the Holy See would almost justify the assumption that persecution of heresy, far from being a matter of conscience, was one of expediency, to be enforced or disregarded as the temporal interests of the papacy might dictate. The Greeks were not only schismatics, but heretics, for, as St. Raymond of Pennaforte proved, schism was heresy, as it violated the article of the creed "*unam sanctam Catholicam ecclesiam.*" We have repeatedly seen that to deny the supremacy of Rome and to disregard its commands was heresy. Boniface VIII., in the bull "*Unam sanctam*," proclaimed it to be an article of faith, necessary to salvation, that every human creature is subject to the Roman pontiff, and he especially includes the Greeks in this. Besides this, there was the Procession of the Holy Ghost from both the Father and the Son, in which Charlemagne forced Leo III. to modify the Nicene symbol, and which the Greeks persistently refused to receive, rendering them heretics on a doctrinal point assumed to be of the greatest importance. Yet the Church, when it seemed desirable, could always establish a *modus vivendi,* and exercise a prudent toleration towards the Greek Church. It was thus in southern Italy, which had been withdrawn from Rome and subjected to Constantinople in the eighth century by Leo the Isaurian during the iconoclastic controversy. In 968 the Patriarch of Constantinople substituted the Greek for the Roman rite in the churches of Apulia and Calabria, and though some resisted, most of them submitted and retained it even after the conquest of Naples by the Normans. Thus in the see of Rossano in 1092, when a Latin bishop was introduced, the people recalcitrated and obtained from Duke Roger permission to retain the Greek rite. This lasted until 1460, when the Observantine Bishop Matteo succeeded in changing it to the Latin rite.*

The Greek churches, which long continued to exist throughout the Slavic and Majjar territories, were subjected to greater pressure, though it was fitful and intermittent. In 1204 Andreas II. of Hungary applied to Innocent III. to appoint Latin priors for the Greek monasteries in his dominions. In the settlement of 1233, after the kingdom had been placed under interdict, an oath was exacted of Bela IV. that he would compel all his subjects to render obedience to the Roman Church, and Gregory IX. forthwith summoned him to enforce his promise with regard to the Wallachians, who were addicted to the Greek rite. In 1248 we find Innocent IV. sending Dominicans to Albania to convert the Greeks, and it would indicate that persuasion rather than force was relied upon, when we see these missionaries empowered to grant the ecclesiastics dispensation for all irregularities, including simony. A hundred years later Clement VI. and Innocent VI. were more energetic, and ordered the prelates of the Balkan Peninsula to drive out all schismatics, calling in the aid of the secular arm if necessary. We have already seen how fruitless were the efforts to exterminate the Cathari in these regions, and that the only result of the effort to enforce uniformity of faith was to facilitate the advance of the Turkish conquest.†

The possessions of the Crusaders in the Levant offered a more complex problem. Although Innocent III. had protested against the conquest of Constantinople in 1204, when it was successful he

---

* S. Raymondi Summ. I. vi. i.—i. Extrav. Commun. I. viii.—Lib. Carolin. iii. 1, 3.—Harduin. Concil. IV. 131, 453–4, 747, 775, 970.—Hartzheim Concil. German. I. 390–6.—Eymeric. p. 325.—Tocco, L'Eresia nel Medio Evo, pp. 389–90.—C. 9, 11, Extra, i. xi.

When Sigismund of Austria, in his quarrel with Nicholas of Cusa over the bishopric of Brixen, refused to observe the interdict cast on his territories, Pius II., in 1460, summoned him to trial within sixty days as a heretic, because his disobedience showed him to be notoriously guilty of that heresy of heresies, disbelief in the article of the Creed, "*Credo in unam sanctam Catholicam et Apostolicam ecclesiam*" (Freher et Struv. II. 192).

† Innoc. PP. III. Regest. vii. 47.—Batthyani Legg. Eccles. Hung. II. 355-6.— Ripoll I. 70–1, 186.—Wadding. ann. 1351, No. 8; ann. 1354, No. 4, 5.

was ardent in his recognition of the mysterious wisdom of God in thus overthrowing the Greek heresy, and he took prompt action to secure the utmost advantage to be expected from it. He ordered the crusaders to suspend all priests ordained by Greek bishops, and to provide Latin priests for the churches seized, taking care that their property was not dissipated. A hungry horde of clerics speedily precipitated itself on the new possessions, embarrassing those in charge, and Innocent, in answer to inquiries, advised that only those who brought commendatious letters should be allowed to officiate in public. Thus, in the Latin kingdoms of the East a new hierarchy was imposed upon the churches, but the people were not converted, and an embarrassing situation arose concerning which no clearly defined policy could be preserved.*

Strictly speaking, all schismatics and heretics were under *ipso facto* excommunication, but this could be disregarded if it was politic to do so, as when, in 1244, Innocent IV., in sending Dominican missionaries to the Greeks, Jacobines, Nestorians, and other heretics of the East, gave full authority to participate with them in all the offices of religion. Where the Greek churches were independent efforts were made to win them over by persuasion and negotiation, as in the mission sent in 1233 by Gregory IX. to Germanus, Patriarch of Nicæa, and in 1247 by Innocent IV. to the Russians; but when these endeavors failed there was no hesitation in resorting to force, and the disappointed Gregory preached a crusade for the purpose of reducing the schismatics to obedience. So, in 1267, when the measureless ambition of Charles of Anjou, inflamed by the conquest of Naples, dreamed of reconquering Constantinople, his treaty with the titular emperor, Baldwin II., recites the uniting of the Eastern Empire with the Church of Rome as the impelling motive. Charles's enterprise was postponed by the submission of Michael Palæologus at the Council of Lyons in 1274, but this only stirred up rebellion among his subjects; Michael Comnenus was placed at the head of the party sustaining the national church, and war broke out in 1279. Although Charles hastened to take advantage of this, the Sicilian Vespers, in 1283,

---

* Innoc. PP. III. Regest. VII. 2–12, 121, 152–4, 164, 203–5; IX. 243–6; X. 49–51.

gave him ample occupation at home, and his projects were, per-force, laid aside.*

In the territories subjected to Latin domination the conditions were somewhat different. It was impossible to uproot the native Church, and the two rites were necessarily permitted to coexist, with alternations of tolerance and persecution, of persuasion and coercion. In 1303 Benedict XI., when ordering the Dominican prior of Hungary to send missionaries to Albania and other prov-inces, speaks of the Latin churches and monasteries in a manner to show that the two rites were allowed side by side, and only intrusions of the Greeks were to be resisted. Documents which chance to have been preserved concerning the kingdom of Cyprus illustrate the perplexities of the situation and the varying policy pursued. In 1216 Innocent III. reduced the bishoprics of the island from fourteen to four—Nicosia, Famagosta, Limisso, and Baffo—and provided in each a Greek and Latin bishop for the respective rites, which was an admission of equality in orthodoxy. Forty years later we find the Greek monasteries subjected to the Latin Archbishop of Nicosia, and there seems to have been some ascendency claimed by the Latin prelates, for in 1250 the Greek archbishop petitioned Innocent IV. for permission to reconstitute the fourteen sees and consecrate bishops to fill them; that they should all be independent of the Archbishop of Nicosia, and that all Greeks and Syrians be subjected to them and not to the Latins. This prayer was rejected. Alexander IV. gave an express power of supervision to the Latin prelates, which naturally led to quar-rels, and at times the Greeks were treated as heretics by zealous churchmen and by those whose authority was set at nought, as we learn from some appeals to Boniface VIII. in 1295. John XXII. energetically endeavored to extirpate certain heresies and heretical practices of the Greeks, but seems to have allowed the regular observance of their rites. Yet about the same time Bernard Gui, in his collection of inquisitorial formulas, gives two forms of abjuration of the Greek errors and reconciliation from the ex-communication pronounced by the canons against the schismatic

---

* C. 35 Decr. P. ii. Caus. xxiv. Q. 9.—Berger, Registres a'Innoc. IV. No. 573, 1817.--Raynald. ann. 1233, No. 1-15.—Epistt. Sæculi XIII. T. I. No. 725 (Pertz). —Buchon, Recherches et Matériaux, pp. 31, 40-2.

Greeks, showing that the inquisitors of the West were accustomed to lay hold of any unlucky Greek who might be found in the Mediterranean ports of France. Their fate was doubtless the same in Aragon, for Eymerich does not hesitate to qualify them as heretics. The persecuting spirit grew, for about 1350 the Council of Nicosia, although it allowed the four Greek bishops of Cyprus to remain, still ordered all to be denounced as heretics who did not hold Rome to be the head of all churches and the pope to be the earthly vicar of Christ, and in 1351 a proclamation was issued ordering all Greeks to confess once a year to a Latin priest and to take the sacrament according to the Latin rite. If this was enforced, it must have provided the Inquisition with abundant victims, for in 1407 Gregory XII. defined that any Greek who reverted to schism after participating in orthodox sacraments was a relapsed, and he ordered the inquisitor Elias Petit to punish him as such, calling in if necessary the aid of the secular arm.*

The Venetians, when masters of Crete, endeavored to starve out the Greek Church by forbidding any bishop of that rite to enter the island, and any inhabitant to go to Constantinople for ordination. Yet, in 1373, Gregory XI. learned with grief that a bishop had succeeded in landing, and that ordination was constantly sought by Cretans in Constantinople. He appealed to the Doge, Andrea Contareni, to have the wholesome laws enforced, but to little purpose, for in 1375 he announced that nearly all the inhabitants were schismatics, and that nearly all the cures were in the hands of Greek priests, to whom he offered the alternative of immediate conversion or ejection.†

---

* Theiner Monument. Slavor. Meridional. I. 120.—Berger, Registres d'Innoc. IV. No. 2058, 4053, 4750, 4769.—Barb. de' Mironi, Hist. Eccles. di Vicenza II. 102.—Thomas, Registres de Boniface VIII. No. 613–4.—Raynald. ann. 1318, No. 57.—Ripoll II. 172, 482.—B. Guidon. Practica P. II. No. 9; P. v. No. 11.—Eymeric. p. 303.—Harduin. VII. 1700, 1709, 1720.

The relations between the races in the Levant were not such as to win over the Greeks. A writer of the middle of the thirteenth century, who was zealous for the reunion of the churches, repeatedly alludes to the repulsion caused by the tyranny and injustice of the Latins towards the Greeks. Even the lowest of the former treated the Greeks with contempt, pulling them by the beard and stigmatizing them as dogs.—Opusc. Tripartiti P. II. c. xi., xvii. (Fascic. Rer. Expetend. et Fugiend. II. 215, 216, 221).

† Raynald. ann. 1373, No. 18; ann. 1375, No. 25.

Efforts so spasmodic were of course unavailing. So far from suppressing the Greek Church it was found that many Catholics living in a schismatic population became perverts. To this, in 1449, Nicholas V. called the attention of the inquisitor of the Greek province, telling him that although the Oriental rite was praiseworthy, it must be kept distinct from the Latin, and that all such cases must be coerced, even if the assistance of the secular arm was necessary. There was scant encouragement for the Inquisition in those lands, however, for when, in 1490, Innocent VIII. appointed Frà Vincenzo de' Reboni as Inquisitor of Cyprus, where there were many heretics, and ordered the Bishops of Nicosia, Famagosta, and Baffo each to give him a prebend for his support, there was so energetic a remonstrance from the prelates that Innocent withdrew the demand. From all this it is evident that in its relations with the Greek Church Rome was governed by policy; that it could exercise toleration whenever the occasion demanded, and that the Inquisition was practically quiescent in its dealings with these heretic populations, although their heresy was of a dye so much deeper than that of many sectaries who were ruthlessly exterminated.*

During the Middle Ages there were few greater pests of society than the *quæstuarii*, or pardoners—the sellers of indulgences and pardons, who wandered over the face of Europe with relics and commissions, with brazen faces and stout lungs, vending exemptions from penance and purgatory, and prospective admission to paradise; telling all manner of lies, and at once disgracing the Church and impoverishing the credulous. Sometimes they were the authorized agents of Rome or of a bishop of a diocese; sometimes they farmed out a district for a fixed price or for a portion of the spoils; sometimes they merely bought from the curia or a local prelate the letters which authorized them to ply their trade.

---

* Raynald. ann. 1449, No. 10.—Ripoll IV. 72.

In 1718 the congregation of the Propaganda permitted the erection of a Greek episcopate in Calabria, to supply the spiritual needs of the Greek population. The Greeks in the Island of Sicily complained of the expense of sending their youths to Calabria or to Rome for ordination, and in 1784, at the instance of Ferdinand III., Pius VI. authorized the establishment of another Greek bishop in Palermo.—Gallo, Codice Ecclesiastico Siculo, IV. 47 (Palermo, 1852).

Tetzel, who stirred the indignation of Luther to rebellion, was only a representative of a horde of vagabonds who for centuries had fleeced the populations and had done all in their power to render religion contemptible in the eyes of thinking men. The Dominican Thomas of Cantimpré bitterly compares the trifling sums which purchased salvation from papal emissaries collecting funds for the Italian wars of the Holy See with the endless labors and austerities of his brethren and of the Franciscans—the sleepless vigils and the days spent in ministering to the spiritual needs of fellow-creatures, without obtaining assured pardon for their sins. The character of these peddlers of salvation is summed up in a tract presented to the Council of Lyons in 1274 by Umberto de' Romani, who had resigned the generalate of the Dominican Order in 1263. He declares that they expose the Church to derision by their lies and filthiness; they bribe the prelates and thus obtain what privileges they want; the frauds of their letters of pardon are almost incredible; they find a fruitful source of gain in false relics, and though they collect large sums from the people, but little inures to the ostensible objects for which the collections are made.*

These creatures were not to be reached by the ordinary jurisdiction, for they either bore papal commissions or those of the bishop of the diocese; their trade was too profitable to all parties to be suppressed, and the only way of curbing their worst excesses seemed through the Inquisition. Accordingly the Inquisition had hardly been fully organized when Alexander IV. had recourse to it for this purpose, and included in the powers conferred on inquisitors that of restraining the *quæstuarii* and of forbidding their

---

* Th. Cantimprat. Bonum Universale, Lib. II. c. 2.—Humb. de Roman. Tract. in Concil. Lugdun. P. III. c. 8. (Martene Ampl. Coll. VII. 197). Cf. Opusc. Tripart. P. III. c. viii. (Fascic. Rer. Expetend. et Fugiend. II. 227).

William Langland sets forth the popular appreciation of the *Quæstuarii* with sufficient distinctness—

> "Here preched a Pardonere as he a prest were,
> Broughte forth a bulle with bishopes seles,
> And seide that hym-selfe myghte asoilen hem alle
> Of falshed of fastyng of vowes ybroken.
> Lewed men leued hym well and lyked his wordes . . .
> . . . Were the bischop yblissed and worth bothe his eares
> His seel shulde not be sent to deceyue the peple."
>
> Piers Plowman, Prologue, 68–79.

preaching. This was repeated by successive popes; it came to be embodied in the canon law, and was customarily included in the enumeration of duties recited in the commissions issued to inquisitors. A tithe of the energy shown in hunting down Waldenses and Spirituals would have effectually suppressed the worst features of this shameful traffic, but that energy was wholly lacking. In all the annals of the Inquisition I have met with but a single case, occurring in 1289, when Berenger Pomilli was brought before the inquisitor Guillaume de Saint-Seine. He was a married clerk of Narbonne, who stated that for thirty years he had followed the trade of *quæstuarius* in the dioceses of Narbonne, Carcassonne, and elsewhere, collecting the alms of the pious for the building of churches, bridges, and other objects. He was wont to preach to the people during the celebration of mass, and confessed to telling the most outrageous lies—that the cross which Christ carried to the place of crucifixion was so heavy that it would be a burden for ten men; that when the Virgin stood at the foot of the cross it bent over so that she kissed the Saviour's hands and feet, after which it arose again, and many fables concerning purgatory and the liberation of souls—the latter, which were the real frauds of his trade, being prudently suppressed in the official report of his confession. A question as to his belief in these stories revealed to him his danger, for to admit it would have been to stamp himself a heretic. He humbly replied that he knew that he had been habitually uttering lies, but he told them to move the hearts of his hearers to liberality, and he at once begged to be penanced. What penance was awarded him does not appear.*

That trials of this sort were rare is evident from the complaint of the Council of Vienne, in 1311, that these vagabonds were in the habit of granting plenary indulgences to those who made donations to the churches which they represented, of dispensing from vows, of absolving for perjury, homicide, and other crimes, of relieving their benefactors from a portion of any penance assigned them, or the souls of their relations from purgatory, and granting immediate admission to paradise. All this was forbidden for the future, but the Inquisition was no longer relied upon to coerce the par-

---

* C. xi. § 2 Sexto v. ii.—Bern. Guidon. Practica P. v. (Ed. Douais, p. 199).—Eymeric. pp. 107, 564.—Coll. Doat, XXVI. 314.

doners to obedience; the bishops were ordered to take the matter in hand and punish the evil-doers. They proved as inefficient as might have been expected. The abuse continued until it became the proximate cause of the Reformation, after which the Council of Trent abolished the profession of pardoner, avowedly because it was the occasion of great scandal among the faithful, and that all efforts to reform it had proved useless.*

More important was the nonfeasance of the Inquisition with respect to simony. This was the corroding cancer of the Church throughout the whole of the Middle Ages—the source whence sprang almost all the evils with which she afflicted Christendom. From the highest to the lowest, from the pope to the humblest parish priest, the curse was universal. Those who had only the sacraments to sell made a trade of them. Those whose loftier position gave them command of benefices and preferment, of dispensations and of justice, had no shame in offering their wares in open market, and preferment thus obtained filled the Church with mercenary and rapacious men whose sole object was to swell their purses by extortion and to find enjoyment in ignoble vices. Berthold of Ratisbon, about the middle of the thirteenth century, preaches that simony is the worst of sins, worse than homicide, adultery, perjury, but it now so crazes men that they think through it to serve God.† Instinctively all eyes turned to the Holy See as the source and fountain of all these evils. A quaint popular satire, current in the thirteenth century, shows how keenly this was felt:

" Here beginneth the Gospel according to the silver Marks. In those days the pope said to the Romans: When the Son of Man shall come to the throne of our majesty, first say to him: Friend, why comest thou? And if he continue to knock, giving you nothing, ye shall cast him into outer darkness. And it came to pass that a certain poor clerk came to the court of the lord pope and cried out, saying: Have mercy on me, ye gate-keepers of the pope, for the hand of poverty hath touched me. I am poor and hungry, I pray you to help my misery. Then were they wroth and said: Friend, thy poverty perish with thee; get thee behind me Satan, for thou knowest not the odor of money. Verily, verily, I say unto thee that thou shalt not enter into the joy of thy Lord until thou hast given thy last farthing.

---

* 2 Clement. v. ix.—Concil. Senonens. ann. 1485, Art. II. c. 8 (D'Achery, I. 758). —C. Trident. Sess. xxi. De Reform. c. 9.

† Bertholdi a Ratispona Sermones, Monachii, 1882, p. 93.

" Then the poor man went away and sold his cloak and his coat and all that he had, and gave it to the cardinals and gate-keepers and chamberlains. But they said: What is this among so many? And they cast him beyond the gates, and he wept bitterly and could find nought to comfort him. Then came to the court a rich clerk, fat and broad and heavy, who in his wrath had slain a man. First he gave to the gate-keeper, then to the chamberlain, then to the cardinals; and they thought they were about to receive more. But the lord pope, hearing that the cardinals and servants had many gifts from the clerk, fell sick unto death. Then unto him the rich man sent an electuary of gold and silver, and straightway he was cured. Then the lord pope called unto him the cardinals and servants, and said unto them: Brethren, take heed that no one seduce you with empty words. I set you an example; even as I take, so shall ye take." *

Vainly the intrepid energy and inflexible will of Hildebrand in the eleventh century strove to extirpate the ineradicable curse. It only grew wider and deeper as the Church extended its powers and centralized them in the Holy See. Simony was recognized in the canon law as a heresy, punishable as heresy with perpetual seclusion, and as such was justiciable by the Inquisition. With that organization at the command of the Holy See the untiring energy which through so many generations pursued the Cathari and Waldenses could in time have cured this spreading ulcer and purified the Church, but the Inquisition was never instructed to

---

* Carmina Burana, Breslau, 1883, pp. 22-3.—This was a favorite theme with the poetasters of the time—

" Cardinales ut prædixi   Petrus foris, intus Nero,
     novo jure crucifixi   intus lupus, foris vero
     vendunt patrimoniam.   sicut agni ovium " (Ib. p. 18),

and this pervaded the whole Church—

" Veneunt altaria,
venit eucharistia
cum sit nugatoria
gratia venalis."—(Ib. p. 41).

The honest Franciscan, John of Winterthur, attributed all the evils which oppressed the Church to its venality—

"Ecclesiam nummus vilem fecit meretricem,
Nam pro mercede scortum dat se cupienti.
Nummus cuncta facit nil bene justitia,
Cunctis prostituens pro munere seque venalem,
Singula facta negat vel agit pro stipite solo;
Divino zelo nulla fere peragit."

Vitodurani Chron. ann. 1343.

prosecute simoniacs, and there is no trace in its records that it ever volunteered to do so. In fact, had any overzealous official attempted such uncalled-for work he would speedily have been brought to his senses, for simony was not only the direct source of profit to the curia in the sale of preferment, but indirectly so in the sale of dispensations to those who had incurred its disabilities. It seems almost a contradiction in terms to speak of the Holy See issuing dispensations for heresy, and yet this was habitual. Legates and nuncios, when despatched abroad, were empowered to gather a harvest among the faithful by issuing dispensations for all manner of disabilities and irregularities, and among these simony is conspicuously noted. This ceased when John XXII. systematized the sale of absolutions and drew everything to the papal penitentiary, when pardon for simony in a layman could be had for six grossi, in a cleric for seven, and in a monk for eight. It is easy to see why the Inquisition was not used to suppress a heresy so profitable in every aspect. Indeed, while under the canon law it was held to be a heresy, yet it was practically never treated as such. Guillaume Durand, in his *Speculum Juris*, written in 1271, gives formulas for the accusation, by private individuals, of simoniacal bishops and priests and monks, but neither he nor his numerous commentators make the slightest allusion to it as subject to the procedure against heresy.*

---

* C. 7, 20, 21 Decr. P. ii. Caus. 1, Q. 1.—Th. Aquin. Summ. Sec. Sec. Q. 100, Art. 1.—Gloss. Bernardi; Gloss. Hostiens. (Eymeric. pp. 138, 143, 165).—Eymeric. p. 318.—Berger, Registres d'Inn. IV. No. 2977, 3010, 4668, 4718.—Thomas, Reg. de Boniface VIII. No. 547, 554, 557-8, 644, 726, 747.—Taxæ Sac. Pœnitent. Ed. Friedrichs, p. 35; Ed. Gibbings, p. 3 (cf. Van Espen, Dissert. in Jus Canon. noviss. P. iii. p. 699).—Durandi Specul. Juris Lib. iv. Partic. iv. Rubr. *de Simonia.*

Clement IV. was exceptional in seeking to repress the acquisitiveness of the curia. When, in 1266, Jean de Courtenai was elected Archbishop of Reims, and encumbered his see with a debt of twelve thousand livres to pay the Sacred College, Clement promptly excommunicated him and summoned him to reveal the names of all who participated in the spoils. Yet Clement had no scruple in following the example of his predecessor, Urban IV., in the negotiations which resulted in the crusade of Charles of Anjou against Manfred. Simon, Cardinal of S. Cecilia, sent to France for the purpose, was furnished with special powers to dispense for defects of age or birth or other irregularities in the acquisition of benefices, for holding pluralities, and for marriage within the prohibited grades,

It would be impossible to exaggerate the corruption which from this cause interpenetrated every fibre of the Church, filling benefices with ignorant and worldly men, eager to wring from the unfortunates committed to their cure the sums with which they had bought the preferment. Stephen Palecz, in a sermon preached before the Council of Constance, declares that there is scarce a church in Christendom free from the stain of simony, owing to the desperate struggle of all kinds of men to obtain the honors, wealth, and luxury attending an ecclesiastical preferment, and resulting in the promotion of the ignorant, weak, and wicked, who could not find employment as shepherds or swineherds. So unblushing was the venality of the Holy See that dialecticians and jurists of high authority seriously argued that the pope could not commit simony. This is scarce surprising when popes were found who could do a sharp stroke of business, like Boniface IX. In want of money to pay his troopers and defray the cost of his vast buildings, he suddenly deposed nearly all the prelates who chanced to be at the papal court, and many absent ones, or he translated them to titular sees, and then sold to the highest bidder the places thus vacated. Many unlucky ones, who were unable to buy back their preferment, wandered around the court without bread to eat, and the confusion and discord caused in many provinces was indescribable. Theodore a Niem, to whom we are indebted for this fact, was himself a papal official for thirty-five years, and knew whereof he spoke when he compared the splendid liberality of the German prelates with the stingy avarice of the Italians, who gave nothing in charity, but bent their whole energies to enriching themselves and their families. But when they die, he says, the collectors of the apostolic camera seize the whole spoil, and through this depredation and rapine it would be impossible to exaggerate the destruction of the Italian cathedrals and monasteries, which are left almost tenantless. As for the camera itself, its officials have hard heads and stony bosoms, and hearts more impenetrable to mercy than steel itself. They are as pitiless to Christians as Turks or Tartars could be, stripping all newly pro-

and was instructed to distribute these favors so as to remove obstacles to the enterprise (Urbani PP. IV. Epistt. 32–35, 40, 64–5, 68; Clement. PP. IV. Epistt. 8, 19, 20, 41, 383.—*ap.* Martene Thesaur. II.).

moted prelates of everything. If the latter cannot pay their demands, forbearance for a time is sold at an immoderate price under terrible oaths, and if anything has been kept back for the expenses of the homeward journey it is extorted, so that whoever escapes from their clutches can truly say, *Cantabit vacuus coram latrone viator.* If you go there to pay a thousand florins and a single one is light, you are not allowed to depart till you have replaced it with a heavier one, or made good in silver twice the deficiency. And if, within a year, the promised sum is not paid, the bishop becomes a simple priest again, and the abbot a simple monk. Never satiated, the proper place of these officials is with the infernal furies, with the harpies, and with the unsatisfied Tantalus. Poggio, who was papal secretary for forty years, describes the applicants for preferment as worthy of these officials. They were idle, ignorant, sordid men, useless for all good purposes, who hung around the curia, clamoring for benefices or any other favor which they could get. Another papal official tells us that Boniface IX. filled the German sees with unfit and useless persons, for he who paid the most obtained the preferment. Many paid ten times more than it had cost their predecessors, for some archbishoprics fetched forty thousand florins, others sixty thousand, and others eighty thousand.*

---

* Von der Hardt, I. xvi. 841.—D'Argentré I. ii. 228.—Theod. a Niem de Schismate Lib. ii. c. xiv. ; Ejusd. Nemor. Unionis Tract. vi. c. 36, 37, 39.— Poggii Bracciol. Dialogus contra Hypocrisim.—Gobelini Personæ Cosmodrom. Æt. V. c. 85.

The question as to the possibility of a pope committing simony was long under discussion. At the Council of Lyons, in 1245, Guiard, Bishop of Cambrai, was asked by a cardinal if he believed it possible, when he rendered a most emphatic answer in the affirmative (Th. Cantimprat. Bonum Universale, Lib. ii. c. 2). Thomas Aquinas not only asserts it, but adds that the higher the position of the offender the greater the sin (Summ. Sec. Sec. Q. 100, Art. 1, No. 7). Yet the venality of the Holy See was too notorious for concealment, and arguments were framed to prove that the pope had a right to sell preferments, for which see the *Aureum Speculum Papæ*, P. ii. c. 1, written in 1404, under Boniface IX., and the laborious effort of William of Ockham to controvert the assertion. The ingenious methods of the curia to extract the last penny from applicants are described in P. i. c. v. of the Speculum. The author has no hesitation in pronouncing the curia to be in a state of damnation (Fascic. Rer. Expetend. et Fugiend. II. 63, 70, 81, 461). All who deplored the condition of the Church instinctively turned to the Holy See as the source of corruption and demoralization. Nothing can well

It was in vain that Gerson proved that the papal demand of first-fruits of preferments was simony. It was in vain that the councils of Constance and of Siena complained and protested, and that of Basle endeavored to frame reformatory regulations. Equally vain was the attempt of Charles VII. and the Emperor Albert II. in the Pragmatic Sanctions of 1438, against the protests of Eugenius IV., to declare the annates and first-fruits to be simony. The papal system was too strong for its grasp to be thrown off, and up to the time of the Reformation simony continued to be the all-pervading curse.*

In addition to this source of infection from above there was an equally potent cause of demoralization from below in the immunity enjoyed by the clergy from secular jurisdiction. Not only were the people scandalized by seeing clerical homicides and criminals of all sorts set free after the mockery of a trial in the ecclesiastical courts, but the impunity thus enjoyed drew into the ranks of the Church hosts of vile and worthless men, who sought in the tonsure security from justice.†

Under such a system it is easy to conceive the character of the prelates and priests with which the Church was everywhere afflicted.

---

be conceived more terrible than the account of it given about this time by Cardinal Matthew of Krokow in his tract *De Squaloribus Romanæ Curiæ* (Ib. II. 584–607).

* Gersoni Tract. de Symonia.—D'Argentré I. II. 234.—Goldast. Constit. Imp. I. 402.

In *La déploration de l'Église militante* of Jean Boucher, in 1512, simony is described as the chief source of trouble—

> "Ceste sixte gloute et insatiable
> Du sanctuaire elle a fait ung estable,
> Et de mes loys coustume abhominable.
> Ha, ha, mauldicte et fausse symonie !
> Tu ne cessas jamais de m'infester . . . .
> Pour ung courtault on baille ung bénéfice ;
> Pour ung baiser ou aultre malefice
> Quelque champis aura ung evesché ;
> Pour cent escus quelque meschant novice,
> Plein de luxure et de tout aultre vice,
> De dignitez sera tout empesché."

(Bull. de la Soc. de l'Hist. du Prot. Français, 1856, pp. 268–9).

† Vaissette, Éd. Privat, X. Pr. 242, 254.—See the author's "Studies in Church History," 2 Ed. pp. 210 sqq.

Making some allowance for rhetorical enthusiasm, the invective of
Nicholas de Clemangis must be received as true.   As for the bishops, he says, as they have to spend all the money they can raise
to obtain their sees, they devote themselves exclusively to extortion, neglecting wholly their pastoral duties and the spiritual welfare of their flocks ; and if, by chance, one of them happens to
pay attention to such subjects, he is despised as unworthy of his
order.   Preaching is regarded as disgraceful.   All preferment and
all sacerdotal functions are sold, as well as every episcopal ministration, laying on of hands, confession, absolution, dispensation ;
and this is openly defended, as they say they have not received
gratis, and are not bound to give gratis.   The only benefices bestowed without payment are to their bastards and jugglers.   Their
jurisdiction is turned equally to account.   The greatest criminals
can purchase pardon, while their proctors trump up charges against
innocent rustics which have to be compounded.   Citations under
excommunication, delays and repeated citations, are employed,
until the most obstinate is worn out and forced to settle, with
enormous charges added to the original trifling fine.   Men prefer
to live under the most cruel tyrants rather than undergo the judgments of the bishops.   Absenteeism is the rule.   Many of the
bishops never see their dioceses ; and these are more useful than
those who reside, for the latter contaminate their people by their
evil example.   As no examination is made into the lives of aspir-
ants to the priesthood, but only as to their ability to pay the stip-
ulated price, the Church is filled with ignorant and immoral men.
Few are able to read.   They haunt the taverns and brothels, consuming time and substance in eating, drinking, and gambling ;
they quarrel, fight, and blaspheme, and hasten to the altar from
the embraces of their concubines.   Canons are no better ; since,
for the most part, they have bought exemption from episcopal
jurisdiction, they commit all sorts of crimes and scandals with
impunity.   As for monks, they specially avoid all to which their
vows oblige them—chastity, poverty, and obedience—and are licentious and undisciplined vagabonds.   The Mendicants, who pretend to make amends for the neglect of duty by the secular clergy, are pharisees and wolves in sheep's clothing.   With incredible
eagerness and infinite deceit they seek everywhere for temporal
gain ; they abandon themselves beyond all other men to the pleas-

ures of the flesh, feasting and drinking, and polluting all things with their burning lusts. As for the nuns, modesty forbids the description of the nunneries, which are mere brothels, so that to take the veil is equivalent to becoming a public prostitute.[*]

We might suspect this to be the exaggeration of a soured ascetic if it were not for the unanimous testimony of all who describe the condition of the Church from the thirteenth century on. When St. Bonaventura defended the Mendicants against the charge of assailing, in their sermons, the vices of the secular clergy, he denied their doing so for the reason that any such arraignment would be superfluous; and, moreover, that if they were to unveil the full turpitude of the clerical class these would all be expelled, and there would be no hope of seeing their places more worthily filled, for the bishops would not select virtuous men. To do so, moreover, would deprive the people of all faith in the Church, and heresy would become uncontrollable. In another tract he declares that almost all priests were legally incapable of performing their functions, either through the simony attendant on their ordination or through the commission of crimes entailing suspension and deprivation. It was not infrequent, he says, for priests to persuade women that there was no sin in intercourse with a clerk.[†]

In 1305 Frederic of Trinacria, in a confidential letter to his brother, Jayme II. of Aragon, says that he has been led to doubt whether the Gospel was divine revelation or human invention, for three reasons. The first is the character of the secular clergy, especially of the bishops, abbots, and other prelates, who are destitute of all spiritual life, and are pestiferous in their influence through the public display of their wickedness. The second reason is the character of the regular clergy, and especially of the Mendicants, whose morals and lives stupefy all observers; the are so alienated from God that they justify the seculars and the laity by the comparison; their wickedness is so notorious that he fears that some day the people will rise against them, for they bring infection into every house which they frequent. The third

---

[*] Nic. de Clemangis de Ruina Ecclesiæ, cap. xix.–xxxvi.

[†] S. Bonaventuræ Libell. Apologet. Quæst i.; Tractatus quare Fr. Minores prædicent.

reason is the negligence of the Holy See, which of old, as we are told, used to send legates through the kingdoms to look after the condition of religion; but now this is never done, and they are sent only for worldly objects. We see, he says, that it labors without ceasing to slay schismatics, but we never see it solicitous to convert them. The eloquence of Arnaldo de Vilanova was required to persuade Frederic that all this was compatible with the truth of Christianity, and he undertook to introduce a reformation in his own kingdom, commencing with himself.*

Marsiglio of Padua may be a suspected witness when he assumes, as a universally recognized fact, the corruption of the mass of ecclesiastics. They despoiled the poor, they were insatiable in their greed, and what they wrung from their flocks was wasted in debauchery. Boys, unlettered men, unknown persons, were promoted to benefices, and the bishops, by their example, carried to destruction more souls than they saved by their teaching. But his contemporary, Alvaro Pelayo, the Franciscan penitentiary of John XXII., is beyond suspicion, and he describes the Church of his time as completely secularized. There is no act of secular life in which priests and monks are not busy. As for the prelates, he can only compare them to the fabled Lamia, with a human head and the body of a beast—a monstrous fury which tears its own offspring to pieces and destroys all within its reach. The prelates, he says, give no teaching to their people, but flay and rend them. The bread due to the poor is lavished on jesters and dogs. Faith and justice have abandoned the earth; there is no humanity or kindness; the voracious flame of wrath and envy destroys the Church and skins the poor with fraud and simony. Scripture and the canons are regarded as fables. Through the iniquity of the priests and prelates the evils gather, for they publicly pervert the law, they render false judgments, they add blood to blood, for many perish through their frauds and machinations. They gloss and declare the law as they choose. The doctors and prelates and priests shed the blood of the just. They take the broad path that leads to destruction, and will not enter, nor permit others to enter, the narrow way that conducts to eternal life. This description is fully borne out by a letter of Benedict XII. to

---

* Pelayo, Heterodoxos Españoles, I. 721-3, 735-6.

the Archbishop of Narbonne, describing the utter demoralization of the clergy of his province, so lately purified of heresy by the tireless labors of the Inquisition.*

Benedict's well-intentioned effort at reformation was fruitless, and after his death matters only became worse, if possible. Under Clement VI. vices of all kinds flourished more luxuriantly than ever. In 1351 a Carmelite, preaching before the pope and cardinals, inveighed against their turpitude in terms which terrified every one, and caused his immediate dismissal.   Shortly afterwards a letter was affixed to the portals of the churches addressed to the pope and his cardinals.   It was signed Leviathan, Prince of Darkness, and was dated in the centre of hell.   He saluted his vicar the pope and his servants the cardinals, with whose help he had overcome Christ; he commended them for all their vices, and sent them the good wishes of their mother, Pride, and their sisters, Avarice, Lust, and the rest, who boast of their well-being through their help.   Clement was sorely moved, and fell dangerously sick, but the writer was never discovered.   When Clement died, the next year, a majority of the cardinals were disposed to cast their votes for Jean Birel, Prior of the Grande Chartreuse, but the Cardinal of Périgord warned them that their favorite had such zeal for the Church, and was a man of such justice, equity, and disregard of persons, that he would speedily bring them back to their ancient condition, and that in four months their coursers would be converted into beasts of burden.   Frightened at this prospect, they incontinently elected Innocent VI.†

These stories are verified by Petrarch's descriptions of the papal court at Avignon, wherein even his glowing rhetoric fails to satisfy the vehemence of his indignation, while the details which he gives to justify his ardor are unfit to repeat.   It is the Western Babylon, and nothing which is told of Assyria or Egypt, or even of Tartarus, can equal it, for all such are fables by comparison.   Here you find Nimrod and Semiramis, Minos and Rhadamanthus, Cerberus consuming all things, Pasiphaë under the bull, and

---

* Marsil. Patav. Defensor Pacis II. xi. Cf. cap. xxiii., xxiv.—Alvar. Pelag. de Planct. Eccles. Lib. II. Art. vii.—Baluz. et Mansi, III. 24–5.

† Chron. Glassberger ann. 1335.—Albert. Argentinens. Chron. ann. 1351.— Hist. Ordin. Carthus. (Martene Ampl. Coll. VI. 187).

her offspring, the monster Minotaur. Here you see confusion, blackness, and horror. It is not a city, but a den of spectres and goblins, the common sink of all vices, the hell of the living. Here God is despised, money is worshipped, the laws are trodden under foot, the good are ridiculed till there scarce is one left to be laughed at. A deluge is necessary, but there would be no Noah, no Deucalion to survive it. Avignon is the woman clothed in purple and scarlet, holding the golden bowl of her abominations and the uncleanness of her fornications. He returns to the subject again and again with undiminished wrath, and he casually alludes to one of the cardinals as a man of a nobler soul, who might have been good had he not belonged to the sacred college. The mocking spirit of Boccaccio is equally outspoken. From the highest to the lowest, every one in the papal court is abandoned to the most abominable vices. The sight of it converts a Jew, for he argues that Christianity must be of God, seeing that it spreads and flourishes in spite of the wickedness of its head.*

Gregory XI. was the fiercest persecutor of heresy in the fourteenth century, incessantly active against Brethren of the Free Spirit, Waldenses, and Fraticelli. He could boast that even as his namesake and prototype, Gregory IX., had founded the Inquisition, so he had restored it and had extended it into Germany. Yet, with all this zeal for compelling unity of faith, St. Birgitta was divinely commissioned to convey to him this message from the Lord:

"Hear, O Gregory XI., the words I say to thee, and give unto them diligent attention! Why dost thou hate me so? Why are thy audacity and presumption so great against me that thy worldly court destroys my heavenly one? Proudly thou despoilest me of my sheep. The wealth of the Church which is mine, and the goods of the faithful of the Church, thou extortest and seizest, and givest to thy worldly friends. Thou takest unjustly the store of the poor and lavishest it without shame on thy worldly friends. What have I done to thee, O Gregory? Patiently have I suffered thee to rise to the high-priesthood, and I have foretold to thee my will by letters divinely sent to thee, warning thee of

---

* Petrarchi Lib. sine Titulo Epistt. vii., viii., ix., xii., xvi.—Decamerone, Giorn. I. Nov. 2.

Petrarch's wrath at the papal court is explicable if there is truth in the disgusting story alleged in explanation of the enigmatical allusions in his Canzone XXII.—"*Mai non vo' più cantar com' io soleva.*"

the salvation of thy soul, and reproaching thy recklessness. How then dost thou repay my many favors? Why in thy court dost thou suffer unchecked the foulest pride, insatiable avarice, wantonness execrable to me, and all-devouring simony? Moreover, thou dost seize and carry away from me innumerable souls, for well-nigh all who go to thy court thou plungest into the fire of hell. . . . . Gird up thy loins, then, and fear not. Arise and bravely seek to reform the Church which I have purchased with my blood, and it will be restored to its former state, though now a brothel is more respected than it is. If thou dost not obey my command, know verily that thou wilt be condemned, and every devil of hell will have a morsel of thy soul, immortal and inconsumable."

In another vision St. Birgitta was ordered to represent to the pope the deplorable state of all orders of the clergy. Priests were rather pimps of the devil than clerks of God. The monasteries were well-nigh abandoned, mass was only celebrated in them intermittently, while the monks resided in their houses and had no shame in acknowledging their offspring, or wandered around, frequently clad in armor under their frocks. The doors of the nunneries were open night and day, and they were rather brothels than holy retreats. Such is the burden of St. Birgitta's repeated revelations, and nothing that Wickliff or Huss could say of the depravity of the clergy could exceed the bitterness of her denunciation.*

The inspiration of St. Catharine of Siena was equally outspoken. In her letters to Gregory XI., Urban VI., and the dignitaries who listened respectfully to her enunciations of the voice of God, her constant theme is the corruption of every rank in the hierarchy and the immediate necessity for reform. To Gregory she announces that God will sharply rebuke him if he does not cleanse the Church of its impurities; God demands of him to cast aside lukewarmness and fear, and to become another man, that he may eradicate the abundance of its iniquity. To Urban she says that it is not possible for him to put an end to the evil everywhere committed throughout Christendom, and especially by the clergy, but at least he can do what lies within his power. The prelates she describes as caring for nothing but pleasure and ambition; they

---

* Revelat. S. Brigittæ Lib. i. c. 41; Lib. iv. c. 33, 37, 142.

St. Birgitta was canonized in 1391 by Boniface IX., and after the Schism was healed this was confirmed in 1419 by Martin IV. Both popes ascribe her revelations to the Holy Ghost.

are infernal demons carrying off the souls of their subjects, they are wolves and traffickers in the divine grace. As for the priests, they are the exact opposites of what they should be, injuring all who come in contact with them; all their lives are corrupt, and they are not worthy to be called men, but, rather, beasts, wallowing in filth and indulging in all the wickedness craved by their bestial appetites; they are not guardians of souls, but devourers, delivering them up to the Wolf of Hell.* All these warnings fell upon deaf ears, and the Church, during the Great Schism, plunged, if possible, deeper into the pit of abominations.

In 1386 Telesforo, the hermit of Cosenza, could only explain the Schism by the wealth and worldliness of the clergy, whom God could only reform by stripping them of their temporalities and thus forcing them to live according to the gospel. Although Henry of Hesse disputed the prophetic gifts of Telesforo, he, too, had no hesitation in ascribing the Schism to the simony, avarice, pride, luxury, and vanity of the Church, and he can only explain it by God sometimes in his wrath allowing his servants to act according to their own evil desires. Even should the Schism be healed, he can only look forward to the Church falling from bad to worse until the coming of Antichrist. This he anticipates speedily, for all the prophetic signs are present in the extreme iniquity of the world. The insatiable avarice and ambition of clergy and laity will lead them to support any one who promises them worldly advantage, and they will unite in aiding Antichrist to conquer the world. Bad as were the attacks of heresy, he says, the peace now enjoyed by the Church after overcoming the heretics is even worse, for in it the evil spirits succeed in excluding virtues and substituting vices—a significant admission from an enthusiastic churchman of the result of the labors of the Inquisition.†

---

* Epistole della Santa Caterina da Siena, Lett. 9, 13, 14, 15, 17, 18, 21, 35, 38, 39, 41, 44, 50, 91, etc. (Milano, 1843).

† Telesphori de magnis Tribulationibus (Venet. 1516, fol. 11).—Henrici de Hassia Lib. contra Thelesphori Vaticinia c. i., ii., x., xx., xxxvi., xxxvii., xli., xlii., (Pez, Thesaur. Anecd. T. I. P. ii.).

Henry wrote a letter to the princes of the Church in the name of Lucifer, Prince of Darkness and Emperor of Acheron, similar to that which agitated Clement VI. in 1351 (Pez, Dissert. p. lxxix.).

These deplorable statements are confirmed by the supplication of the Council of Pisa in 1409 to Alexander V., and by the reformers who gathered around the Council of Constance in hopes of seeing it fulfil its functions of purifying the Church in its head and members—John Gerson, Cardinal d'Ailly, Cardinal Zabarella, Bernhardus Baptizatus, Theodoric Vrie. I have already quoted Nicholas de Clemangis, and need only say that the others were equally outspoken and equally full of detail, while the reformatory projects drawn up for consideration by the council are eloquent as to the evils which they were designed to remove. At first Sigismund and the Germans, with the French and English nations, were united in demanding that reformation should precede the election of a pope in place of the deposed John XXIII., but the close alliance formed between Sigismund and Henry V. alienated the French; by a skilful use of this they were won over, and the prospects of reform grew so desperate that Sigismund seriously contemplated seizing all the cardinals, as the main obstacle to the wished-for action, and removing them from Constance. On learning this, far from yielding, they put on their red hats and wore them in the streets as a token of their readiness to undergo martyrdom, and a paper was drawn up stigmatizing the English and Germans as Wickliffites and Hussites. The Germans responded in a vigorous protest, officially describing the condition of the Church in terms as decided as those employed by Nicholas de Clemangis. For this state of things they hold the Holy See solely responsible, for they date back these abuses to a time, a century and a half before, when the increasing pretensions of the curia enabled it to infect all Christendom with its vices, and they allude with special horror to the use of the papal penitentiary, worse than ordinary simony, whereby crimes were taxed in proportion to their heinousness and villainous traffic was made in sin. The Church, they concluded, had forfeited the reverence of the laity, which regarded it with contempt, as rather Antichristian than Christian. The steadfast attitude of the Germans, however, was weakened by the death of their strongest ally, Robert Hallam, Bishop of Salisbury, and two of Sigismund's most trusted prelates were bribed to betray the cause. The Archbishop of Riga, who was tired of his constant quarrels with the Teutonic knights, was promised the rich bishopric of Liége, and the Bishop of Coire was promised the archbishopric of Riga. The opposition crumbled away, and Martin V. was elected. The French quickly saw their mistake, and appealed to Sigismund, who curtly referred them to the pope whom they had chosen, and who now had full power of granting or refusing reform. The council hurriedly adjourned after passing a few canons of little worth, and providing for a succession of general councils at short intervals.*

We have seen how reform was skilfully eluded at the Council of Siena in 1424. At Basle it fared no better. In 1435 Andreas, Bishop of Minorca, addressed to the Cardinal-legate Cesarini an exhortation in which he said, "Evils, sins, and scandals have so increased, especially among the clergy, that, as the prophet says, already accursed lying and theft, and adultery and simony, and murder and many other crimes have deluged the earth. . . . The avarice and lust of domination and the foul and abominable lives of the ecclesiastics are the cause of all the misfortunes of Christendom. The infidel and the heretic say that if the Christian faith and gospel law were true and holy, the prelates and priests would not live as they do, nor would the spiritual rulers work such confusion and scandal in Christendom without instant punishment from the Lord Jesus Christ, the founder of the gospel and the Church." Bishop Andreas further urged that the council condemn by an irrefragable decision the impious doctrine of some canonists that the pope cannot commit simony. Two years later, in 1437, John Nider, the Dominican, declared that the general reformation of the Church was hopeless, on account of the wickedness of the prelates and the lack of good-will of the clergy. Partial reforms might be practicable, but even in this the difficulty was almost insuperable. The council, he said, in its six years of existence had been unable to reform a single nunnery, although aided by all the force of the secular power.†

The council, indeed, attempted some reformation, but Eugenius IV. and his successors refused to observe its canons. Even in Germany and France the old abuses were reinstated, with their de-

---

* Libellus Supplex oblatus Papæ in Concilio Pisano (Martene Ampl. Coll. VII. 1124–32).—Von der Hardt, IV. 1414, 1417–18, 1422–3, 1426–7, 1432.—Rymer, X. 433–6.—Gobelini Personæ Cosmodrom. Æt. VI. cap. 96.

† Andreæ Gubernac. Concil. P. II., III., v. cap. 2 (Von der Hardt, VI. 175, 179, 209).—Nideri Formicar. Lib. I. c. vii.

plorable consequences. The writers of the period are as emphatic
as their predecessors in describing the superabounding and universal turpitude of the Church during the remainder of the century.
That they do not exaggerate may be assumed from one or two instances. In 1459 there died at Arras, at the age of eighty, Nicaise
le Vasseur, canon and head of the chapter of Arras. He not only
had daughters and committed incest with them, but also with a
daughter-granddaughter whom he had by one of them. Yet so
blunted was the moral sense of Church and people that, as we are
told, this monster officiated *"très honorablement"* in divine service
on all feasts and holidays, and the only comment of the chronicler
is that he did it most becomingly. When, in 1474, the death of
Sixtus IV. was received in Rome with a pæan of joy, people commented not so much upon his selling benefices to the highest bidder and his other devices of extorting money, as upon the manner
in which he rewarded the boys who served his unnatural lusts by
granting to them rich bishoprics and archbishoprics. Under such
men as Innocent VIII. and Alexander VI., there could only be
deeper degradation expected. Julius II. was a *condottiere* rather
than a priest; but when political exigencies led him to summon
the Lateran Council, earnest souls like Jacob Wimpfeling permitted themselves to hope that he would set bounds to the moral
plague which pervaded all the churches. When he died, and Leo
X. conducted the labors of the assembled fathers, Gianfrancesco
Pico della Mirandola addressed him an epistle describing the evils
for which reformation was requisite. It is a repetition of the old
complaints. The worship of God was neglected, the churches were
held by pimps and catamites; the nunneries were dens of prostitution, justice was a matter of hatred or favor; piety was lost in
superstition; the priesthood was bought and sold; the revenues
of the Church ministered only to the foulest excesses, and the people were repelled from religion by the example of their pastors.
The author of a little anonymous tract printed about the year 1500
feels obliged to prove by laborious citations that fornication is forbidden to the clergy, and he attributes the contempt generally entertained for the Church to the openly scandalous lives of its members. To appreciate fully the effect on the popular mind of this
degradation of the Church, we must keep in view the supernatural
powers claimed and exercised by the priesthood, which made it the

arbiter of every man's destiny, for salvation depended not so much on individual desert as on the ministrations of those who controlled the sacraments. How benumbing was this influence on the moral faculties is visible in the confession of Anna Miolerin, one of the Tyrolese witches burned in 1506, where the spread of witchcraft is attributed to the sensual and drunken priests who are unable to confess their penitents properly, or to baptize children, so that the latter, unprotected by the sacrament, are easily betrayed to Satan. The priests, she says, ought to baptize children reverently and repeat all the words of the ceremony.*

As for monasticism, Abbot Trithemius gives us a vigorous sketch of its demoralization. The great Benedictine Order, the mother and exemplar of the rest, had been founded on a wise and comprehensive system, including productive labor in the fields and religious observances in the houses: but he tells us that the monks when abroad were idle and vain, and when inside the walls were abandoned to carnal delights, with nothing of decorous to show but the habit, and even this was mostly neglected. No one thought of enforcing the forgotten discipline. The monasteries had become stables for clerks, or fortresses for fighting-men, or markets for traders, or brothels for strumpets, in which the greatest of crimes was to live without sin. The abbots thought of nothing but of satisfying their appetites and vanities, their lusts, their ambition, and their avarice, while the brethren were monks only in name, and were vessels of wrath and sin. A confirmatory glimpse at the interior life of these establishments is afforded by Angelus Rumpherus, elected Abbot of Formbach in 1501, in his account of his immediate predecessor, Leonhard, who had ruled the abbey since 1474. He was especially fond of using torture, of which he had infinite ingenious varieties at his service. Unable to endure his tyranny, a monk named Engelschalk, a man of good natural parts and disposition, fled, but was taken sick and brought back. He

---

* Fascic. Rer. Expetend. et Fugiend. I. 68, 417; II. 105 (Ed. 1690).—Herm. Ryd de Reen de Vita Clericor. (Ib. II. 142).—Mém. de Jacques du Clercq, Liv. III. ch. 43.—Steph. Infessuræ Diar. Urb. Roman. ann. 1474 (Eccard. Corp. Hist. II. 1939).—Wimpfeling de vita et moribus Episcoporum, Argentorati, 1512.—De Munditia et Castitate Sacerdotum (*sine nota*, sed Parisiis c. 1500).—Rapp, Die Hexenprocesse und ihre Gegner aus Tirol, p. 148.

was thrown into the dungeon of the abbey, a building without light and ventilation, except a narrow slit through which to pass in food. Here he died, without even the viaticum, his request for a confessor being refused, and when, as he was dying, the abbot and some of the monks entered, the blood flowed copiously from his nose, showing that they were his murderers.*

Under the guidance of a Church such as this, the moral condition of the laity was unutterably depraved. Uniformity of faith had been enforced by the Inquisition and its methods, and so long as faith was preserved, crime and sin were comparatively unimportant except as a source of revenue to those who sold absolution. As Theodoric Vrie tersely puts it, hell and purgatory would be emptied if enough money could be found. The artificial standard thus created is seen in a revelation of the Virgin to St. Birgitta, that a pope who was free from heresy, no matter how polluted by sin and vice, is not so wicked but that he has the absolute power to bind and loose souls. There are many wicked popes plunged in hell, but all their lawful acts on earth are accepted and confirmed by God, and all priests who are not heretics administer true sacraments, no matter how depraved they may be. Correctness of belief was thus the sole essential ; virtue was a wholly subordinate consideration. How completely under such a system religion and morals came to be dissociated is seen in the remarks of Pius II. quoted above, that the Franciscans were excellent theologians, but cared nothing about virtue.†

This, in fact, was the direct result of the system of persecution embodied in the Inquisition. Heretics who were admitted to be patterns of virtue were ruthlessly exterminated in the name of Christ, while in the same holy name the orthodox could purchase

---

* Joann. de Trittenheim Lib. Lugubris de Statu et Ruina Monast. Ord. c. i., iii. —Angeli Rumpheri Hist. Formbach. Lib. ii. (Pez, I. iii. 446, 451-2).

This is by no means a solitary case. In 1329 the Abbot of La Grasse was by a judgment of the Parlement of Paris deprived for life of *haute justice,* and the abbey condemned in a fine of thirty thousand livres to the king and six hundred livres damages to victims, for murders committed, illegal tortures, and other crimes.—A. Molinier, Vaissette, Éd. Privat, IX. 417.

† Gersoni de Reform. Eccles. c. xxiv. (Von der Hardt, I. v. 125-8). — Theod. Vrie Hist. Concil. Constant. Lib. iv. Dist. vii.—Revel. S. Brigittæ Lib. vii. cap. vii.

absolution for the vilest of crimes for a few coins. When the only unpardonable offence was persistence in some trifling error of belief, such as the poverty of Christ; when men had before them the example of their spiritual guides as leaders in vice and debauchery and contempt of sacred things, all the sanctions of morality were destroyed and the confusion between right and wrong became hopeless. The world has probably never seen a society more vile than that of Europe in the fourteenth and fifteenth centuries. The brilliant pages of Froissart fascinate us with their pictures of the artificial courtesies of chivalry; the mystic reveries of Rysbroek and of Tauler show us that spiritual life survived in some rare souls, but the mass of the population was plunged into the depths of sensuality and the most brutal oblivion of the moral law. For this Alvaro Pelayo tells us that the priesthood were accountable, and that, in comparison with them, the laity were holy. What was that state of comparative holiness he proceeds to describe, blushing as he writes, for the benefit of confessors, giving a terrible sketch of the universal immorality which nothing could purify but fire and brimstone from heaven. The chroniclers do not often pause in their narrations to dwell on the moral aspects of the times, but Meyer, in his annals of Flanders, under date of 1379, tells us that it would be impossible to describe the prevalence everywhere of perjuries, blasphemies, adulteries, hatreds, quarrels, brawls, murder, rapine, thievery, robbery, gambling, whoredom, debauchery, avarice, oppression of the poor, rape, drunkenness, and similar vices, and he illustrates his statement with the fact that in the territory of Ghent, within the space of ten months, there occurred no less than fourteen hundred murders committed in the bagnios, brothels, gambling-houses, taverns, and other similar places. When, in 1396, Jean sans Peur led his crusaders to destruction at Nicopolis, their crimes and cynical debauchery scandalized even the Turks, and led to the stern rebuke of Bajazet himself, who as the monk of Saint-Denis admits, was much better than his Christian foes. The same writer, moralizing over the disaster of Agincourt, attributes it to the general corruption of the nation. Sexual relations, he says, were an alternation of disorderly lusts and of incest; commerce was nought but fraud and trickery; avarice withheld from the Church her tithes, and ordinary conversation was a succession of blasphemies. The Church, set

up by God as a model and protector for the people, was false
to all its obligations. The bishops, through the basest and most
criminal of motives, were habitual accepters of persons; they anointed themselves with the last essence extracted from their flocks, and
there was in them nothing of holy, of just, of wise, or even of
decent. Luke Wadding is a witness above suspicion; his conscientious study of original sources entitles his opinions to weight,
and we may accept his description of Italy in the early part of
the fifteenth century: "At that time Italy was sunk in vice and
wickedness. In the Church there was no devotion, in the laity no
faith, no piety, no modesty, no discipline of morals. Every man
cursed his neighbor; the factions of Guelf and Ghibelline flood-
ed the streets of the towns with fraternal blood, the roads were
closed by robbers, the seas infested with pirates. Parents slew
with rejoicing their children who chanced to be of the opposite
faction. The world was full of sorcery and incantations; the
churches deserted, the gambling-houses filled." The testimony is
too uniform to explain it away with the assumption that it represents only the disenchantment of puritanism. Æneas Sylvius
was no puritan, and his adventurous life had made him, perhaps,
better acquainted with the whole of Christendom than any other
man of his time, and in 1453 he says: "It is for this that I dread
the Turks. Whether I look upon the deeds of princes or of prelates I find that all have sunk, all are worthless. There is not one
who does right, in no one is there pity or truth. There is no
recognition of God upon earth; you are Christians in name, but
you do the work of heathen. Execration and falsehood and
slaughter and theft and adultery are spread among you, and you
add blood to blood. What wonder if God, indignant at your acts,
places on your necks Mahomet, the leader of the Turks, like another Nebuchadnezzar, for you are either swollen with pride, or
rapacious with avarice, or cruel in wrath, or livid with envy, or in-
cestuous in lust, or unsparing in cruelty. There is no shame in
crime, for you sin so openly and shamelessly that you seem to
take delight in it." To what extent the Church was responsible for this may be judged by the terrible condition of Rome
under Innocent VIII. as pictured in the diary of Infessura. Out-
rages of all kinds were committed with impunity so long as the
criminal had wherewith to compound with the papal chancery;

and when Cardinal Borgia, the vice-chancellor, was reproached with this, he piously replied that God did not desire the death of the sinner, but that he should pay and live. A census of the public women showed them to number sixty-eight hundred, and when the vicar of the city issued a decree ordering all ecclesiastics to dismiss their concubines, Innocent sent for him and ordered its withdrawal, saying that all priests and members of the curia kept them, and that it was no sin.*

This was the outcome of the theocracy whose foundation had been laid by Hildebrand in the honest belief that it would realize the reign of Christ on earth. Power such as was claimed and exercised by the Church could only be wielded by superhuman wisdom. Human nature was too imperfect not to convert it into an instrumentality for the gratification of worldly passions and ambition, and its inevitable result was to plunge society deeper and deeper into corruption, as unity of faith was enforced by persecution. In this enforcement, as I have said, faith became the only object of supreme importance, and morals were completely subordinated, tending naturally to the creation of a perfectly artificial and arbitrary standard of conduct. If, to win the favor of Satan, a man trampled on the Eucharist believing it to be the body of Christ, he was not liable to the pains of heresy; but if he did so out of disbelief, he was a heretic. If he took interest for money believing it to be wrong, he was comparatively safe; if believing it to be right, he was condemned. It was not the act, but the mental process, that was of primary importance, and wilful wrong-doing was treated more tenderly than ignorant conscientiousness. Thus the divine law on which the Church professed to be founded was superseded by human law administered by those who profited by its abuse. As Cardinal d'Ailly tells us, the doctors of civil law regarded the imperial jurisprudence as more binding than the commands of God, while the professors of canon law taught that the papal decretals were of greater weight

---

* Alvar. Pelag. de Planctu Eccles. Lib. II. Art. i., ii. — Meyeri Annal. Flandriæ Lib. XIII. ann. 1379. — Religieux de S. Denys, Hist. de Charles VI. Liv. XVI. ch. 10; Liv. XXXV. ch. 8.—Wadding. ann. 1405, No. 7.—Æn. Sylvii opp. inedd. (Atti della Accad. dei Lincei, 1883, pp. 558-9).—Steph. Infessuræ Diar. (Eccard. II. 1988, 1996-7).

than Scripture. Such a theocracy, practically deeming itself as superior to its God, when it had overcome all dissidence, could have but one result.*

When we consider, however, the simple earnestness with which such multitudes of humble heretics endured the extremity of outrage and the most cruel of deaths, in the endeavor to ascertain and obey the will of God in the fashioning of their lives, we recognize what material existed for the development of true Christianity, and for the improvement of the race, far down in the obscurer ranks of society. We can see now how greatly advanced might be the condition of humanity had that leaven been allowed to penetrate the whole mass in place of being burned out with fire. Unorganized and unresisting, the heretics were unable to withstand the overwhelming forces arrayed against them. Power and place and wealth were threatened by their practical interpretation of the teachings of Christ. The pride of opinion in the vast and laboriously constructed theories of scholastic theology, the conscientious belief in the exclusive salvation obtainable through the Church alone, the recognized duty of exterminating the infected sheep and preserving the vineyard of the Lord from the ravages of heretical foxes, all united to form a conservatism against which even the heroic endurance of the sectaries was unavailing. Yet there are few pages in the history of humanity more touching, few records of self-sacrifice more inspiring, few examples more instructive of the height to which the soul can rise above the weaknesses of the flesh, than those which we may glean from the fragmentary documents of the Inquisition and the scanty references of the chroniclers to the abhorred heretics so industriously tracked and so pitilessly despatched. Ignorant and toiling men and women — peasants, mechanics, and the like — dimly conscious that the system of society was wrong, that the commands of God were perverted or neglected, that humanity was capable of higher development, if it could but find and follow the Divine Will; striving each in his humble sphere to solve the inscrutable and awful problems of existence, to secure in tribulation his own salvation, and to help his fellows in the arduous task—these forgotten martyrs of

---

* Pet. Alliacens. Principium in Cursum Bibliæ (Fascic. Rer. Expetend. II. 516).
—Bernardi Comens. Lucerna Inquis. s. v. *Hæresis*, No. 21.

the truth drew from themselves alone the strength which enabled them to dare and to endure martyrdom. No prizes of ambition lay before them to tempt their departure from the safe and beaten track, no sympathizing crowds surrounded the piles of fagots and strengthened them in the fearful trial; but scorn and hatred and loathing were their portion to the last. Save in cases of relapse, life could always be saved by recantation and return to the bosom of the Church, which recognized that even from a worldly point of view a converted heretic was more valuable than a martyred one, yet the steadfast resolution, which the orthodox character-ized as satanic hardening of the heart, was too common to excite surprise.*

This inestimable material for the elevation of humanity was plucked up as tares and cast into the furnace. Society, so long as it was orthodox and docile, was allowed to wallow in all the wickedness which depravity might suggest. The supreme object of uniformity in faith was practically attained, and the moral con-dition of mankind was dismissed from consideration as of no impor-tance. Yet the incongruity between the ideal of Christianity and its realization was too unnatural for the situation to be permanent. In the Church as well as out of it there was a leaven working. While St. Birgitta was thundering her revelations in the unwill-ing ears of Gregory XI., William Langland, the monk of Malvern, sharpened his bitter denunciations of friar and prelate by remind-

---

* It would scarce seem possible that, in the full light of the nineteenth century, men could still be found hardy enough to defend the position of the Church tow-ards heretics, but it is a sign of the progress of humanity that this is no longer done by justifying the irrefragable facts of history, but by boldly denying them. In a recent work by M. le Chanoine Claessens, "Camérier secret de Sa Sainteté," who informs us that after long and serious study of the original sources he writes with scrupulous impartiality and with the calmness befitting history, we are told that the penalty of the Church for public and obstinate heretics is simply ex-communication, and that it has never allowed itself to employ any direct con-straint, whether for the conversion of Jews and Pagans or to bring back wan-dering Christians to unity. At the same time he is careful to make the reserva-tion that the Church possesses an incontestable right to use physical means to compel those who have been baptized to fulfil the obligations thus assumed.— Claessens, L'Inquisition et le régime pénal pour la répression de l'hérésie dans les Pays-Bas du passé, Tournhout, 1886, p. 5.

ing the common-folk that love and truth were the sole essentials
of Christianity—

> "Loue is leche of lyf and nexte owre lorde selve,
> And also the graith gate that goth in-to heuene;
> For-thi I sey as I seide ere by the textis,
> Whan alle tresores ben ytryed treuthe is the beste.
> Now haue I tolde the what treuthe is, that no tresore is bettere,
> I may no lenger lenge the with, now loke the owre lorde!"
>
> (VISION, I. 202–7.)

All such warnings, however, were disregarded, and in the hour of
its unquestionable supremacy the sacerdotal system, which seemed
impregnable to all assaults and to have no assailants, was on the
eve of its overthrow.   The Inquisition had been too successful.
So complete had been the triumph of the Church that the old
machinery was allowed to become out of gear and to rust for
want of daily use.   The Inquisition itself had ceased to inspire its
old-time terror.   For a century it had little to do save an occasional foray upon the peasants of the Alpine valleys, or an extortion on the Jews of Palermo, or the fomenting of a witchcraft craze.   It no longer had the stimulus of active work or the
opportunity of impressing the minds of the people with the certainty of its vengeance and the terrors of its holocausts.

At the same time the Great Schism had inflicted a serious blow
upon the veneration entertained for the Holy See by both clergy
and laity, which found expression in the great councils of Constance and Basle.   Dexterous management, it is true, averted the
immediate dangers threatened by these parliaments of Christendom, and the Church remained in theory an autocracy instead of
being converted into a constitutional monarchy, but nevertheless
the old unquestioning confidence in the vicegerent of God was
gone, while the aspirations of Christendom grew stronger under
repression.   The invention of printing came to stimulate the spread
of enlightenment, and a reading public gradually formed itself,
reached and influenced by other modes than the pulpit and the
lecture-room, which had been the monopoly of the Church.   No
longer was culture virtually the sole appanage of ecclesiastics.
The New Learning spread among a daily increasing class the
thirst for knowledge and the critical spirit of inquiry, which in-

sensibly undermined the traditional claims of the Church on the veneration and obedience of mankind.

Save in Spain, where racial divisions furnished peculiar factors to the problem, everything conspired to disarm the Inquisition and render it powerless when it was most sorely needed. Orthodox uniformity had been so successfully enforced that the popes of the fifteenth century, immersed in worldly cares beyond the capacity of the Inquisition to gratify, scarce gave themselves the trouble to keep up its organization; and, save when some madness of witchcraft called for victims, the people and the local clergy made no demand for vindicators of the faith. Scholastic quarrels, for the most part, were settled by the universities, which arrogated to themselves much of the jurisdiction of the Holy Office; and the episcopal ordinaries seemed almost to have forgotten the functions which were theirs by immemorial right.

Although German orthodoxy had been so uniform that the Inquisition there had always been weak and unorganized, yet Germany was the inevitable seat of the revolt. In England and France the power of a monarchy, backed by a united people, had set some bounds to papal aggression and assumption. In Italy the pope was regarded more as a temporal prince than as the head of the Church, and the Ghibellines had never hesitated to oppose his schemes of political aggrandizement. In Germany, however, the papal policy of disunion and civil strife had proved fatally successful, and since the untimely death of Louis of Bavaria there had been no central power strong enough to defend the people and the local churches from the avarice and ambition of the representatives of St. Peter. Luther came when the public mind was receptive and insubordinate, and when there was no organized instrumentality for his prompt repression. As I have already pointed out, his scholastic discussion as to the power of the keys seemed at first too insignificant to require attention; when the debate enlarged there were no means at hand for its speedy suppression, and, by the time the Church could marshal its unwieldy forces, the people had espoused his cause in a region where, as the Sachsenspiegel shows, there was no hereditary or prescriptive readiness to venerate the canon law. The hour, the place, and the man had met by a happy concurrence, and the era of modern civilization and unfettered thought was opened, in spite of the fact that the reformers were as rigid as the orthodox in setting bounds to dogmatic independence.

The review which we have made of the follies and crimes of our ancestors has revealed to us a scene of almost unrelieved blackness. We have seen how the wayward heart of man, groping in twilight, has under the best of impulses inflicted misery and despair on his fellow-creatures while thinking to serve God, and how the ambitious and unprincipled have traded on those impulses to gratify the lust of avarice and domination. Yet such a review, rightly estimated, is full of hope and encouragement. In the unrest of modern society, where immediate relief is sought from the mass of evils oppressing mankind, and impatience is eager to overturn all social organization in the hope of founding a new structure where preventable misery shall be unknown, it is well occasionally to take a backward view, to tear away the veil which conceals the passions and the sufferings of bygone generations, and estimate fairly the progress already effected. Human development is slow and irregular; to the observer at a given point it appears stationary or retrogressive, and it is only by comparing periods removed by a considerable interval of time that the movement can be appreciated. Such a retrospect as we have wearily accomplished has shown us how, but a few centuries since, the infliction of gratuitous evil was deemed the highest duty of man, and we learn how much has been gained to the empire of Christian love and charity. We have seen how the administration of law, both spiritual and secular, was little other than organized wrong and injustice; we have seen how low were the moral standards, and how debased the mental condition of the populations of Christendom. We have seen that the Ages of Faith, to which romantic dreamers regretfully look back, were ages of force and fraud, where evil seemed to reign almost unchecked, justifying the current opinion, so constantly reappearing, that the reign of Antichrist had already begun. Imperfect as are human institutions to-day, a comparison with the past shows how marvellous has been the improvement, and the fact that this gain has been made almost wholly within the last two centuries, and that it is advancing with accelerated momentum, affords to the sociologist the most cheering encouragement. Principles have been established which, if allowed to develop themselves naturally and healthfully, will render the future of mankind very different from aught that the world has yet seen. The greatest danger to modern society lies in the impatient theorists who desire to reform the world at a blow, in place of aiding in the struggle of good with evil under the guidance of eternal laws. Could they be convinced of the advance so swiftly made and of its steady development, they might moderate their ardor and direct their energies to wise construction rather than to heedless destruction.

A few words will suffice to summarize the career of the mediæval Inquisition. It introduced a system of jurisprudence which infected the criminal law of all the lands subjected to its influence, and rendered the administration of penal justice a cruel mockery for centuries. It furnished the Holy See with a powerful weapon in aid of political aggrandizement, it tempted secular sovereigns to imitate the example, and it prostituted the name of religion to the vilest temporal ends. It stimulated the morbid sensitiveness to doctrinal aberrations until the most trifling dissidence was capable of arousing insane fury, and of convulsing Europe from end to end. On the other hand, when atheism became fashionable in high places, its thunders were mute. Energetic only in evil, when its powers might have been used on the side of virtue, it held its hand and gave the people to understand that the only sins demanding repression were doubt as to the accuracy of the Church's knowledge of the unknown, and attendance on the Sabbat. In its long career of blood and fire, the only credit which it can claim is the suppression of the pernicious dogmas of the Cathari, and in this its agency may be regarded as superfluous, for those dogmas carried in themselves the seeds of self-destruction, and higher wisdom might have trusted to their self-extinction. Thus the judgment of impartial history must be that the Inquisition was the monstrous offspring of mistaken zeal, utilized by selfish greed and lust of power to smother the higher aspirations of humanity and stimulate its baser appetites.

APPENDIX.

I.

CONFESSION OF A HARBORER OF SPIRITUALS.

(Doat, XXVII. fol. 7 sqq.)

This is one of twenty-two similar cases. The statements have every appearance of being drawn up to lay before an assembly of experts.

Johannes de Petra, sartor, filius quondam Guillelmi de Petra oriundus de parrochia Vallis diocesis Mimatensis, habitator Montispessulani, sicut per ipsius confessionem in judicio sub anno Domini MCCC vigesimo sexto mense Novembris et Januarii factam, legitime nobis constat a tribus vel quatuor annis ante tempus confessionis factæ per eum de infrascriptis contra Guillelmum Verrerii de Narbona et Petrum Dayssan de Biterris pro hæresi fugitivos in domo propria multo tempore receptavit, cum eis comedit et bibit, et ad diversa loca in eorum societate ivit, multosque alios fugitivos et alios de credentia beguinorum combustorum etiam in dicta domo sua vidit, et cum eis comedit et bibit frequenter, et etiam fratrem Raimundum Johannis apostatam ab ordine minorum et a fide fugitivum in dicta domo propria ad prandendum invitavit, sibique comedere et bibere de suis bonis dedit, in festo fratris Petri facto per eos in Montepessulano interfuit et comedit, aliasque multipliciter et diversimode cum ipsis fugitivis et quibusdam aliis de credentia beguinorum conversatus fuit non cum omnibus simul et semel, sed diversis vicibus, aliquando cum uno, alias cum duobus vel pluribus, sicuti veniebant, sciens eos esse tales. Item ab eis fugitivis et beguinis seu aliquibus eorum errores infrascriptos audivit, videlicet : quod beguini qui fuerant condemnati et combusti in Narbona, Capitestagno, Biterris, Lodeva et Lunello et alibi fuerant boni homines et catholici, et fuerant indebite et injuste condemnati, et quod erant sancti et martyres gloriosi ; et idem audivit a quodam quem nominat dici de fratribus minoribus Massiliæ combustis, videlicet quod erant injuste condemnati, et quod erant mortui sancti martyres gloriosi, et erant in Paradiso, et quod tenuerant sanctam vitam et bonam, et viam veritatis et paupertatis, et quod propter hoc inquisitores condemnabant eosdem. Item audivit ab eodem quem nominat quod dominus papa qui nunc est non est verus papa sicut fuit Sanctus Petrus nec habet illam potestatem quam Dominus Jesus Christus dederat beato Petro, quodque si fuisset verus papa non consentiret nec sustineret quod dicti beguini et fratres minores condemnarentur qui tenebant viam Dei et veritatis. Item quod cardinales et alii prælati ecclesiæ Romanæ sustinebant et faciebant prædictas condemnationes propter favorem et timorem dicti domini papæ, dicens ipse Joannes quod inductus per dictum hominem prædictos errores credidit, scilicet dictos condemnatos credidit fuisse injuste condemnatos et esse sanctos et martyres gloriosos et esse in Paradiso, credidit etiam quod dominus papa non esset verus papa propter condemnationem prædictorum, sicut a prædicto homine et pluribus aliis quos nominat se asserit audivisse, et fuit in credentia prædictorum errorum ab illo tempore citra, quo prædictus homo sibi prædictos errores dixit usque ad illud tempus quo fuit in Montepessulano arrestatus de mandato inquisitoris, et tunc pœnituit ut asserit, de prædictis. Item audivit a quibusdam, scilicet a predicto Guillelmo Verrerii et aliis quod si unus homo fecisset votum eundi ad Sanctum Jacobum quod melius faceret si daret pecuniam illam quam expendere posset in via pauperibus latitantibus et non aliis qui publiæ mendicabant, quia S. Jacobus vel aliquis alius sanctus non indiget oblationibus quæ sibi offerebantur. Item quod si unus homo promiserit alicui sancto vel beatæ Mariæ virgini unam candelam vel ejus valorem, daret pauperibus, et hoc credidit ipse loquens et in ipsa credentia stetit per unum annum vel quasi sicut dixit; committens prædicta a prædicto tempore citra celavit ea nec confiteri voluit, donec captus est et longo tempore sub arresto positus et denique in muri carcere detentus fuit, et contra proprium juramentum de prædictis celavit et negavit expressius a principio veritatem, nec dictos fugitivos detexit nec capi procuravit, dicens se pœnitere.

II.

BULL OF JOHN XXII. ORDERING THE TRANSFER OF PIERRE TRENCAVEL.

(Archives de l'Inquisition de Carcassonne.—Doat, XXXV. fol. 18.)

Johannes episcopus servus servorum Dei dilecto filio Michaeli Monachi de ordine fratrum minorum inquisitori hæreticæ pravitatis in partibus Provinciæ auctoritate apostolica deputato salutem et apostolicam benedictionem. Ex insinuatione dilecti filii Joannis de Prato de ordine fratrum prædicatorum inquisitoris hæreticæ pravitatis in partibus Carcassonensibus auctoritate apostolica deputati nuper accepimus quod Petrus Trencavelli de Aurilhat Biterrensis diocesis, qui olim de crimine hæresis delatus et vehementer suspectus captus extitit et in muro inquisitionis Carcassonæ positus et detentus, de quo muro postmodum temerariis dicitur ausibus aufugisse, quodque factis subsequente rite processibus contra eum, ipsoque reperto de crimine hujusmodi culpabili et resperso, in sermone publico Carcassonæ de eodem fuit crimine condemnatus tanquam hæreticus, necnon Andræa ejusdem Petri filia, de prædicto crimine vehementer suspecta et etiam fugitiva, mancipati tuis carceribus detinentur. Cum autem negotio fidei expediat quod præfati Petrus et Andræa, ut de aliis per ipsos ut fertur infectis, ipsorumque fautoribus in eis partibus possit haberi certitudo plenior, inquisitori restituantur prædicto, nos qui negotium hujusmodi ubique cupimus, Domino cooperante, prosperari, præfati inquisitoris in hac parte supplicationibus inclinati, discretioni tuæ per apostolica scripta mandamus quatinus eidem inquisitori vel ejus certo nuncio prædictos Petrum Trencavelli et Andræam filiam ejus restituere, cessante difficultatis obstaculo, non postponas. Datum Avenione decimo secundo Kalendas Aprilis, Pontificatus nostri anno undecimo. (21 Mar. 1327.)

III.

SENTENCE OF NAPROUS BONETA.

(Doat, XXVII. fol. 95.)

In nomine Patris et Filii et Spiritus Sancti, Amen. Cum nos fratres Henricus de Chamayo Carcassonæ et P. Bruni Tholosanus inquisitores, et Hugo Augerii et Durandus Catherini commissarii supradicti per inquisitionem legitime factam invenimus et per confessionem vestram fatam in judicio legitime nobis constat quod tu Naprous Boneta filia quondam Stephani Boneti de Sancto Petro de la Cadiera diocesis Nemausensis, habitatrix Montispessulani, contra veram fidem catholicam et ecclesiam Romanam sacrosanctam, potestati et auctoritati sanctæ sedis apostolicæ et domini summi pontificis detrahendo, de potestate et auctoritate ipsius vicarii Domini nostri Jesu Christi ac sacrosanctæ ecclesiæ principatum et fundamentum indissolubile, et claves ac sacramenta blasphemando et quantum in te est totaliter enervando, et male ac perverse sentiendo de fide, plures articulos sacris canonibus contrarios, hæreticales et erroneos sustinuisti et adhuc sustinere niteris animo pertinaci, sicque tam graviter in crimine hæreseos deliquisti prout est tibi lectum et recitatum intelligibiliter in vulgari; idcirco nos inquisitores et commissarii antedicti, præfati illius vestigiis inhærentes qui non vult mortem peccatoris, sed majus ut convertatur et vivat, te Naprous Boneta prædictam tantos et tam enormes errores et hæreses, ut præmittitur sustinentem et defendere volentem protervia improba et anima pertinaci, sæpe ac sæpius caritative prius per nostrum ꝑrædecessorem multipliciter monitam et rogatam iteratis vicibus, nihilominus ꝑ quisivimus, rogavimus, monuimus et per probos viros religiosos et sæculares moneri et rogari salubriter et humiliter fecimus ut a prædictis erroribus resilire et eos revocare verbo et animo ac etiam abjurare velles, redeundo fideliter et veraciter ad sanctæ matris ecclesiæ unitatem quæ claudere non consuevit, imo potius aperire gremium ad eam redire volenti; tu vero monitiones et requisitiones hujusmodi et preces admittere hactenus recusasti et adhuc etiam recusas tuæ sævitiæ inhærens et insuper asserens te velle in ipsis erroribus et hæresibus, quos veros et catholicos asseris, vivere atque mori, nolens nostris et peritorum proborumque virorum in sacra scriptura et in utroque jure doctorum consilio credere, quoquomodo attento per nos, et viso per experientiam manifestam quod per impunitatis audaciam fiunt qui nequam fuerunt quotidie nequiores, ex nostro compulsi officio, ad quod cum diligentia exercendum ex præcepto sanctæ obedientiæ obligamur, nolentes sicuti nec debemus tam nefanda et totæ ecclesiæ et fidei catholicæ obviantia periculosissime ulterius tolerare, de multorum virorum religiosorum et sæcularium peritorum in utroque jure super præmissis consilio præhabito diligenti, Deum habentes præ oculis, sacrosanctis evangeliis. Jesu Christi positis coram nobis ut de vultu Dei nostrum prodeat judicium et rectum appareat coram Deo, oculique nostri videant æquitatem, hac die loco et hora præsentibus per nos peremptorie assignatis ad audiendum diffinitivam sententiam, sedentes pro tribunali, Christi nomine invocato, te Naprous, in et cum his scriptis pronuntiamus, judicamus et declaramus esse hæreticam et hæresi-archam impœnitentem et in tua duritia pertinacem, et ecclesia non habeat quid ulterius faciat de talibus, te, tanquam hæreticam et hæresiarcham impœnitentem et obstinatam relinquimus curiæ sæculari, eamdem curiam rogantes, prout suadent canonicas sanctiones, ut tibi vitam et membra citra mortis periculum illibata conservet.

IV.

CONFESSION OF A FRATICELLO OF LANGUEDOC.

(Doat, XXVII. fol. 202.)

Frater Bartholomeus Bruguiere, sicut per ipsius confessionem sub anno Domini MCCCXXVIII. mense Februarii factam in judicio, legitime nobis constat, quod quibusdam quos nominat dixit: *Loquamur de istis papis*, intelligendo sicut dixit, de Domino Joanne Papa XXII. et de illo Italico, sic intruso, et subjunxit in veritatem: "Modo dum Missam celebrabam, et fui in illo puncto in quo est orandum pro Papa nostro, steti ibi aliquandiu rogitans et hesitans pro quo istorum Paparum orare debuerem, et dum sic stetissem per aliquod spatium, non procedens ultra, cogitavi quod unus illorum ecclesie regimen usurpabat, alio existente vero Papa, et idcirco volui quod oratio mea esset pro illo qui juste regimen Ecclesie tenebat, quicunque esset ille." Nec dixit quid determinasset se ad unum nec ad alium predictorum. Item dixit duobus fratribus predicatoribus: "Vos alii fratres habetis bonum tempus in isto Papa in istis partibus, et fratres nostri malum, sed in Lombardia cum illo Papa Italico est totaliter contrarium." Dixit enim quod audiverat quod in creatione illius Pape italici fuerunt septuaginta prelati. Item dum citatus veniret ad inquisitoris penitentiam et jurasset ad sancta Dei Evangelia certa hora in ejus presentia comparere, hoc non obstante non comparuit, sed abscondit se nolens venire ad inquisitoris mandatum. Item frequenter audivit multos fratres sui ordinis qui dicebant quod bene staret, quod Deus daret Domino Joanni Pape tales facendas quod de negotiis illius ordinis non recordaretur, quia videbatur dictis fratribus quod dictus dominus Papa non haberet aliquid pungere vel restringere nisi ordinem eorumdem, et dixit seipsum dixisse predicta cum aliis; causam suam et dictorum fratrum quare ista dicebant assignavit, quia dominus Papa revocaverat constitutionem per quam dicebant procuratores suos esse procuratores ecclesie Romane. Item dixit quod audivit frequenter a multis fratribus sui ordinis fratrem Michaelem quondam suum ministrum generalem esse injuste depositum et excommunicatum. Item dixit quod dum semel predicabat dixit ista verba: "Dicitur quod habemus duos Papas, et tamen ego credo unum esse verum Papam," et, aliquibus verbis interjectis, subjunxit hec verba: "Teneant se ergo cum fortiori." Item dixit quod dum semel in magna societate fratrum diceret: "Utinam iste Antipapa esset de ordine predicatorum, vel de statu alio" respondit unus de fratribus: "Plus volo quod dictus Antipapa sit de ordine nostro, quia si esset de statu alio, tunc nec ipsum nec istum Joannem Papam haberemus amicum, et tandem istum Italicum habemus amicum." Cujus dicto applauserunt omnes presentes dicentes: "Bene comedit se et rodit semetipsum modo iste Papa Joannes;" et videbatur ipsi qui loquitur, sicut dixit, quod de ruina, infortuniis ecclesie que Domino Joanni pape contingebant, tempore sui regiminis, multum gaudebant. Hec omnia audivit ipse qui loquitur, nec revelavit. Item, mense Maii sequenti, ipse predicta verba que debuit dicere in sermone, videlicet: "Habemus duos Papas, teneamus nos cum fortiori" revocat tanquam falso confessata per eumdem, quam confessionem fecerat, sicut dixit, metu carceris et catene et jejunii et aque, de quibus sibi plurimi minabantur ut dixit. Premissa omnia alia asserit esse vera, dixit tamen quod, istis non obstantibus, nunquam credidit quin dominus noster Papa Joannes XXII. esset verus Papa. Postque, anno quo supra, die nona Septembris, sentiens et videns se convictus per testis super verbis predictis in ipso sermone prolatis, rediit ad confessionem predictam, et ab ipsa revocatione penitus resilivit et se supposuit misericordie Inquisitoris.

(Doat, XXXV. fol. 87.)

Joannes episcopus, servus servorum Dei, dilecto filio Inquisitori heretice pravitatis in partibus Carcassonensibus, auctoritate apostolica deputato, salutem et apostolicam benedictionem. Exposuit nobis dilectus filius Raimundus de Ladots ordinis fratrum minorum, ejusdem ordinis procurator generalis, quod licet Bartholomeus Brugerie olim predicti ordinis jamdudum, suis culpis et delictis exigentibus, per dilectum filium Geraldum Ottonis ipsius ordinis generalem ministrum ab eodem ordine fuerit per sententiam deffinitivam expulsus, tu tamen ipsum ratione criminis heresis de qua se respersum reddidit et convictum, cum habitu dictorum fratrum detines tuis carceribus mancipatum; sane quia in opprobrium redundaret fratrum et ordinis predictorum si dictus Bartholomeus postquam sic expulsus extitit ab eorum ordine ipsorum habitum in carceribus gestaret predictis, discretioni tue per apostolica scripta mandamus quatenus habitum ejusdem Bartholomei prefato procuratori vel dilecto filio guardiano fratrum ejusdem ordinis Carcassone studeas quantocius assignari. Datum Avenione decimo sexto Kalendas Octobris, Pontificatus nostri anno quintodecimo (16 Sep. 1331).

V.

Extracts from the Sentence of Cecco d'Ascoli.

Senza nissuna opressione di forza per sua libera e spontanea voluntà costituito dinanzi a noi in giudizio disse e confessò che mentre che fu citato e ricevuto per il religioso e reverendo Fr. Lamberto del Cordiglio del Ordine de' Predicatori, inquisitore dell' eretica pravità della Provincia de Lombardia comparse dinanzi a lui e confessò in giudizio che elli aveva detto e dogmatizato publicamente, leggendo che un uomo poteva nascere sotto la Costellazione che necessariamente fosse rico o povere e d' esser decapitato o appiccato, se Iddio non mutasse l'ordine della natura, nè altrimenti potesse essere parlando della potenza di Dio ordinata, overo ordinario, benchè per potenza assoluta di Dio potesse essere altrimenti.

Ancora che aveva detto in una certa sua lezione che dal segno dell' ottava sfera nascono homini felici di divinità, i quali si chiamo *dijnabet*, i quali mutano le leggi secondo più o meno, come fu Moyse, Ermete Mello e Simone Mago.

Ancora che egli aveva detto e dogmatizato perchè Cristo figliolo di Dio ebbe nella sua nascita la Libra nel decimo grado d' essa per ascendente, che per ciò doveva essere giusta la sua morte per destinazione, e doveva morire di quella morte e modo che mori, e perchè Cristo ebbe il Capricorno nell' angolo della terra però nacque in una stalla, e perchè ebbe lo Scorpione in secondo grado, però doveva esser povero, e perchè l' istesso Cristo ebbe Mercurio in Gemmini in casa propria nella nona parte del cielo, però doveva avere scienza profonda data sotto metafora.

Ancora perchè aveva detto che l' istesso Anticristo era per venire in forma di buon soldato et accompagnato nobilmente, ne verrà in forma di poltrone, come venne Cristo accompagnato da poltroni—

— Ancora disse e confessò che doppo la predetta abiurazione e penitenza . . . confessò d' aver osservato le costellazioni de' corpi celesti e che secondo il corso della stel a crede che nascono i costumi degli huomini e azioni e fini e che secondo queste cose giudicò nel comprare e vendere per argomentare il bene e schifare il male, et ancora nel fare essercizij et altre azzioni umane.

Ancora disse e confessò che quando fu interrogato da un certo fiorentino rispose che credeva esser vere quelle cose che si contengono nell' arte magica o Negromantia, e replicando il medesimo fiorentino che se fosse vero i principi e potenti huomini nel mondo acquisterebbero tutto, rispose e disse che non s'acquistano perchè non sono in tutto il mondo tre astrologi che sappiano servirsi bene di quell' arte, e questo disse aver detto per se medesimo perchè fecce più in quell' arte astrologica che alcun altro che fosse stato da Tolomeo in qua—

— Pronunciamo in questi scritti il predetto Maestro Cecco eretico a sentire questa sentenza, e costituto in nostra presenza di essere ricaduto nella eresia abiurata e di essere stato relasso, e per questo doversi rilassare al giudizio secolare, e lo rilasiamo al nobil soldato e cavaliere illustrissimo signor Jacopo da Brescia Vicario fiorentino di questo ducato presente e recipiente, che lo debba punire con debita considerazione, e di più che il suo libretto e scritto superstizioso pazzo e negromantico fatto dal detto Maestro sopra la sfera, pieno di eresie falsità e ingane, et un cert' altro libretto volgare intitolato Acerbo, il nome del quale esplica benissimo il fatto, avenga che non contenga in se maturità o dolcezza alcuna Cattolica, ma v' abbiamo trovato molte acerbità eretiche e principalmente quando v' include che si appartengono alla virtù e costume che riduce ogni cosa alle stelle come in causa, e dannando i loro dogmi e dottrine e riprovandoli deliberiamo e comandiamo per sentenza doversi abbrucciare, et al eretico

desiderando toglier la vena della fonte pestifera per qualsivoglia meato deri-
vino—

— Il sopradetto Signor Vicario immediatamente e senza dilazione mandando
per il capitano e sua famiglia il predetto Maestro Cecco al luogo della giustizia
dinanzi ad una moltitudine grande radunata di popolo in quel luoga, lo fece abbrucciare come richiedevano li suoi errori, sino alla morte sua penale, et a terrore
et esempio di tutti gli altri, come riferiscono di aver visto con li proprij occhij
Signor Vandi dal Borgo, Borghino di Maestro Chiarito dal Prato, Manovello di
Jacopo, e Giovanni Serafino, familiari dell' Uffizio andando all' istesso luogo, come
in Firenze e publico e per evidenza del fatto manifesto.

VI.

Sentence of a Carmelite Sorcerer.

(Archives de l'Inquisition de Carcassone.—Doat, XXVII. fol. 150.)

In nomine Domini amen. Quoniam nos frater Dominicus Dei gratia et apostolicæ sedis Appamiæ episcopus et fratres Henricus de Chamayo Carcassonæ et
P. Bruni Tholosanus ordinis prædicatorum inquisitores hæreticæ pravitatis in
regno Franciæ auctoritate apostolica deputati, per tuam confessionem propriam
in judicio legitime factam coram reverendo patre in Christo domino Jacobo tunc
Appamiæ episcopo nunc vero sedis apostolicæ cardinalis,* et postmodum coram
nobis per te recognitam, et etiam duobus vicibus confirmatam legitime invenimus et nobis constat quod tu, frater Petrus Recordi ordinis beatæ Mariæ de Car-
melo a quinque annis ante confessionem per te factam in judicio de infrascriptis
et citra diversis temporibus et locis, diabolico seductus consilio et libidinis ar-
dore succensus, voto castitatis quod in professione tui ordinis emiseras, pro do-
lor! violato, multa gravia et enormia commisisti sortilegia hæresim sapientia,
modis et conditionibus variis et abominabilibus, etiam recitatione indignis, et
inter alia quinque imagines cereas diversis temporibus succesive fecisti et fabri-
casti, multas et diversas dæmonum conjurationes et invocationes dicendo dum
dictas imagines fabricabas, et quamplurima venenosa etiam immiscendo, et san-
guinem bufonis terribili et horribili modo extractum infra dictas imagines in-
fundendo et ipsas imagines supra unam tabulam tapazeto vel panno coopertam
prostratas de sanguine narium tuarum in ventre spargendo et etiam de saliva
tua immiscendo, intendens per hoc diabolo sacrificare, quas imagines sic factas
et aliis modis recitatione indignis ponebas clandestine in limine hospitiorum ali-
quarum mulierum quas cognoscere volebas carnaliter, et de quarum numero tres
isto modo habuisti et carnaliter cognovisti et duas alias cognovisses carnaliter
nisi de loco ad locum per ordinem tuum transmissus fuisses; et cognitis eisdem

---

* Jacques Fournier (subsequently Benedict XII.) was made Cardinal of S. Prisca in
the creation of December 18, 1327, but he had been previously translated from the see
of Pamiers to that of Mirepoix (Ciacconii Vit. Pontif. Ed. 1677, II. 424). Pierre Recordi's
trial must, therefore, have endured for at least several years.

mulieribus et cum eis actu luxuriæ perpetrato dictas imagines recipiens easdem
in flumine jaciebas et unum papilionem dabas diabolo in sacrificium, et ejusdem
diaboli præsentiam per ventum aut alias sentiebas, credens dictas imagines ha-
bere virtutem astringendi dictas mulieres ad amorem tui vel si consentire nollent
per dæmones affligendi, et in dicta credentia stetisti per sex annos vel circa usque
captus fuisti.   Item quamdam de imaginibus prædictis in ventre percussisti, et
inde sanguis exivit.   Item cuidam personæ quam sciebas esse de hæresi culpa-
bilem, in muro de Alemannis detentæ favorem impertivisti quamdam cedulam
manu tua scriptam cum qua se defenderet scribendo et tradendo eidem, et multa
alia sortilegia commisisti quæ prolixum esset referre et audientibus forte tædio-
sum.   Multociens in confessionibus tuis variasti et revocasti eas sæpius contra
juramentum proprium temere veniendo.   Demum tamen ad cor rediens ad istas
confessiones pristinas redeundo et eas ratificando et approbando tanquam veras,
dixisti te corde et animo pœnitere et velle redire ad viam veritatis, et sanctæ
matris ecclesiæ unitatem, supponens te humiliter misericordiæ ejusdem sanctæ
matris ecclesiæ ac nostræ et petens absolutionis beneficium a sententia excommunicationis, quam pro præmissis culpis incurreras tibi per nos misericorditer
impendi, offerendo te paratum portare et complere humiliter pro posse pœnitentiam quam pro prædictis et aliis per te commissis tibi duxerimus injungendam.
Idcirco nos episcopus et inquisitores præfati, attenta gravitate culparum tuarum
prædictarum et aliarum quæ commisisti, et revocationes varias quas fecisti, con-
siderantes rectæ intentionis oculo quod si talia nefanda crimina transires im-
pune, forsitan ad eadem vel similia imposterum iteranda facilius relabereris et
mala malis ultimaque pejora prioribus aggregares ; quodque si austeritatem jus-
titiæ et rigorem apud te vellemus cum totali severitate judicialiter exercere
gravibus pœnis et quasi insupportabilibus punire deberes, quia tamen ecclesia
non claudit gremium redeunti humiliter misericordiam et gratiam postulanti,
æstimantes et per experientiam æstimantes te corde bono et intentione non ficta
demum fuisse confessum, et recognovisse de te et aliis veritatem, necnon toto
posse ad promotionem negotii inquisitionis existens in carcere cum quibusdam
personis de hæresi culpabilibus et delatis, veritatem super dicto crimine celan-
tibus et confiteri nolentibus, ad confitendum multipliciter induxisti multaque
gravia quæ ab ipsis audiveras revelare curasti, de quibus in fidei negotio et dictæ
inquisitionis officio bonum spirituale non modicum provenit et in futurum etiam
provenire poterit, Domino annuente, propter quod majori gratia et misericordia
te reddidisti in hoc casu spiritualiter digniorem, et insuper pensato dicti ordinis
tui honore, cui quantum bono modo poterimus deferre volumus, et ipsius confu-
sionem effugere, gratiose in facto hujusmodi procedentes, te præfatum fratrem
Petrum Recordi a sententia excommunicationis qua ligatus eras pro culpis prædictis, abjurata primitus per te in judicio coram nobis omni imaginum talium in-
debita fabricatione, adoratione, et dæmonum sacrificiis et immolatione, ac credentia sortilegiorum aliorum quorumcumque hæreticam sapientium pravitatem,
et aliam quamcumque et specialiter omnem fautoriam hæreticorum et etiam hæresim necnon credentiam et receptationem et fautoriam sortilegorum et hæreticorum quorumcumque, de peritorum consilio super hoc habito misericorditer

duximus absolvendum, et sedentes pro tribunali, sacrosanctis Dei evangeliis positis coram nobis, ut de vultu Dei nostrum prodeat judicium, et oculi nostri videant æquitatem rectum quoque appareat coram ipso, hac die loco et hora præsentibus tibi per nos peremptorie assignatis, de prædictorum peritorum consilio, in et cum his scriptis, per hanc nostram diffinitivam sententiam dicimus et pronunciamus te fuisse sortilegum ac immolatorem dæmonum et fautorem hæreticorum et te tanquam talem et corde non ficto ut asseris pœnitentem et ad sinum matris ecclesiæ reversum, et nostris mandatis obedire paratum, promittentemque pro posse tuo complere pœnitentiam tibi per nos injungendam in et cum eisdem præsentibus scriptis te primitus omni sacerdotali et quocumque alio ecclesiastico seu clericali ordine dicimus et decernimus degradandum, et te sicut præmittitur postquam degradatus fueris ad agendum pœnitentiam pro commissis ex nunc pro tunc et ex tunc pro nunc ad perpetuum carcerem in Tholosano conventu tui ordinis tibi per nos deputatum sententialiter condemnamus et etiam adjudicamus; in quo quidem carcere in vinculis et compedibus ferreis detineri et panem et aquam dumtaxat pro omni cibo et potu tibi ministrari volumus et mandamus, ut ibidem perpetuo peccata tua defleas et panem pro cibo doloris et aquam pro potu tribulationis habeas et recipias patienter; ita quod vivere inibi sapiat tibi mortem, et mors quam ibi tuleris tibi vitam tribuat sempiternam. Verum si, quod absit et Deus avertat, te in posterum antequam ad dictum carcerem venias vel in ipso fueris intrusus, diabolico instinctu fugere contigerit vel ipso carcere modo quolibet exire vel frangere absque nostro speciali mandato vel licentia et negligere aut non complere pœnitentiam prædictam tibi per nos impositam, volumus, ordinamus, et præsentis scripti serie declaramus absolutionem per nos et gratiam tibi factam penitus esse nullam, et te tanquam impœnitentem ficteque et dolose conversum, pristinæ excommunicationis vinculo fore totaliter irretitum. Porro, ne priores et fratres dicti conventus ubi fueris in carcere detrusus negligenter aut scienter te permiserint evadere vel licentiam dederint evadendi, vel procurantibus assenserint, opem vel auxilium dederint scienter, protestamur eisdem et auctoritate qua fungimur nobis et nostris in officio successoribus potestatem specialiter reservamus procedendi contra ipsos et eorum quemlibet prout de jure, stylo, cursu, usu et privilegiis inquisitionis fuerit procedendum; retinemus autem nobis et nostris in hoc officio successoribus liberam potestatem et auctoritatem mutandi in dicta pœnitentia, et eam mitigandi vel minuendi, vel ipsam totaliter remittendi, si et quando et prout de peritorum consilio nobis visum fuerit faciendum, et in favorem tui ordinis super degradatione actualiter facienda de speciali gratia dispensamus, et dictam degradationem facere nec fieri volumus ob reverentiam ordinis memorati. Lata fuit hæc sententia anno Domini MCCC vicesimo octavo, die Martis in crastino festi Sti. Marcelli (17 Jan. 1329), indictione XII., pontificatus SS^{mi} patris et domini, Domini Joannis divina providentia papæ XXII. anno decimo tertio, in aula episcopali urbis Appamiæ, præsentibus venerabilibus et discretis viris (sequuntur 43 nomina), testibus... et notariis....

VII.

BULL OF JOHN XXII. REMOVING SORCERY FROM THE JURISDICTION
OF THE INQUISITION.

(Archives des Frères-prêcheurs de Toulouse.—Doat, XXXIV. fol. 181.)

Johannes episcopus servus servorum Dei venerabilibus fratribus archiepis-
copo tholosano ejusque suffraganeis et dilecto filio inquisitori hæreticæ pravitatis in regno Franciæ per sedem apostolicam deputato, Tholosæ residenti, salutem
et apostolicam benedictionem. Dudum venerabilis frater noster Guillelmus
episcopus Sabinensis scripsit tibi, fili inquisitor, de mandato nostro per suas litteras in hac forma : Guillelmus miseratione divina episcopus Sabinensis religioso
viro inquisitori hæreticæ pravitatis in partibus tholosanis salutem in Domino
sempiternam. Sanctissimus pater noster et dominus, dominus Johannes divina
providentia papa vicesimus secundus optans ferventer maleficos infectores gregis
Dominici effugare de medio domus Dei, vult, ordinat, vobisque committit quod
auctoritate sua contra eos qui dæmonibus immolant vel ipsos adorant aut homa-
gium ipsis faciant, dando eis in signum cartam scriptam seu aliud quodcumque ;
vel qui expressa pacta obligatoria faciunt cum eisdem, aut qui operantur vel
operari procurant quamcumque imaginem vel quodcumque aliud ad dæmonem
alligandum seu cum dæmonum invocatione ad quodcumque maleficium perpe-
trandum, aut qui sacramento baptismatis abutendo imaginem de cera seu re alia
factam baptizant, sive faciunt baptizare, seu alias cum invocatione dæmonum
ipsam fabricant quomodolibet, aut faciunt fabricari, aut si scienter baptismus
seu ordo vel confirmatio iterantur. Item de sortilegis et maleficis qui sacramento
eucharistiæ seu hostia consecrata necnon et aliis sacramentis ecclesiæ, seu ipsorum
aliquo, quoad eorum formam vel materiam utendo eis in suis sortilegiis seu male-
ficiis abutuntur, possitis inquirere et alias procedere contra ipsos, modis tamen
servatis qui de procedendo cum prælatis in facto heresis vobis a canonibus sunt
præfixi. Ipse namque dominus noster præfatus potestatem inquisitoribus datam
a jure quoad Inquisitionis officium contra hæreticos, necnon et privilegia, ad
prætactos casus omnes et singulos ex certa scientia ampliat et extendit quoadus-
que duxerit revocandum. Nos itaque præmissa omnia vobis significamus per
has nostras patentes litteras de præfati Domini nostri Papæ speciali mandato
facto nobis ab ipso oraculo vivæ vocis. Datum Avenione die vicesima secunda
mensis Augusti anno Domini MCCC vicesimo, pontificatus prædicti Domini
Papæ anno quarto. Sane noviter intellecto quod errores et abominationes in
eisdem litteris comprehensi in partibus illis, de quibus in litteris ipsis habetur
mentio, adhuc vigent, nos cupientes super ipsis, ne deinceps pullulent, plenius
providere, discretioni vestræ præsentium tenore committimus et mandamus quatinus omnes inquisitiones quas auctoritate litterarum hujusmodi, vos, fratres Archiepiscope et suffraganei, prout quemlibet vestrum tangit, et tu inquisitor præfate, cum singulis eorumdem insimul, vel tu inquisitor solus per teipsum incho-
astis, si completæ non fuerint, vos, Archiepiscope et suffraganei, quilibet vestrum
videlicet in sua diocesi per se vel alium, quem ad huc deputandum duxeritis, et

tu inquisitor prædicte, insimul celeriter compleatis; quas postquam comple-
veritis una cum illis quæ jam per te solum, præfate inquisitor, forsitan sunt completæ, nobis sub vestris sigillis fideliter interclusas quanto citius poteritis trans-
mittatis, ut eis visis quid faciendum sit tam super illis de quibus fuerit inquisi-
tum, quam super omnibus cæteris de quibus nondum est inceptum inquiri, plenius
et certius, auctore Domino, disponamus. Tu vero, inquisitor prædicte, super illis
de quibus adhuc inquirere non cœpisti prætextu dictarum litterarum, nisi forsan
aliud a nobis receperis in mandatis, te nullatenus intromittas. Per hæc autem
non intendimus vobis vel vestrum alicui, quantum ad illa quæ a jure vobis alias
sunt permissa, in aliquibus derogari. Datum Avinione secundo Nonas Novembris, pontificatus nostri anno decimo quinto (Nov. 4, 1330).

VIII.

Decision of the Council of Venice Concerning the Witches of Brescia.

(Archivio di Venezia, Misti Cons. X. Vol. 44, p. 7.)

1521 Die 21 Martii in Cons. X. cum additione. É sta sempre instituto del
religiosissimo stato nostro in scontar li heretici et extirpar cussi detestando
crimine, siccome nella promission del Serenissimo Principe et capitular de con-
seieri nei primi capituli se leze. Dal che sine dubbio è processa la protectione
che sempre el Signor Dio ha havuta della Republica nostra come per infinite
experientie de tempo in tempo se ha veduto. Unde essendo in questa materia
de i strigoni et heretici da proceder cum gran maturità però l' andarà parte che
chiamado nel collegio nostro el Rev.mo Legato intervenendo i capi di questo conseio li sia per el Ser.mo Prencipe nostro cum quelle grave et accomodate parole
pareranno alla sapientia de sua serenità dechiarito quanto l' importi che questa
materia sia cum maturità et justicia rite et recte et per ministri che manchino
de ogni suspitione tractata et terminata in forma che iuxta la intention et de-
siderio nostro tutto passi iuridicamente et cum satisfaction dell' honor del Signor
Dio et della fede catholica. E però ne par debino esser deputadi ad questa inquisitione uno o doi Reverendi Episcopi insieme cum uno venerabile Inquisitor
i qual tutti siano de doctrina, bontà et integrità prestanti ac omni exceptione
majores: Azò non se incorri nelli errori vien ditto esser seguiti fin questo jorno
et unitamente cum doi excellenti doctori de Bressa habbino a formar legitime i
processi contra i dicti strigoni et heretici. Formati veramente i processi (citra
tamen torturam) siano portati a Bressa dove per i predicti cum la presentia et in-
tervento de ambi li Rectori nostri et cum la corte del Podestà et quattro altri
Doctori de Bressa della qualità sopradicta: siano lecti essi processi facti cum al
dir etiam i rei et intender se i ratificheranno i loro dicti o se i voranno dir altro
nec non far nove examinatione o repetitione et etiam torturar se cussi indicia-
ranno. Le quel cose facte cum ogni diligentia et circumspectione se procedi
poi alla sententia per quelli a chi l' appartien, iuxta el conseio dei sopranominati.
Ala execution de la qual servatis omnibus premissis et non aliter, sia dato el

brachio secular; et questo che se ha a servar neli processi da esser formati nel advenir sia medesimamente servato et exequito neli processi formati per avanti; non obstante che le sententie fusseno sta facte sopra de quelli. Preterea sia efficacemente parlato cum dicto Rev^{mo} Legato e datogli cargo che circa la spese da esser fatte per la inquisitione el facci tal limitatione che sia conveniente e senza extorsion o manzarie come se dice esser sta facte fin al presente. Sed in primis se trovi alcun expediente che lo appetito del danaro non sia causa de far condennar o vergognar alcuno senza aver cum minima culpa sicome vien divulgato finhora in molti esser seguito. Et die cader in considerazione che quelli poveri di Valcamonica sono gente simplice et de grossissimo inzegno et che hariano non minor bisogno de predicatori cum prudente instructione della fede catholica che de persecutori cum animadversione essendo uno tanto numero de anime quante se ritrovano in quelli monti e vallade.

Demum sia suaso el R^{mo} Legato a la deputation de alcune persone idonee qual habbino ad reveder et investigar le manzarie et altre cose mal fatte che fusseno sta commesse fin questo jorno ne la inquisitione, et che habbino ad syndicar et castigar quelli che havesseno perpetrati de i mancamenti che si divulgano cum murmuration universale. Et questo sia facto de presenti senza interposition de tempo per bon exemplo de tutti.

Et ex nunc captum sit: che da poi facta la presente execution cum el R^{mo} Legato se vegni a questo Conseio per deliberar quanto se havrà ad scriver alli Rectori nostri de Bressa et altrove sicome sarà indicato necessario. Et sia etiam preso che tutte le pignoration ordinate et facte da poi la sospension presa a dì XII Dicembre proximo preterito in questo conseio siano irrite et nulle ne haver debbino alcuna executione.

De parte—24. De non—1. Non sinceri—2.

IX.

CONFESSION OF A PARDONER.

(Doat, XXVI. fol. 314.)

Anno Domini MCCLXXXIX quinto Kalendas Aprilis, Berengarius Pomilli clericus uxoratus de Narbona predicator questuarius citatus comparuit Carcassone coram fratre Guillelmo de Sancto Secano inquisitore, et juratus super sancta Dei evangelia dicere veritatem, requisitus per dictum inquisitorem sponte recognovit et dixit quod officium questuarii exercuerat pro fabrica pontium et ecclesiarum et pro aliis negotiis triginta annis vel circa in diocesi Carcassone et Narbone et quibusdam aliis. Dixit etiam quod in diocesi Carcassonensi infra annum pluries predicavit publice clero et populo, dum missa solemniter celebrabatur, et inter alia predicavit ut dixit quod qui daret ei pro hospitali Sancti Johannis unam poneriam bladi pro dicta mensura haberet triginta missas. Item dixit quod crux, in qua pependit Dominus Jesus Christus et quam portavit in suis humeris, erat adeo magna et tanti ponderis quod decem homines essent onerati de ea portanda. Item dixit quod cum beata Virgo staret ad pedem crucis, ad

preces ipsius crux inclinata est ad eam versus terram, et ipsa osculata est pedes
et manus filii sui dum penderet in dicta cruce, et iterato crux se erexit. Dixit
etiam quod beata Maria Magdalena quandocumque esset peccatrix et exposita
operibus luxurie, non tamen se exponebat hominibus effectu libidinis vel de-
siderio voluptatis carnalis, sed cum ipsa vocaretur Maria et Christus debebat
concipi et nasci de Maria, credebat quod Christum debebat concipere et parere,
et se diversis hominibus exponebat. Dixit etiam se predicasse quedam fabulosa
de Purgatorio et de liberatione animarum benefacto eleemosinarum et Missarum,
que tamen in scriptura reperiuntur, sed dixit se a bonis hominibus audivisse; et
ista predicavit in presentia fratris Berengarii de ordinis hospitalis sancti Johannis
qui moratur Narbone. Requisitus si predicta que superius scripta sunt credit et
credidit esse vera, respondit quod non, sed falsa et mendosa et erronea, sed ea
predicavit ut moveret homines quod darent sibi aliquid. Dixit etiam quod predicta predicavit in ecclesiis de Podio - nauterio, de Aragone, de Villasicca, de
Sancta Eulalia, de Comelano, de Monteclaro, de Roffiaco. Inquisitus si intelligit
Latinum, respondit quod non. Super quibus petivit penitentiam et indulgentiam
quam predictus inquisitor voluerit sibi injungere. Hec deposuit coram predicto
inquisitore, presentibus fratribus Petro de Leva, Petro Regis, Joanne de Felgosio,
ordinis fratrum predicatorum, et me Raimundo de Malveriis, notario inquisitionis
qui hec scripsi et recepi.

INDEX

THE END.